# BEA NETTLES

# Bea Nettles
# HARVEST OF MEMORY

EDITED BY
Jamie M. Allen and Olivia Lahs-Gonzales

WITH ADDITIONAL TEXTS BY
Bea Nettles and Amy L. Powell

GEORGE EASTMAN MUSEUM

UNIVERSITY OF TEXAS PRESS, AUSTIN

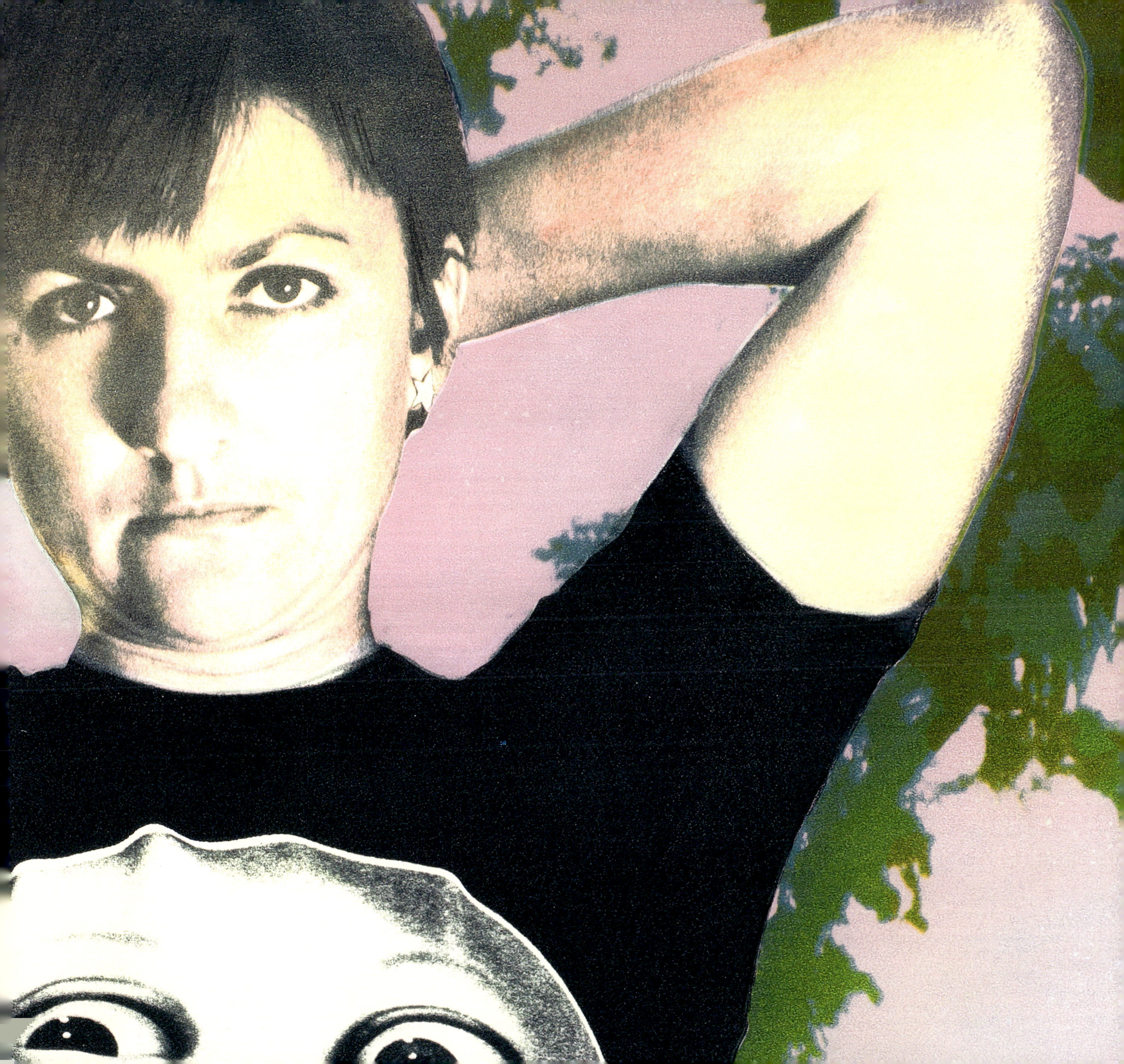

Publication of this book has been supported in part by the George Eastman Museum Publishing Trust Endowment, which was established by Thomas Gosnell and Richard Menschel with funds donated by Thomas and Georgia Gosnell and the Horace W. Goldsmith Foundation.

The book is published to accompany the exhibition *Bea Nettles: Harvest of Memory*, co-organized by the George Eastman Museum and Sheldon Art Galleries.

Exhibition venues
Sheldon Art Galleries, St. Louis, Missouri, October 5–December 30, 2019
George Eastman Museum, Rochester, New York, January 31–June 14, 2020
Krannert Art Museum, University of Illinois at Urbana-Champaign, Champaign, Illinois, August 27–November 28, 2020

The exhibition is supported in part by the National Endowment for the Arts and the Missouri Humanities Council.


Printing and color separations
by Dr. Cantz'sche
Druckerei Medien GmbH, Germany
First edition, 2019



∞ The paper used in this book meets the minimum requirements of ANSI/NISO Z39.48-1992 (R1997) (Permanence of Paper).

Library of Congress Cataloging-in-Publication Data

Names: Nettles, Bea, 1946– artist, writer of supplementary textual content. | Allen, Jamie M., editor. | Lahs-Gonzales, Olivia, editor. | Powell, Amy L., writer of supplementary textual content. | Sheldon Art Galleries, host institution. | George Eastman Museum, host institution. | Krannert Art Museum, host institution.
Title: Bea Nettles : harvest of memory / edited by Jamie M. Allen and Olivia Lahs-Gonzales ; with additional texts by Bea Nettles and Amy L. Powell.
Description: First edition. | Austin : University of Texas Press, 2019. | This book is published on the occasion of the exhibition Bea Nettles: Harvest of Memory, presented by Sheldon Art Galleries, St. Louis, Missouri, October 5–December 30, 2019; George Eastman Museum, Rochester, New York, January 31–June 14, 2020; Krannert Art Museum, Champaign, Illinois, August 27–November 28, 2020. | Includes bibliographical references and index.
Identifiers: LCCN 2018061124
ISBN 978-1-4773-1925-3 (cloth : alk. paper)
Subjects: LCSH: Nettles, Bea, 1946—Exhibitions. | Photography, Artistic—Exhibitions.
Classification: LCC TR647.N446 N48 2019 | DDC 770.74/ 77866—dc23
LC record available at https://lccn.loc.gov/2018061124

# CONTENTS

# FOREWORD

In December 1970 our museum opened the exhibition *Images and Swamp Dreams . . . Works by Bea Nettles*. At that time, Nettles was just settling into Rochester's vibrant photography community, which included Thomas Barrow, Betty Hahn, Harold Jones, Nathan and Joan Lyons, John Pfahl, and Robert Sobieszek, among many others. Nearly fifty years later, we at the George Eastman Museum are delighted to collaborate with the Sheldon Art Galleries in St. Louis to survey Nettles's career through a retrospective exhibition.

Nettles has worked in various media, including photography, printmaking, bookmaking, painting, and drawing. Her innovative application of photography expanded our understanding of the many ways it can be used to create a work of art. Nettles and a small group of her contemporaries paved the way for artists to move fluidly among media and to freely create mixed-media works.

Because photography has become an integral part of many contemporary artworks that defy simple categorization, it is important that the Eastman Museum's photography collection—which spans the medium's history from its inception to the present—include a strong selection of works by Bea Nettles. We celebrate the artist's extraordinary generosity to our museum, which now holds 145 of her artworks, twenty-three of her rare or handmade books, and each of her twelve trade books.

As a major repository of her work, our collection allows scholars to study outstanding examples from every major period of her oeuvre—from her first undergraduate course to her current gravestone poetry books. Through our online collections database and our photography study center, these works are both digitally and physically accessible to the public.

This publication and the accompanying exhibition will be milestones in the understanding and appreciation of Bea Nettles and her artworks, and we hope that they will serve as the foundation for future scholarship on and exhibition of the work of this pioneering artist. This book project was supported in part by the George Eastman Museum Publishing Trust Endowment.

Bruce Barnes, PhD
RON AND DONNA FIELDING DIRECTOR
GEORGE EASTMAN MUSEUM

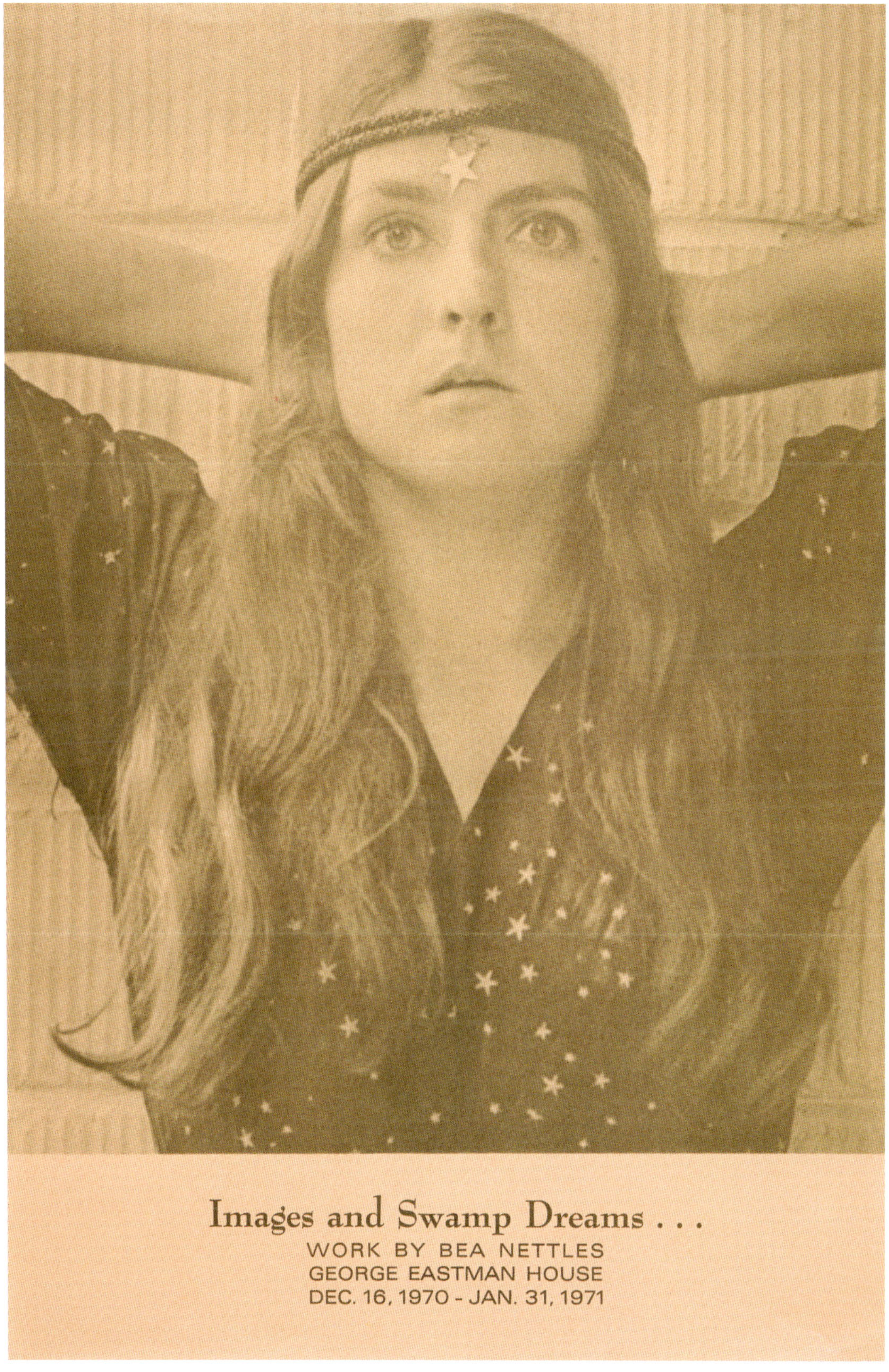


Exhibition poster for
*Images and Swamp Dreams . . .* ,
George Eastman House,
December 16, 1970–January 31, 1971

# PREFACE

Long before such words were an active part of the contemporary art lexicon, Bea Nettles was a multimedia artist who expanded the definition of photography. She used alternative photographic processes to create layered and textured autobiographical works that included self-portraiture; investigations of her body and its relationship to nature and the landscape; and examinations of mothering, loss, and aging.

However, while the many extant exhibit reviews and articles about Nettles reveal an artist who has received steady recognition for over fifty years, her groundbreaking work has not given her the renown that many male photographers of her generation have received at this stage in their careers. Though her photographs have been included in many important surveys, including Naomi Rosenblum's *World History of Photography* (1984) and Anne Tucker's *The Woman's Eye* (1973), her experimental methods and themes have hitherto not garnered her a large-scale retrospective monograph or a major museum retrospective.

This book and its accompanying exhibition, jointly organized by the George Eastman Museum in Rochester, New York, and the Sheldon Art Galleries in St. Louis, Missouri, seek to create a wider audience for Nettles by bringing together works from the 1960s to the present day. The book's three essays illuminate different aspects of her long and influential career. Jamie M. Allen, cocurator of the exhibition, provides an in-depth overview of the trajectory of Nettles's practice, tracing her roots in painting and printmaking to the evolution of her use of alternative processes and important contributions to the production of artist's books, and considers Nettles's recent projects in which she mines gravestones for surnames that she uses to construct visual poems. My essay looks specifically at the way motherhood influenced Nettles's artistic path when her children were young and shows how the challenges of this period led to bodies of work that speak both personally and more broadly to the experiences of working women everywhere. Amy L. Powell, curator of modern and contemporary art at the Krannert Art Museum, in Champaign, Illinois, considers Nettles's artistic output in the context of the institutions in which she operated as a student and then later as a longtime educator. Powell situates Nettles's work in the context of the institutional world of photography and discusses how her art served to upend established traditions while forging pathways that align with performative feminist practice.

This project seeks to place Nettles's artistic practice in a wider public arena, one that articulates and illuminates the unique experiences found in the inner lives of women.

Olivia Lahs-Gonzales
DIRECTOR (2001–2019)
THE SHELDON ART GALLERIES, ST. LOUIS

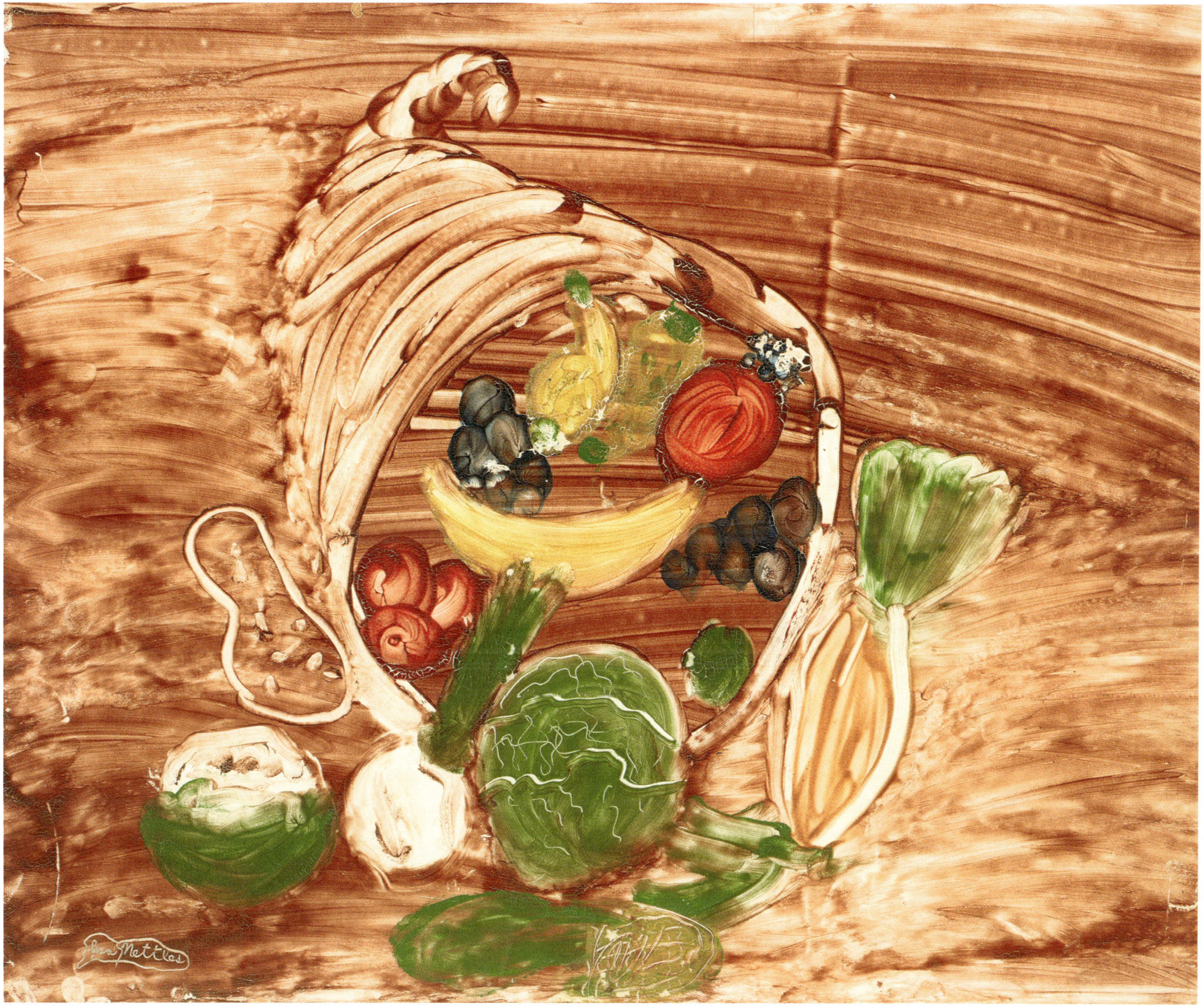

*Cornucopia*,
finger painting Bea Nettles
created in elementary school

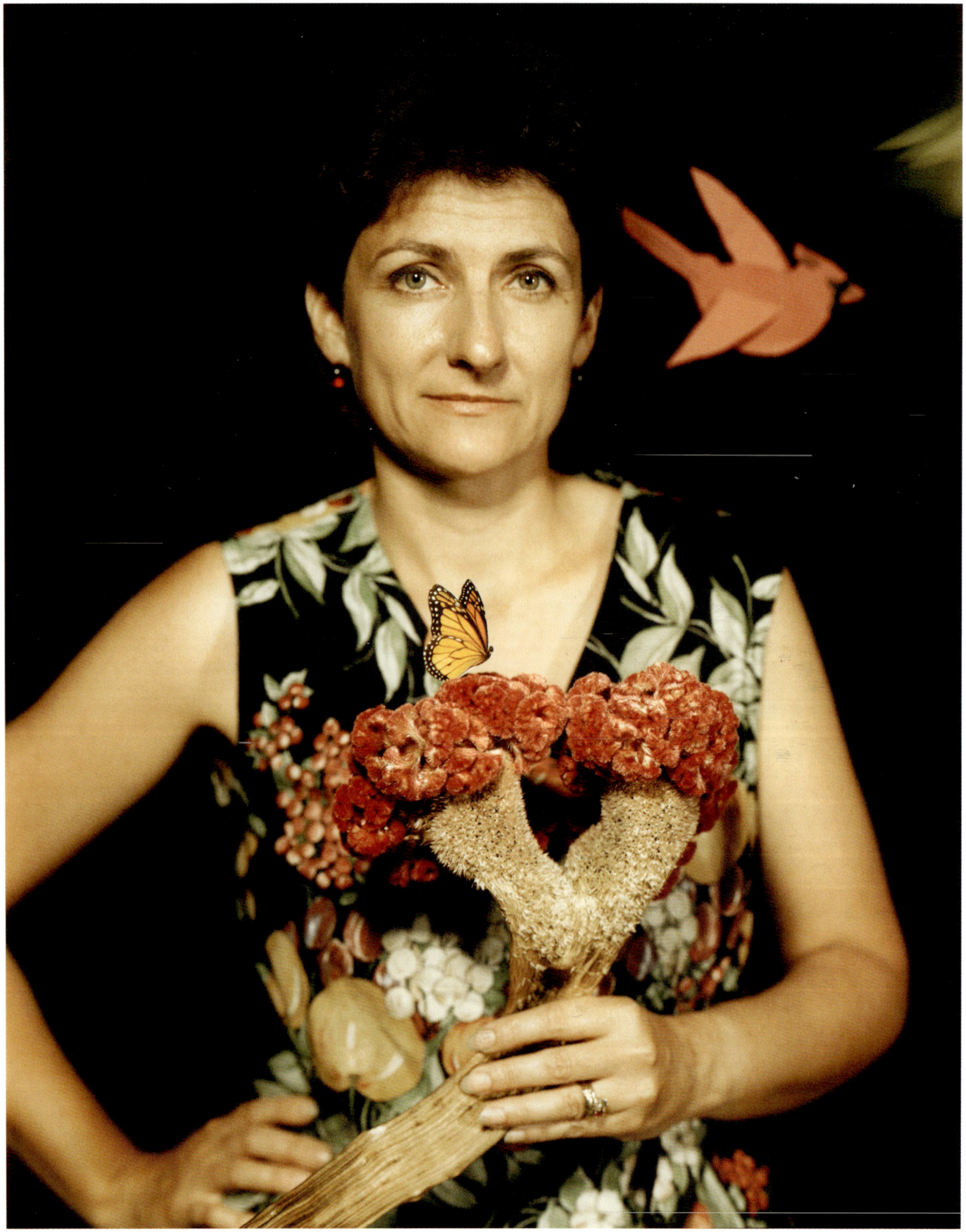

*Flower Dress*, 1987,
dye diffusion transfer print

# ACKNOWLEDGMENTS

My family's participation has always been critical to my work, starting with my parents, Grace and Victor, and my siblings, Victor, Jack, Elizabeth, and Connie, and continuing with my steadfastly supportive husband, Lionel Suntop, and my creative children, Rachel and Gavin. My main mentors, Robert Fichter and Keith and Flo Hatcher, also deserve special recognition.

Thank you, Olivia Lahs-Gonzales, Jamie Allen, and Amy Powell, for your thoughtful writing and all of your hard work.

Bea Nettles

---

On behalf of the Sheldon Art Galleries and the George Eastman Museum, I would like to express our profound gratitude to those who made *Bea Nettles: Harvest of Memory* a reality.

First and foremost, our thanks to Bea Nettles, a woman of generous spirit who welcomed the authors into her home and studio, encouraging conversation about the role of women in artistic practice, work environments, and the home.

Additional thanks to Bea's husband, Lionel Suntop, and to her children, Rachel and Gavin.

We are pleased to have partnered with the University of Texas Press for this book, and we benefited from the guidance and skills of David Hamrick, director; Allison Faust, assistant to the director; Robert Kimzey, managing editor; and Dustin Kilgore, design and production manager. Our colleagues at the press have, once again, produced a beautiful book that recognizes the breadth of photographic history through the importance of Bea Nettles's work.

We wish to thank our collaborators at the Sheldon Art Galleries, particularly Olivia Lahs-Gonzales, director (2001–2019), for taking on this ambitious project with our institution. She shared her time and energy in bringing this book and exhibition to fruition, for which we will be forever grateful. For their support work on the project, we would further like to thank, also at the Sheldon galleries, Paul Reuter, program advisor; Peter Palermo, executive director; Rebecca Gunter, gallery coordinator and education manager; Paula Lincoln, gallery assistant; Quintin Reed, director of operations; Michael Murphy, facilities assistant; Chris Peimann, marketing director; Sarah Samples, marketing and publicity coordinator; Christina Cacciatore, development assistant; and Connor Pearson, development and marketing assistant.

To our colleagues at the Krannert Art Museum, in Champaign, Illinois, thank you for making your collections available for this project and for your early enthusiasm for hosting the exhibition. We are proud to have worked with Amy L. Powell, curator of modern and contemporary art, who kindly shared her research and whose essay places Bea's life and work into context. Thanks also to the museum's director, Jon L. Seydl, for supporting this idea even though it was already under way on his first day of work at the museum, and to Kimberly Sissons, collection manager, for making the collection available for research, photography, and travel.

Our thanks also go to Kiley Reed Black, Will Arnold, Chris Bonner, and David Akins at the School of Art + Design at University of Illinois for their assistance in using the school's studio and equipment to image objects for this project.

The Eastman Museum is fortunate to have a talented staff that works tirelessly to make our institutional visions possible. First and foremost I would like to thank our director, Bruce Barnes, who immediately saw the importance of Nettles's career. In particular, we wish to thank Amy Schelemanow, director of publishing and design, for coordinating the museum's efforts on this publication; Molly Tarbell and Amy Slentz, for sharing their keen senses for detail and design across many rounds of review; Elizabeth Chiang, for traveling to Champaign-Urbana to photograph Nettles's works and for putting in countless hours making match prints so that the reproductions in this book truly represent these complex objects; and Lauren Lean, for bringing together files of these unique objects from several collections so that this book could represent the whole of Nettles's work.

In the Department of Photography, I am fortunate to be supported by many wonderful colleagues. My fellow curatorial staff, including Lisa Hostetler, Heather Shannon, William Green, and Meghan Jordan, serve as a sounding board for ideas and were my first-round editors for this book. Without their feedback and assistance, no project here would be possible, and I am proud to work with each of them. Our collection managers, Ross Knapper and Rachel Andrews, have made Nettles's photographs accessible by cataloging and housing them, and I am grateful for the care they take with every object in the collection. And many thanks to the staff in our Richard and Ronay Menschel Library, including Ken Fox, Deborah Mohr, and Stephanie Hofner.

Additional thanks to our colleagues throughout the museum, including Sarah Evans, registrar; David Howe, assistant registrar; Kate Meyers Emery, manager of digital engagement; and Nick Marshall, manager of exhibitions and programs. Thanks as well to our exhibitions team, including Andrew Salomone; Taina Meller, conservator; Zach Long, assistant conservator; Emily Phoenix, chief object preparator, and her team, including Bonnie Hodul and Cory Card;

Lisa Ann Seischab, vice president of development; Karly Marshall, assistant director of development; Eliza Kozlowski, director of marketing and engagement; Kellie Fraver, public relations manager; and, in our IT department, Julie Brubaker, Ory Ballenger, and Matthew Shepard.

Additional thanks to Erin Fisher for her research assistance in the preliminary phases of the project.

We wish to thank the following individuals: Linda Connor, Betty Hahn, Joanne Leonard, Barbara Raymond, and Robert Fichter. We would also like to thank our colleagues at other institutions who provided assistance related to this project: Jennifer Belt and Diana Edkins, at Art Resource; Hayley Blomquist and Janet Hicks, at the Artists Rights Society; Leslie Squires, Shandi Wagner, and Emily Weirich, at the Center for Creative Photography; Lauren Tent, at CEPA Gallery; Grace Pamperien and Taylor Pecktal, at Crystal Bridges Museum of American Art; Nelda Damiano and Kristen Zimmerman, at the Cummer Museum of Art and Gardens; Dannyl Dolder, Erich Schroeder, and Robert Sill, at the Illinois State Museum; Raven Amiro, at the National Gallery of Canada; Becky Simmons, at the Rochester Institute of Technology Archive Collections; Daniel Burge, Al Carver-Kubik, and Jennifer Jae Gutierrez, at the Image Permanence Institute, Rochester Institute of Technology; Julie Dunn-Morton, at the St. Louis Mercantile Library, University of Missouri–St. Louis; Susanne Belovari and Olivia M. Hagedorn, at the University of Illinois Urbana-Champaign; Adam Doskey and Dennis Sears, at the Rare Book and Manuscript Library, University of Illinois at Urbana-Champaign; Carol McCusker, Erin Gordon, Liz Rogers, and Jessica Uelsmann, at the Harn Museum of Art, University of Florida, Gainesville; and Stephen Lockwood, at the University of New Mexico Art Museum.

On a personal note, I wish to thank Kiley, David, Holden, and Lucille Black for allowing me into their home each time I visited Illinois; it is wonderful to come back to a home filled with light, love, dance parties, and jousting matches.

I also am forever grateful to Al Carver-Kubik for the continuous support that you offer in my life and for answering all my pesky photography-process questions.

In addition to acknowledging those thanked by the George Eastman Museum, Olivia Lahs-Gonzales and those at the Sheldon Art Galleries, St. Louis, would like to thank Terry Suhre, director of Gallery 210 and a research professor at the University of Missouri–St. Louis, for providing initial contact information and encouraging the project. They would also like to thank the National Endowment for the Arts and Missouri Humanities Council for their support of the project and, finally, the George Eastman Museum for collaborating on the project and producing this beautiful, in-depth publication.

Jamie M. Allen
STEPHEN B. AND JANICE G. ASHLEY ASSOCIATE CURATOR
GEORGE EASTMAN MUSEUM

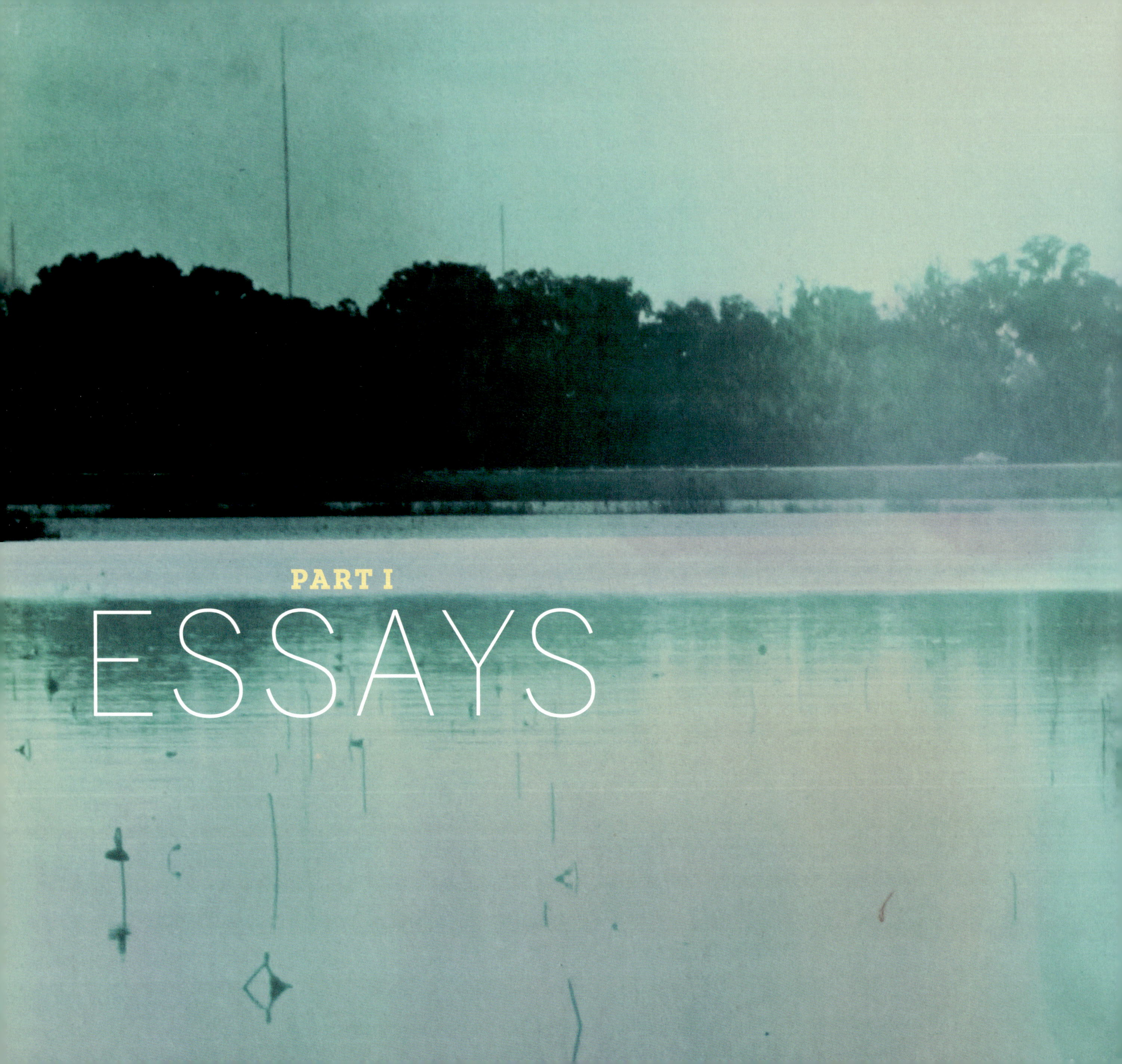

PART I

# ESSAYS

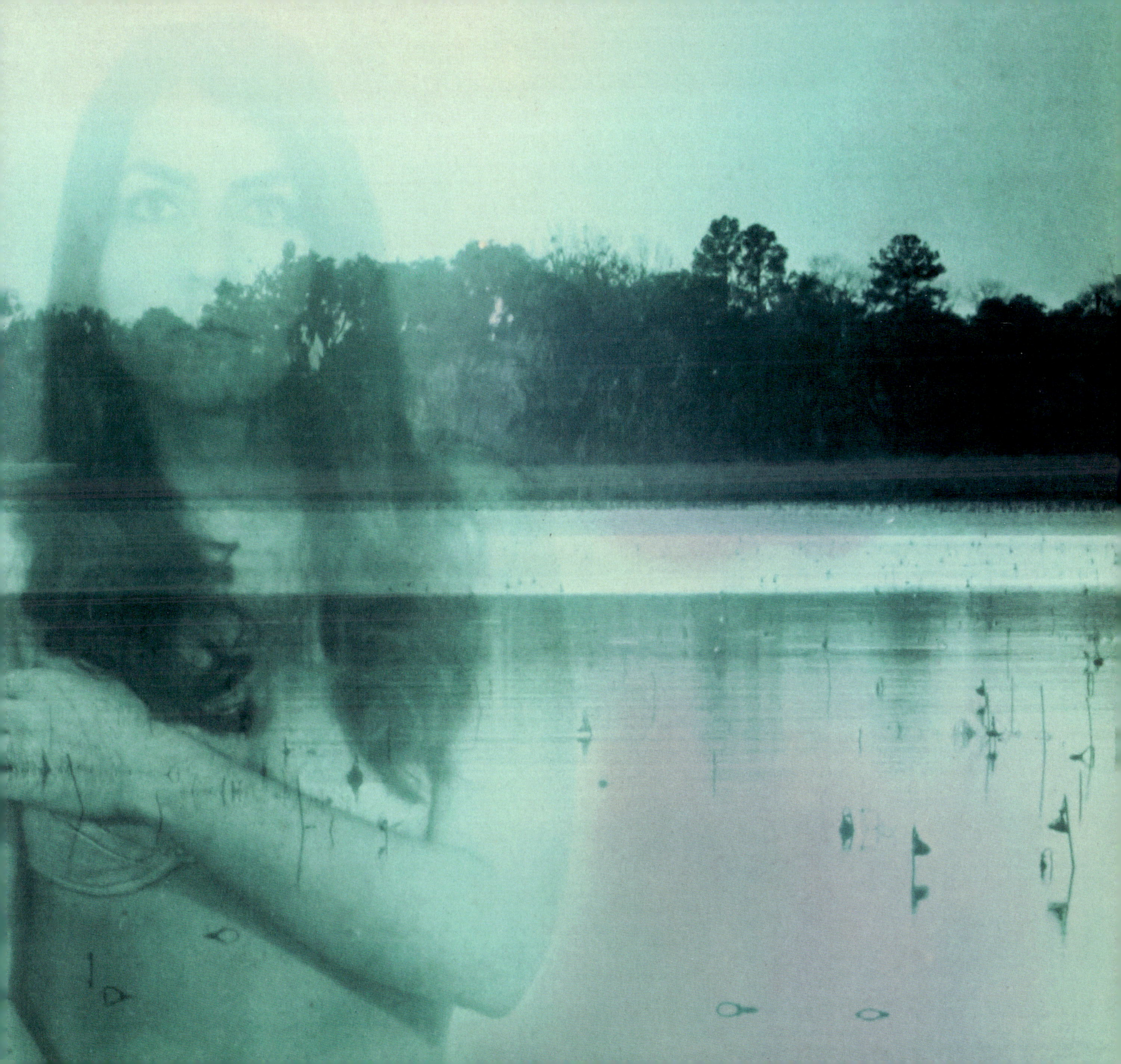

# OVERCOMING CONSTRAINTS

Jamie M. Allen

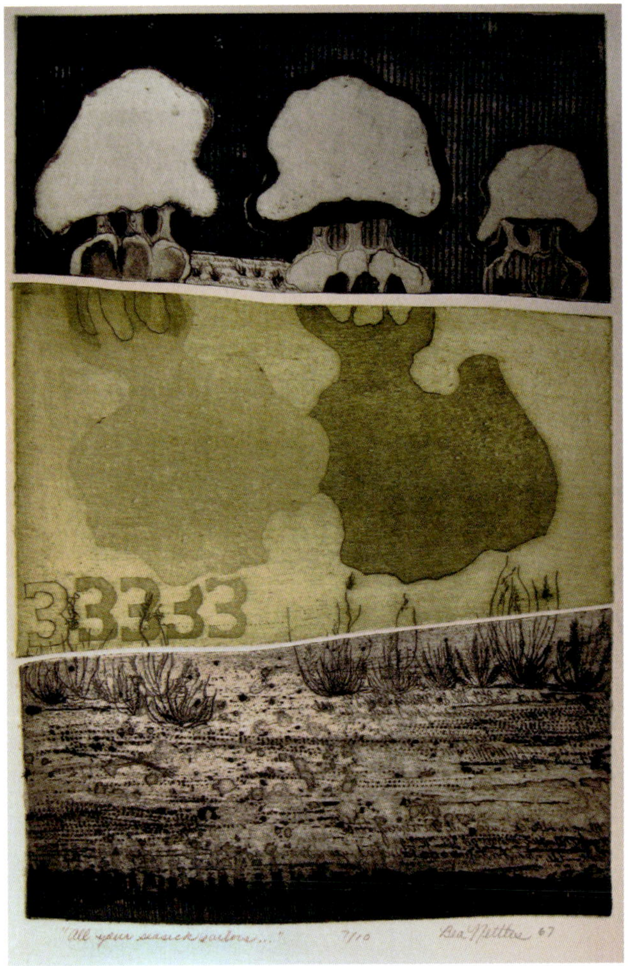


FIGURE 1.1. *All your seasick sailors*, spring 1967, etching

Throughout her career, Bea Nettles has explored the narrative potential of photography through constructed images. Her artistic practice is experimental, combining craft and photography through diverse techniques, including the use of large-format, pinhole, and simple snapshot cameras;[1] fabric; stitching; hand-coloring; alternative photographic processes; printmaking; and the book and card deck formats. Her imagery evokes metaphors that reference key stages in the lives of women. Often autobiographic, Nettles's photographs address themes of place, landscape, dreams, mythology, family, motherhood, aging, and the passage of time.

Now more than fifty years into her career, Nettles remarks that she was constantly working with and against constraints, including those related to money, time, and space; the available technology; and the work-life balance of motherhood, teaching, and artistic career.[2] Yet in reviewing Nettles's work, one can see these constraints as catalysts of experimentation, driving forces that not only imposed limitations but also, and equally, allowed for exploration and freedom. Her actions place her at the forefront of postmodern photography. She pushed the boundaries of acceptable finished photographic work and, through her teaching career, shared her knowledge, practice, methods, and approaches with others. As Nettles has written her autobiography in multiple editions of her book *The Skirted Garden*, my essay explores the arc of Nettles's life and career by examining how these constraints influenced her work in terms of narrative themes and her use of various mediums.

According to Nettles, her "professional career" began in 1970 with the display of her work at the Museum of Modern Art and the completion of her graduate work at the University of Illinois. Yet the foundations of her photographic vision can be found prior to this date;[3] her work about her family began when she was a child. Nettles remembers having two cameras: one that she received at the age of ten from her grandmother and a second—a Kodak Brownie camera—that she won at the age of thirteen.[4] Her first rolls of film are snapshots of her family, which she valued and saved. As the themes of passing time, childhood, family, and home became common throughout her work, she used these images, along with snapshots of her young self made by friends and family members, in many projects. These early snapshot negatives are not the only images that she revisits; for Nettles, every negative may be subjected to repeated use, time and time again and in various media.

During her undergraduate work at the University of Florida, Gainesville (fall 1964–spring 1968), Nettles studied painting and printmaking. Her subjects were primarily landscapes, sometimes populated with trees, stacked one on top of another in a collage-like fashion (fig. 1.1), or depicted from varying vantage points, such as that of an airplane window. These early works transform the seemingly everyday landscapes into mythic localities steeped in longing, mystery, and memory. During her senior year, Nettles took her first photography course, with Robert Fichter (fig. 1.2).[5] Her early photographs are continuations of the work she was already producing—collaged, flattened landscapes—with colors (sepia, blue, yellow, and red) derived from toning (for an example of this, see p. 58). These layered images are both the foundation on which Nettles subsequently built her practice and of the beginning of her creating photographic memories that translate the places she visits into mythic locales.

During her undergraduate education, she was also introduced to the Penland School of Crafts, in the Blue Ridge Mountains of North Carolina.[6] Nettles returned to Penland repeatedly throughout her career as a student, teacher, and artist in residence. In the summer of 1968, waiting to begin graduate school, Nettles stayed at Penland, making new work and teaching a course. There she created *Self Totem* (1968; p. 59), a work inspired by Esphyr Slobodkina's *Caps for Sale*, a children's story of a hat vendor who piles his wares atop his head. *Self Totem* lays the foundations for several themes prevalent in Nettles's work: inspiration from literary sources, self-portraiture, and a strong use of color. With its lack of constraints—no need to cook or clean and few teaching or prep hours required—Penland provided a place where Nettles could make new images, explore new concepts, and ultimately regroup. Her often referenced *Mountain Dream Tarot* deck started here in the summer of 1970, and during various residencies at Penland, she conceived of several books and series, including *Complexities*, *Turning 50*, and *Return Trips*.

While attending graduate school at University of Illinois at Urbana-Champaign (fall 1968–spring 1970), Nettles continued to add to her image-making arsenal. While studying painting and printmaking, she began to use materials and techniques often identified with women's work, such as fabric, sewing, and hand-coloring. One example is her constructed landscape *The Skirted Garden* (1969; p. 61), which incorporates a red skirt that Nettles found at a thrift shop. In the painting, the fabric acts as a physical skirt covering a portion of the work. When the work hung in her studio, Nettles found that many viewers could not resist lifting the skirt, so she added an underlayer—a satin slip complete with

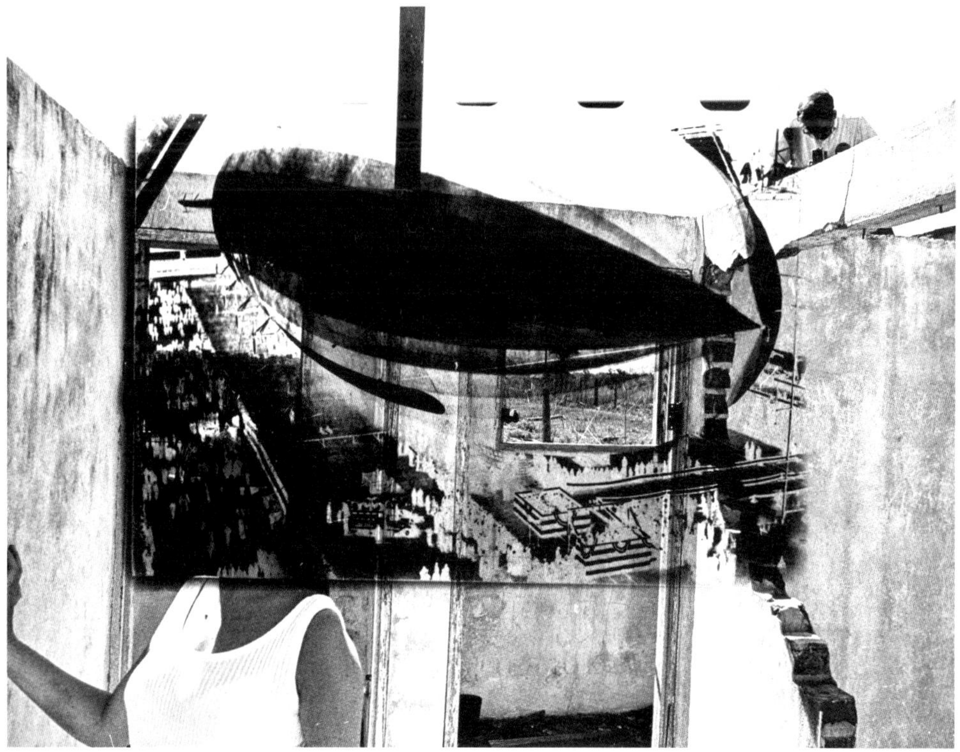

**FIGURE 1.2.** Robert Fichter (American, b. 1939), *Untitled*, 1967, gelatin silver print

lace trim—and signed the piece underneath.[7] Viewing this from a modern-day vantage, Nettles might seem to have been making a feminist statement, particularly with the addition of the slip, but this was not her intention. Instead, she wanted to draw connections between clothing and the landscape, as soft billowy folds of fabric become the foreground. The work is also filled with humor; in her view, the skirt—and more so the slip—changed how viewers interacted with the work.[8]

Nettles used these methods—sewing and hand-coloring in particular—to solve limitations that she faced in her photographic work. She drew on her grandmother's quilting methods, for example, to stitch together her toned photographs. While she also continued to combine images in the darkroom, this new technique of constructing images with machine stitching added physicality to her flat images, much as adding cloth to the surface of a painting had done in *The Skirted Garden*. Eventually she was able to procure photo linen, which allowed her to print directly on cloth. She then used a sewing machine to stitch added details, bestowing an extra dimensionality to her essentially two-dimensional works (for an example of this, see p. 69).

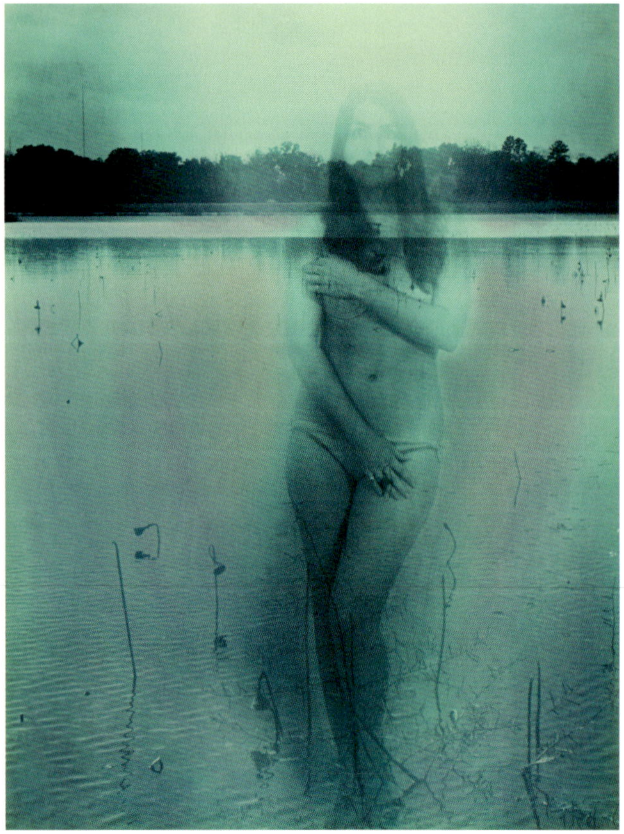

**FIGURE 1.3.** *Lake Lady*, February 1970, gelatin silver print with applied color

Her bank of images grew while her themes expanded during this period. She increasingly included self-portraits in her work; drew upon mythological figures, such as Eve; and created images that recalled Florida, home, and family. One work that combines all three of these subjects is *Lake Lady* (February 1970; fig. 1.3). Nettles portrays herself as Venus, who is born not of sea foam but from the algal bloom lapping at the lake's edge. Because Nettles created this image by printing two different negatives on the same piece of paper, Lake Lady both emerges from and blends into the lake, a symbol of home for Nettles, who grew up in the swamplands of northern Florida. Yet in her image, the goddess—one who is known to have great powers—emerges shyly from the landscape; she appears caught off-guard by our gaze, having not yet found her abilities to woo men and master her surroundings.

Nettles's bodies of work in all media began to merge into one artistic vision, and her thesis exhibition included a number of photographic works alongside her quilted paintings and etchings on fabric, as well as more sculptural furniture and mirror pieces. While Nettles had already been using her painting and drawing skills to add color and detail to her photographs, she also used her photographs in her printmaking (for an example of this, see p. 64). As audience participation became important in Nettles's graduate school work, she created mixed-media works with pieces of furniture (particularly cabinets and mirrors) serving as the basis for single works. Inspiration from Joseph Cornell's boxes (see fig. 1.4) can be seen in works such as *Swamp Box: Birth of Venus* (1969; p. 68, see detail in fig. 1.5), a glass-front cabinet that contains tiers (shelves) of landscapes made of cloth, prints, and photographs, along with sewn elements and a photographic self-portrait. Nettles portrays another Floridian Venus, born in a swamp of lily pads rather than sea foam, inhabiting a watery landscape alongside an alligator, and surrounded by palm trees. Traditionally Venus is depicted nude and sometimes demurely hiding herself in classical works, yet Nettles's Venus is fully clothed and confidently displays her sexuality.

Two of Nettles's works were included in Peter Bunnell's landmark exhibition *Photography into Sculpture*, which opened at MoMA on April 8, 1970, just before Nettles's thesis defense.[9] The exhibition, which later traveled to eight venues—including the University of Illinois's Krannert Art Museum in the fall of 1970, after Nettles's graduation—brought together photographs that had characteristics of sculptural practice and emphasized the materiality of the photographic object.[10] In the press release, Bunnell stated that the exhibition "embraces concerns beyond those of the traditional print, or what may be termed 'flat' work, and in so doing seeks to engender a heightened realization that art in photography has to do with interpretation and craftsmanship rather than mere record making."[11] For Nettles, who was making extremely personal work that was considered "bizarre and radical" by some members of her Champaign-Urbana community, this level of recognition led her to feel that she had made it as an artist.[12]

Just after graduation, Nettles returned to the Penland School of Crafts as a teacher and visiting artist.[13] While working there, she continued to print photographs on fabric and began what has become one of her most notable works, *Mountain Dream Tarot* (1975; p. 118). Inspired by the symbols found in Arthur Edward Waite's *Pictorial Key to the Tarot* and after visualizing the project in a dream, Nettles spent the next five years photographing her family and friends, including members of the Penland community, and assembling photomontages that display the symbolism of the tarot.[14] She also took a number of self-portraits in a star dress, images that recur periodically in her work (pp. 77, 79, and 88).

In August 1970 Nettles moved to Rochester, New York, to take a teaching position at Nazareth College. After spending her days teaching drawing, painting, design, and photography, Nettles would return home and try to find the energy to work on her personal pieces. Facing such time constraints, she made small photo-collages by sewing together layers of toned gelatin silver prints and transparencies. She created several books, each a three-ring binder with photo collage pages. *Neptune and Lake Lady . . . a series* (1970; pp. 70–75),

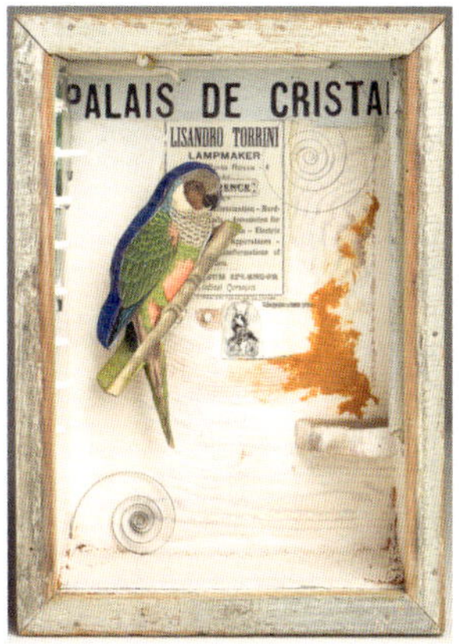


**FIGURE 1.4.** Joseph Cornell (American, 1903–1972), *Untitled (Palais de Cristal)*, ca. 1953, wood box construction: printed paper collage, glass, and metal

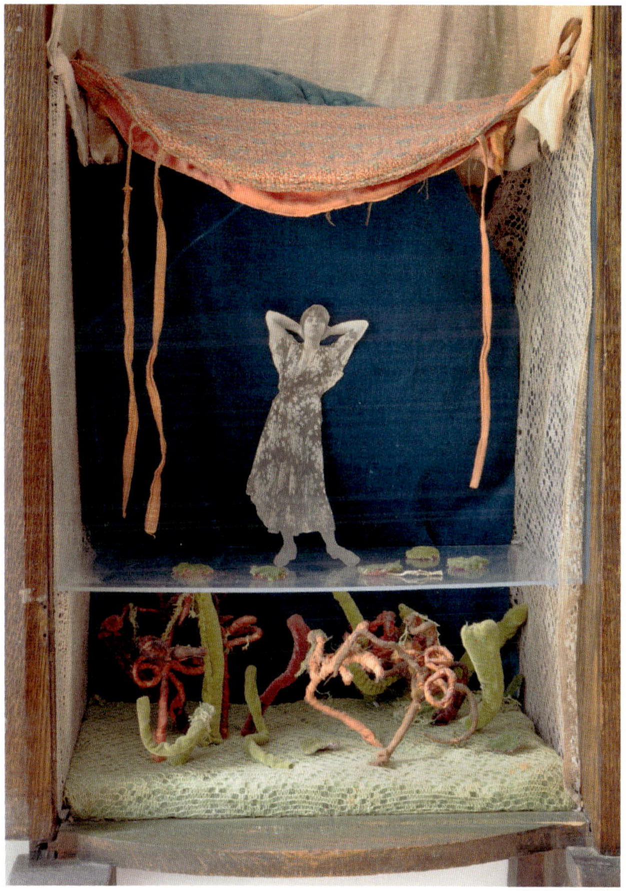

**FIGURE 1.5.** Detail of *Swamp Box: Birth of Venus*, 1969

one of her earliest book projects, contains dreamlike juxtapositions that draw on mythological themes. The imagery in this book recalls the story of any powerful relationship, but for Nettles, the book ultimately foretold the breakup of a relationship in which she was involved at the time. Nettles places herself into the narrative by using self-portraits that often gaze directly at the viewer, serving as a comment on the "male gaze."

While working at the Rochester Institute of Technology (RIT) during the 1971–1972 school year, Nettles created several works composed of toned photographs stitched into vinyl hearts filled with liquid colored to resemble Kool-Aid.[15] For Nettles, these ephemeral and fragile objects represented growing older and losing one's innocence, sometimes through references to the onset of menstruation and at other times by referring to romantic breakups. The hearts were, in many ways, meant to burst. An example of this came in 1972, after Nettles had moved to Philadelphia to teach at the Tyler School of Art. Two *Koolaid Heart* works were on display when someone could not resist pressing the frame, bursting the heart and causing the liquid to drip out onto the mat, wall, and floor. While many believed this action was intentionally planned, Nettles explained, "Hearts sometimes burst, but I hadn't expected it to happen there."[16]

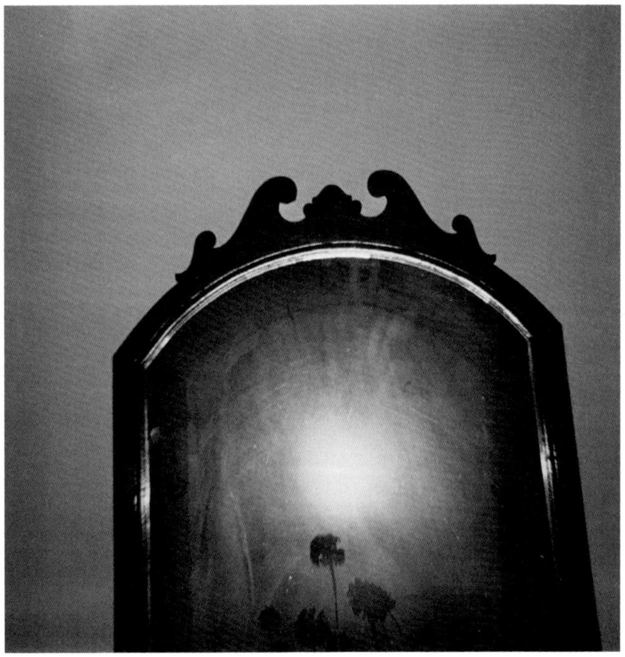

**FIGURE 1.6.** *Escape*, 1972, digital positive from original negative

This sense of chance occurrence entered into Nettles's work again in the summer of 1972, when her camera jammed and she turned to a 3M Revere Automatic 500 snapshot camera.[17] As Anne Tucker discusses in *The Woman's Eye*, "With her cheaper camera there was a certain lack of control—what was seen in the viewfinder and what was isolated through the lens was [*sic*] not exactly the same—which she liked."[18] While this initially simplified the process of taking pictures, Nettles carefully selected and sequenced the images into several series of gelatin silver prints. In her series *Escape*, Nettles explores her longing for home and her desire to escape the area of Philadelphia where she was then living.[19] This series also displays another important trope in Nettles's work: the inclusion of her previous works in later photographs. Her 1971 piece *Plastic Sky*, which consisted of ortho film transparencies and bird feathers sewn between sheets of vinyl, appears in two works from this sequence (pp. 90 and 91). This work and another, showing a mirror with palm trees screen-printed onto it (*Escape*, 1972; fig. 1.6), act as dreamlike escapes within Nettles's Philadelphia apartment in this body of work, embodying memories of home until reality transports her there later in the sequence.

Nettles originally assembled each sequence from this time period into three-ring binders or notebooks, but in 1973 she began to produce hand-assembled offset-lithographic books with screen-printed covers. The first two were based on photographic sequences made with her simple snapshot camera: *Events in the Water* (1973; p. 92) and *Events in the Sky* (1973; p. 96). The third, *The Imaginary Blowtorch* (1973; p. 104), combined self-portraits with images of family and incorporated periodic images on transparent pages, which allowed Nettles to actively recombine images as the reader interacted with the book.[20] *The Imaginary Blowtorch*, as well as her 1974 book *The Elsewhere Bird* (p. 106), extended her artistic practice of embracing the written word by including poems by her mother, Grace Nettles. By mass producing her books, Nettles hoped to reach a wider audience with her dreamlike yet squarely autobiographical work.[21] After returning to Rochester in 1974 to be with her husband, Lionel Suntop, Nettles continued to make offset books and printed her first card decks—*Mountain Dream Tarot* (1975) and *Swamp Lady* (1975)—which draw on mythological figures and create seemingly endless narratives when rearranged.

By the summer of 1975, Nettles had also returned to making photographic prints, employing processes that allowed her to work in her own backyard, without the need of a darkroom. Working again with layers of images, Nettles constructed cyanotype and Van Dyke prints that recalled her memories of living in Florida. In 1976 she began to teach again at RIT and received a grant from the New York State Council on the Arts that allowed her to explore a commercially available photographic medium called Kwik-Print.[22] A modification of the gum bichromate process, Kwik-Print allowed photographers to expose and manipulate multiple image layers and to select from a number of different pigments for each exposure. While Nettles used only the standard colors (cyan, magenta, and yellow), she mixed them like paint to formulate her own color palette for each work;[23] this permitted Nettles to expand her palette into bright pinks, yellows, blues, greens, and reds. Nettles also utilized the ability to apply and manipulate multiple layers of images on one sheet, building complex collage-like images. In a sense, Kwik-Print gave Nettles an extended color palette that otherwise could have been obtained only through hand-coloring paired with an ability to print a seamlessly constructed image. As Nettles became known for her work with alternative photographic processes, she regularly taught workshops about them and wrote the book *Breaking the Rules: A Photo Media Cookbook* (1977; reprinted in 1988 and 1999).

During these years, images of the moon began to enter her work. For Nettles, the moon became a symbol of fertility, for it traces a woman's menstrual cycle through its phases, waxing to full (prepuberty to maturity) and then waning (menstruation and menopause). This symbol can be prominently seen in her series *Flamingo in the Dark* (1976–1982). In 1978 Nettles gave birth to her daughter, Rachel. Now a mother, teacher, and artist, Nettles learned to balance her time and energies. By 1980, when her son, Gavin, was due, she began to realize that her methods for building layered images in the darkroom were impractical, since her time in the darkroom was often interrupted. She constructed a pinhole camera and used nearby objects and subjects—her daughter's toys, a backyard garden, dinner plates, snapshots, herself, and her children. The resulting body of work, *Close to Home* (1980–1982), comprises still lifes often seen from a child's vantage of the world. (These topics are explored further in Olivia Lahs-Gonzales's essay in this book, along with plates dated 1978 to 1983).

Nettles's husband, Lionel, was a founding member of Light Impressions, a firm based in Rochester, that became the main distributor of Kwik-Print materials shortly after Nettles began using the process.[24] In the summer of 1982, Nettles faced a dilemma when Lionel was "voted out" of the business. Nettles quickly felt that she could no longer use what had become her signature process.[25] Her first body of work after she quit using Kwik-Print was *Rachel's Holidays*. For this series, Nettles began to collaborate with her daughter to construct still lifes and plan images. She learned how to print using several different color photographic processes by taking a course offered by one of her colleagues at RIT and then printed the series using the labor-intensive dye imbibition process.[26] *Rachel's Holidays* (1984) was completed just before the family moved to Champaign-Urbana, where Nettles was to be the chair of the photography program at the University of Illinois. After her move, life circumstances prompted Nettles to once again shift her working practice, for she no longer had a darkroom equipped to make dye imbibition prints. She instead took advantage of access to an etching studio, producing a series of still lifes about the "fears and innocent delights" of her children.[27] The photographic base images incorporate her children's drawings and constructions, documenting their creations, which had become the landscape surrounding Nettles. Again, Nettles manipulated the narrative of her finished series, *Landscapes of Innocence* (1985), through careful sequencing, hand-working the printing plates, and using slightly tinted inks.

By the end of 1985, Nettles had moved to a house where she could build a darkroom. She began to use a 4 x 5 camera and started receiving film from the Polaroid Corporation in exchange for prints.[28] Once again, this support changed her working practice. Nettles found that the Type 55 film, which created both a small proof print and a negative, allowed her to be more agile in both the studio and the darkroom, for she could use the contact print to make adjustments to her still lifes and lighting while retaining good negatives at the end of each studio session. For her imagery, she continued to draw on narratives from her own life, creating her series *Life's Lessons* (1986). She first printed these works as photo-etchings, creating triptychs that explore luck, money, and the prevailing fear of lost or stolen children (pp. 180–185). After an invitation to use the 20 x 24 camera at Polaroid's studio in New York, Nettles was able to expand her photographic practice away from etchings and back to photographic images. Nettles envisioned a series of images of her and her children, as well as still lifes depicting such everyday subjects as bread, snapshots, and toys. In some cases, the images would have other information (conveyed by, say, a child's handwriting, hand-drawn map, or homework) overlaid on a portrait of Nettles or one of her children. Because it was not practical to take her children to New York with her, Nettles went to the Polaroid studio armed with props as well as finished 16 x 20–inch gelatin silver prints (mostly those that included portraits of her children), from which she made one-of-a-kind Polaroid prints. *Life's Lessons: A Mother's Journal* (1990) was printed as a self-published book, a format that Nettles began to use more frequently beginning in 1988 with her work *Corners*. By this era, Nettles was adept at laying out her books digitally to produce the exact layout she envisioned.

As Nettles's daughter neared puberty, Nettles returned to the subject of the moon and menstrual cycles. Her work *Faces/Phases* (1989; fig. 1.7) confronts this subject head on. Accompanied by a small brochure titled *The Moon Sisters* (1990), *Faces/Phases* depicts her daughter, Nettles herself, and Nettles's mother, each of whom was the appropriate age to represent the three parts of a woman's menstrual life: menarche (the onset of menstruation), menstruation, and menopause. In 1991 Nettles followed this work with her card deck *28 Days* (p. 196), which illustrates a typical

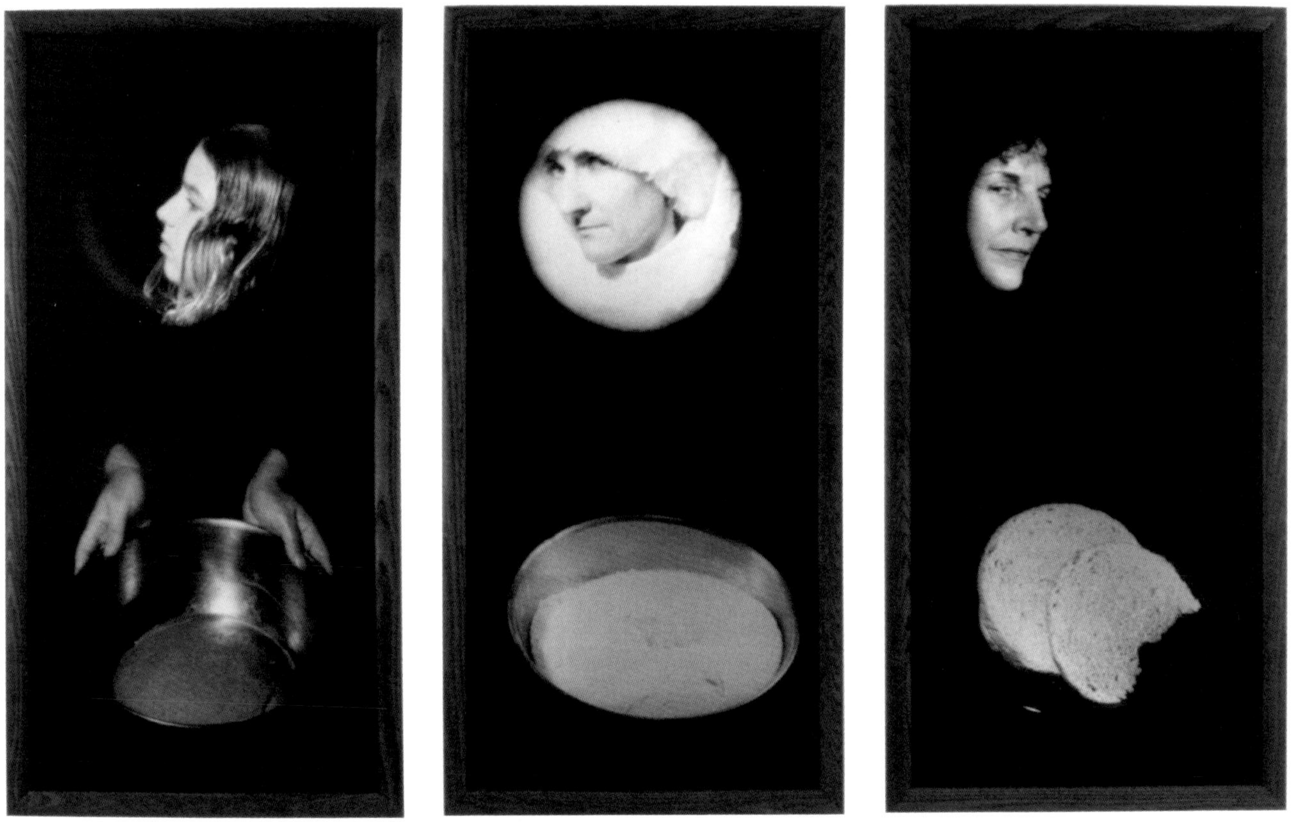

**FIGURE 1.7.** *Faces/Phases*, 1989, gelatin silver prints

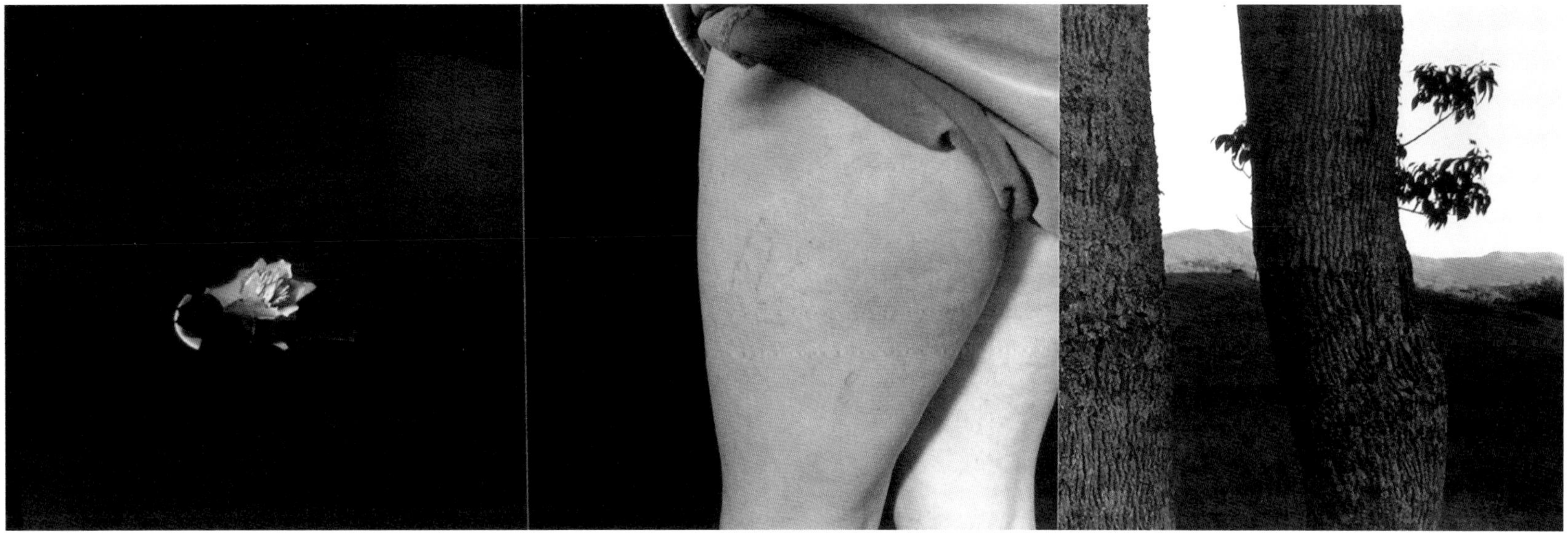

**FIGURE 1.8.** *Tulip Poplar*, 1995, gelatin silver prints

twenty-eight-day menstrual cycle through stark and sometimes humorous images. As her children grew, Nettles's struggles with balancing her roles of mother, teacher, and artist culminated in her book *Complexities* (1992), which is discussed in Olivia Lahs-Gonzales's essay in this book.

After completing *Complexities*, Nettles experienced what she terms a "dry spell."[29] She began stringing together images in her sketchbook. Inspired by the realization that she would soon be turning fifty years old, Nettles set about arranging the groupings into her past, present, and future. This quickly became her book *Turning 50* (1995), which was followed by an exhibition of these works as prints in 1996, when she turned fifty.[30] In these groupings, she experimented with the way signifiers in each photograph modify others in the grouping. In *Tulip Poplar* (1995; fig. 1.8), Nettles groups a flower, her bare legs, and the trunk of a tree at Penland. The combination of the softness of the petal and the sturdiness of the tree trunks plays on the image of Nettles's legs; they are at once grounded and revealing themselves to the viewer. In the book, the accompanying text discusses how being at Penland earlier in the year had changed her experience of the place: "The dogwood and tulip poplar were blooming. For more than twenty summers I had passed these modest trees unaware of their true identities." In the photograph, the experience of the place also affects her understanding of herself.

In her series *Return Trips* (1999–2008), Nettles constructs composite images to evoke memories of particular places, tracing her life's journeys as she physically and mentally returns to them. In this series, the triptych arrangement of images along the top draws on religious paintings that Nettles viewed while in Italy. The often existential imagery echoes her reflections on her own life as she travels, as well as her struggle to find meaning in the simplicity of daily existence. Even though she was now working in an era when photographs may easily be manipulated with tools such as Photoshop, Nettles grouped her unmanipulated images to convey a sense of time, space, and memory through her composite imagery.

While making her series *Return Trips* (as well as several artist's books), Nettles faced what might best be termed the roller coaster of life. She had moments of great joy: she visited Europe with her sister Elizabeth and again with her daughter, she celebrated her mother's eightieth birthday, and Rachel and Gavin accompanied her to Penland. She also bore great hardships: she was forced to step down as chair of the photography department at the University of Illinois, she was diagnosed with cancer, and both her parents passed away. These personal experiences surface in her work from this time. We see the delight of riding in a gondola (fig. 1.9), her aging father (p. 211), and her hairless head following chemotherapy and radiation (p. 222). Yet Nettles continued to draw on her vast archive of images to create new works, such as *Mermaid* (1999; fig. 1.10), which uses *Head Crowned* (November 1969; p. 65), or *Light House* (2001; p. 217), which incorporates a plate from *Events in the Water* (1972; p. 94). Ultimately, Nettles's work continues to consider what constitutes family and home over the course of a lifetime, relaying universal themes through personal memories.

Her life events in the 1990s and 2000s also prompted Nettles to return to producing handmade books. In 1999 she began to develop course descriptions for book arts classes, and in 2002 she attended her first meeting of the Paper and Book Intensive, a yearly two-week meet-up where book and paper artists can learn new skills from one another. Her works

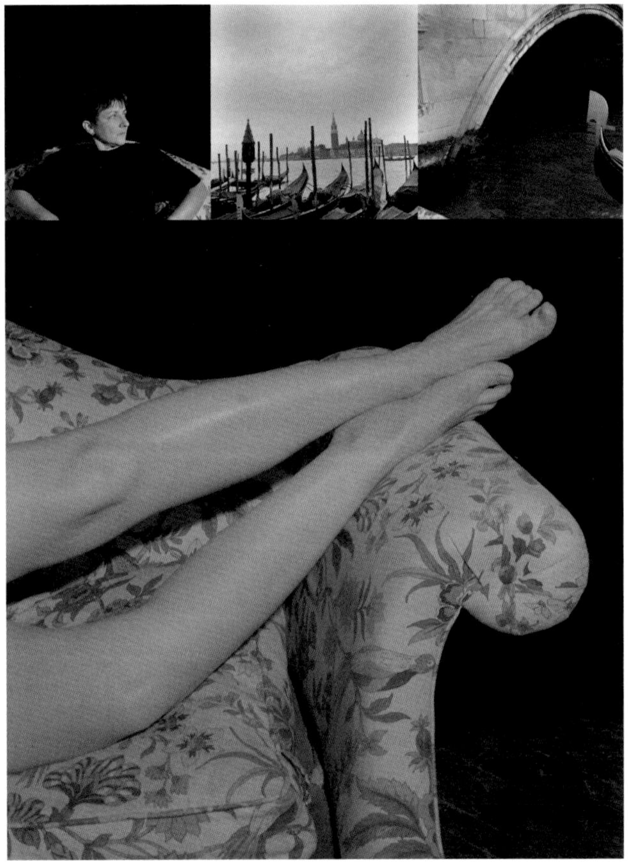

**FIGURE 1.9.** *Gondola*, 1999, from *Return Trips*, gelatin silver print

ranged from simple progressions of her aging self, as in *The Observer* (2005; p. 224), to investigations of Norse mythology told through colorful images, handmade papers, and carefully worded poems, as in *Mind & Memory* (2007; p. 228).

In 2010 Nettles began photographing surnames she found on tombstones, assembling a vast collection of names that work also as ordinary words. She uses this collection to write stories and poems that are printed as books; she also creates card decks with them. Nettles sets her own constraints for each project, always limiting herself to proper grammar and spelling but sometimes adding other rules. For instance, in her work *Hawk/Dove* (2013; p. 244), each name is drawn from the tombstone of an American veteran. Her book works explore the intersection of history and language through universal themes such as seasonal changes, war and peace, and the cardinal directions, while her card decks highlight funny and often poignant observations about the English language, as in the cases of surnames doubling as occupations; antonyms; homonyms; or famous pairings, such as Fred and Ginger (which evokes Fred Astaire and Ginger Rogers) or salt and pepper. In these works, Nettles points to the power of photographic images as symbols, metaphors, and signifiers that photographers can use to speak about the world around them. In her earlier works, visual symbols/images/pictures served as these signifiers, but during this later period, Nettles reduced her photographic images to a small set of linguistic symbols—literally words—which she uses to construct narratives that demonstrate the nuances and absurdities of the English language.

On the slipcover to her 2016 work *Dante Enters Hell* (p. 250), Nettles writes that it is a "'plot' summary" of Dante's *Inferno*.[31] While other works, such as *The Nymph of the Highlands* and *Mind & Memory*, bring together images and text to convey stories from varying cultures and points in time, *Dante Enters Hell* relies solely on language as a visual cue. Here Nettles's drastically simplified version of Dante's tale is made with a limited vocabulary but remains stunningly graphic, with the words bringing about visual images specific to each reader's own pictorial language.

In contrast, works such as *Edge of Summer Lake* (2015; p. 248) nearly omit words altogether. With the exception of the title, the book is a purely visual work.[32] Not unlike

Nettles's painted and photographic landscapes, the book envelops the reader in color and texture, acting as a window into Nettles's memory of a specific place. In many ways, this book functions in counterpoint to *Dante Enters Hell*, as the readers' minds are left to create free associations with their own memories of places and times. These ideas may be in the form of visual or verbal signifiers (pictures or words), sounds, smells, or feelings (both emotional and physical). While one reader may perceive a sense of calm, others may feel a sense of panic or dread as they experience the deserted and quiet landscape.

With patience and persistence, Nettles has produced a body of work showing the cohesive vision of an artist interpreting the worlds that she inhabits and transforming them into works of art. Whether the piece is a narrative book, a poem, or a visual work, Nettles allows her viewers to enter her private world. Her themes are those of an ordinary woman struggling to find a balance between self/work and family/life. This woman travels the path of every woman, emerging as a confident girl and slowly progressing to become a wiser woman who both relishes her journey and questions the lessons she has learned along the way. Through her work, Nettles has recorded herself as a mythological character—inspired by the eons of women who have come before her—to blaze her own path through an ever-changing garden. While her path is one that steadily unfurls in new and unimaginable ways, she creates an opening for future generations of women, mothers, poets, and makers to overcome their constraints and transform their own dreams into realities.

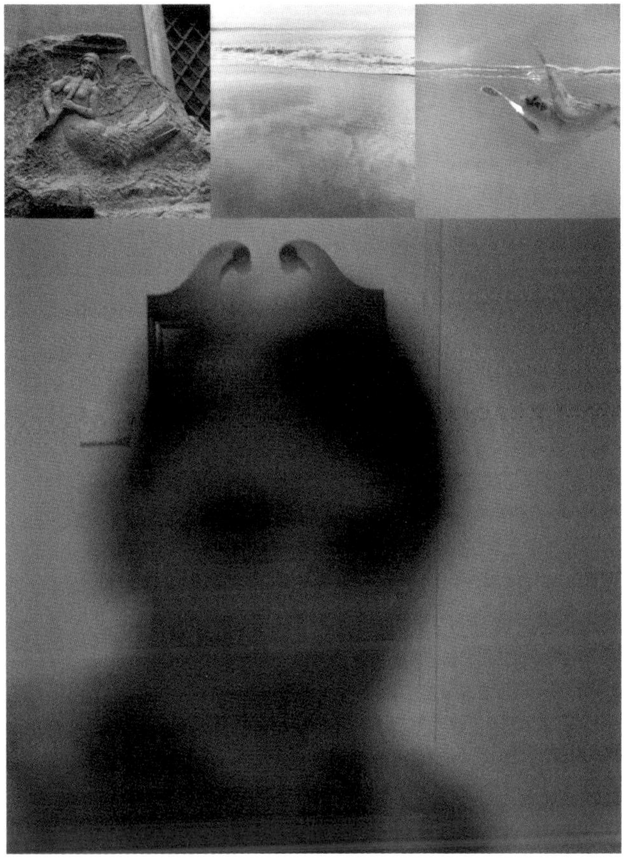

**FIGURE 1.10.** *Mermaid*, 1999, from *Return Trips*, inkjet print

## Notes

1. For a period of time beginning in 1972, Nettles used a 3M Revere Automatic 500 that she had received as a gift. A simple box camera, it was designed to be an easy-to-use snapshot camera using 126 cartridge roll film. Nettles liked that the device left plenty of room for chance in the resulting images; it had a range finder, so the actual frame of the image differed slightly from what the photographer saw through the viewfinder when she released the shutter. In addition, the camera's uncoated plastic lens, nonadjustable shutter speed, fixed aperture, and optional flash cube lent the images it produced an informal innocence that Nettles embraced.
2. Nettles in a discussion with the author on August 16, 2018, at Nettles's home in Urbana, Illinois.
3. Bea Nettles, "Introduction," *The Skirted Garden: Forty-Five Years of Images* ([Urbana, IL]: self-published, 2015; distribution, Morrisville, NC: Lulu).
4. See Nettles's text in her book *Family Remembrances: 50 Years of Florida Family Portraits* ([Urbana, IL]: self-published, 2006).
5. This would have been in the fall of 1967.
6. Nettles took a lithography course during the summer of 1967, and returned after graduation in 1968 to take a photography course taught by Robert Fichter. Nettles, *Skirted Garden*, 2.
7. Nettles, *Skirted Garden*, 1; author's conversations with the artist.
8. Author's conversations with the artist.
9. Mary Statzer, "Bea Nettles," in *The Photographic Object 1970* (Oakland: University of California Press, 2016), 174.
10. Mary Statzer, "Conversation with the Curator, Peter Bunnell," in *The Photographic Object 1970*, 21; and Museum of Modern Art, press release for *Photography into Sculpture*, April 8, 1970.
11. MoMA, press release for *Photography into Sculpture*, April 8, 1970, 1.
12. Statzer, "Bea Nettles," 172.
13. Nettles has continued her involvement with Penland throughout her career, teaching photographic and book arts there.
14. For more on this work, please read Nettles's "Mountain Dream Tarot" in this volume, p. 117.
15. The "Kool-Aid" in these cases was simply water dyed to resemble the drink.
16. Nettles, *Skirted Garden*, 12.
17. For more on this, see Nettles, "Fall 1972," *The Skirted Garden*, 13–14; and Anne Tucker, "Bea Nettles," in *The Woman's Eye*, ed. Anne Tucker (New York: Knopf, 1973), 155. See note 1 for information on the 3M Revere Automatic 500 camera.
18. Tucker, "Bea Nettles," 155.
19. This series is discussed in-depth and reproduced in Tucker, "Bea Nettles," 155–169.
20. The foundations of this, as well as the use of cutaways, can be seen in Nettles's earlier three-ring binder books, such as *Bruises and Other Collections*, located in the collection of the Center for Creative Photography, Tucson, Arizona, and partially reproduced in illustrations accompanying Amy Powell's essay in this book.
21. Nettles, *Skirted Garden*, 15; each of these books was produced in an edition of 100, with the exception of *The Elsewhere Bird*, of which 120 copies were made. Her husband was president of Light Impressions, a distributor based in Rochester, New York, that carried Nettles's books in its catalog, helping her reach a wider audience.
22. Nettles discusses this product in her book *The Skirted Garden*, explaining how she encouraged Direct Reproductions Corporation of Brooklyn, New York (the manufacturer), to test their Kwik-Proof product for permanency; after the product was improved, it was renamed "Kwik-Print." According to a Light Impressions brochure, "Kwik-Print was developed in the 1940s as a material for graphic artists to make color proofs from color separation negatives" (*Kwik-Print: A Unique Printmaking Process for Sophisticated Color* [Rochester, NY: Light Impressions, ca. 1983]). Nearly all sources compare Kwik-Print, a proprietary product, to the gum bichromate (aka

gum dichromate) process, where the paper is coated with pigmented gum arabic that has been made light-sensitive with chromium salts; when exposed to light, the coating hardens yet remains water-soluble in unexposed areas. Unlike that process, however, Kwik-Print involved printing on specially formulated vinyl sheets, which helped to eliminate the staining, shrinkage of the substrate material, and thus registration issues commonly noted by gum bichromate printers who tried to print full-color images onto one sheet. The product could be used on sized artist papers, but Nettles has noted that she never printed any of her own finished works that way, preferring the ease of the vinyl sheets. While the product offered the standard cyan (medium blue), magenta, and yellow (lemon yellow) color palette used for full-color printing, a wide variety of other colors were also available.

**23.** Author's conversation with the artist in September 2018.

**24.** Light Impressions was established in 1969. It became the exclusive distributor for Kwik-Print products in 1977 according to Sylvie Pénichon's *Twentieth-Century Color Photographs: Identification and Care* (Los Angeles: Getty Conservation Institute, 2013), 109.

**25.** Nettles, *Skirted Garden*, 28.

**26.** Nettles, *Skirted Garden*, 29.

**27.** Nettles, *Skirted Garden*, 31.

**28.** Nettles, *Skirted Garden*, 33.

**29.** Author's conversation with the artist in August 2018.

**30.** This exhibition was held at I-space Gallery in Chicago, Illinois, in the fall of 1996, and closed on November 11 of that year.

**31.** Here, as in many of these works, her words purposefully become puns as she points to the plots where the names were photographed as well as the outcome of her work. Bea Nettles, *Dante Enters Hell* (Urbana, IL: self-published, 2016), back cover.

**32.** Here the title acts as the title of an artwork displayed on a label next to a piece in a museum rather than a narrative in a book, so one could say the book is devoid of text.

# BEA NETTLES
## ARTIST/MOTHER

Olivia Lahs-Gonzales

*Though it is truly gratifying to witness the beginnings of a recognition of the experiences of women, the experience of women as mothers remains largely unheard and unseen in any public forum. Mothers may talk among themselves whenever possible, but the content of these conversations is not of value in the larger society. We generally see and hear of mothers as either idealized or derogatory stereotypes, with little evidence of the complexity and potency of the experience from a mother's point of view. How is it that such a large and important group of people, whose concerns are fundamental to the survival of the species, can be culturally invisible?*[1]

—**SANDRA MATTHEWS,** INTRODUCTION TO *BEA NETTLES, LIFE'S LESSONS: A MOTHER'S JOURNAL* (1990)

Women artists have had to overcome much to fulfill their ambitions to be recognized artists, and they still struggle to be acknowledged at the same level as their male counterparts. At the same time, motherhood has never been conducive to the pursuit of artistic expression, in part because making art has been neither a socially acceptable profession nor always a safe practice. Indeed, it is often seen as an impractical and selfish pursuit. Though the rise of feminism has made it more acceptable for women in some professions to have both meaningful relationships with their children and careers, the realities of life as an artist—particularly an economically successful one—present numerous pitfalls. These include having to move the family across the country for a teaching job every few years or even simply managing time in the studio between school and day-care pickups, 1950s-era summer camp schedules, and breakfast meetings scheduled before a school's official drop-off time. Then there is the question of museum real estate, which has favored large-scale paintings and monumental sculptures (most often made by men) whose subjects are abstract, emotionally detached, and hardly ever about family, women's issues, or parenting (unless the subject celebrates the idealized myth of the mother as Madonna). In the established institutions of the art world, subjects related to motherhood are often considered too "sentimental" or "emotional."[2] Throughout her career, Bea Nettles faced such criticisms, beginning in her early days as a student and continuing in later years, as is revealed in several reviews of her work that faulted it for being "too personal."[3] The women who have made art about what it is to be a woman or a mother are often left out of the history; when they are recognized at all, their works are more often found in specialized thematic publications or in segregated "Women's Art" museums.

Much of Bea Nettles's works from the late 1960s and 1970s centered on self-investigation and celebrated her body's power and fecundity. Walled gardens and cabinets figured frequently during this period and were a reference to wombs, privacy, and the internal.[4] In particular, *Swamp Box: Birth of Venus* (1969; p. 68) is a womblike work that employs an antique wooden cabinet into which Nettles has placed images of a Florida landscape and a self-portrait as Venus, goddess of fertility, beauty, and victory. Other early works that deal with the physicality of fertility are her *Koolaid Heart* works (1972) and *The Nymph of the Highlands* (1974). The *Koolaid Heart* works, about "losing one's Koolaid innocence" and beginning menstruation,[5] each consist of a heart-shaped sewn vinyl pocket filled with water in the acid-bright colors of the popular drink over a portrait of the artist or one of her sisters, Elizabeth and Connie (see pp. 84–85). *The Nymph of the Highlands* (p. 110), one of Nettles's early illustrated books, is a creation myth written by her sister Connie—a story that would foreshadow later works by Nettles that deal with birth and creation.

Though her body as an element of nature and symbol of power was an already visible theme in her works from the 1960s, after her marriage to Lionel Suntop in 1974, self-portraits with moon imagery and other statements that reference birth and cycles of life came to play a more prominent role. Powerful self-portraits that incorporate moon imagery reflect Nettles's awareness of her body as a powerful vessel for giving life. In these layered Kwik-Print compositions, such as *Florida Moonrise* (1977), *Tropical Moonrise* (1977), and *Moon and Dish* (1977; p. 140), she associates the monthly cycle of the moon with a woman's menstrual cycle, linking the rhythm of her body with the orbit of our closest natural satellite. Nettles wrote, "I've always been attracted to the moon and the imagery associated with it. I continue to discover additional meaning in these images. The full moon for me symbolized fertility, the monthly cycles of the moon echoing the monthly menstrual cycle. Self-portraits as a full moon were made prior to my first pregnancy when I felt fertile and in my prime."[6] These photographs presaged her coming pregnancy, but she acknowledges that they were not made overtly to address a desire to have children. She would revisit these themes again in the late 1980s, when she used the imagery to speak about the cycle of womanhood.

When Nettles became pregnant, she created several self-portraits that revealed her changing body. She viewed this period as a time of mixed emotions—of trepidation, awe, and wonder—and was fascinated that her body "knew what to do."[7] These images would not become fully formed works until a year after the birth of her daughter, Rachel. In *Gifts* (1979; p. 143), she juxtaposes her nude body with a photograph of herself as a child at Christmas holding a watch. Nettles remembers: "The unfocused portrait of myself pregnant reminded me of an earlier snapshot taken on a Christmas morning. In the snapshot, I was shyly and proudly displaying the grown-up watch that I had been given. As a pregnant woman, I felt somewhat the same mixture of

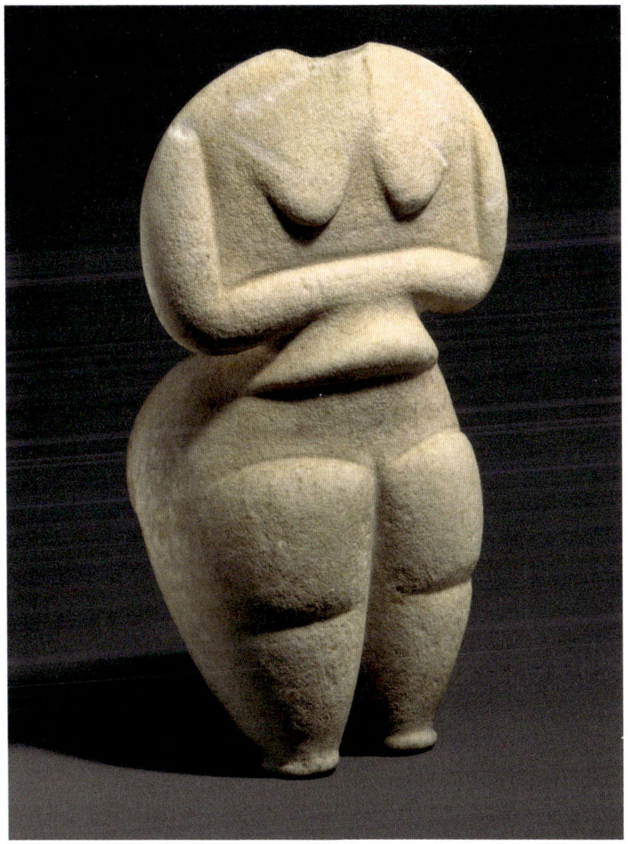

**FIGURE 2.1.** Statuette of a woman, steatopygous, ca. 4500–4000 B.C., marble, Final Neolithic, Cycladic (Metropolitan Museum of Art, New York, bequest of Walter C. Baker, 1971)

emotion having been given a gift and giving one at the same time."[8] In this construction, Nettles filled the frame with a photograph of her pregnant form that she purposefully blurred to evoke an iconic symbol rather than a documented reality. The resulting image recalls ancient fertility figures (fig. 2.1). "Women are truly heroic. Our bodies are capable of performing the miraculous, giving birth, and then producing milk. These emotions and realizations began to surface in my work," Nettles would recall.[9] Other works in the series, such as *Reflection Pool II* (1979; p. 149), *Three Bluebirds* (1978) and *Sea Oats* (1979), similarly treat the body as an element of power, linking it to nature and the landscape.

**FIGURE 2.2.** *Star Collage*, 1979, from *Flamingo in the Dark*, gum bichromate print with applied color

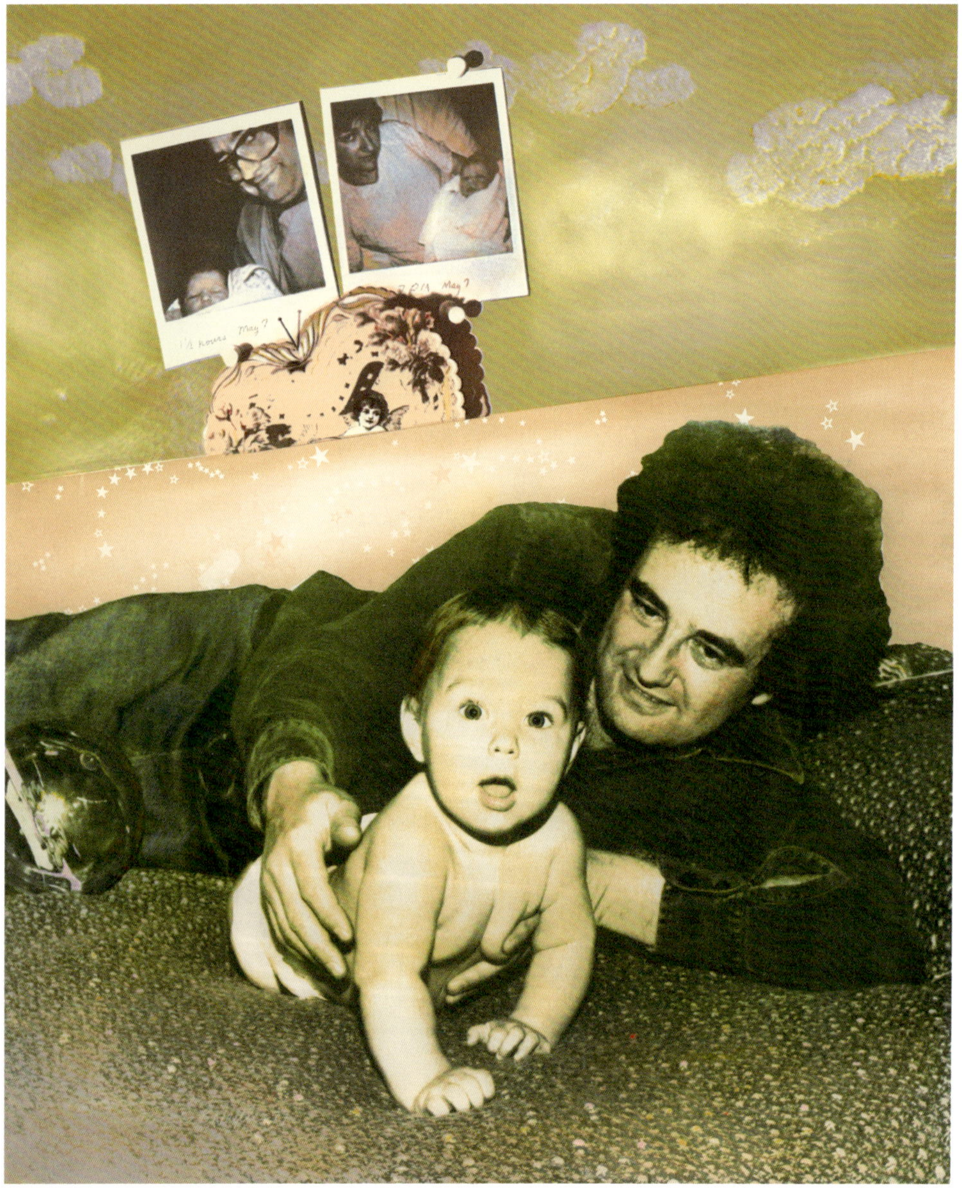

In the year after she gave birth, Nettles almost immediately returned to teaching at the Rochester Institute of Technology (RIT), but with a reduced class load. She would bring Rachel to work and employed a sitter while she taught classes and worked in the studio. In subsequent years, she arranged for day care but spent much of her time traveling back and forth from the classroom to the day-care center so she could spend time with her daughter.

Before Rachel's birth and during her infancy, Nettles began work on the autobiographical series *Flamingo in the Dark*, a fantastical journey through landscapes populated by old family photographs. A section of the series deals with her pregnant body, the birth of her first child, and the joys and anxieties of motherhood. Her husband, Lionel, also appears in several images. *Second Week* (1978; p. 147) and *Star Collage* (1979; fig. 2.2) show him to be a devoted father, cradling and interacting with his new daughter.

Nature and the landscape are recurring threads throughout Nettles's career. In *Seventh Month* (1978; p. 146), Nettles overlays her pregnant figure with an image of hills used in another work, *Flyin Princess* (1978; p. 266), and texture created by superimposing an image of a chenille bedspread.[10] The Kwik-Print process and ortho film negatives allowed for seamless image juxtapositions long before Photoshop was invented. In *Seventh Month*, Nettles *becomes* the landscape—a "mother earth" figure whose baby bump echoes the undulating hills in the distance. Several other compositions from the same period also place her new baby in the landscape. The ease with which multiple images could be layered and superimposed with the Kwik-Print process allowed Nettles to create imaginative metaphoric works in which her baby seems immersed in the lush landscape. *R and Delphiniums* (1978; fig. 2.3) is one such image; here, baby Rachel seems almost engulfed by the vegetation that surrounds her.

*Rachel in the pines* (1978; p. 145) places more emphasis on the figure of the baby, who is centered in the frame. She seems to be part of the landscape that is her mother's body. Nettles, subsumed and attenuated, becomes a backdrop of hills and valleys or perhaps a throne on which the child rests. This photograph brings to mind "hidden mother" photographs, a practical nineteenth-century studio practice where a baby is placed in the mother's lap and the mother is covered with a cloth to act as an anonymous support and backdrop (fig. 2.4).[11] In Nettles's photograph, the baby, though now outside the womb, is still cradled and protected by her mother's figure. She uses the same negative of pine trees again in *Young B in Pines* (1979; p. 150), creating a link between her own childhood self and her daughter and thus bridging generational experiences.

Nettles, through the Kwik-Print process, transforms photographs like ones most of us know and have in our own albums into rich cinematic moments to which we can relate on a more universal level. *Rachel and the Bananaquit* (1979; fig. 2.5), a jubilant composition that was used on the poster and book cover for the 1987 Aperture exhibition *Mothers and Daughters: That Special Quality*, uses a photograph taken by her husband, Lionel, on a vacation in the Virgin Islands. As she does in *Rachel in the pines*, baby Rachel throws up her hand in a gesture of happiness and triumph. A kind of emblem for the joys of motherhood, this image celebrates a special moment of freedom from the cares and pressures of the world. Estelle Jussim, in her essay in *Mothers and Daughters*, elaborates: "Here is the mother-daughter combination before the pressures of growing up intervene, before competition emerges, before sexuality threatens, before illness or separation or divorce or social disaster can overpower this captivating *joie de vivre*."[12]

By 1980 Nettles was teaching full-time and felt overwhelmed by the detritus that constitutes motherhood—the clutter of toys and clothes—and the lack of time for sustained concentration.[13] In 1981 she gave birth to her son, Gavin, so that she was now navigating life and artistic labor with two small children. At this time, Nettles discontinued the elaborate multiple negative process she had used in previous series and instead resurrected a large-scale, 16 x 20 pinhole camera that she had made in 1977, which she redesigned with help from a colleague so that it would be easier to manage.[14] A sabbatical that year enabled her to pursue a new project aptly titled *Close to Home*. In this body of work,

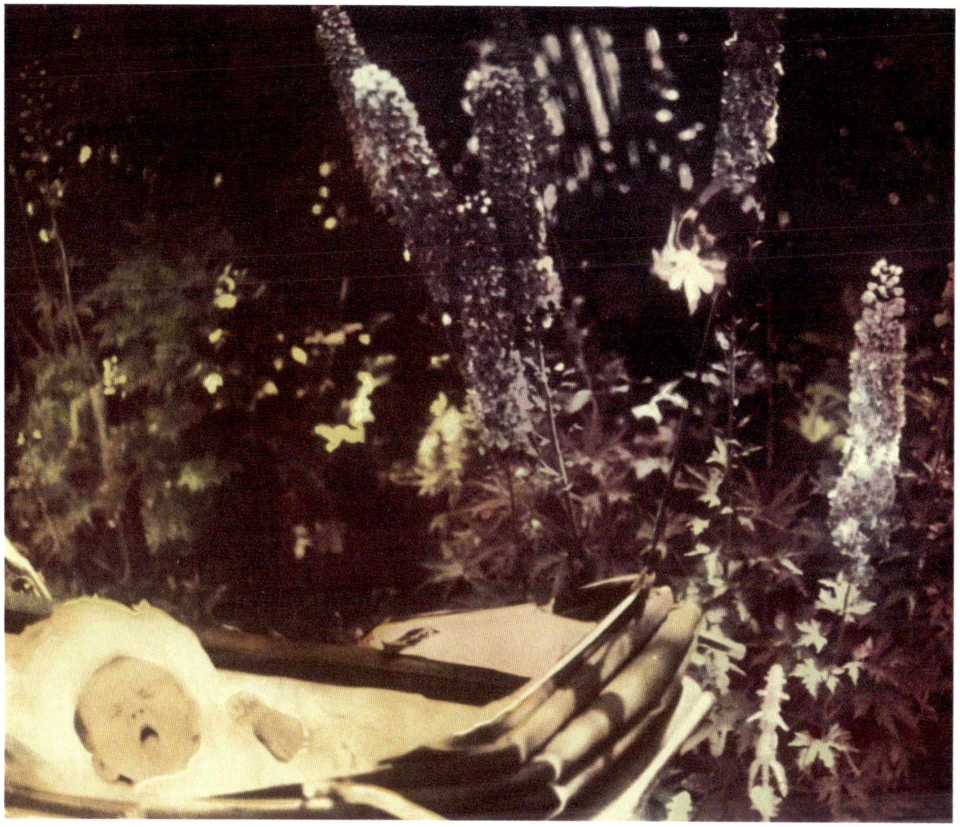

**FIGURE 2.3.** *R and Delphiniums*, 1978, from *Flamingo in the Dark*, gum bichromate print with applied color

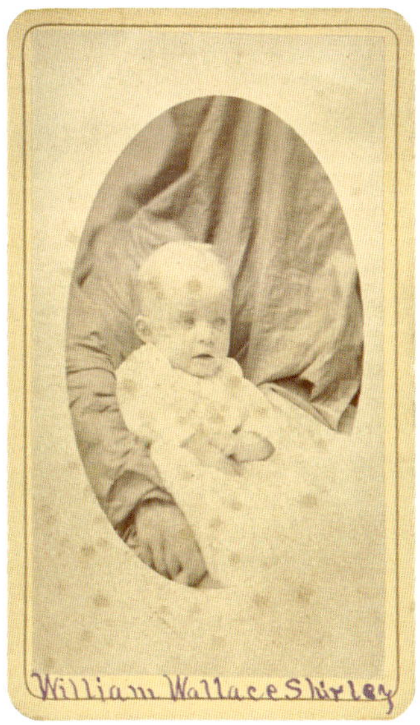


**FIGURE 2.4.** John E. James (American, d. 1881), *William Wallace Shirley*, ca. 1865, albumen silver print

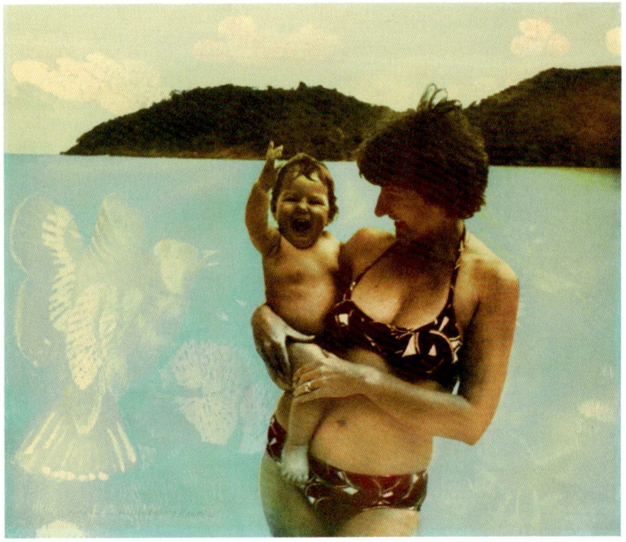

**FIGURE 2.5.** *Rachel and the Bananaquit*, 1979, from *Flamingo in the Dark*, gum bichromate print with applied color

she expanded on ideas that she had introduced in earlier works, such as *Bathroom Corner* (1978; fig. 2.6) and *Crib View* (1978; fig. 2.7), both from *Flamingo in the Dark*. *Bathroom Corner*, a tableau that records a conference of toys in her bathroom, and *Crib View*, which she photographed from a child's point of view, both presage the tableaux that she would erect and photograph, sometimes with the help of her daughter, in *Close to Home* (1980–1982), in selected color works from 1983, and in *Rachel's Holidays* (1984). She found this method of working more compatible with life with small children because the works she made were constructed and captured in a single negative.

In these years, Nettles hired a sitter so she could work in the darkroom or made prints while her children were napping. In addition to creating an easier workflow, the technique used for the photographs in *Close to Home* allowed Nettles to escape from the daily rigors of motherhood: she solved the problem of the overwhelming clutter that comes with having children by making the trappings central to her creative process.

In these works, she also found excitement in the optical possibilities of the pinhole camera. Because they have an unlimited depth of field, these cameras can create visual situations that are not possible with a lens-based camera. Small items in the foreground can be made to appear like giants, creating new, fantastical worlds from the ordinary. The images she created by this method also helped her to more fully immerse herself in, and understand, her child's experience of the world. "The images looked the way that I imagined a child might see the world full of looming objects," Nettles explained.[15]

Some of the subjects of this series also address the anxieties faced by both child and mother. Several illustrate her daughter's wishes, nightmares, and fears; one such work is

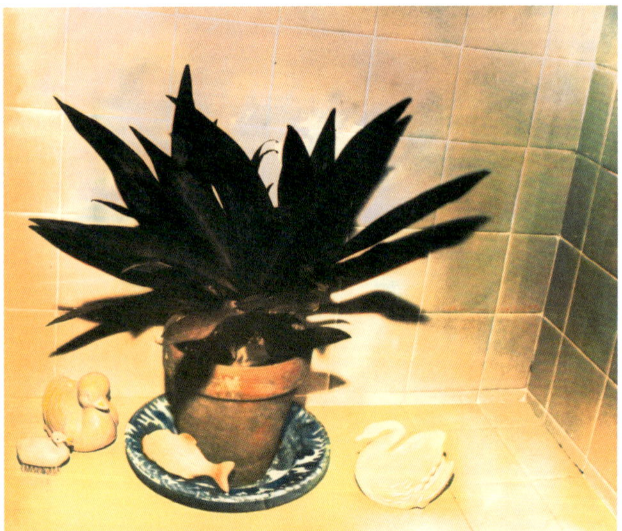

**FIGURE 2.6.** *Bathroom Corner*, December 1978, from *Flamingo in the Dark*, gum bichromate print with applied color

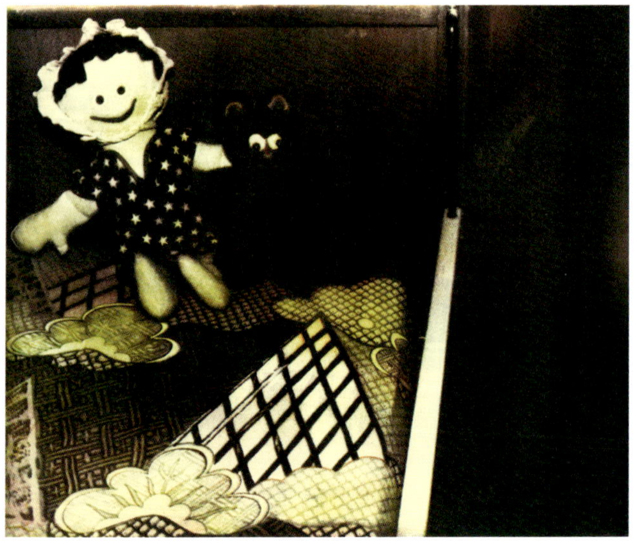

**FIGURE 2.7.** *Crib View*, 1978, from *Flamingo in the Dark*, gum bichromate print with applied color

*Pack Up Your Troubles* (1981; p. 156, an allusion to the World War I song), which speaks to her daughter's occasional frustration with having a little brother. In this work, she imagines her daughter wanting to pack up and send off her little brother in a suitcase with some clothing and an alien squishy toy that caused her distress. Other works in the series, including *Snake through the Window Dream* (1982; fig. 2.8) and *Bad Laughing Frog* (1982; fig. 2.9), illustrate her daughter's nightmares. Both of these images are dark works that speak not only of a child's anxieties but also to a mother's fear of losing her child.

Nettles further examines these feelings in works that reference some of the more disturbing of the classic nursery rhymes, which she applies to her own life. In her version of the "Humpty Dumpty" rhyme (*Humpty Dumpty*, 1982; p. 158), Nettles uses the story to articulate her own feelings of exhaustion, noting that the mother on the package of baby formula she used as a prop in the image looked unrealistically well put-together. "The mother pictured holds a contented baby, has her hair brushed, wears a fresh nightgown . . . a fantasy image. I was often disheveled, stressed, and sometimes so exhausted that I wished I could be like Humpty Dumpty and just jump out of the second-floor bedroom window and call it quits."[16] Nettles is expressing the often unspoken feeling of many a mother who tries to maintain selfhood while balancing the rigors of work and caring for a family.

By the summer of 1983, Rachel was old enough to collaborate with her mother, and they began creating diorama photographs with toys and other objects that were cherished by both. The series, which would become *Rachel's Holidays*, was printed by Nettles with the complicated dye imbibition process that she had learned in a workshop at RIT.

Portraits of Rachel actively engaging in the scene also make up several images in the series. In *Hands and Shells* (1984; fig. 2.10), her daughter's arms in the act of creation become part of the final composition, revealing her role as collaborator. By using blur and often placing her daughter at the edge of the picture plane, Nettles emphasizes her daughter's active presence both in her life and in the art-making process. The blurring also serves as a metaphor for something that virtually all parents know—that these childhood

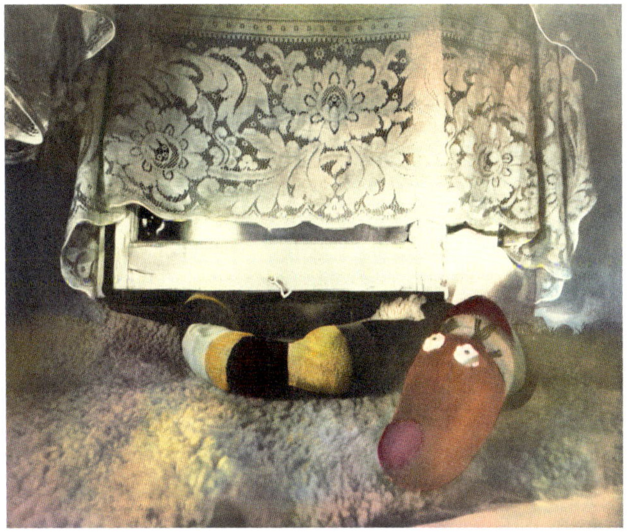

**FIGURE 2.8.** *Snake through the Window Dream*, 1982, from *Close to Home*, gum bichromate print with applied color

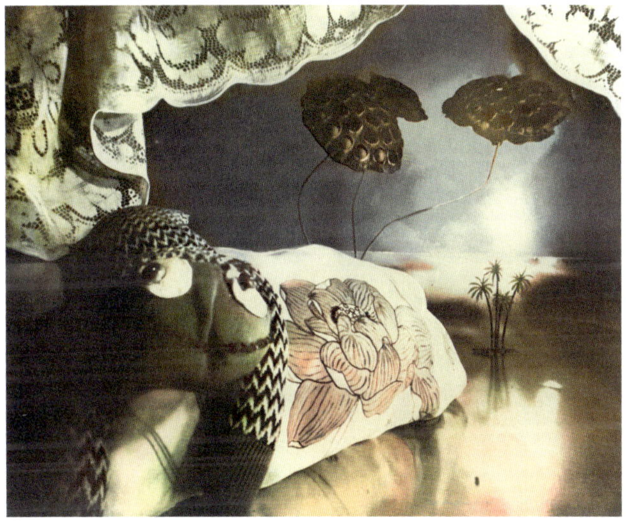

**FIGURE 2.9.** *Bad Laughing Frog*, 1982, from *Close to Home*, gum bichromate print with applied color

FIGURE 2.10. *Hands and Shells*, 1984, from *Rachel's Holidays*, dye imbibition print

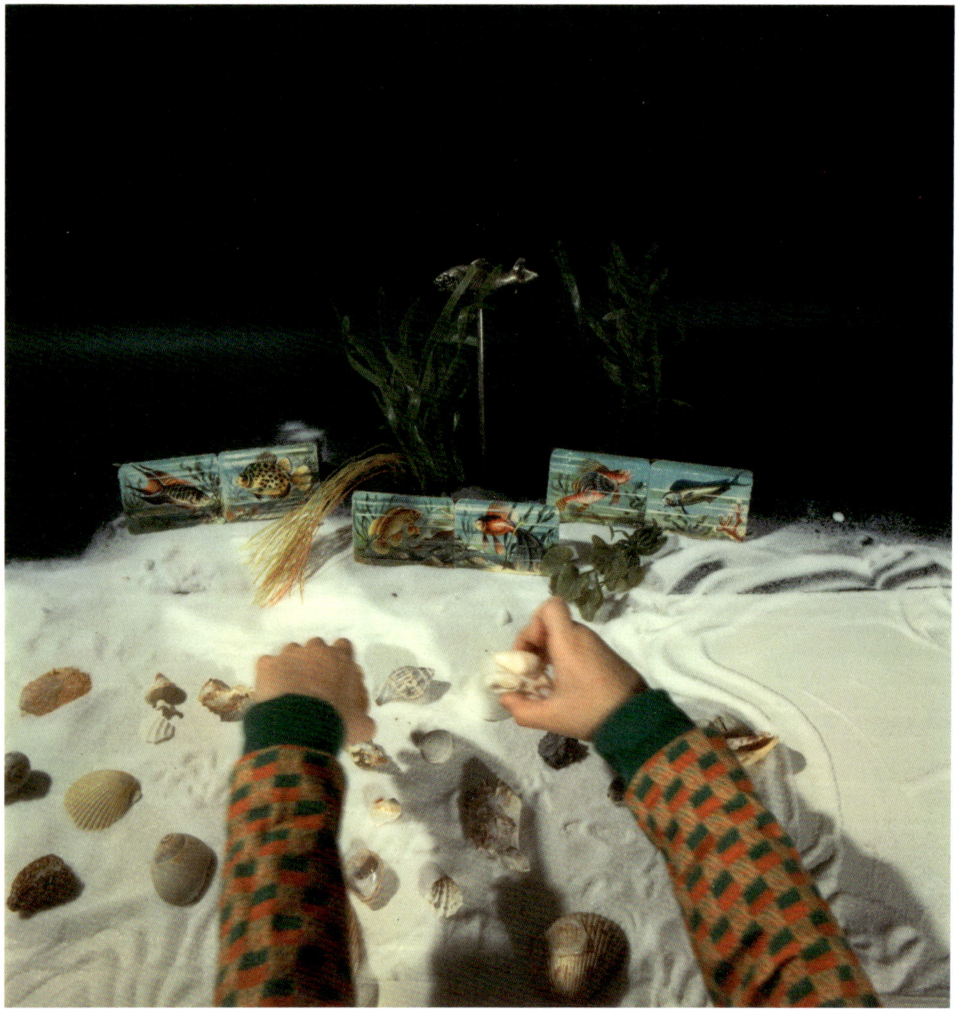

moments are fleeting and precious. Particularly compelling in the series is *String of Hearts* (1984; p. 169), an image of Rachel wearing a red nightgown with a lace collar that was a gift from her grandmother. She holds to her chest a string of hearts that a friend has made for her. The image preserves memories of both a beloved grandparent and a friend.

Her son, who was only three during the making of *Rachel's Holidays*, is not often pictured. Nettles cites a practical reason: "Gavin wiggles," she would recollect. "He's hard to photograph in a tight setting—and being more boisterous, he knocks over the lights."[17] Nettles made a number of photographs outside the *Rachel's Holidays* series that kept to the proscenium theme, expanding on the collaborative image-making process with her daughter and including images of her son with a black eye he had received in day care.[18]

Several photographs in *Rachel's Holidays*, such as *Fish on Shore* (1984; fig. 2.11), depict beach scenes that her daughter constructed with shells and other items found on the sand during their vacation to Sanibel Island. Nettles has often utilized objects made by her children in her constructed images. These objects evoke memories that serve to record her own life and childhood but that attain a broader significance as emblems for more universal states of longing, loss, and active preservation. Parents will be familiar with the kinds of objects found in Nettles's mise-en-scènes. These are the stuff of rainy day, nursery school, and art-room projects that loving parents keep on display for a time to show support for their children's artistic endeavors. In *Rachel's Holidays*, such objects populate and bring to life imagined territories and wishful dreams while simultaneously preserving memories that would otherwise seep and fade.

The only self-portrait in *Rachel's Holidays* is one of Nettles sleeping among some of the props seen in other images. Her daughter had expressed interest in being the photographer, and her mother allowed her to press the cable release. This image (*Bea Sleeping*, 1984; p. 167) places Nettles in a fanciful scenario where she is relieved of her normal sleep-deprived state. The family cat also makes an appearance in several of the photographs, illuminating the sometimes chaotic state of family life when it intersects with making art.

From a practical standpoint, engaging her daughter in her creative process also allowed Nettles the freedom to pursue her work unencumbered in the darkroom. "Rachel was willing to let me print all day Saturday because she knew I'd bring the proof sheets back and share them with her. Her involvement made her more understanding and positive about her mother's taking time to work," Nettles remembers.[19] Unlike other photographers who have made their children the subjects of their photographs, Nettles has collaborated with her children, employing the products of her children's assertions of their own selves in the world (their artistic output) to convey something about their personalities while also sharing her feelings about her own life and motherhood. In this way, she molded her subject matter to successfully negotiate the challenges of simultaneously being a mother and an artist.

When Nettles moved her family from Rochester to Champaign-Urbana in 1984, she no longer had access to a facility where she could print using the dye imbibition process. Instead, she availed herself of the University of Illinois's printmaking studio and in 1985 produced a series of photo-etchings titled *Landscapes of Innocence*. These prints were pulled from etched copper plates that produced an effect similar to that of an aquatint; they were etched by a local company, G. R. Grubb Engraving. Nettles printed the plates in inks that yielded black-and-white images tinted in a range of shades of black, some with pink or greenish casts. She found photo-etching to be a satisfying method for expanding her investigations of "the fears and innocent delights" of her children (now four and seven), as well as her own fears for her children's safety and the safety of all children during a time of social uncertainty.[20] She writes: "These photographs dealt with their concerns at that young age by recording their artifacts, drawings, sculptures, and collections. My concerns as a parent and my anxieties for the future of all children determined the form these images took."[21] The mid-1980s—the Reagan and Thatcher years—were a time of missile tests, domestic and international terrorism, AIDS, wars, and famines. *Rocket*, *Snowmen*, and *Valley of the Shadow* speak to fears about the possibilities of apocalyptic world events, while *Coffee Cup*, *Paperbirds*, and *Headband* document Nettles's life with her children and illustrate their imaginary worlds. Nettles continued her practice of constructing mise-en-scène photographs using artworks and other objects that her children had made, involving them in the process, thereby providing them with a voice in their own representation.

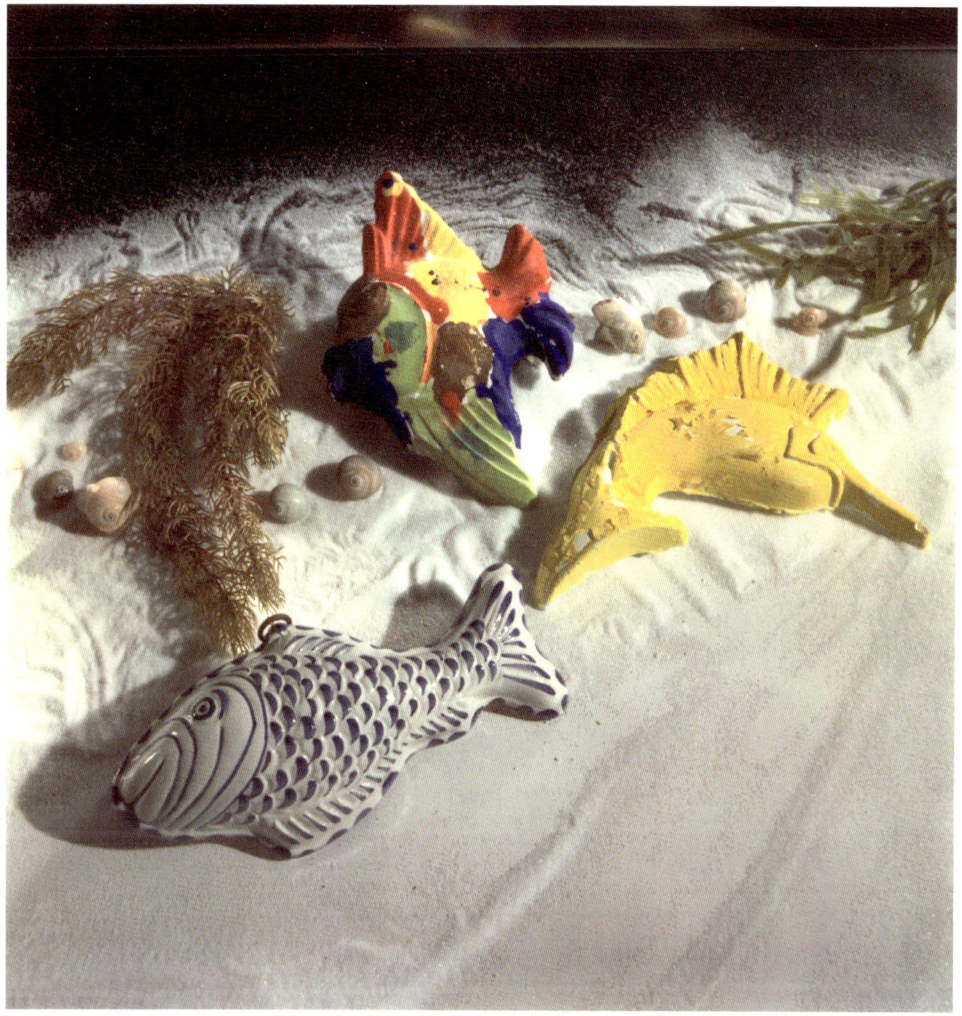

**FIGURE 2.11.** *Fish on Shore*, 1984, from *Rachel's Holidays*, dye imbibition print

*Coffee Cup* (1985; p. 172), like *Bea Sleeping* from the series *Rachel's Holidays*, illustrates Nettles's wish for a break from the chaos of family life. During this time, Nettles saw having a cup of coffee as one of life's great luxuries. The cup in the photograph also contains a spoon that was a meaningful object—it was both a gift she gave to her daughter and a reminder of the spoons her mother used to stir her coffee, thus representing a generational gesture of tribute and remembrance. The domestic scene became a common thread in much of her work during these years, and Nettles incorporated artifacts made by her children as well as family heirlooms and beloved household objects. With the artifacts that her children created, she found a way to make images that articulate ideas revolving around the fear of loss and innocence and the preservation of memory.

An amalgam of the dreams and fears of both the mother and her children is seen in the work *Valley of the Shadow* (1985; p. 177), which depicts a desert landscape strewn with the bodies of cicadas, whose sound was a constant source of fear for her son. Rachel contributed several pieces to this composition, including a felt snake and drawings of a mountain landscape and girl on a bicycle.[22] Nettles positioned the small drawing of the girl so that she seems to be making her way bravely through the foreboding landscape, which is scattered with the bodies of dead cicadas. Throughout her work during this period, we find positive images of her daughter imbued with strength and power.

Though they seem to be an innocent gathering of ceramic figures made and positioned by her daughter—perhaps celebrating winter solstice or another winter holiday—for Nettles, the figures in *Snowmen* (1985; p. 178) also hint at dark subjects, such as the aftereffects of a nuclear blast or the Holocaust. Similarly, *Rocket* (1985; p. 178) can be read as a reference either to space travel or to the hardware of war. In these photographs, Nettles deliberately leaves the subjects open to interpretation. Further, the reductive quality of the tinted black-and-white imagery lends itself well to expressing these fantastical stories, dreams, and fears.

In 1985 Nettles expanded *Landscapes of Innocence*, creating larger prints and triptychs that would become *Life's Lessons* when the Polaroid Corporation provided her with Type 55 film for a 4 x 5 camera that she had begun to use. In these works, she focused on particular parental anxieties, including the fear of losing her children. The triptych form enabled Nettles to enrich her narratives by juxtaposing several images in a kind of filmstrip. In *Hansel and Gretel* (1986; p. 180), she references the terrifying folktale, popularized by the Brothers Grimm, about two children abandoned to their fate by their father and stepmother in dark and treacherous woods, and she uses imagery from the "missing children" milk-carton campaign, which was at its height in the mid to late 1980s, to articulate these very real fears of so many mothers: "Hansel and Gretel terrified me when I was a kid. It scared me to think that a mother could dump her kids in the woods . . . on purpose! Will my daughter and son know not to take candy . . . not to trust the grown-up (Witch)? Forced to use their own wits and good sense, will they escape unharmed?"[23]

*Missing* (1986; p. 182) juxtaposes three photographic etchings: the left side consists of a composition with her son's fingerprint card and a paper chain of children holding hands; the center displays a scene including paper silhouettes of two children, a cereal bowl, glass of milk, and a "missing-child" milk carton in the background; and the image on the right depicts four "missing campaign" milk cartons, with one in a blur being taken away. As Nettles recalls,

> It is a longstanding kindergarten tradition for
> children to make their handprints for their
> moms. What's different now is that they're
> also being fingerprinted by the police.
> Fear of getting stolen is pervasive and very real,
> troubling discussion for the breakfast table.
>
> When the milk carton girl was "Found," Rachel
> was delighted and wanted to know all the
> details of her homecoming. I've quit buying
> milk in those cartons. The endless stream of
> boy-girl-boy-girl was just too much.[24]

In total, she would complete four triptych etchings, the others articulating questions about the best way to speak to her children about money and the concept of luck.

During two invited trips to the Polaroid studios in New York City in 1987 and 1988, Nettles expanded the project, creating a series of metaphoric mise-en-scènes and portraits. Because she was unable to take her children along, she traveled with preprinted photographs of them, over which she had superimposed handwritten texts and drawings made by her children. Out of these visits came such memorable works as *Feminine/Masculine*, *Gavin with the World*, and *Spider Catches Flies*.

The *Life's Lessons* series continues ideas first seen in *Rachel's Holidays* and *Landscapes of Innocence*, which deal with motherhood and the condition of domesticity. In her new work, however, Nettles dispensed with the painterly effects that the color Kwik-Print and photo-etching processes afford. Instead, she rendered stark, realistic images produced by the straight, black-and-white Polaroid photographic process. These images are still tableaux layered with text, but they are rendered in sharp detail, with no hint of romanticism or nostalgia. Dark in its underlying messages, the series lays bare the raw emotions of this mother, who was faced with the "real fears of harm to [her] children at the hands of strangers, concerns for their health (drugs, pollution, AIDS), and the everpresent [*sic*] fear of nuclear destruction."[25] She elucidates:

> This journal begins in my home,
> with images of food and bread.
> As dark thoughts enter my mind like a serpent, I
> think about Rachel and an entry in her school book,
> "I have many friends, but I have no _____."
> She first entered "fun," then changed her answer.
> How sad to feel that you have no fun when you're
> only eight!
> I thought only grownups felt that way.[26]

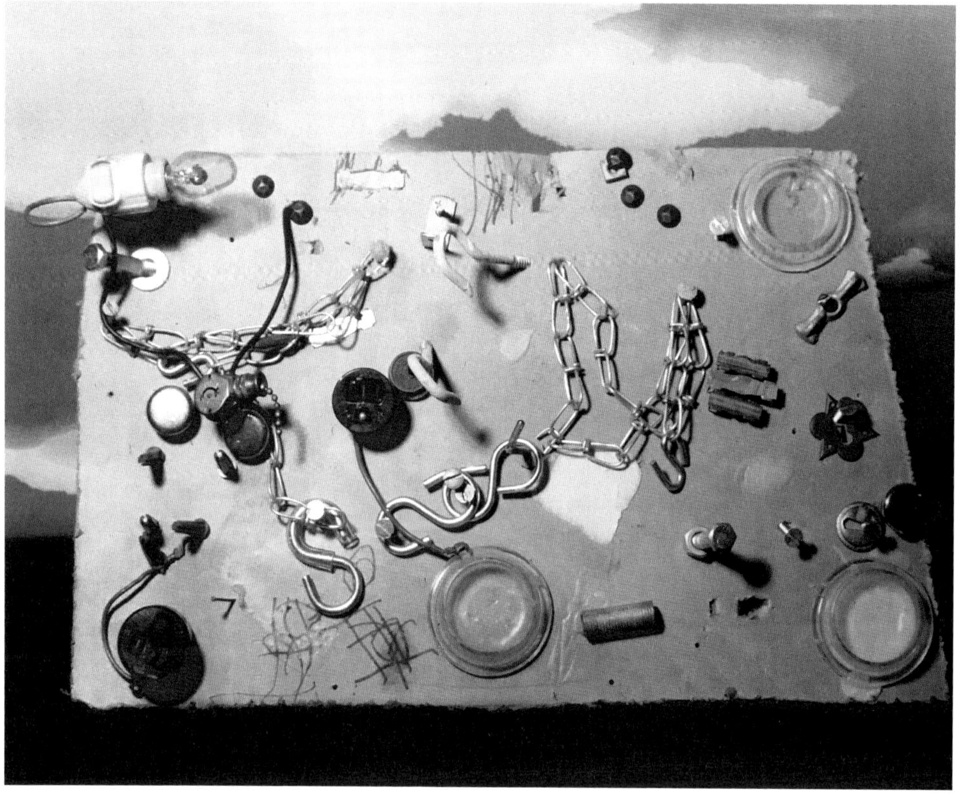

**FIGURE 2.12.** *Gavin's Installation*, May 1986, from *Life's Lessons*, gelatin silver print

This is a mother coming to terms with her children's loss of innocence and their growing awareness of the disappointments and inequalities of life. *Gavin with the World* (1987; p. 189), which shows the face of a slightly unhappy young boy on whose chest is superimposed a hand-drawn world map, is a metaphor for this experience: the weight of the world is etched prematurely on his camouflage sweatshirt.

As Rachel and Gavin grew up and developed their own likes and dislikes, Nettles saw them exposed to and taking on some of the stereotyped gender roles she had sought to avoid. In reaction, Nettles made several works that interrogate stereotyped attributes. In *Feminine/Masculine* (1987; p. 191), Nettles laid an image of her daughter's school assignment about gendered words over her portrait. In some cases, the terms of gendered binaries (feminine/masculine, prince/princess, queen/king, wife/husband, godmother/godfather, heroine/son-in-law) are juxtaposed, interspersed with a few terms that oppose socially established gender roles: "male"

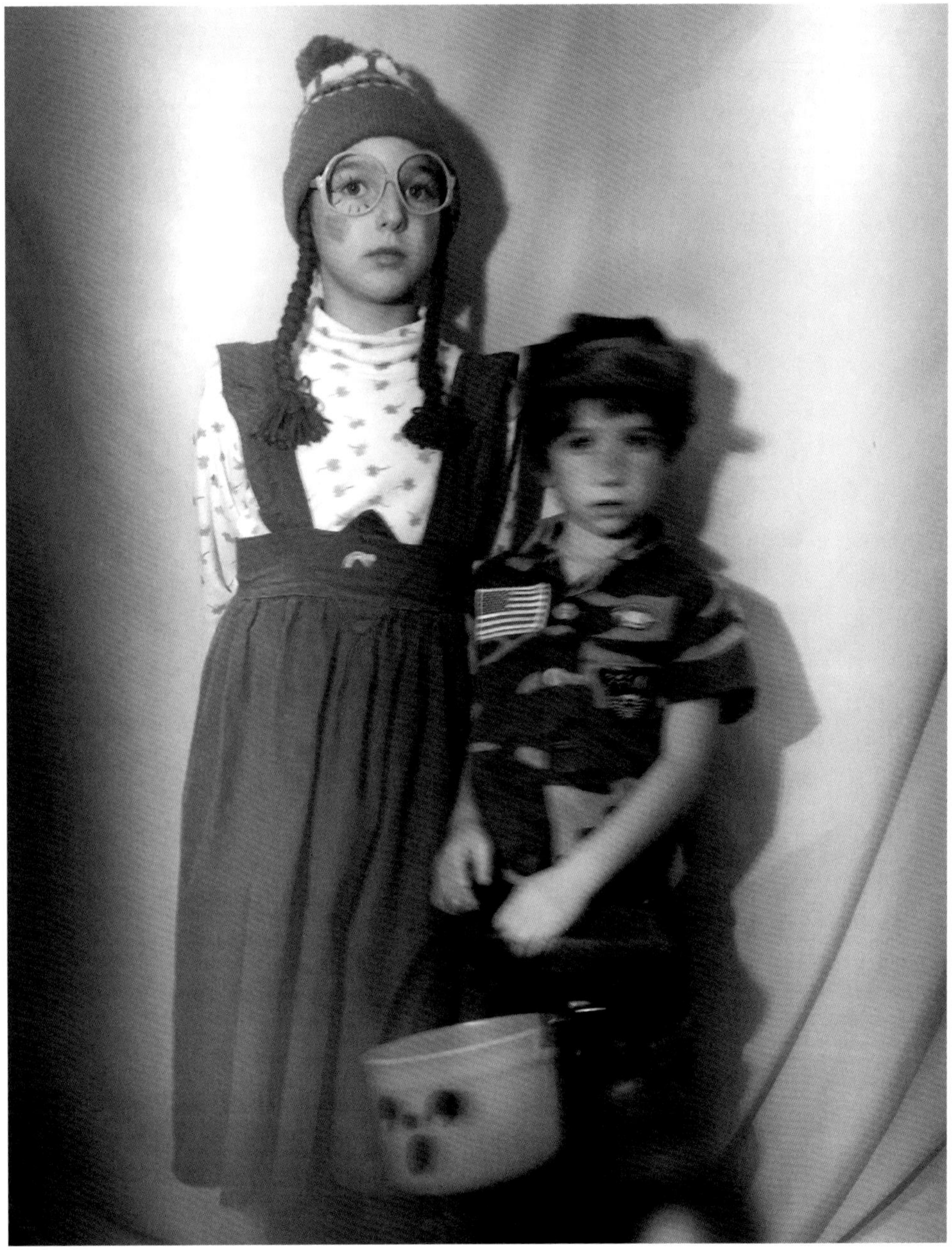

**FIGURE 2.13.** *Trick or Treat*, October 1986, from *Life's Lessons*, gelatin silver print

on the feminine side is coupled with "father" on the masculine side, and "mother" on the feminine side appears across from "female" on the masculine side. Such transgressive associations perhaps indicate only a youthful mistake, but Nettles, in her use of the lesson, creates a powerful statement about gender identification and expectations. The photographs *Gavin's Installation* (1986; fig. 2.12) and *Rachel's Installation* (1987; p. 190) show the gender-specific interests of both children. Gavin's tableau is a collection of chains, bolts, and drawn marks arranged in a kind of Cy-Twombly-meets-Jean-Tinguely composition. Rachel's arrangement, though populated with dolls, shows them with their backs turned to the camera, some lying prone, and all showing their diapers. In this work, Nettles revisits the critique of stereotyped gender roles that she touched on in photographs, circa 1971–1972, where she paired family photos of herself and her brother holding their "feminine" and "masculine" gifts. In *Trick or Treat* (1986; fig. 2.13), we see how these roles still manifest themselves despite illuminated parenting. As Nettles remarks in the text of *Life's Lessons*, it is difficult to get away from these social pressures. "We often talk about the power of advertisement on TV and in stores. The media overpowers our talk," Nettles writes.[27]

Self-portraits make a powerful return in this series, as seen in *Spider Catches Flies*, *Rapunzel Triptych*, and *I Love You*, among others. Self-examination and the self-portrait were always important threads in Nettles's works, but for many years she more often investigated the trappings of motherhood that surrounded and sometimes even buried her. In *Life's Lessons*, self-portraits again become an important part of her work, revealing how she sometimes perceived her role as a mother. *Spider Catches Flies* (1987; p. 187), placed toward the front of the book, is steeped in multiple meanings. On one level, it alludes to the stereotyped patriarchal, Freudian roles imposed on women, who, if not pictured as a Virgin Mary figure, are instead represented as a spider-like hunting female who lures her prey into a trap to be eaten. Nettles articulates another view, however, writing alongside the image:

> The natural laws, such as survival of the fittest,
> are sometimes hard to accept. . . .

> cruel and fascinating lessons. But Nature's way is certainly preferable to the dangerous imbalance caused by humans. We're on the verge of breaking the fragile cycle and I fear for my children's future.[28]

In this context, Nettles the mother can also be regarded as a powerful gatekeeper—the guardian of her children's safety—ready to dispatch anyone who endangers them.

Other challenges that Nettles considers in the book are the effects of rampant consumerism and her own changing body as she ages to become the "witch" rather than the beautiful Rapunzel, a character she had admired in a childhood fairy tale. As she writes in the book:

> The old woman in the story of Rapunzel keeps the young one locked up . . . away from the world and young men. I remember the story well from my childhood. It was probably one of the reasons I grew my hair and wore it long until I turned twenty-one.
>
> The story impressed Rachel as well. She copied it word for word out of one of her books. She made a paper Rapunzel who had a yarn braid, which she used to dangle out of a tower window for the Prince to ascend.
>
> No longer the young Rapunzel,
> I often feel like the witch.[29]

Within this bleak view of the state of the world, the book still closes on a positive note with Nettles's own love, hope, and strength acting as the gifts she gives her children to battle the threats of the world. In the last images, we see the artist/mother first with her hand to her heart, while beside her head lies a small child's chalkboard tablet on which is written "I love you." The penultimate image in the book presents a close-up of her body, obscured in part by a needlepoint made by her daughter, on which appears the word "hope." Nettles would write in closing,

> The strength and sense of honesty that I have came from my parents. Expressing my most urgent concerns through my work helps me to cope with the demands placed upon me. It is my hope that my strength will pass on to my children, helping them to learn life's lessons and survive unbroken and able to contribute something positive to the world.[30]

*Life's Lessons* was in effect a primer for, and love note to, her children and a therapeutic way for her to address the fears and anxieties of motherhood.

In 1992, Nettles published *Complexities*, a diaristic book of black-and-white images and text that speak about the intricacies of being an artist, a mother, and an educator and navigating the societal expectations of women with children. Her introduction to the book was taken from "The Juggling Act," a paper she presented at the Society for Photographic Education conference in March of that year: "All mothers are 'working mothers.' I belong to the majority of American women who also happen to work outside of their homes. For twenty-two years I have been an artist and college professor. What I do involves balancing priorities and making compromise."[31] She went on to speak of her feelings of guilt in taking time with her art and revealed the decisions she made in the public representation of her children. The photographs illustrating the texts combine layered metaphoric works, juxtaposing images of domestic objects and domestic work, such as making bread or washing dishes, with self-portraits (fig. 2.14) and photographs of her husband and children. An image of a hand holding a shell ends the book. Nettles writes, with a list of nouns in an undulating curve across the page,

> And so I reweigh priorities, balance, juggle, think of several spheres (literally) at the same time:
> self
> responsibilities
> exhibitions
> parents
> housework
> happiness
> food
> house
> husband
> garden

love
health
clothing
images
obligations
children
students

> Never in the same order, they are constantly shifting. Winding tight like a top or gyroscope. Spiraling out during growth like a shell.[32]

FIGURE 2.14.
*Juggling*, October 1991, from *Complexities*, gelatin silver print

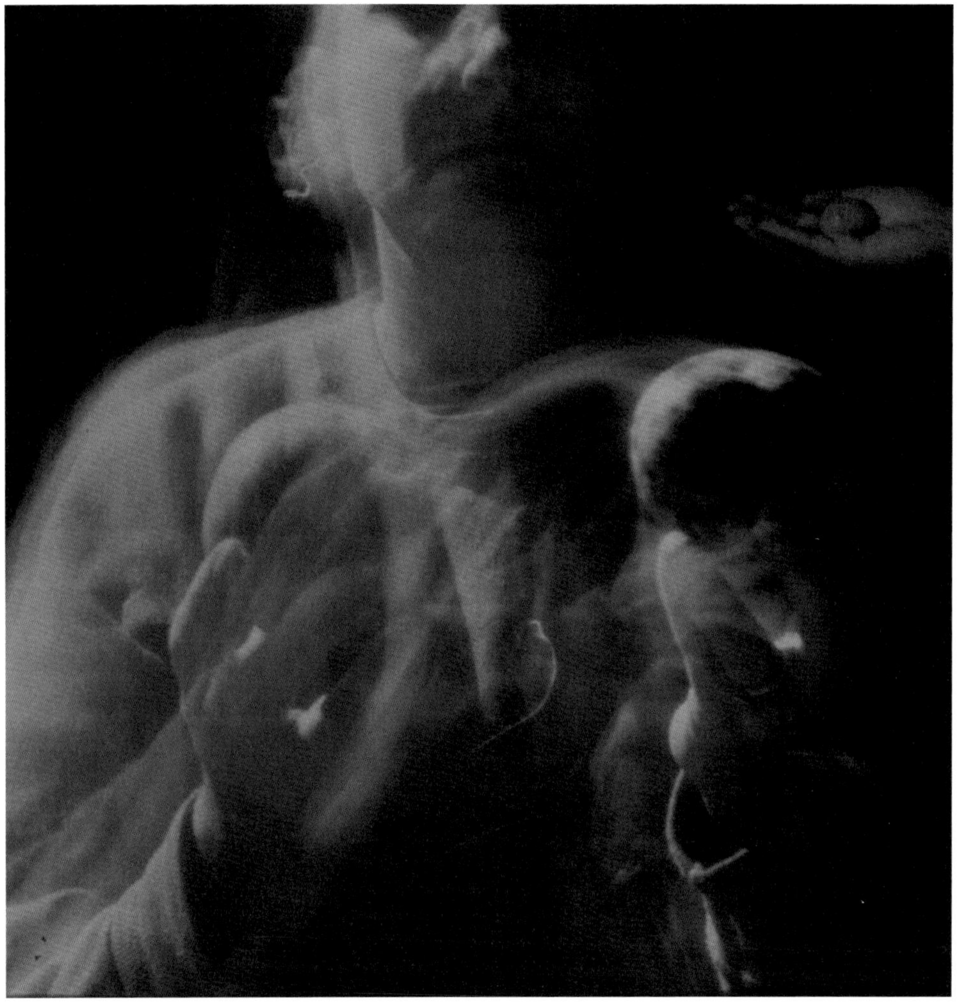

*Complexities* acts as both an autobiography and a manifesto that outlines her thoughts and feelings about being an artist, mother, educator, and wife in today's society.

As her children grew older and more independent, Nettles expanded her vision out into the world again, mounting exhibitions, publishing books, gaining residencies, leading workshops, and traveling. Able to turn inward to examine her own self again as an individual after years of navigating the self as part of a family unit, she produced *Turning 50* and *Memory Loss*, which deal with aging; *Hair Loss*, which speaks of her battle with breast cancer; and, in recent years, a series of poetry books using words garnered from surnames photographed from tombstones—each of these in some way musing on mortality. In the years when she was nurturing her children, Nettles sought to find ways in which she could examine the self in the context of the collective, as the protector and woman of power. Out of necessity, she drove her work in another direction after her children were born. In doing so, she found a rich new visual vocabulary with which to engage her children while simultaneously investigating and developing a part of herself and articulating universal concerns that are shared by virtually all mothers.

## Notes

1. Sandra Matthews, introduction to Bea Nettles, in *Life's Lessons: A Mother's Journal*, preface by Terry Suhre, comments by Bea Nettles (Urbana, IL: Inky Press Productions [self-published], 1990), n.p.
2. See Vicky Goldberg's critique of Nettles's work in "Books: A Touch of Surrealism," *American Photographer*, June 1980, 16.
3. Bea Nettles, *The Skirted Garden: Forty-Five Years of Images* ([Urbana, IL]: self-published, 2015; distribution, Morrisville, NC: Lulu), 3.
4. Nettles, *Skirted Garden*, 2.
5. Nettles, *Skirted Garden*, 11.
6. Nettles, *Skirted Garden*, 23.
7. Nettles, *Skirted Garden*, 24.
8. Nettles, *Skirted Garden*, 24.
9. Nettles, *Skirted Garden*, 24.
10. Bea Nettles, unpublished artist notes titled "Motherhood and Family," June 29, 2018.
11. See more on this in Linda Fregni Nagler, *The Hidden Mother*, (London: Mack Books, 2013).
12. Estelle Jussim, "The Heart of the Ineffable," in "Mothers and Daughters," ed. Olsen, Tillie, Julie Olsen Edwards, and Estelle Jussim, special issue, *Aperture*, Summer 1987, 104.
13. Nettles, *The Skirted Garden*, 26.
14. Bea Nettles, "Close to Home: The Pinhole Project," *On Campus* (published by the Office of Public Affairs of the University of Illinoi–UIUC), March 1984, p. 7.
15. Nettles, *The Skirted Garden*, 26.
16. Nettles, *The Skirted Garden*, 27.
17. Natalie Canavor, "*Rachel's Holidays*," *Popular Photography*, January 1985, 162.
18. Though Rachel appears more often in Nettles's photographs, Gavin makes appearances in the later series *Life's Lessons: A Mother's Journal*, *Complexities*, and *Return Trips*, which were produced in the late 1990s and early 2000s.
19. Canavor, "*Rachel's Holidays*," 162.
20. Nettles, *The Skirted Garden*, 31.
21. Nettles, *The Skirted Garden*, 31.
22. Nettles, unpublished artist notes titled "Motherhood and Family." Rachel eventually earned an advanced degree in textiles.
23. Nettles, *The Skirted Garden*, 34.
24. Nettles, *Life's Lessons*, n.p.
25. Nettles, *Life's Lessons*, n.p.
26. Nettles, *Life's Lessons*, n.p.
27. Nettles, *Life's Lessons*, n.p.
28. Nettles, *Life's Lessons*, n.p.
29. Nettles, *Life's Lessons*, n.p.
30. Nettles, *Life's Lessons*, n.p.
31. Bea Nettles, *Complexities*, (Urbana, IL: Inky Press Productions [self-published], 1992), 2.
32. Nettles, *Complexities*, 40.

# PHOTOGRAPHIC OBJECTS/ INSTITUTIONAL ARTIFACTS

## BEA NETTLES IN CONTEXT

Amy L. Powell

Bea Nettles's Urbana home is enveloped in a collage of earthly and found materials: vegetables on vines covered with netting, brightly colored glass and ceramic shards embedded in stone walkways, and green plants so robust that they allow for an annual digging party where neighbors and friends can remove plantings for their gardens. On one visit, I glimpsed a fern with leaves spray-painted in gold. This seems a perfect picture—a successful (photographic?) image that reflects the sunlight just so but also an indication of Nettles's commitment to world making. Her constant curiosity and fearlessness toward her medium is always grounded in gestures of hospitality and transformation.

Garden metaphors might go far in describing Nettles's photographic practice, which I will view here through the institutional contexts and frictions shaping her work, alongside her persisting and highly influential emphasis on a pedagogy of experimental techniques. While not the direct object of her trowel, the universities, museums, and photography communities with which the artist has been aligned, and to which she has contributed, have made Nettles's photographic objects into institutional artifacts showing how she has long mined, challenged, and refused certain pressures and restrictions. To pay attention to such contexts is to take cues from the work itself, where Nettles's trial-and-error methods—hand-coloring, stitching, etching, and painting with photosensitive chemicals—recuperate the multimedia and chemically experimental origins of photography, thereby challenging any scheme that privileges fine printing techniques. Writing about Nettles's contemporaries Thomas Barrow and Betty Hahn (fig. 3.1), Geoffrey Batchen uses both artists' works—specifically Barrow's scratching out and Hahn's stitching—to reformulate the histories of photography, which must account for handwork.[1]

To consider Nettles's work in its responsiveness to institutions is also to follow her lead as good feminist practice, albeit more out of necessity or common sense than out of

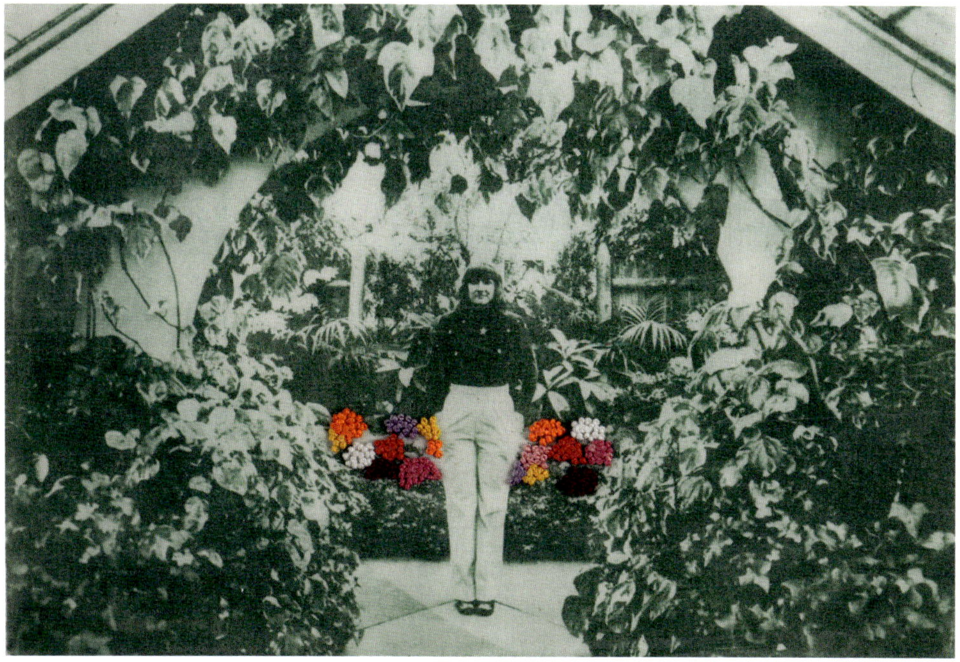

FIGURE 3.1. Betty Hahn (American, b. 1940), *Greenhouse Portrait (Bea Nettles)*, 1972, gum bichromate print on fabric with stitching

political motivation. When asked about feminism's relationship to her work, Nettles has cited two factors: first, the strong women in her family and their endeavors, especially her grandmother's eclectic sewing projects and her mother's poetry; her upbringing, she said, instilled confidence in experimentation. Second were the difficulties of having had only male teachers.[2] Nettles's work is often performative and playful, as when the artist's figure appears in what Melanie Emerson has described as the "tales of our collective memory or imagination: the mother, the nymph, the siren, the witch."[3] But Nettles also applies such a penchant for experimentation to her materials, which she often determined while testing the limits of obstacles she was facing. In a given work, her challenges might include the characteristics of a particular medium, time constraints in the darkroom, career expectations, and the weight of genealogy through a given lineage of instructors.

Abigail Solomon-Godeau helpfully situates women artists practicing photographic self-representation from 1968 to 1980, a task that "takes as its purview the workings of power that shape or inflect representational systems and their technologies."[4] Such power dynamics are evident in Nettles's work, which is unapologetically personal and experimental while fully implicating the politics of representation. Her constructed images are drawn from memory, her recurring imagined personae, dreams, and strong attachments to place and family. In the following, I offer sketches of three sites—and by extension, three bodies of knowledge—where the artist's work entangles most generatively with institutions to reveal the representational systems and technologies on which they depend.

## Illinois

The University of Illinois in the late 1960s was an exciting center for interdisciplinary arts production. Lejaren Hiller, a former chemistry professor who later joined the university's music faculty, had founded the Experimental Music Studio in 1958, and he worked with the artist and musician John Cage when Cage was a visiting faculty member at the Center for Advanced Study, from 1967 to 1969 (though Cage had been a frequent visitor on campus prior to his appointment). Cage staged several of his most notable happenings in Champaign-Urbana, among them *A Passage without Definition* (1967), which featured Salvatore Martirano's

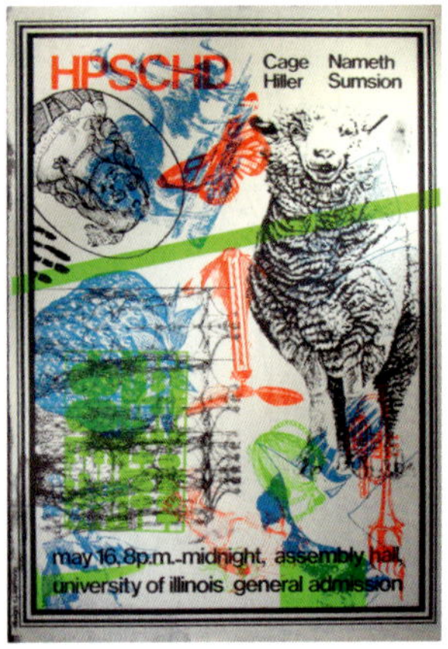


**FIGURE 3.2.** Calvin J. Sumsion with John Cage, Gary Viskupic, and David Eisenman, event poster for *HPSCHD*, a multimedia art performance by John Cage and Lejaren Hiller held on May 16, 1969 at Assembly Hall at the University of Illinois, silkscreen

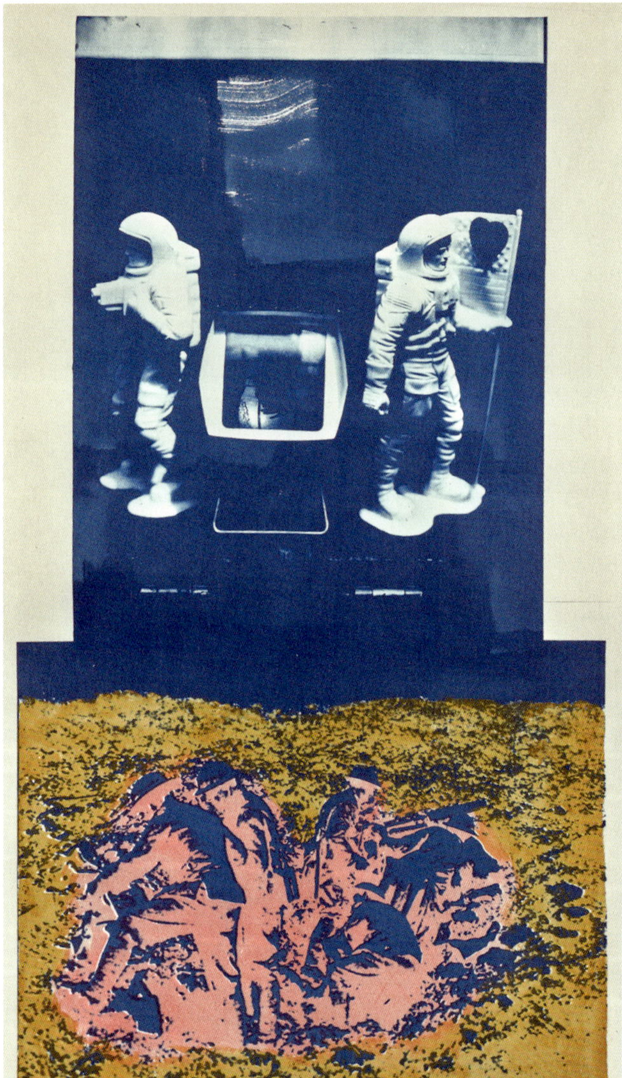

**FIGURE 3.3.** Robert Fichter (American, b. 1939), *Astronaut Still Life*, ca. 1974, cyanotype and gum bichromate print

anti–Vietnam War diatribe *L's GA*; *Musicircus* (1967), held at the university's stock pavilion; and the technologically chaotic and layered *HPSCHD* (1969) at the Assembly Hall (fig. 3.2).[5] The atmosphere surrounding these events more or less extended to pedagogy: in 1969 the systems theorist Heinz von Foerster, along with the biologist Humberto Maturana and the composer Herbert Brün, taught a course on heuristics that produced the *Whole University Catalog*, which compiled various typographic forms to describe the structures of university life.[6] Their effort was modeled on Stewart Brand's countercultural precursor to the internet, the *Whole Earth Catalog*. These few examples, among many others, align Illinois with similar sites for experiments in radical pedagogy, computer science, and performance.[7]

This unconventional creative environment might possibly have framed Nettles's experience in the graduate painting program in the art department at Illinois; however, as the artist recalls, the school maintained separate silos for each artistic discipline, and she felt little influence from the great Midwestern experiments of the time.[8] Painting was located off campus and disconnected from sculpture and printmaking, with each program having distinct visiting artist series and MFA student critiques. Photography did not yet exist as formalized curriculum, though Illinois was an important node in the medium's institutional establishment in the United States. Art Sinsabaugh, formerly a student at the Chicago Institute of Design, implemented basic courses and curated *Six Photographers*, a biennial series surveying contemporary photography at Krannert Art Museum throughout the 1960s while also being a founding member of the Society for Photographic Education.[9]

Sinsabaugh indicates one genealogy for photography at Illinois, a lineage stemming from the instruction of Arthur Siegel and Harry Callahan. Nettles, who arrived in 1968, represents another, having been a student of Kenneth Kerslake, Robert Fichter, and Jerry Uelsmann at the University of Florida and having attended Fichter's workshops at Penland School of Crafts in North Carolina (fig. 3.3). Facing a department culture that discouraged cross-media conversation, an attitude reflected in such bureaucratic decisions as restricting access to the darkroom and other resources to students fully enrolled in specific courses, Nettles improvised:

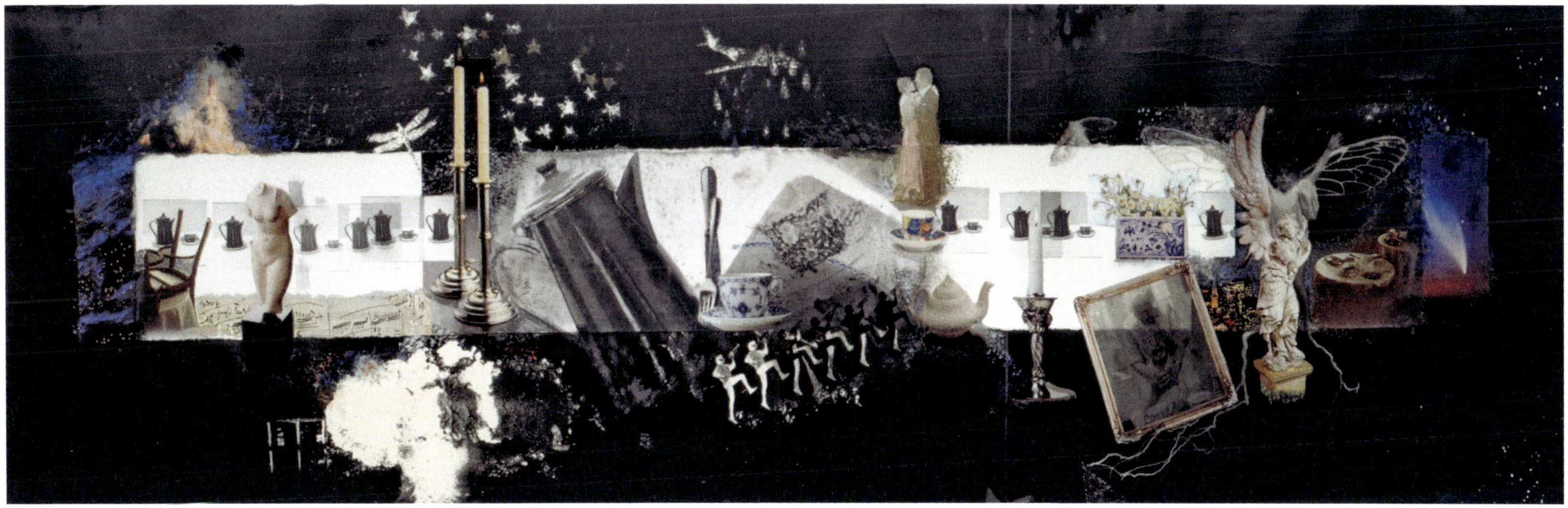

"To keep working, I obtained access to a private darkroom, printing in an unheated basement in a fur coat, with heat tapes under my trays to keep the chemicals from freezing."[10] The somatic image of the artist making her way through the institution is, of course, not an isolated or surprising case among women in the 1960s. One thinks of Joanne Leonard's (fig. 3.4) similarly autobiographical work and writing, or the careers of Nettles's peers Betty Hahn or Barbara Kasten.[11] Yet Nettles persisted at Illinois by applying for a grant toward the construction of a developing lab in the school's printmaking studio. Here, other students could likewise pursue extracurricular and less officially favorable artistic forms, including working with ortho film and screen-printing, thus creating an opportunity for community among experimental artists, however provisional and vexed.

*Imaginary Prairie* (1969; p. 62) is a formative early work that surfaces many of the institution's pressures around medium specificity and what counts as appropriate material for an artist with interests at the intersections of painting, printmaking, photography, and quilting. Nettles made the work using a large copper etching plate she had initially produced under Illinois printmaking faculty member Dennis Rowan. It was her response to Rowan's challenge to his students to create as monumental a work as the press could bear by using an uncut sheet of copper. After making cloth paintings like *The Skirted Garden* (1969; p. 61), Nettles arranged an independent study with supportive painting faculty member Jerry Savage in which she began to experiment even more with sewing. She reprinted the image three times on muslin. The images, stitched together, make a panoramic view of her then-new Illinois home, whose rich black earth initially shocked Nettles, a Florida native. *Imaginary Prairie* is organized by strong horizontal lines that Nettles made by pressing the hems of pillowcases into the etching plate's soft ground. The etching here is blatantly sculptural, a process Nettles likens to gardening.[12] She had acquired hairnets from a downtown Champaign thrift shop, and she sewed them into the surface of the work, where they either stretch in a loose tension or appear as tightly woven protuberances that are somehow integral to their ground. Nettles's other hand-drawn embellishments in the copper plate reproduced to varying degrees in this cloth work, lending a range of tones that are both subtle and overt and require us to really look to discern the differences in the serial image.

Layered and geological, *Imaginary Prairie* intimates tactile knowledge of a place, what Peter Bunnell would later call "tactile materiality" when describing artists' interest in the sculptural aspects of photography.[13] We might also understand it as a wry take on a highly formalist photographic printing technique often assigned to students, who in this case are required to demonstrate a sky completely empty of marks and distinct from a dark foreground showing a

**FIGURE 3.4.** Joanne Leonard (American, b. 1940), *Roots and Wings*, 1988, silver print of photographs and photograms with collage and gouache

landscape or objects.[14] In *Imaginary Prairie*, this compositional gesture, combined with its evocative memory effects, yields a work that manages to be photographic without actually involving photography. It is also an economy of means, one Nettles employed before she could afford the Liquid Light or photo-sensitive linen fabric that would distinguish her photographic objects of the 1970s.[15]

Much later, after her return to Illinois to establish the undergraduate photography degree program in the School of Art + Design, Nettles would make a similar image. *Dinnerplate* (1985; p. 174), from the series *Landscapes of Innocence*, is immersed in domestic life. *Landscapes of Innocence* portrays the artist's young children by examining their fears and delights; the images in the series include insects, rocks, school projects, clay figures with barbed wire, and other elements that Nettles pictured as vignettes, at turns playful and threatening. Nettles photographed the scenes in her home and commissioned G. R. Grubb Engraving, in downtown Champaign, to etch them on copper plates, which she then used to produce the series in the intaglio studio on campus (Nettles's first Urbana home upon her return to Illinois did not have a darkroom).[16] This particular beautiful blue plate had patterns that struck the artist for their suggestion of an intricate landscape, and she pictured it several times. Figure and ground in *Dinnerplate* are ambiguous and markedly different from the 1969 work *Dinnerplate Views* (fig. 3.5) showing the same plate reproduced four times and toned in blue, atop a massive black ground. Objects that resonate with meaning—here one of her few possessions in graduate school during her first time away from home—reappear as different kinds of landscapes, dreamlike recurrences drawn from real life.

**FIGURE 3.5.** *Dinnerplate Views*, July 1969, gelatin silver print

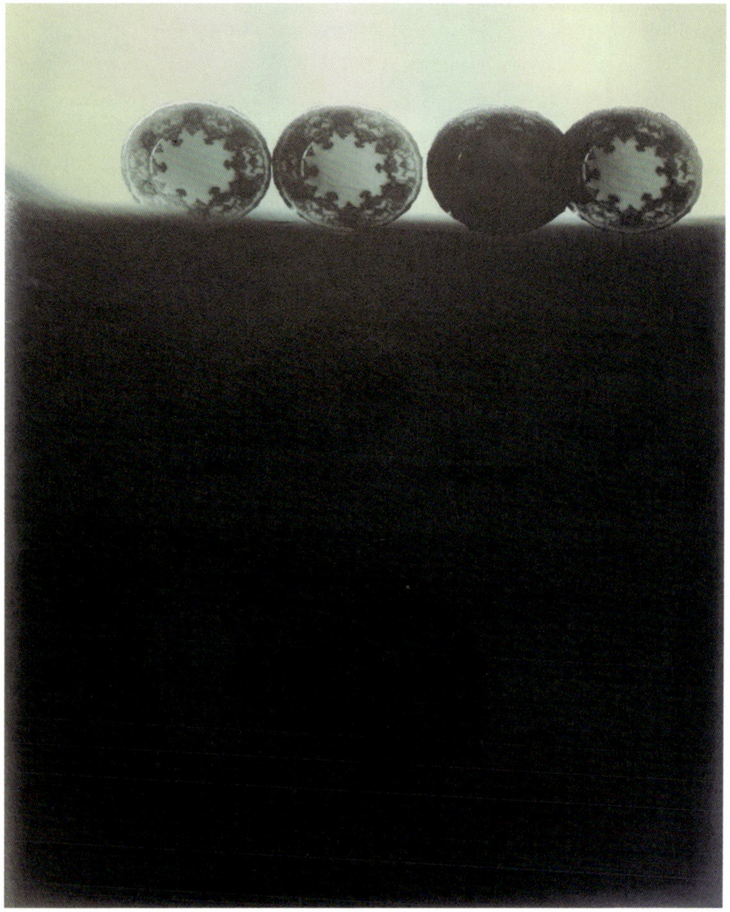

*Star . . . my chevy van* (ca. 1968–1970; fig. 3.6) shows a more precise place: near 1006 West Church Street in Champaign, where the artist lived during her graduate studies. Parked in the Illinois landscape, the white van bears the likeness of a single tree from Florida, which Nettles exposed at varying lengths and in different positions to create a soft image appearing like a windswept Florida palm grove. "Star," the van's name, matched Nettles's moniker from Penland as the queen of stars (she appears in other works wearing a starry dress). The artist's effort directly counters her medium's intended function: *Star . . . my chevy van* is printed on ortho film, which was designed to yield high-contrast products for making screen prints and printing books. Fichter had taught Nettles that applying a different developer to ortho film would achieve a continuous tone, allowing its use in ways other than those the manufacturer had intended.[17] In this work, then, she was experimenting with ortho film's capacities—a completely extracurricular activity in response to her deeply felt cosmology and geography. With areas hand toned in pink and stitching around the perimeter, *Star . . . my chevy van* becomes an autobiographical document of particular times and places but also an object of persistence, a guiding star for the artist as she moved toward picturing the world through her unique expressive lens and ceaseless experimentation.

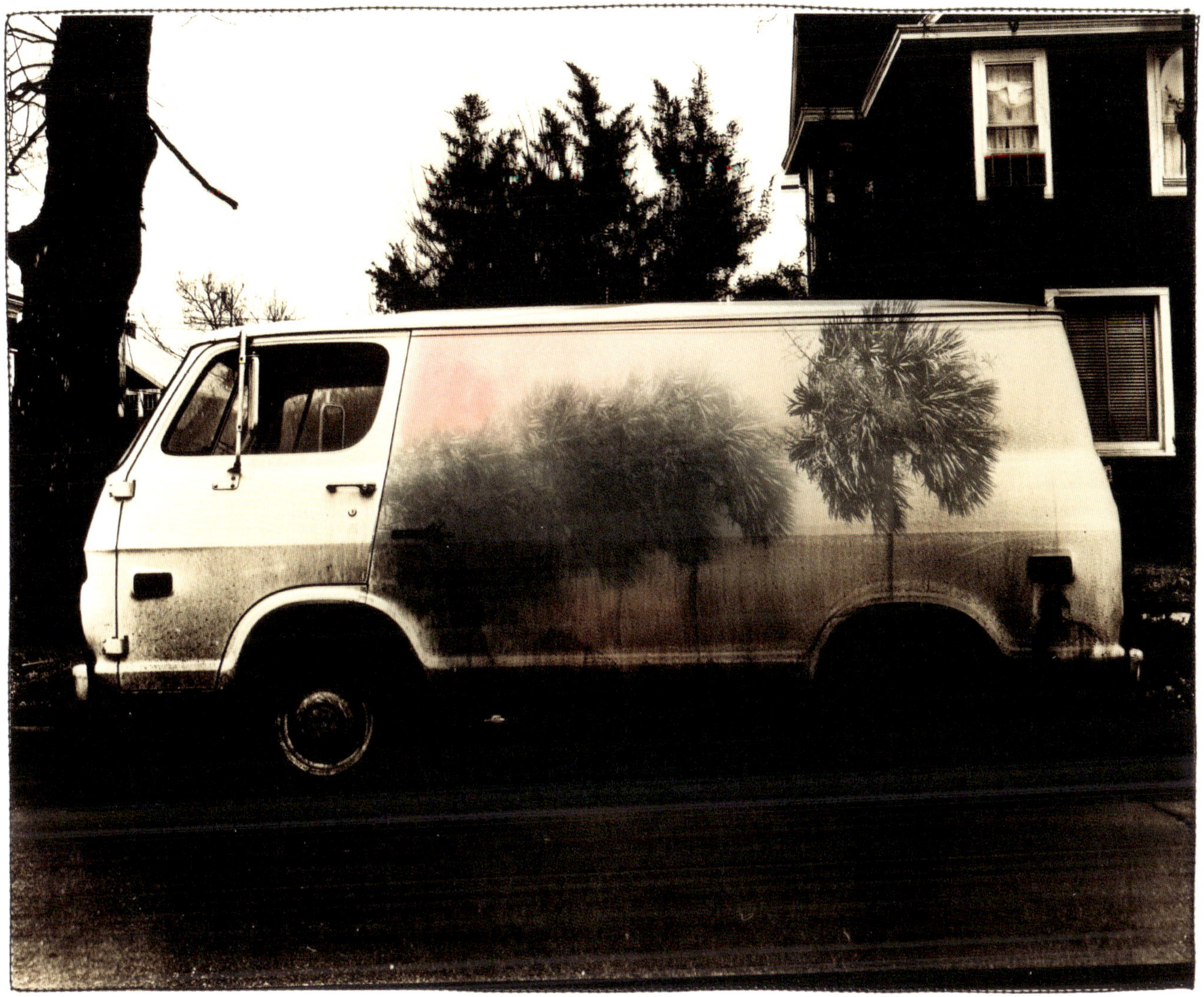

**FIGURE 3.6.** *Star . . . my chevy van*, February 1970, collage with gelatin silver print, ortho film, stitching and applied color

## Breaking the Rules

Nettles's commitment to pedagogy has always bridged the gulf between academic and craft worlds. From 1967, when she was asked to stand in for an absent instructor at Penland, to the years between 1974, when she left the Tyler School of Art, and 1976, when she was hired at the Rochester Institute of Technology (RIT), Nettles kept an extensive notebook of techniques for teaching nonsilver photographic processes in seasonal workshops across the United States. In 1977 she published the first edition of *Breaking the Rules: A Photo Media Cookbook*, all aspects of which she designed while also overseeing its production at Mohawk Printing, an offset printing press in Rochester, New York. Covering ortho film, pinhole cameras, cyanotypes and Van Dyke prints, Kwik-Prints, hand coloring, and much more, *Breaking the Rules* has sold 30,000 copies over the course of three editions, with revisions appearing in 1987 and 1992 (figs. 3.7–3.9). Nettles produced the book while living in Rochester,

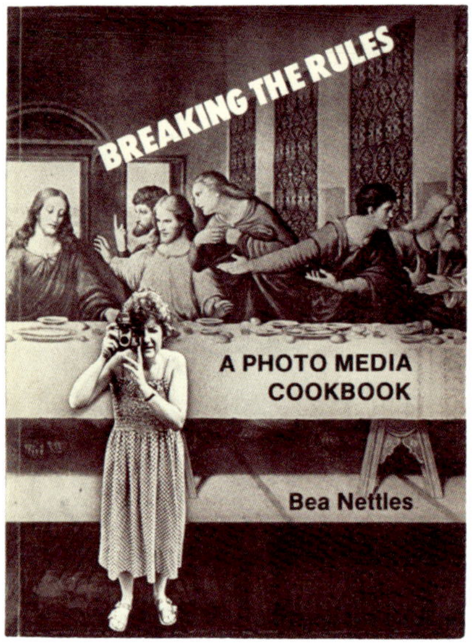


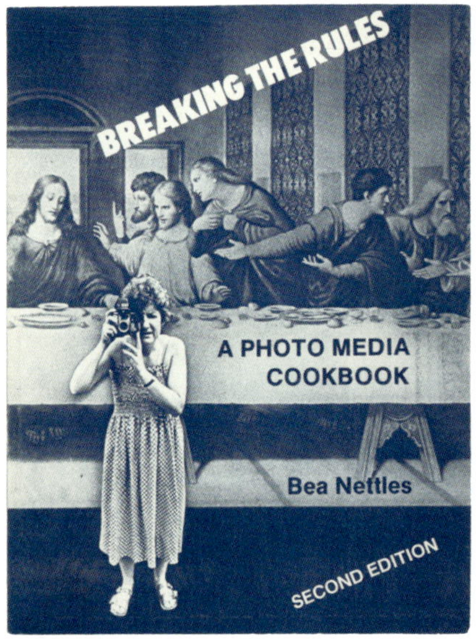


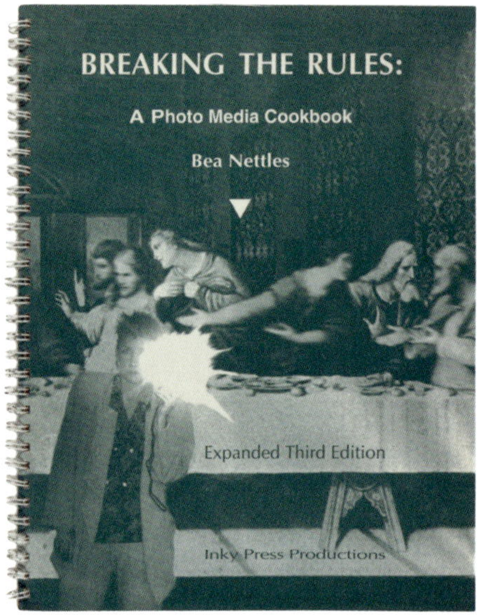


**FIGURES 3.7–3.9** Three covers of Bea Nettles, *Breaking the Rules: A Photo Media Cookbook*, first edition (1977), second edition (1987), and third edition (1992)

when she was making Kwik-Prints, one of the mediums for which she would become particularly well known. The artist appears on the cover in each edition of *Breaking the Rules*, her snapshot camera pointed outward at the reader. The three cover images imply that she is a tourist photographing Leonardo da Vinci's *Last Supper*, in Milan; for the first two editions, Nettles wears a checkered dress and Birkenstock sandals, while in the third, she appears in a nonchalant pose with shorter hair and wearing a collared shirt. Not only is Nettles's instruction of alternative techniques breaking the then-hardened formalist rules of photography, which above all adhered to the conviction that the photograph is truly made at the moment the shutter clicks, but she is blasphemous toward even the most sacred images.[18]

Nettles's humor and tendency toward (at times not so) subtle disruption extended to her nearly all-male colleagues at RIT. In 1980, for the fiftieth anniversary exhibition of work by the School of Photographic Arts and Sciences faculty, all members appeared in a panoramic photograph that doubled as an exhibition card announcement (fig. 3.10). Faculty

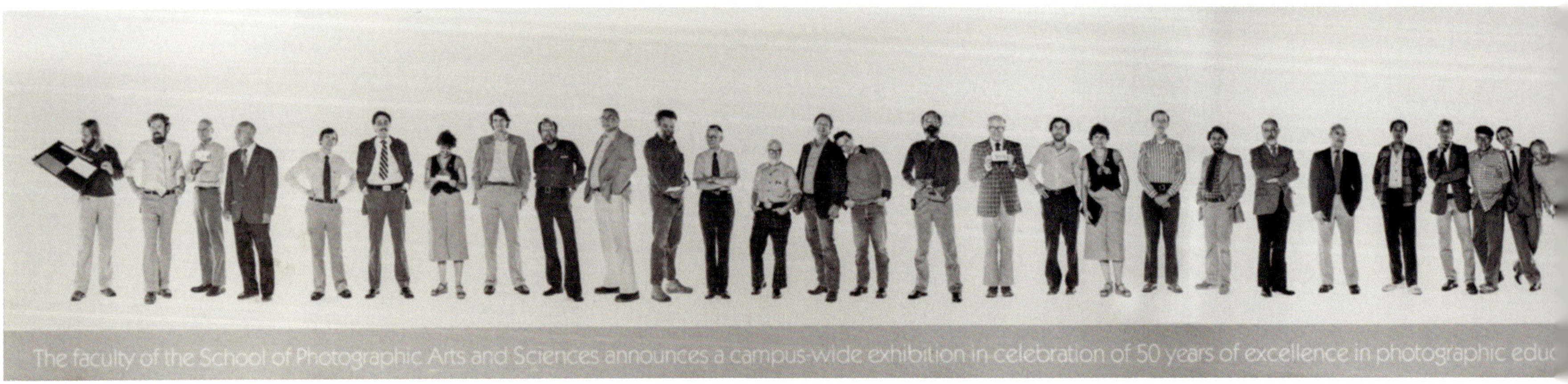

members were scheduled to appear throughout the day, and Nettles and some of her colleagues played a joke by having her stand in for faculty member Kathleen Collins, who was then on sabbatical.[19] Nettles effectively appears twice in the photograph: as herself, smiling at the camera with a notebook under one arm, and as her only female colleague, looking down at a set of notes (yet wearing the same clothes). Apparently no one noticed that the "two" women were in fact the same person, since the announcement was printed and circulated. It is a powerful image, a lineup of the institution's instructors where the dearth of women would have already been evident, but here the marginalization is emphasized graphically. The photograph is an institutional document and serves as a pictorial companion to Nettles's previous stint at RIT, in 1971–1972, when colleagues and critics sometimes confused her with her then-colleague Betty Hahn.[20]

The kinds of challenges to her mixed-media practices that Nettles had experienced as a graduate student in Illinois—if not yet the challenges of gender—were also playing out in the photography departments of museums and universities on the coasts. Nettles's work, along with that of the twenty-two other artists included in Peter Bunnell's 1970 exhibition *Photography into Sculpture*, at the Museum of Modern Art, appeared at a moment of institutional reshaping after the establishment of photography as a fine art worthy of collection by museums. The unsettled ground is evident in the conversations and effects of the exhibition among medium-specific departments at MoMA, whose curators were theorizing photography on its own and in relationship to contemporary art and technology more broadly in the 1960s and 1970s.[21] MoMA's exhibition—along with *California Photographers 1970*, at the University of California, Davis, and *Photographic Synthesis*, at the California College of Arts and Crafts, among others—took the processes and sculptural dimensions of photography as organizing principles instead of considering the medium only for the images it produced, the more prevalent understanding at the time.

Widening our perspective to the questions MoMA has determined through its exhibitions, publications, and collections practices reveals the significant stakes here, since they suggest a broader field for the status of photography as an object and what it is allowed to do: what histories it can draw on, what aesthetic decisions and values are possible, and how it challenges museum departments and lineages as a result. Museum institutions play an undeniable role in conceptualizing what constitutes a photograph, but when we focus specifically on Nettles's work as part of that history, the issues become even knottier (though generative to think with). The dynamics of gender representation; the importance Nettles placed on pedagogy (which directly countered male artists she had known who refused to share their sources); and, though more of a distinction now than in 1970, the ways in which her work connects the worlds of fine and conceptual art with craft—these questions all come to the fore. Significant holdings of Nettles's work are as likely to appear in collections that have focused on the

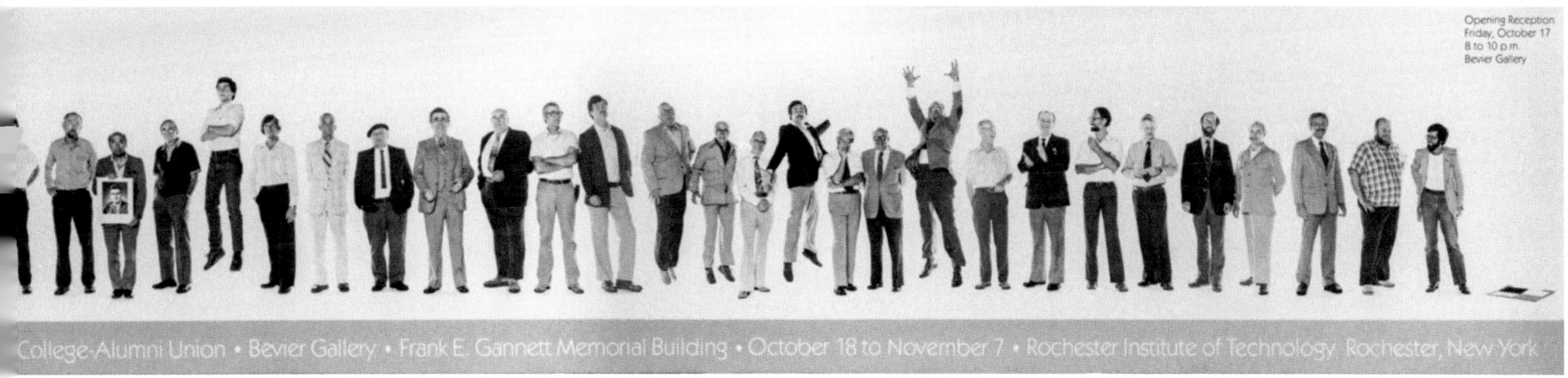


**FIGURE 3.10.** Rochester Institute of Technology art faculty exhibition announcement, 1980

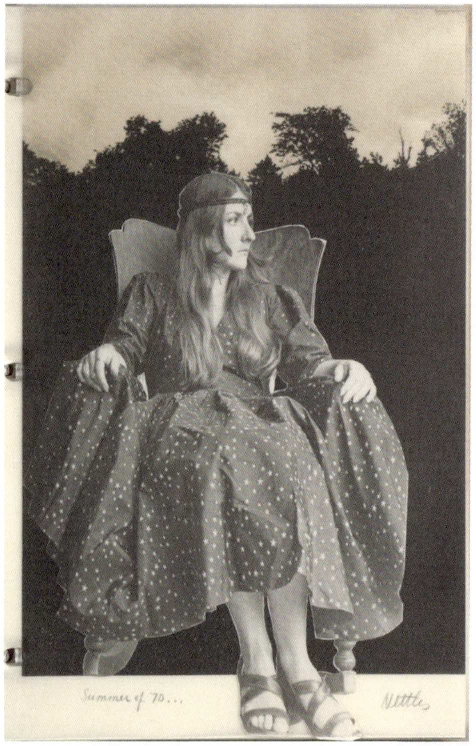

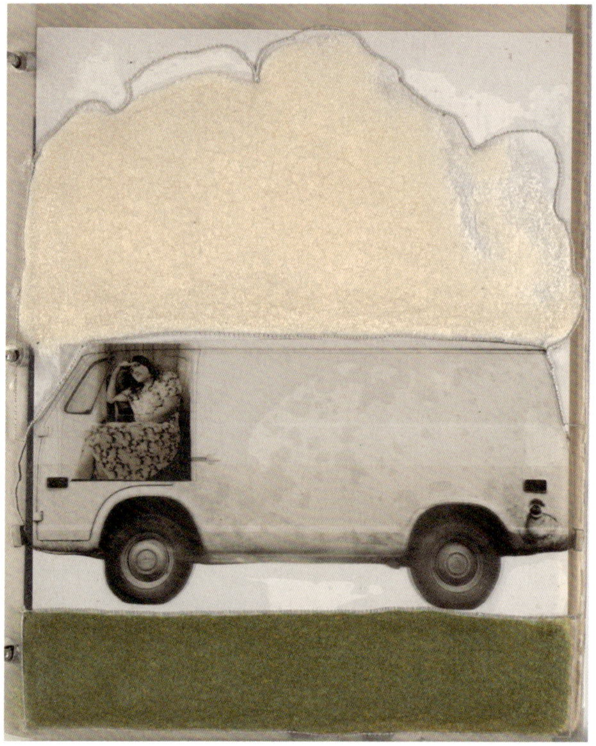

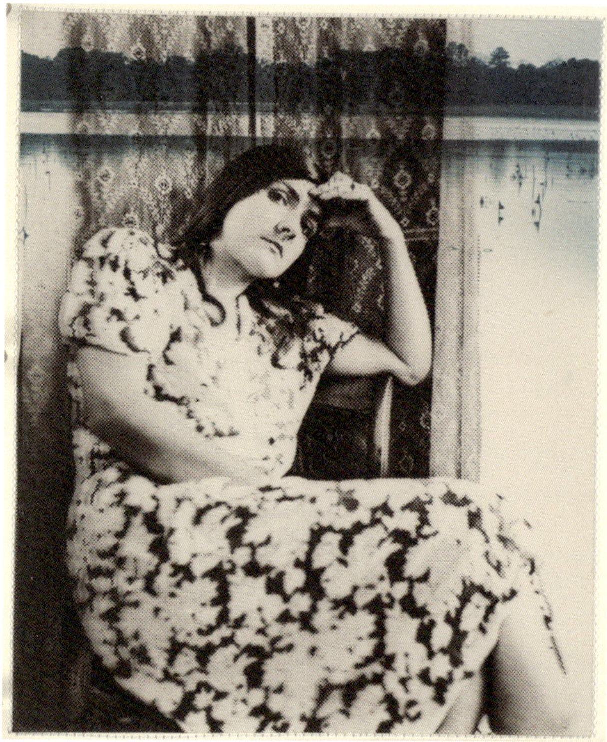

**FIGURE 3.11.** *Summer of 70 . . .*, 1970, from *Bruises and Other Collections*, collage with photographs

**FIGURE 3.12.** *Untitled*, ca. 1970, from *Bruises and Other Collections*, collage with photographs

**FIGURE 3.13.** *Lake Lady*, 1970, from *Bruises and Other Collections*, collage with photographs

craft of photography as they are in those that have centered on the medium as fine art; more accurately, they most likely appear in collections that have not troubled themselves with such distinctions, for example, the Center for Creative Photography and the George Eastman Museum. When her work intersects with institutions, Nettles breaks more rules than just those I have only begun to demonstrate.

## Self-Representation

Because her work is highly self-expressive and sometimes pictures Nettles in personas evoking nature and women's bodies and experiences, one might easily historicize it, deeming it outdated according to one understanding of feminist art practices from the 1960s and 1970s: the notion that such artworks concern themselves with an essential feminine self. Solomon-Godeau has problematized this idea by considering multiple examples of artists using photography to mediate gender and self-representation even while new themes were readily portrayed: pregnancy, lunar cycles, menstruation, breast surgery.[22] Nettles's substantial experimental processes undoubtedly take on some attributes of content; however, to neglect her subject matter and the ways in which Nettles treats self-representation is potentially to miss how her work complicates assumptions of an authentic feminine being and participates in postmodern critiques of the self.

Nettles's *Bruises and Other Collections* (1970; figs. 3.11–3.14) is a notebook of unique collages; like the works *Neptune and Lake Lady . . . a series* (1970), *Ghosts and Stitched Shadows* (1971), and *B and the Birds: A Collection* (1971), all from the early 1970s, it compiles images and various image formats inside a three-ring binder. These works are more easily held in the hand and constitute a unique visual book form indicating Nettles's growing interest in seriality and narrative (though they can also be disassembled and shown as singular works). In *Bruises and Other Collections*,

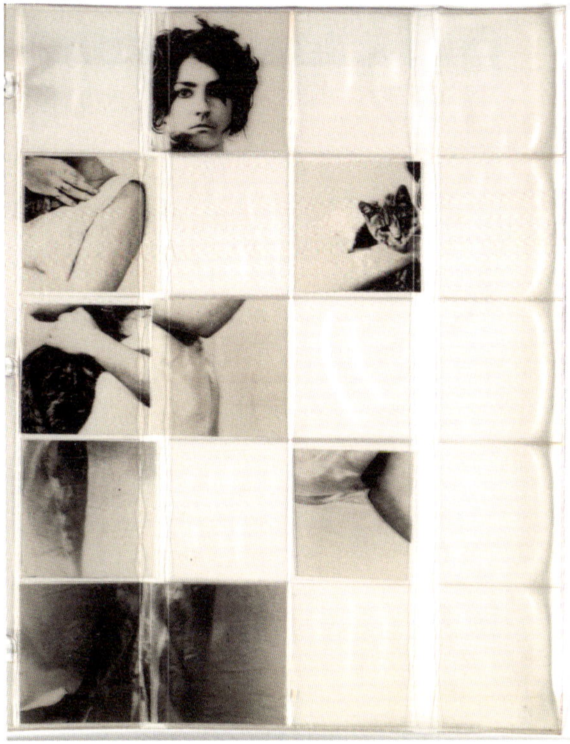

FIGURE 3.14. *Untitled*, ca. 1970, from *Bruises and Other Collections*, collage with photographs

Star, the Chevy van, makes another appearance along with Nettles dressed as the Queen of Stars (figs. 3.11 and 3.12). Both figures are set in indeterminate land(dream)scapes, while star queen Nettles, looking right and toward the subsequent pages, watches confidently as the various other guises of her image unfold. In one, she is seated in a floral print dress and turned sideways but looking directly at the camera, her hand on her forehead, her elbow resting on her chair (fig. 3.13; see also fig. 3.14, where this image appears in the driver's seat of the star van). The decorative patterned backdrop is possibly familiar from other works, yet the studio setting is disrupted by a deep view beyond into a blue-toned photograph of a lake. The image is a positive ortho print made from a 2¼-inch negative and extremely high contrast, in line with ortho film's usual development.[23] It is a constructed image, self-conscious about the way the artist appears while also bringing along ambiguous signs from her memory and personal background.

Another collage page of *Bruises* is on ortho film that Nettles cut into two-inch squares and inserted into a plastic sleeve organizer for 35 mm slides (fig. 3.14). Nettles still looks at the camera, this time holding her beloved first cat, Nimbus. Her image is fragmented and ambiguous—it's not clear how the pieces align, and more than half the plastic squares are empty. She produced this work in response to the experience of applying for jobs, a time when one might feel compartmentalized while one's artwork is shared widely. Here is the self rendered in two-inch squares for assessment and consumption. Nettles's awareness of her appearance extends to her medium, for ortho film's high contrast introduces a mass-media context, however latent and reworked in a notebook binder format. This work could easily be in conversation with the more performance-oriented photographic practices of Eleanor Antin and Hannah Wilke. Like these artists, Nettles is always aware of the camera and its interaction with her persona, and it is here that she takes charge. Her decades-long commitment to self-representation is an incredible document of her career and determination despite—and in reaction to—all the changing constraints and possibilities of medium and time through institutional and family life.

## Coda

Nettles's work retains an alluring and complicating power in its materiality and clear signs of experimentation. She invokes mysterious dream worlds by referencing the long history of photography and makes it personal (and political) by tying everything so unabashedly to her life and her desires. I have attempted to sketch only some of the critical frameworks through which we might understand her work further, which seems particularly useful given the artist's forethought in establishing strong holdings, through gifts and acquisitions, in museum and library collections throughout the United States and Canada. I suspect that many readers will appreciate such contexts, even if they lack the memories, enjoyed by so many, of being nourished in Nettles's and Lionel Suntop's kitchen or under their backyard grape vines or deep in conversation about a pressing matter in any given week. As is evident in the work itself, Nettles cultivates community through the figures and sentiments she gathers and holds close at hand.

## Notes

Special thanks to Bea Nettles for her incredible generosity and institutional memory, and to Allyson Purpura for her insightful comments on a draft of this essay.

**1.** Geoffrey Batchen, "Cancellation," in *The Last Picture Show: Artists Using Photography 1960–1982*, ed. Douglas Fogle (Minneapolis, MN: Walker Art Center, 2003), 177–182.

**2.** See Bea Nettles, *The Skirted Garden: Forty-Five Years of Images* ([Urbana, IL]: self-published, 2015; distribution, Morrisville, NC: Lulu); Mary Statzer, ed. *The Photographic Object 1970* (Berkeley: University of California Press, 2016), 171–175; Anne Tucker, *The Woman's Eye* (New York: Knopf, 1976), 155–157; and Colin Edgington, "In Dream and Soil: A Conversation with Bea Nettles," *Afterimage*, March–April 2017, 15–19.

**3.** Melanie E. Emerson, "Bea Nettles: Performing Identity through Mystical Storytelling," *Journal of Artists Books*, Spring 2018, 15.

**4.** Abigail Solomon-Godeau, "The Woman Who Never Was: Self-Representation, Photography, and First-Wave Feminist Art," in *WACK! Art and the Feminist Revolution, ed. Lisa Gabrielle Mark* (Los Angeles, CA: Museum of Contemporary Art; Cambridge, MA: MIT Press, 2007), 338.

**5.** For more on the experimental art and music environment at Illinois, see David Rosenboom, "'2 + 2 = green': Innovation in Experimental Music at the University of Illinois," in *The University of Illinois: Engine of Innovation*, ed. Frederick E. Hoxie (Urbana: University of Illinois Press, 2017), 121–134; Branden W. Joseph, "*HPSCHD*—Ghost or Monster?," in *Experimentations: John Cage in Music, Art, and Architecture* (New York: Bloomsbury, 2016), 173–204; and Elizabeth Surles, "John Cage at UIUC," library.illinois.edu/mpal/about/exhibits/ johncage (accessed August 26, 2018).

**6.** Heinz M. Von Foerster, *The Whole University Catalog* (Rantoul, IL: Rantoul Press, 1969), spinelessbooks.com/wholeuniversity (accessed August 26, 2018).

**7.** For more on 1960s radical pedagogy centered on counterculture in the United States, see, for example, Janet Sarbanes, "A Community of Artists: Radical Pedagogy at CalArts, 1969–72," eastofborneo.org, June 5, 2014, eastofborneo.org/articles/a-community-of-artists-radical-pedagogy-at-calarts-1969-72 (accessed August 27, 2018); Maurice Stein, Larry Miller, and Marshall Henrichs, *Blueprint for Counter Education* (Garden City, NY: Doubleday, 1970; repr., New York: Inventory Press, 2016); and Andrew Blauvelt, ed., *Hippie Modernism: The Struggle for Utopia* (Minneapolis, MN: Walker Art Center, 2015).

**8.** Though she did attend *HPSCHD* (Bea Nettles, conversation with the author, July 9, 2018).

**9.** Keith F. Davis, *American Horizons: The Photographs of Art Sinsabaugh* (New York: Hudson Hills, 2004), 11–12.

**10.** Nettles, *The Skirted Garden*, 1. Nettles also mentions this story in Statzer, *The Photographic Object*, 171–172.

**11.** See Joanne Leonard, *Being in Pictures: An Intimate Photo Memoir* (Ann Arbor: University of Michigan Press, 2008); Steve Yates, ed., *Betty Hahn: Photography or Maybe Not* (Albuquerque: University of New Mexico Press, 1995); and Alex Klein, ed., *Barbara Kasten: Stages* (Philadelphia: Institute of Contemporary Art, 2015).

**12.** Bea Nettles, conversation with the author, June 2, 2017.

**13.** Peter Bunnell, "Photography into Sculpture," reprinted in *Degrees of Guidance: Essays on Twentieth-Century American Photography* (New York: Cambridge University Press, 1993), 164.

**14.** On formalist printing techniques learned at the Institute of Design, see Davis, *American Horizons*. For a feminist and historical assessment of such concerns among this particular lineage of Chicago photographers, see Abigail Solomon-Godeau, "The Armed Vision Disarmed: Radical Formalism from Weapon to Style," *Photography at the Dock: Essays on Photographic History, Institutions, and Practices* (Minneapolis: University of Minnesota Press, 1991), 52–84.

**15.** Bea Nettles, *Breaking the Rules: A Photo Media Cookbook*, 2nd ed. (Urbana, IL: Inky Press Productions [self-published], 1987), 1–2.

**16.** Bea Nettles, conversation with the author, June 2, 2017.

**17.** Bea Nettles, conversation with the author, July 23, 2018.

**18.** Nettles's commitment to self-publishing extended to the careful documentation of her career. Two editions of *The Skirted Garden* remain authoritative chronologies of the artist's work and abundantly helpful as sources of information. Nettles produced these books in the early days of desktop publishing and was supported by the Women, Information Technology and Scholarship (WITS) group at Illinois. On WITS, see Sharon Irish, "Hierarchies in the Circuitry: Women, Information Technology and Scholarship (WITS) at Illinois," technologystories.org/hierarchies-in-the-circuitry-women-information-technology-and-scholarship-wits-at-illinois (accessed August 26, 2018).

**19.** Kathleen Collins went on to head the Kansas City Art Institute from 1996 to 2011.

**20.** "Even in some mainstream media, Betty Hahn and I were mixed up and reviewed as Bea Hahn and Betty Nettles. There were teachers at RIT who never learned my name. They called me Betty after she left. We're two different women. It's worth learning our names" (qtd. in Statzer, *The Photographic Object*, 175.

**21.** See especially Statzer, *The Photographic Object*.

**22.** Solomon-Godeau, "The Woman Who Never Was."

**23.** Nettles made a contact negative from this positive print and then used the negative to make a photo screen print in a work titled *Interior Exterior* (1969).

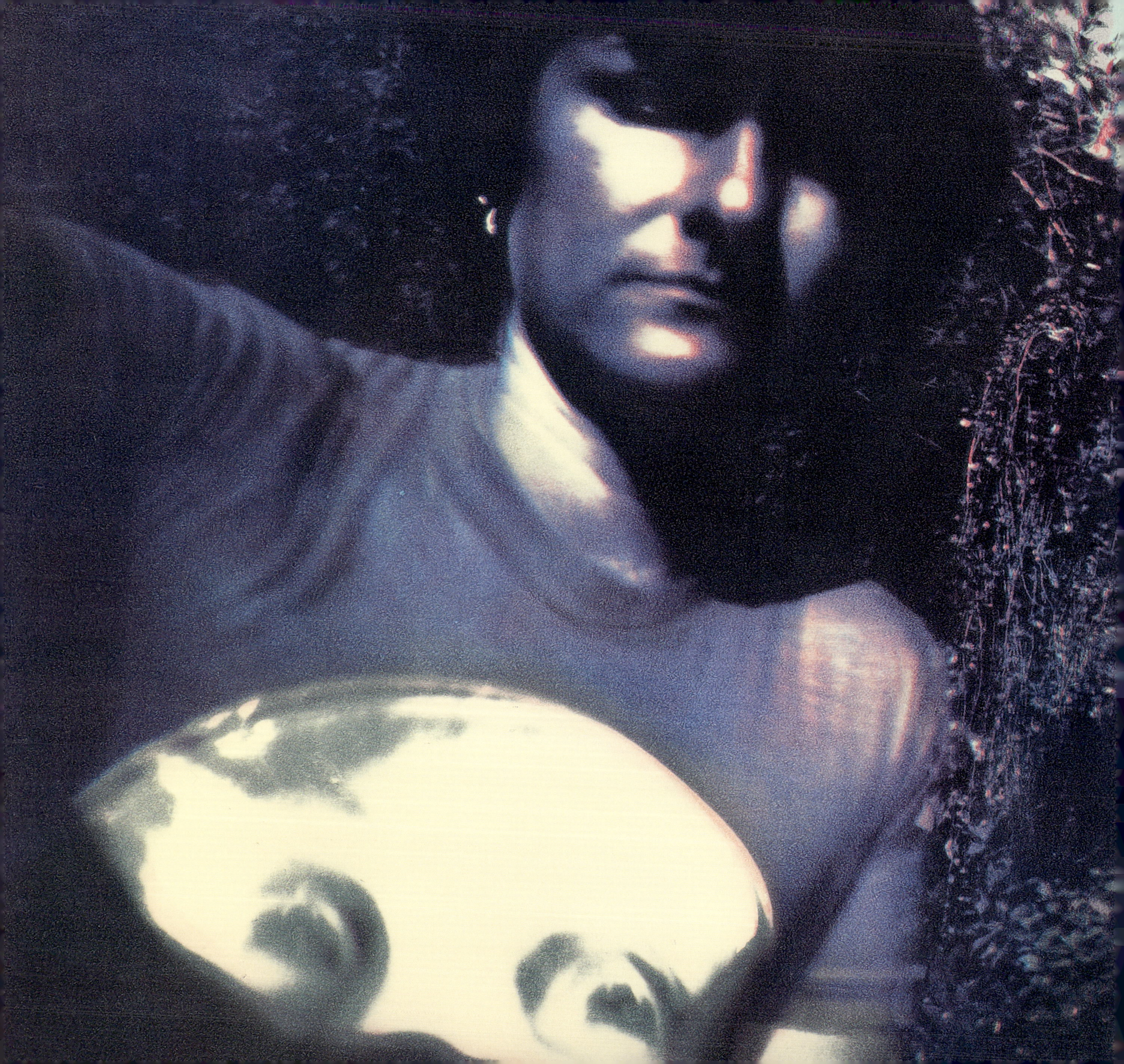

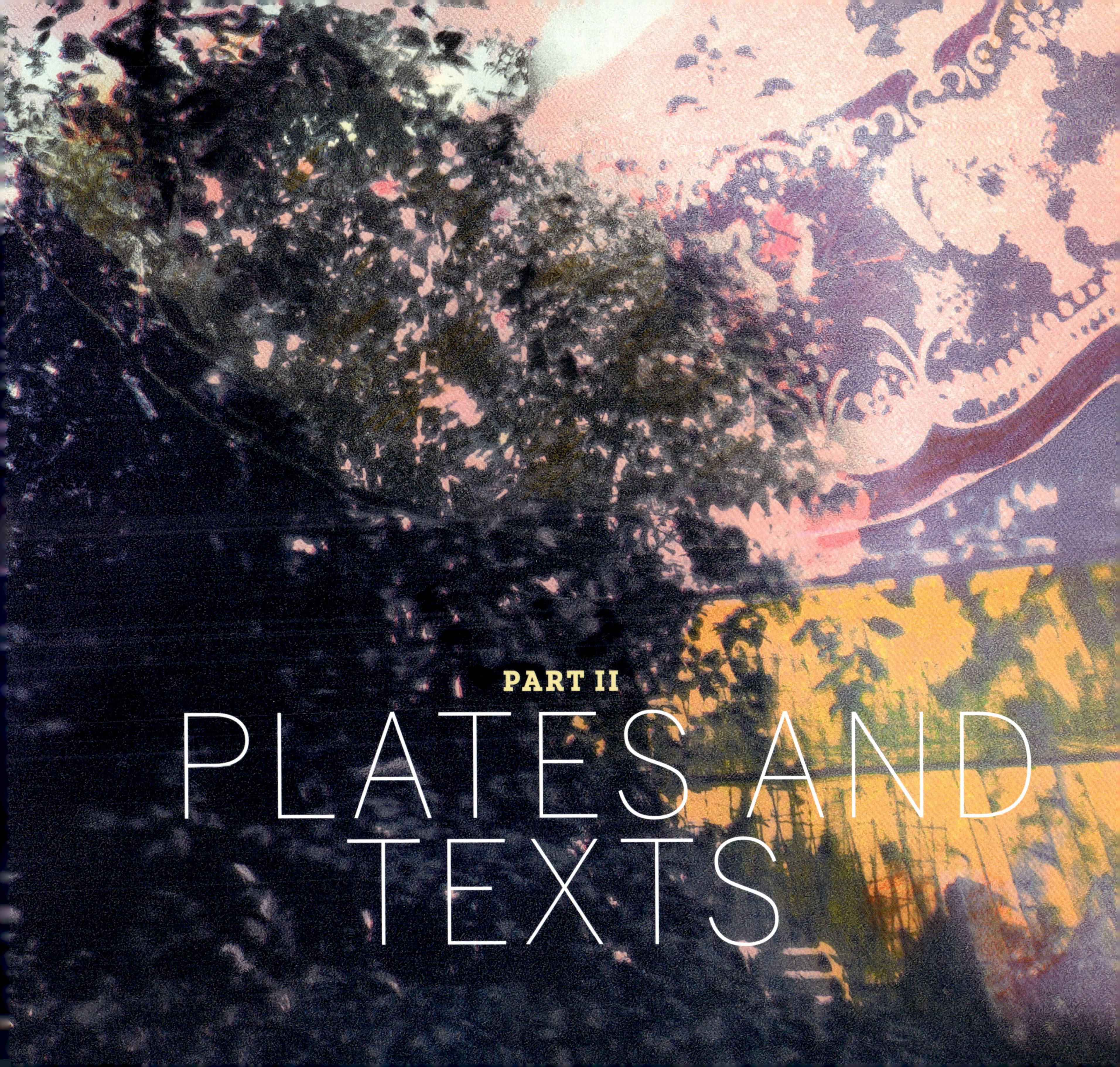

# PART II
# PLATES AND TEXTS

# OPENING STATEMENT

I see my career as a spiral with my ideas always circling and picking up reflections of earlier thoughts.

**BEA NETTLES** *THE SKIRTED GARDEN: 20 YEARS OF IMAGES* (1990)

# 1968-1975

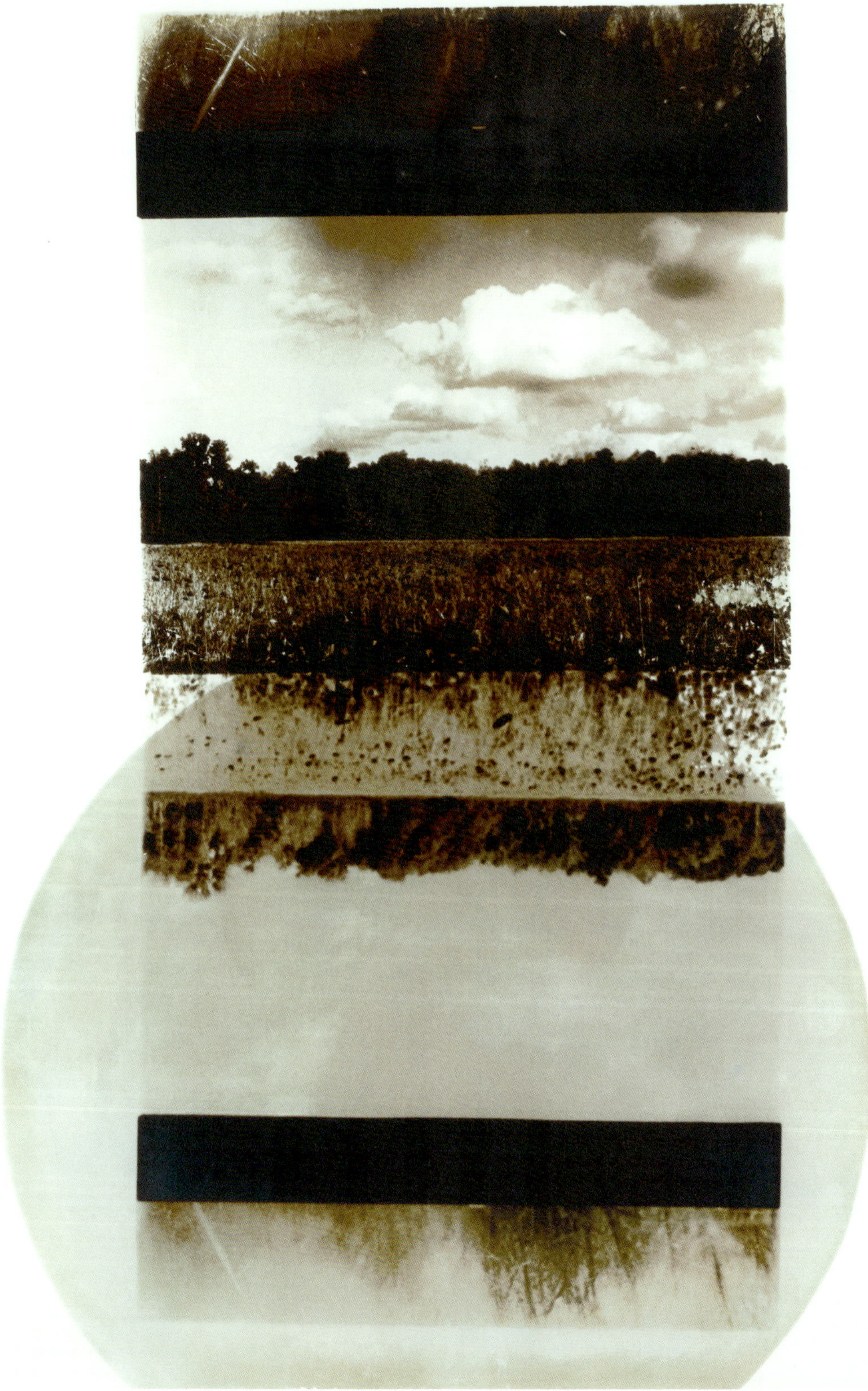

< *Toned Totem*, 1968, gelatin silver print

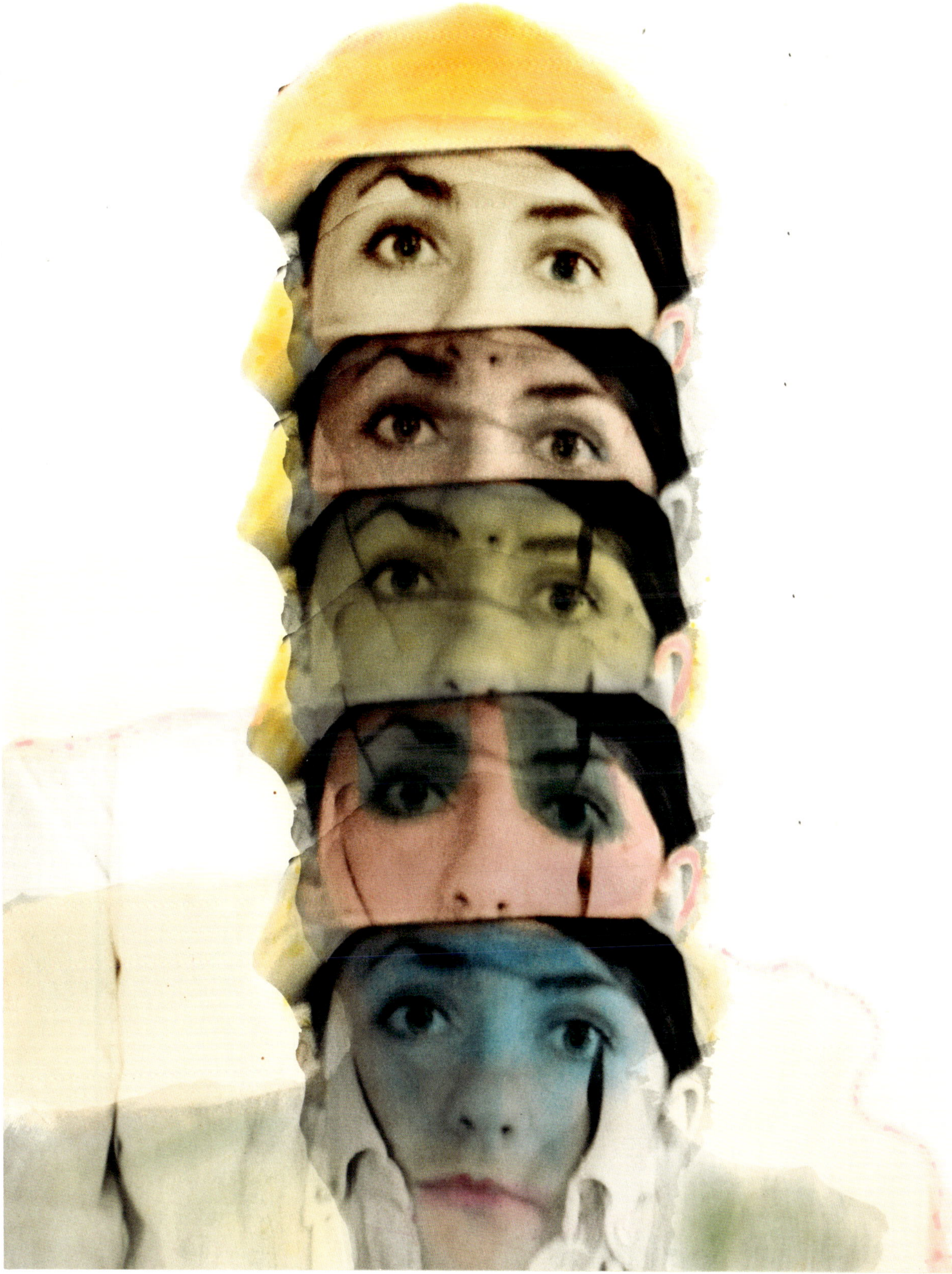

> *Self Totem*, July 1968, gelatin silver print with applied color

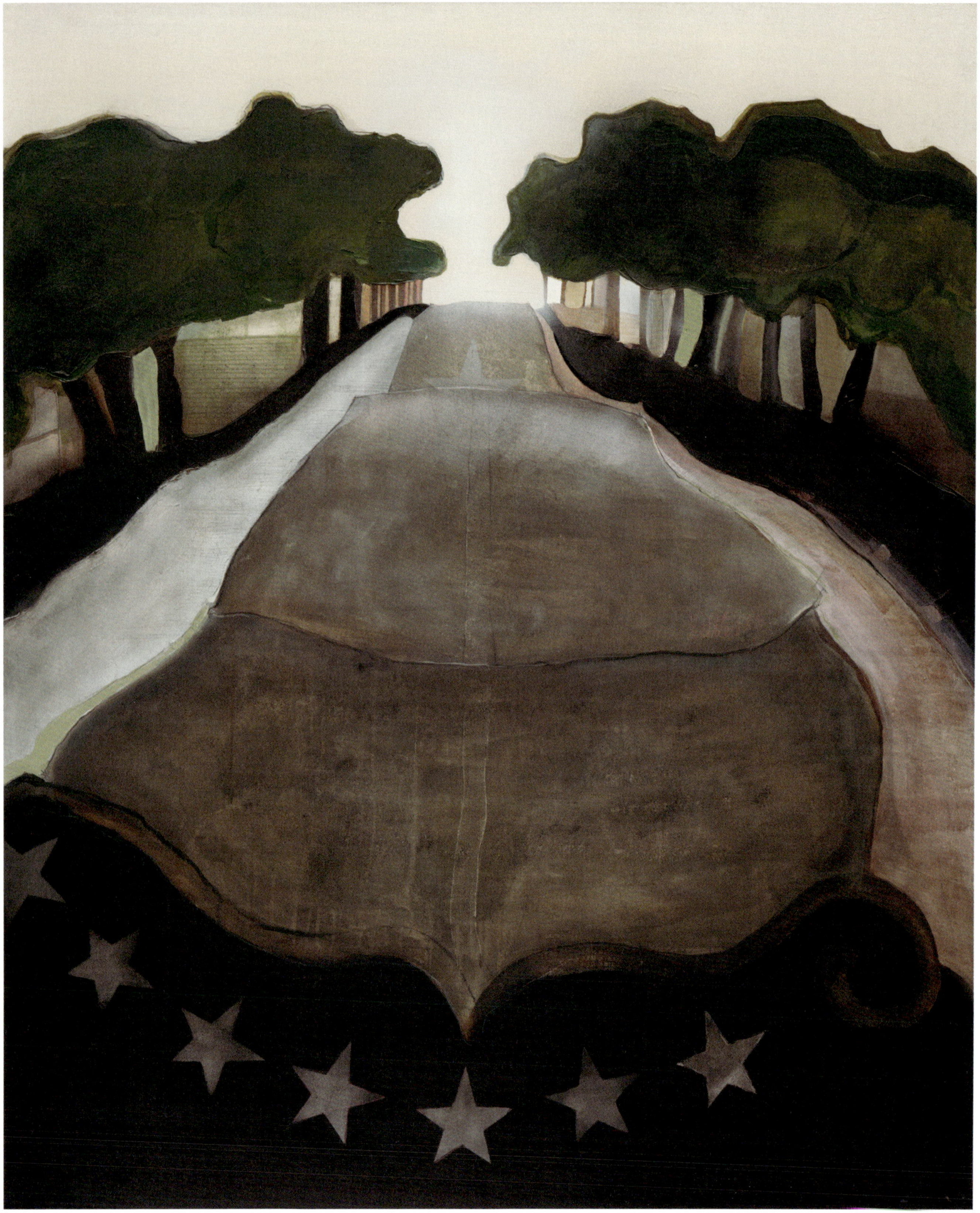

< *Springfield Ave . . . 5:00*, October 1968, acrylic paint on canvas

> *The Skirted Garden*, 1969, fabric skirt, nylon stockings, lace, felt, canvas, and other painted fabrics

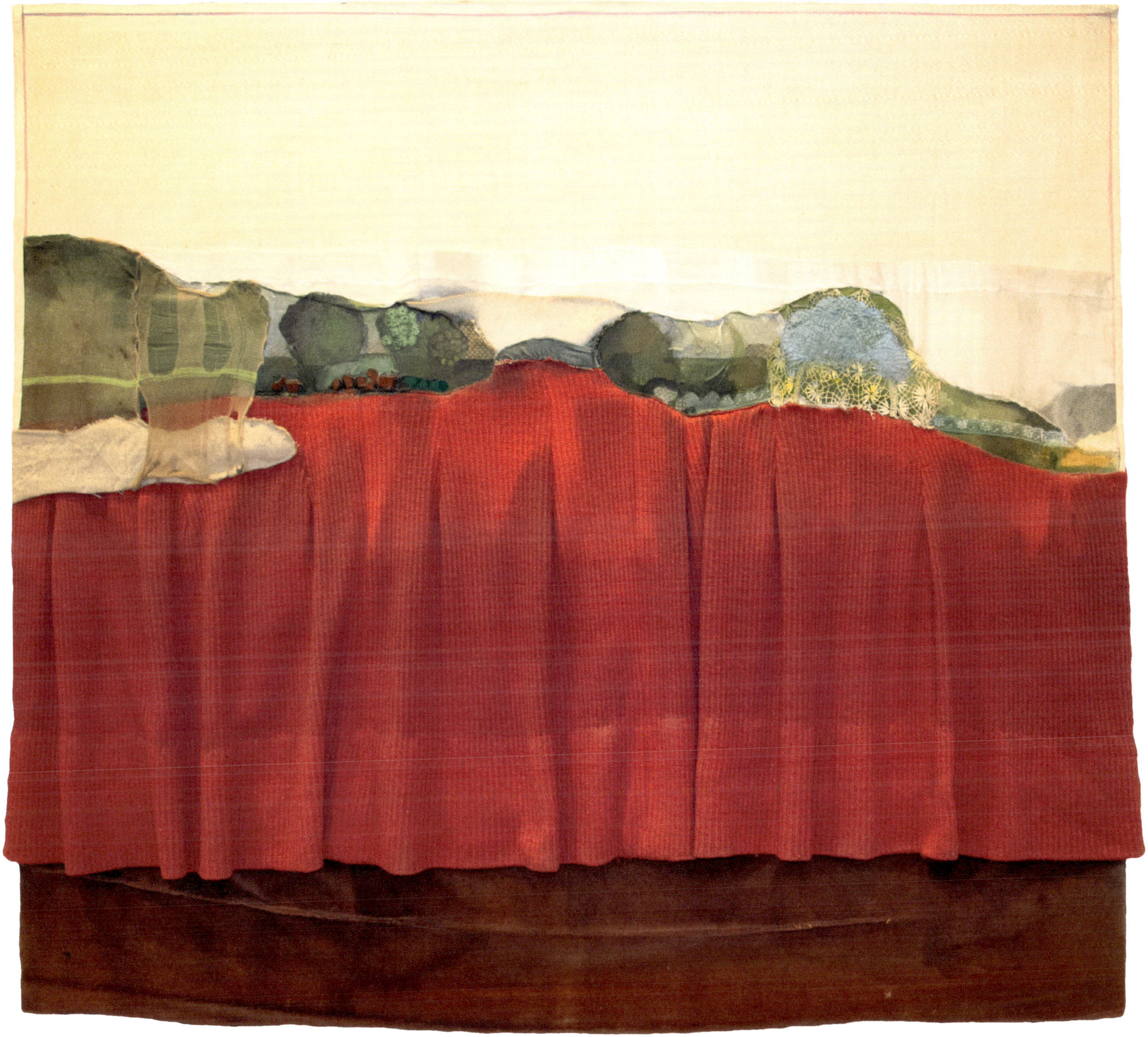

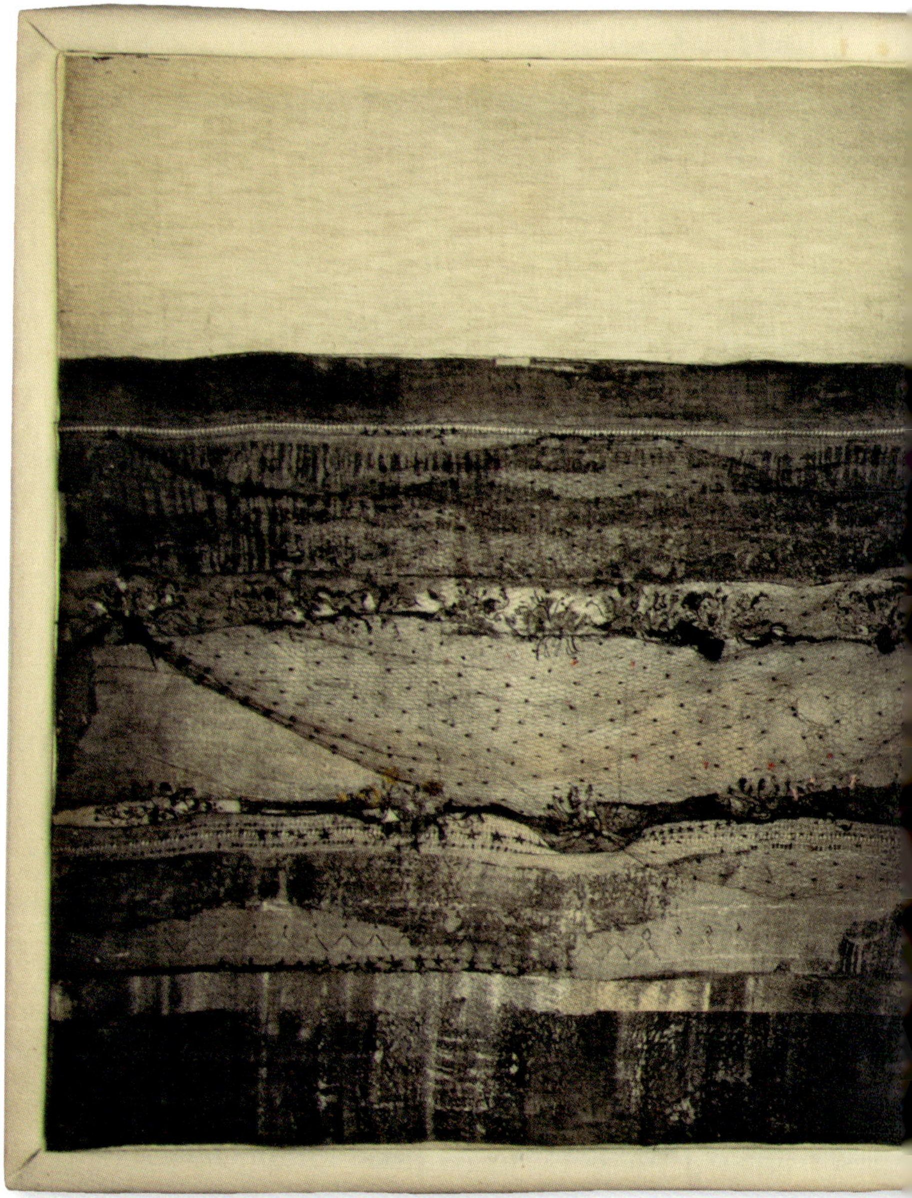

> *Imaginary Prairie*, July 1969, etchings on muslin

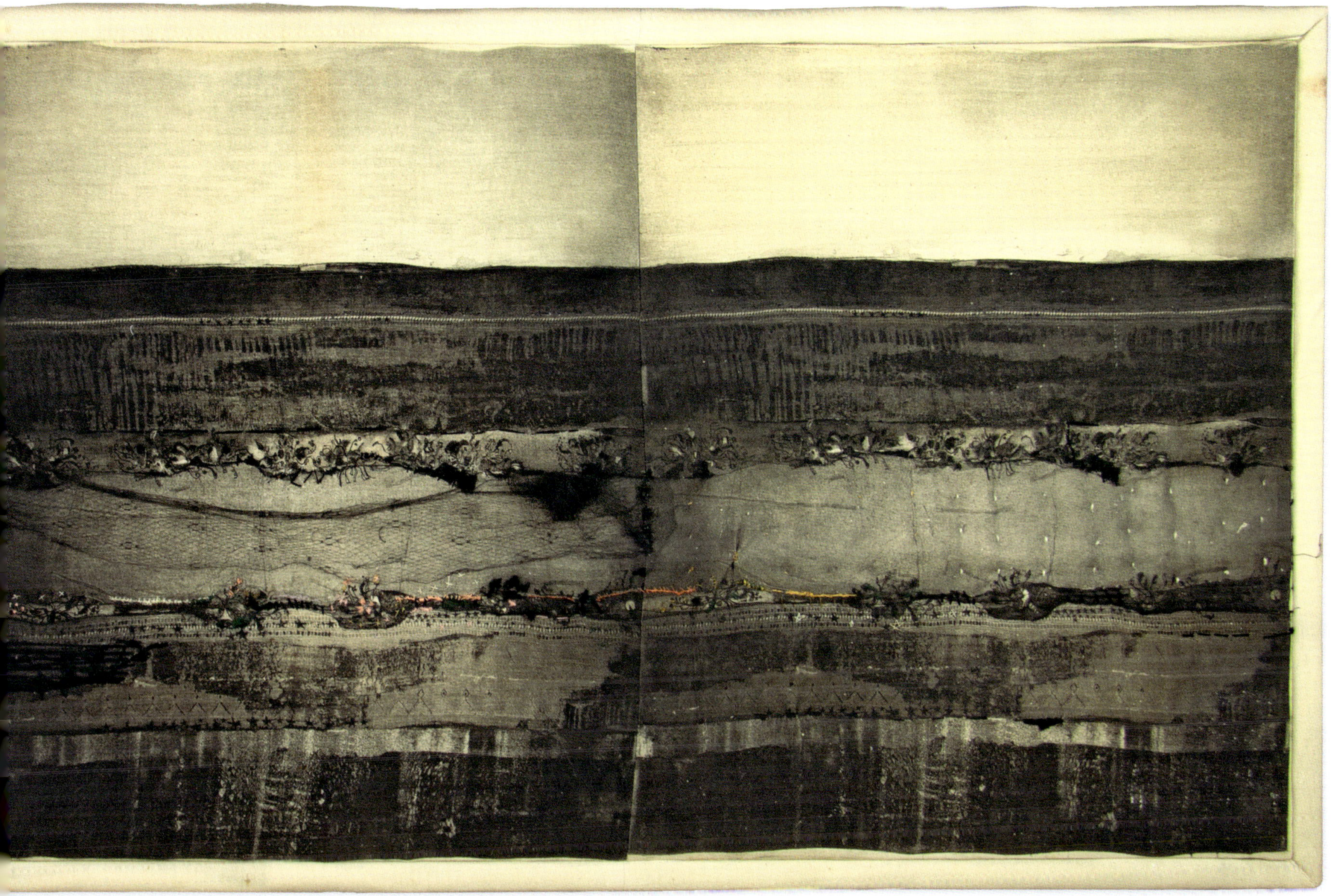

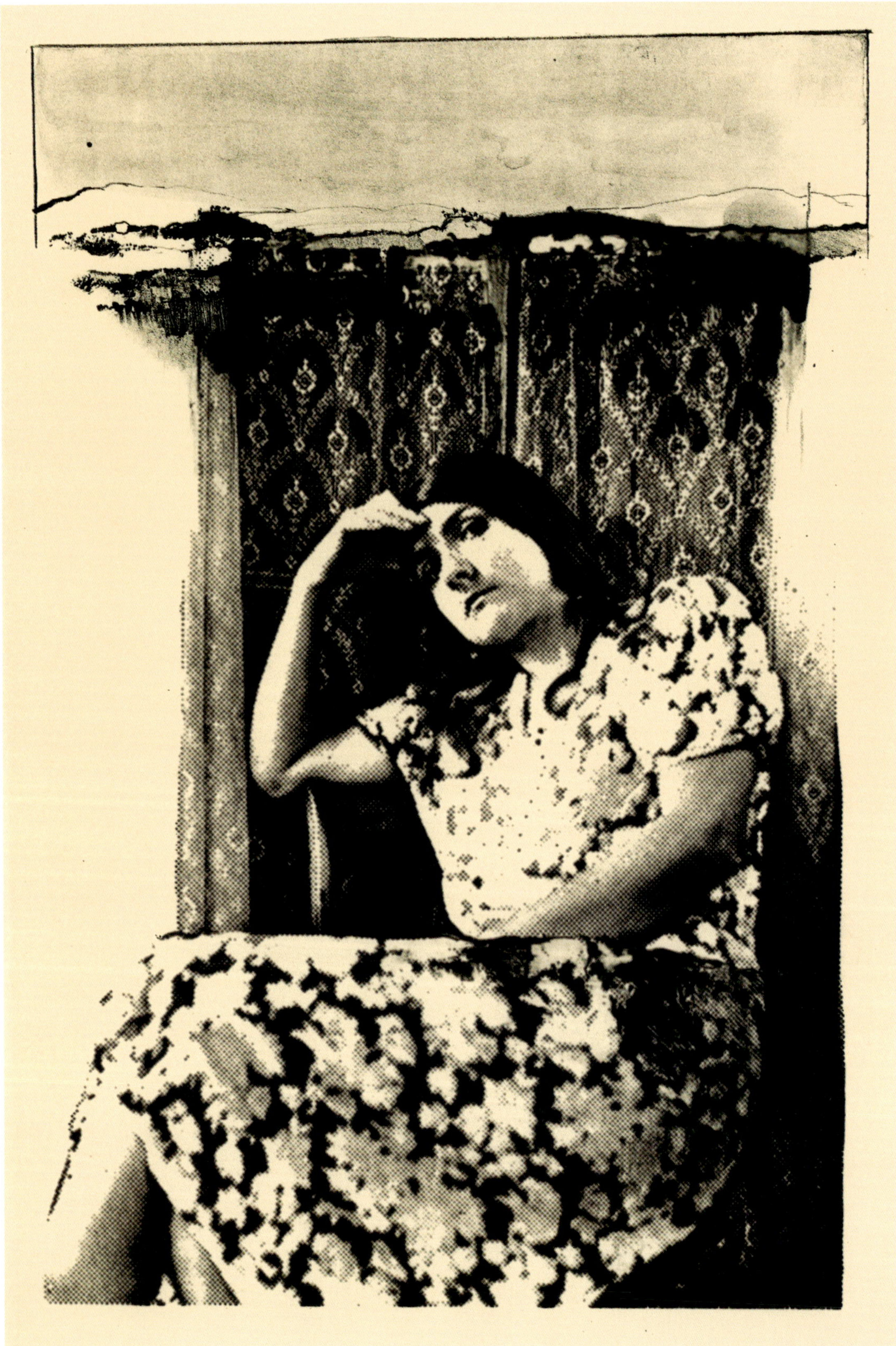

< *Interior Exterior*, October 1969, lithograph (based on screen print)

> *Head Crowned*, November 1969, gelatin silver print

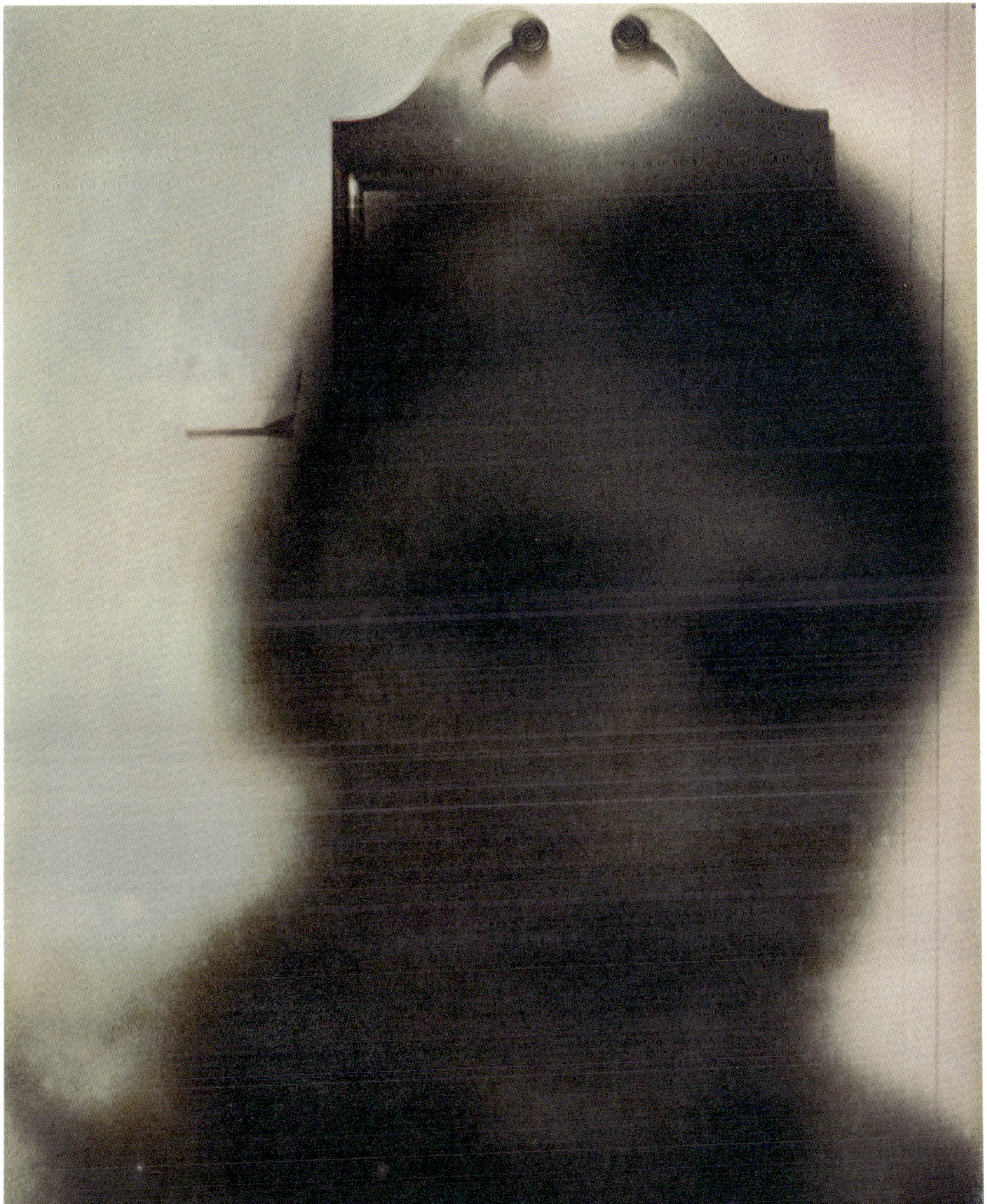

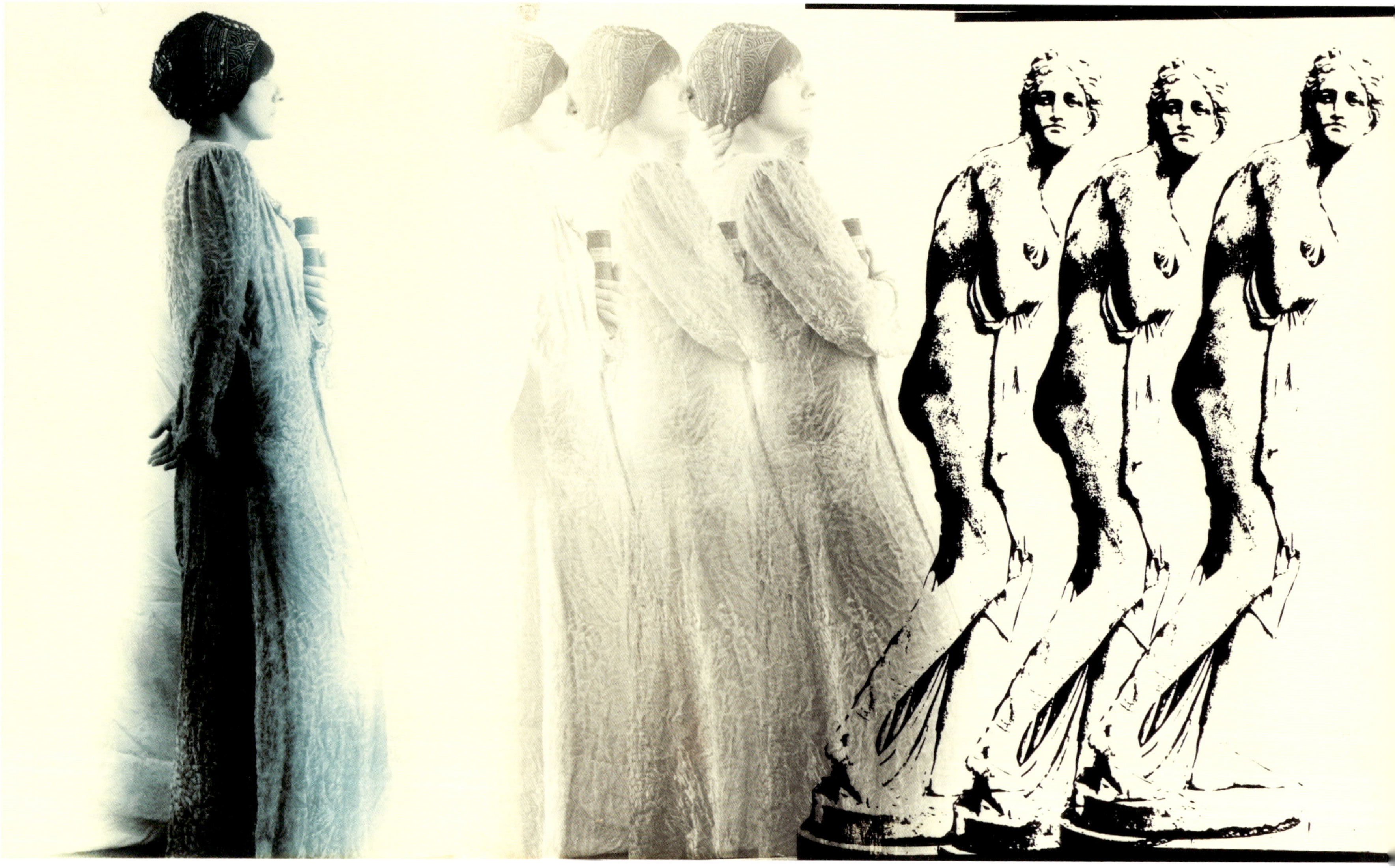

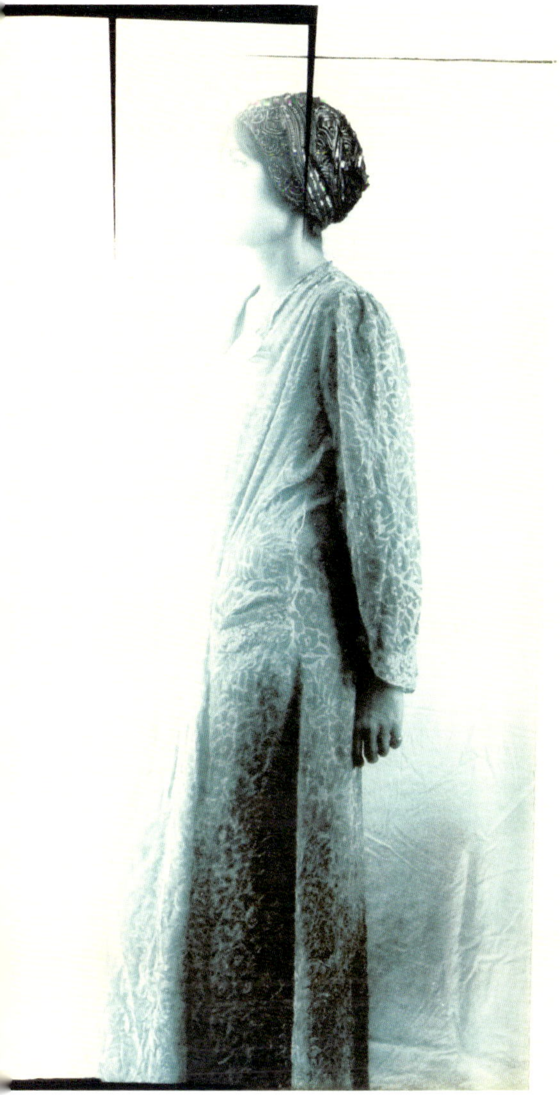

< *Triple Goddess*, November 1969, collage with gelatin silver prints

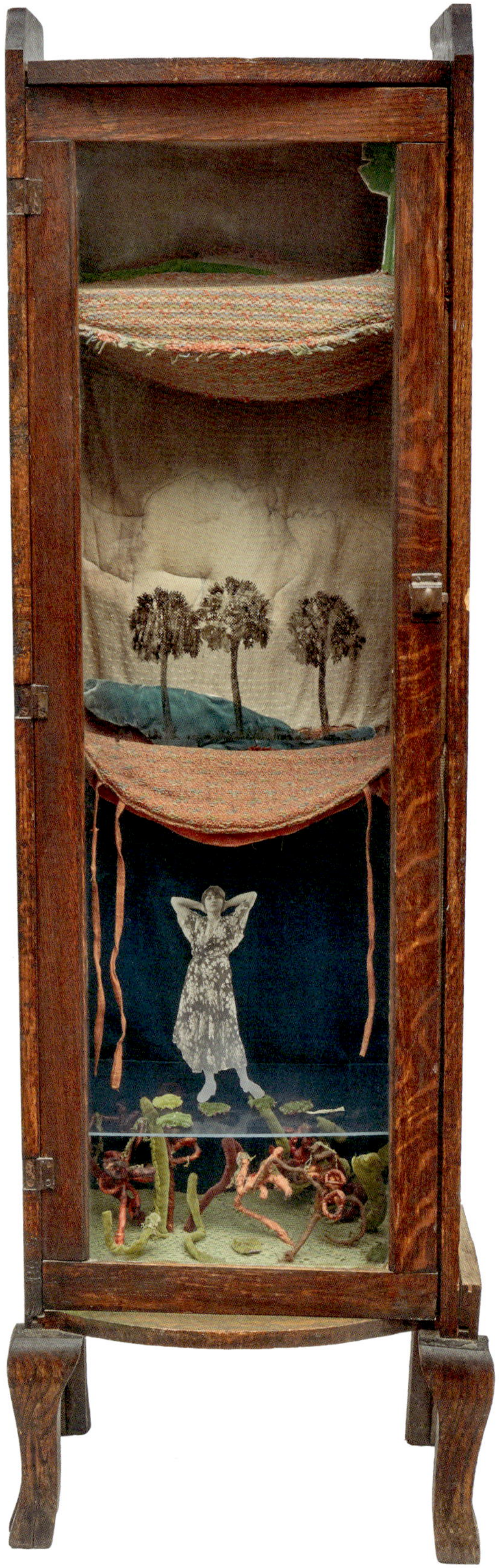

< *Swamp Box: Birth of Venus*, 1969, oak cabinet with mixed media interior

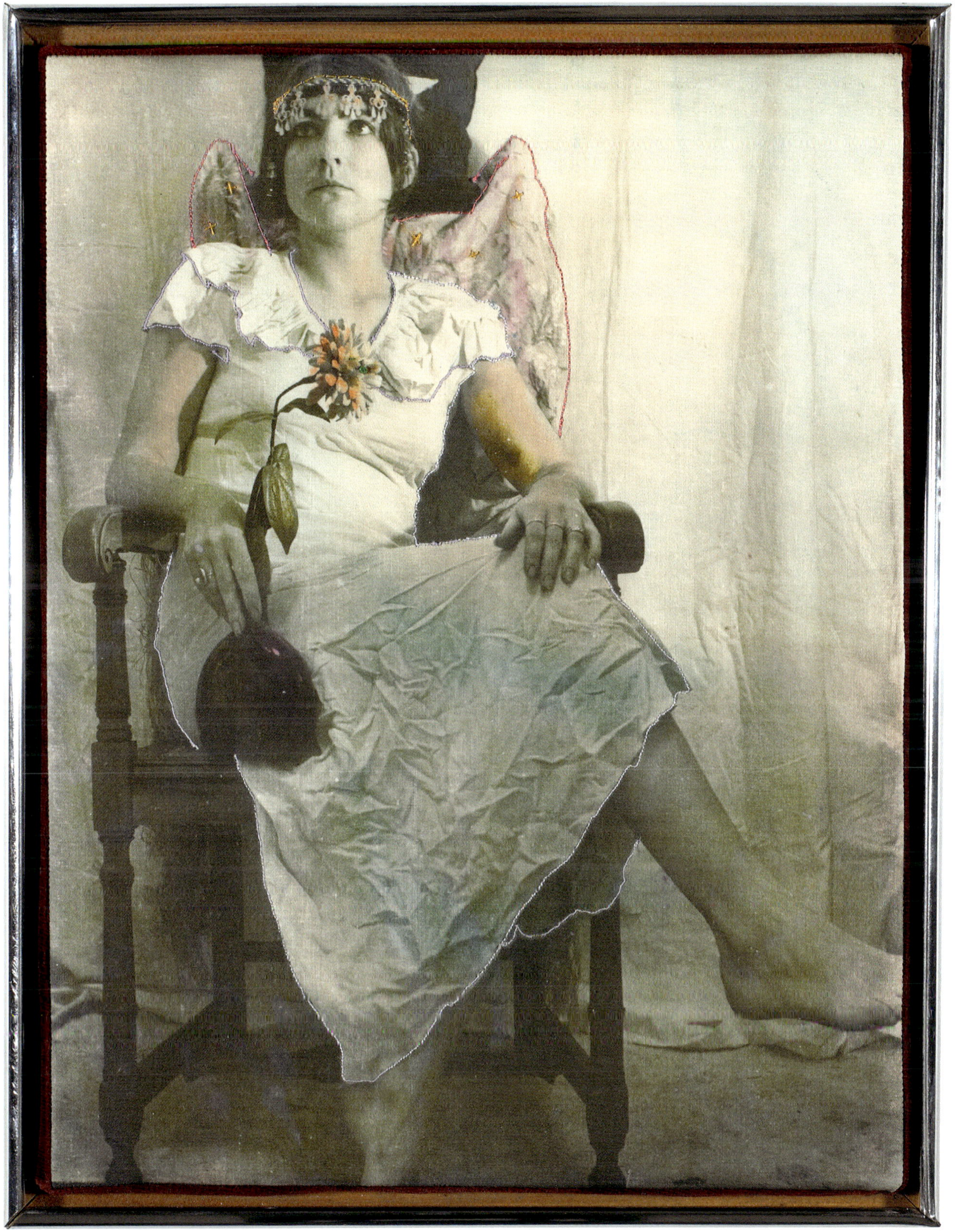

> *Queen of Pentacles*, April 1970, gelatin silver photo linen with applied color, stitched, padded, stretched over wood in aluminum frame

Neptune and Lake lady .. a series
Nettles Winter 71

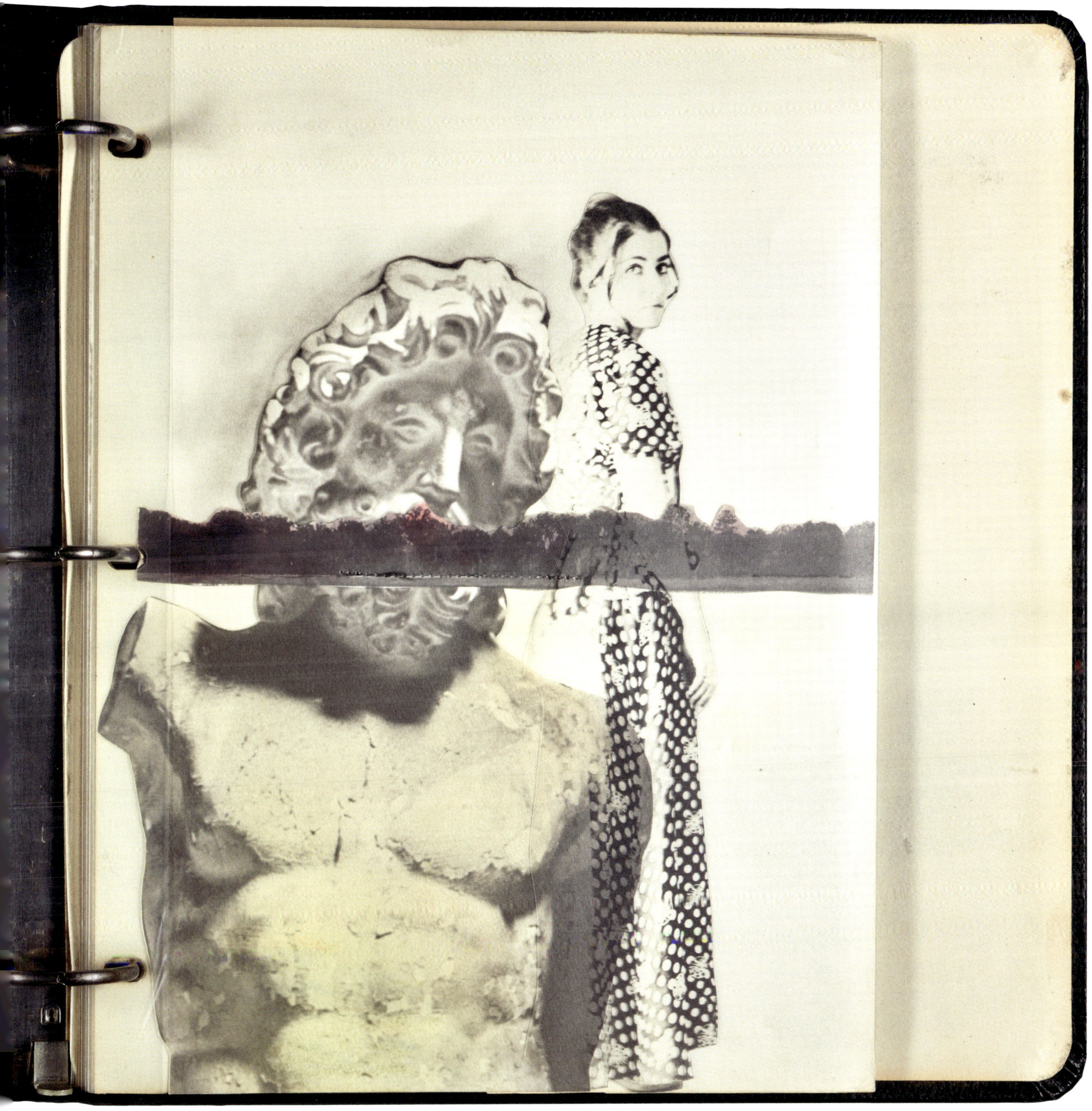

‹ ***Neptune and Lake Lady . . . a series***, 1970, bound volume with gelatin silver prints, ortho film, polyester film, stitching, and applied color

*Neptune & Lotus Lady*, October 1970

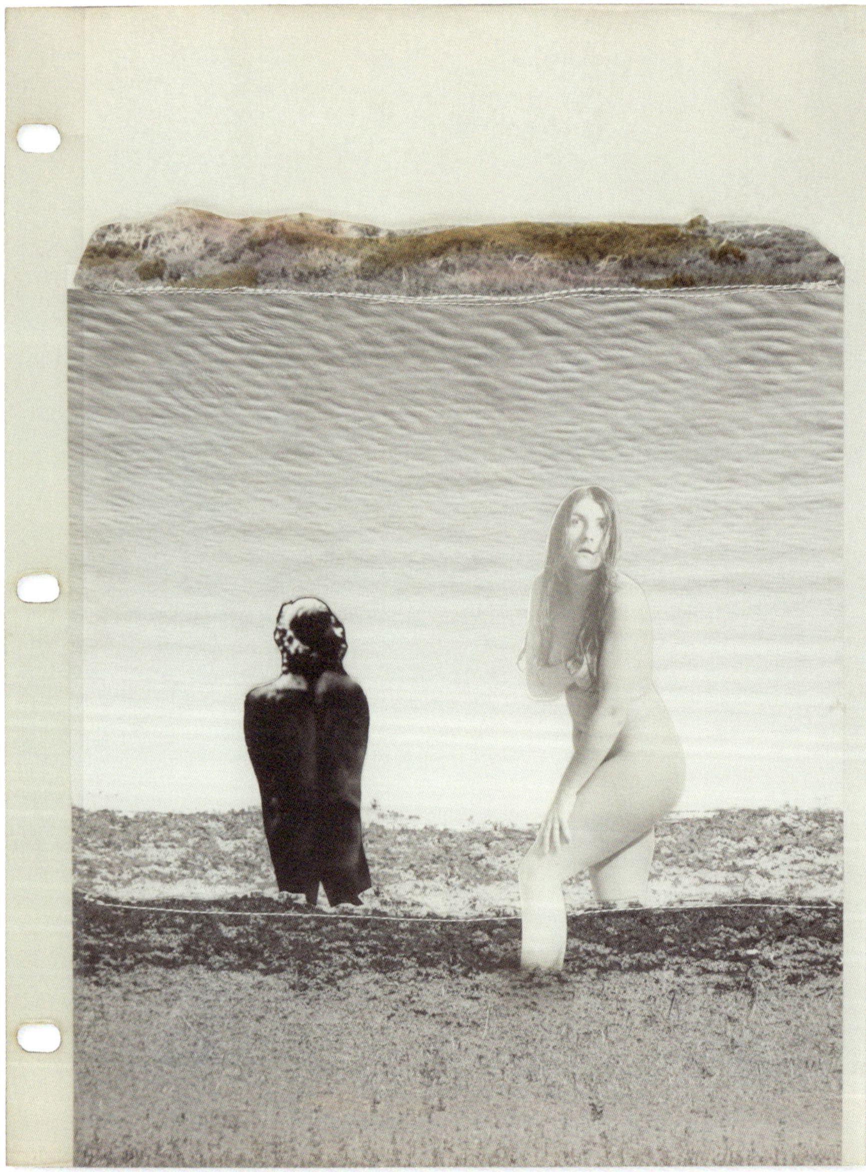

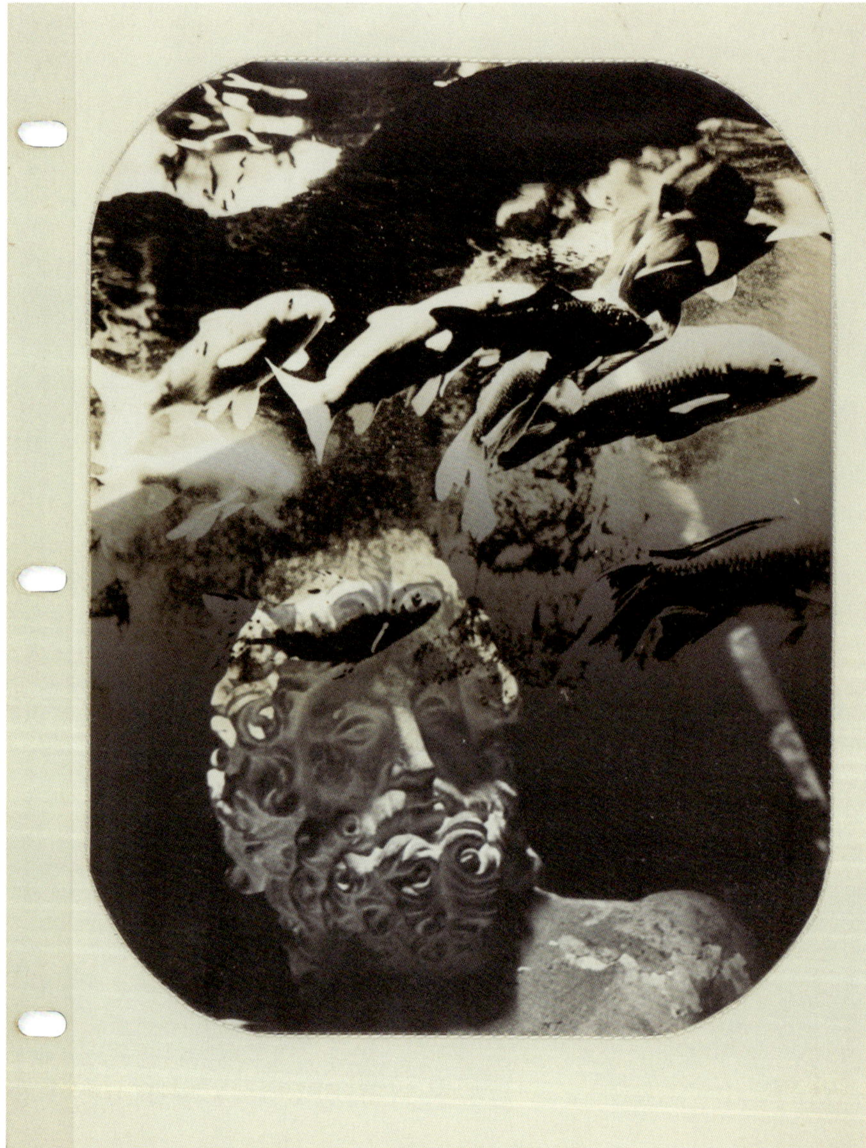

> ***Neptune and Lake Lady . . . a series***

*Lake Edge*, 1970

*Head and Fish*, 1970

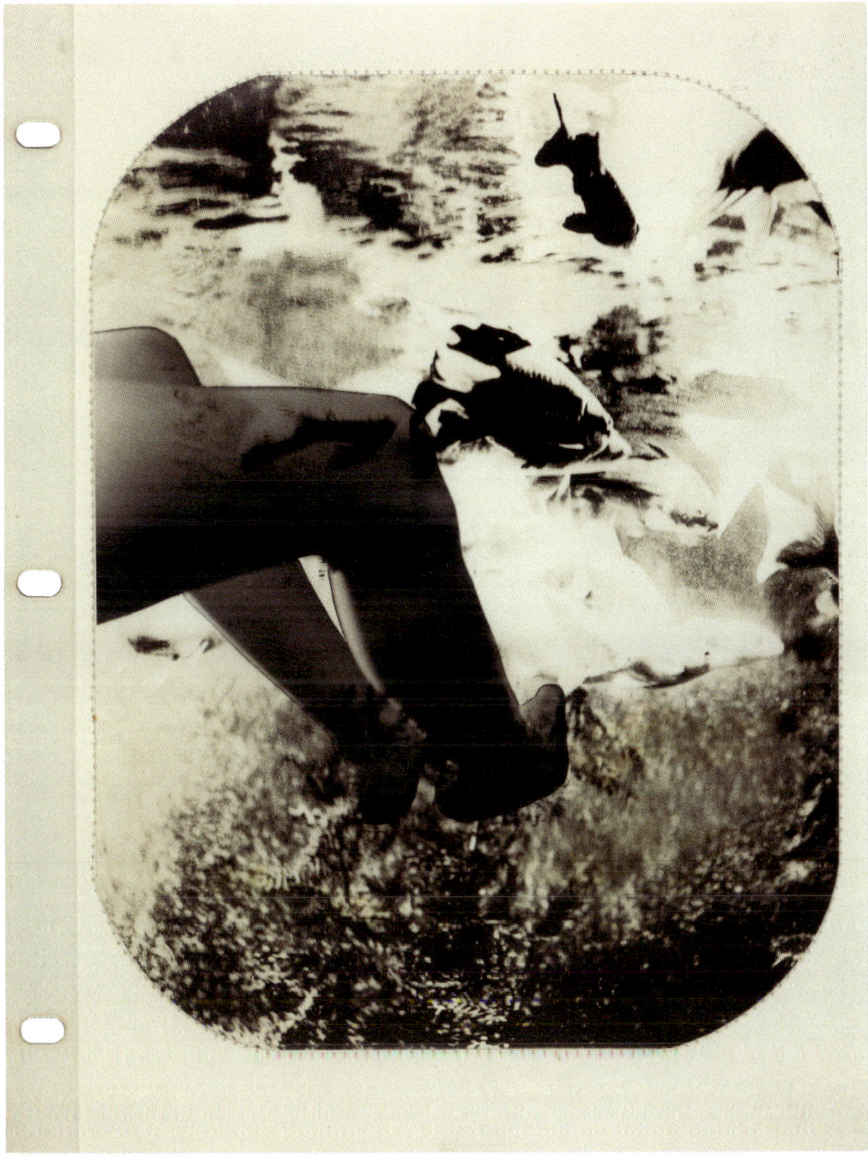

*Lake Lady Legs*, December 1970

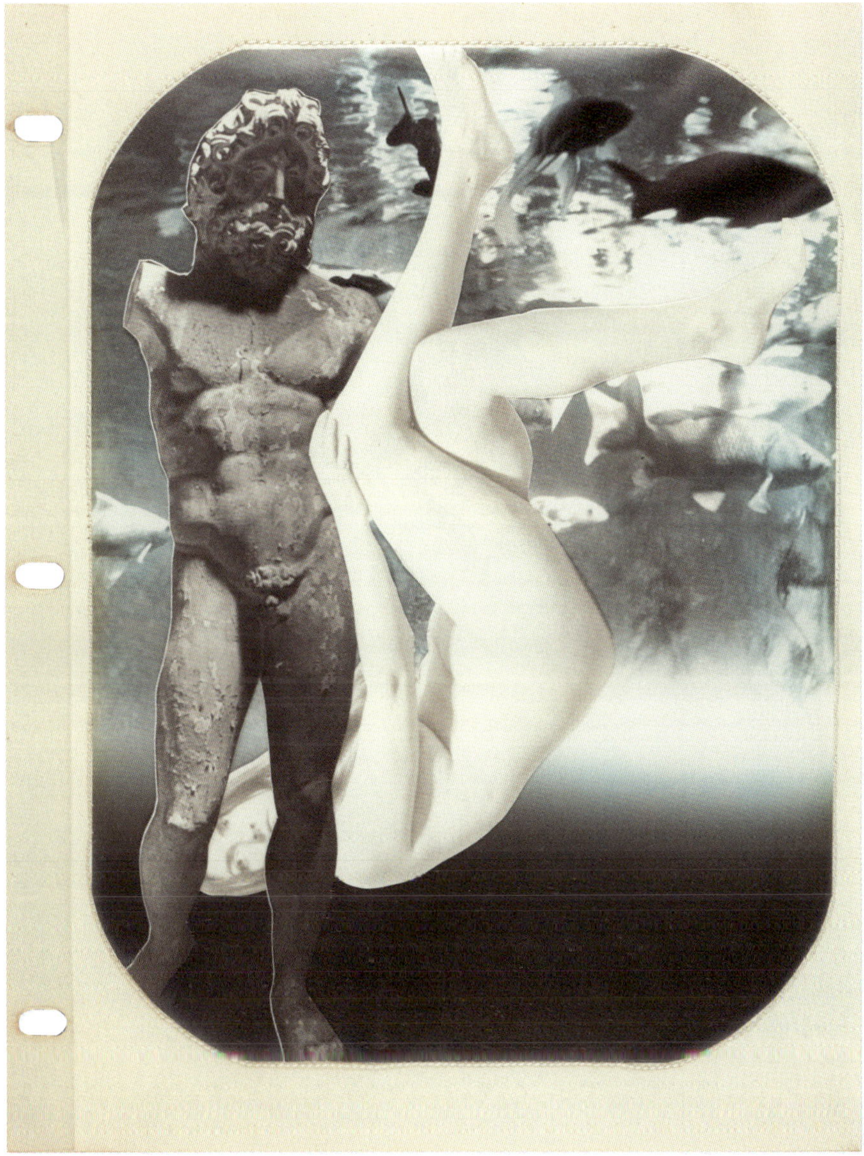

*Figures Intertwined*, 1970

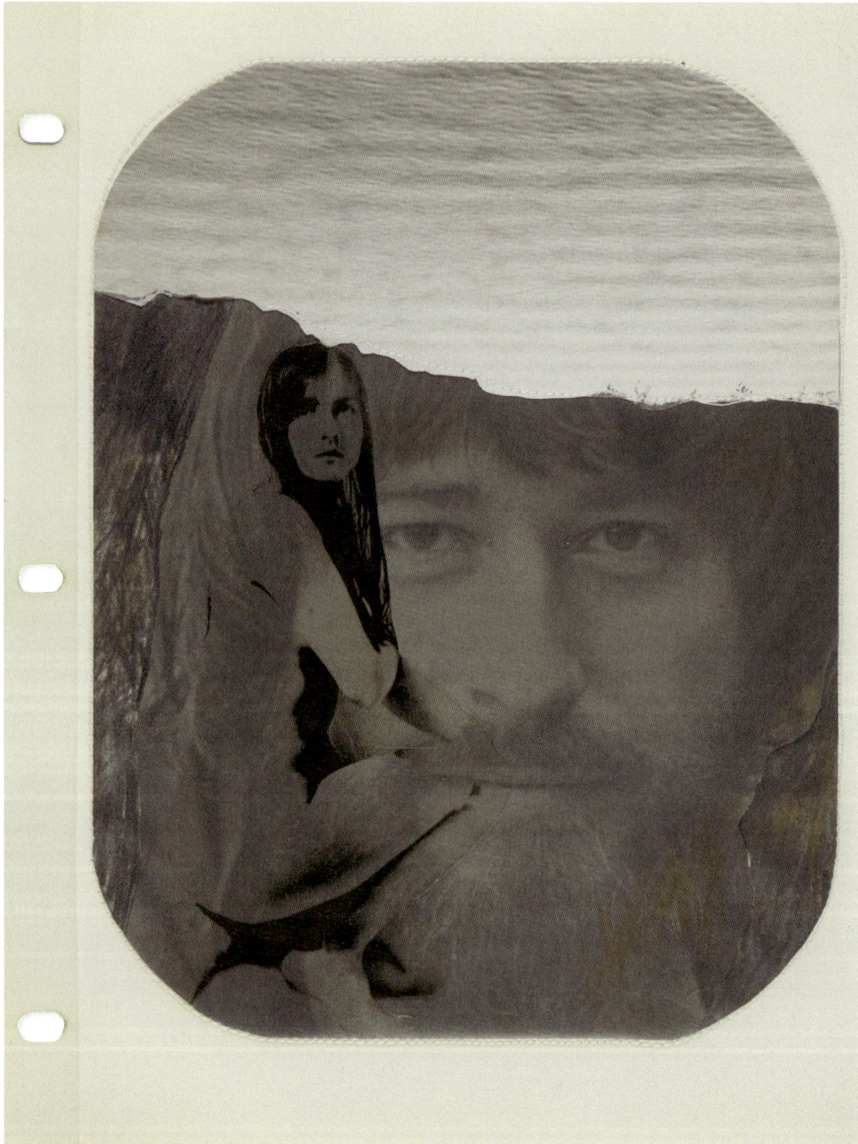

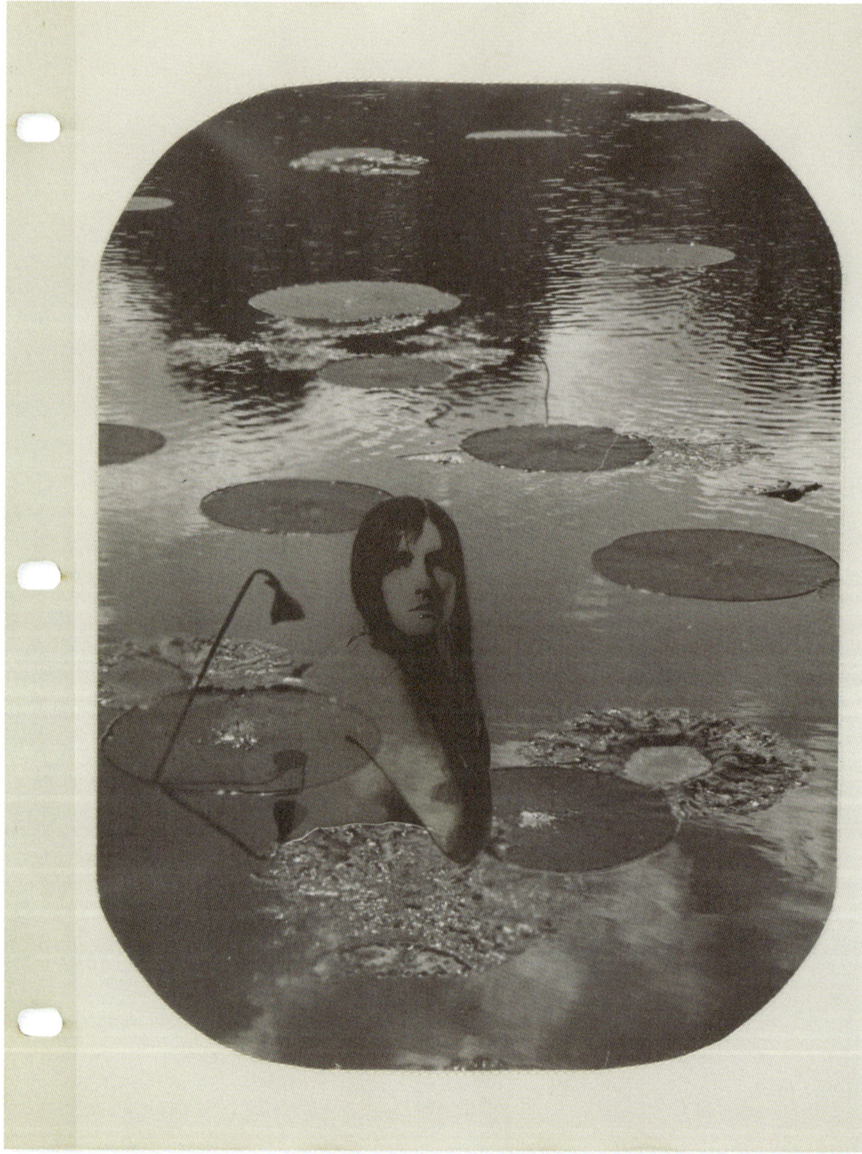

> ***Neptune and Lake Lady . . . a series***

*RJ*, 1970

*B out of Lilies*, 1970

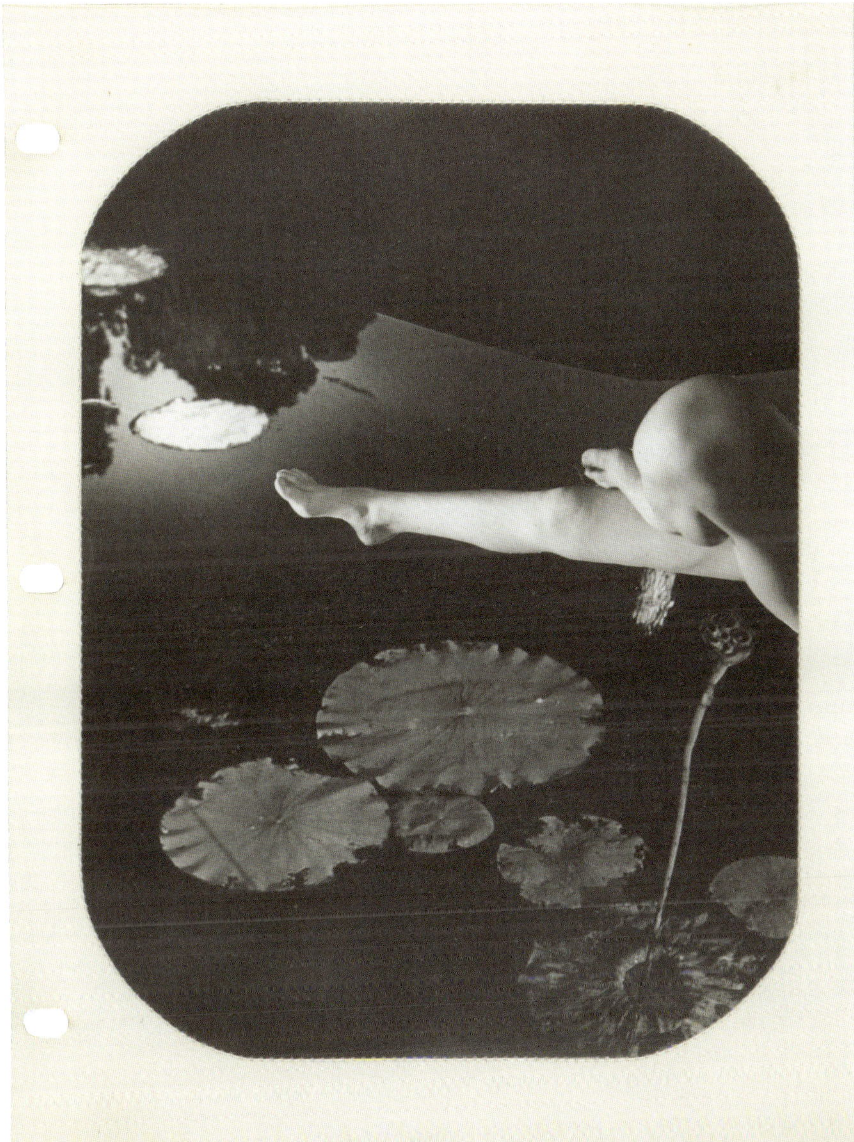

*Lady Legs*, 1970

> *Evenin* . . . , August 1970, collage with gelatin silver prints, stitching, and applied color

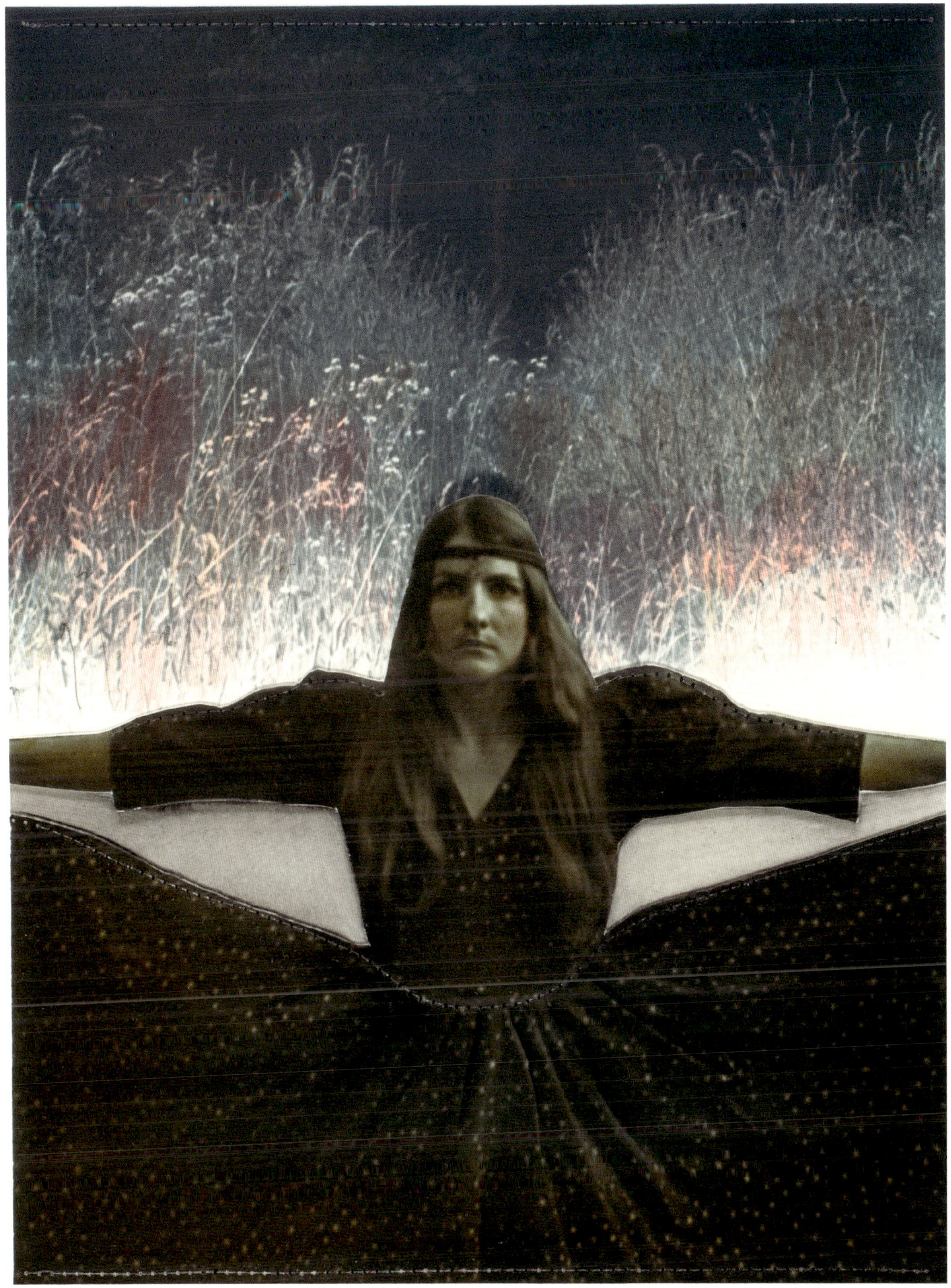

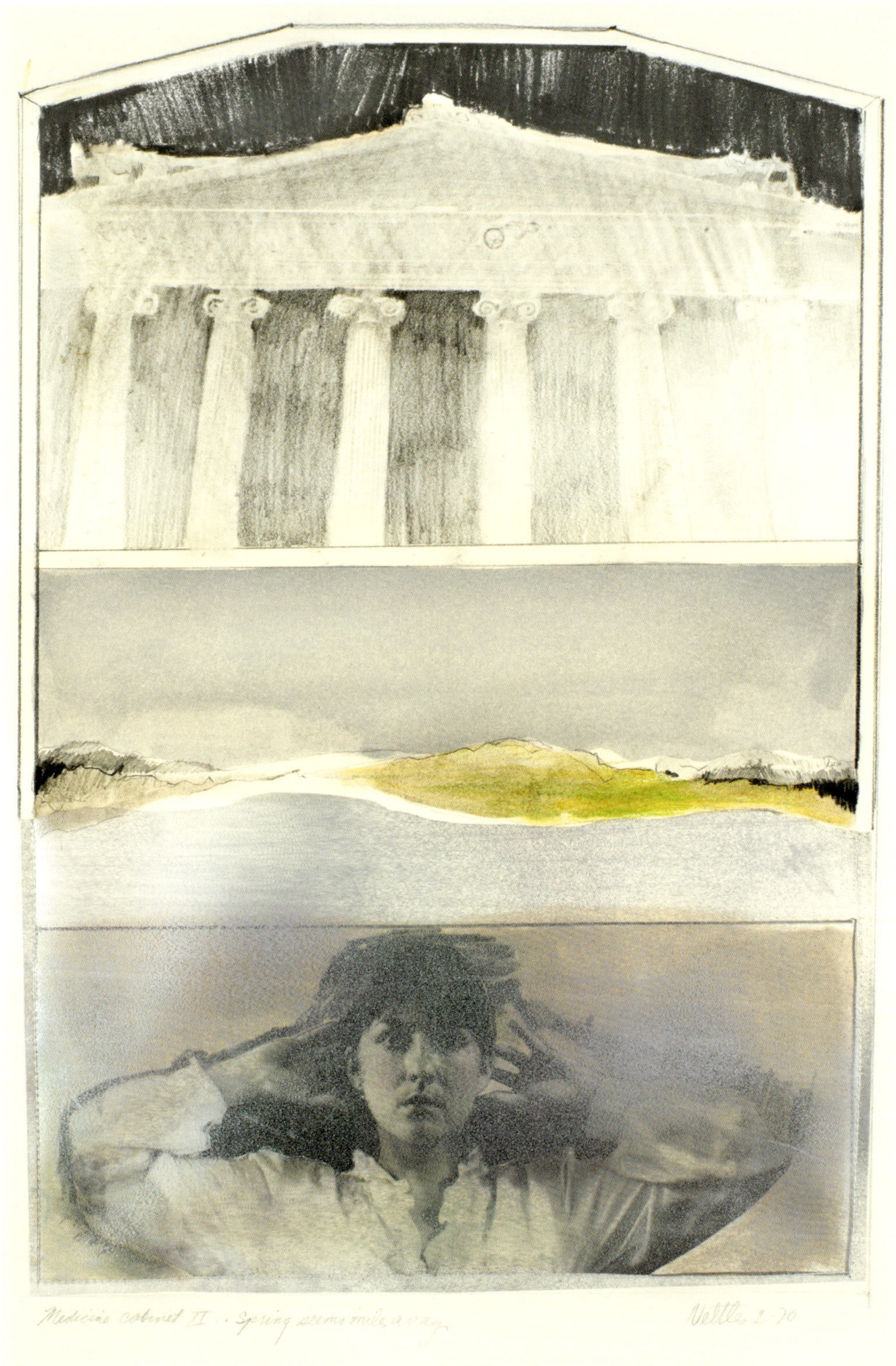


< *Medicine Cabinet II . . . Spring seems miles away*, 1970, collage with gelatin silver prints, magazine transfers, polyester film, and applied color

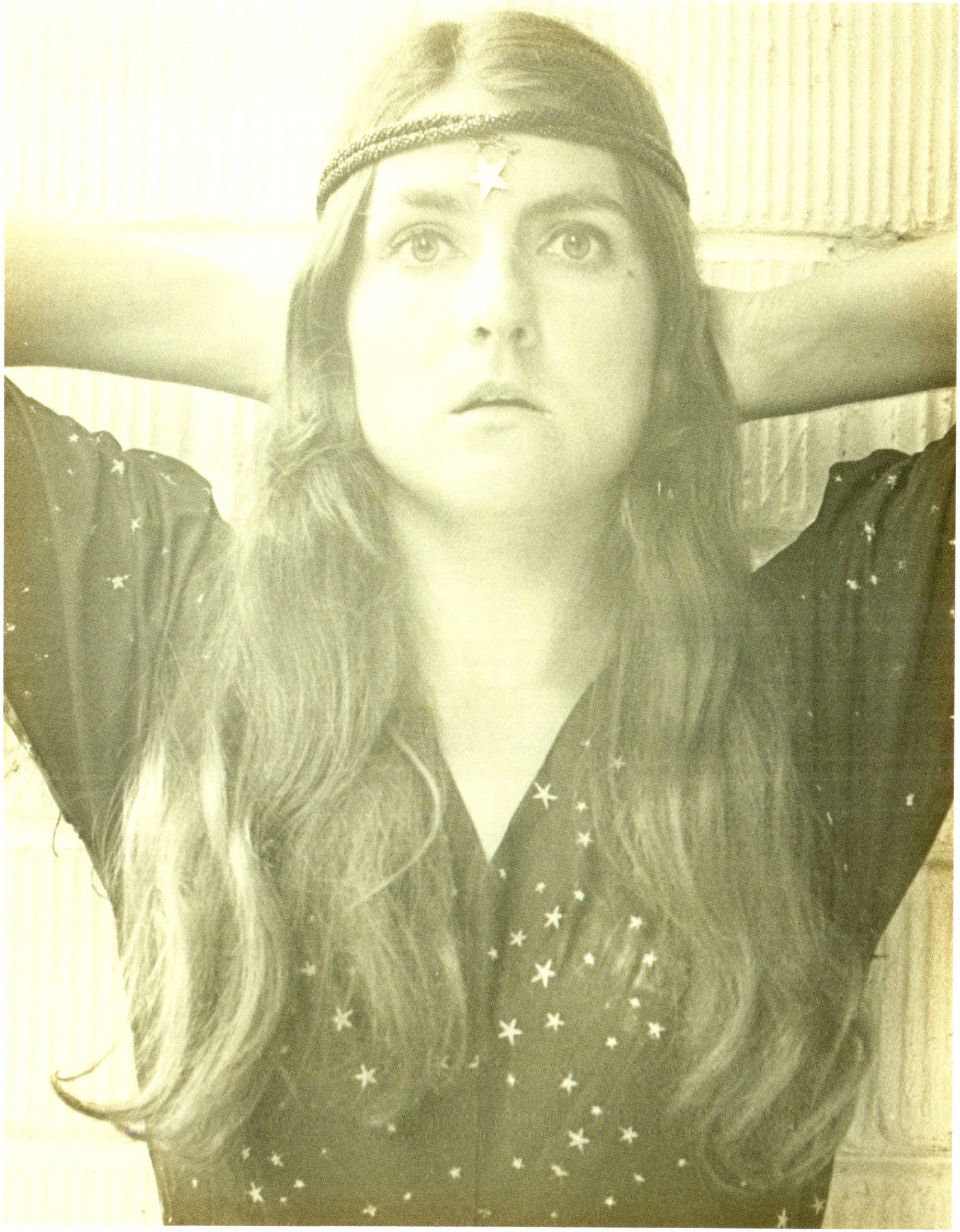

> *Star Lady*, August 1970, gelatin silver print

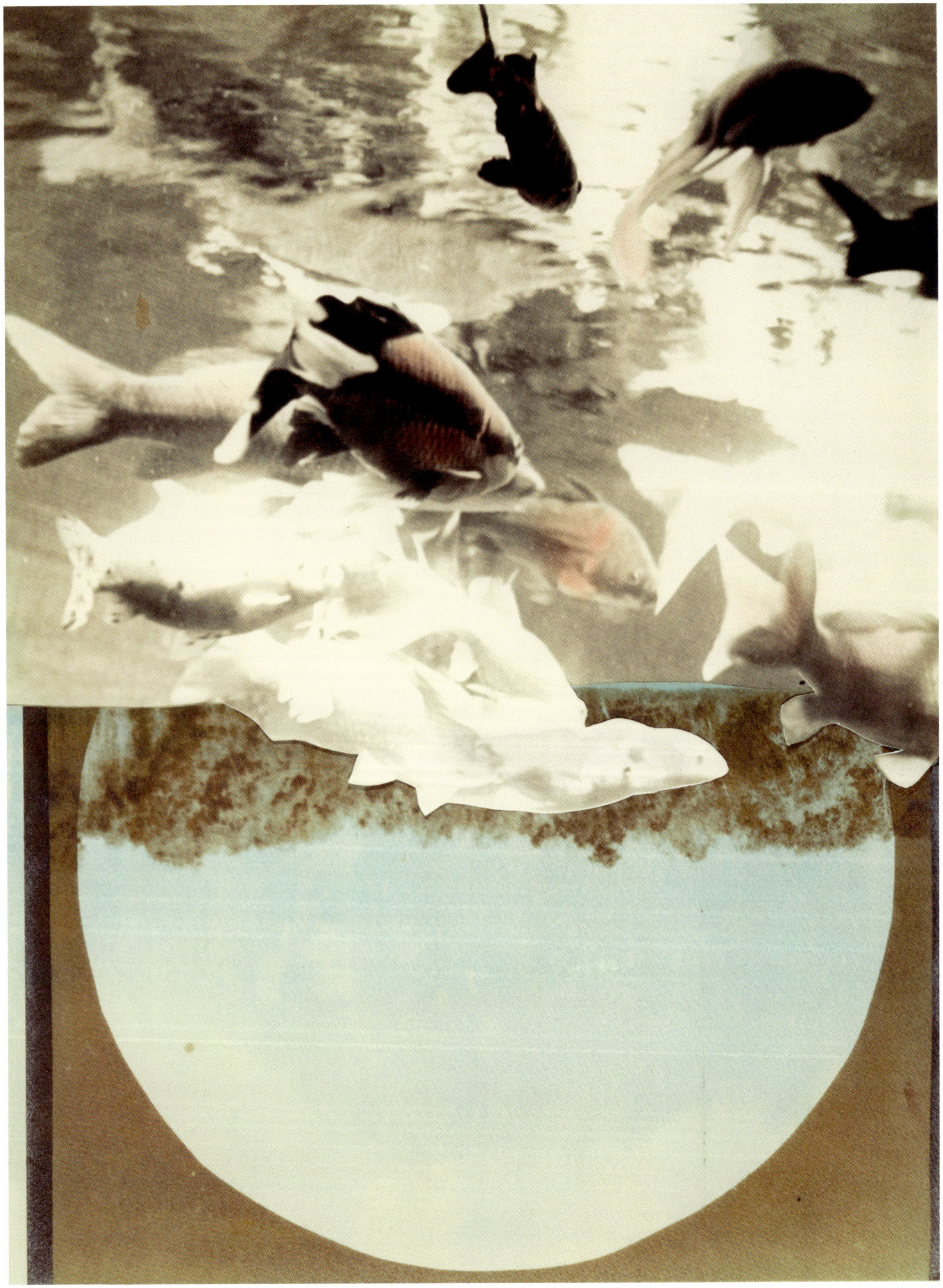

> *Skyfish*, October 1970, collage with gelatin silver prints and applied color

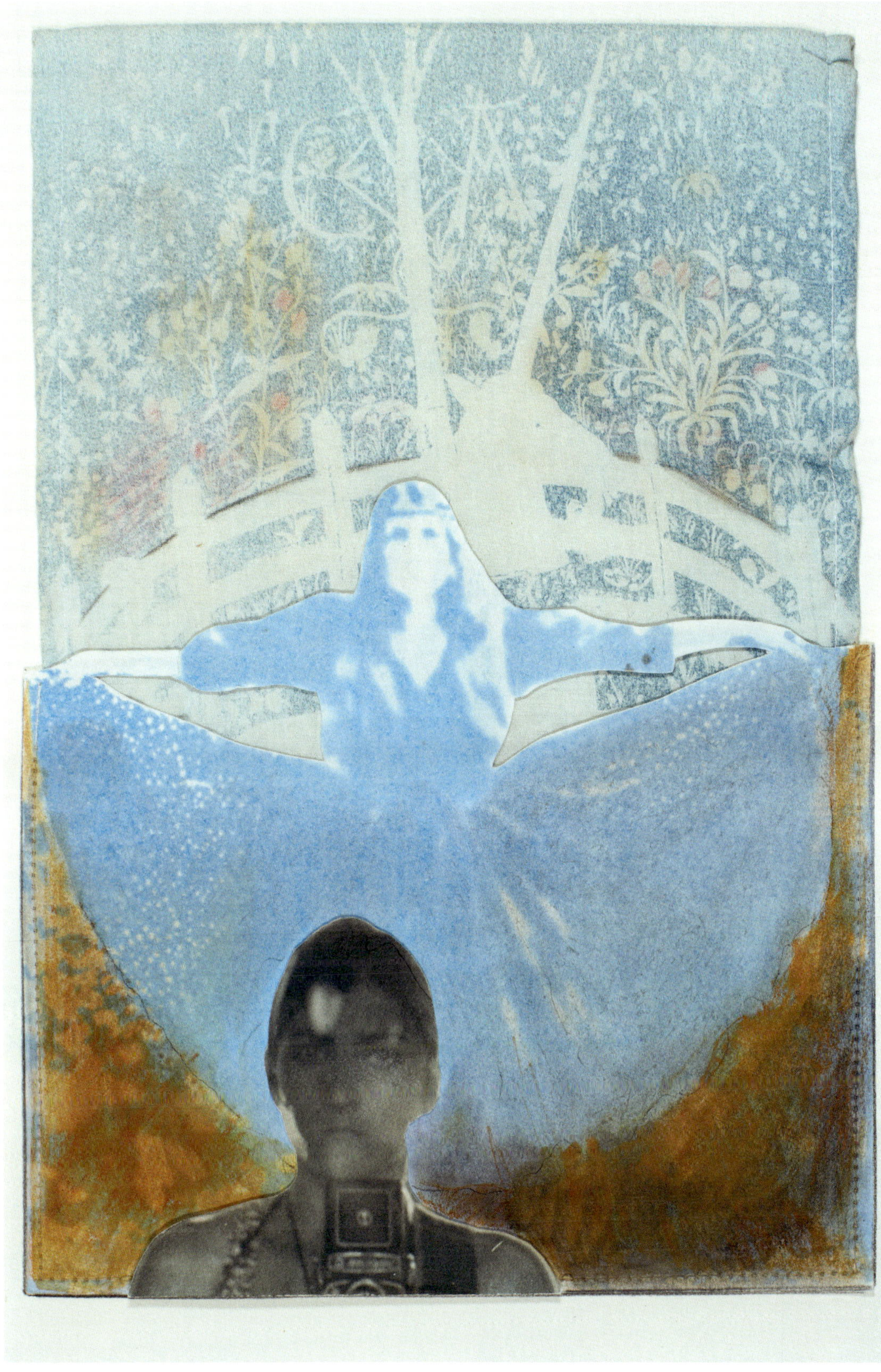

> *Unicorn Tapestry*, January 1972, collage with cyanotypes on cotton fabric and paper, silver gelatin print, stitching and applied color

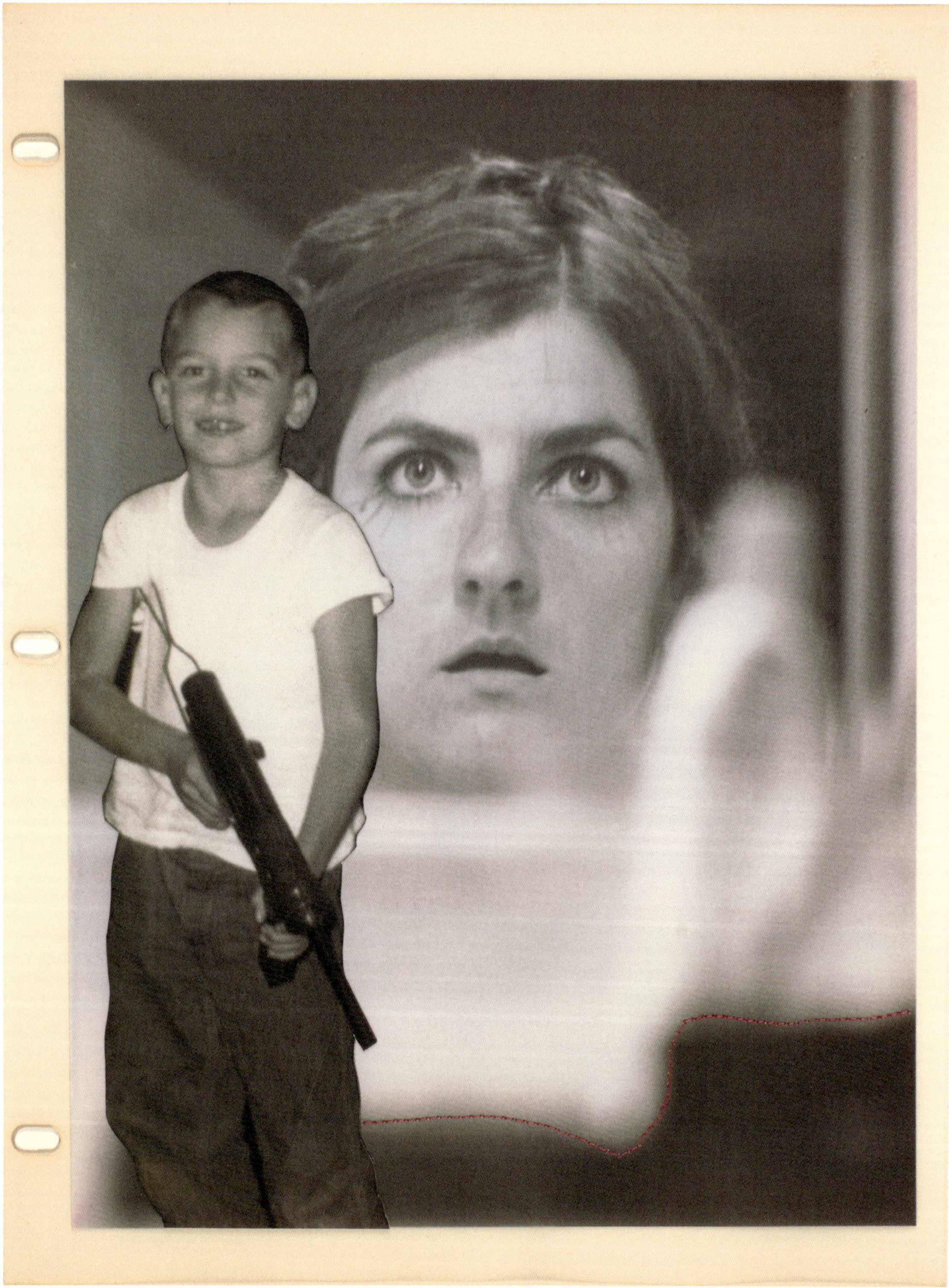

< *Xmas Gun II*, 1971, from *Ghosts and Stitched Shadows*, collage with gelatin silver prints, polyester film and stitching

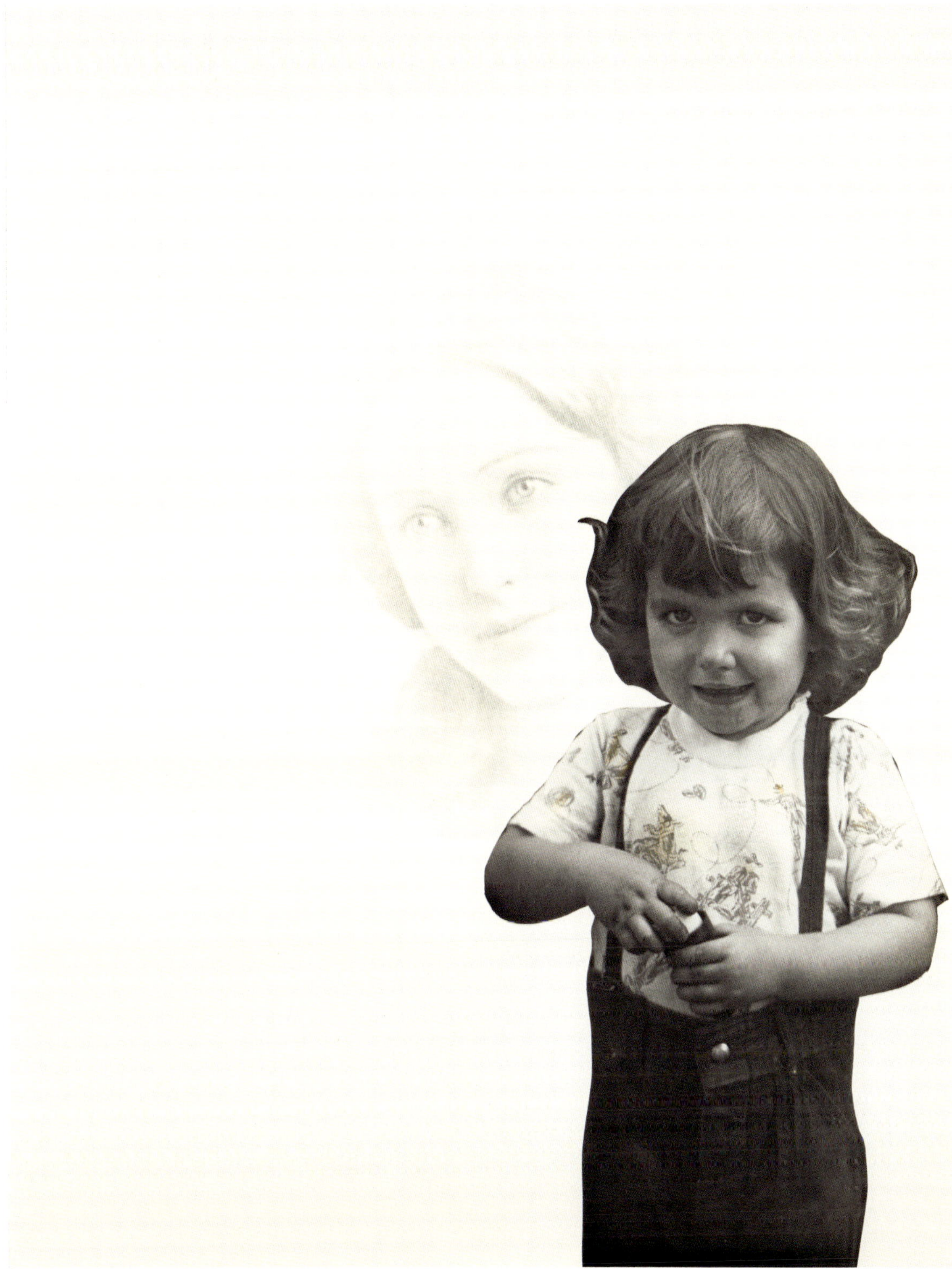

> *B and Venus*, May 1971, collage with gelatin silver prints and applied color

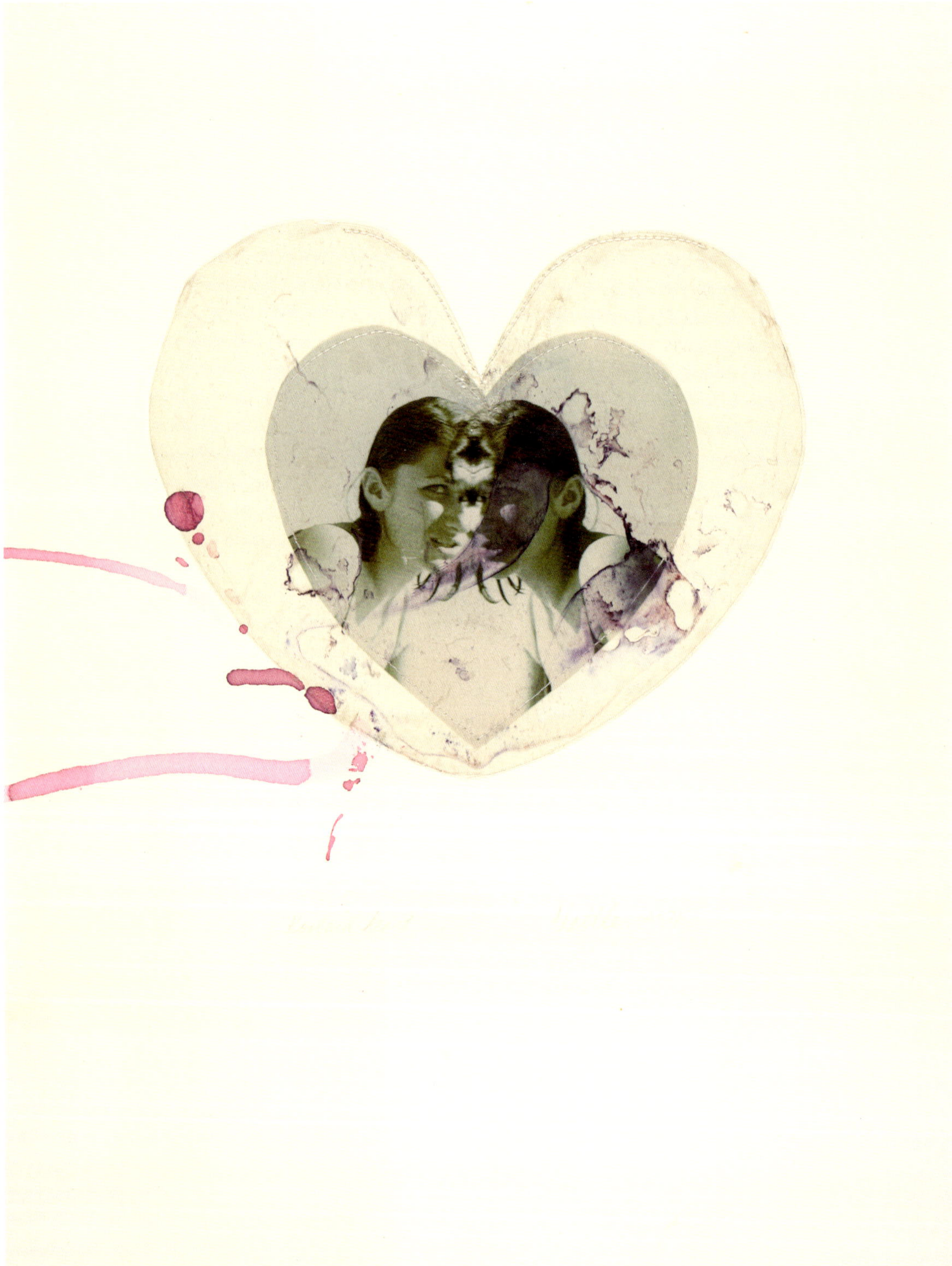

< *Koolaid Heart*, October 1971, gelatin silver print with stitched vinyl overlay that once contained colored liquid

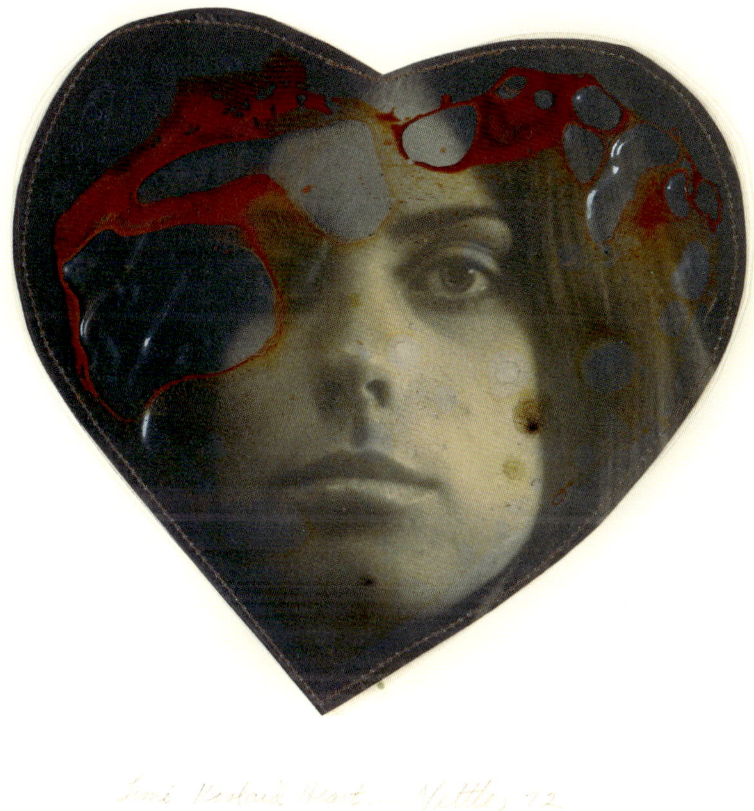

> *Lime Koolaid Heart*, 1972, gelatin silver print with stitched vinyl overlay that once contained colored liquid

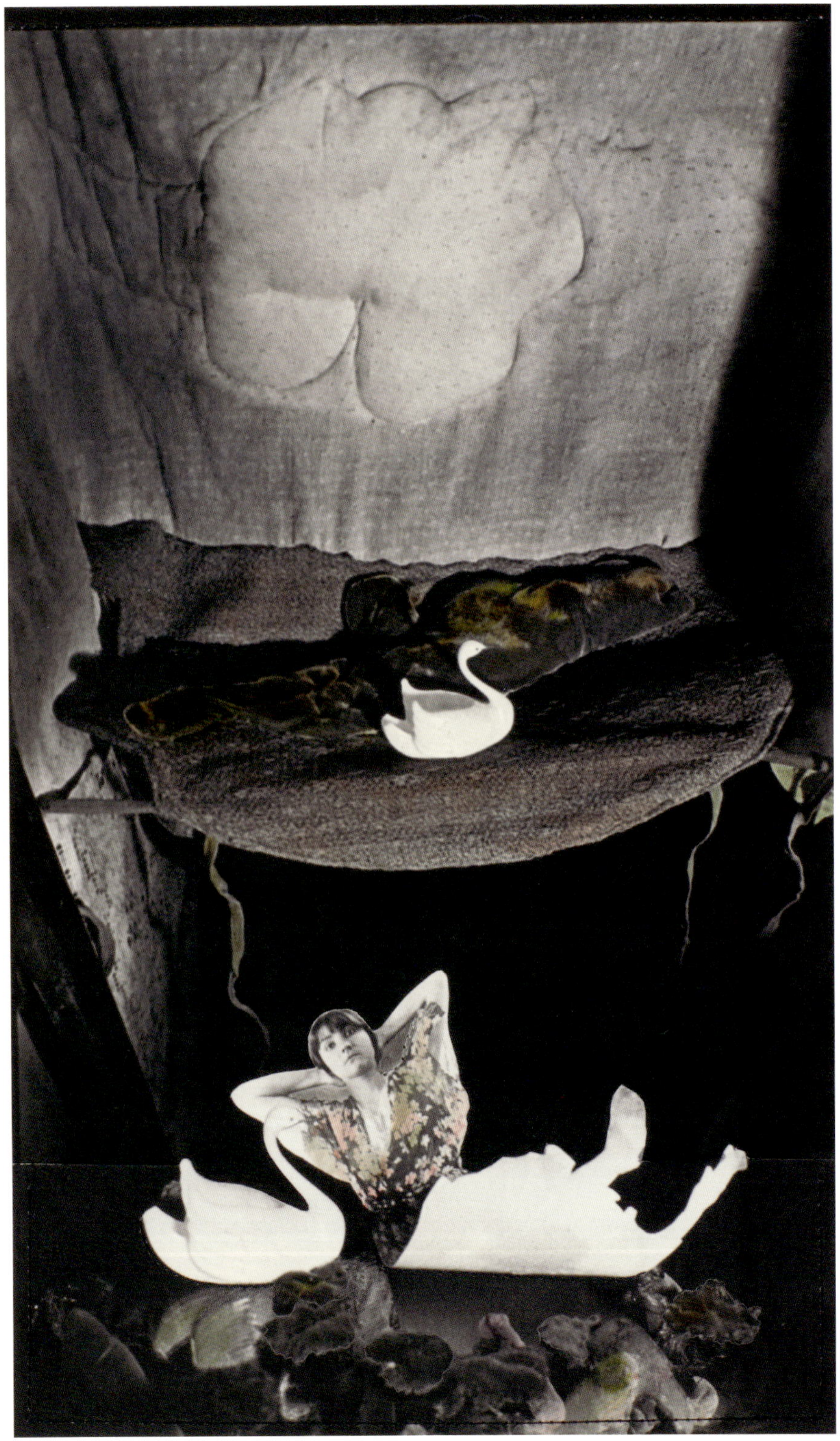

< *Swan Totem*, 1972, collage with gelatin silver prints and applied color

> *Sister in the Garden with Birdbaths*, January 1972, silver emulsion on cloth, stitching, gelatin silver print enclosed in stitched vinyl, embroidery and applied color

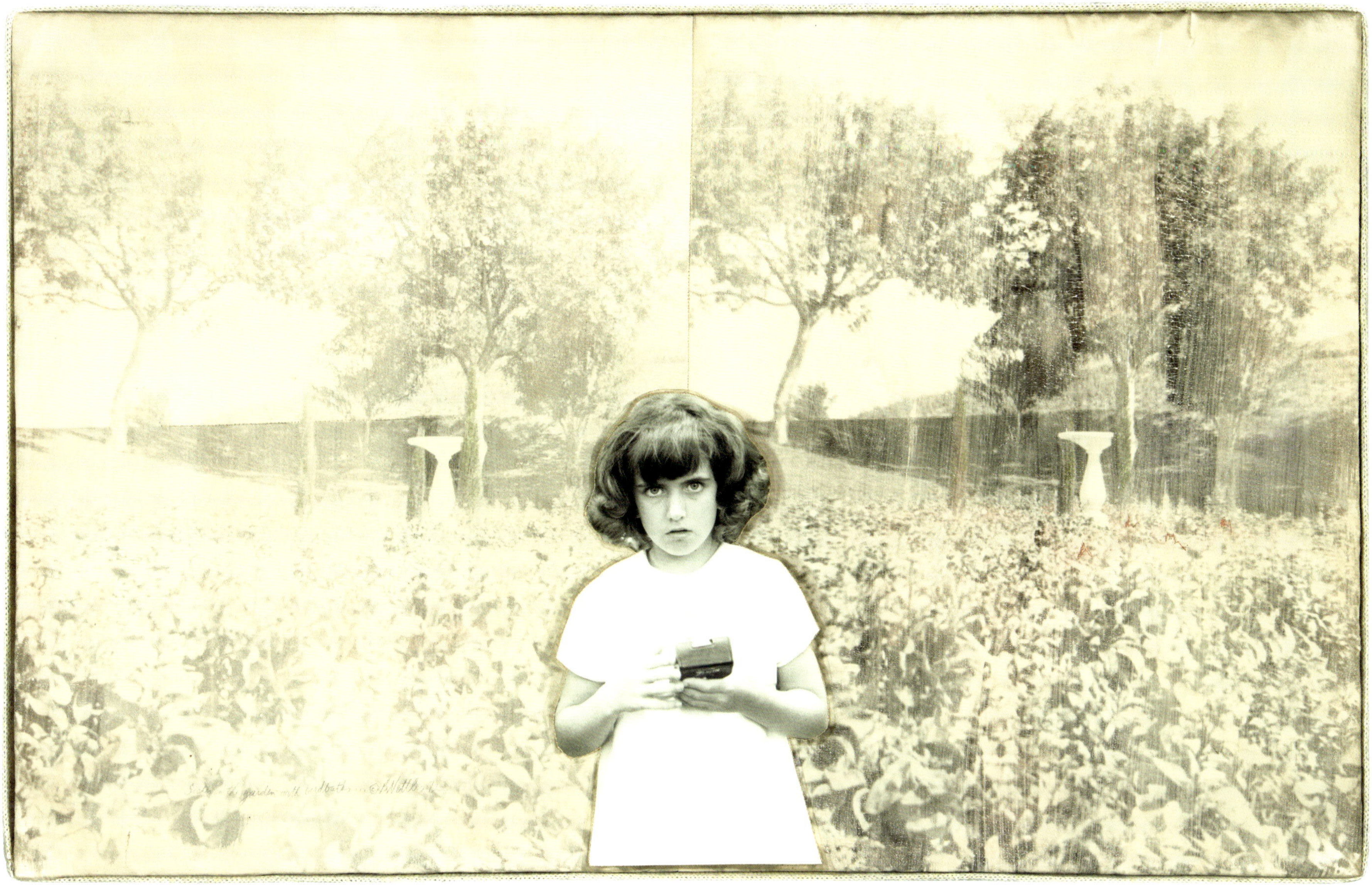

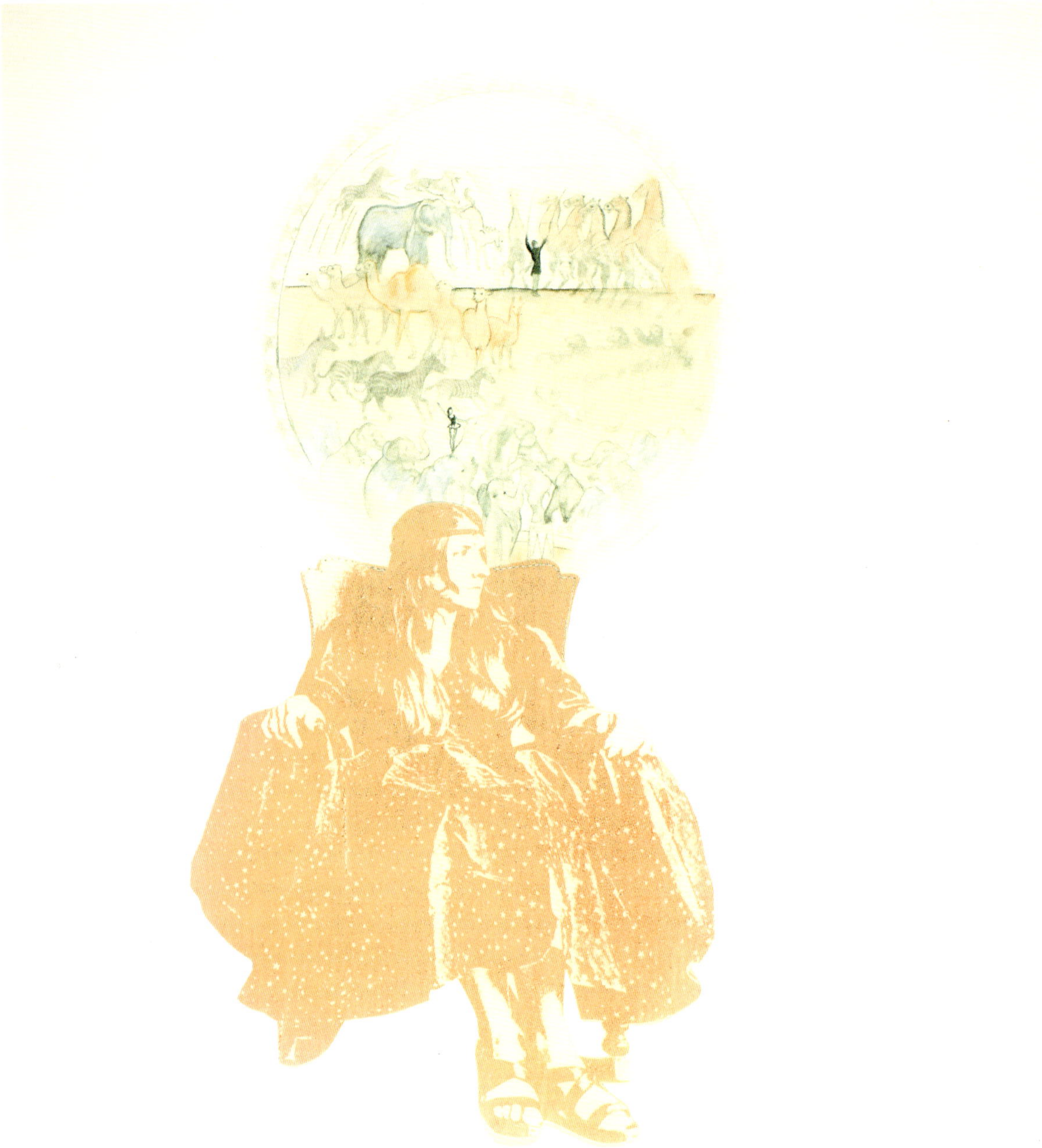

< *Circus Day*, February 1972, collage with gum bichromate print, magazine transfer and applied color

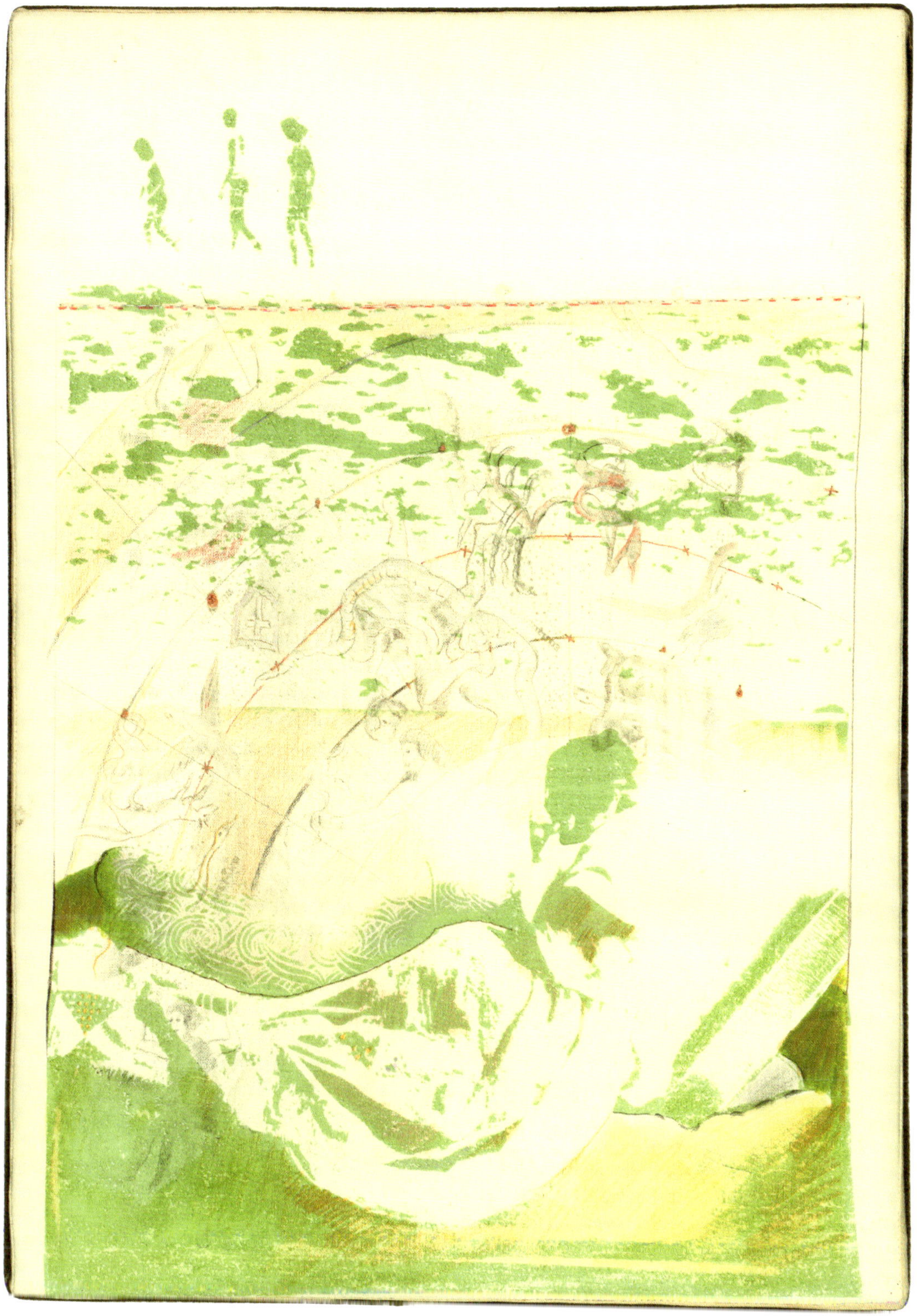

> *Beach & constellations—dream series*, February 1972, gum bichromate print with newspaper transfer and applied color on sized cotton

> Both images
*Escape*, 1972,
gelatin silver prints

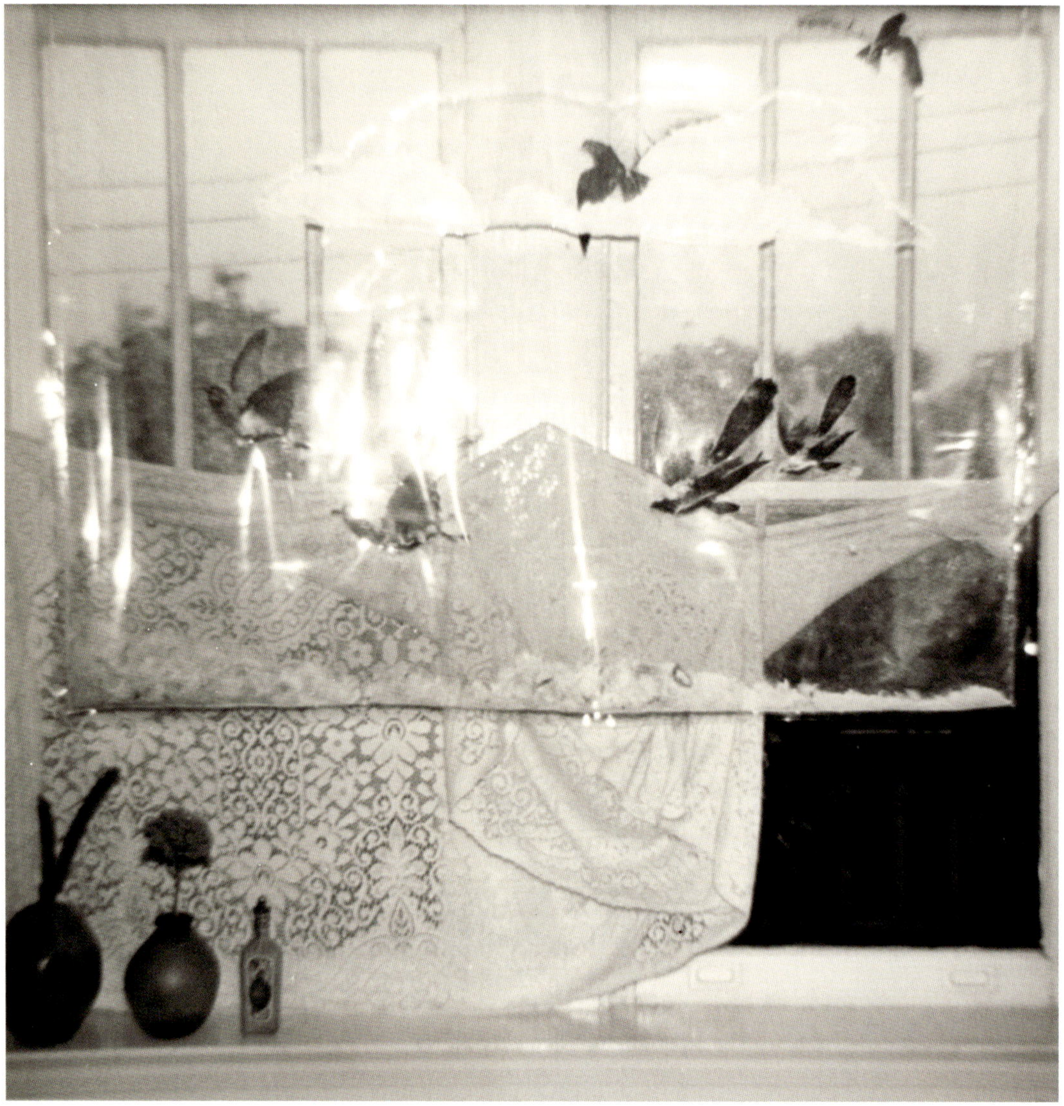

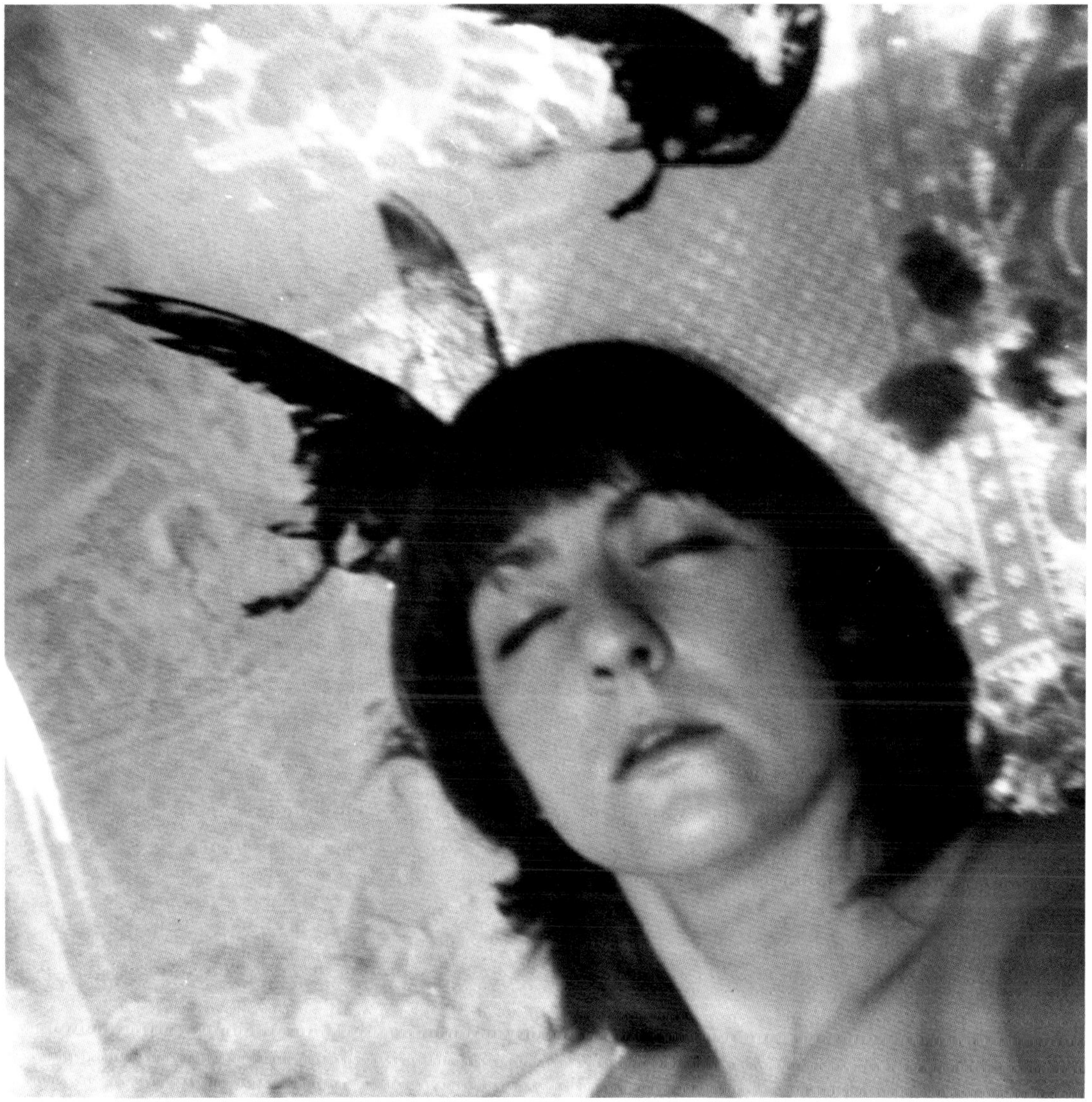

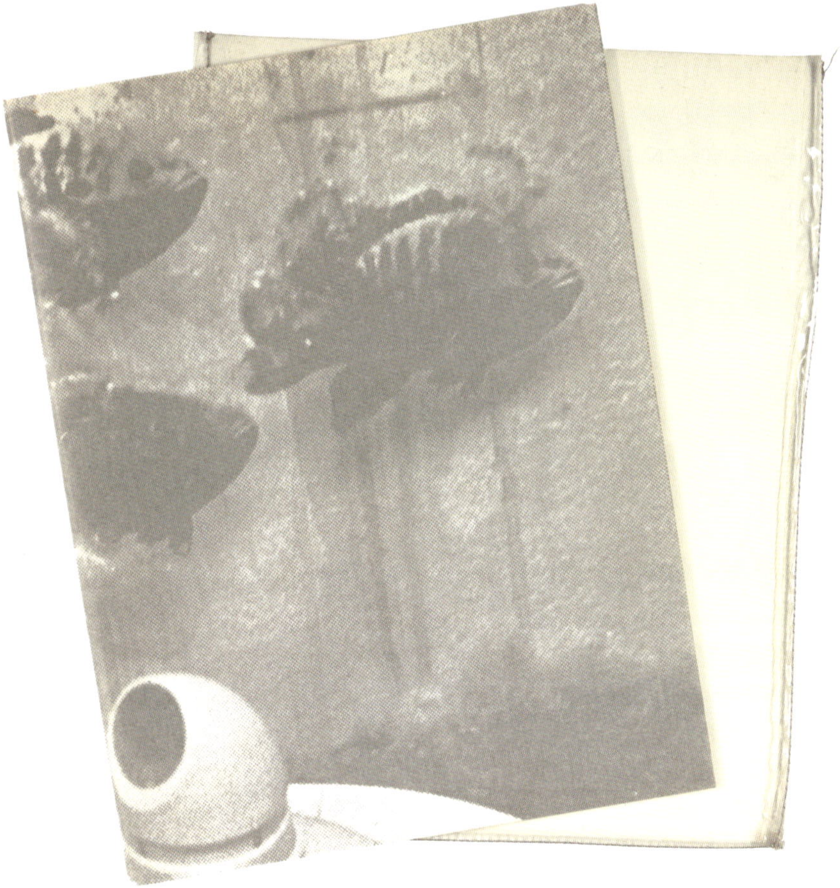

> *Events in the Water*, 1973,
book with screen-print cover,
offset lithographs, and vinyl slipcase

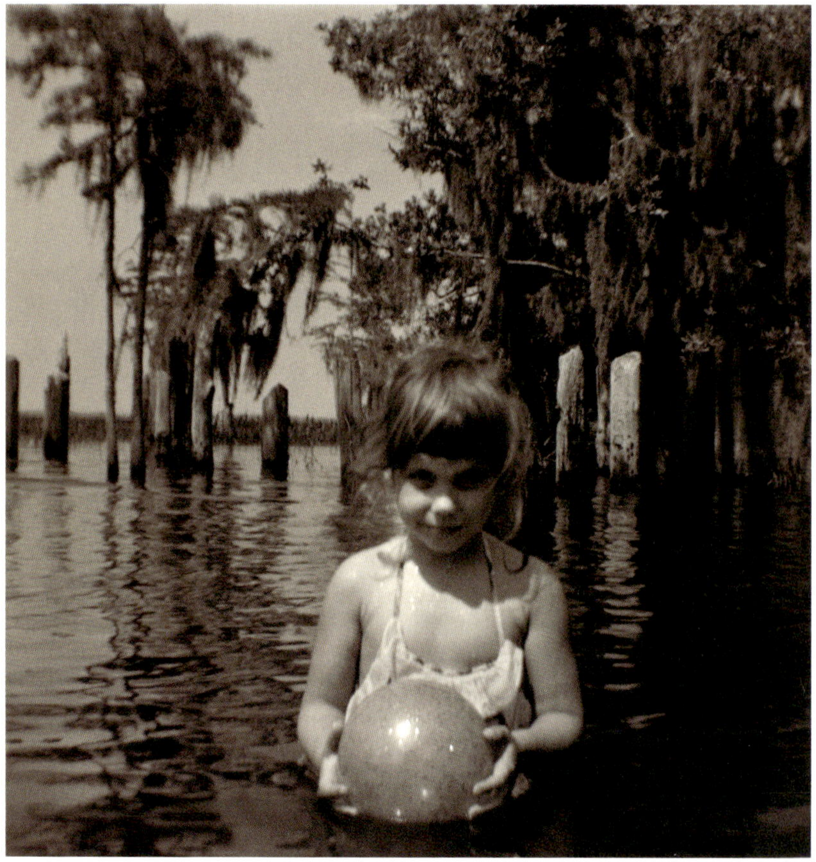

All images *Events in the Water*, 1972, gelatin silver prints

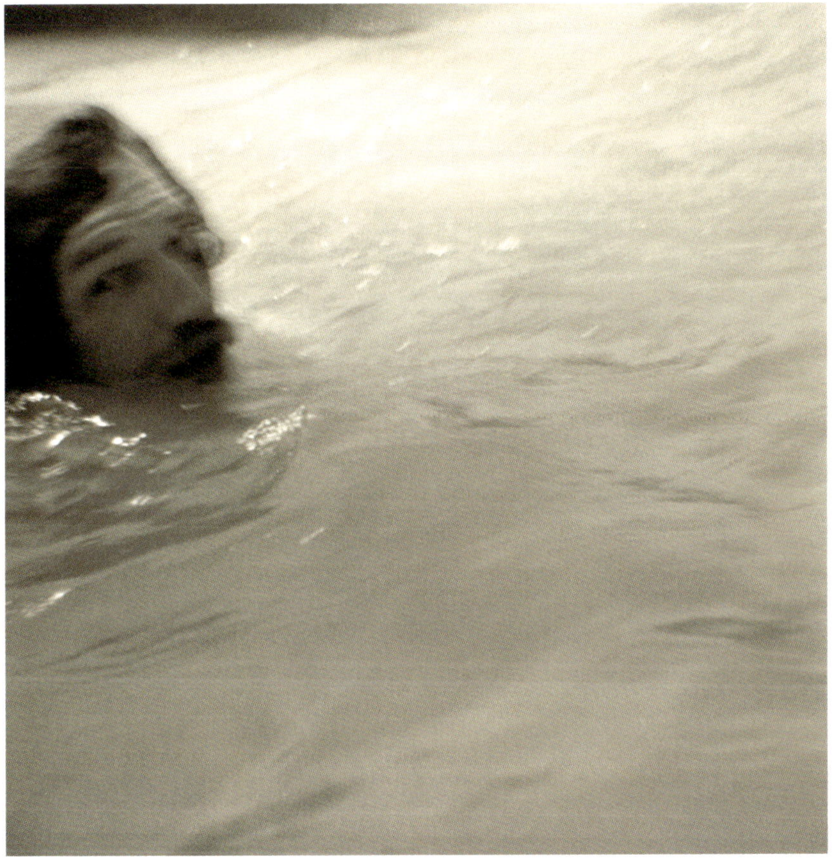

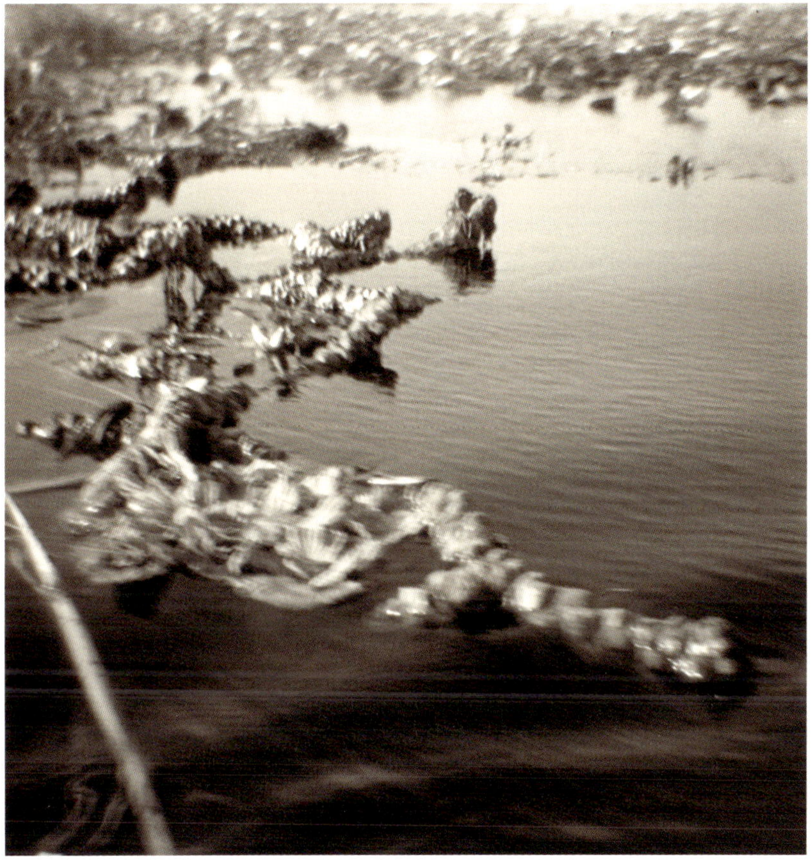

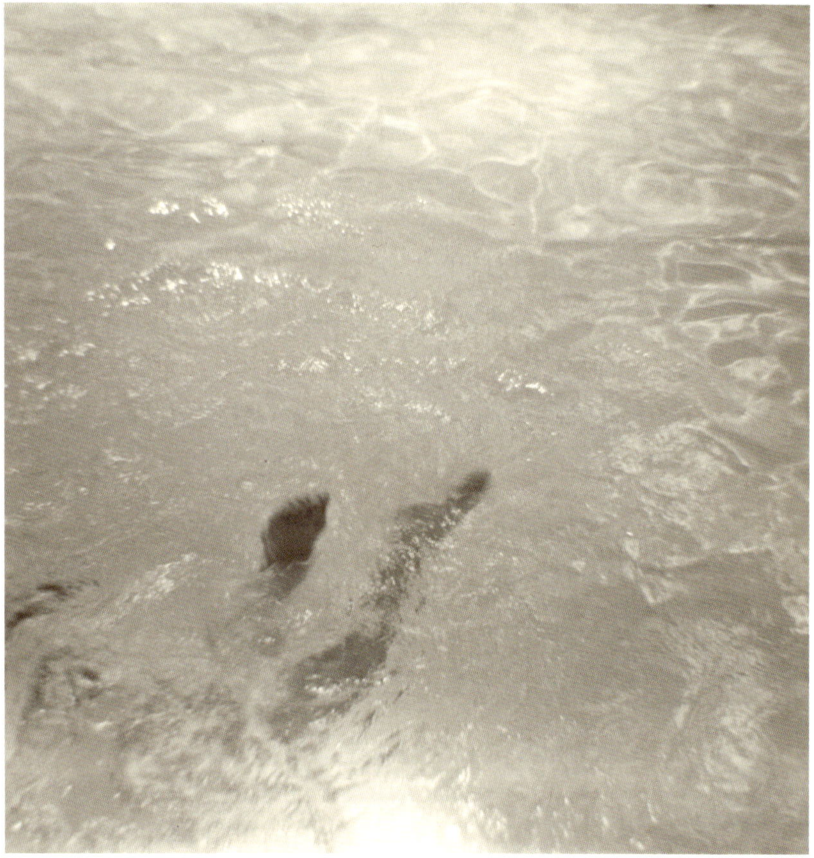

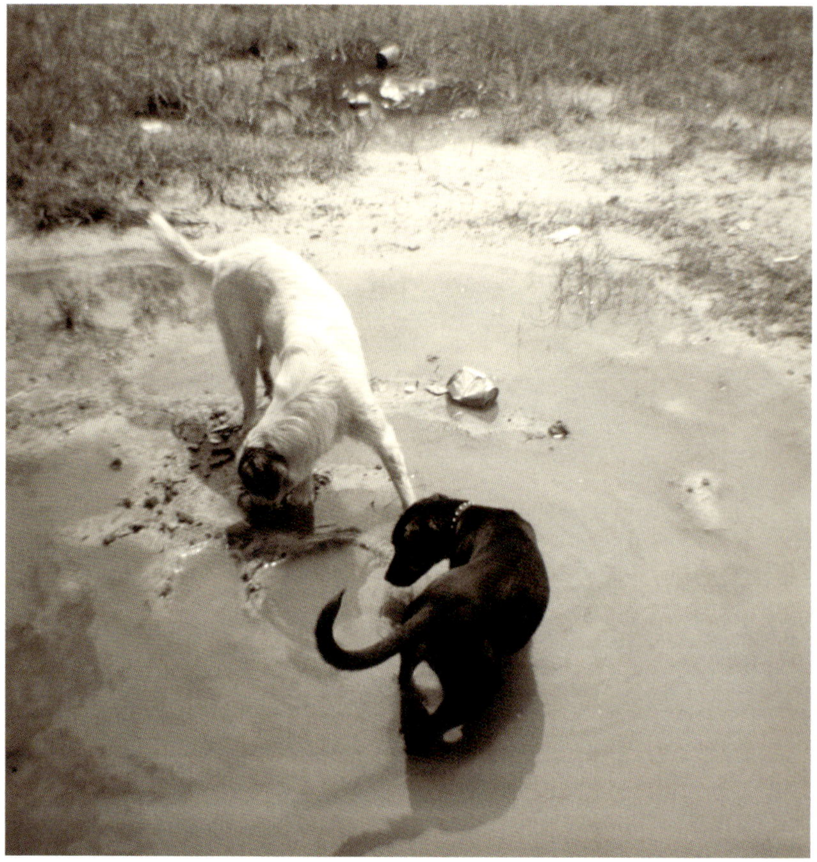

All images *Events in the Water*, 1972, gelatin silver prints

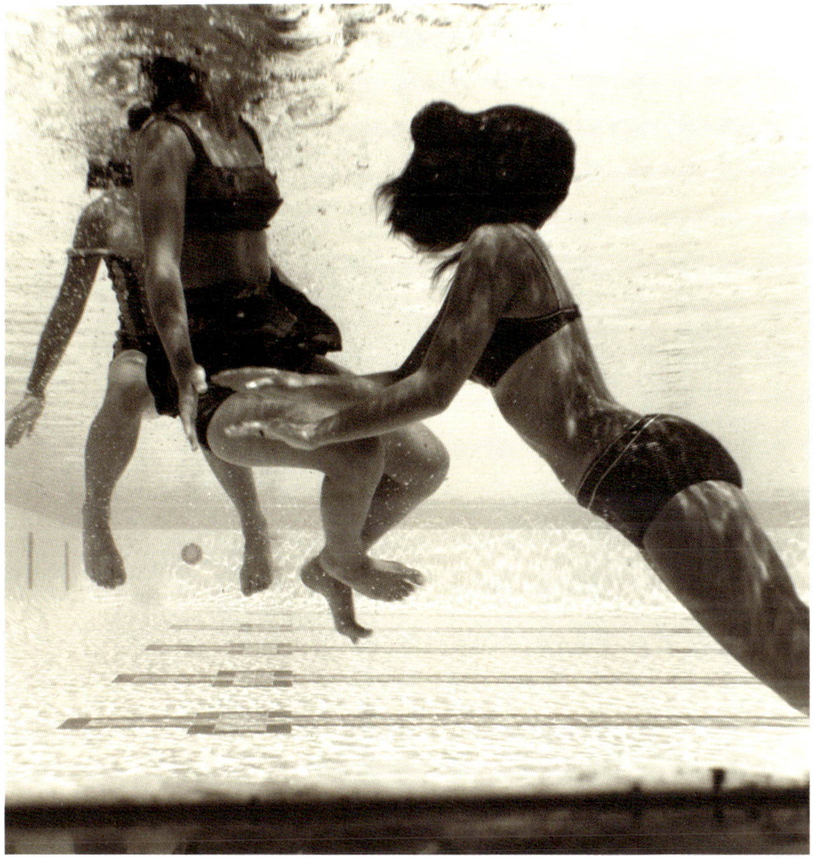

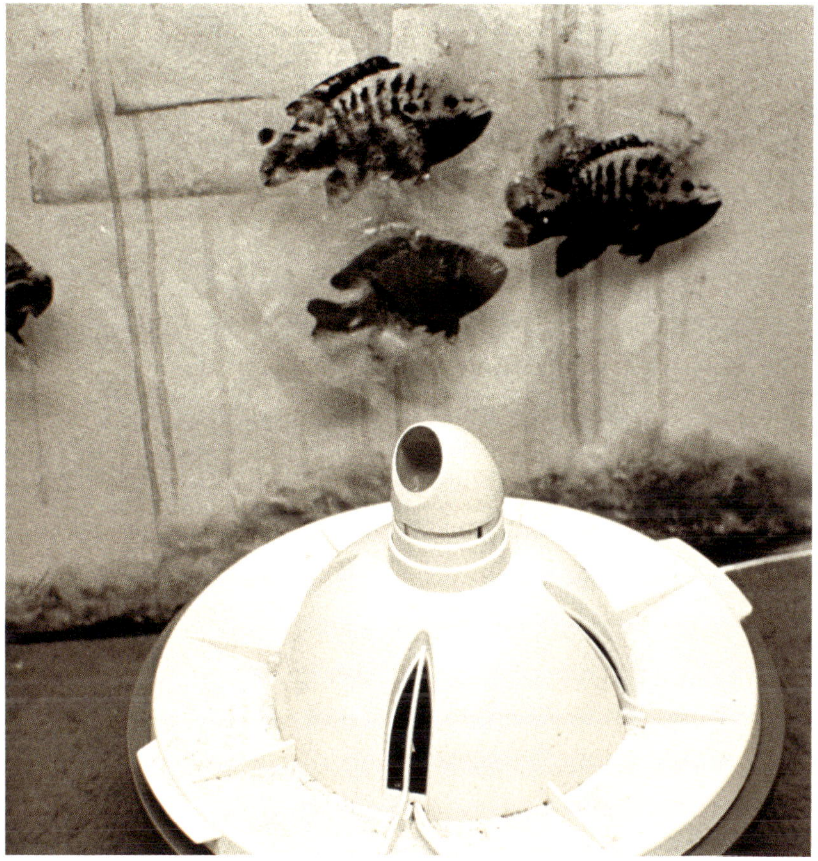

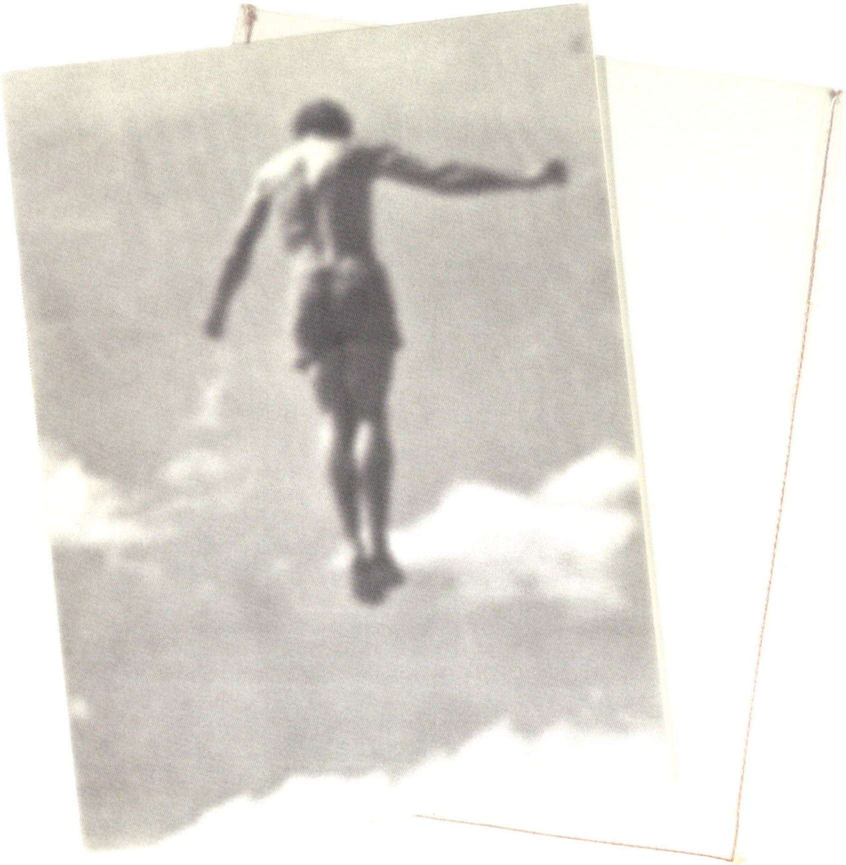

> *Events in the Sky*, 1973, book with screen-print cover, offset lithographs, and vinyl slipcase

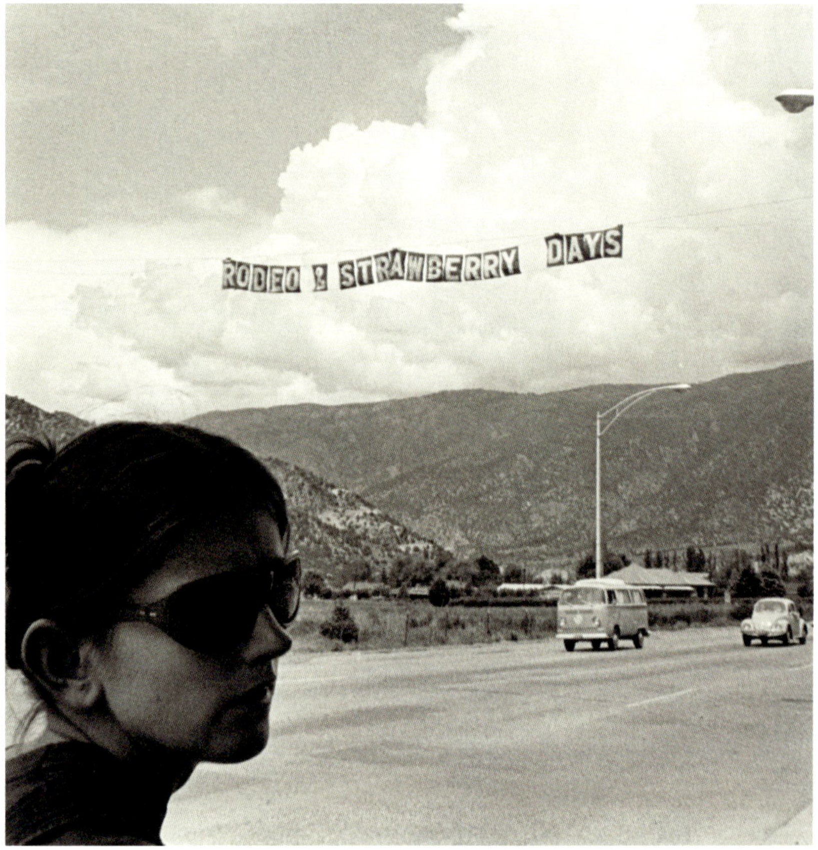


All images *Events in the Sky*, 1973, gelatin silver prints

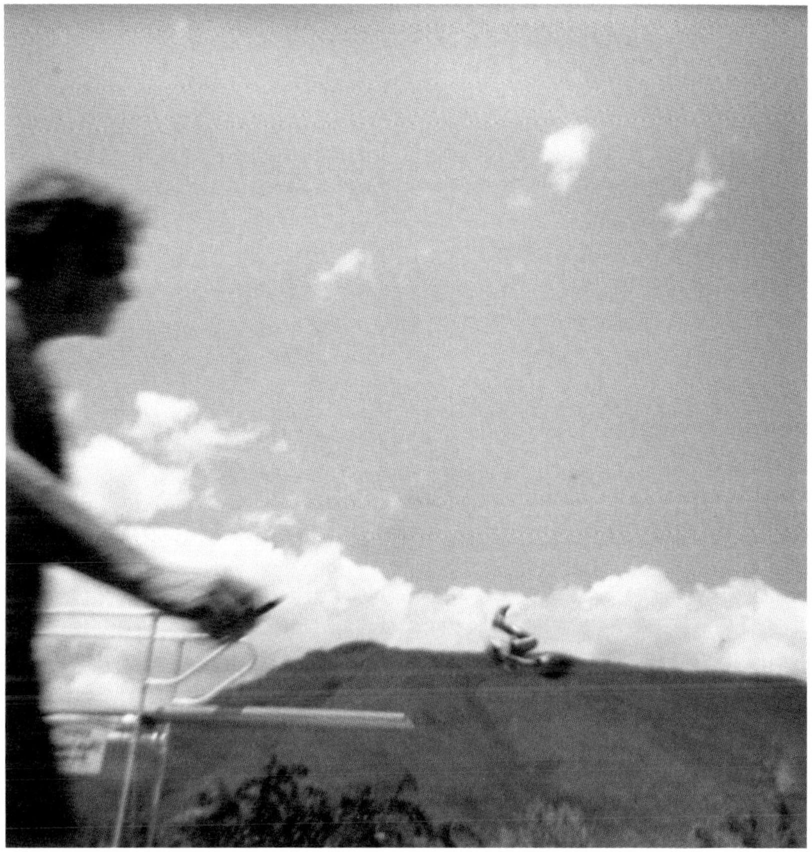

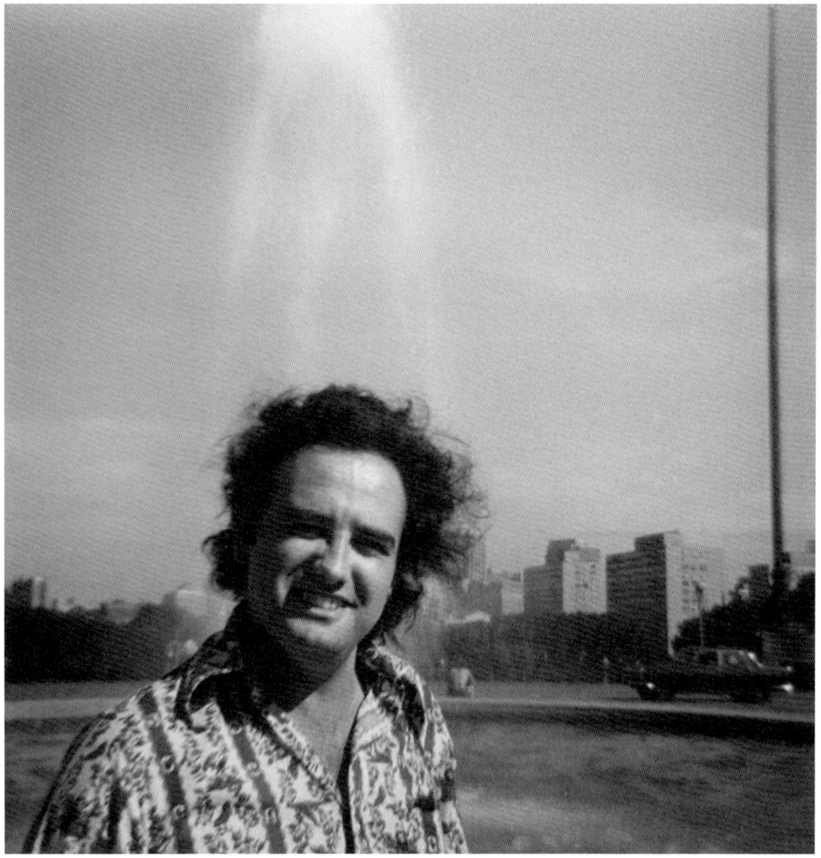

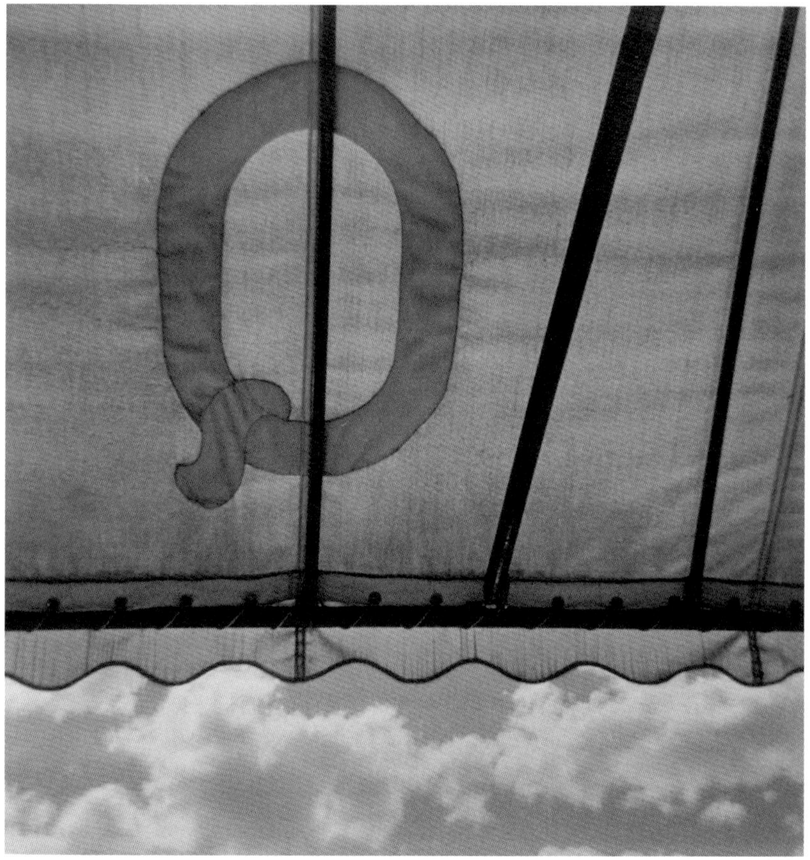

All images *Events in the Sky*, 1973, gelatin silver prints

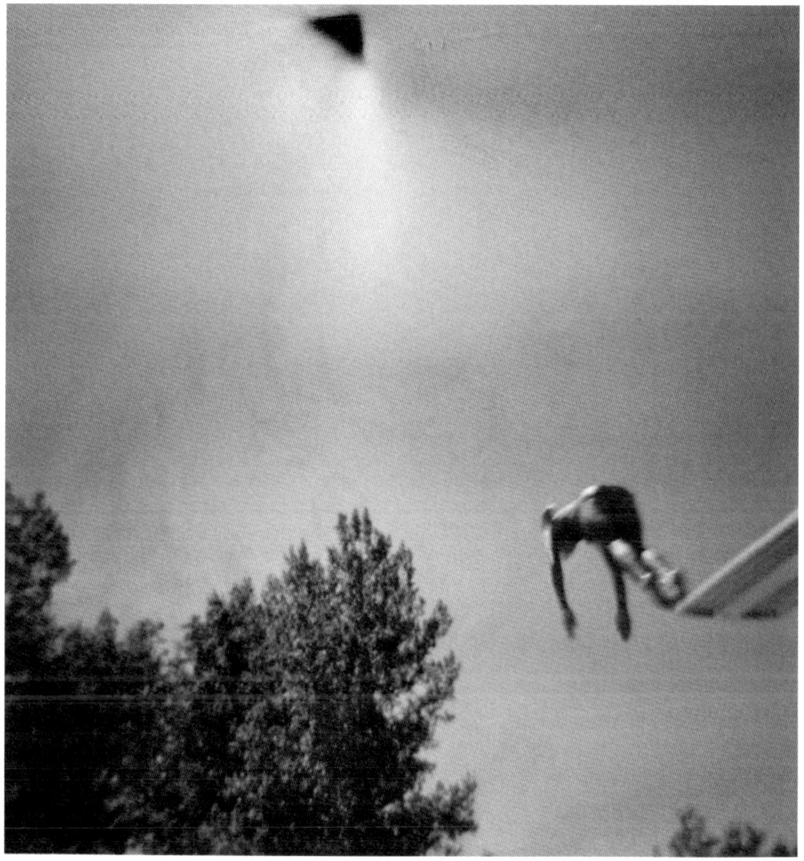

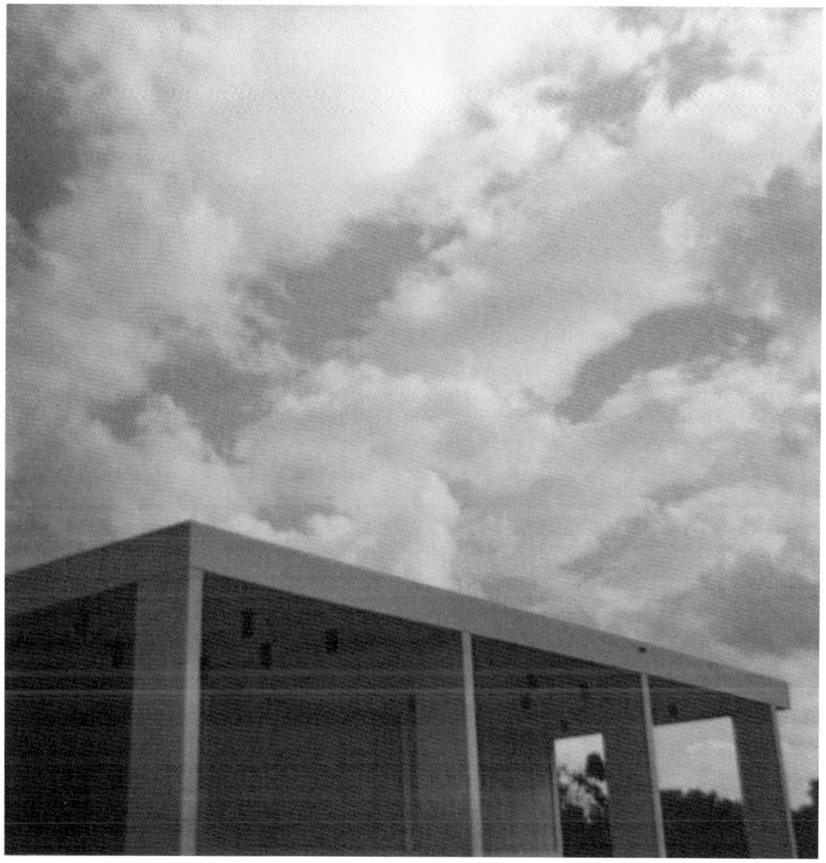

> All images *Feasts and Feats*, 1973, gelatin silver prints

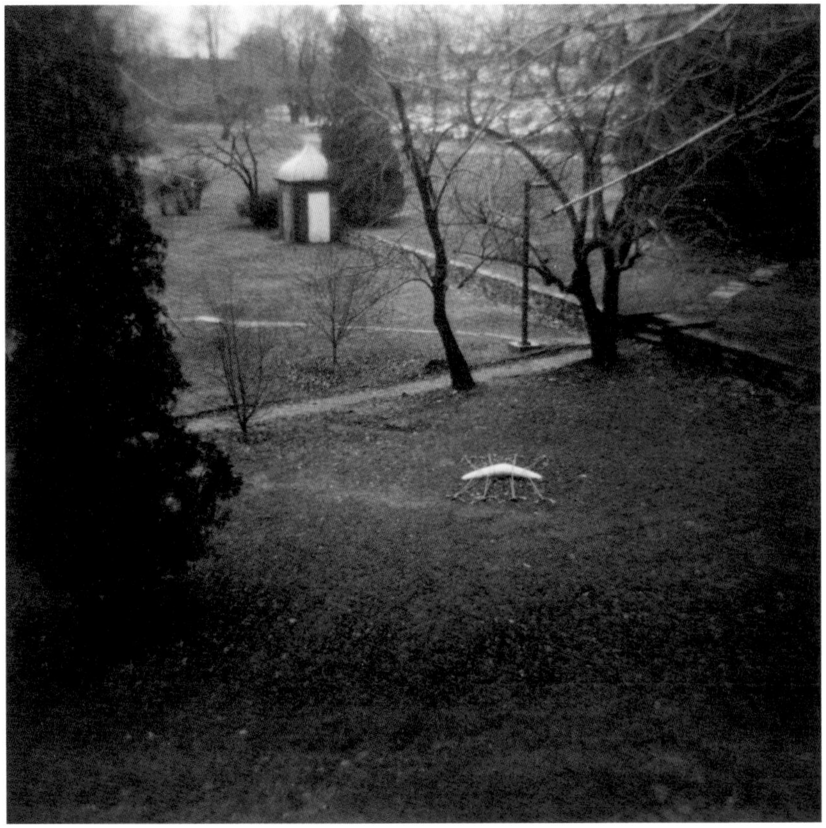

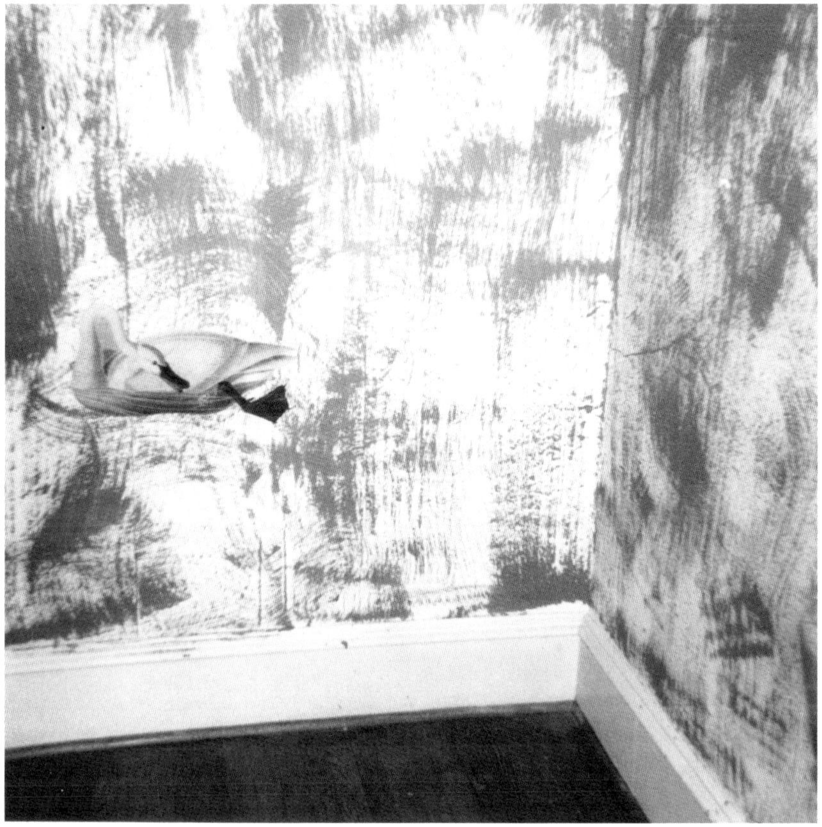

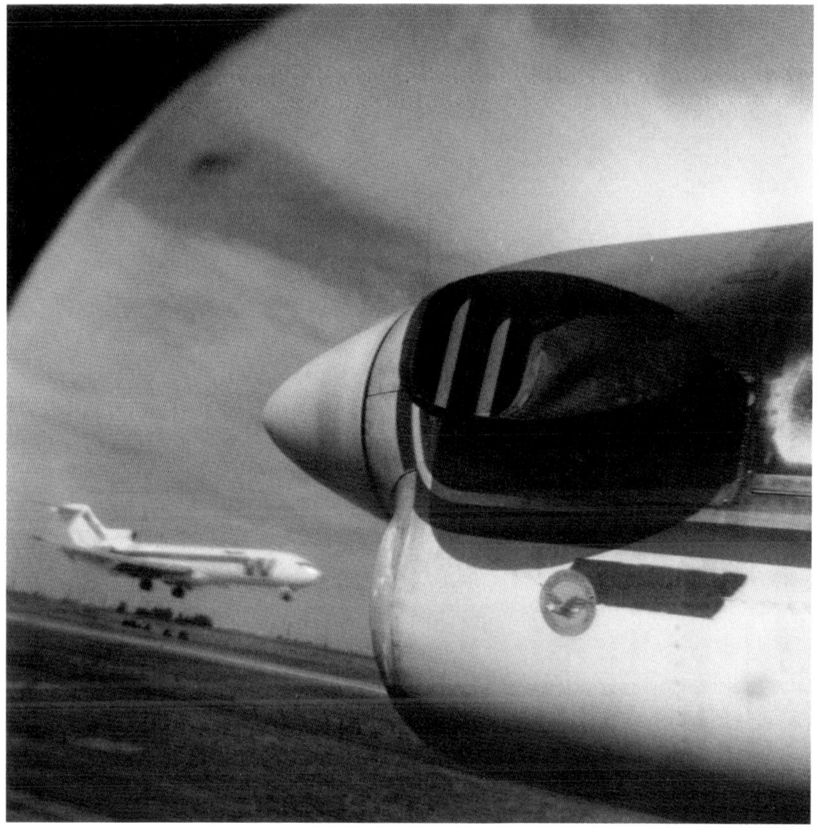

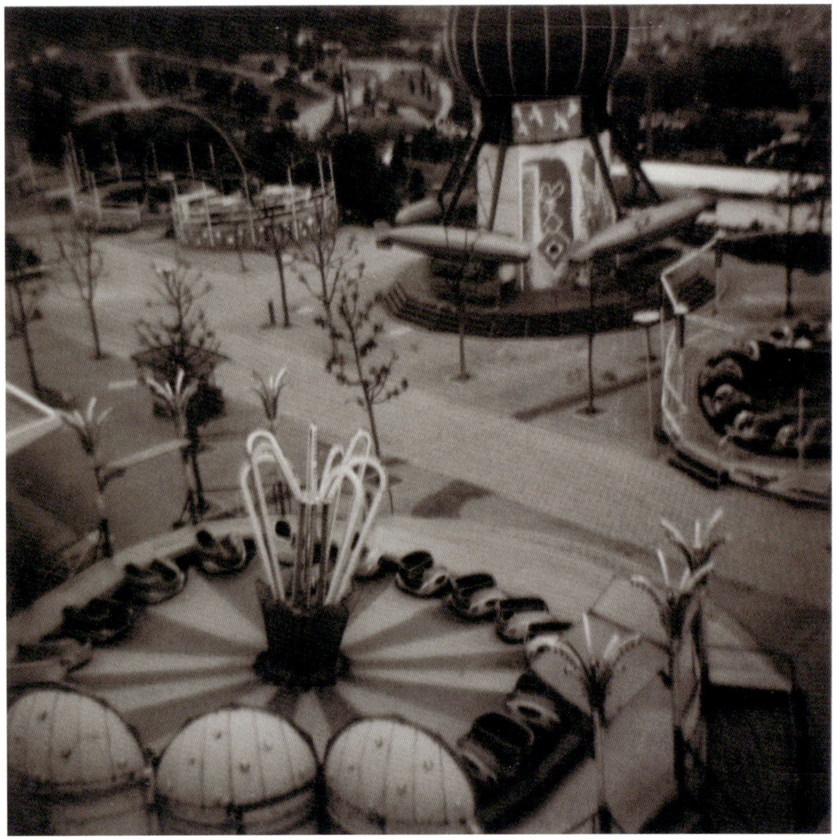

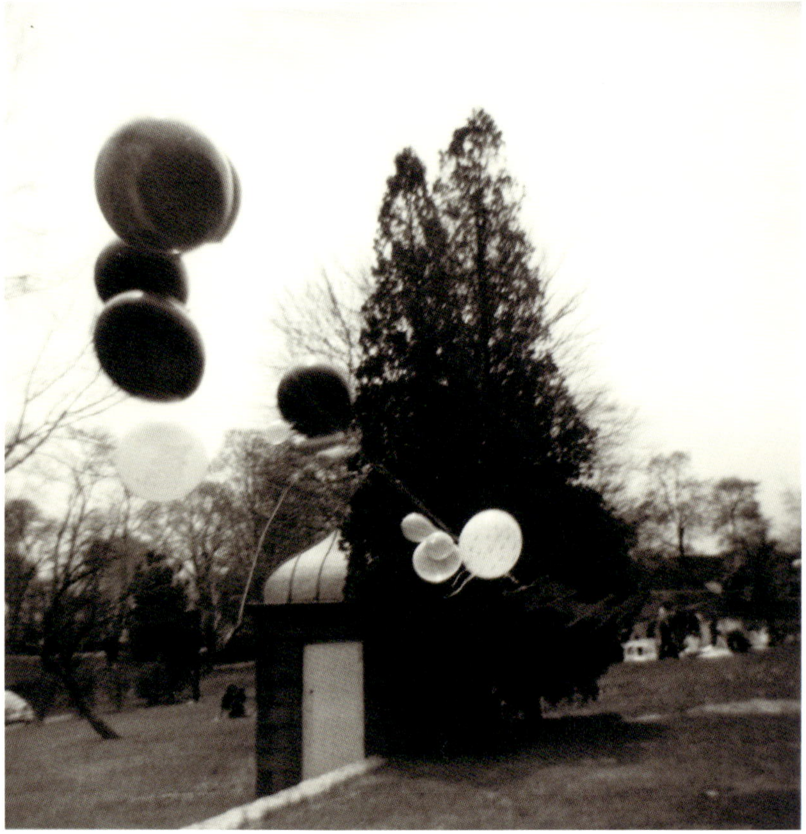

> All images *Feasts and Feats*, 1973, gelatin silver prints

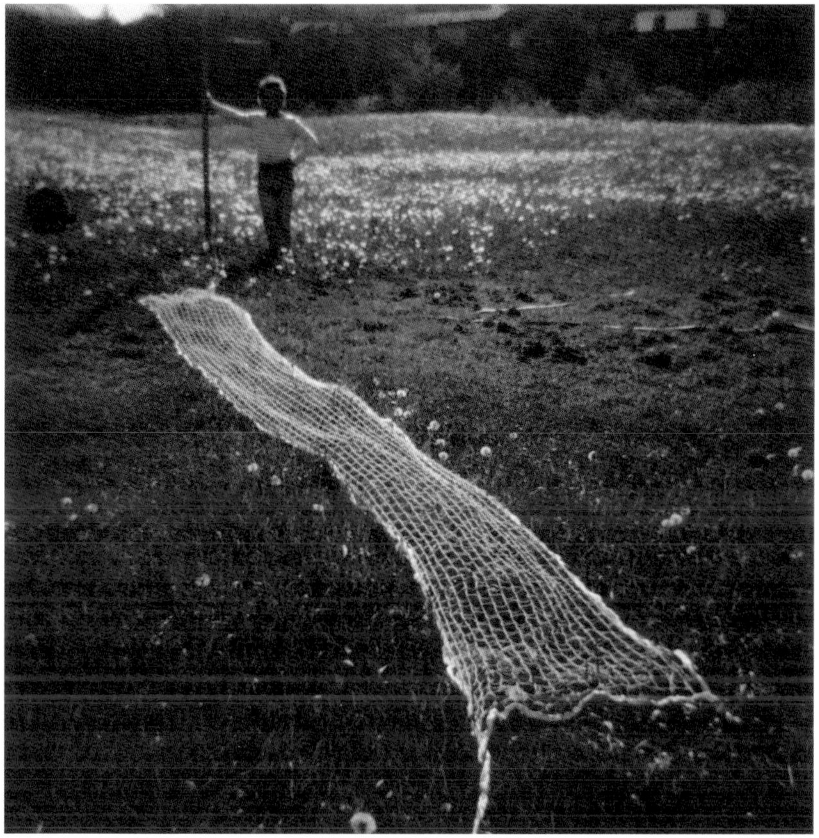

> *The Imaginary Blowtorch*, 1973, book with offset lithographs, screen prints, applied color, polyester film, tissue paper and sewn white vinyl lace slipcase; poetry by Grace Nettles

The artist who does not know
That God has no creed;
That justice lives outside the law,
That peace is an embattled and scarred condition;
That love needs no keyring;
And that though man has bred a friendly kind of wolf,
The original still runs free, and dangerous,
Exactly as the artist must..
That one,
Without that knowledge,
Is like a palm tree without wind:

No lift.

No sway.

No ballet.

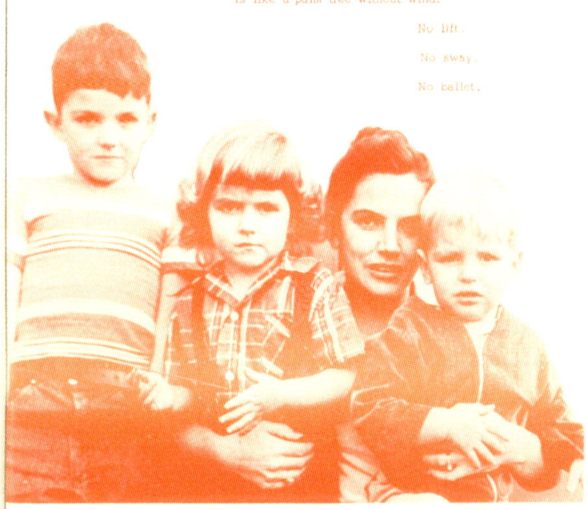

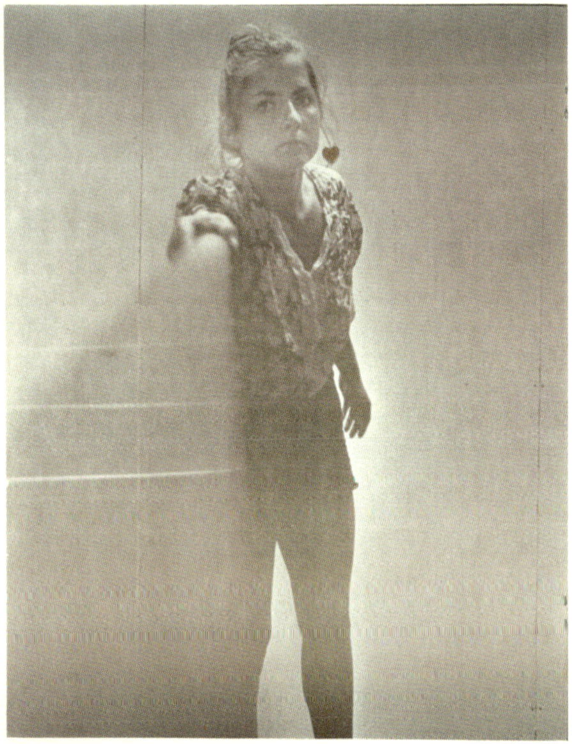

THE IMAGINARY BLOWTORCH

It is always 3:00 A.M. in the clearing
In the briarpatch of the mind.
One-way tunnels lead out all around,
Converging on another clearing
Where something monstrous sits,
Waiting.
It is the Swallowing Woman,
The one who will not die.

But you know this.
And so you say to your other self
(the earned companion..
The listener who always gets the point..
A tough character if there ever was one):
"Out with your imaginary blowtorch now!
And burn those tunnels shut!"

And when the daylight comes,
You're still holding out.
Not a scratch on you.

Only just a little bit blue
On a green morning.

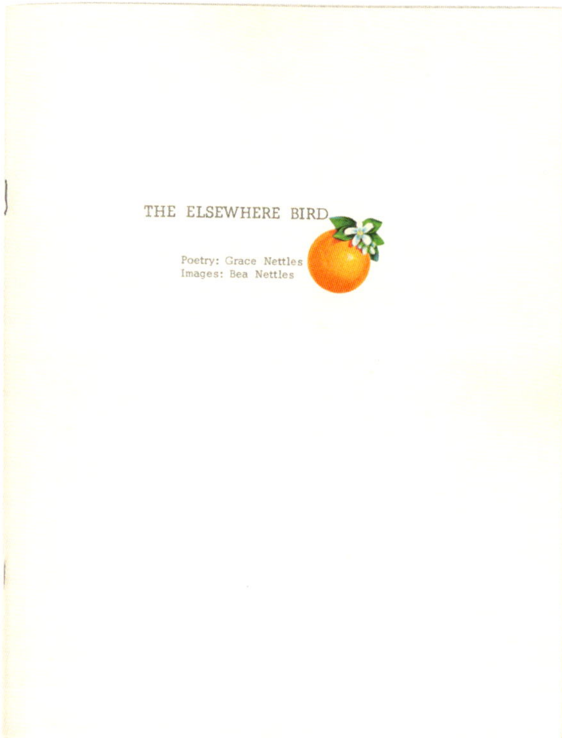


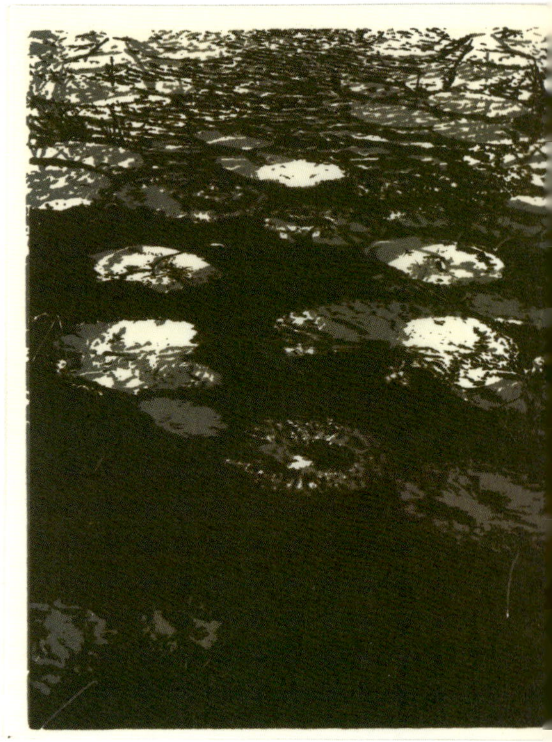

> *The Elsewhere Bird*, 1974, book with offset lithographs, screen prints, applied color, fabric, polyester film, tissue, gummed orange sticker, and sewn orange vinyl slipcase; poetry by Grace Nettles

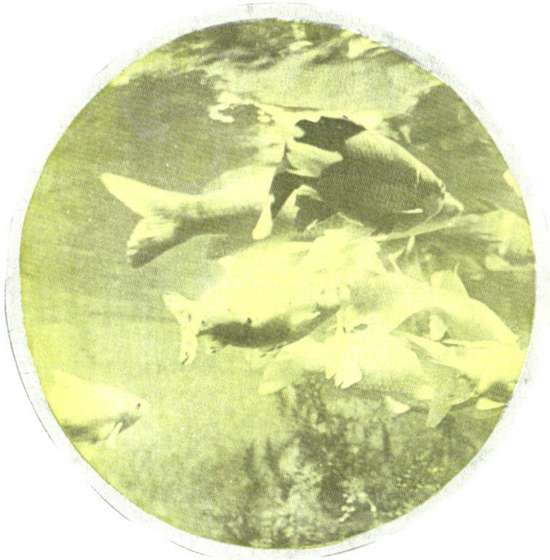

CHANT OF YOUR JAMAICAN RAINBOW SPRINGS UNDERWATER BOAT TRIP GUIDE

Now ladies and gentlemennnn
SEE your feeshsh!
Your bluegill, your bream, your eel,
Your shiners, your turtle, your panfeesh
And your BEEG
BASSSS.

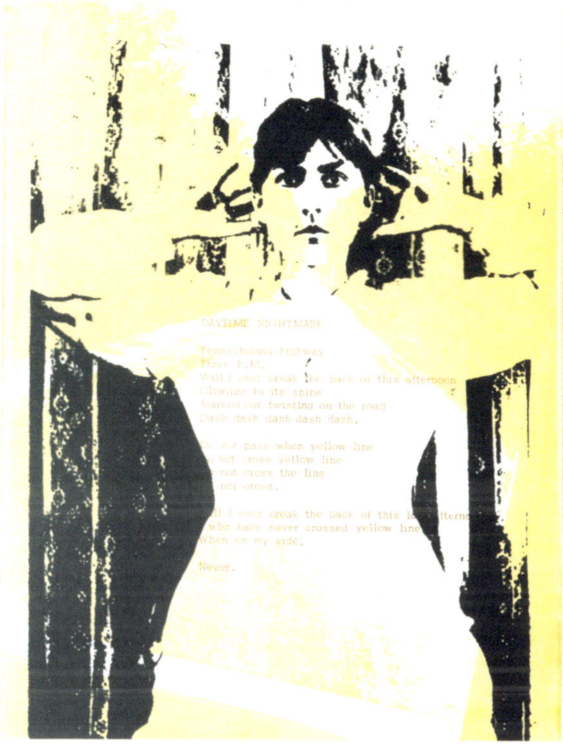


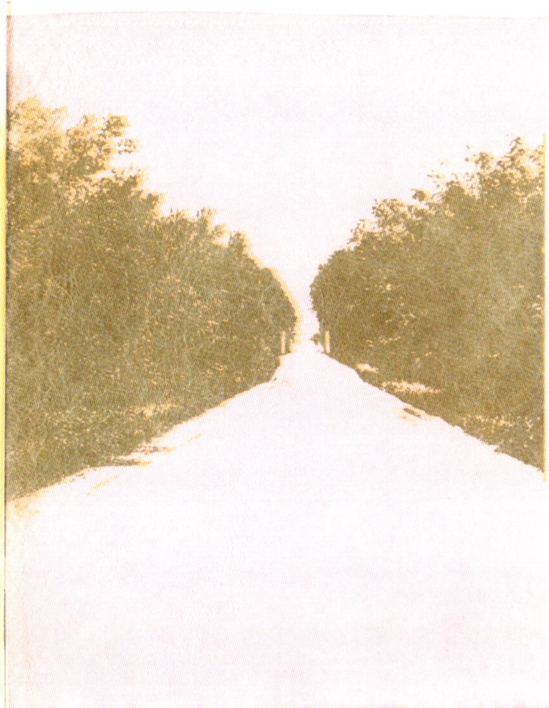

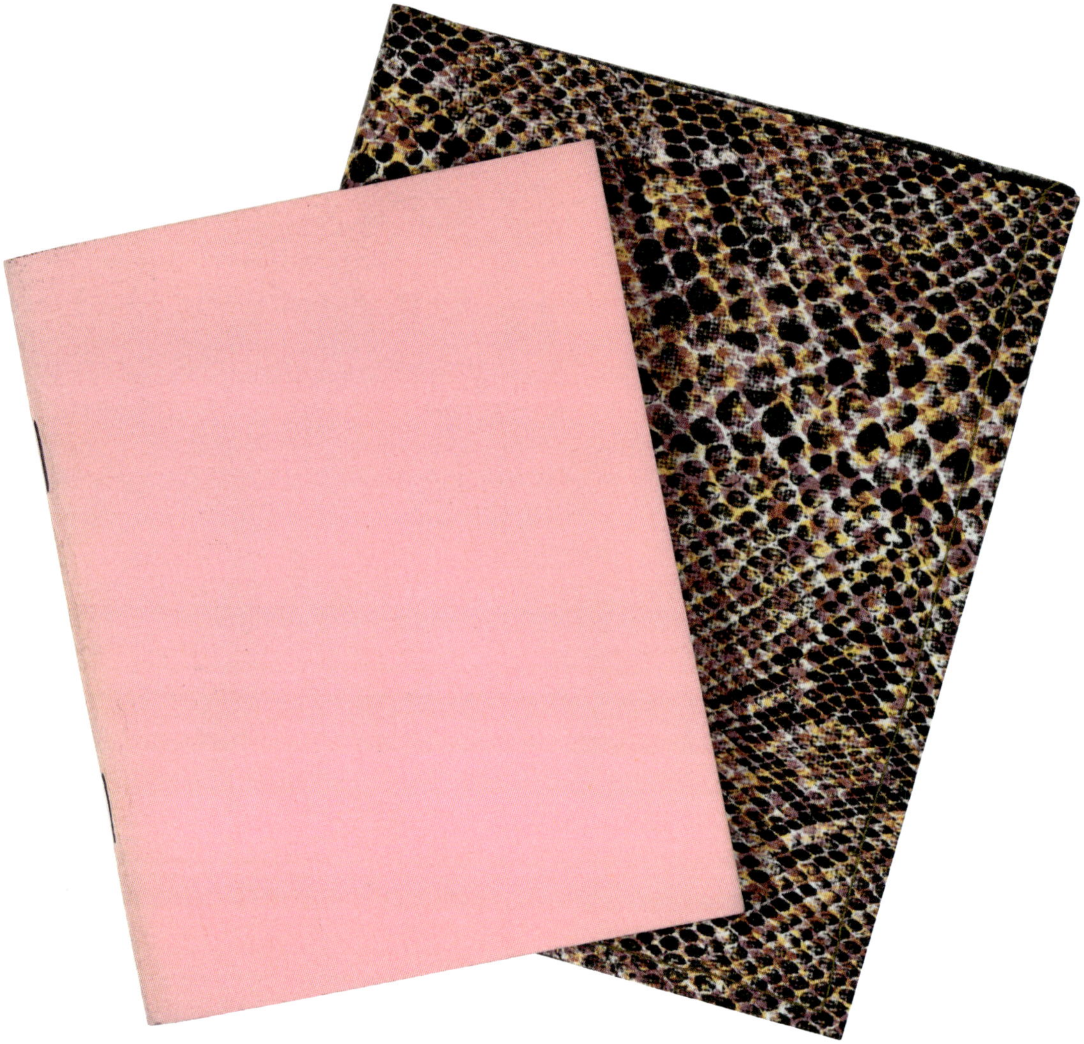

> *A is for Applebiting Alligators*, 1974, book with lavender paper cover, offset lithographs, screen prints, and mock-alligator vinyl slipcase

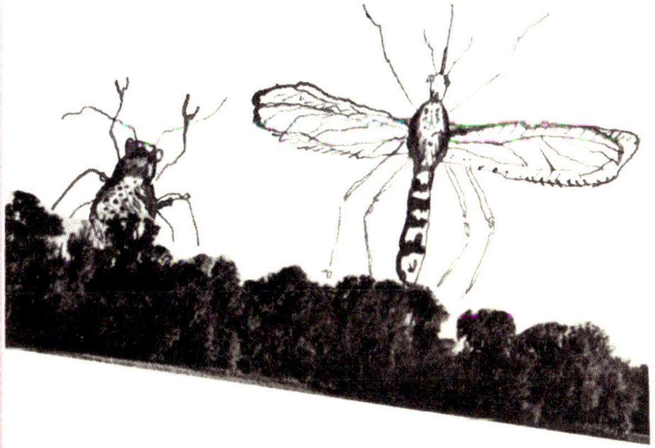

B is for
Buzzy Bugs

C is for Cuddly Cats

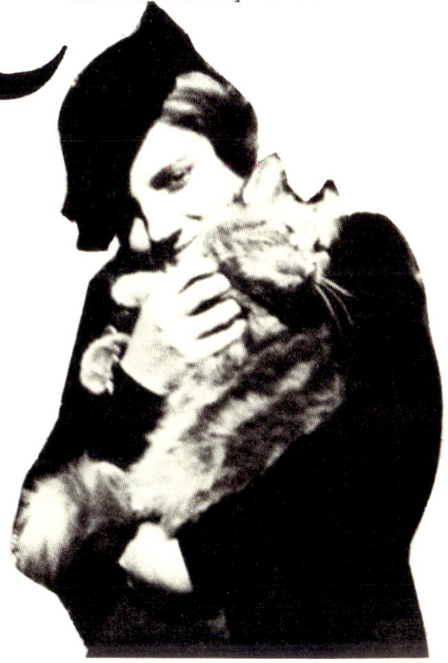

J is for a Jumping Joker

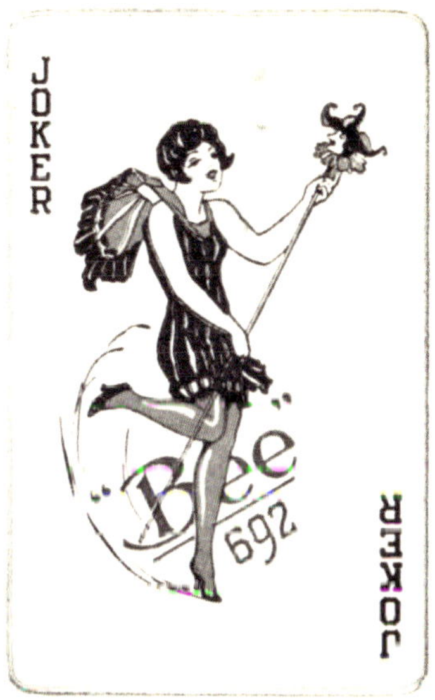


K is for the Kindest King

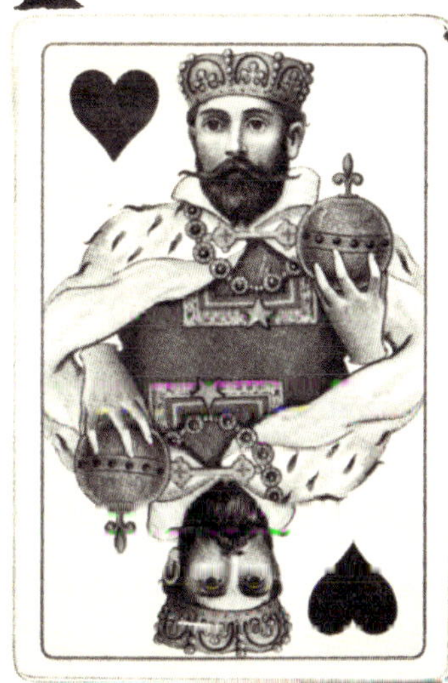

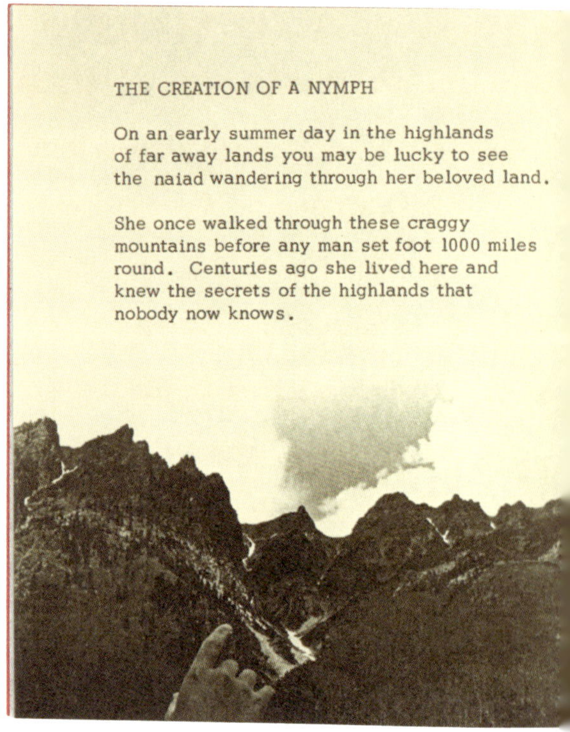
THE CREATION OF A NYMPH

On an early summer day in the highlands of far away lands you may be lucky to see the naiad wandering through her beloved land.

She once walked through these craggy mountains before any man set foot 1000 miles round. Centuries ago she lived here and knew the secrets of the highlands that nobody now knows.

> *The Nymph of the Highlands*, 1974, book with burgundy mock-velvet cover, offset lithographs, screen print, polyester sheets, tissue paper, and opaque green vinyl slipcase with water swirl pattern; story by Connie Nettles at age thirteen

She was beautiful yet as you would picture her. She had long black flowing hair that talked to the wind.
Her gowns were of the riches of the mountains,
her shoes of the crystal clear waters,
her voice of the early morning dew.

Her face was featureless yet her body was soft and gentle.

She was made
of the mountains
and the mountains
were to be made of her.

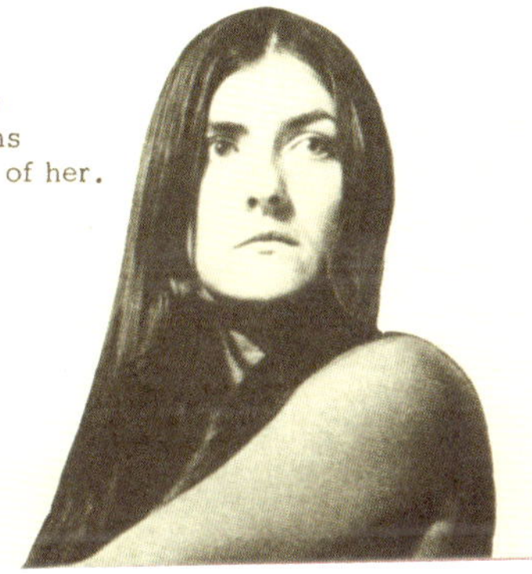

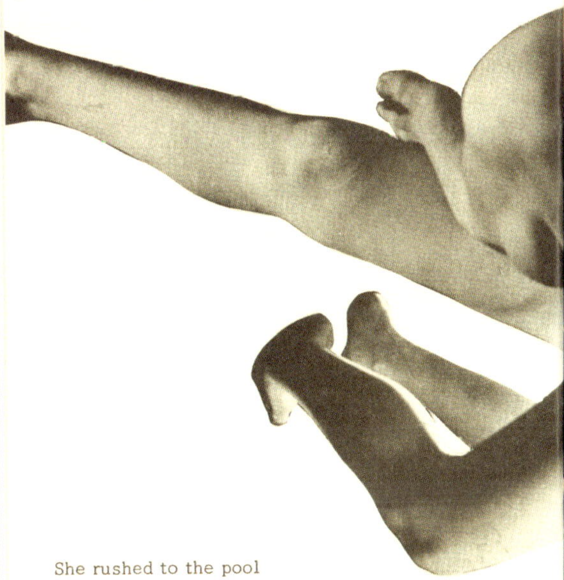

She rushed to the pool
and swam to the very bottom where instead of finding two creatures she found one. A handsome creature at that. They immediately fell in love and as they swam to the top hand in hand they saw a brilliant light shining.

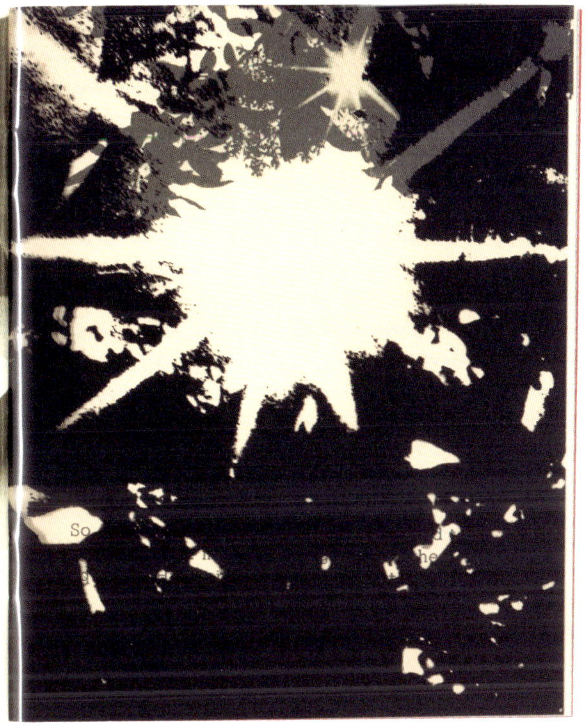

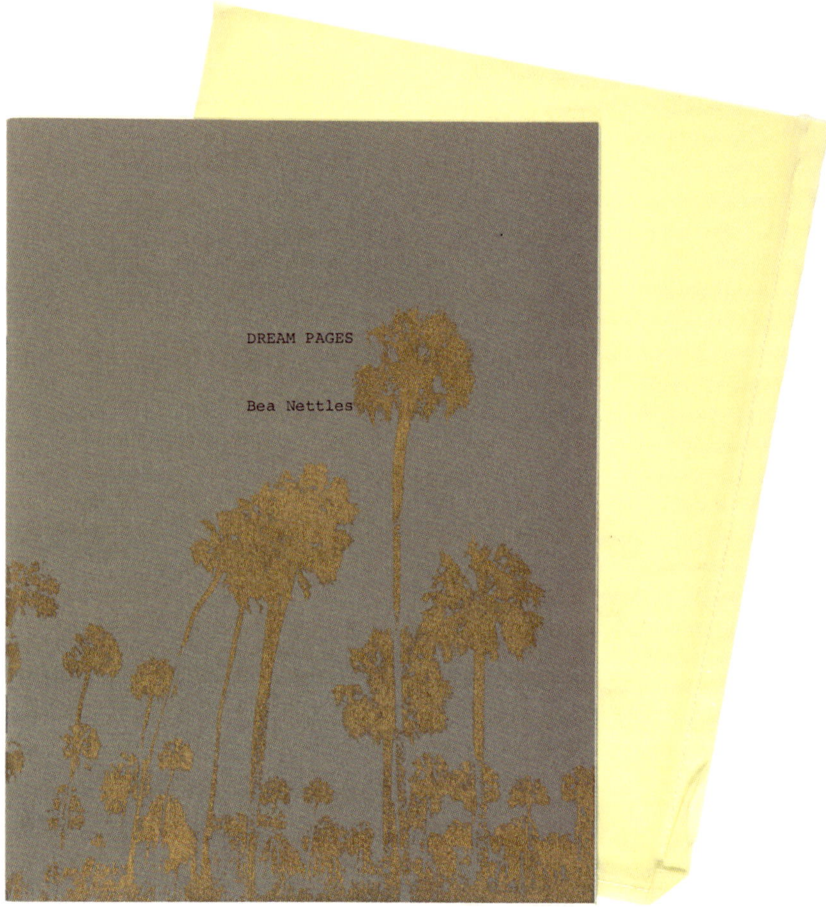


> *Dream Pages*, 1975, book with grey cover with gold screen print, offset lithographs, screen prints, and pale-yellow vinyl slipcase

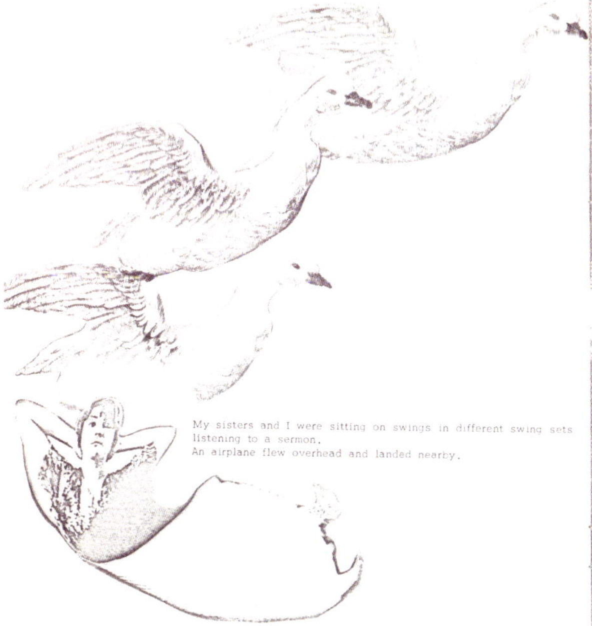

My sisters and I were sitting on swings in different swing sets
listening to a sermon.
An airplane flew overhead and landed nearby.

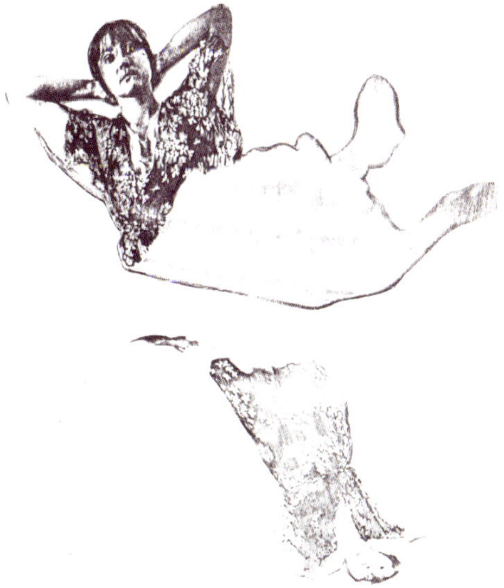

During the day at the beach I swung in a huge swing...
over the ocean, getting tan and seeing everything that was going on below.
Sometimes I would quit swinging to draw.

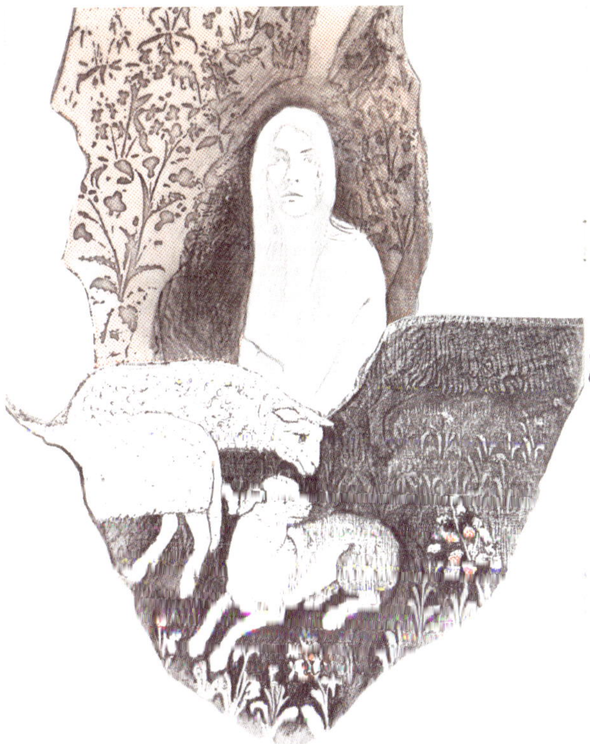

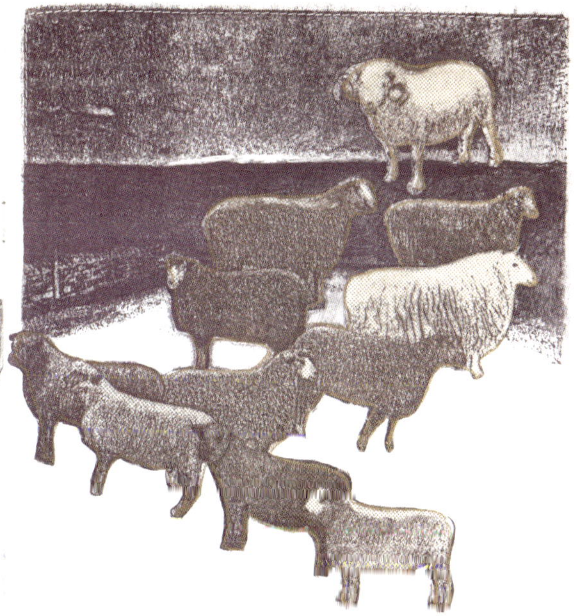

I dreamed of the winter and summer kings and queens.
I [illegible] queen [illegible] small dark and slim.
A buxom blonde woman was the summer queen and every summer
she gave birth to herds of golden sheep.
As winter came they would thunder away over the hills.......

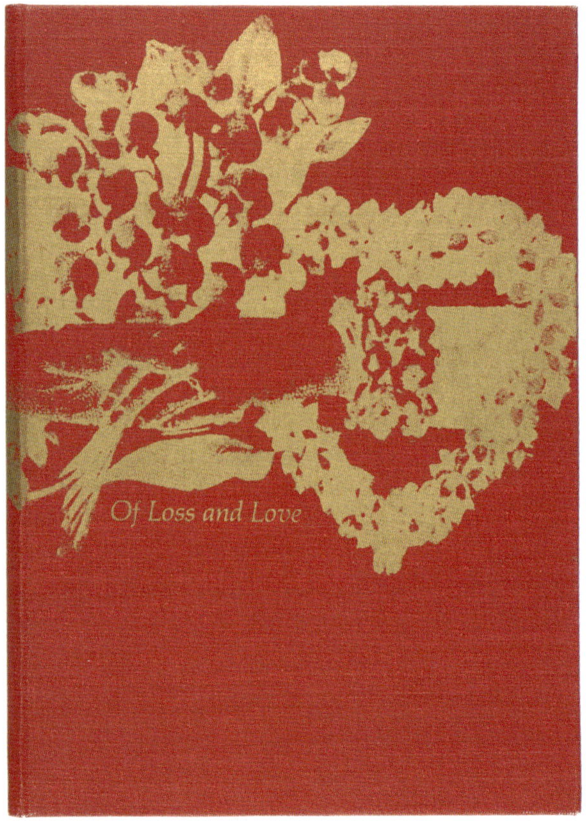


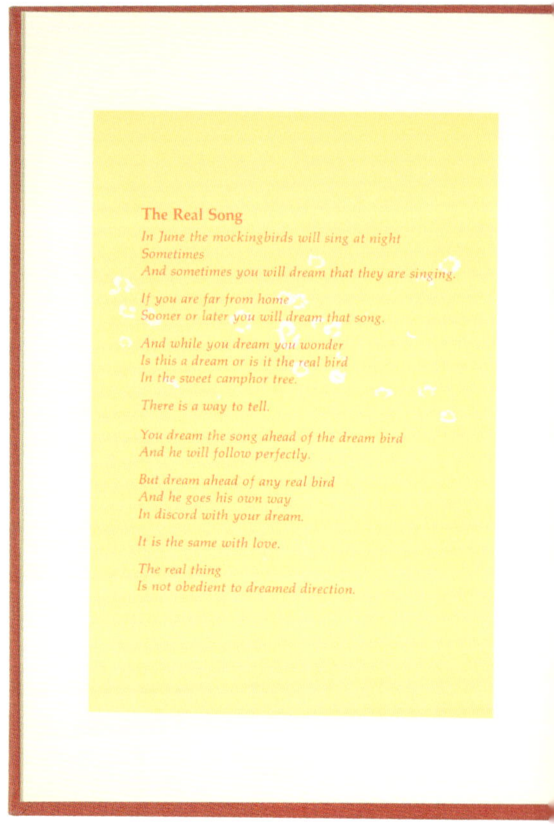


> *Of Loss and Love*, 1975, book with red cover with gold screen print, offset lithographs; poetry by Grace Nettles

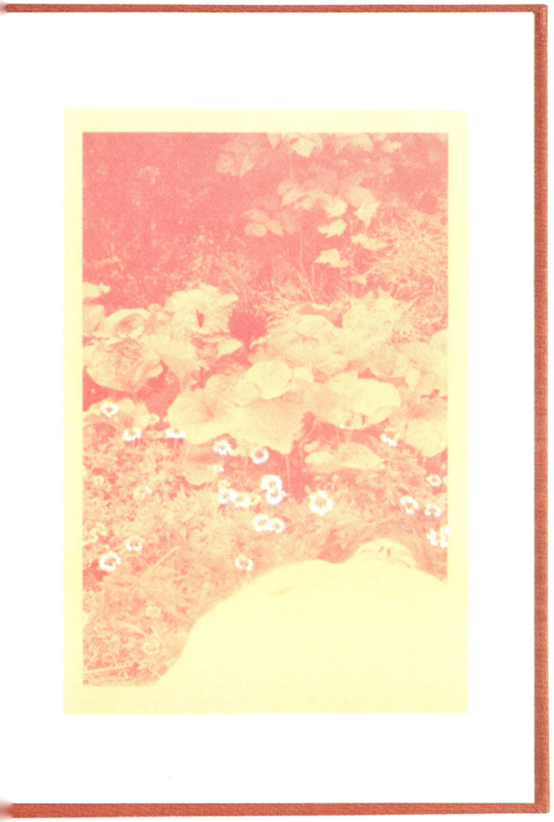

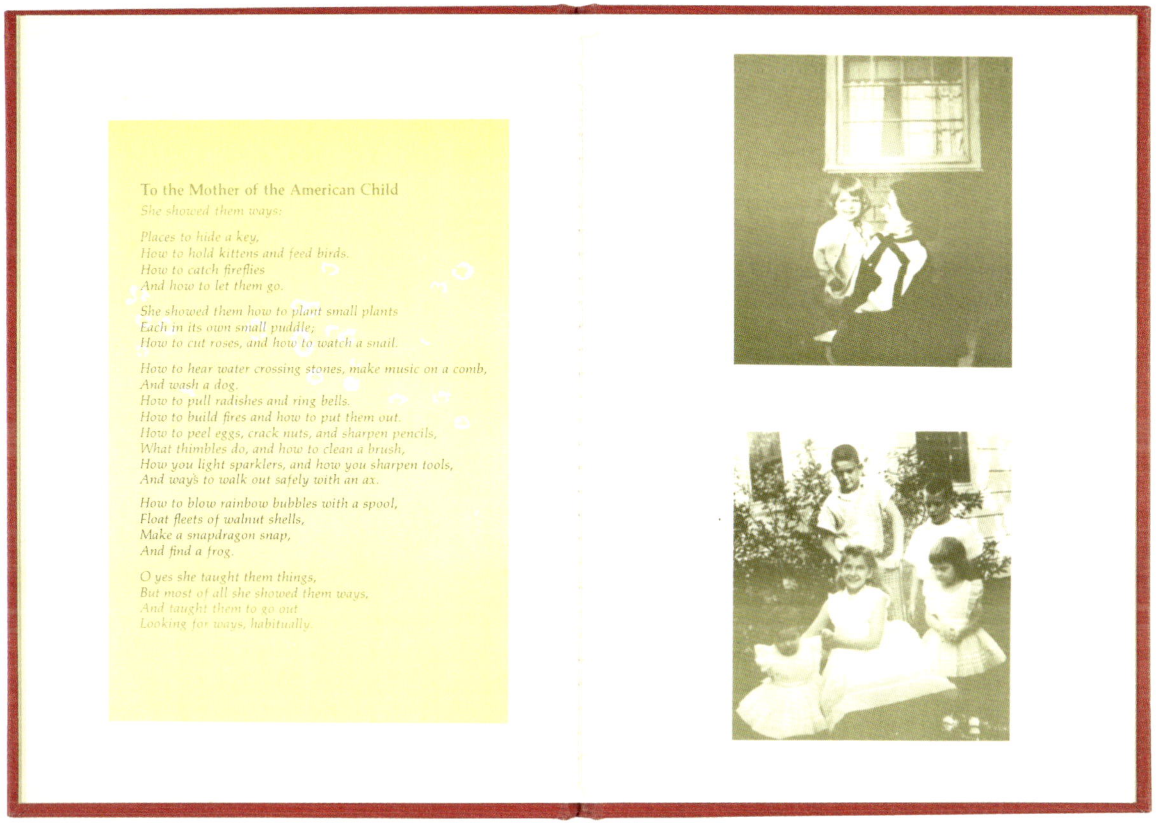

To the Mother of the American Child

*She showed them ways:*

*Places to hide a key,*
*How to hold kittens and feed birds.*
*How to catch fireflies*
*And how to let them go.*

*She showed them how to plant small plants*
*Each in its own small puddle;*
*How to cut roses, and how to watch a snail.*

*How to hear water crossing stones, make music on a comb,*
*And wash a dog.*
*How to pull radishes and ring bells.*
*How to build fires and how to put them out.*
*How to peel eggs, crack nuts, and sharpen pencils,*
*What thimbles do, and how to clean a brush,*
*How you light sparklers, and how you sharpen tools,*
*And way's to walk out safely with an ax.*

*How to blow rainbow bubbles with a spool,*
*Float fleets of walnut shells,*
*Make a snapdragon snap,*
*And find a frog.*

*O yes she taught them things,*
*But most of all she showed them ways,*
*And taught them to go out*
*Looking for ways, habitually.*

# MOUNTAIN DREAM TAROT

Fresh out of graduate school, I spent the summer of 1970 at Penland, teaching and working for the school. One morning I woke up and began to arrange sessions with models to create a photographic tarot card deck. The idea had come to me in a dream, hence the name *Mountain Dream Tarot*. I was familiar with tarot cards through a recently read book containing line drawings of the cards. Working from these, I located models and props and set to work—work that took me five years and several returns to Penland's studios and the surrounding landscape, where the majority were shot. My family also served as models.

People were selected not only because they physically resembled the drawings in the cards but in some cases because they were connected with the card in some other way—for example, the artist who made the cups or a person who owned a bird or a horse. The photographs often utilized the experimental darkroom techniques needed to make wands fly through the air and cups hover in the clouds. In some cases, negatives were retouched or the photographic prints were painted.

In 1975 I was ready to publish the deck with a printer in Rochester, New York. They printed and cut the cards, and I then collated sets, rounded the corners, and placed them in custom-made boxes. Several cards were reproduced in Stuart Kaplan's *The Encyclopedia of Tarot* (1978) as probably the first photographic treatment of all seventy-eight cards in a genre that has been in existence for over five hundred years. By the end of the 1970s, the edition of 800 was sold out.

In August 2001 it was reissued. For this deck I was able to scan the images and alter them digitally. I wished to retain the original character of the deck, but changes were so easy that I couldn't resist making a few. I added my son and daughter as the Page of Swords and Cups, respectively, while they were students at Penland, very near the age I was when I began the project.

In 2012, after the second edition sold out, I created a print-on-demand version. I had to adjust the aspect ratio of the cards, and I further retouched them. It is possible now to create a different version of the deck each time it is ordered, allowing it to continue to evolve.

**BEA NETTLES**

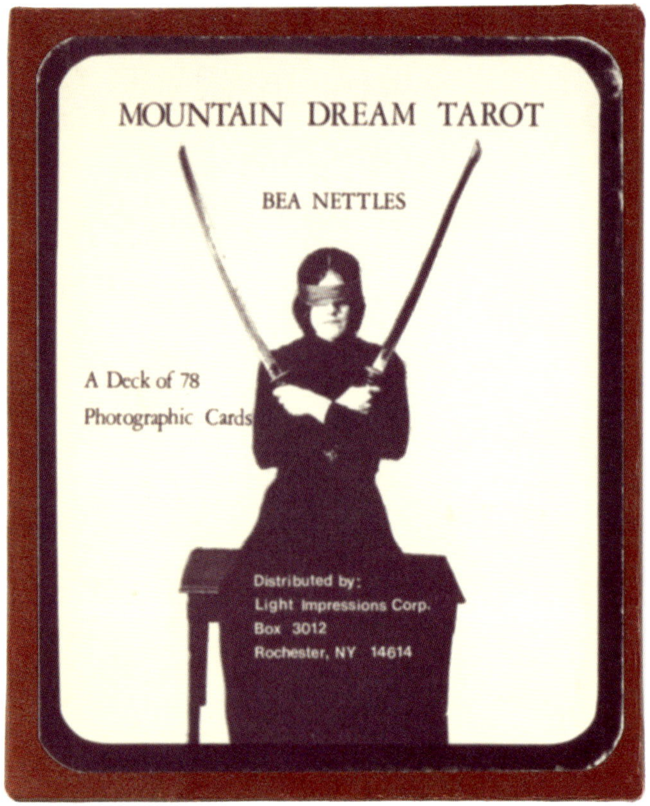


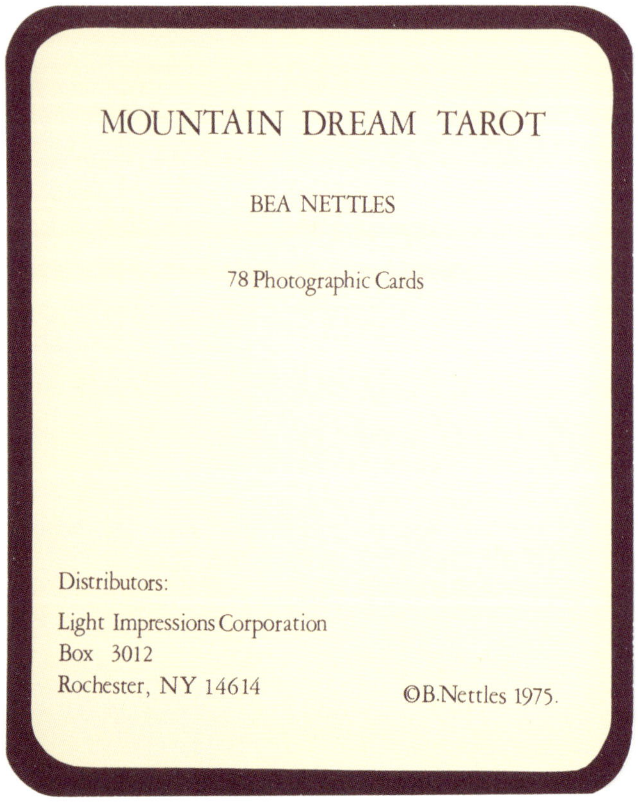


> *Mountain Dream Tarot*, 1975,
card deck with offset lithographs

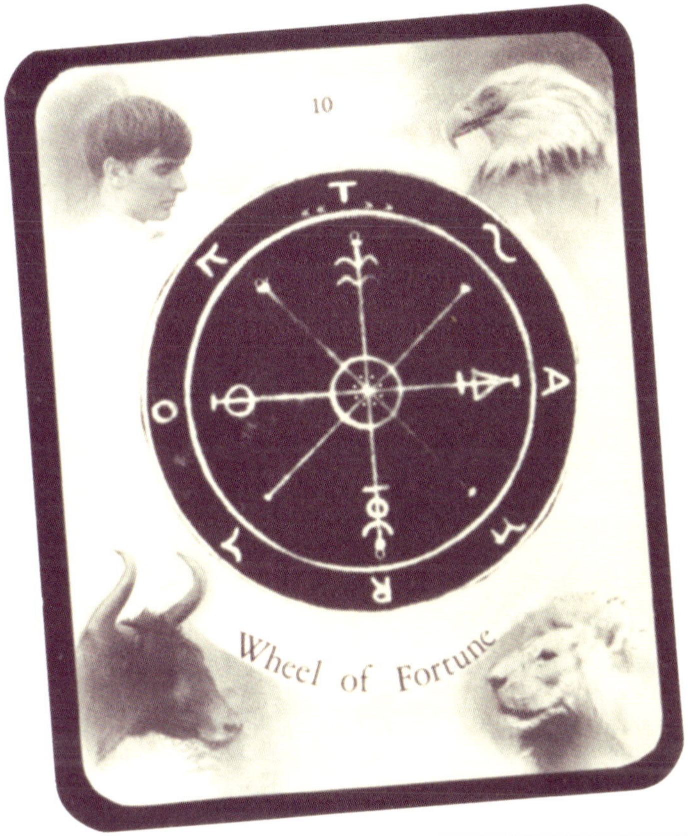
10
T
A
R
O
Wheel of Fortune

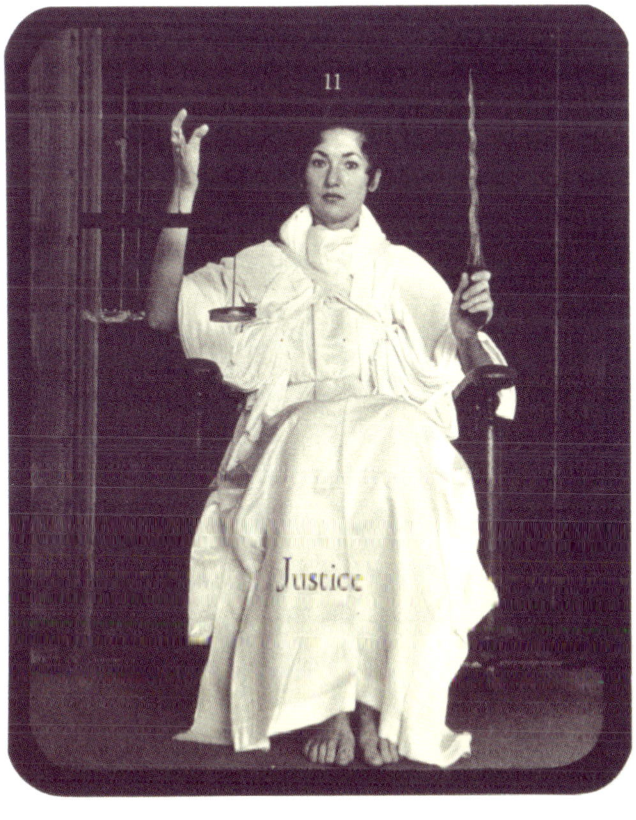
11
Justice

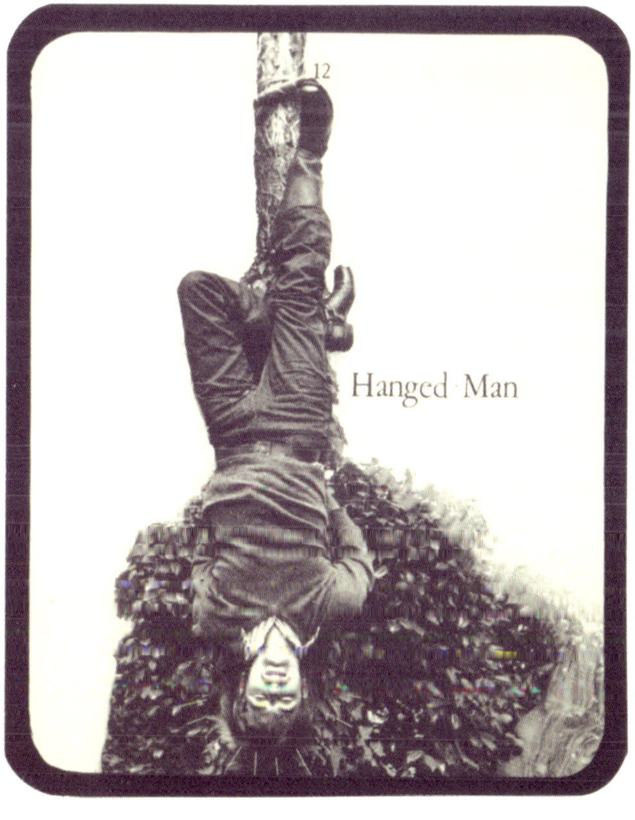
12
Hanged Man

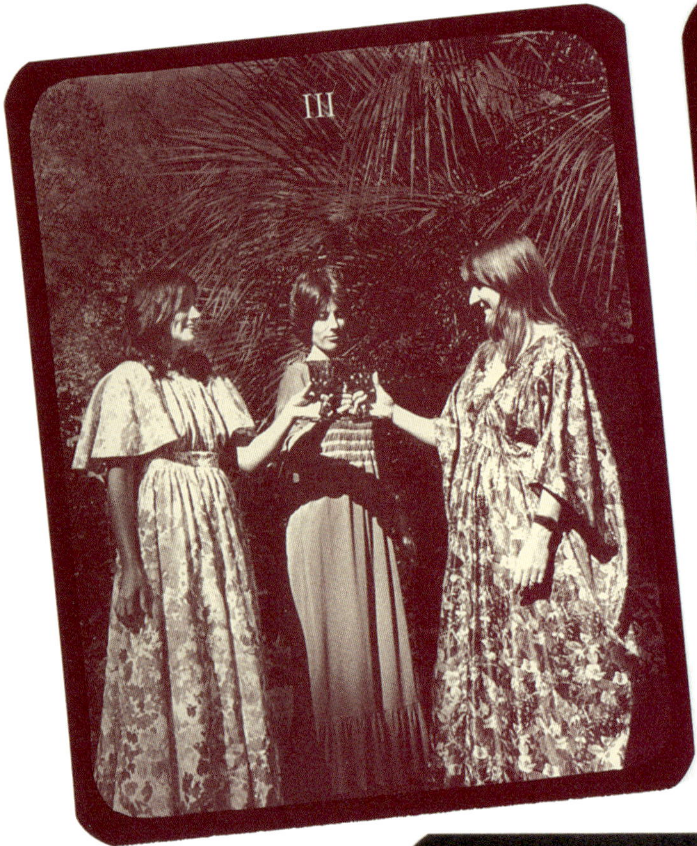
III

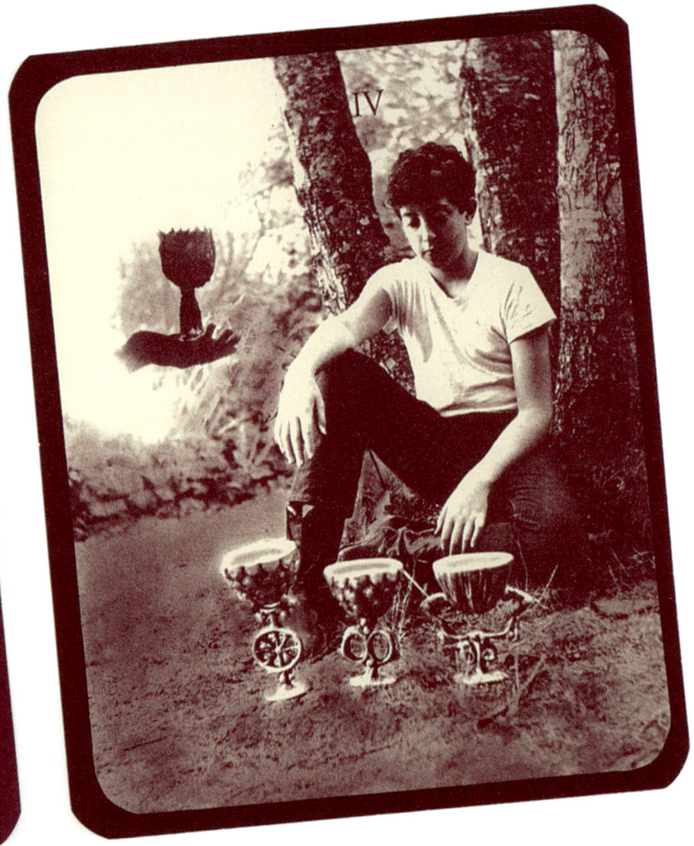
IV

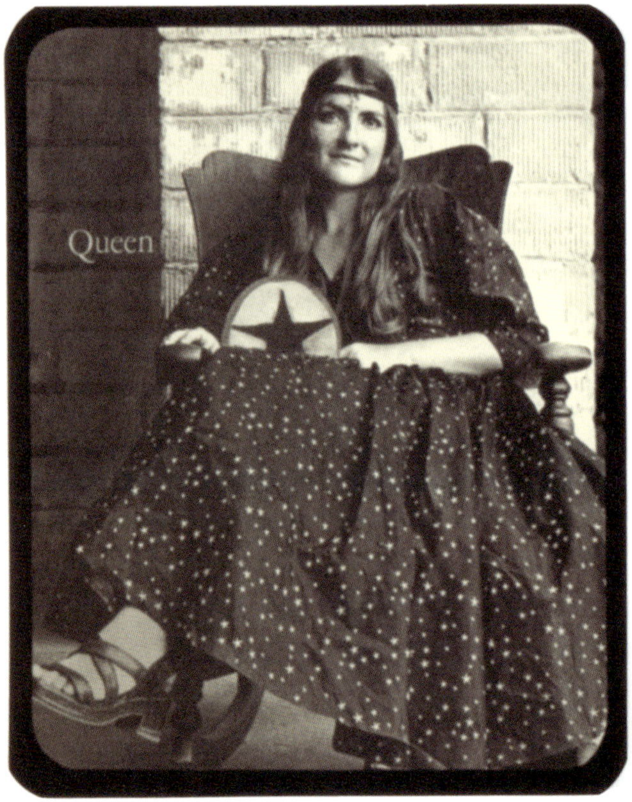
Queen

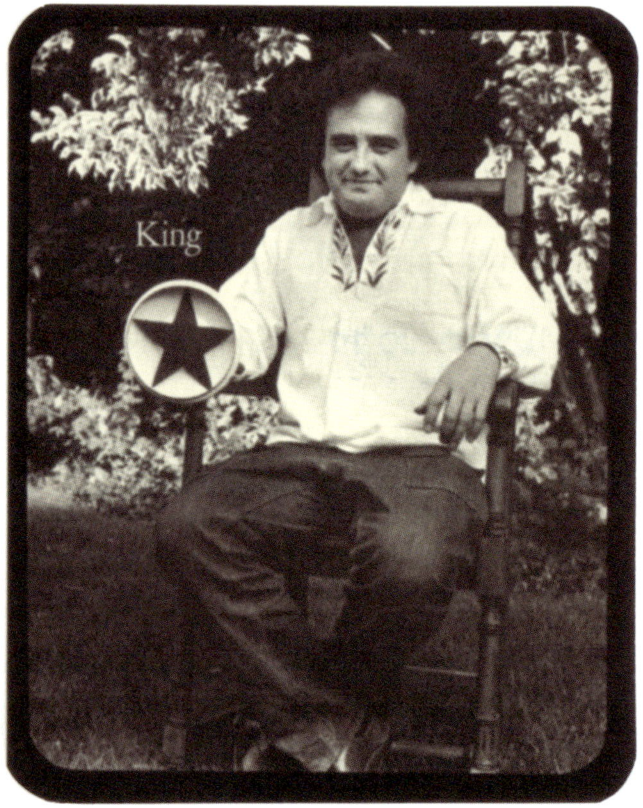
King

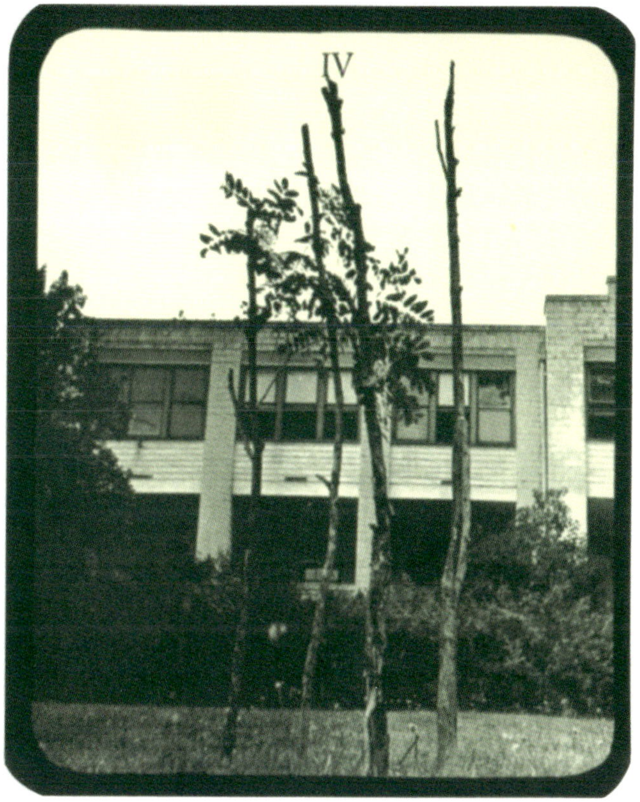
IV

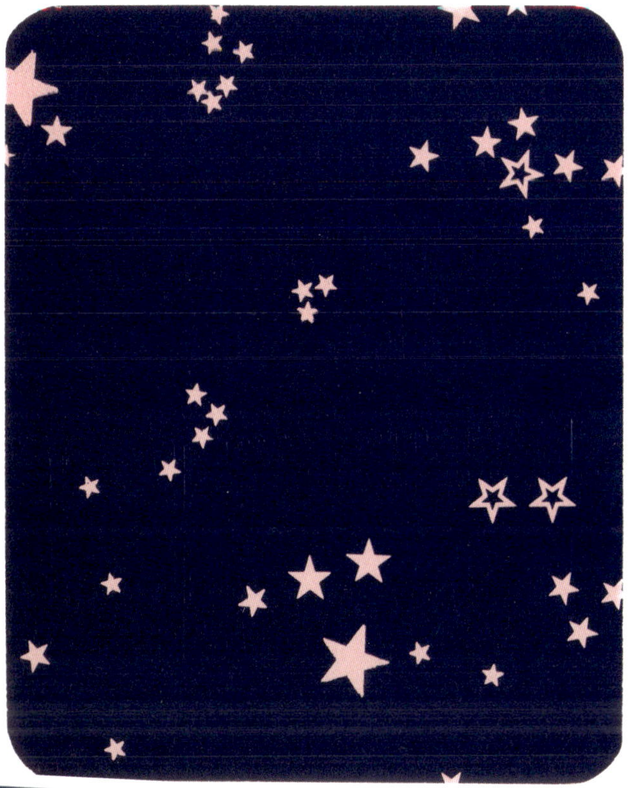

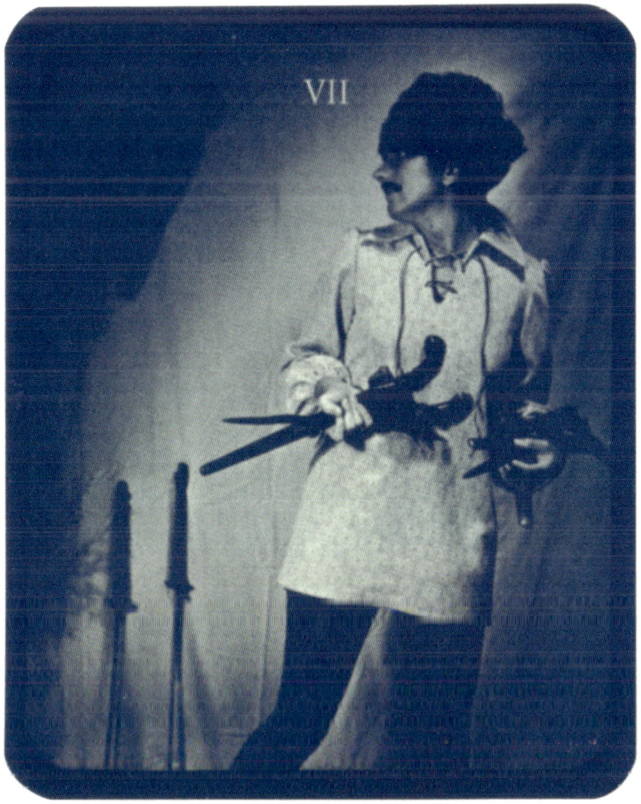
VII

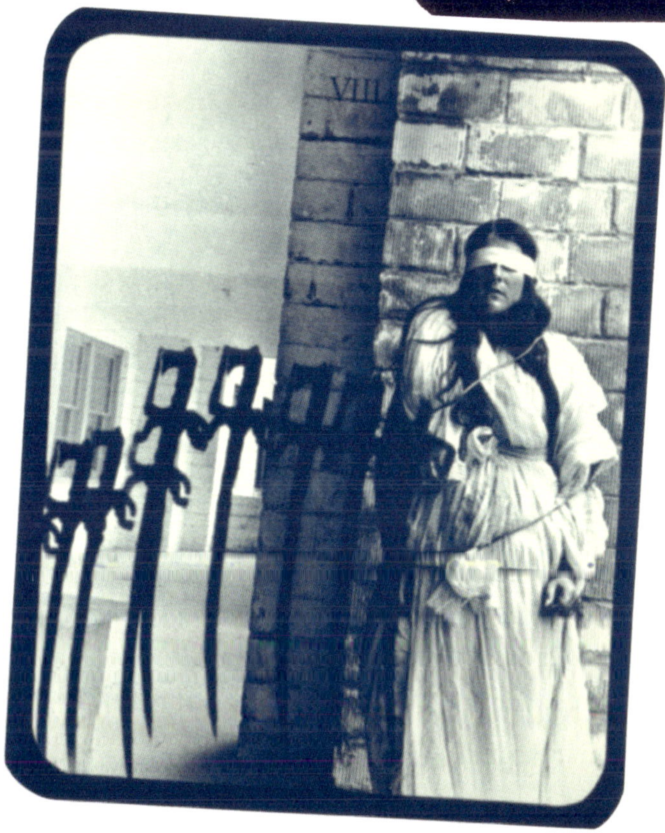
VIII

# 1975–1992

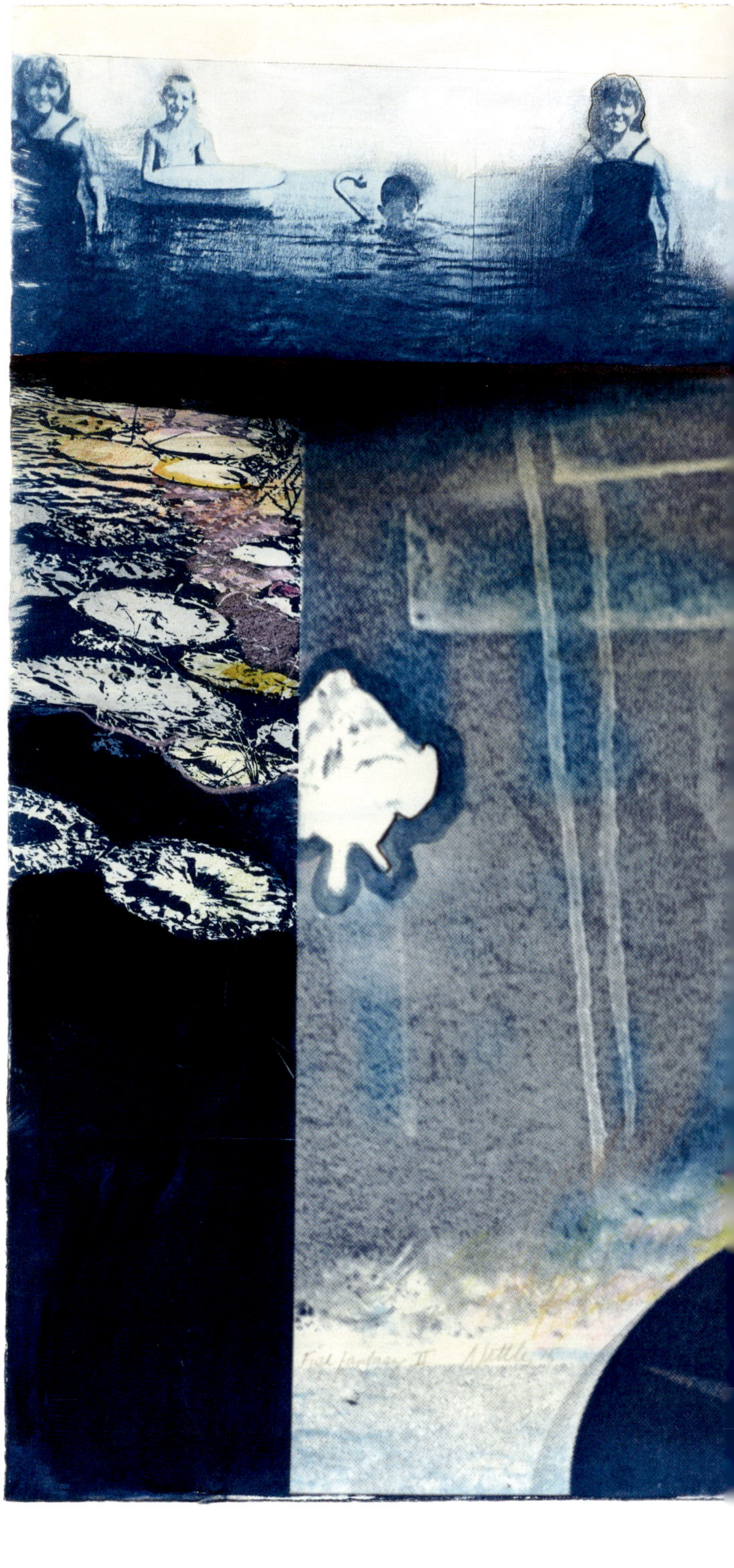

> *Fish Fantasy II*, 1975,
cyanotype with applied color

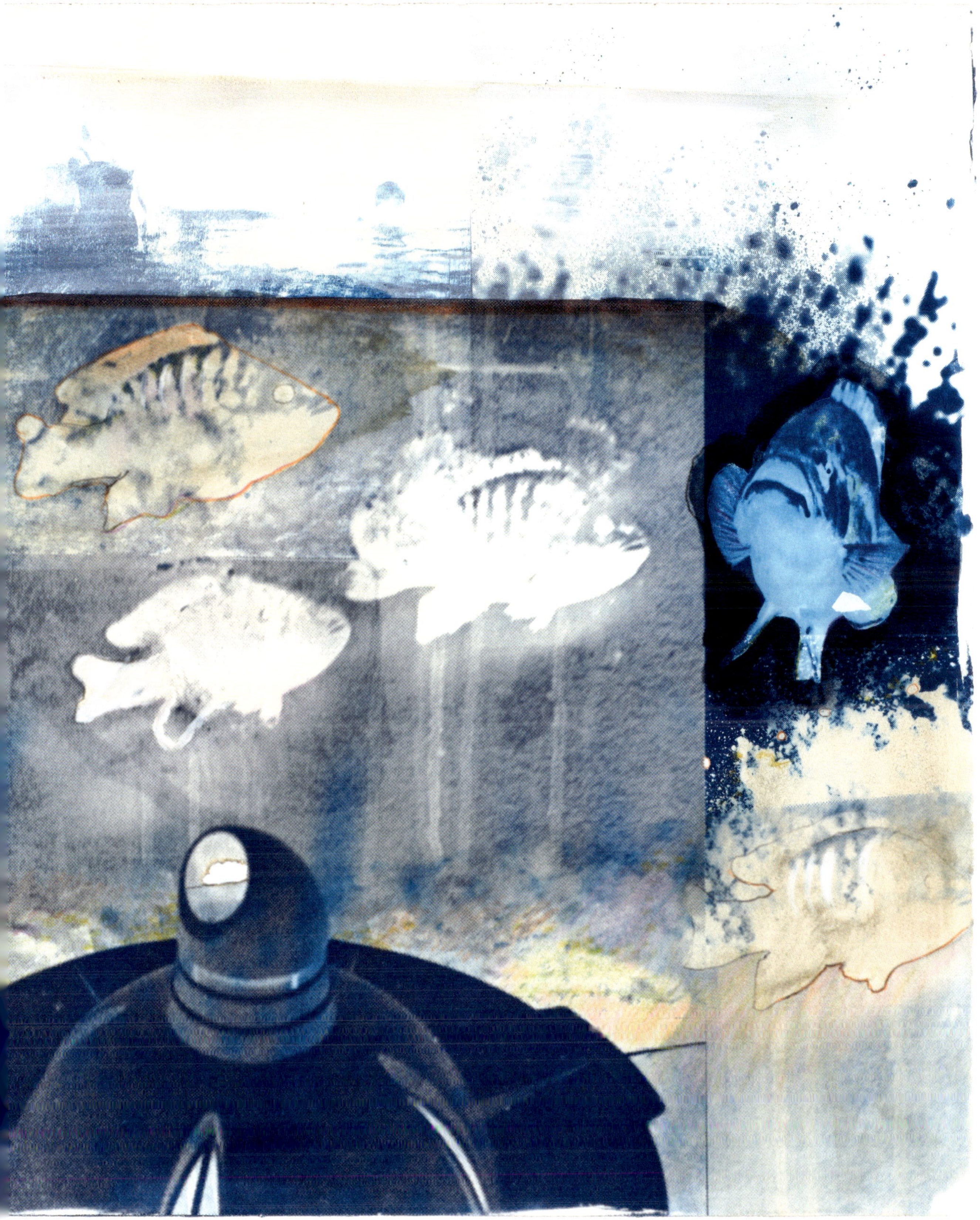

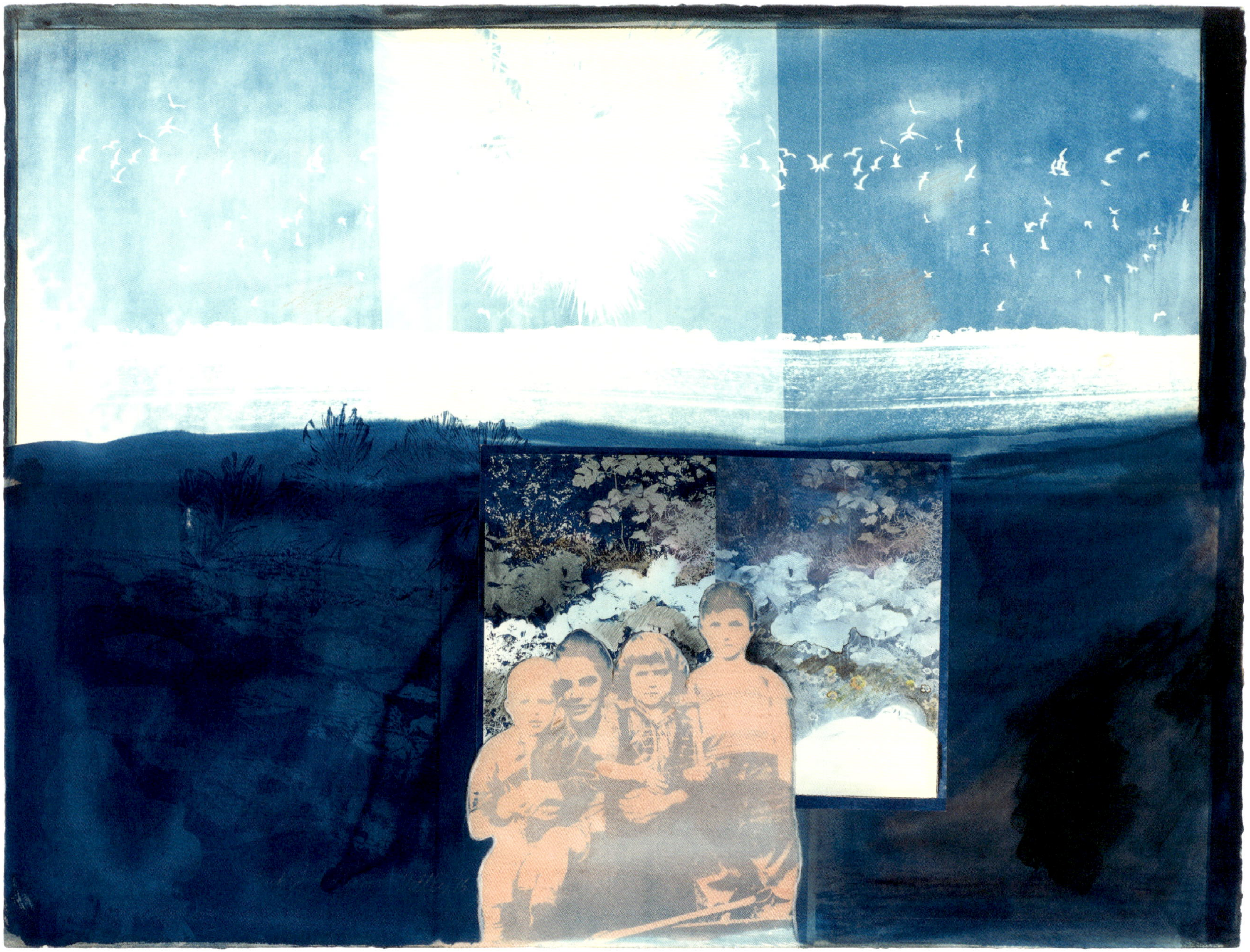

> *Backyard Dream*, 1975, collage with cyanotypes, stitching and applied color

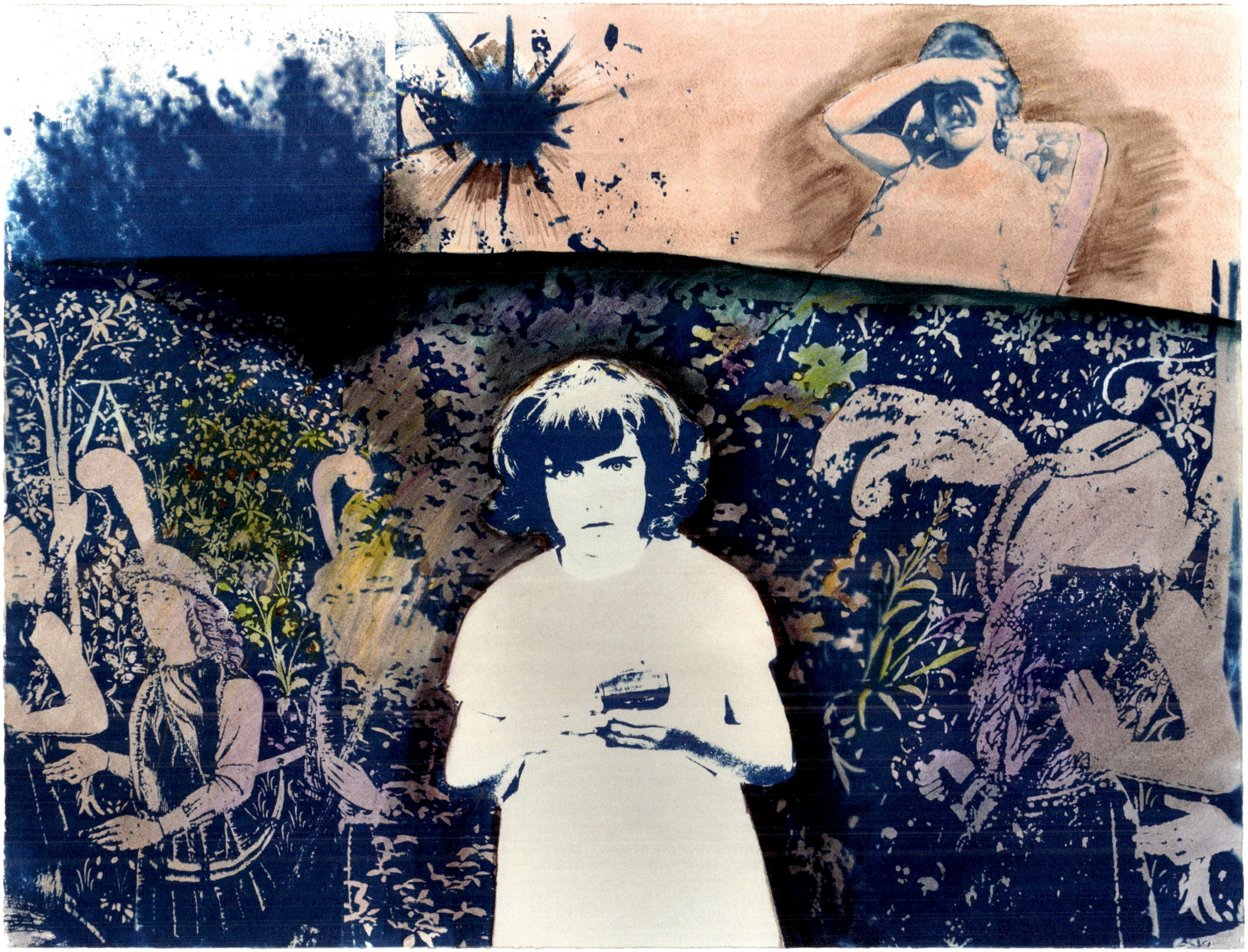

> *Golden Evenin*, 1975, cyanotype with applied color

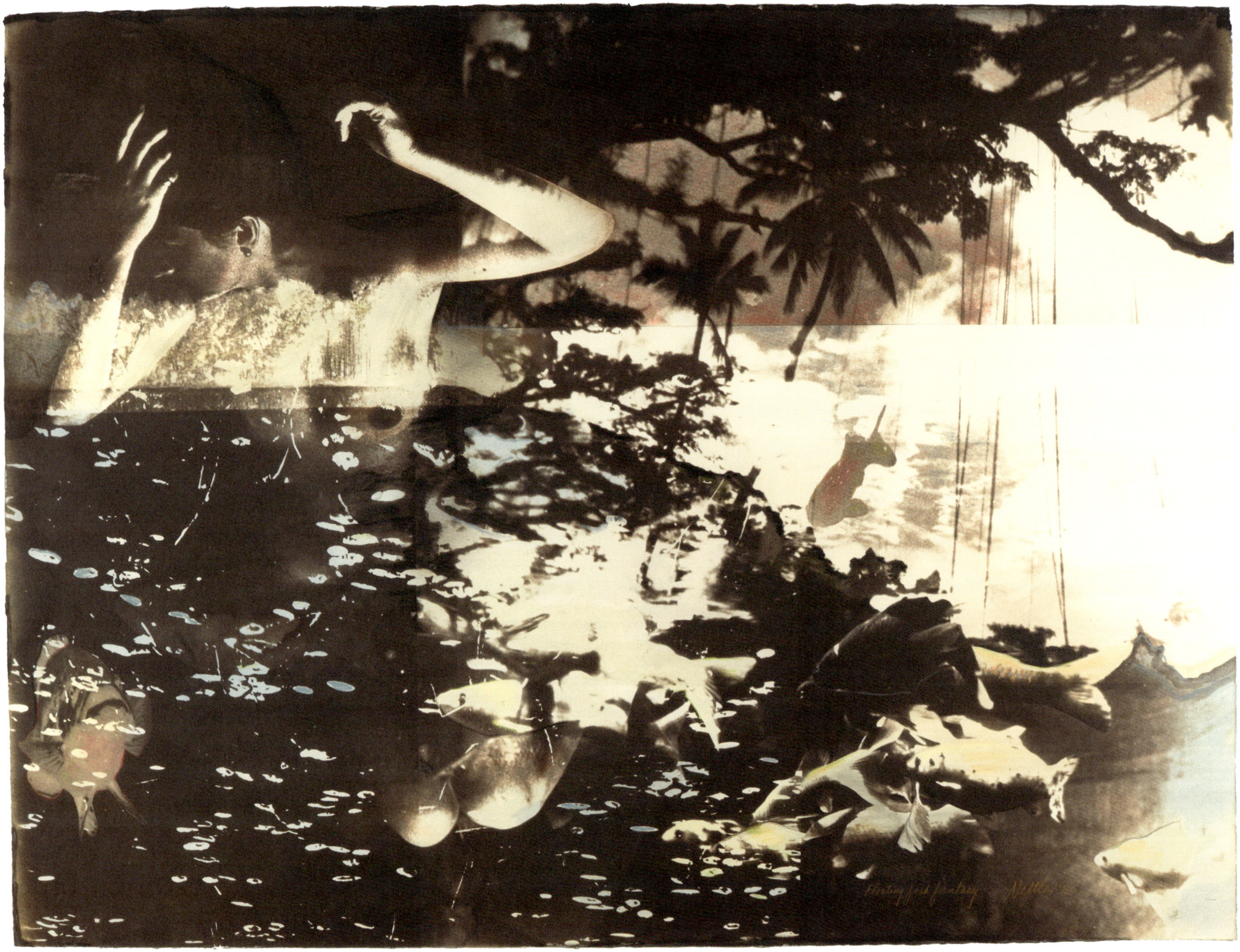

> *Floating Fish Fantasy*, 1976,
Van Dyke print with applied color

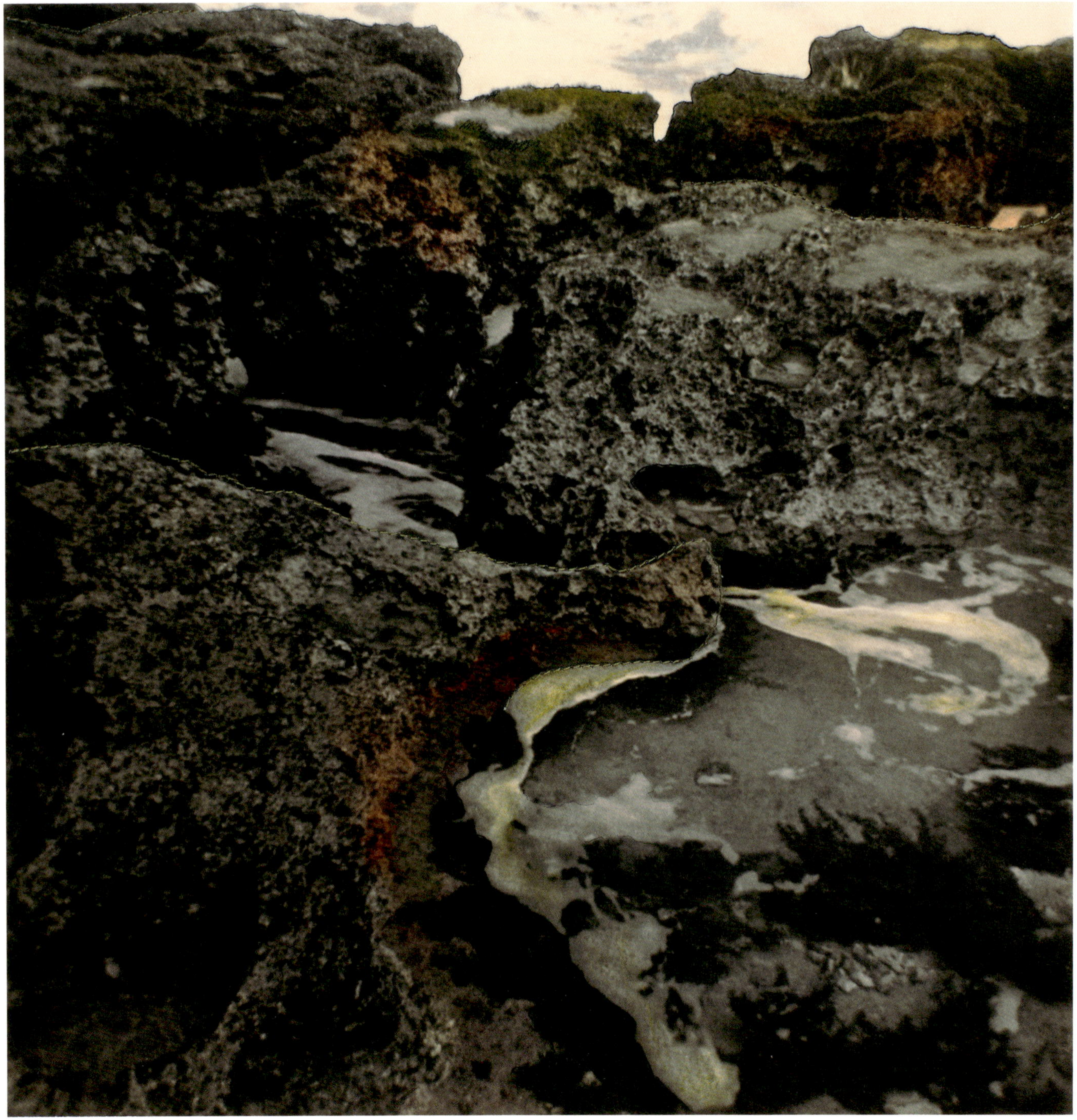

> ***Warm Weather Wishes***

*Tidal Pool*, 1975, gelatin silver print with applied color and machine stitching

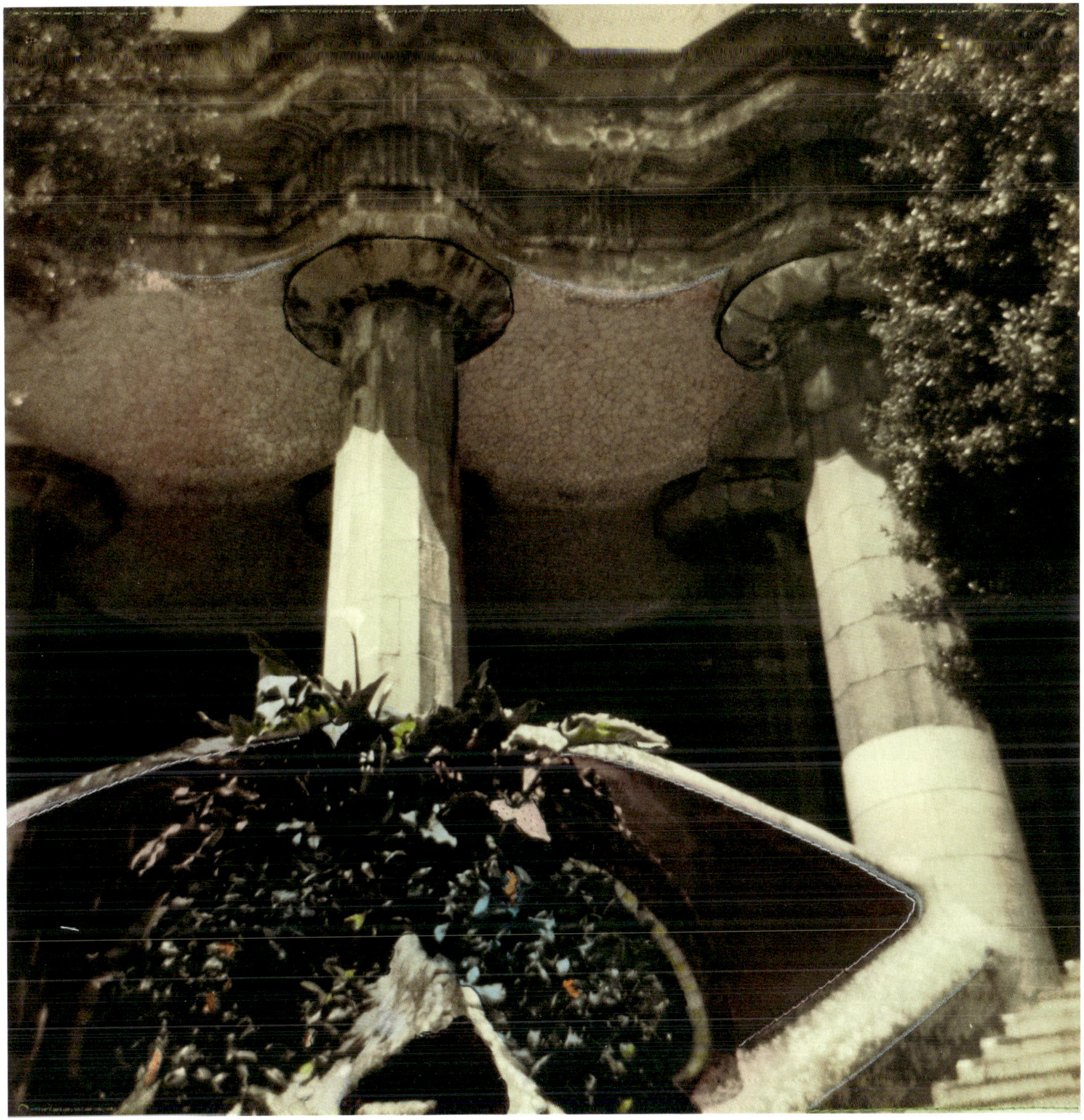

*Barcelona II*, 1975, gelatin silver print with applied color and machine stitching

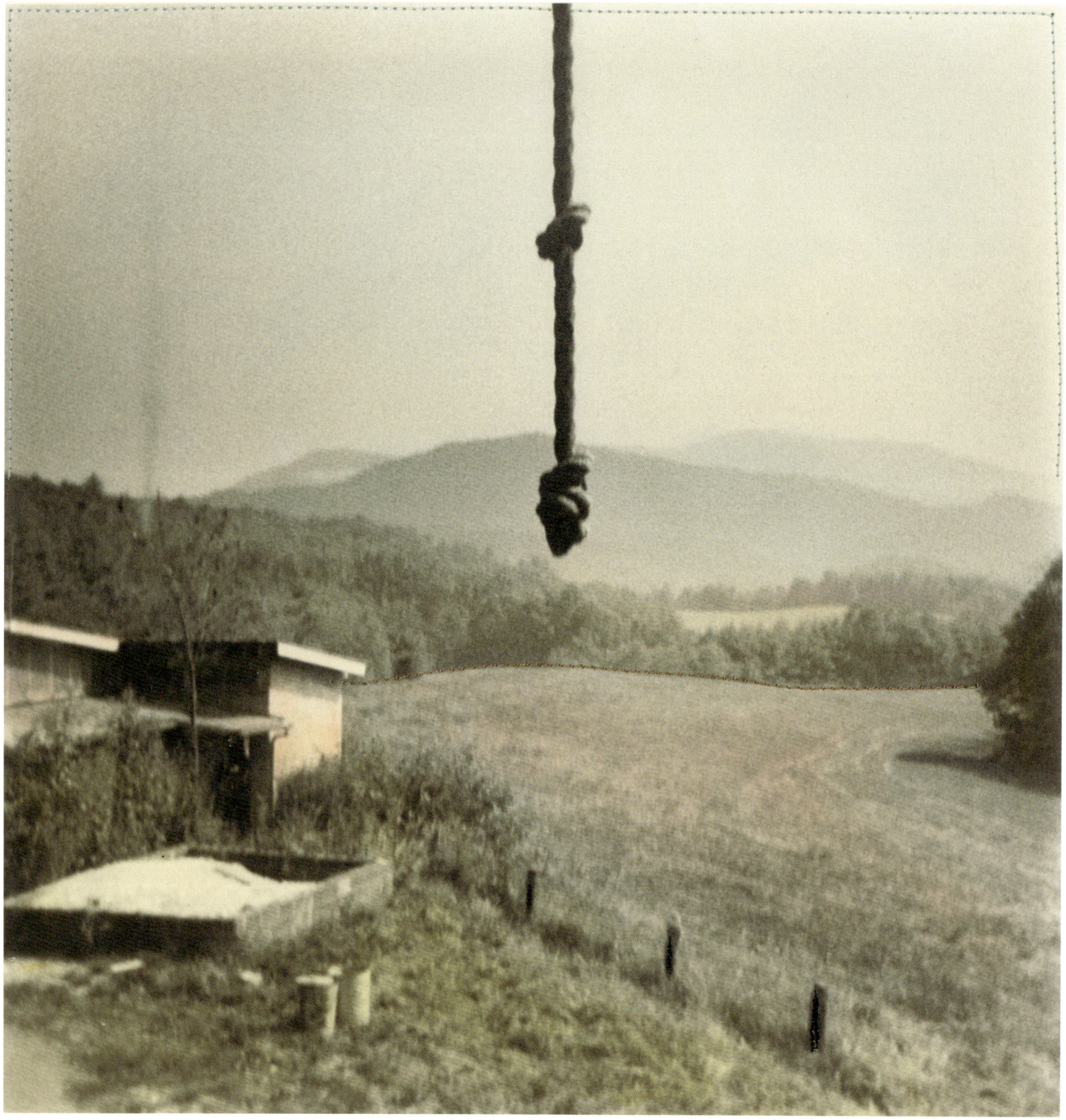

> ***Warm Weather Wishes***

*Rope Trick*, 1977, gelatin silver print with applied color and machine stitching

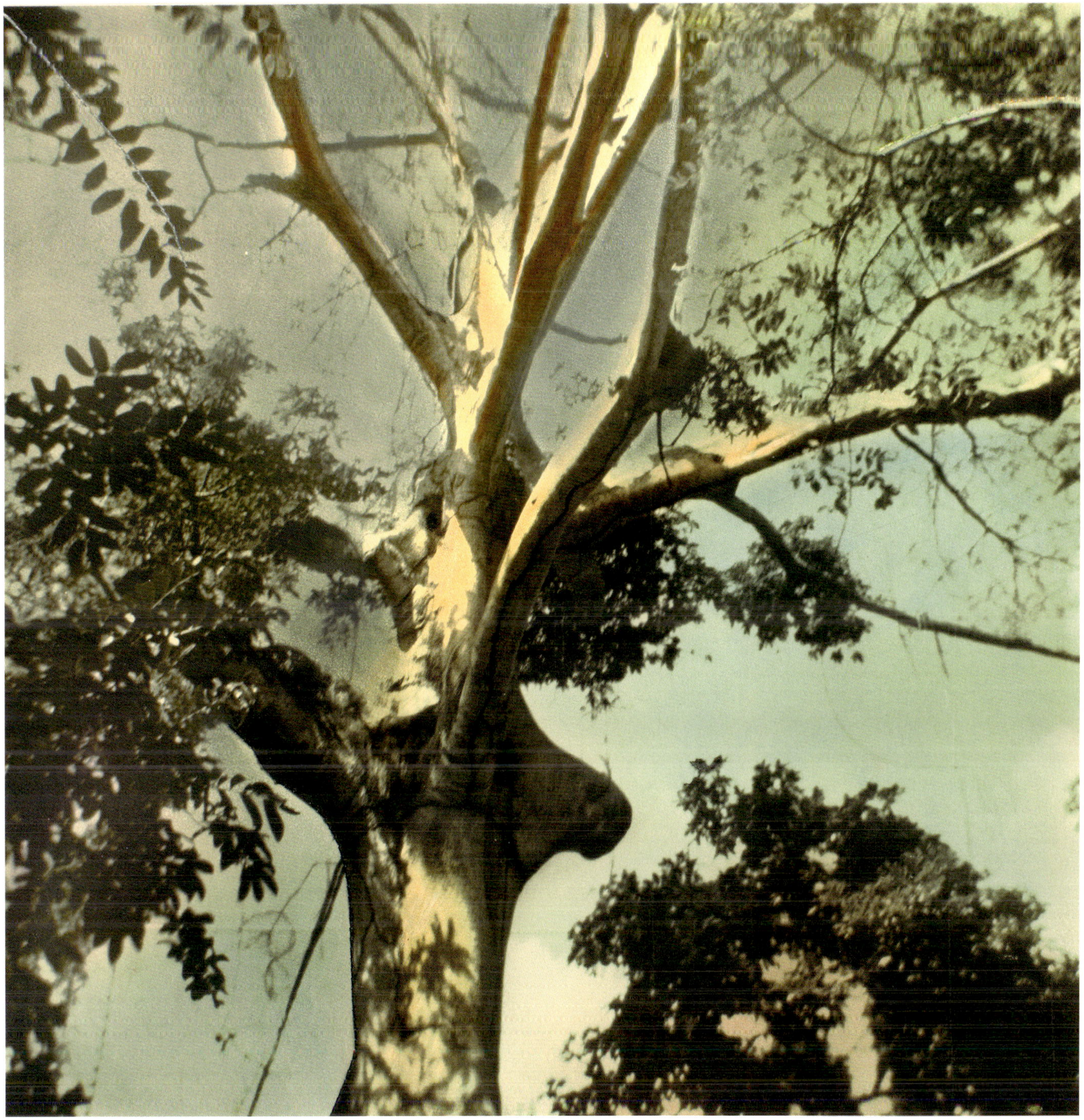

*Rackham Tree*, 1977, gelatin silver print with applied color and machine stitching

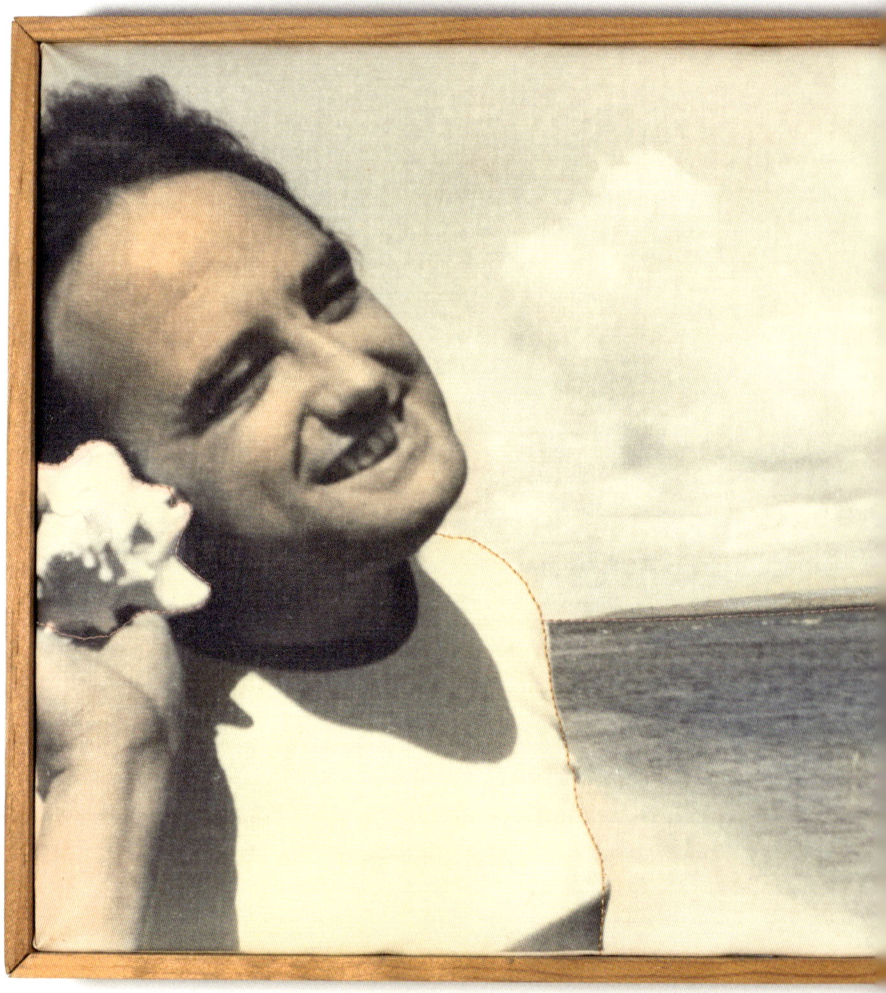

> *Seaside Portrait*, 1977, gelatin silver photo linen with applied color, embroidery, stitching, and wood

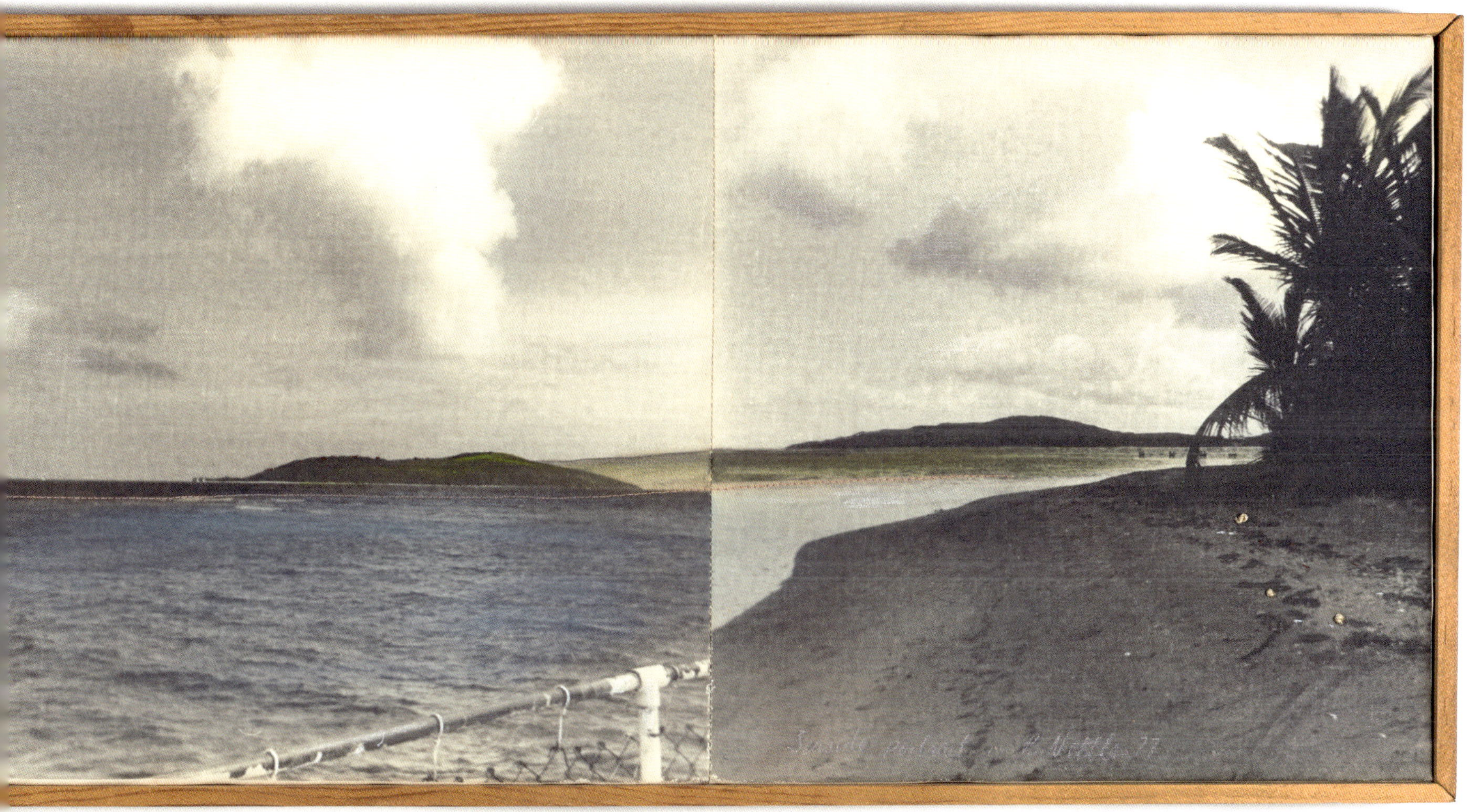

> ***Flamingo in the Dark***

*Tropical Childhood*, 1976, gum bichromate print with applied color

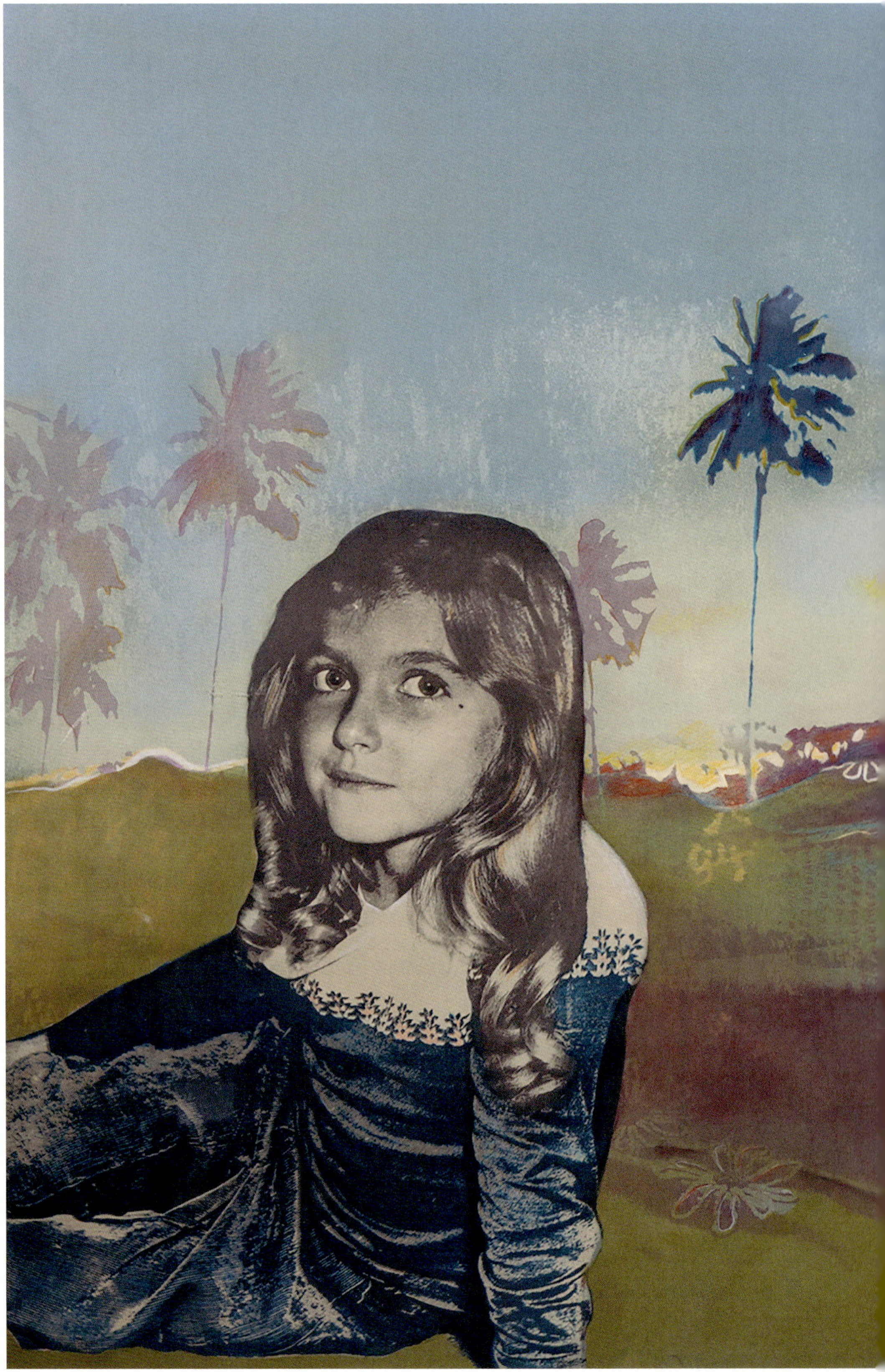

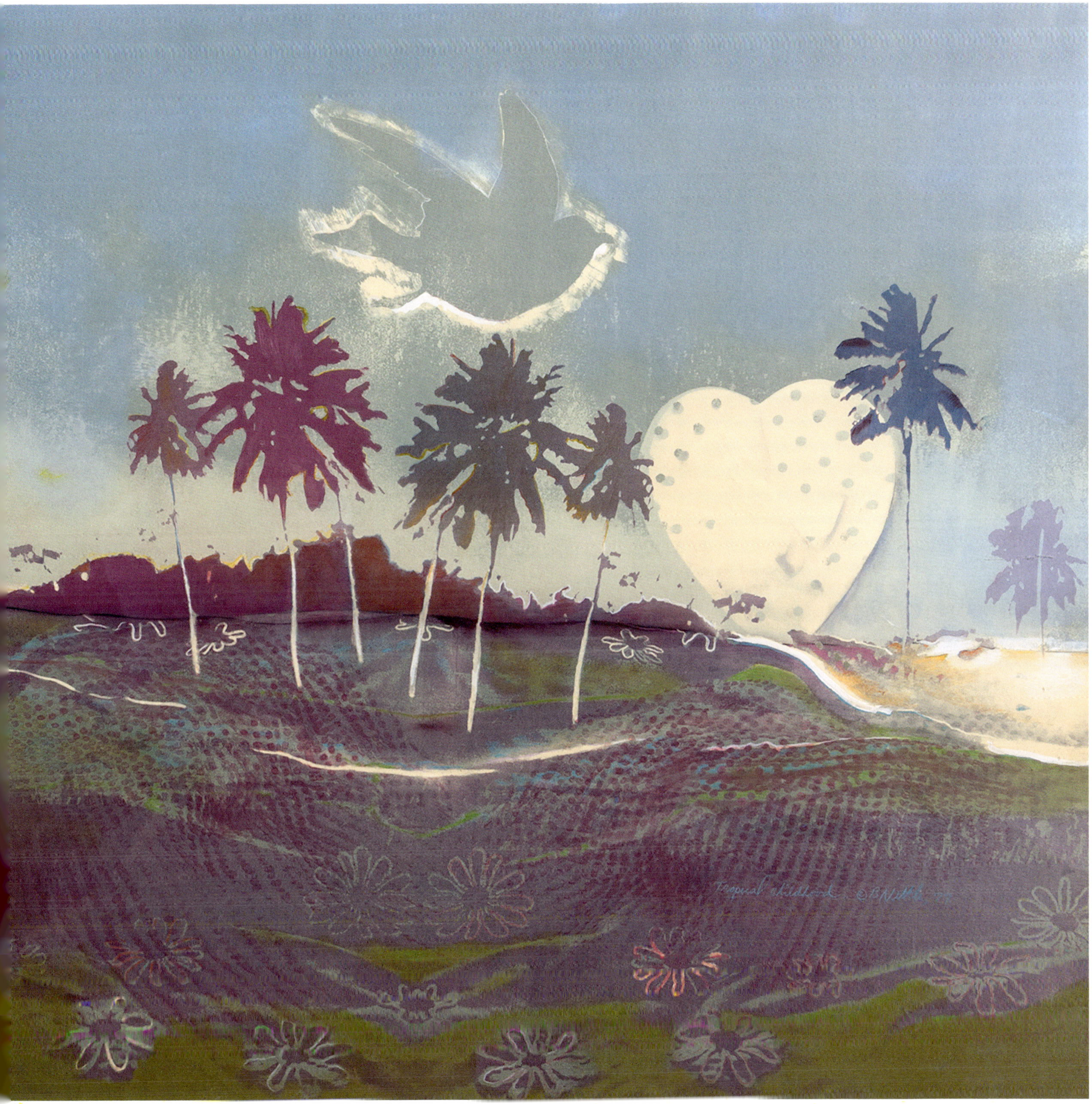

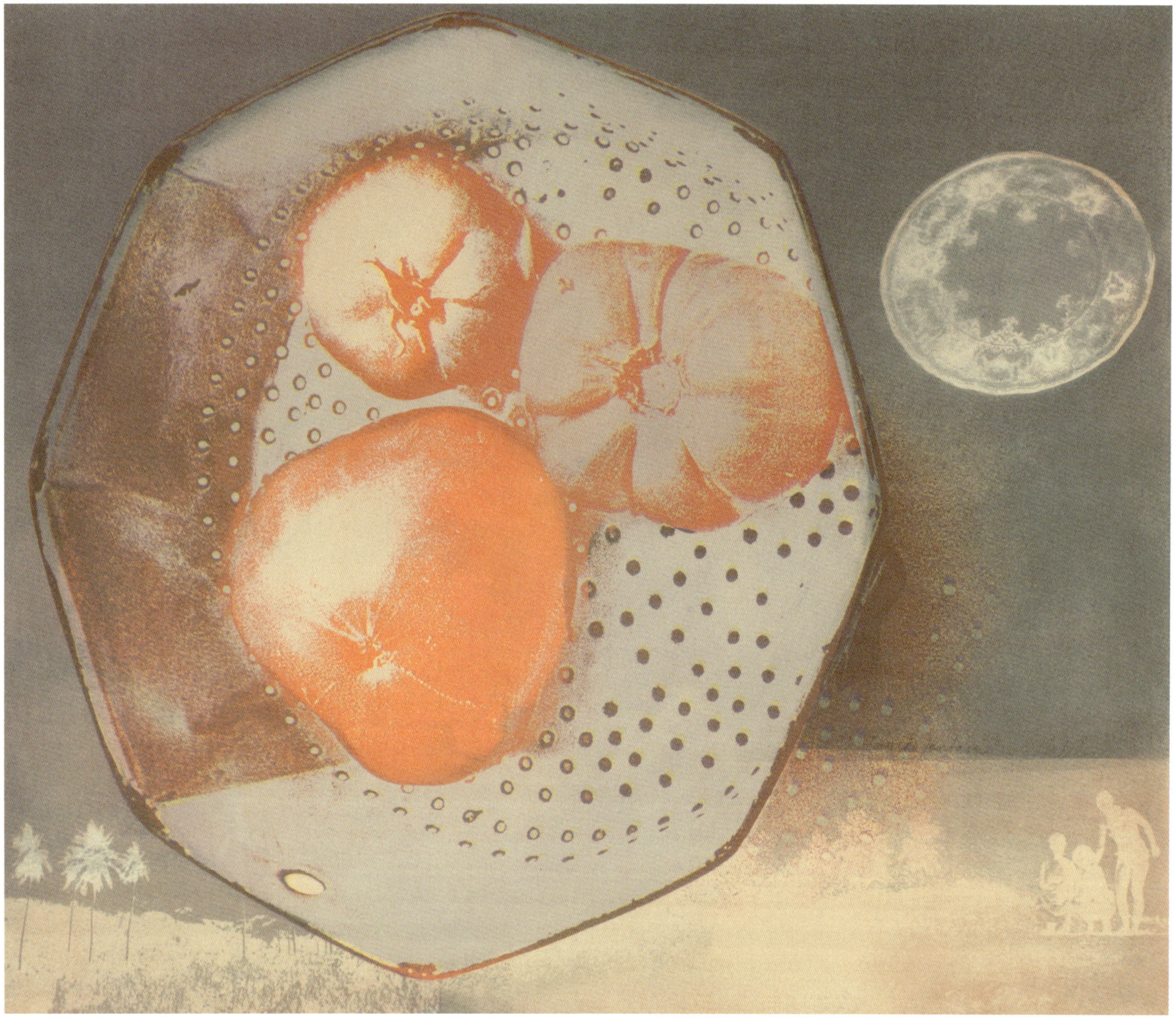

> ***Flamingo in the Dark***

*Tomato Fantasy*, 1976, gum bichromate on vinyl with applied color

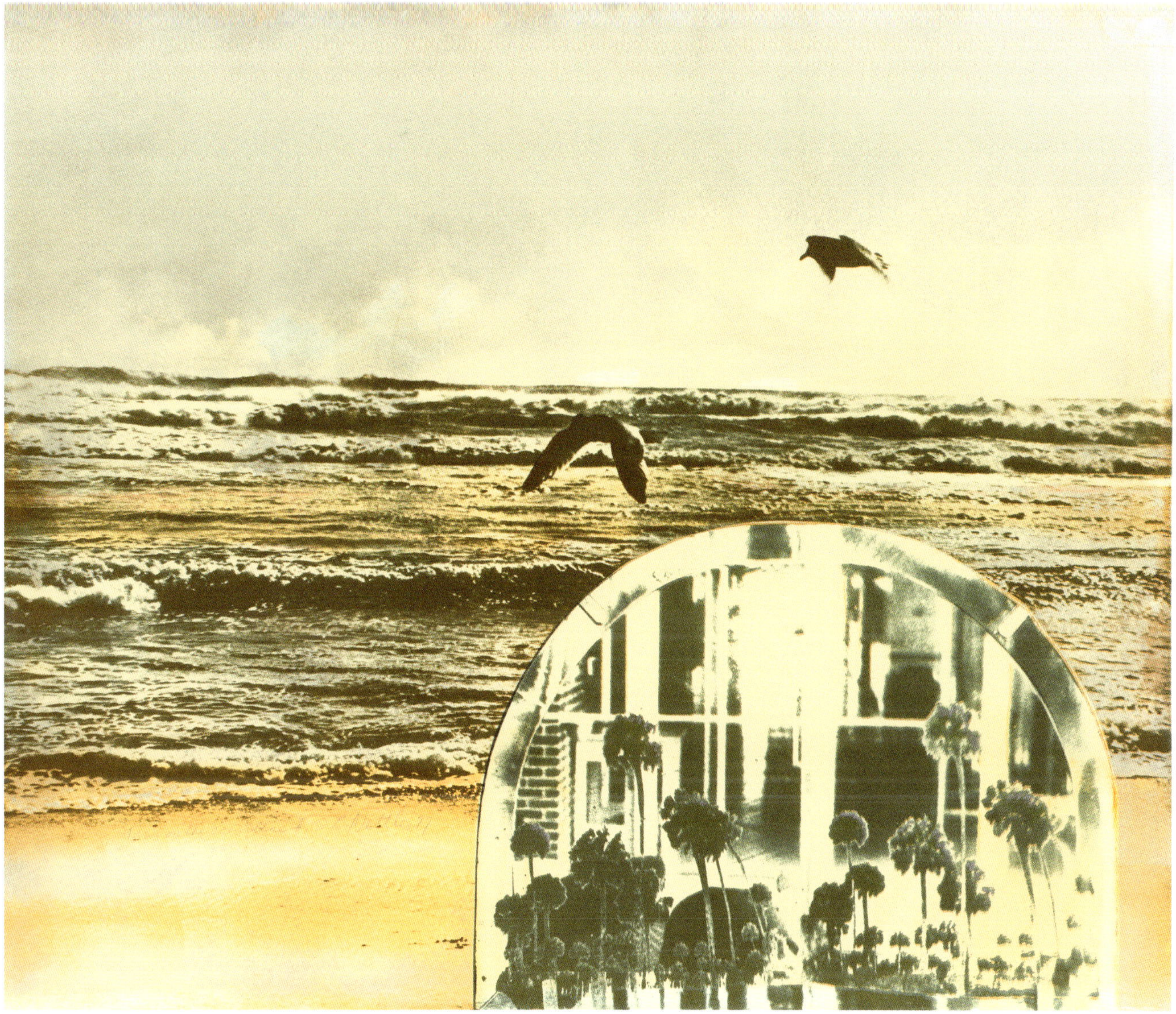

*Mirror on Coastline II*, 1976, gum bichromate print with applied color

> ***Flamingo in the Dark***

*Flyin Princess*, November 1978, gum bichromate prints with applied color

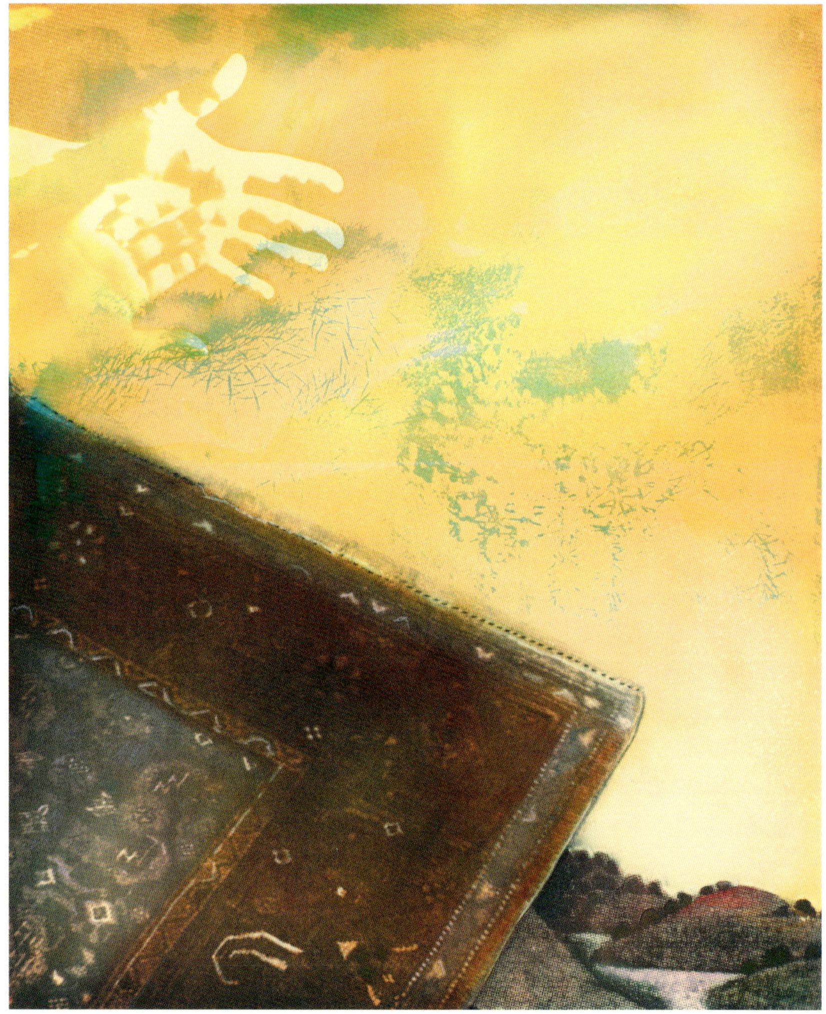

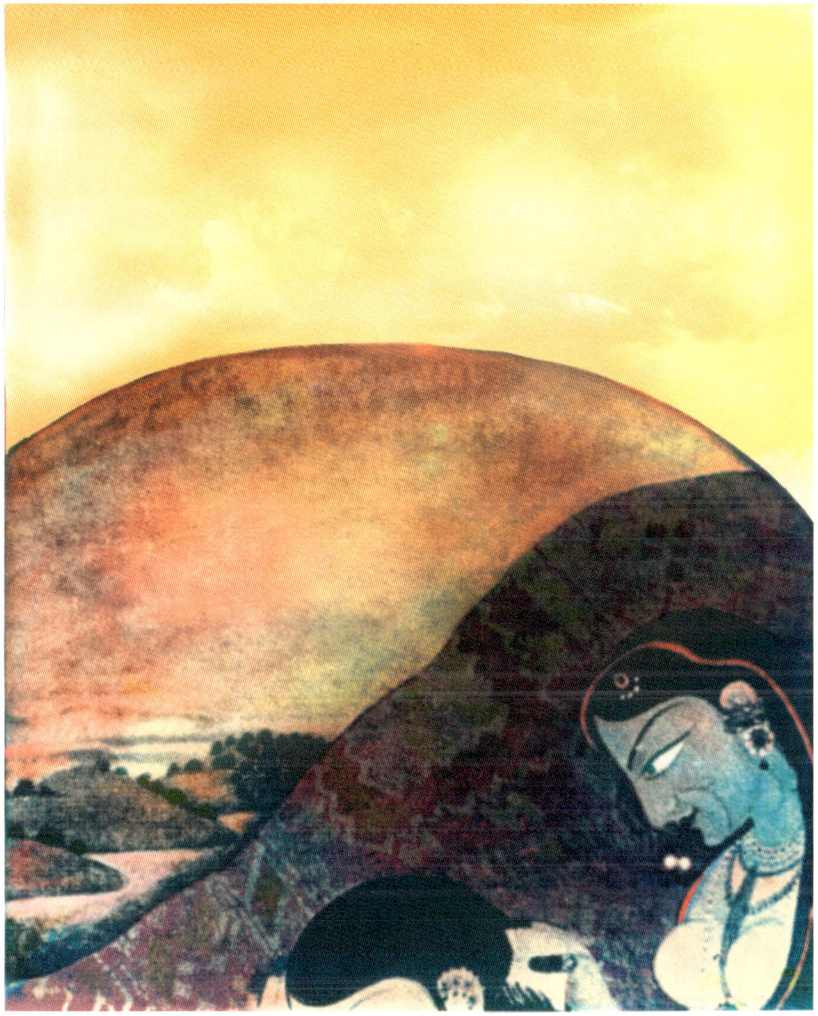

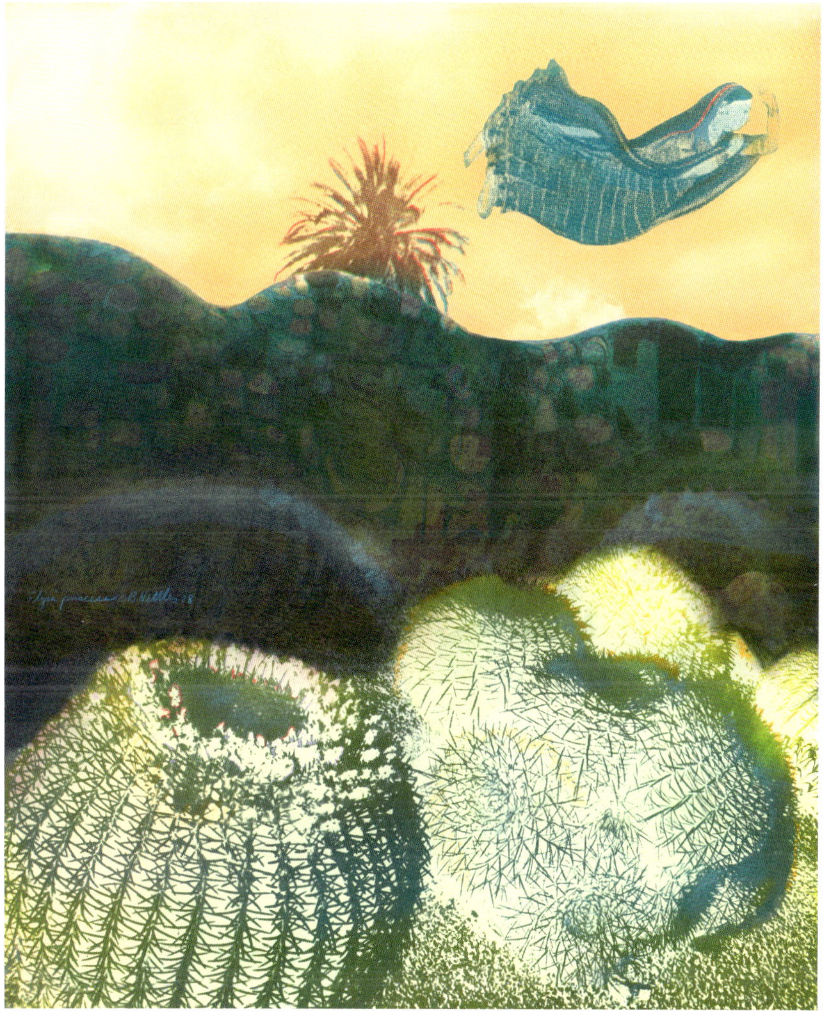

> ***Flamingo in the Dark***

*Moon and Dish*, 1977, gum bichromate prints with applied color

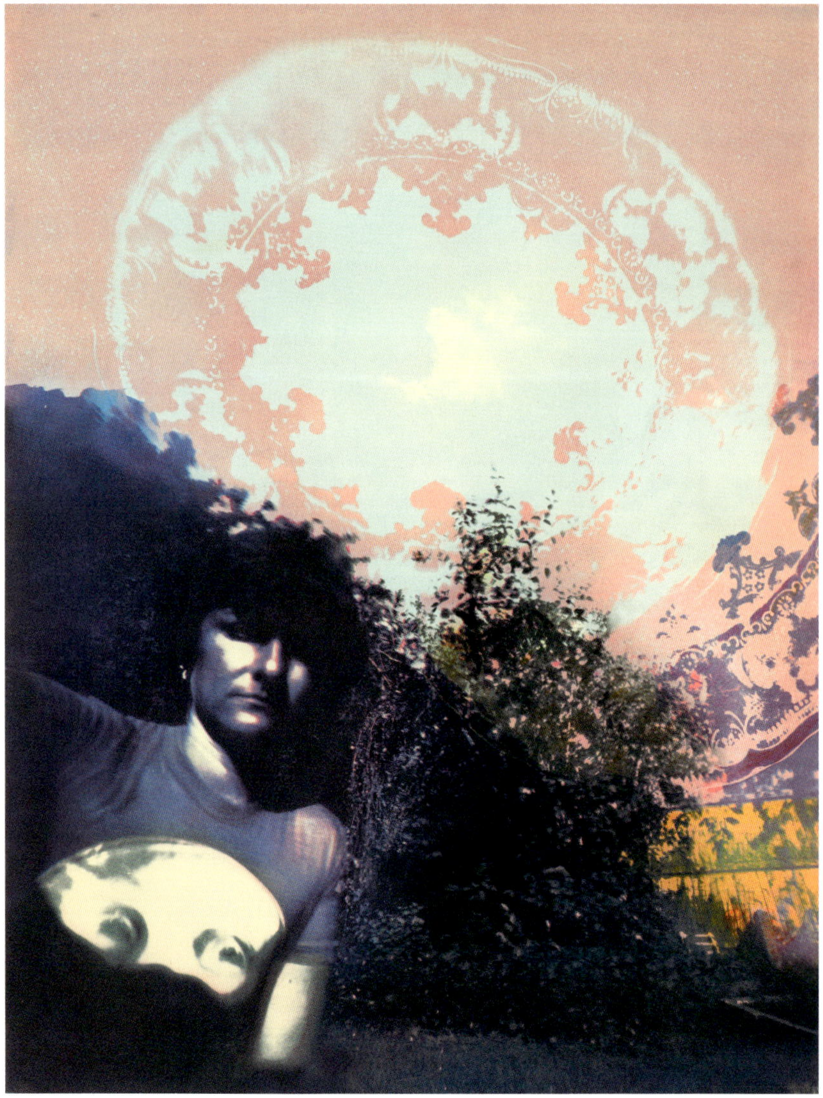

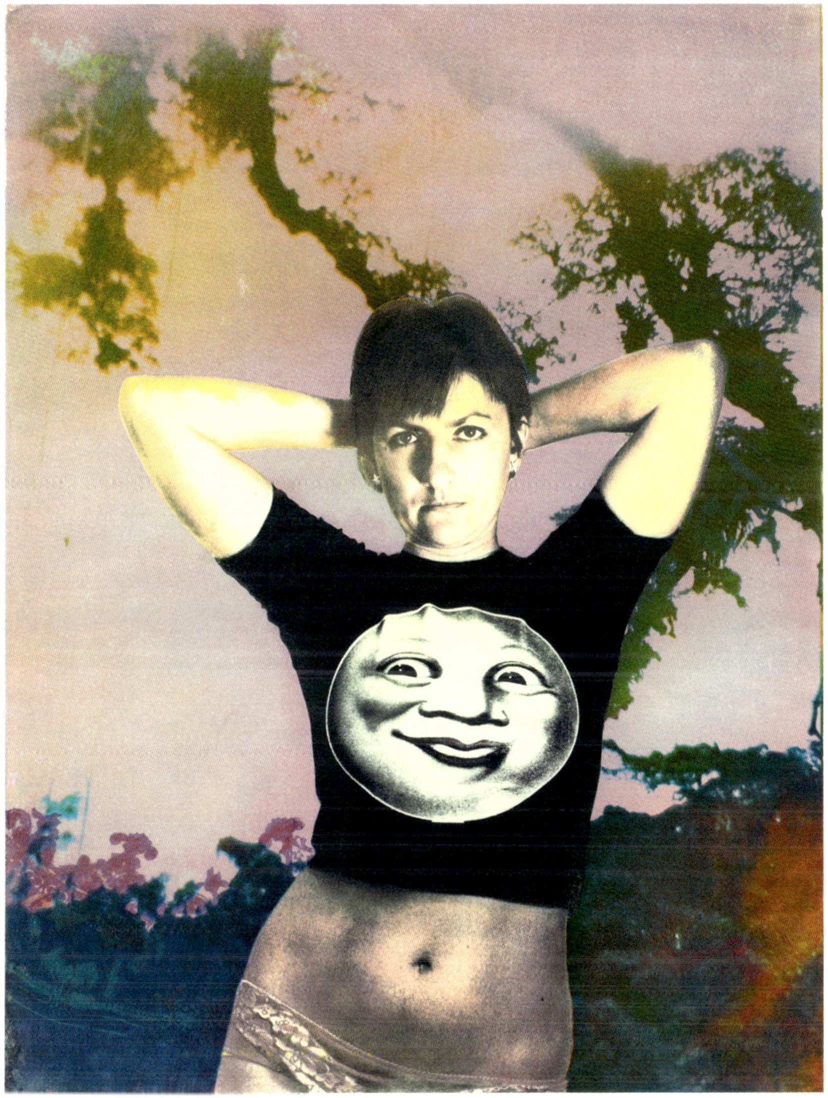

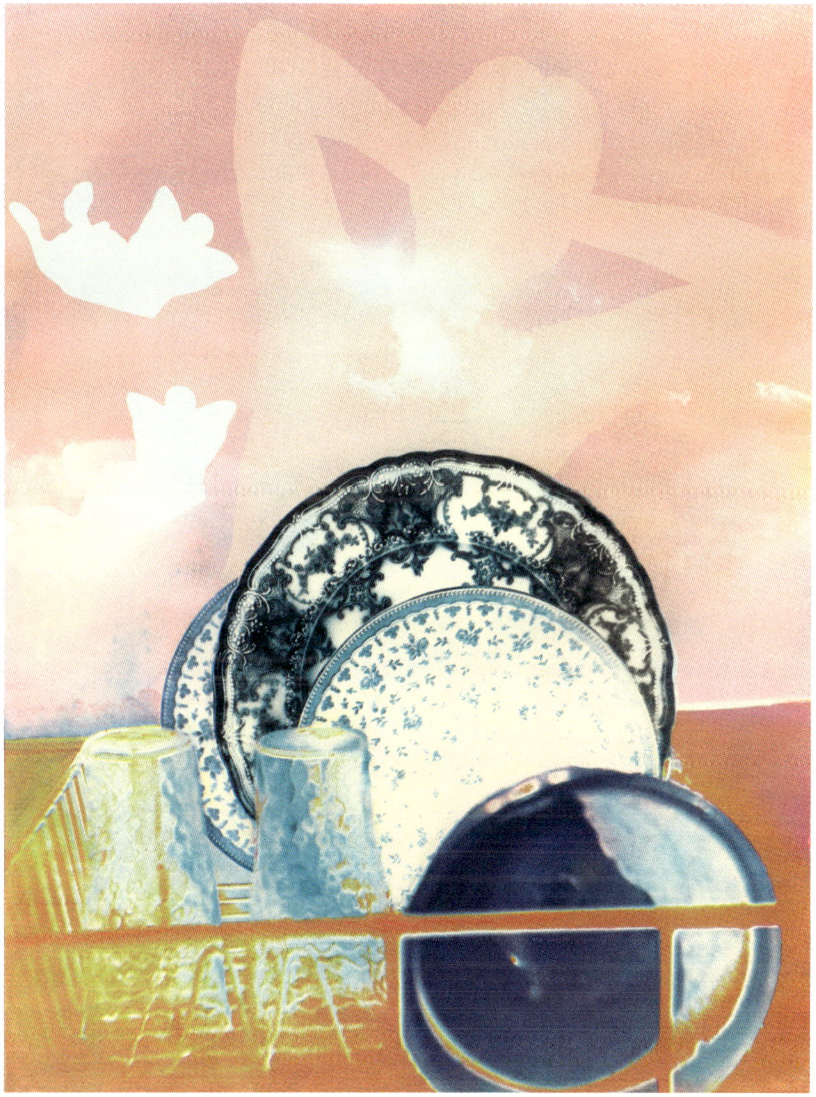

> ***Flamingo in the Dark***

*Gifts*, 1979, gum bichromate print with applied color

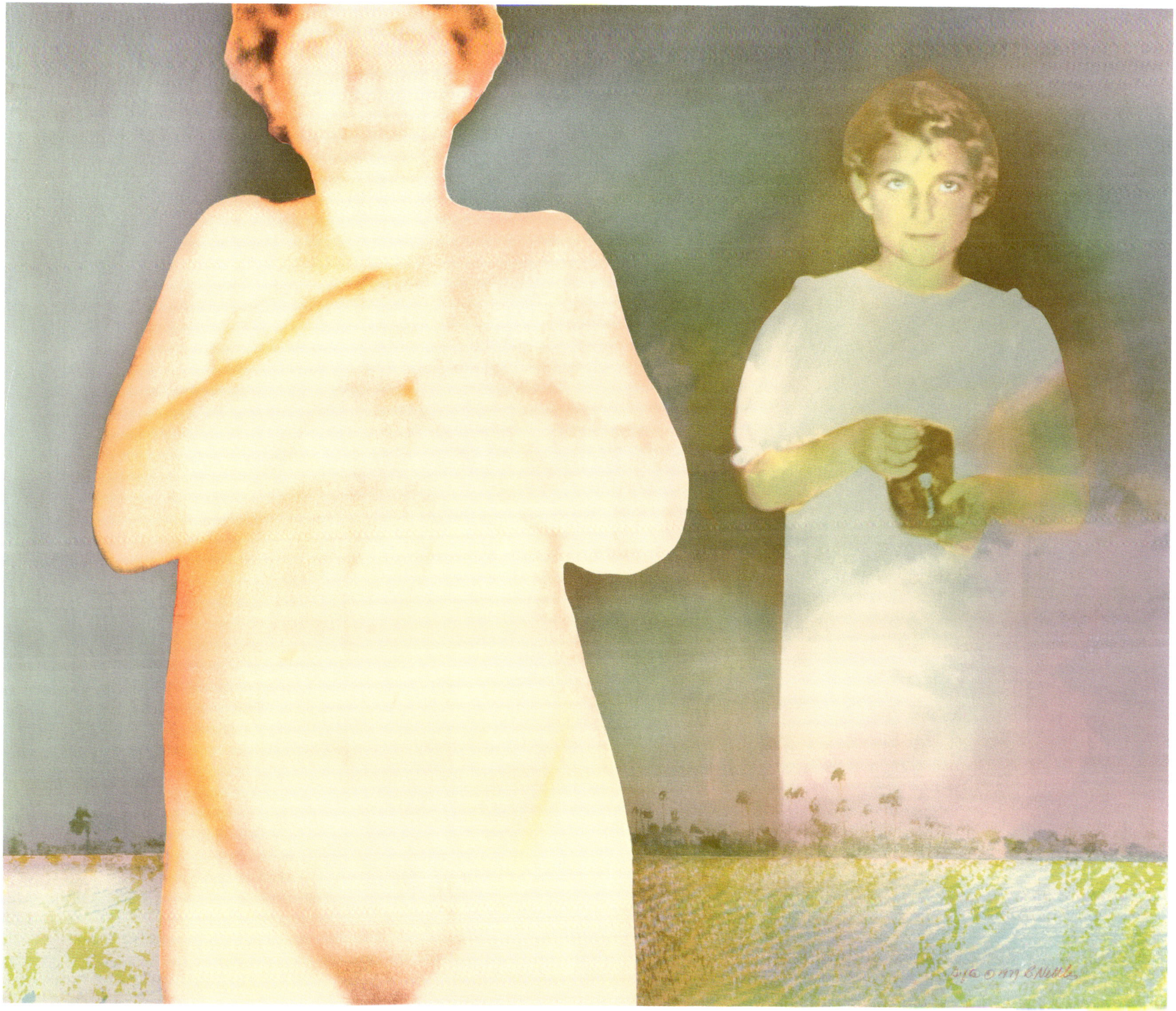

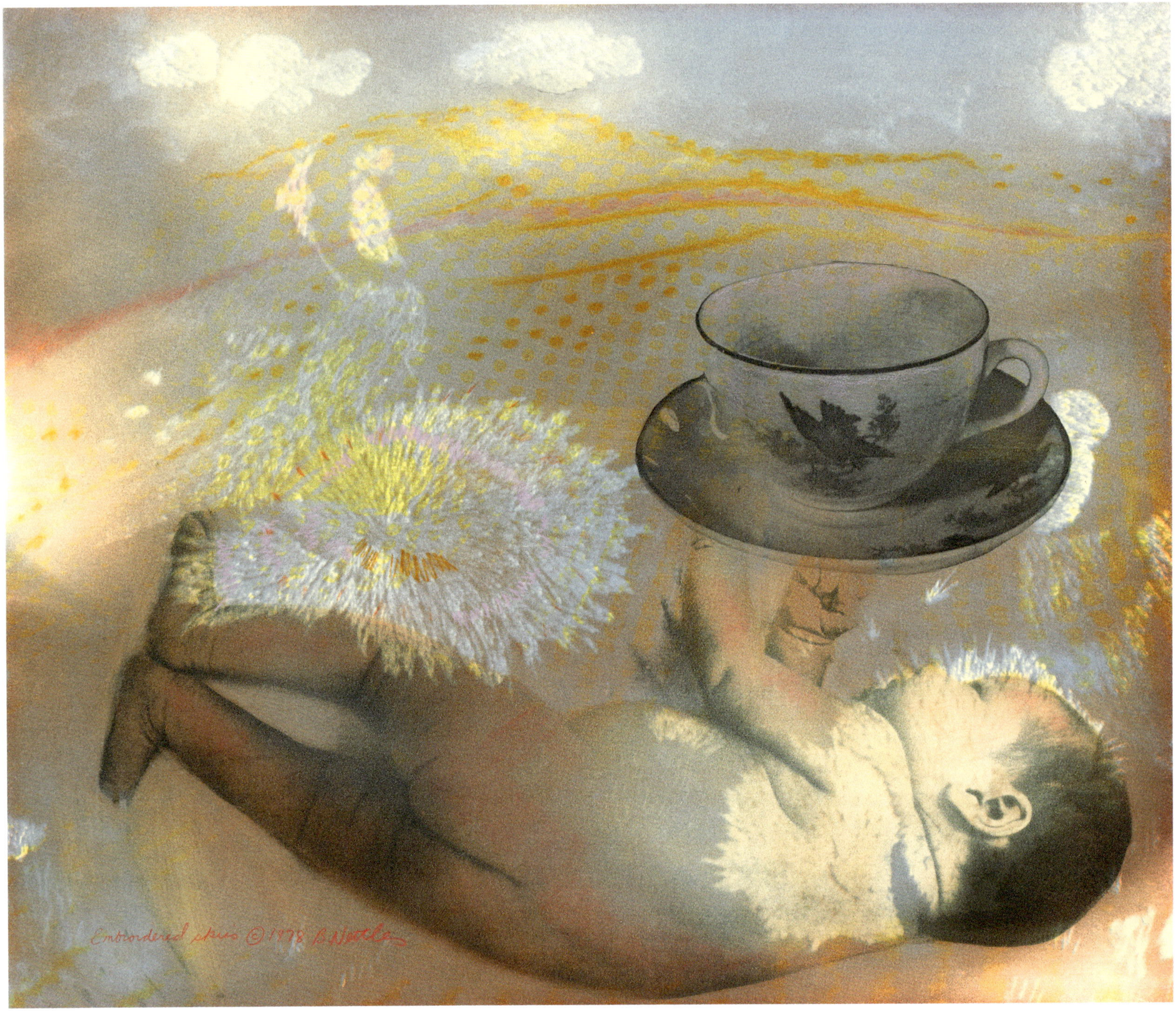


> ***Flamingo in the Dark***

*Embroidered Skies*, 1978, gum bichromate print with applied color

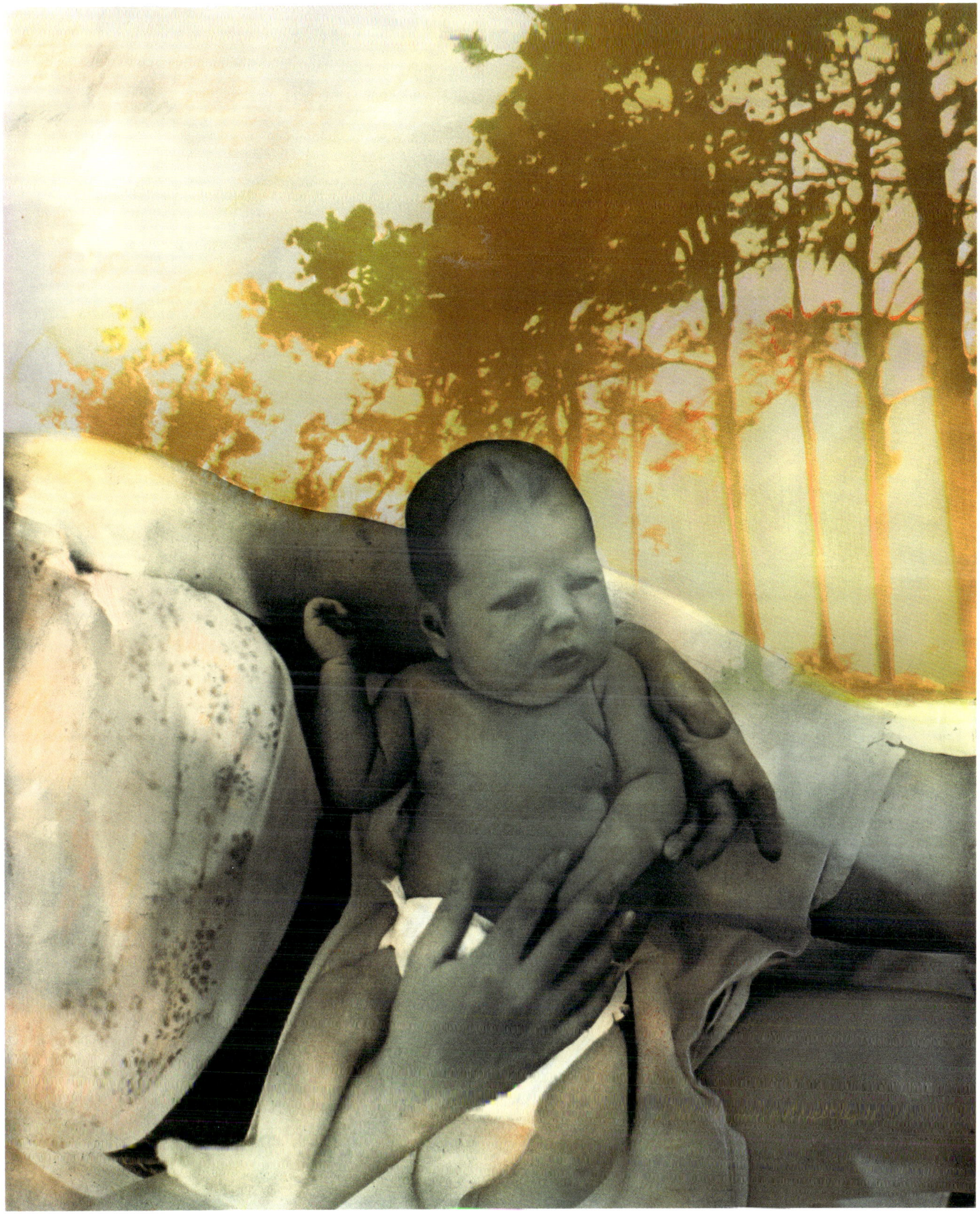

*Rachel in the pines*, 1978, gum bichromate print with applied color

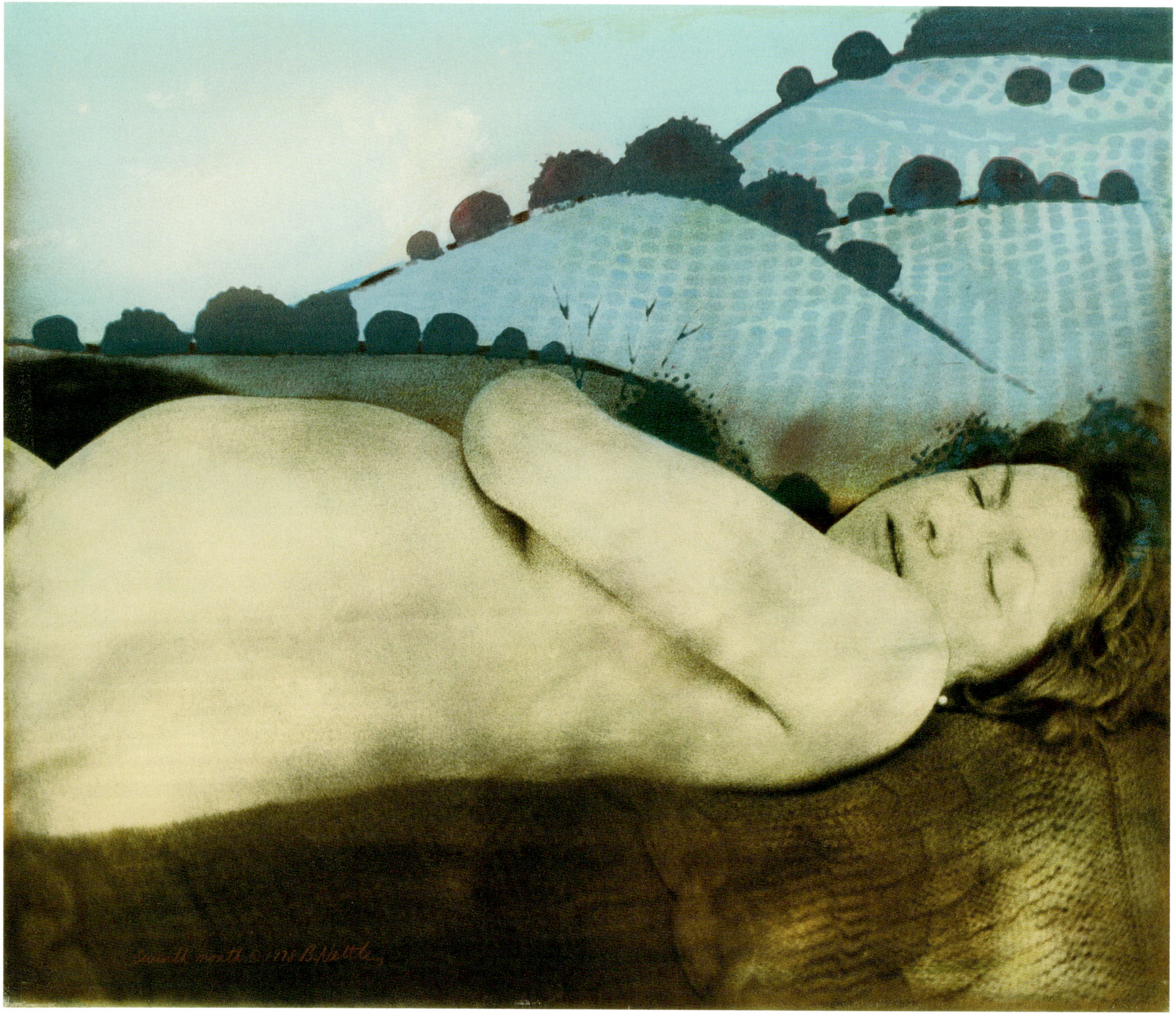

> ***Flamingo in the Dark***

*Seventh Month*, 1978, gum bichromate print with applied color

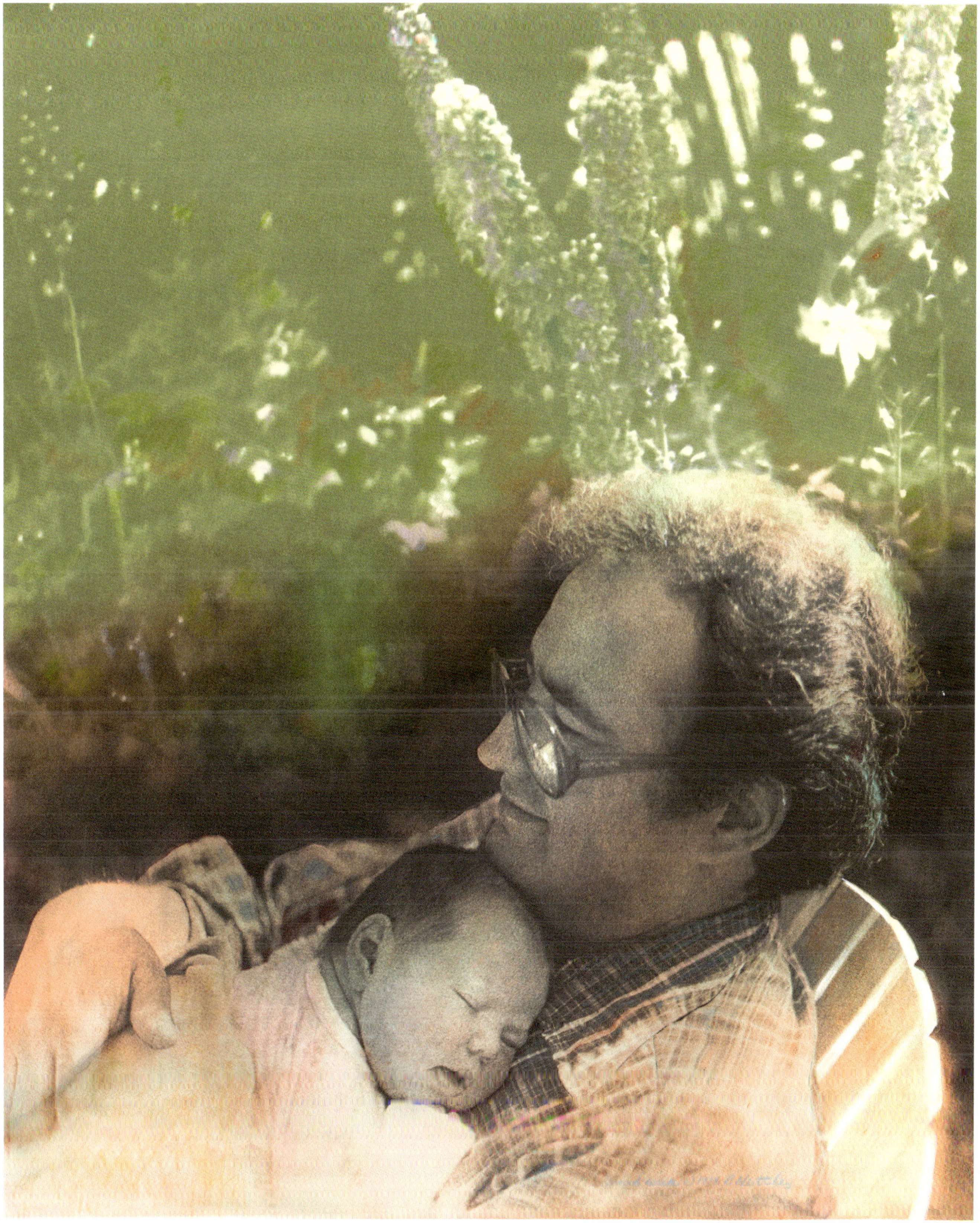

*Second Week*, 1978,
gum bichromate print with
applied color

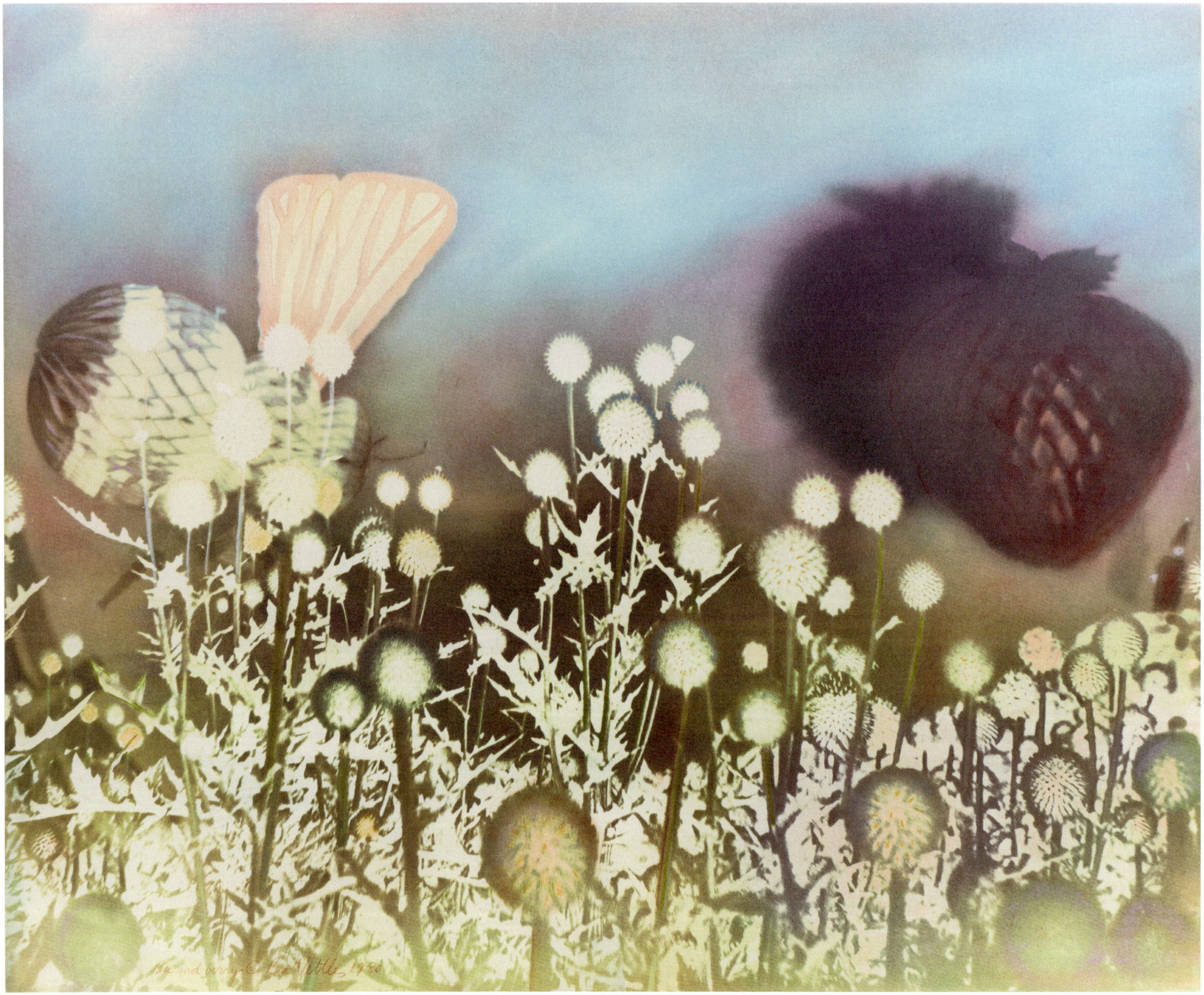

> ***Flamingo in the Dark***

*Bee and Berry*, 1980, gum bichromate print with applied color

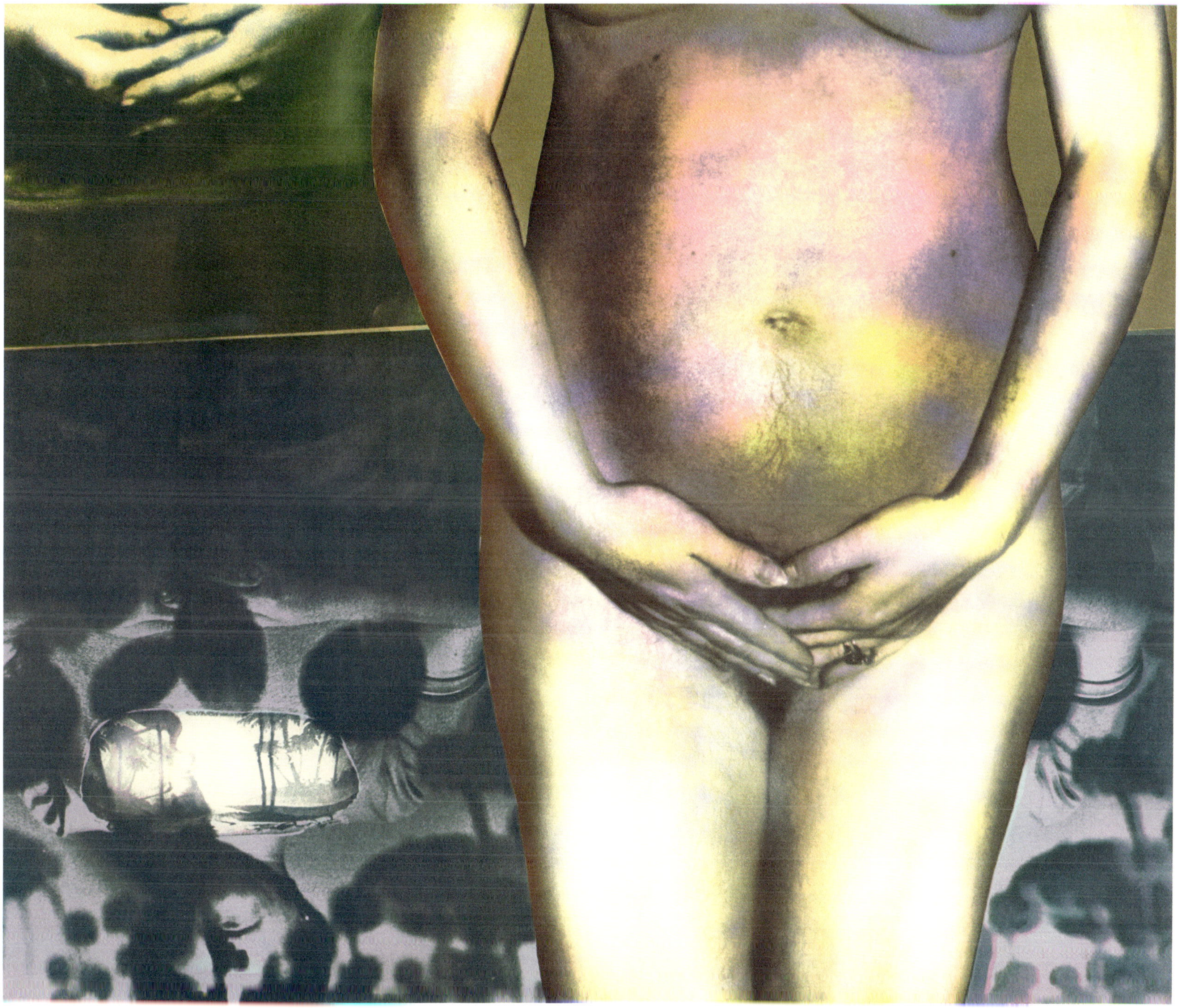

[illegible]
bichromate print with applied color

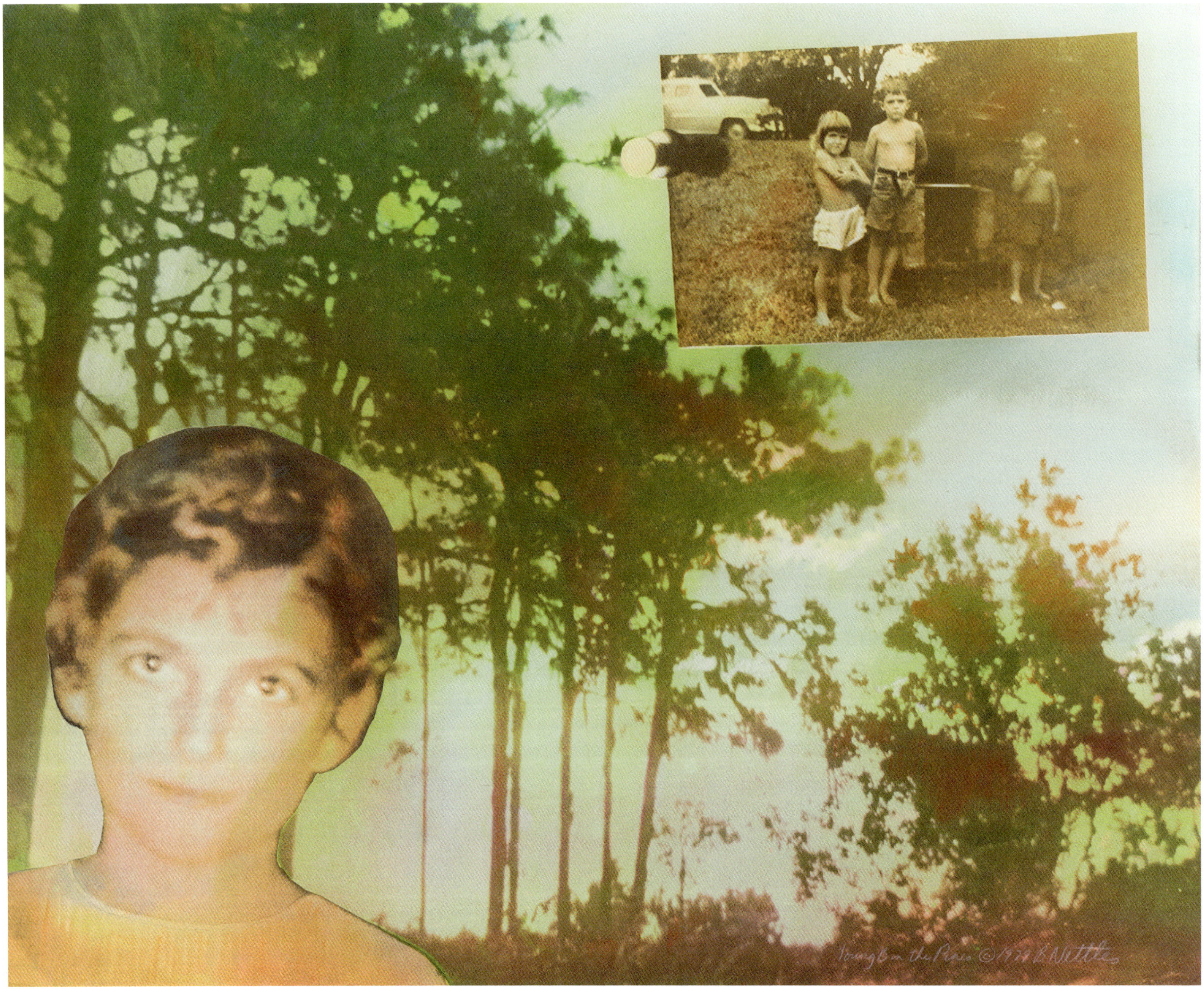


> ***Flamingo in the Dark***

*Young B in Pines*, 1979, gum bichromate print with applied color

> ***Close to Home***

*Dish and Spoon*, 1980,
gum bichromate print with
applied color

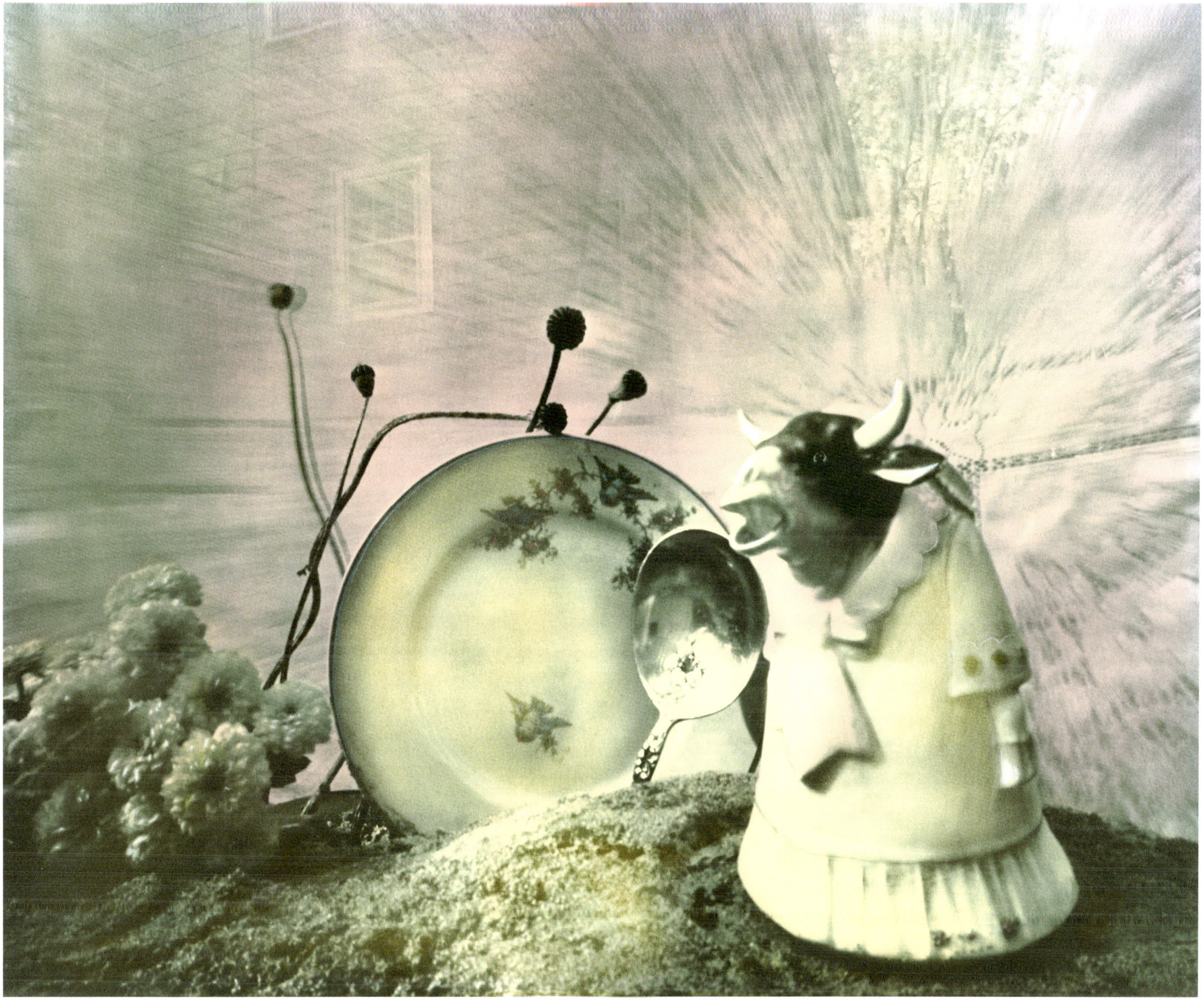

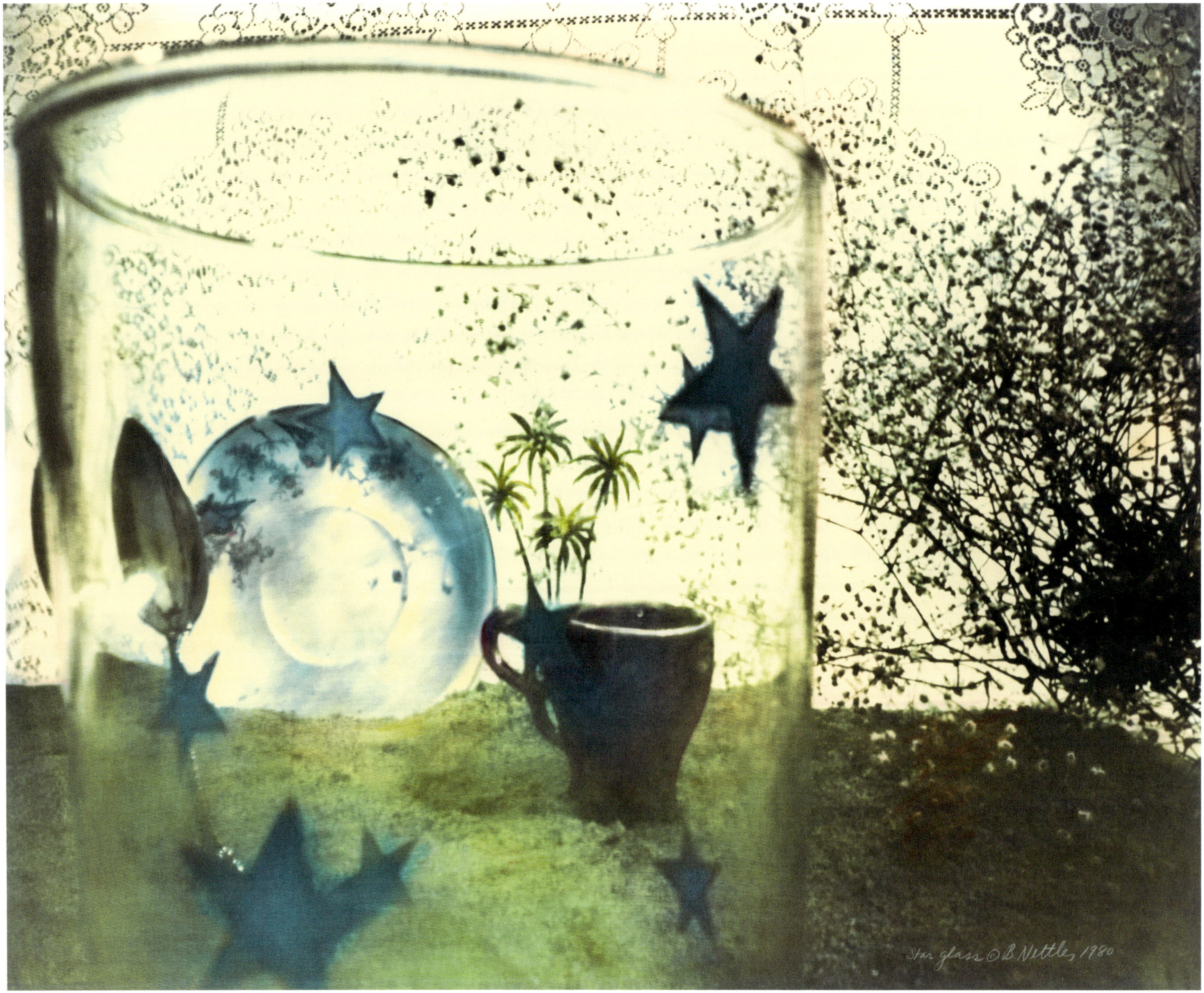


> ***Close to Home***

*Star Glass*, 1980, gum bichromate print with applied color

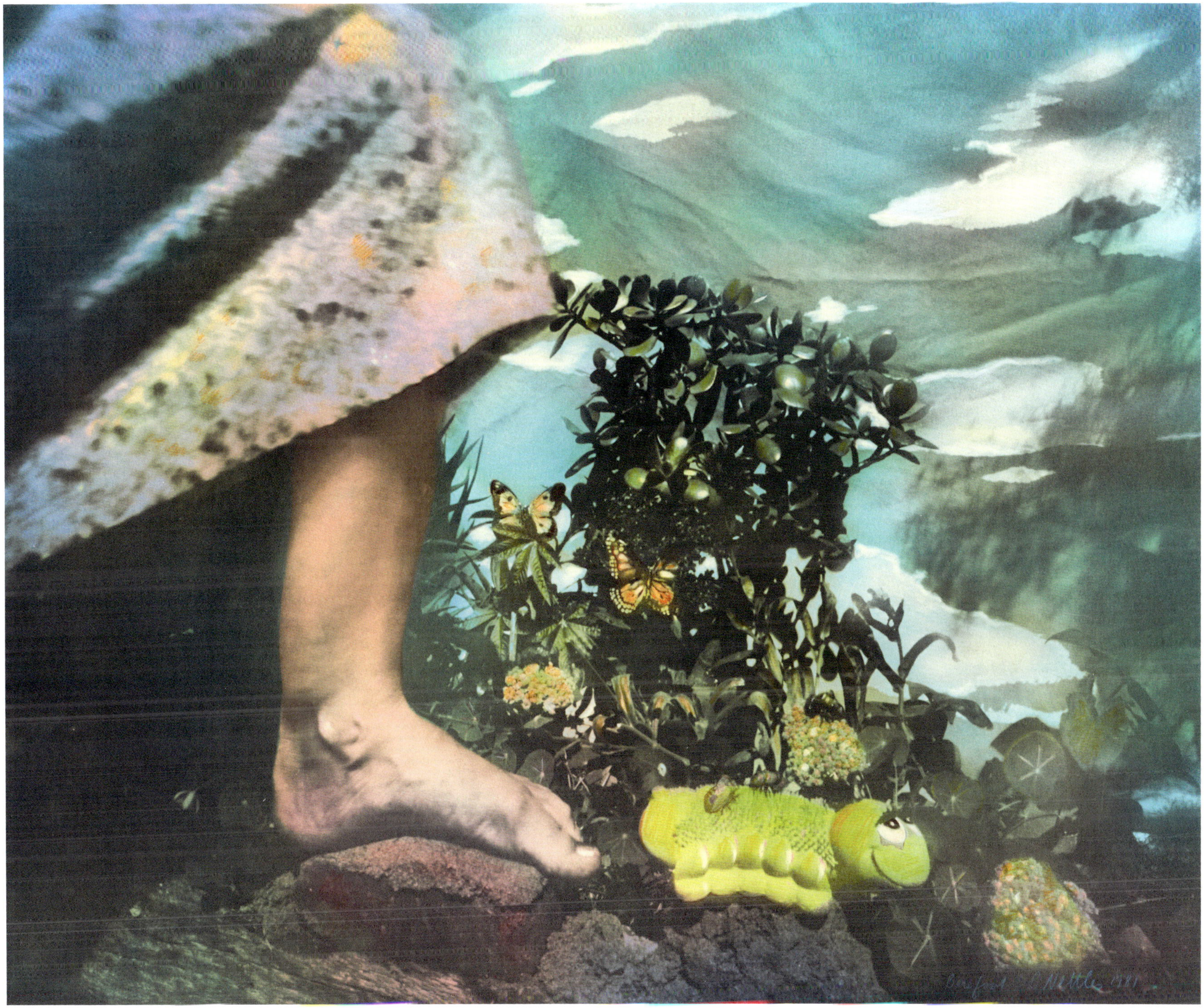

*Barefoot*, 1981, gum bichromate print with applied color

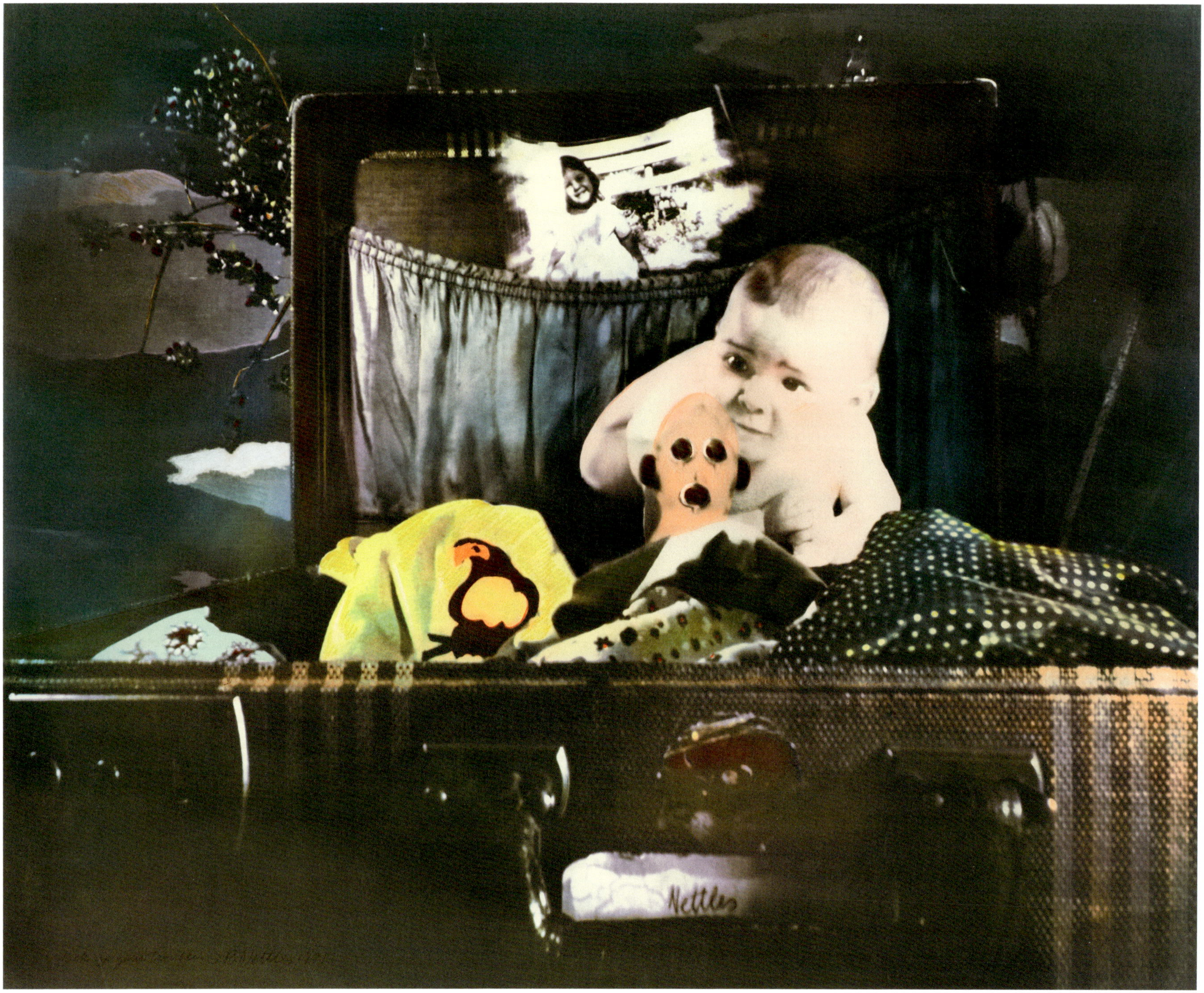

> **_Close to Home_**

*Pack Up your Troubles*, 1981, gum bichromate print with applied color

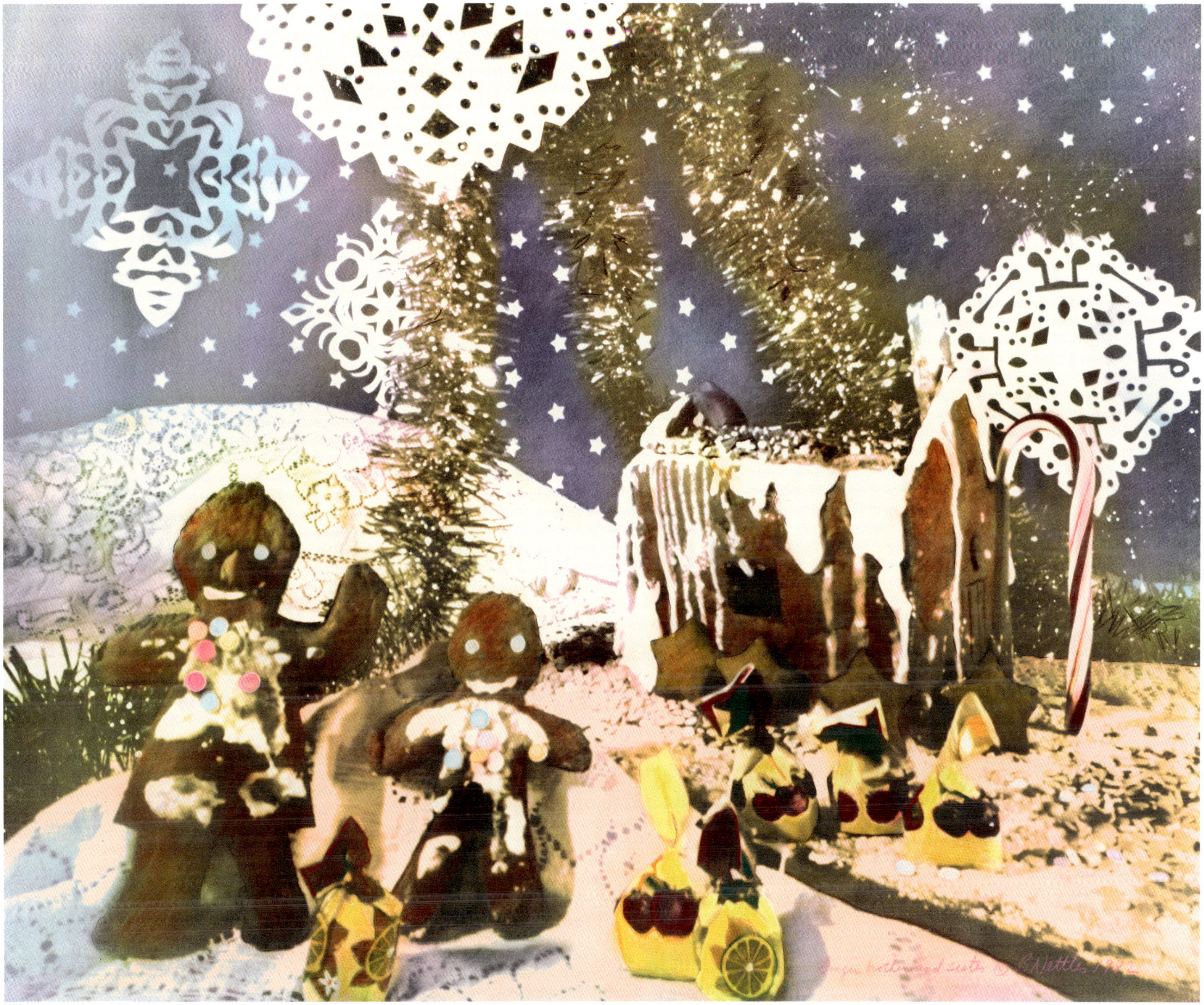

*Ginger Brother and Sister*, 1982,
gum bichromate print with applied color

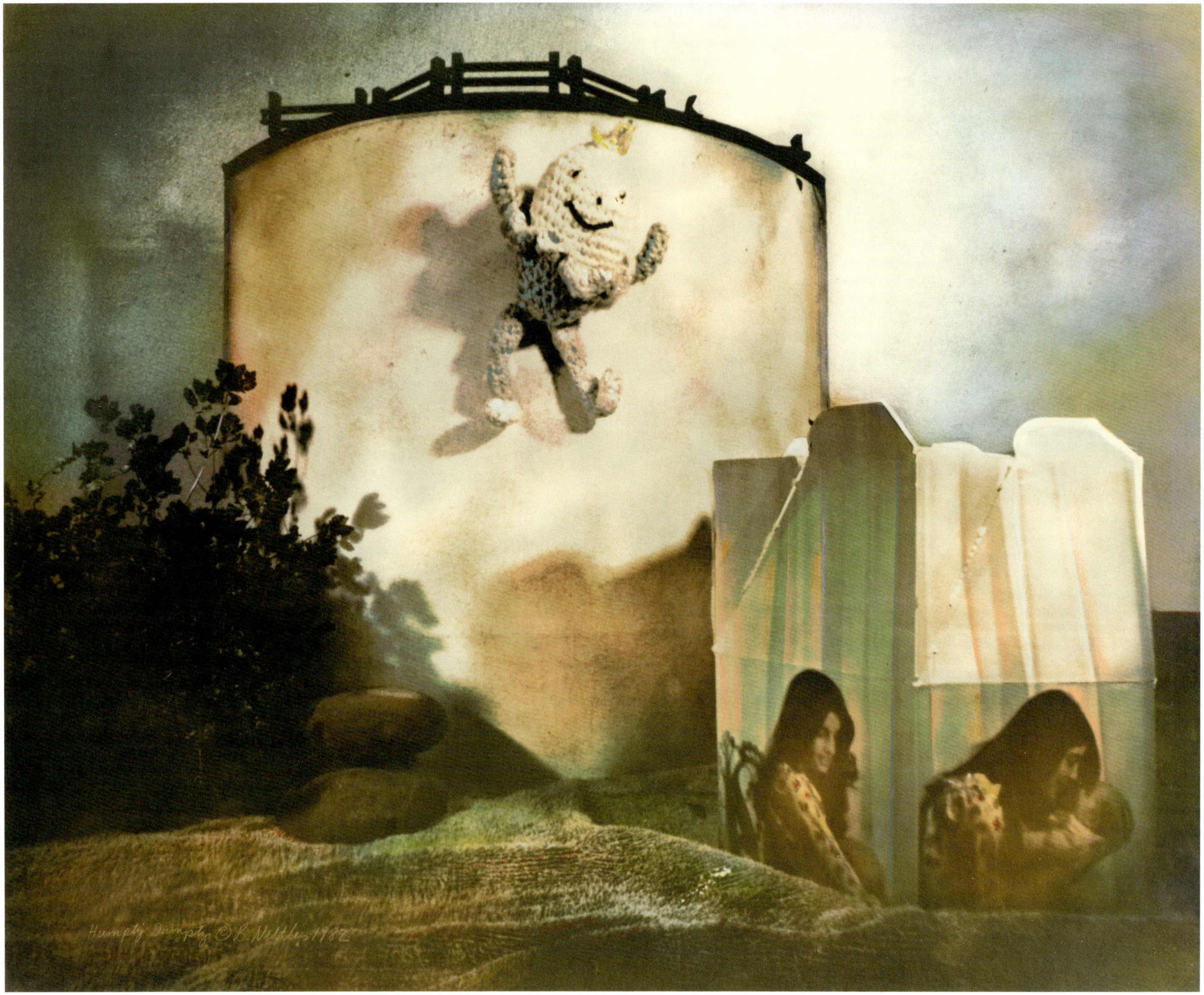


> ***Close to Home***

*Humpty Dumpty*, 1982,
gum bichromate print with
applied color

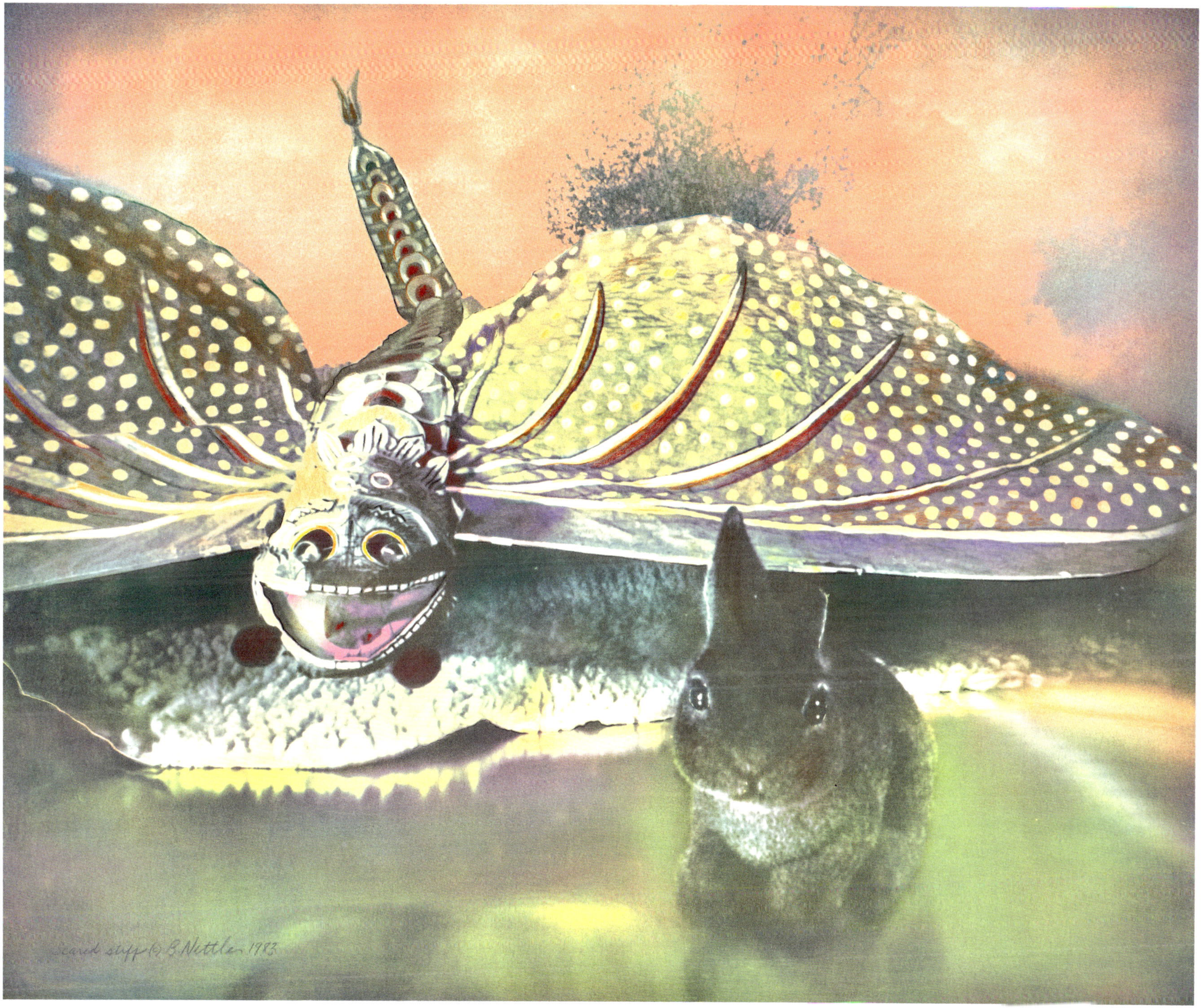


*Scared Stiff*, 1983, gum bichromate print with applied color

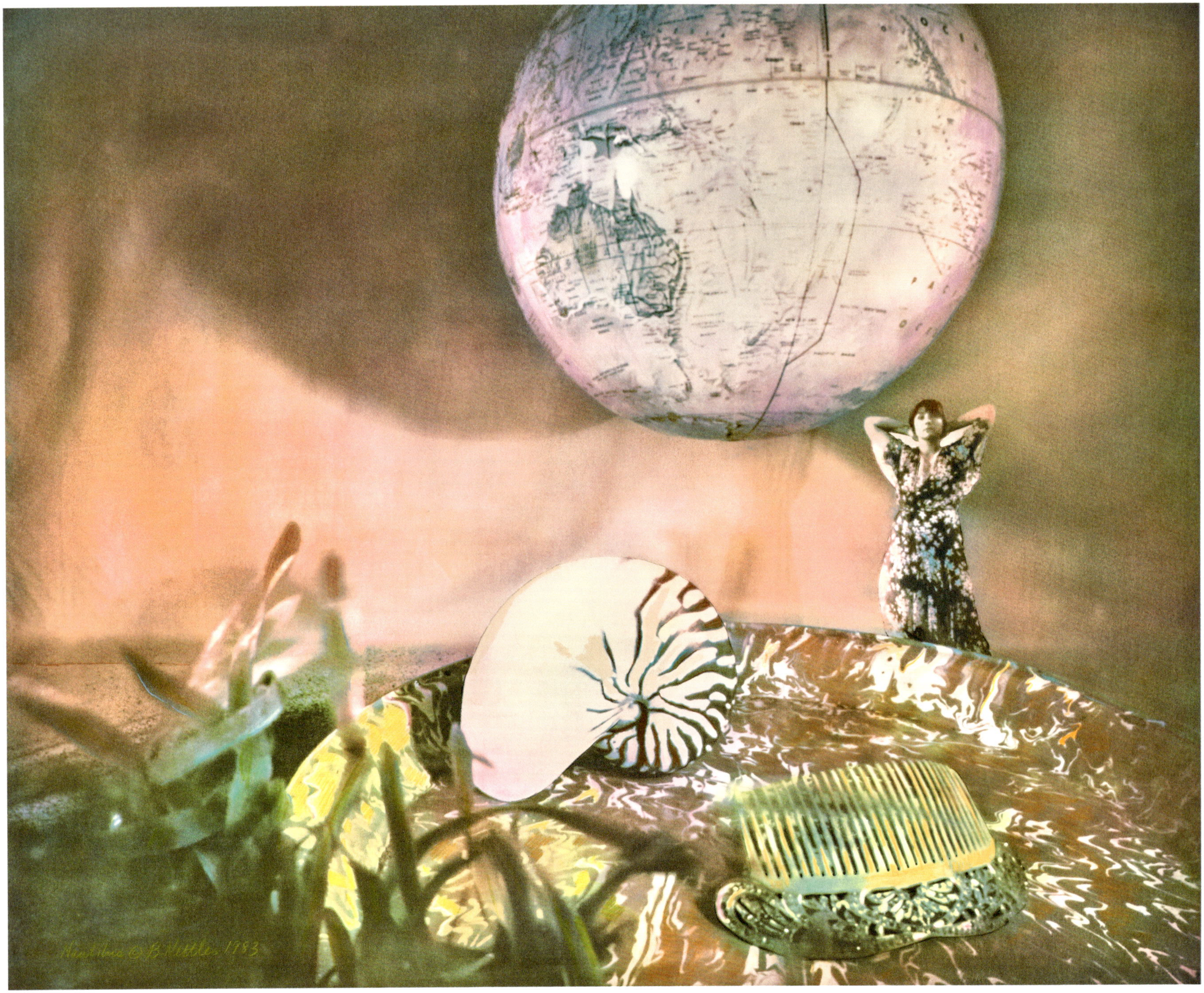

> ***Close to Home***

*Nautilus*, 1983, gum bichromate print with applied color

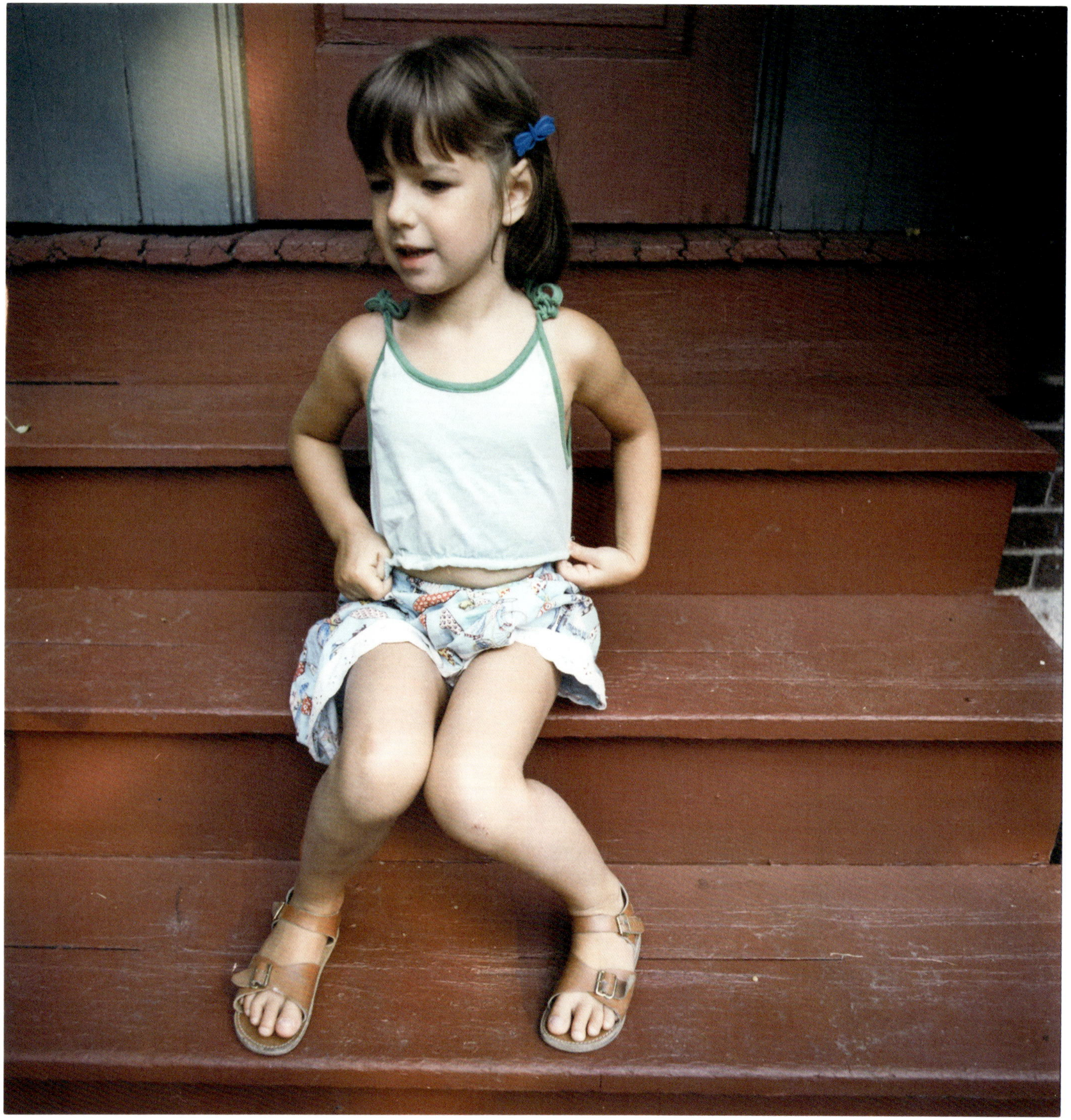

< *Rachel . . . Rochester Back Steps*, July 1983, dye imbibition print

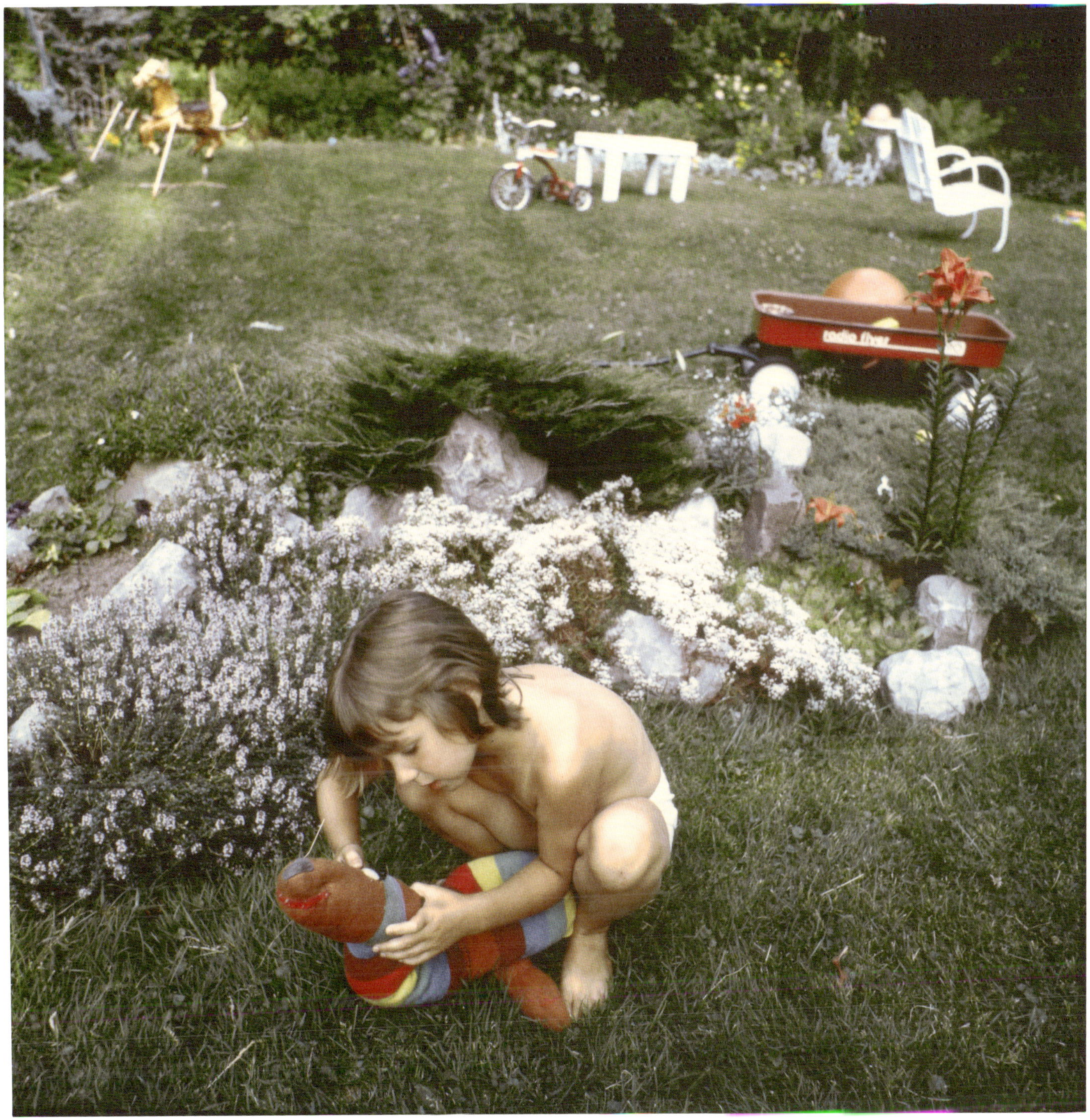


> *R and Snake . . . ,* July 1983, silver dye bleach print

> ***Rachel's Holidays***

*Bridge*, 1984,
dye imbibition print

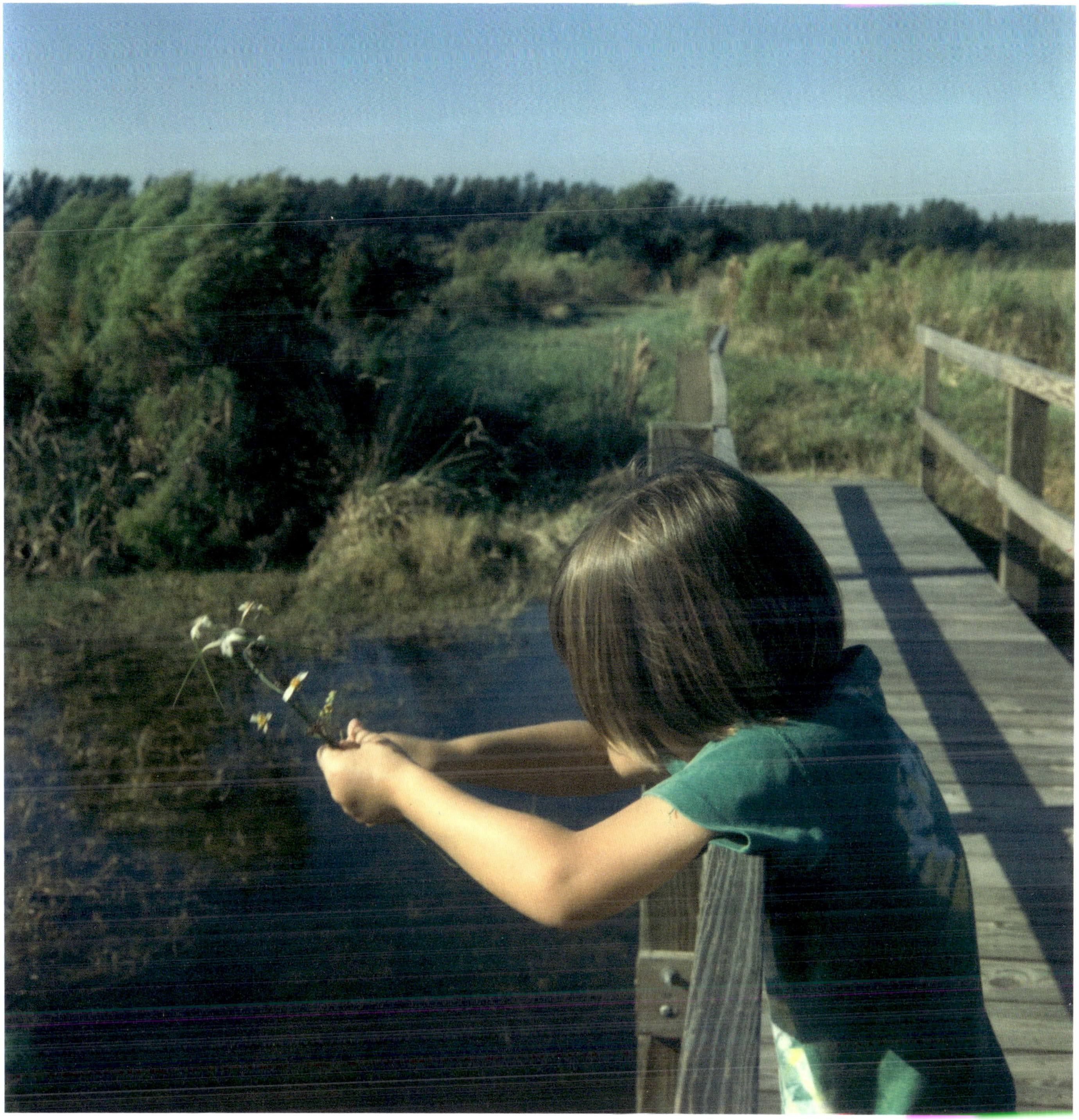

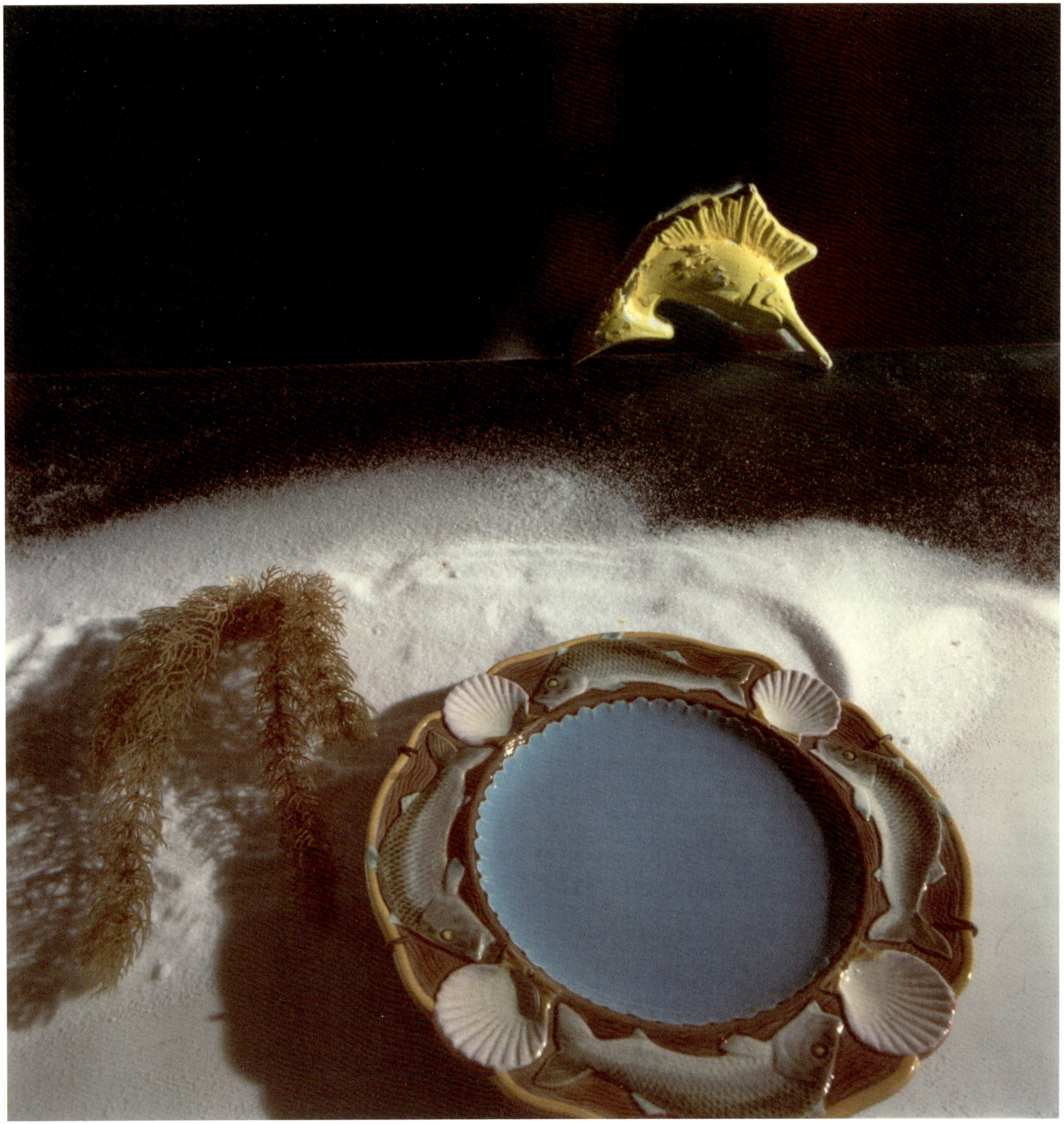

> ***Rachel's Holidays***

*Swordfish*, 1984,
dye imbibition print

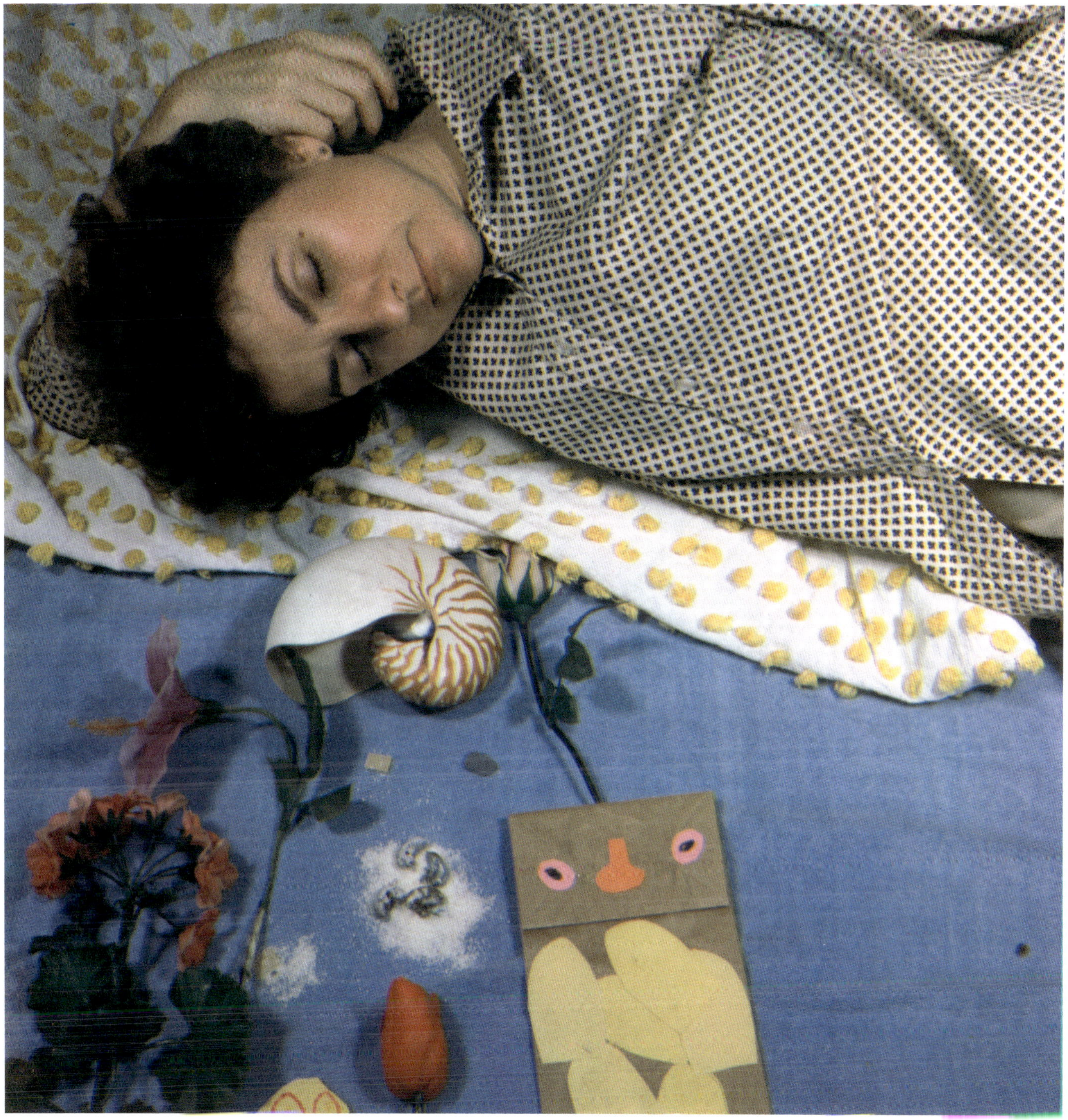

*Bea Sleeping*, 1984,
dye imbibition print

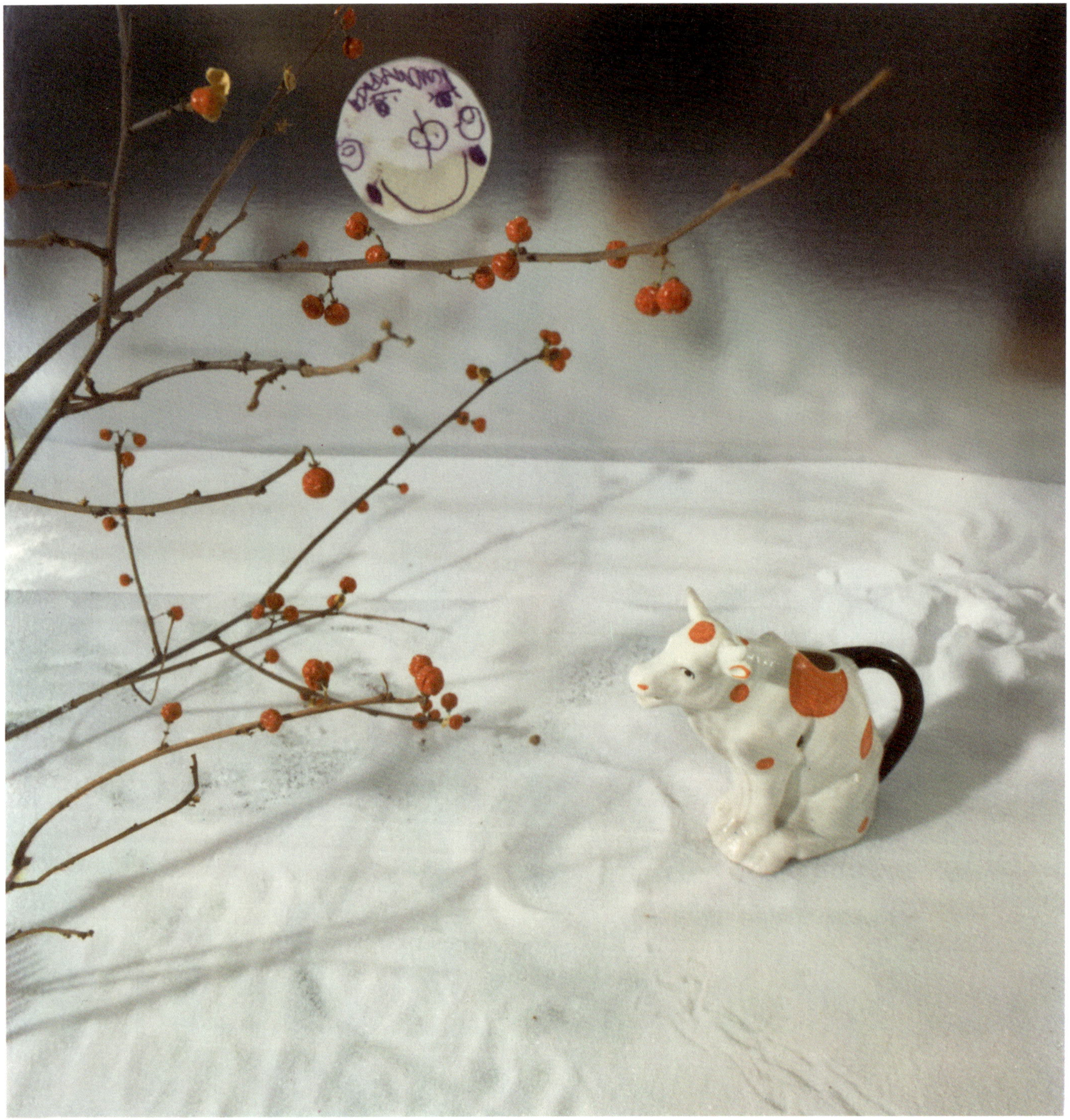

> ***Rachel's Holidays***

*Cow*, 1984,
dye imbibition print

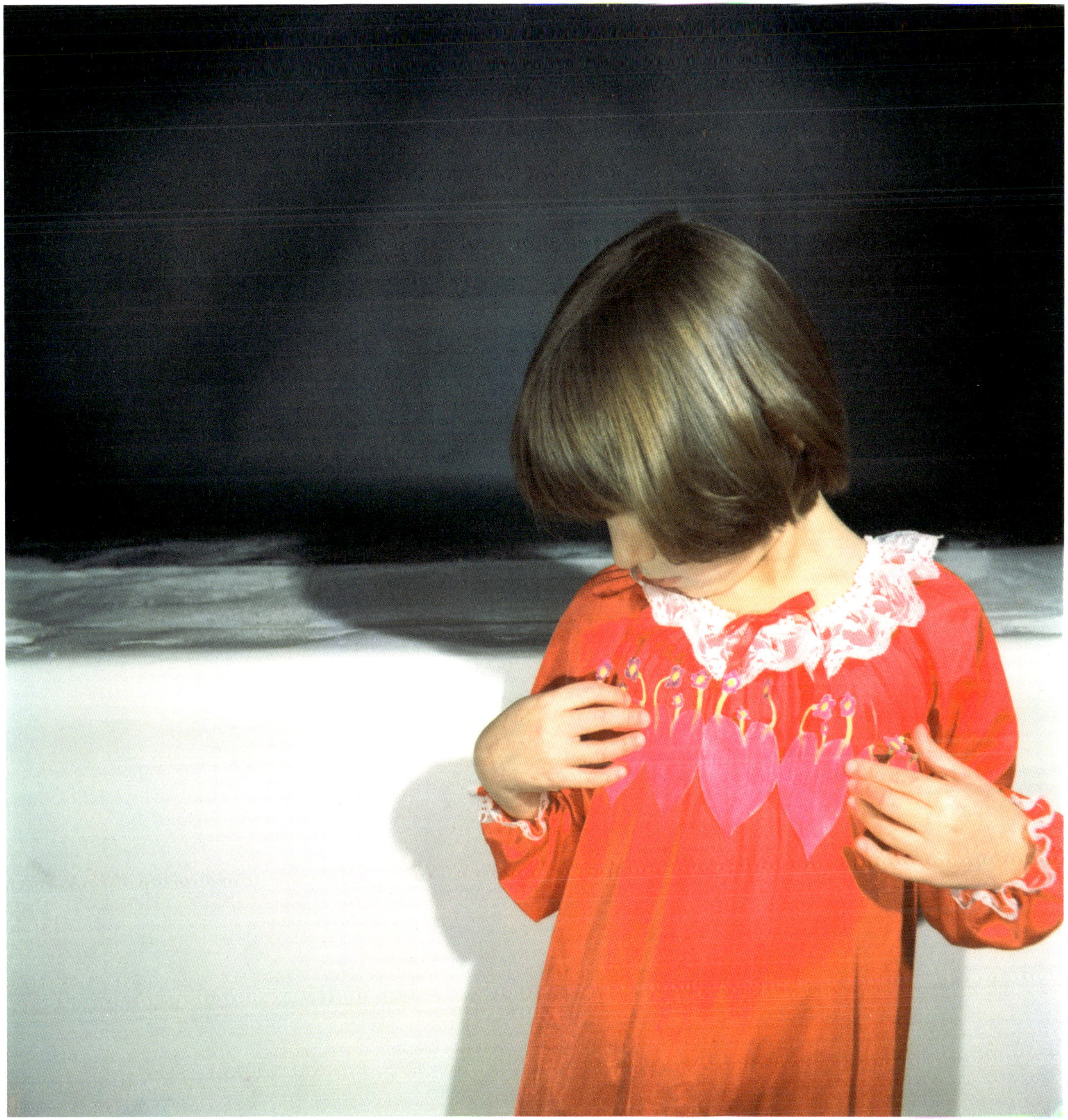

*String of Hearts*, 1984,
dye imbibition print

> ***Landscapes of Innocence***

*Paperbirds*, 1985,
photographic etching

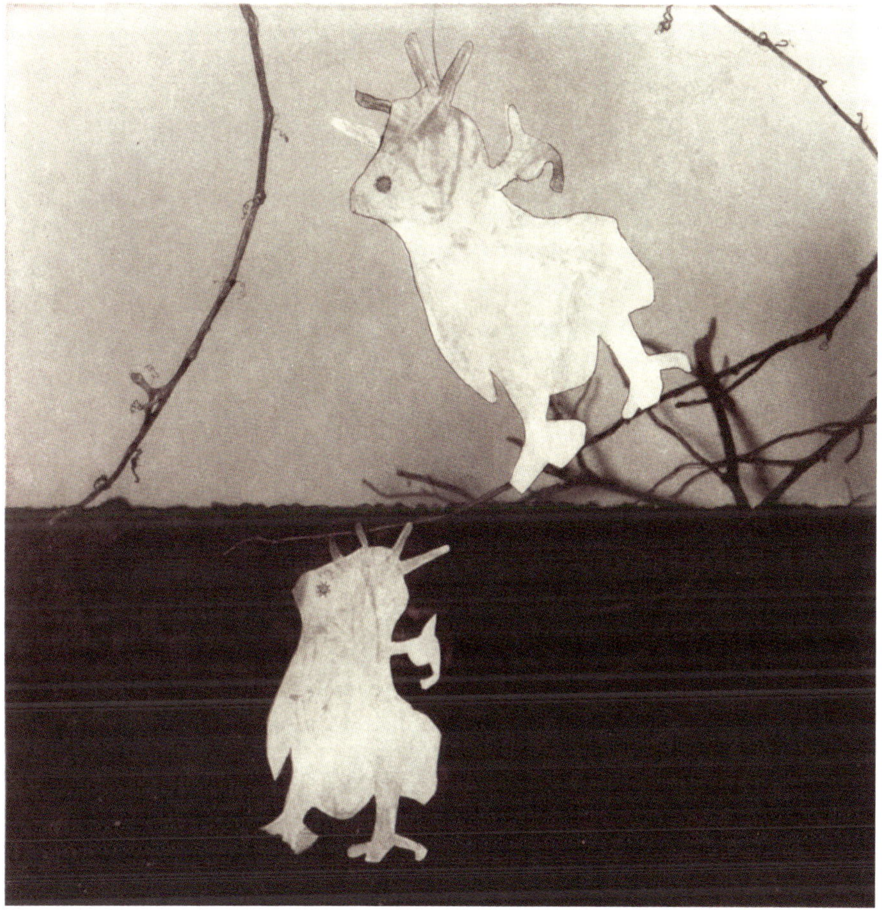

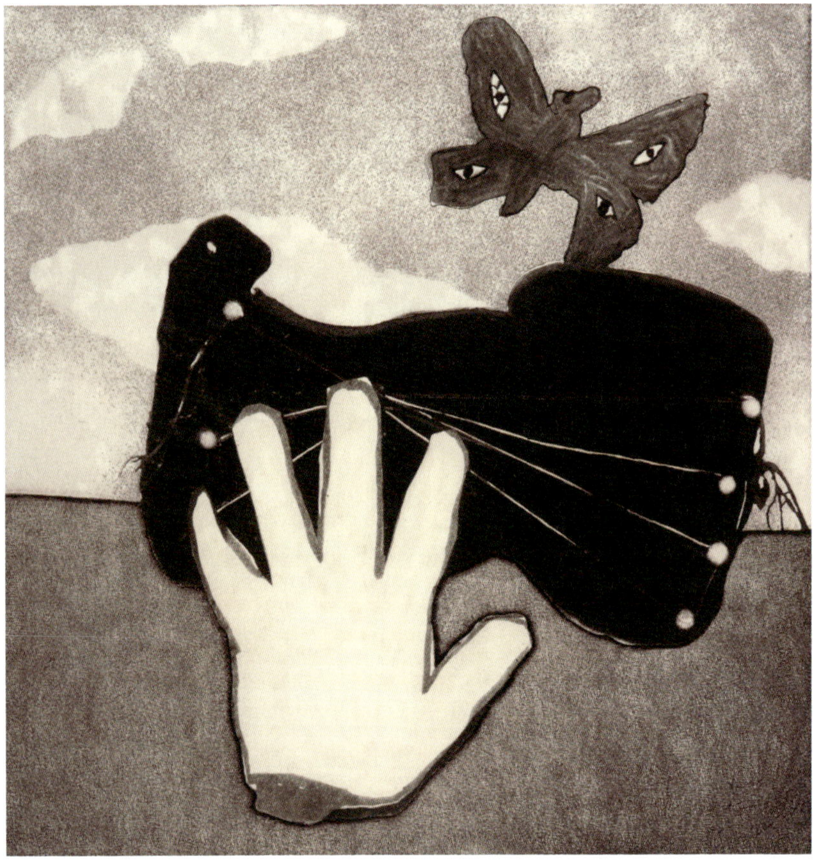

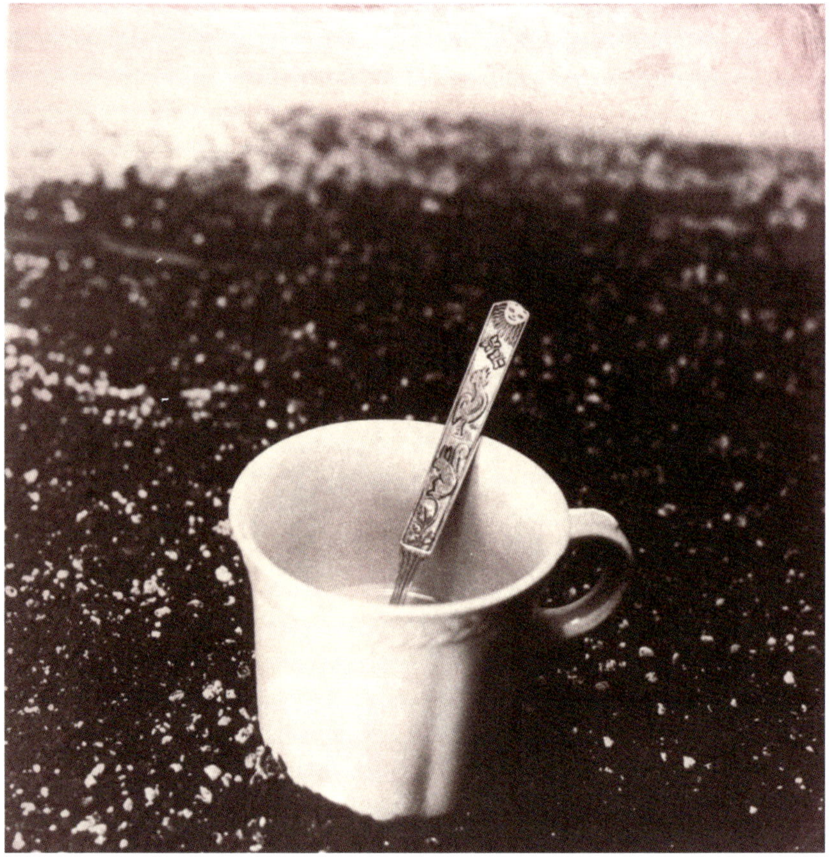

> ***Landscapes of Innocence***

*Making Music*, 1985,
photographic etching

*Coffee Cup*, 1985,
photographic etching

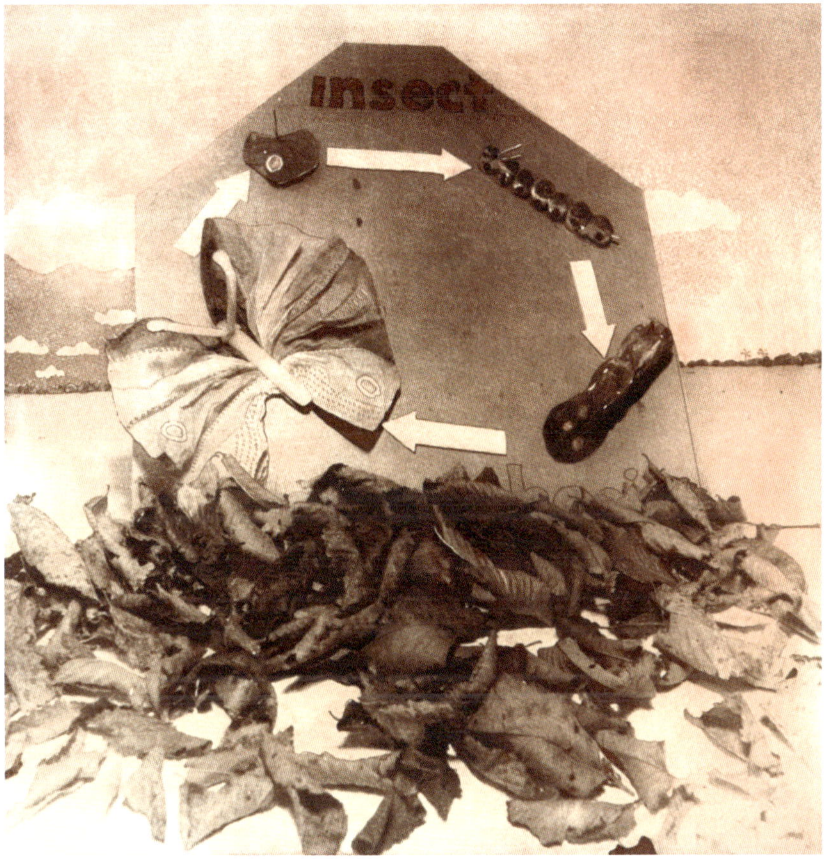


*Metamorphosis*, 1985,
photographic etching

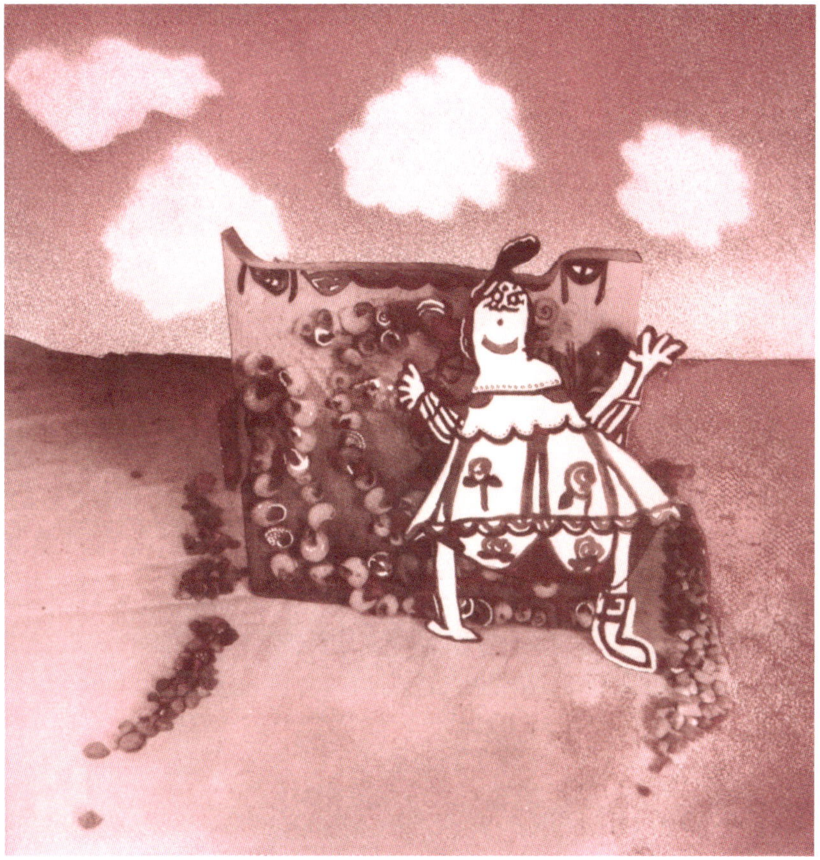

*Rose Lady*, 1985,
photographic etching

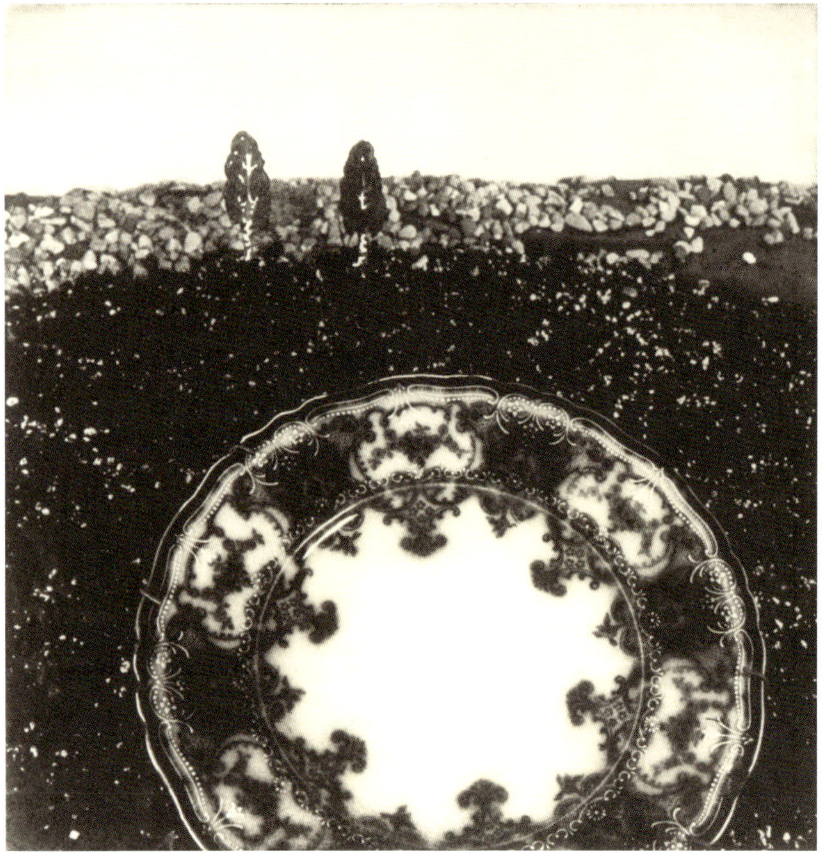

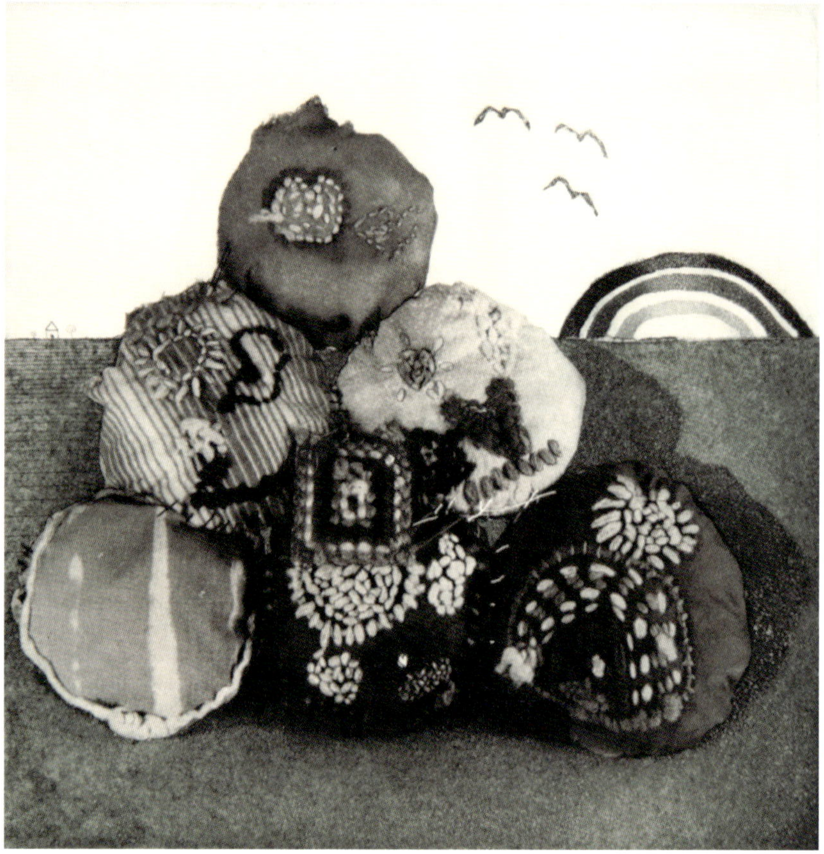

> ***Landscapes of Innocence***

*Dinnerplate*, 1985,
photographic etching

*Embroidery*, 1985,
photographic etching

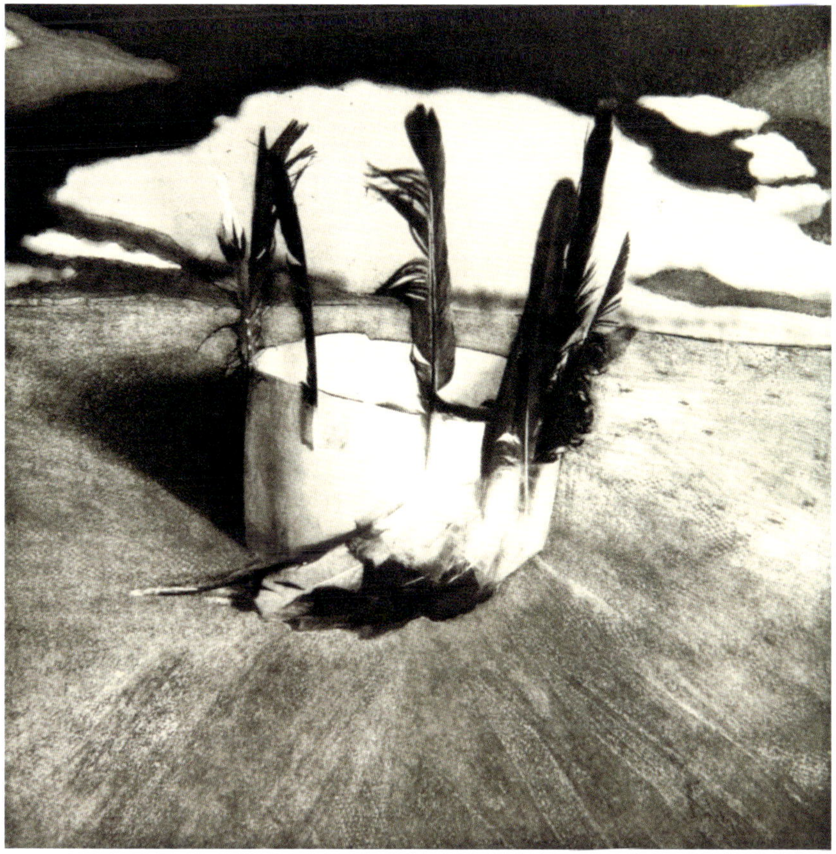

*Headband*, 1985,
photographic etching

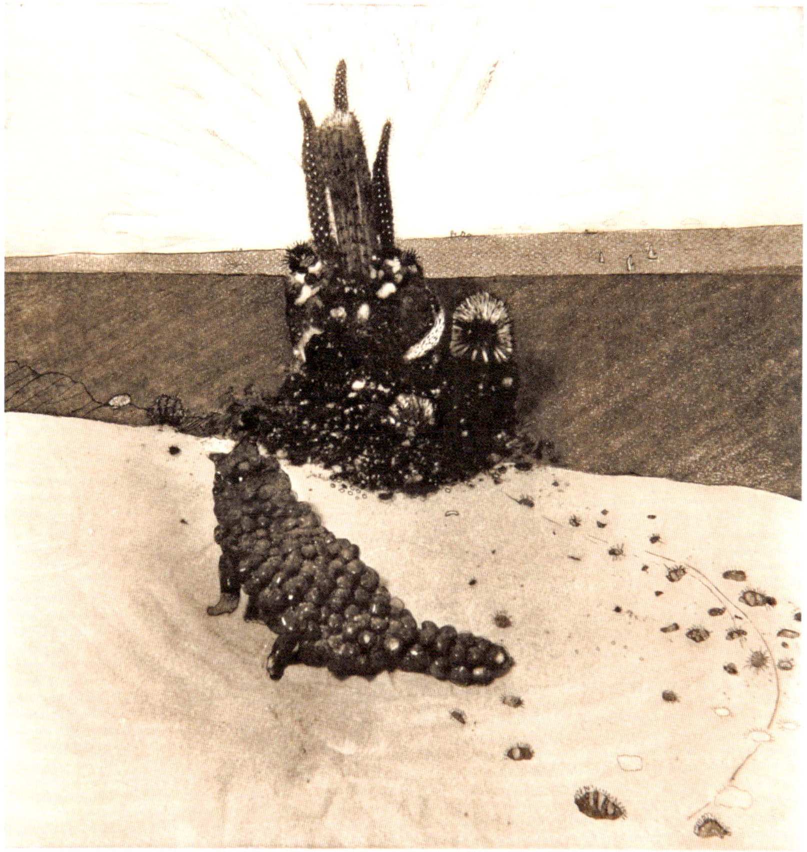

*Desert Blast*, 1985,
photographic etching

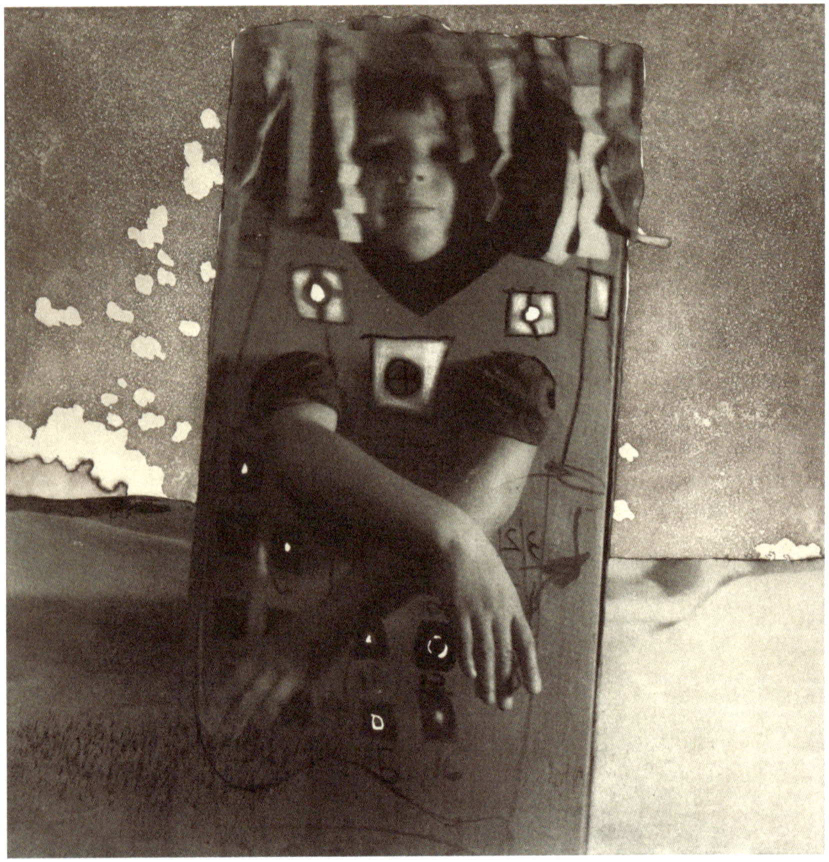

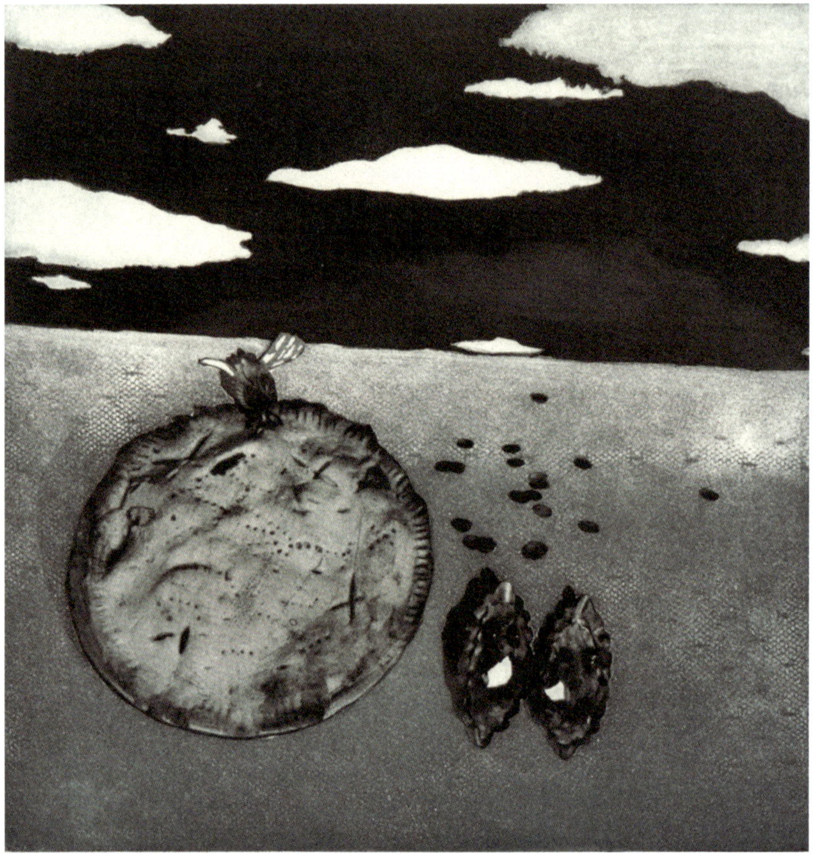

> ***Landscapes of Innocence***

*Robot*, 1985,
photographic etching

*Pie and Sky*, 1985,
photographic etching

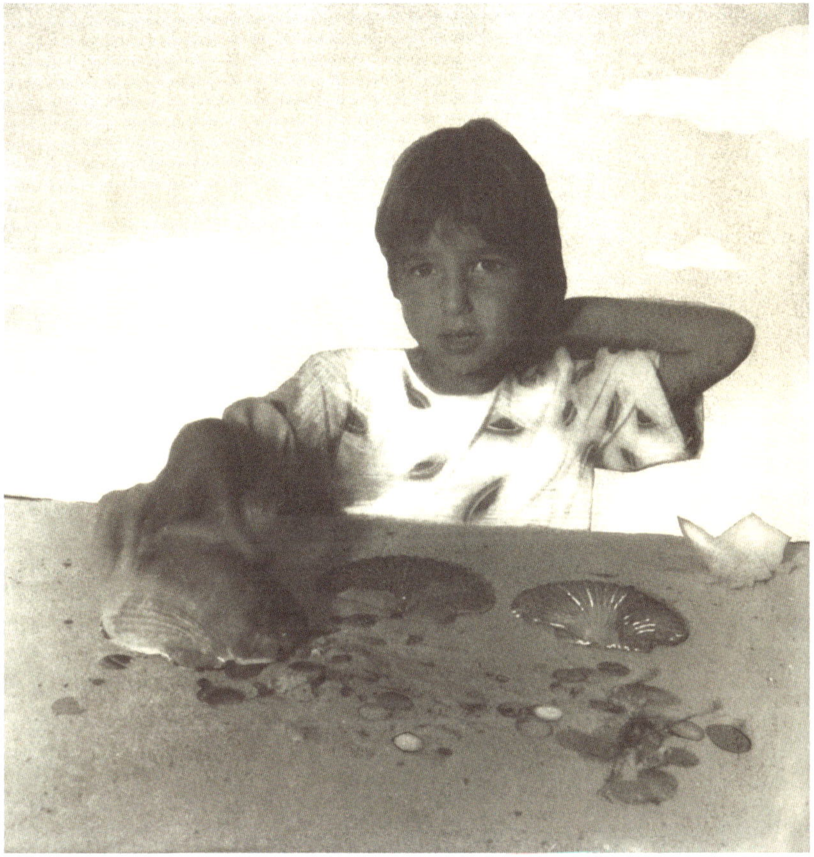

*Shell Game*, 1985,
photographic etching

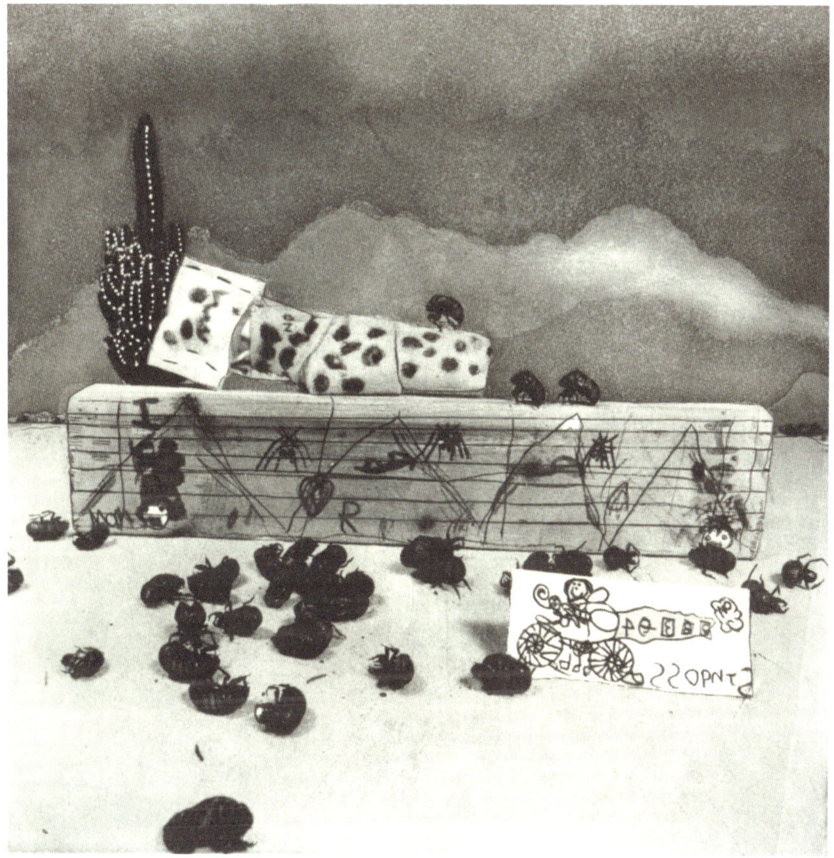

*Valley of the Shadow*, 1985,
photographic etching

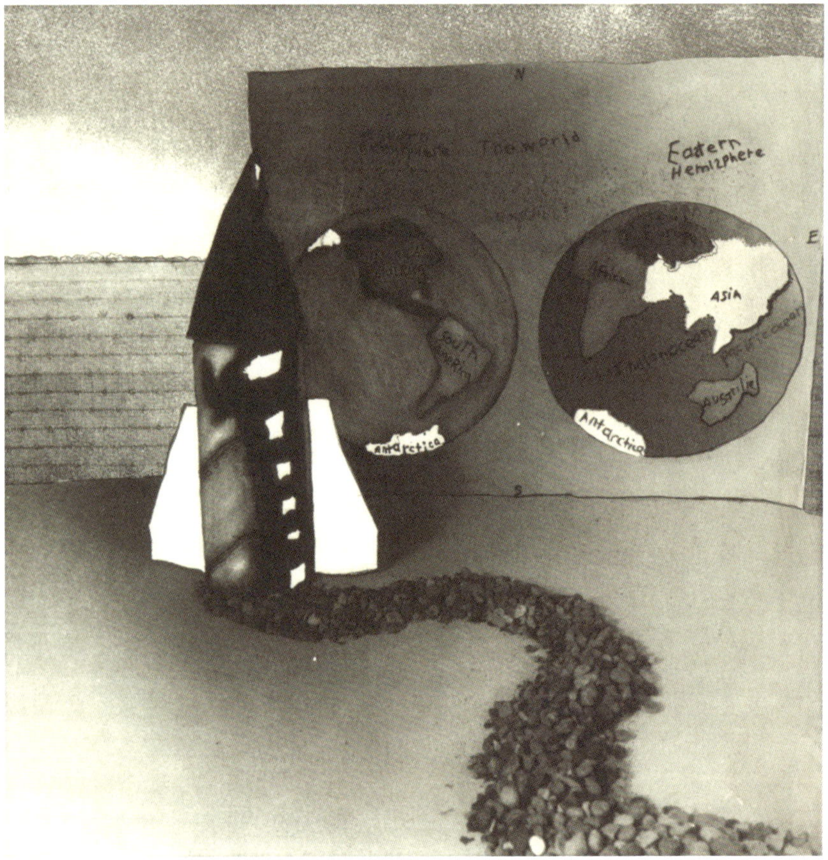


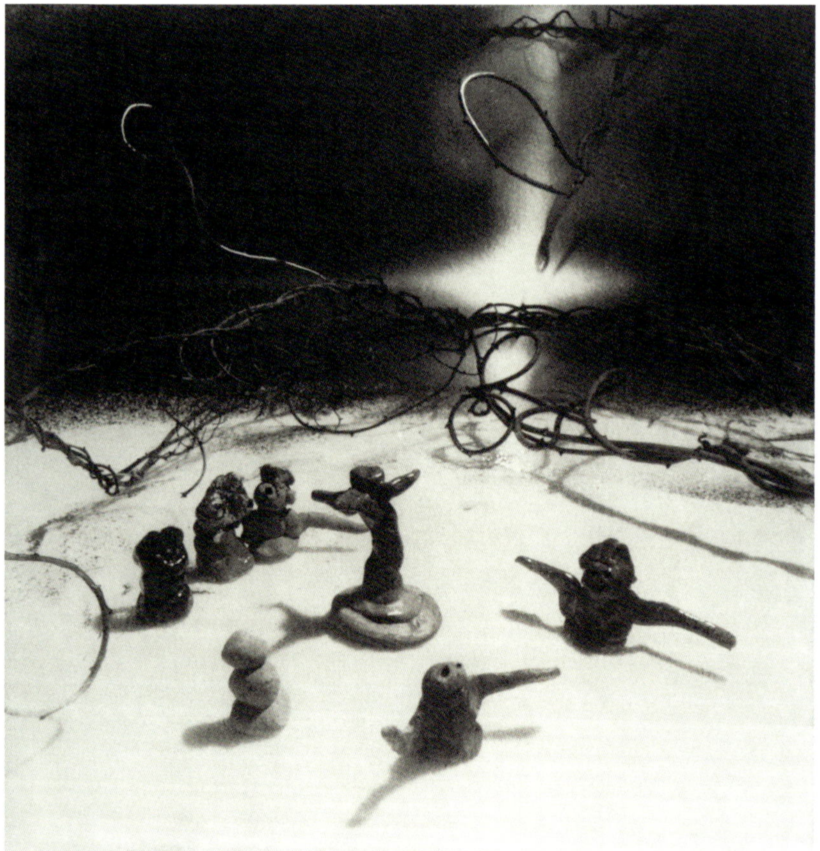

> ***Landscapes of Innocence***

*Rocket*, 1985,
photographic etching

*Snowmen*, 1985,
photographic etching

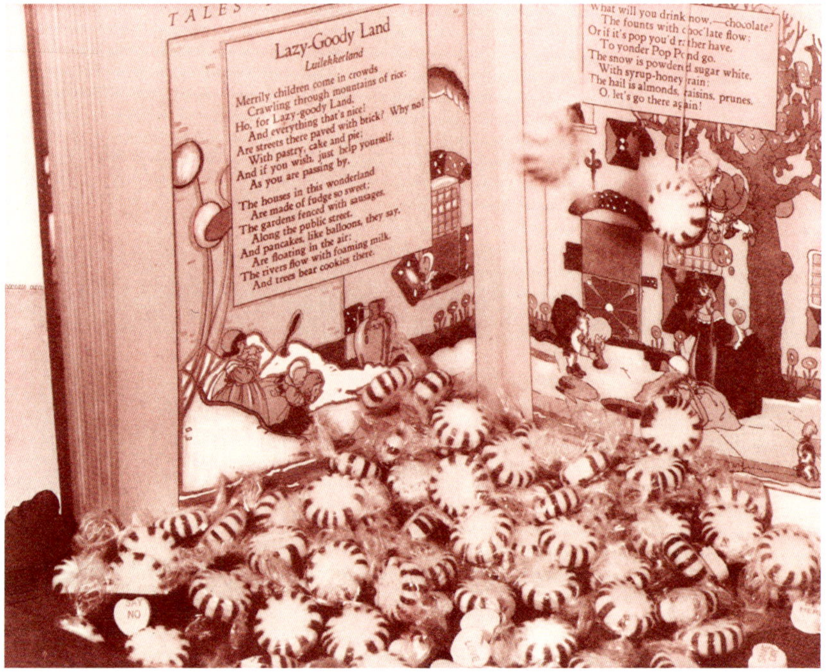


> ***Life's Lessons***

*Hansel & Gretel*, 1986,
photographic etchings

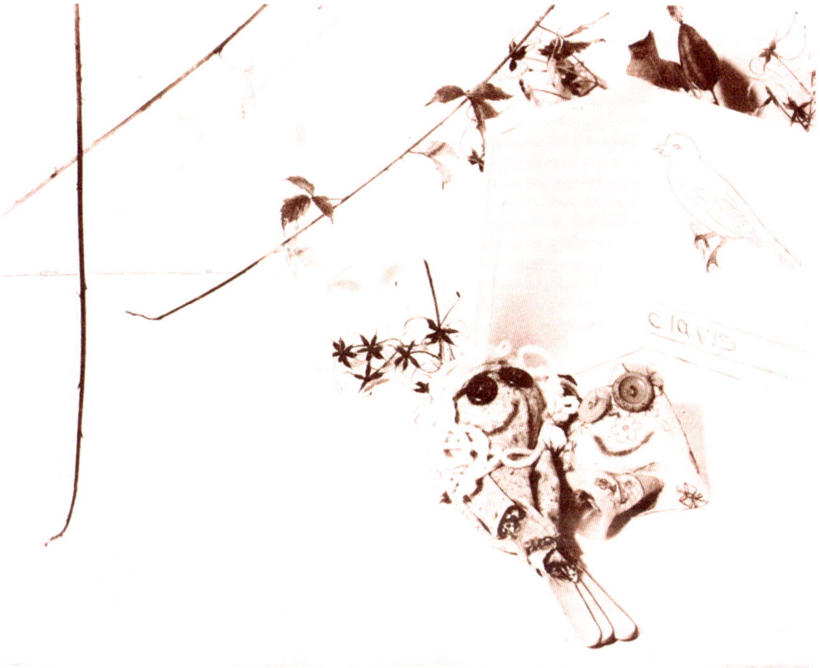

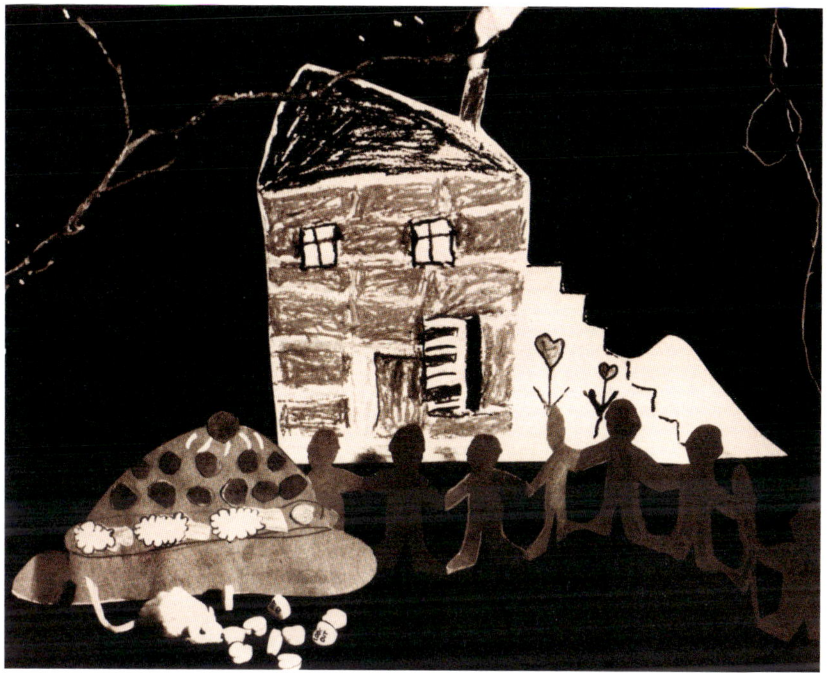

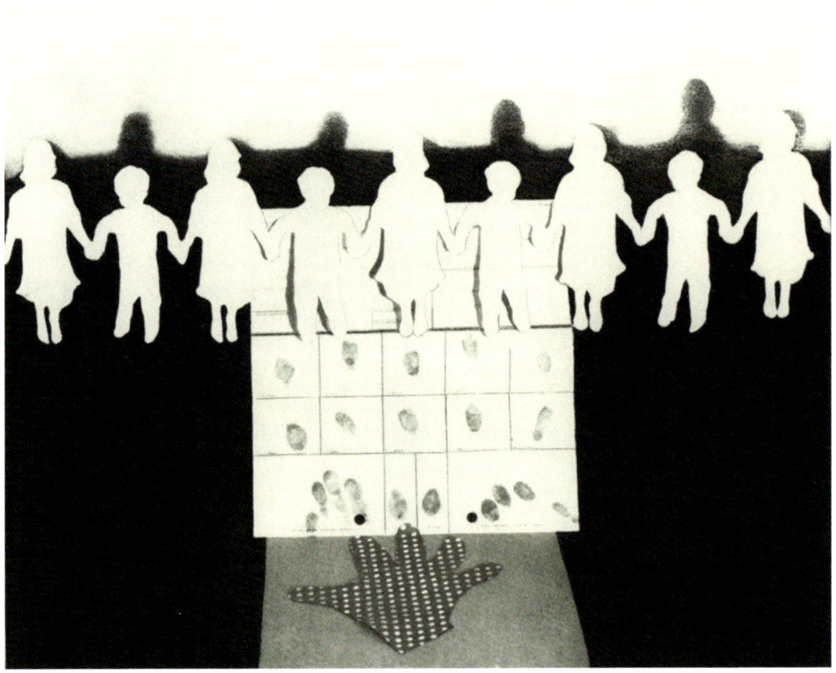

> ***Life's Lessons***

*Missing*, 1986,
photographic etchings

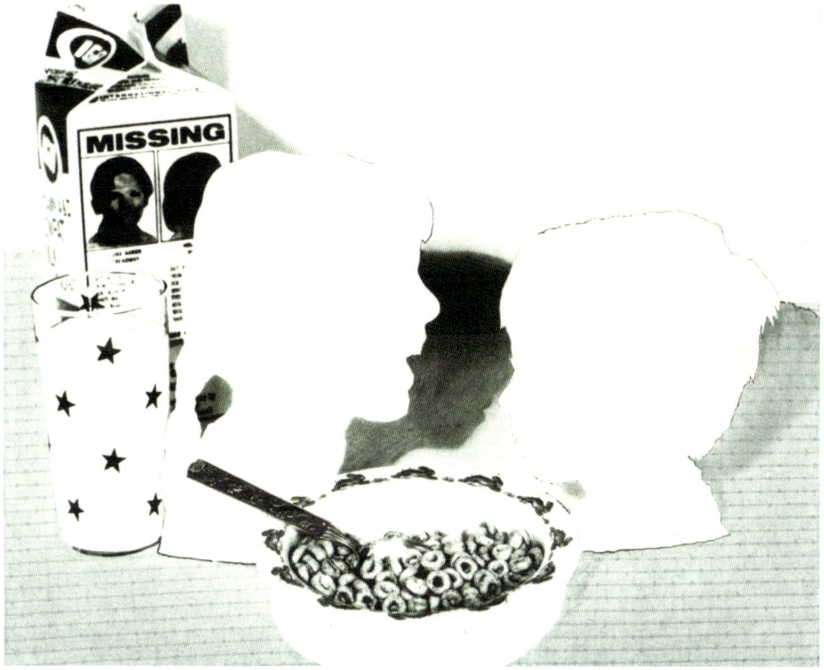
MISSING

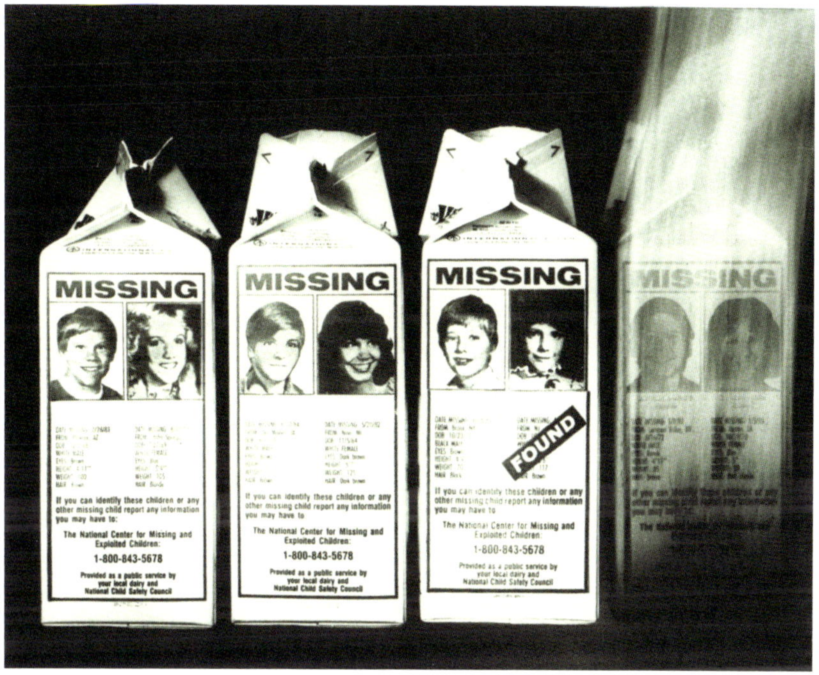
MISSING
If you can identify these children or any other missing child report any information you may have to:
The National Center for Missing and Exploited Children:
1-800-843-5678
Provided as a public service by your local dairy and National Child Safety Council
FOUND

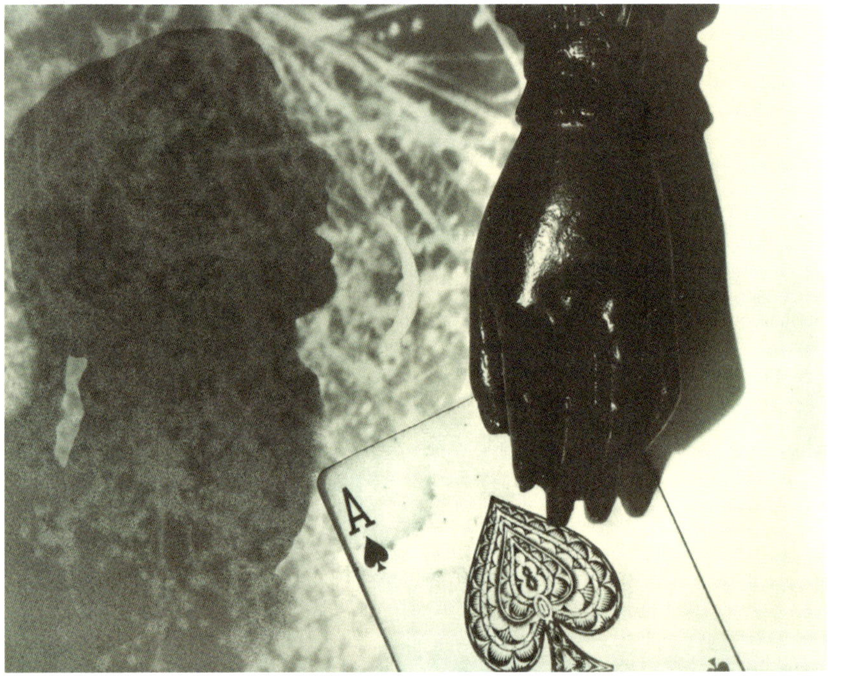

> ***Life's Lessons***

*Luck*, 1986,
photographic etchings

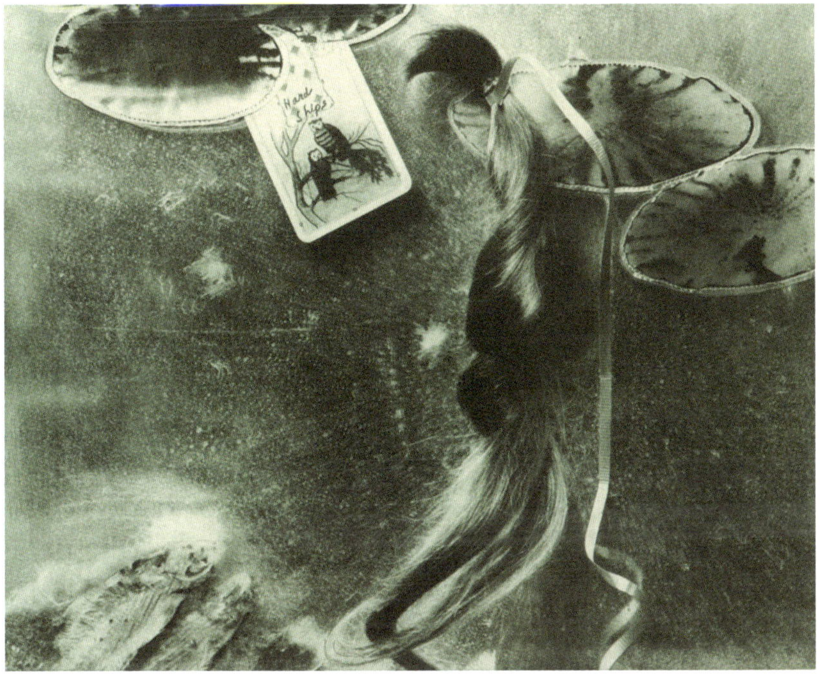

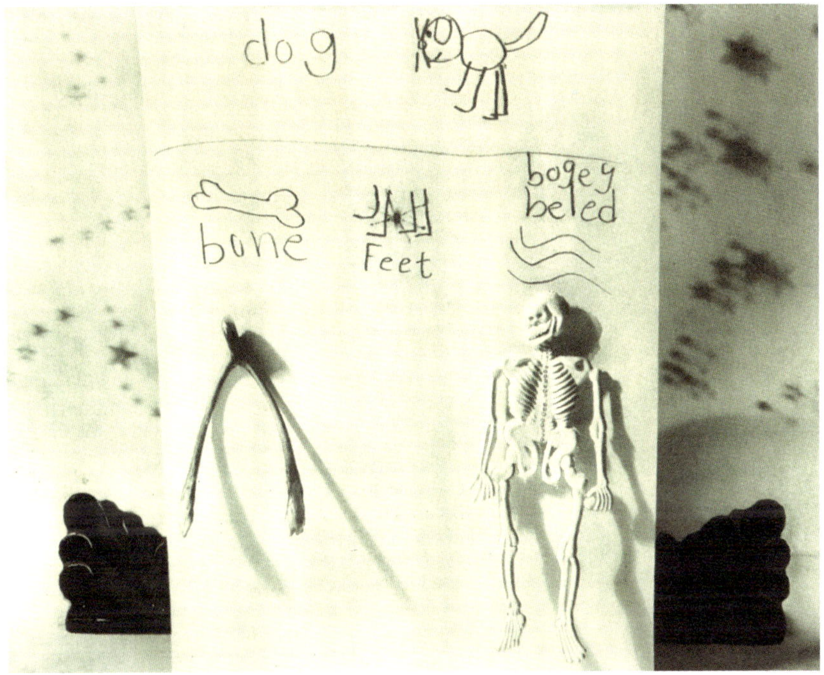
dog
bone
Feet
bogey
beled

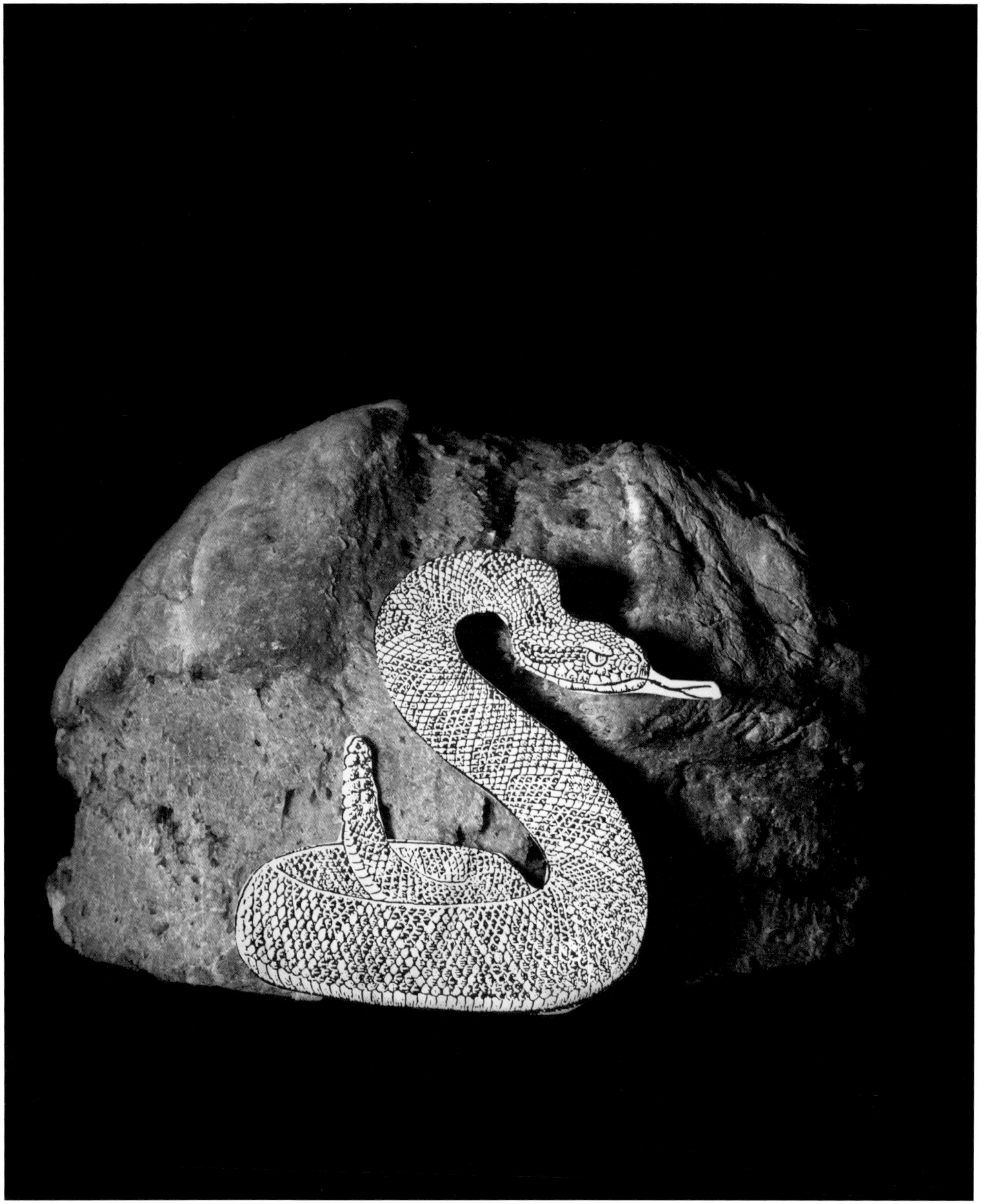

> ***Life's Lessons***

*Bread/Snake*, 1987–1988, diffusion transfer print

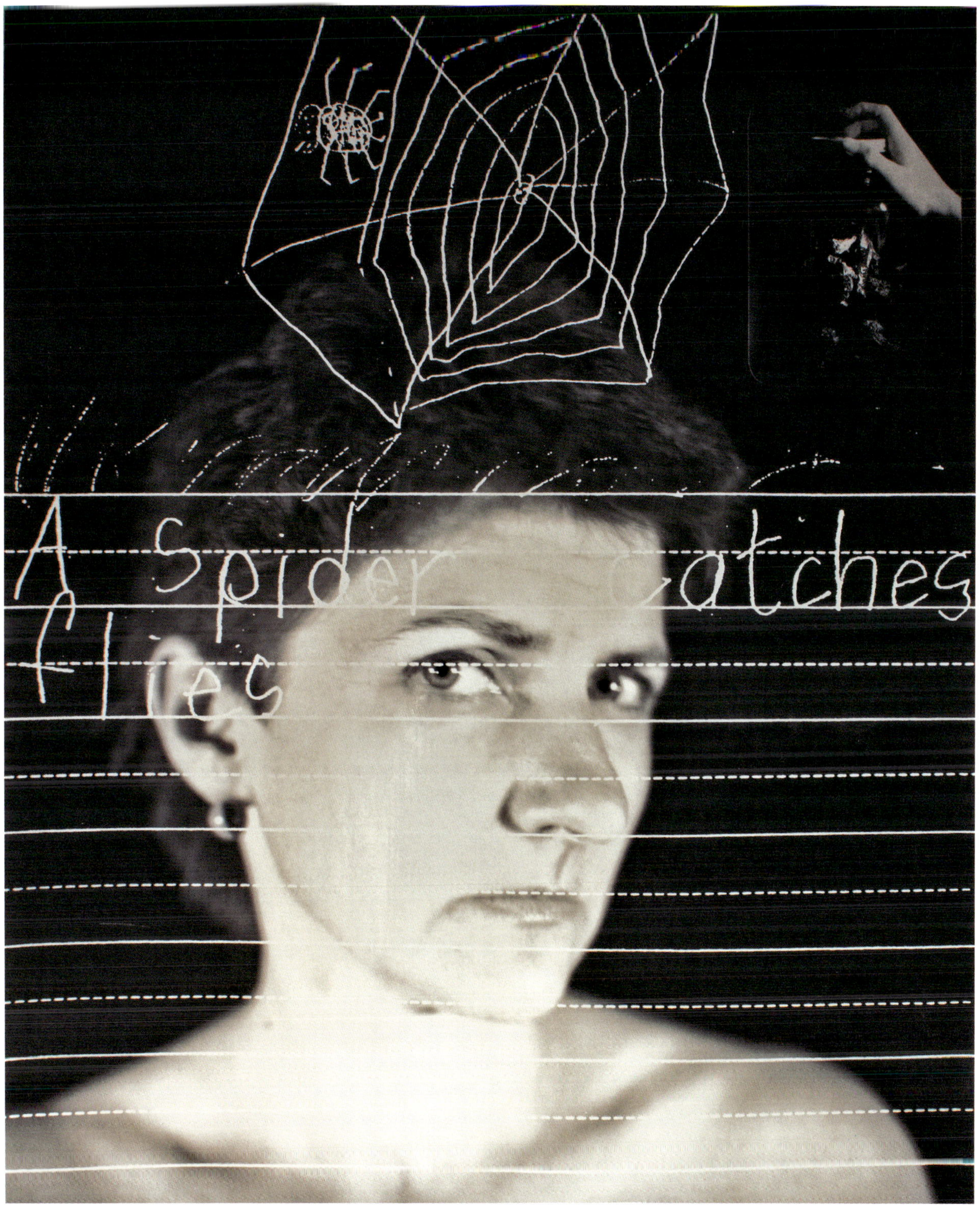


*Spider Catches Flies*, 1997,
diffusion transfer print

*Gavin with the World*, 1987,
gelatin silver print

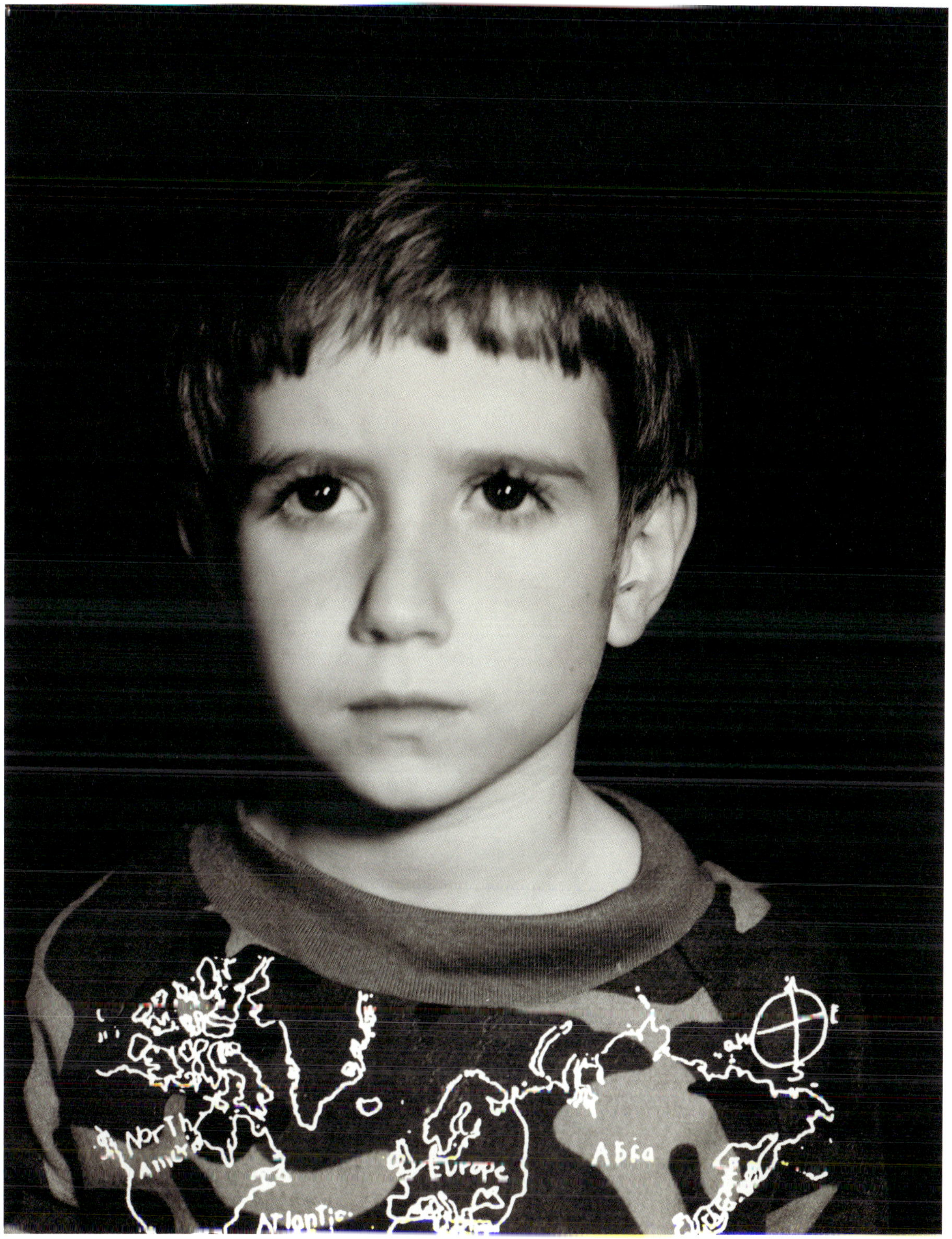

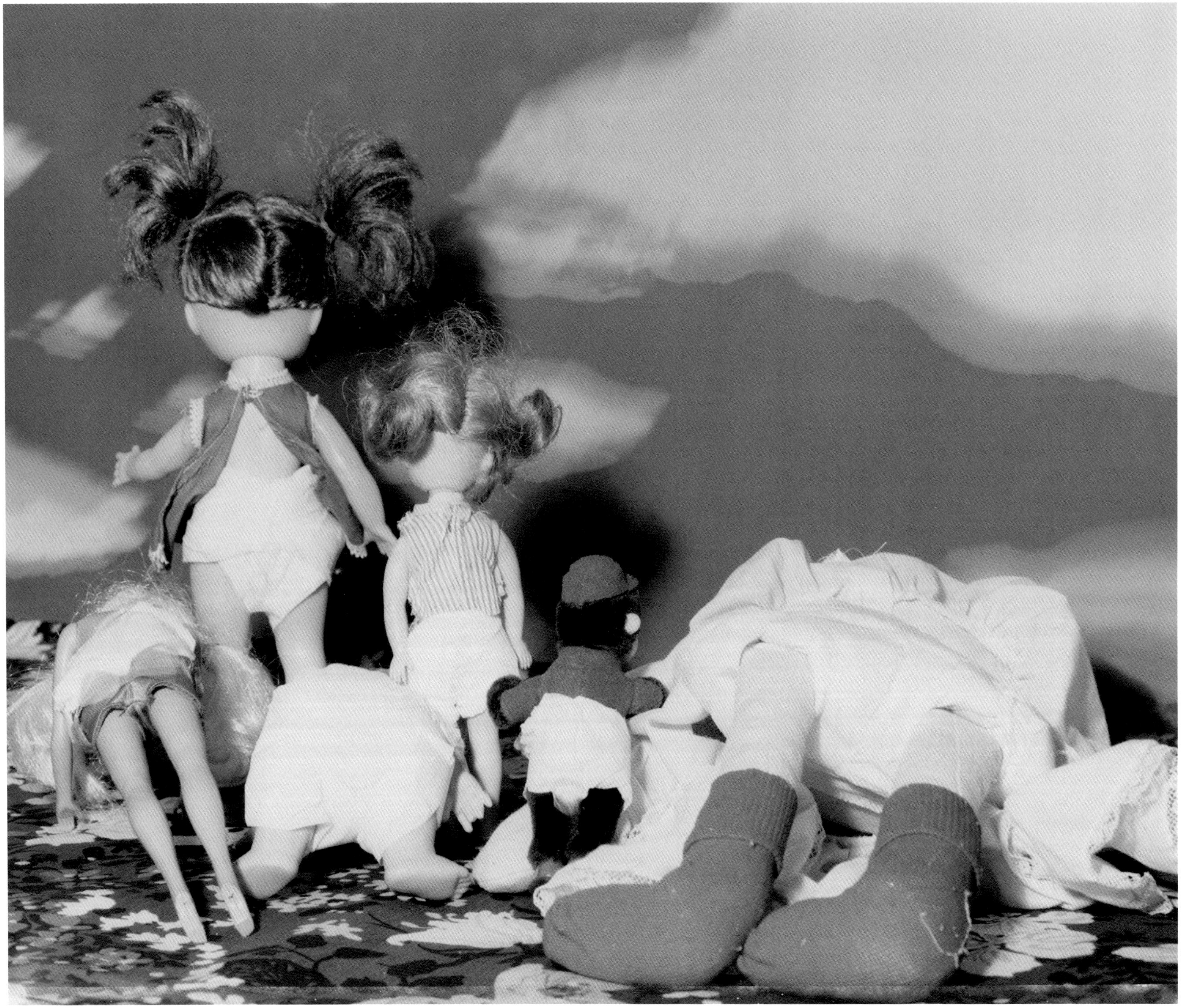

*Rachel's Installation*, 1987,
gelatin silver print

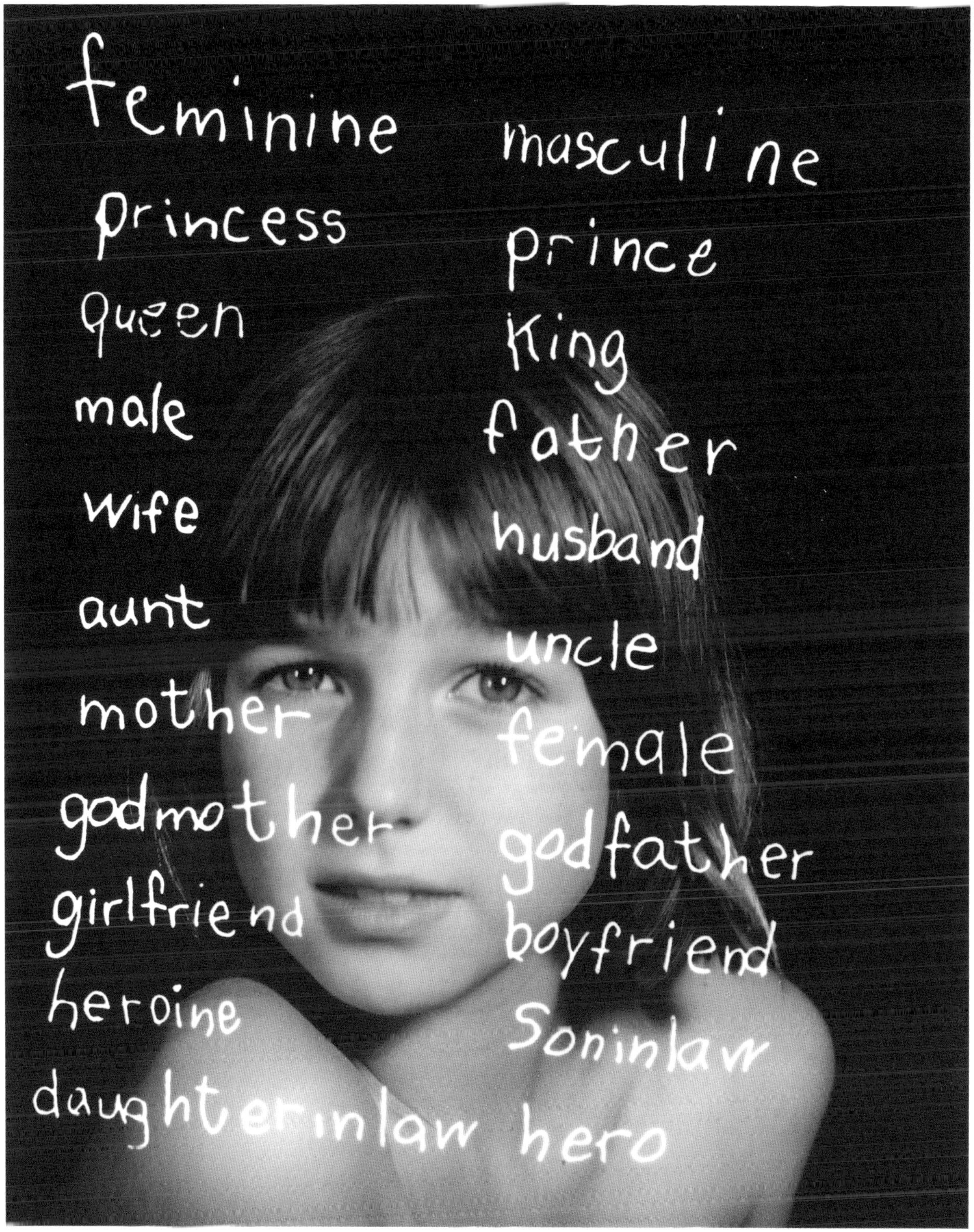


*Feminine/Masculine*, 1987,
gelatin silver print

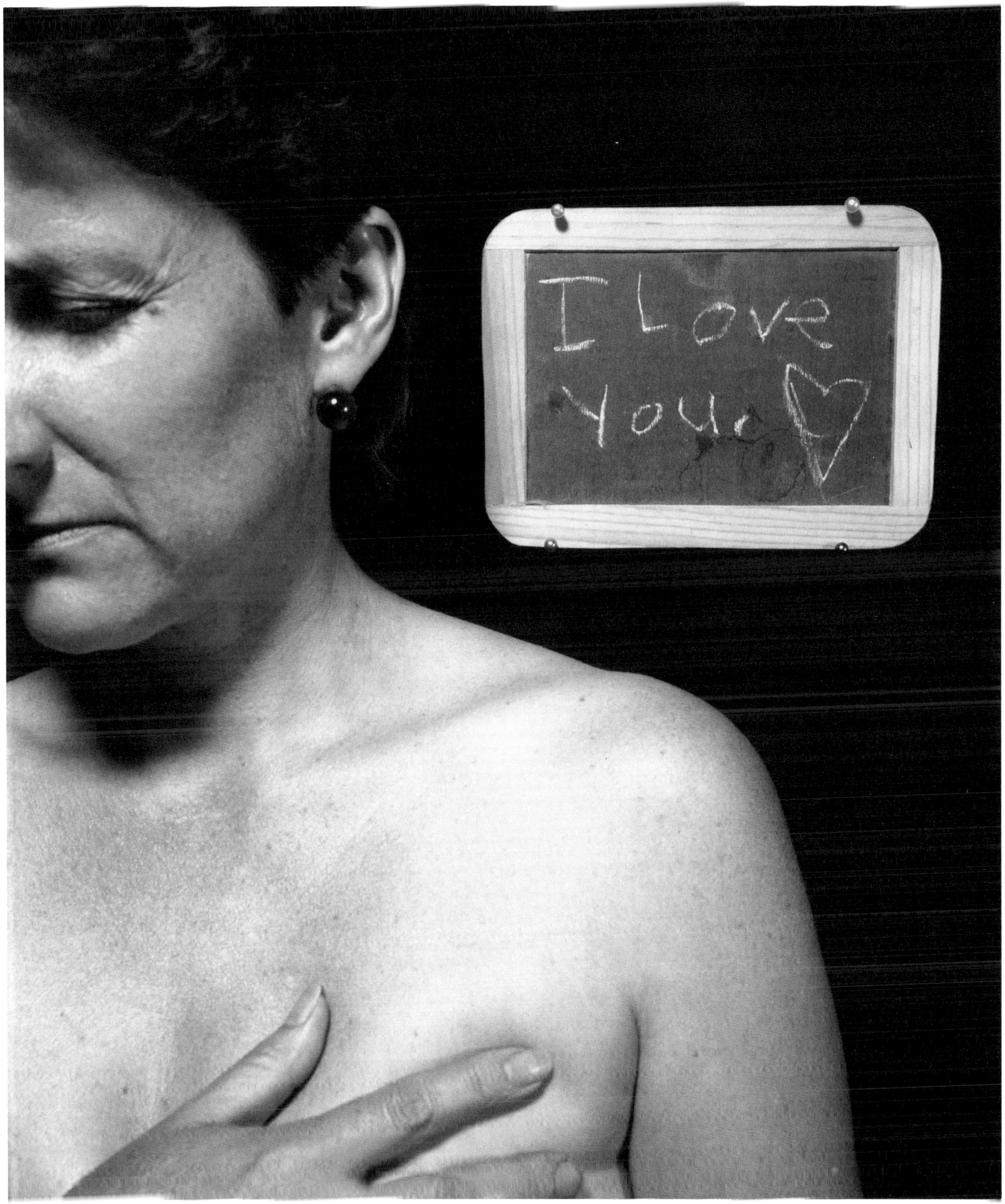


> ***Life's Lessons***

*I Love You*, 1987,
diffusion transfer print

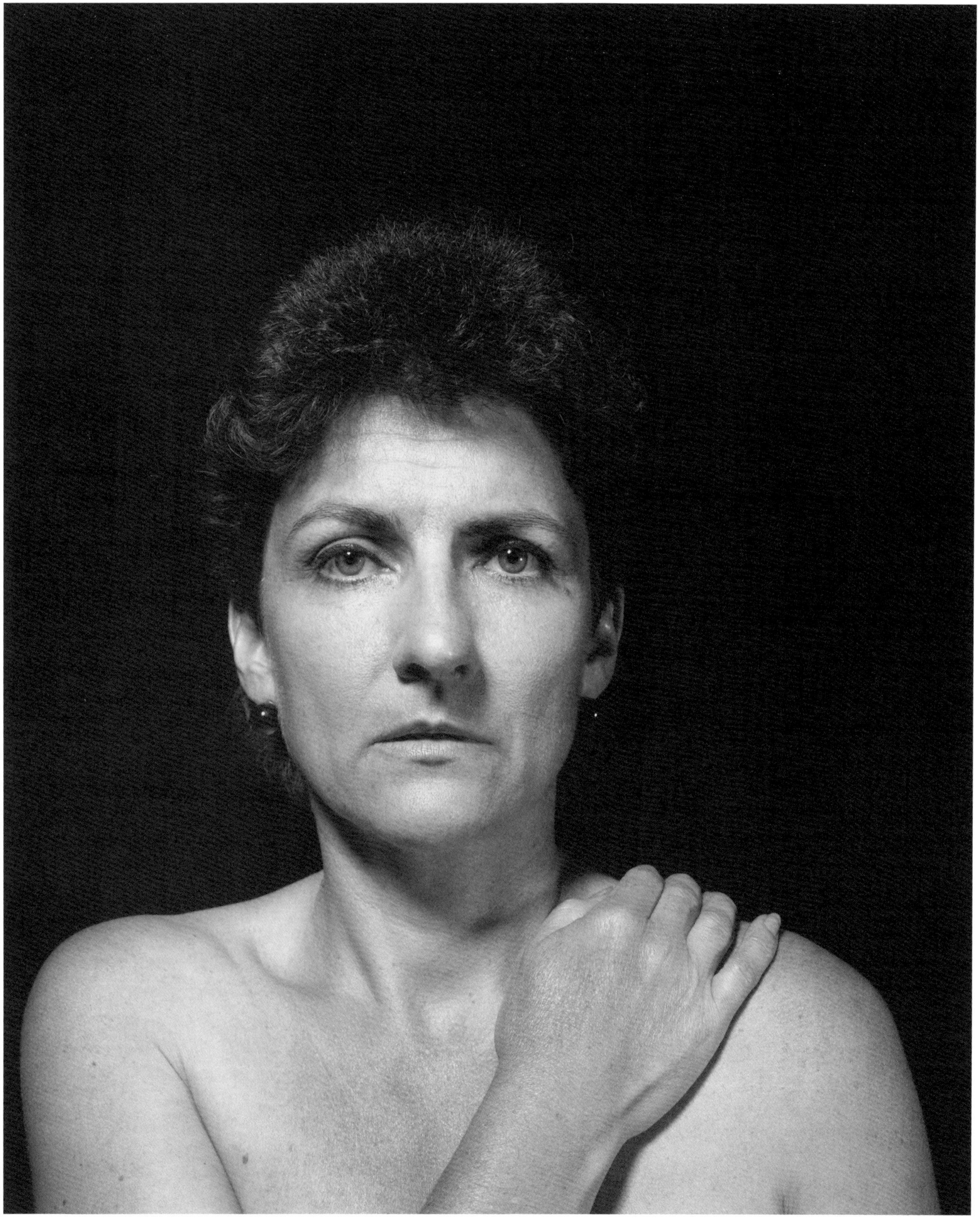

< ***Life's Lessons***

*Final Portrait*, 1987, diffusion transfer print

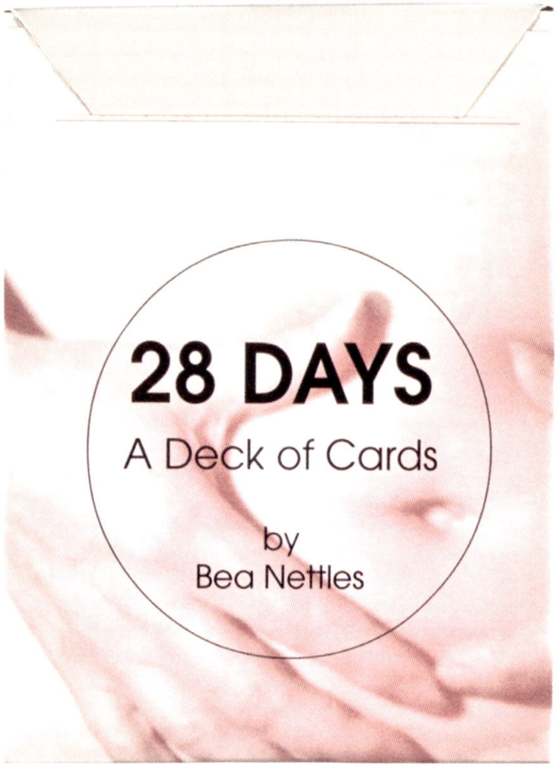


> *28 Days: A Deck of Cards*, 1991, card deck with offset lithographs

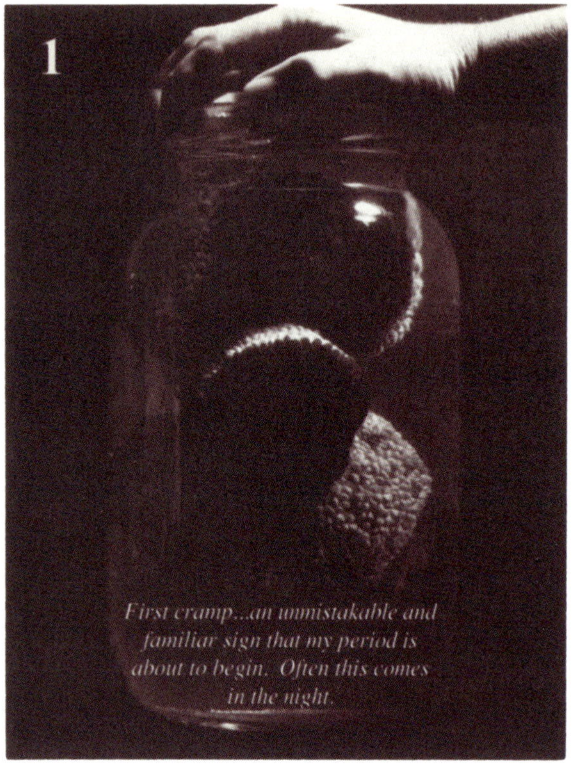


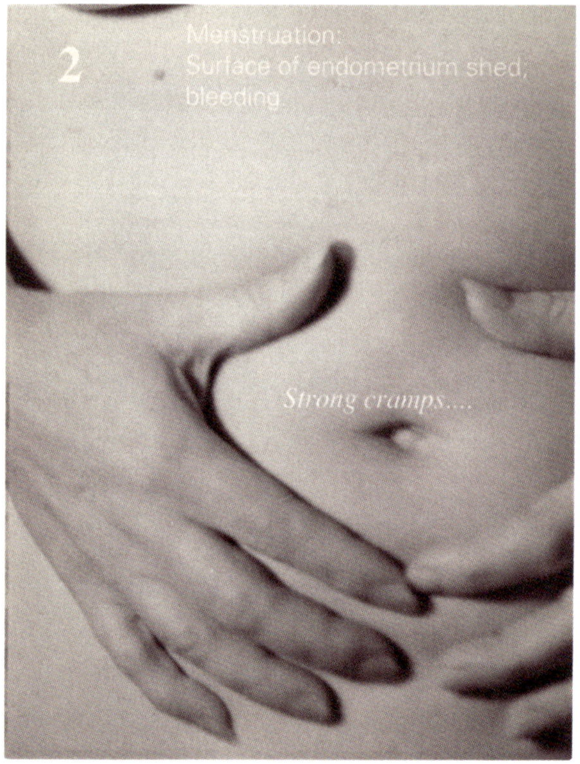

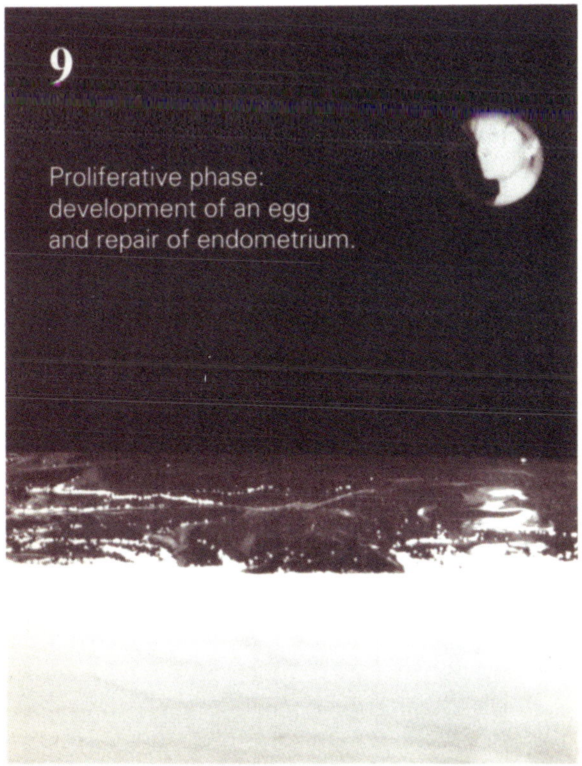
9
Proliferative phase: development of an egg and repair of endometrium.

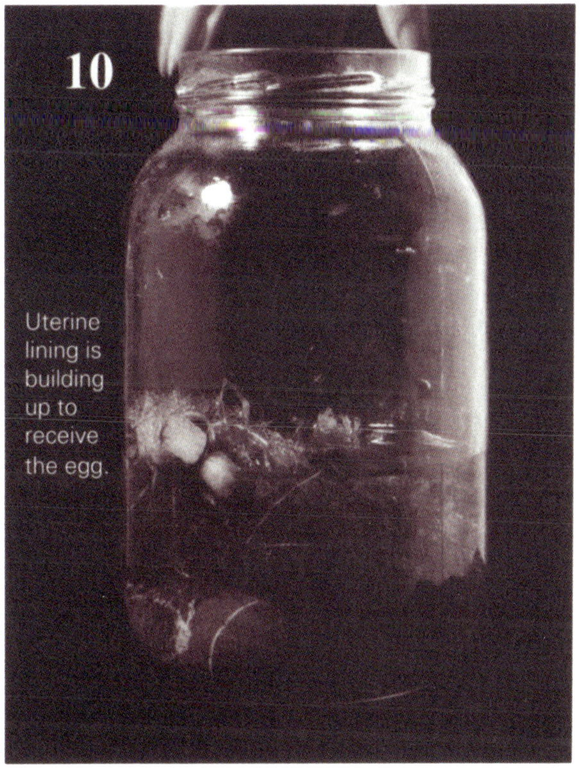
10
Uterine lining is building up to receive the egg.

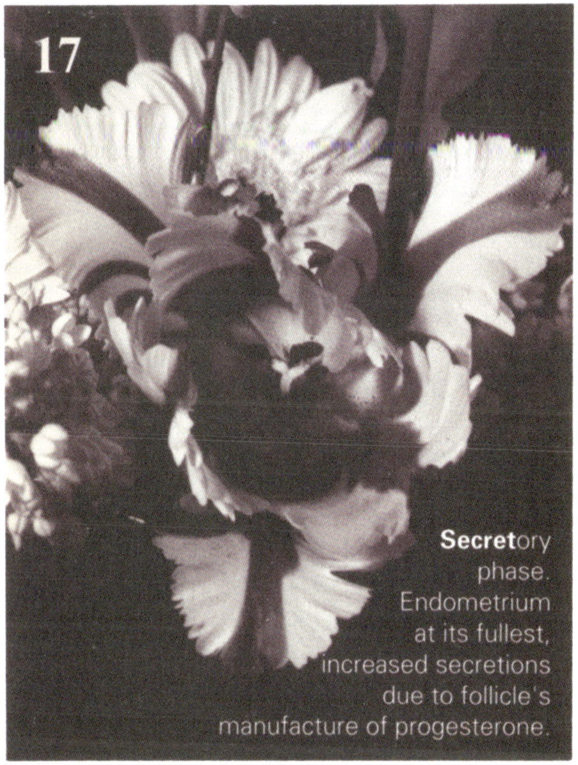
17
**Secret**ory phase. Endometrium at its fullest, increased secretions due to follicle's manufacture of progesterone.

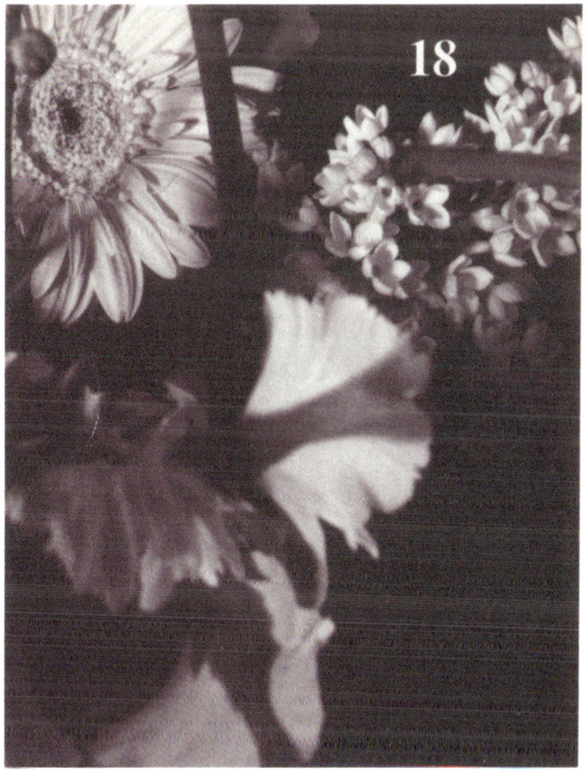
18

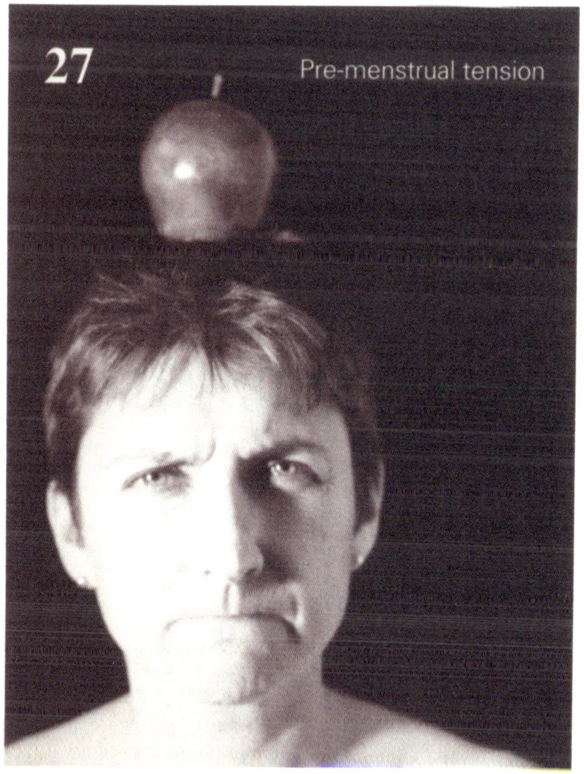
27
Pre-menstrual tension

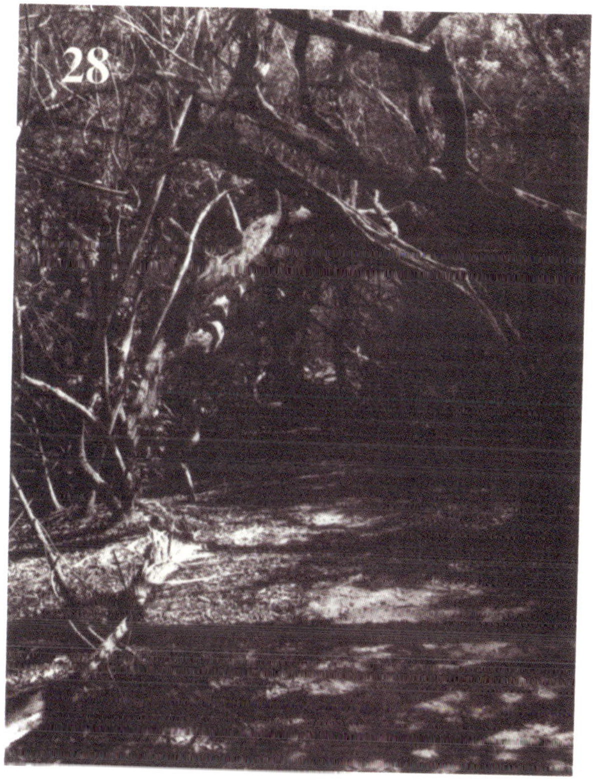
28

All mothers are "working mothers." I belong to the majority of American women who also happen to work outside of their homes. . . . What I do involves balancing priorities and making compromise. I function despite frequent interruptions, piecing things together in patches of time. My roles as artist, teacher, and mother can at times enhance each other, at times compete. . . .

I learned the ways that women cope primarily from my mother. Her ability to take a nap amid a sea of confusion impressed me. Other things she taught were organization and an appreciation of quality, which in her case ranged from house cleaning, polishing brass, and arranging flowers to singing in a strong, clear voice. She taught me to respect my intelligence. She returned to graduate school when her last child started kindergarten, and then began to commute to teach in a nearby college. . . .

During these years of my mother's commuting, I lived at home and got my sisters off to school before I went to class in the university's art department. My sophomore year I was told that I would never make it into graduate school unless I was twice as good as the male candidates. This warning was a shock, as until then I had never consciously noticed discrimination. I had seen how difficult things had been for my mother in graduate school, but I felt immune, that it wouldn't be a problem for me. I worked very hard. I did go to graduate school. I got my first teaching job in 1970, married at twenty-seven, and had children in my early thirties. I am glad that I waited until I was professionally established, as motherhood is a permanent state and a tremendous commitment.

When asked what I am, I say I'm an artist. Trying to balance art with teaching, I have often felt frustrated by the lack of time to do both well. . . . Life got much more complex when I became a mother. . . .

Something new entered the making of art: an undeniable sense of *guilt*, that I really should be with my children. . . . It is difficult for artists to feel appreciated. This feeling of defensiveness is compounded for artists who are mothers. . . .

In my privileged situation, I enjoy the flexibility of teaching with planned sabbaticals and summers off. I arrange my teaching schedule so that I can be home when my children get out of school. Many working women are not so lucky. We all function surrounded by two strong stereotypes. First, there is the "working woman" who "has it all," the executive type whose hair flies as she breezes off to her exciting job with briefcase in her hand and baby on her hip. In reality, women are still mainly in low-paying positions and make about seventy cents to the male dollar. The opposite stereotype is the cocooning stay-at-home wife. She burns scented potpourri, hangs wreaths, and drinks solitary cups of coffee. Our culture pays lip service to her but doesn't appreciate her labor enough to pay for it.

Those stereotypes, combined with the attitude that one cannot be a good mother and a good artist and a good teacher, make my triple career even more difficult. It is also a dangerous arena—if one makes photographs of one's own naked children, for example. I have had to struggle with the demarcation between our family's private life and what I will make public. I have drawn a line beyond which I'm not willing to drag my family members. I feel more comfortable revealing myself and have returned to creating self-portraits for this very reason.

Despite its complexities, motherhood has been a galvanizing experience for me. The work of mothering creates special types of thinking. For the artist-teacher who chooses to become a mother there are advantages. Mothers are the original teachers.

I am interested in the idea of home, and especially housework. Despite the backlash against women, I doubt that we will return to the traditional household. Housework must still be done. Whoever does it is worthy of our genuine appreciation. Men and children must truly share in the creation of the home space. Fathers need to spend more time with their children. Women have the right to fully develop their talents. We must take care that our creative energies are not drained by endless demands. We must not succumb to disparagement and stereotyping that sidetrack us into subordinate roles. Rather, we must use these intrusions, these small voices in our heads, this ability to quilt and improvise, along with our organizational skills and learned balancing act. Through our art, teaching, and very lives, let us confirm our cycles, the magic of our bodies, our abilities to make a whole out of parts. Let us celebrate the complexities.

**BEA NETTLES** ADAPTED FROM *COMPLEXITIES* (1992)

COMPLEXITIES

# 1995–2011

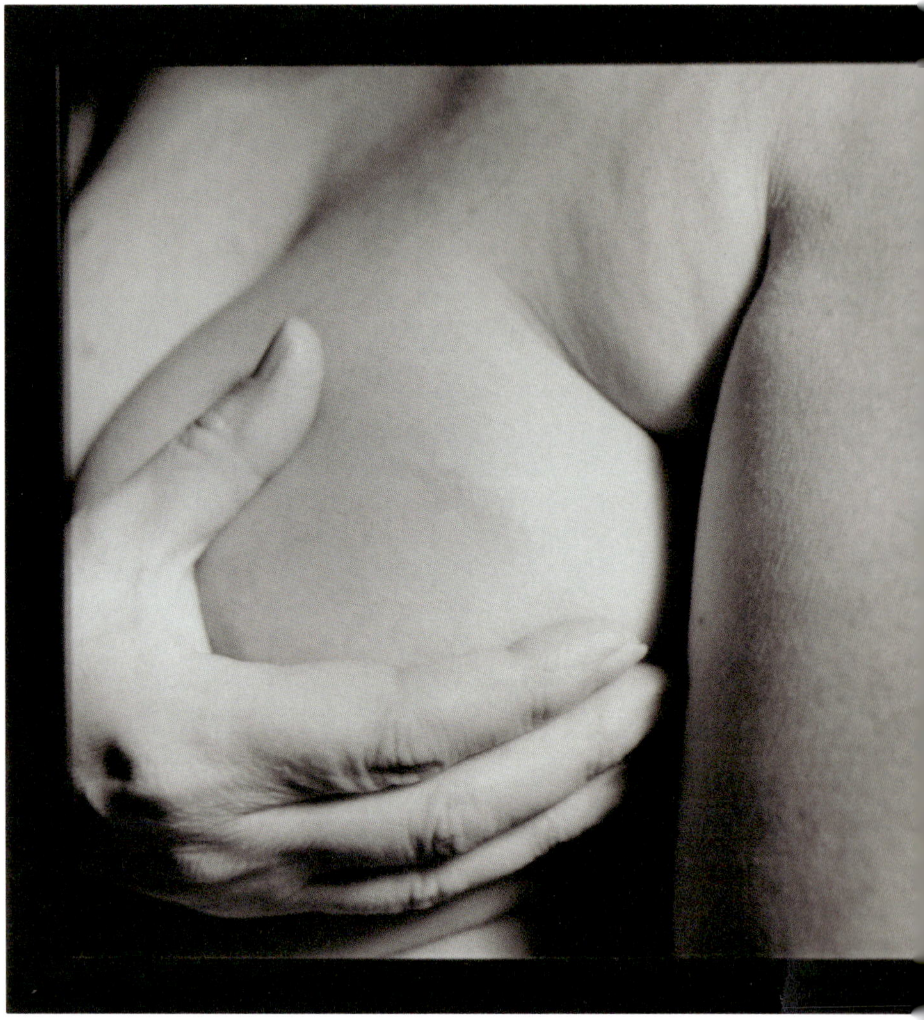

> *Pincushion*, 1995, from *Turning 50*, gelatin silver prints with black wood frame

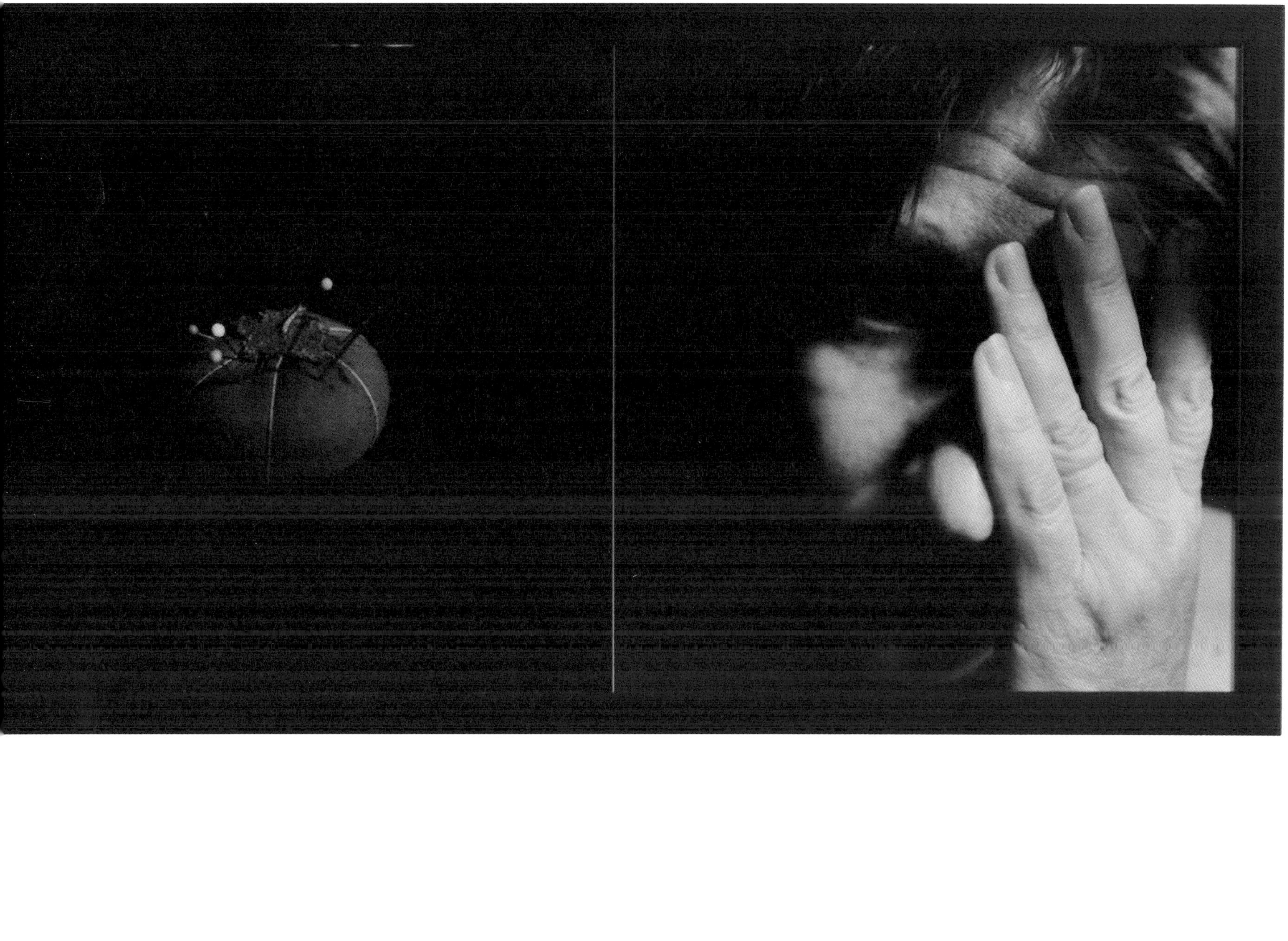

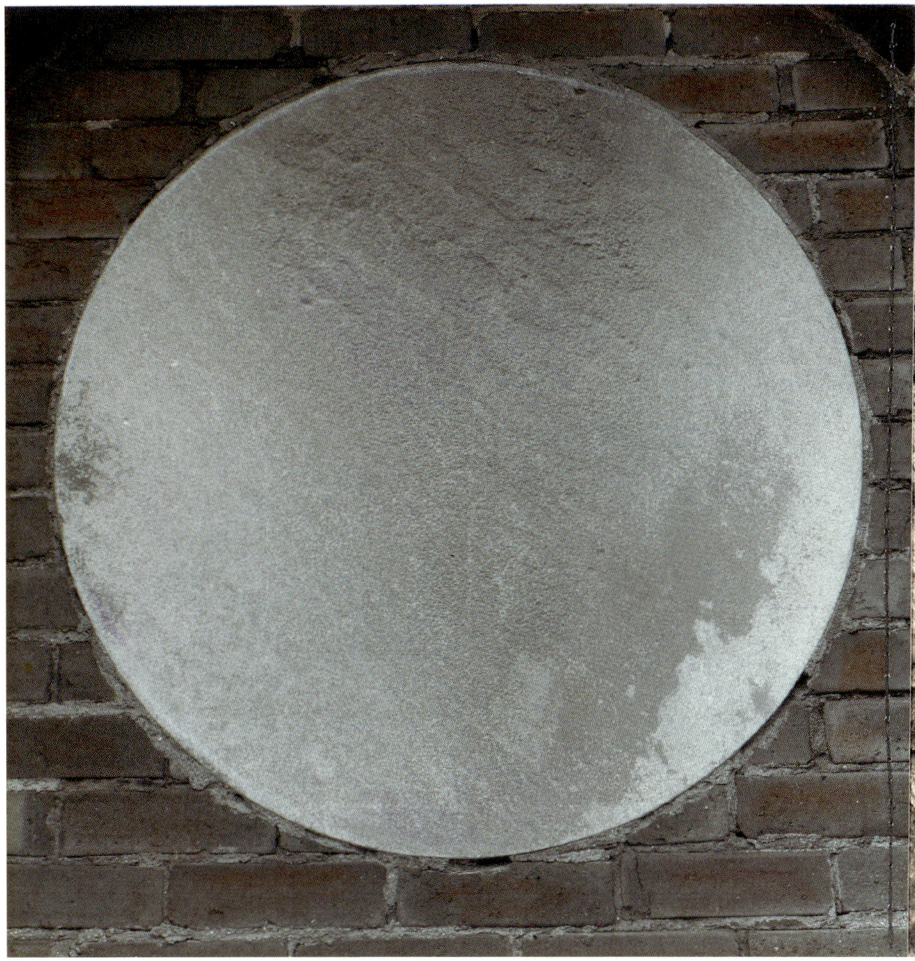

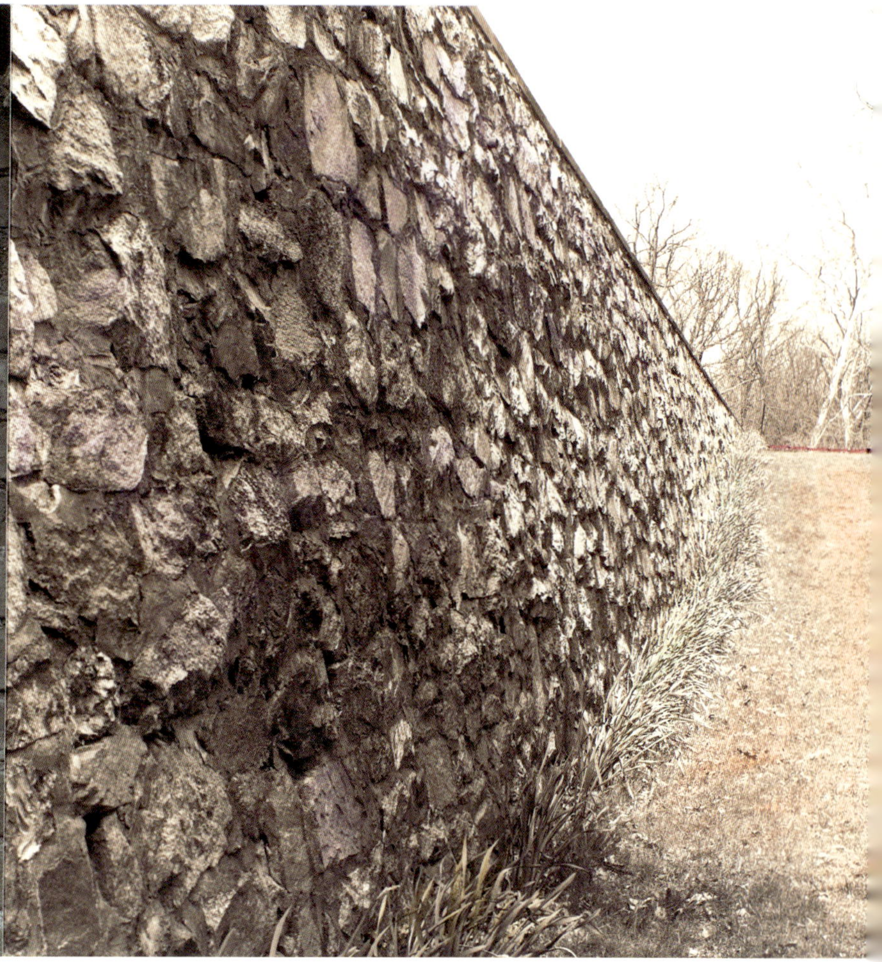

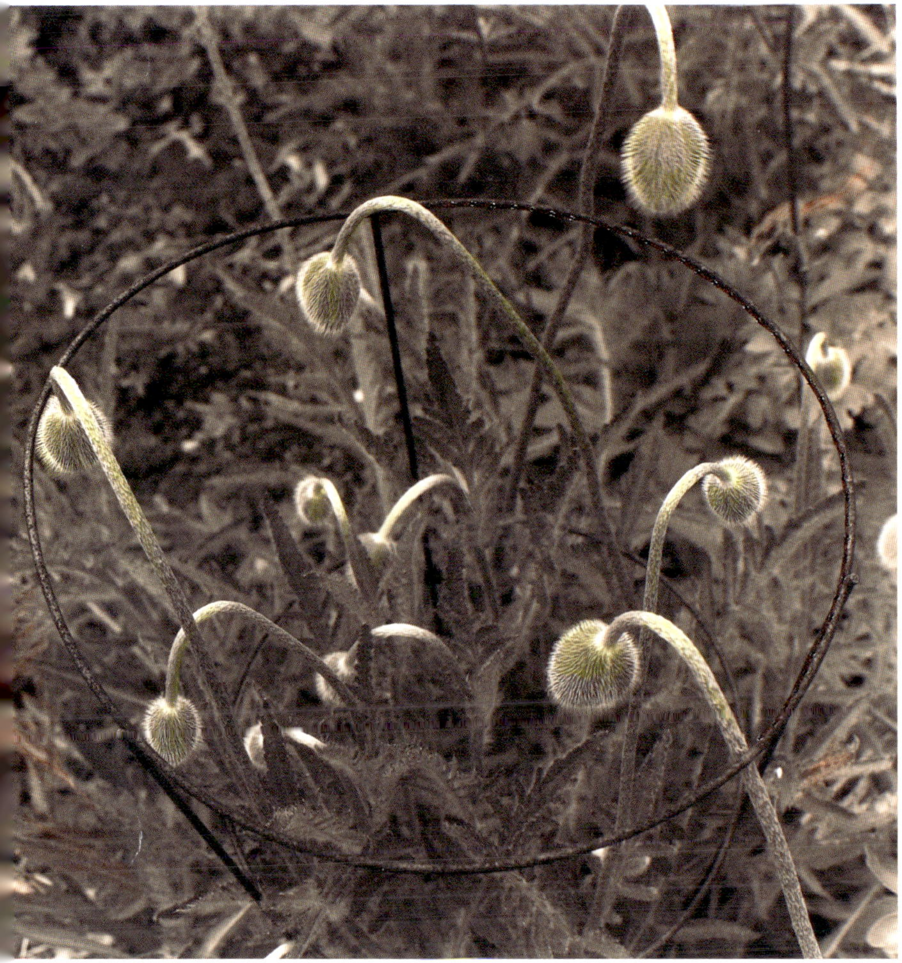

< *Allerton Park*, July 1997, gelatin silver prints with stitching and applied color

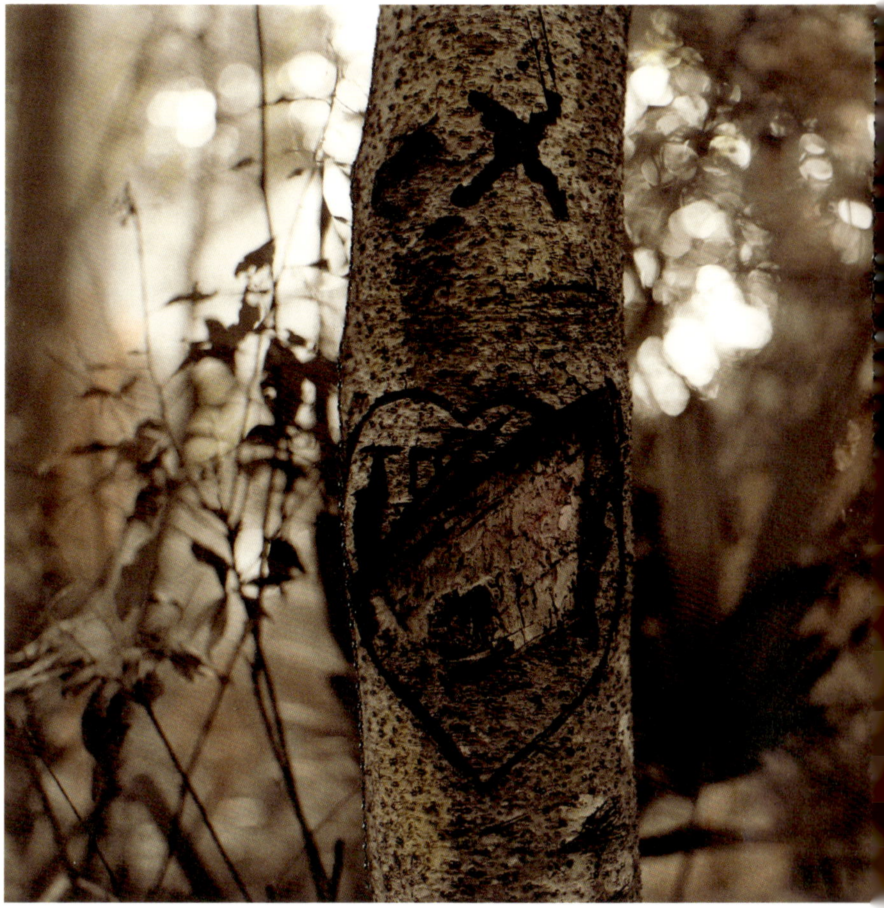

> *Carved Heart*, July 1997, gelatin silver prints with stitching and applied color

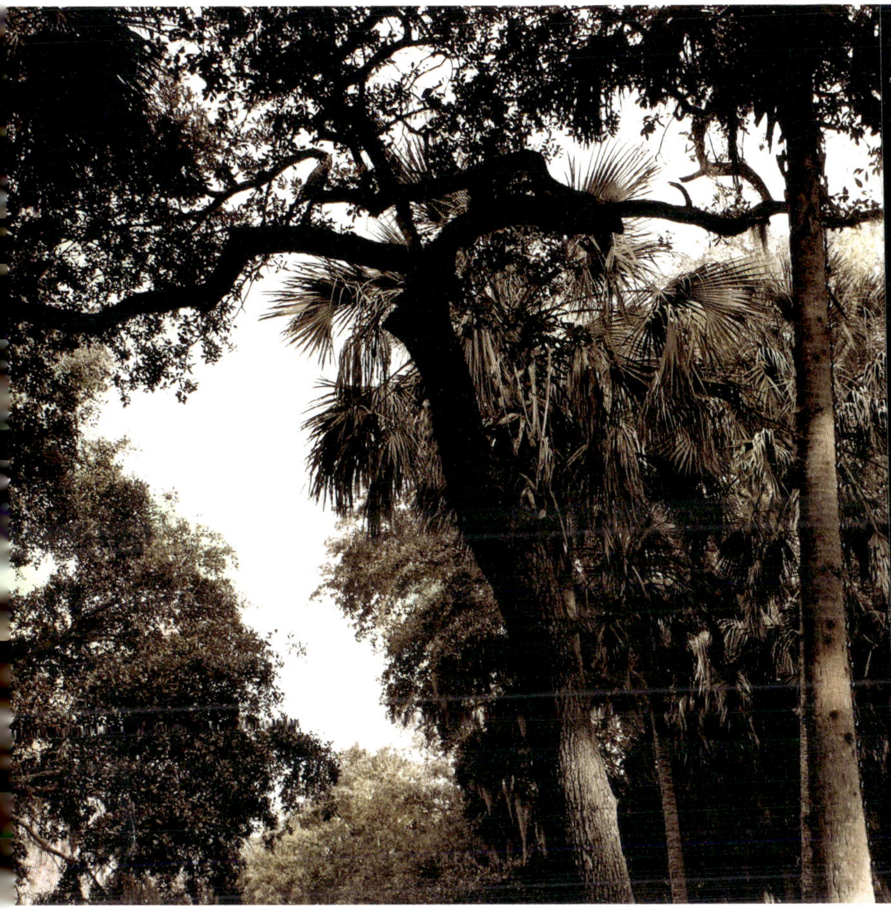

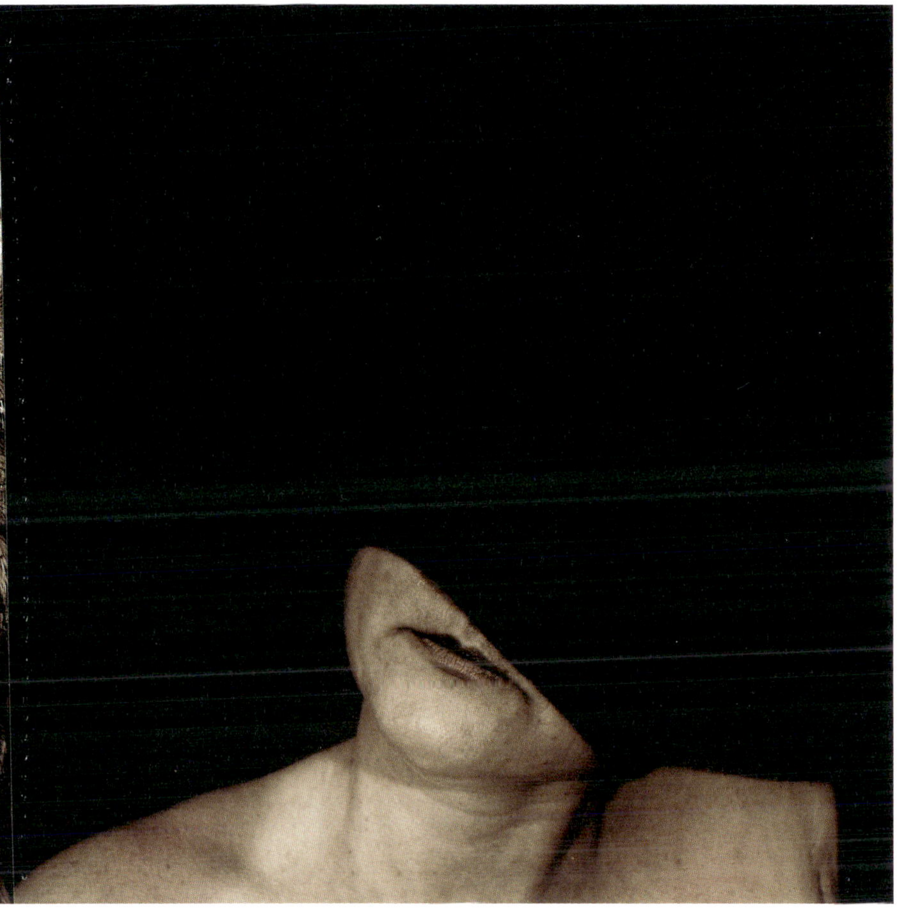

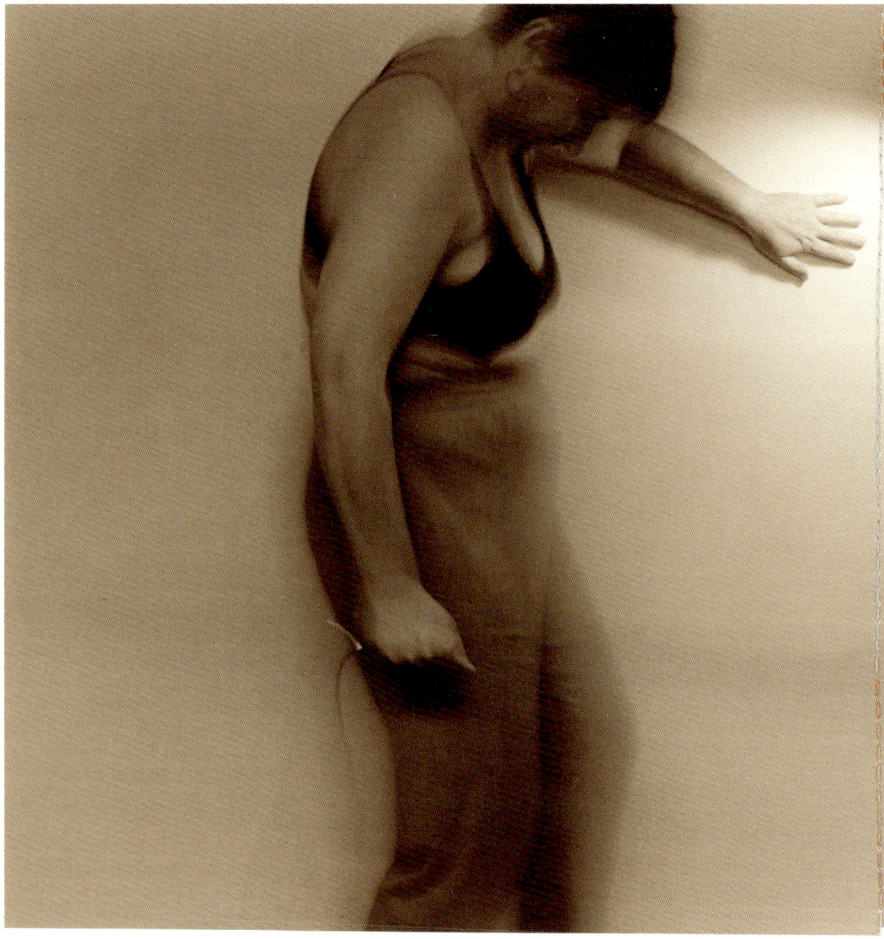

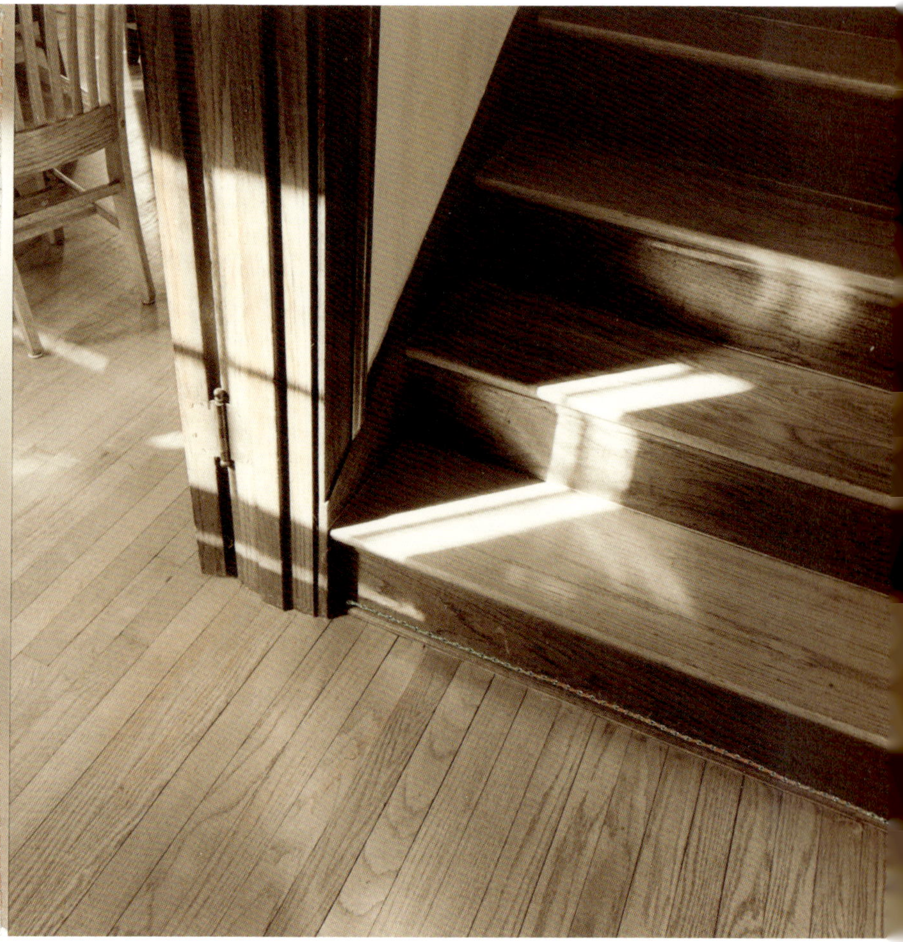

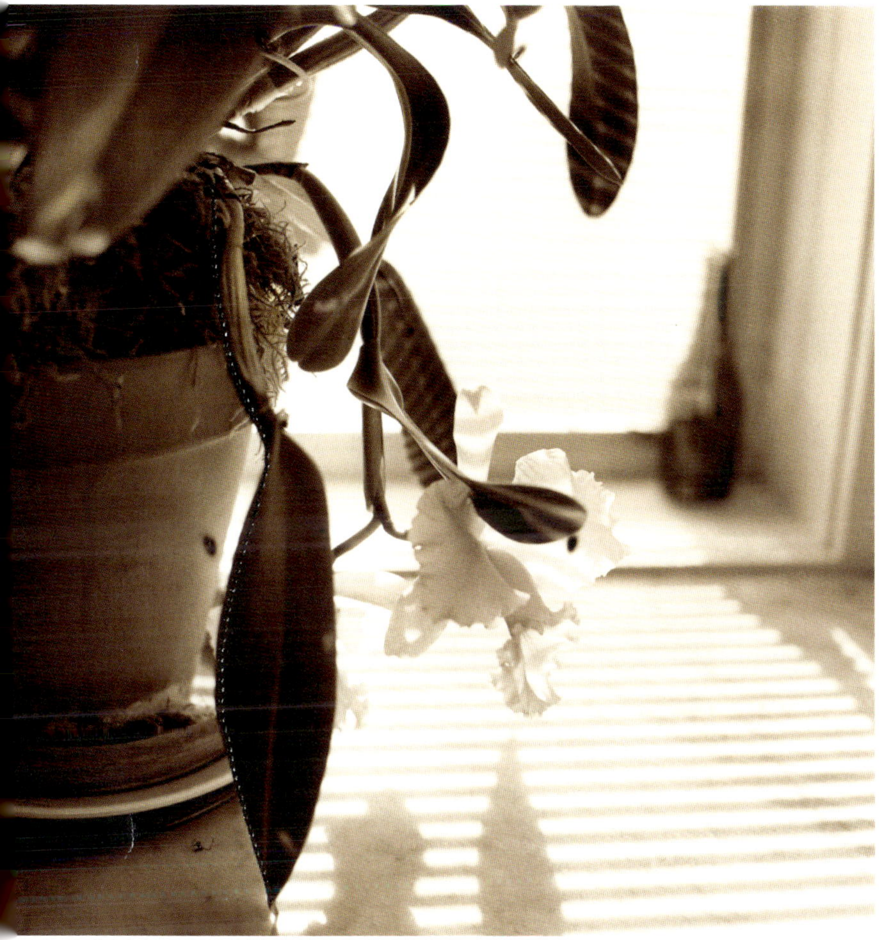

< *Stairway*, July 1997, gelatin silver prints with stitching and applied color

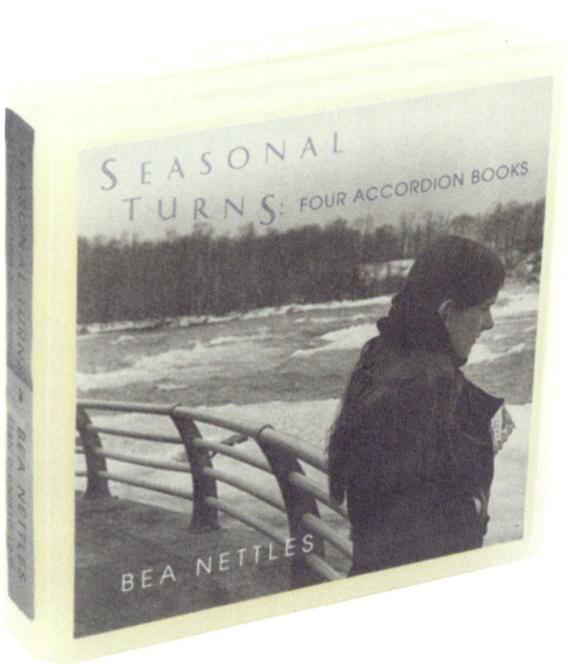


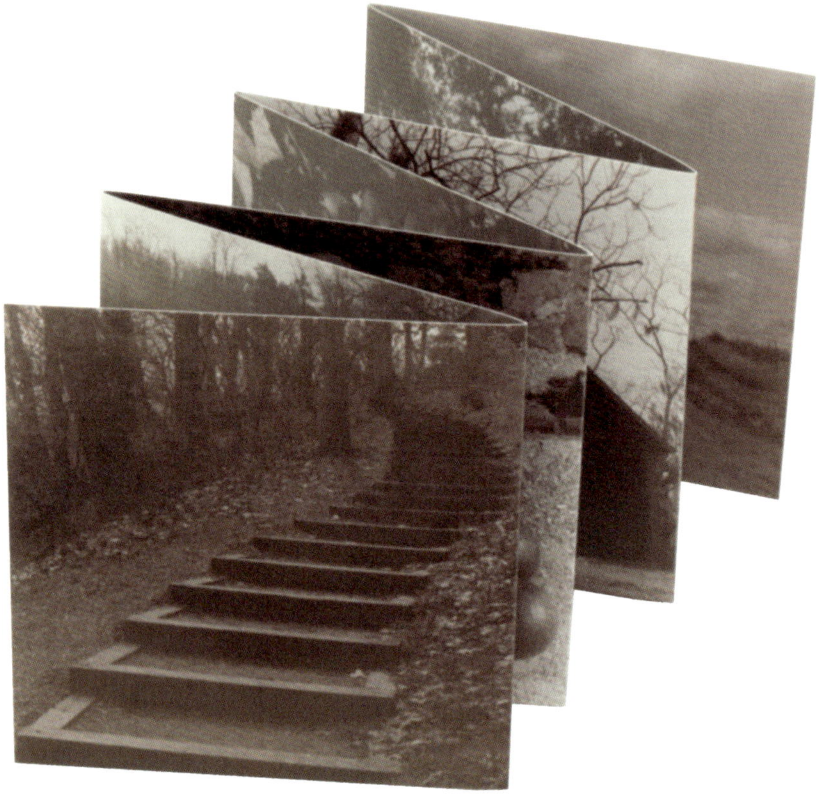

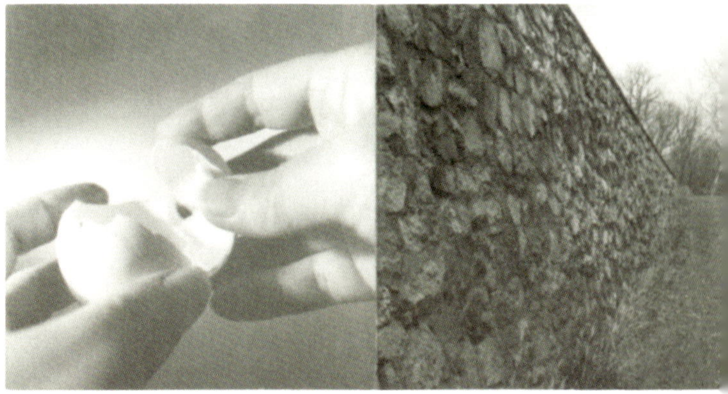

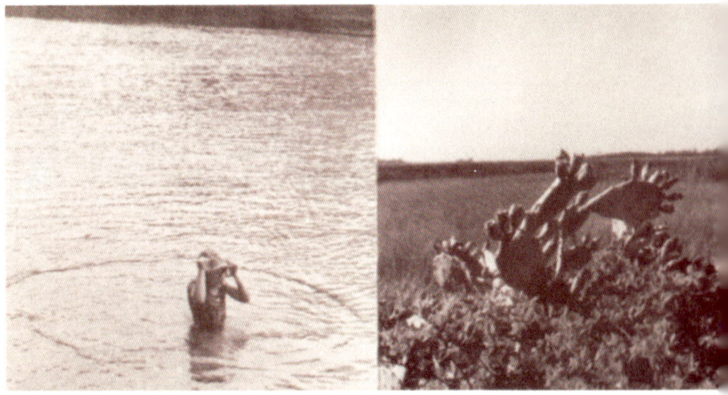

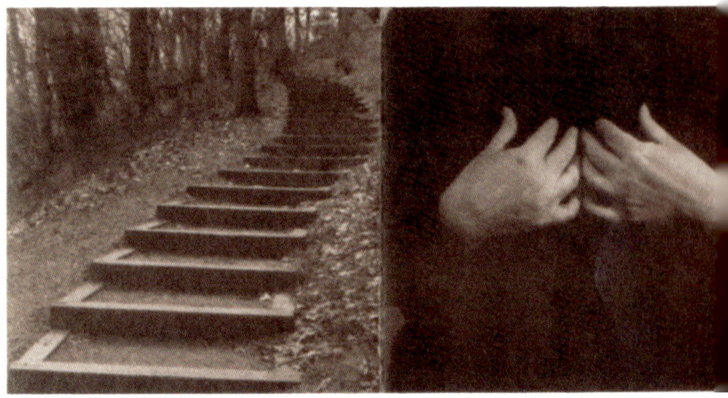

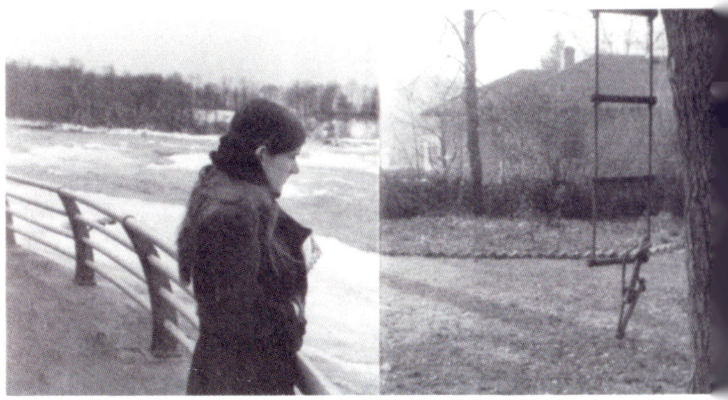

> *Seasonal Turns: Four Accordion Books*, 1998, four books with offset lithographs in plastic case

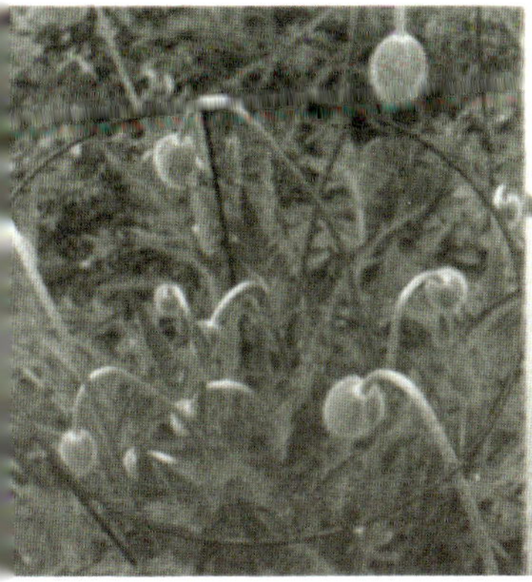
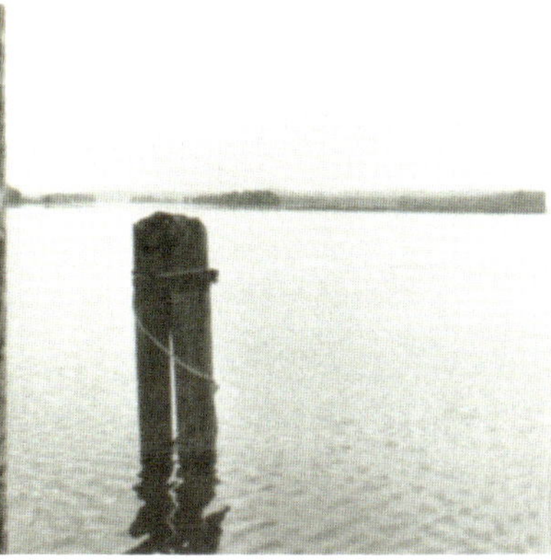

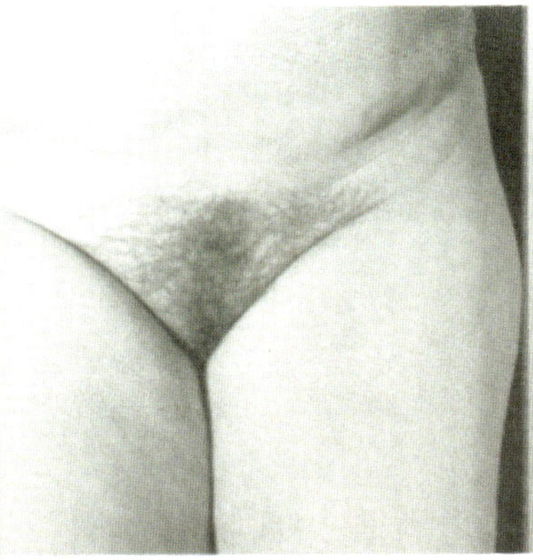
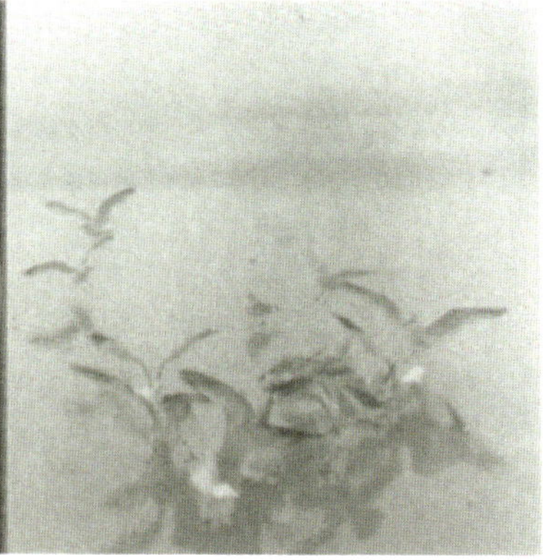
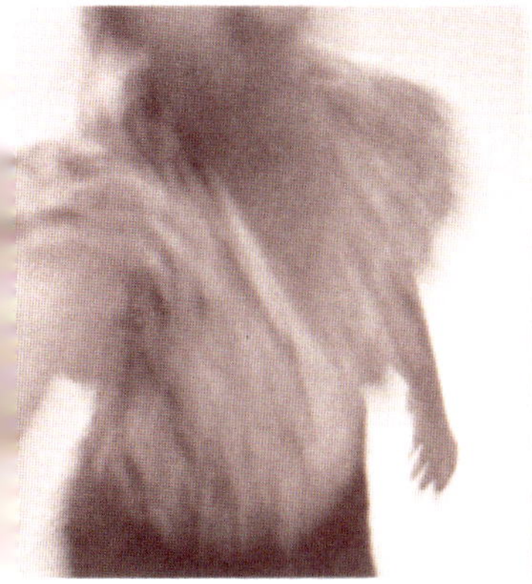
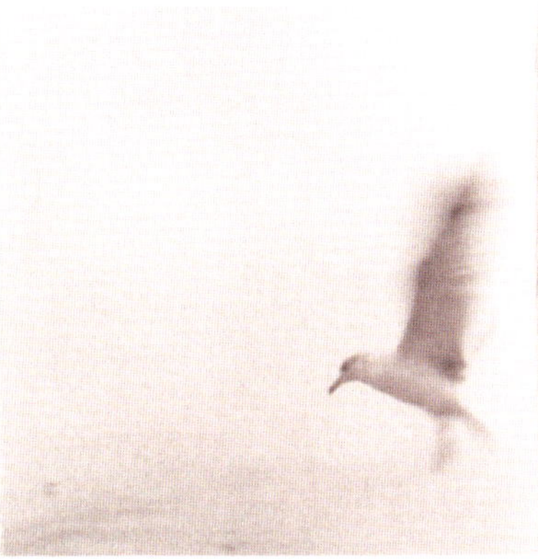
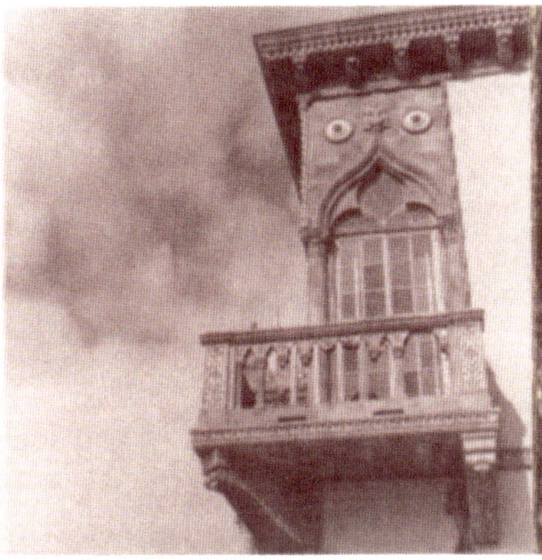
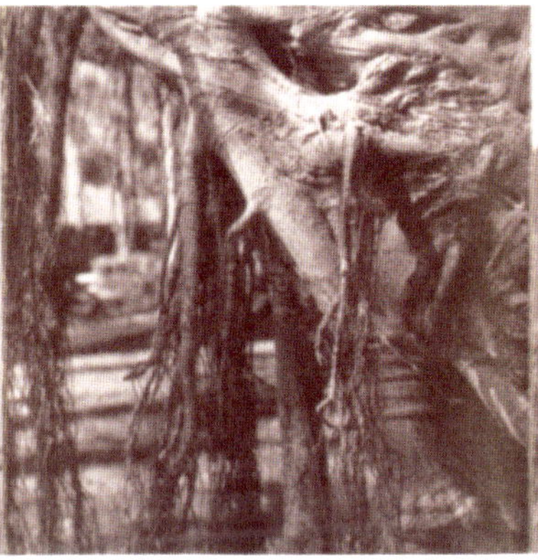
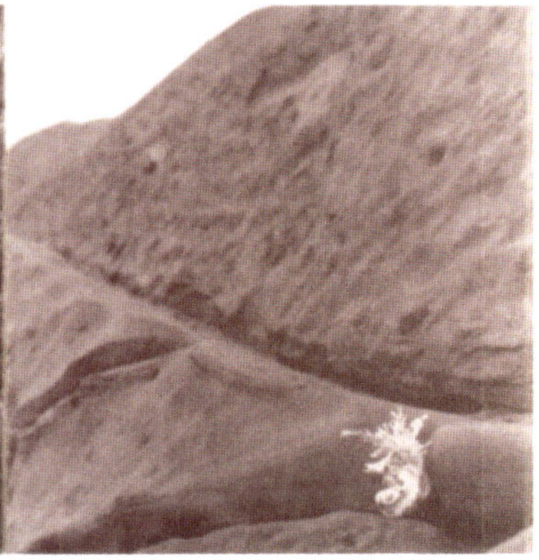
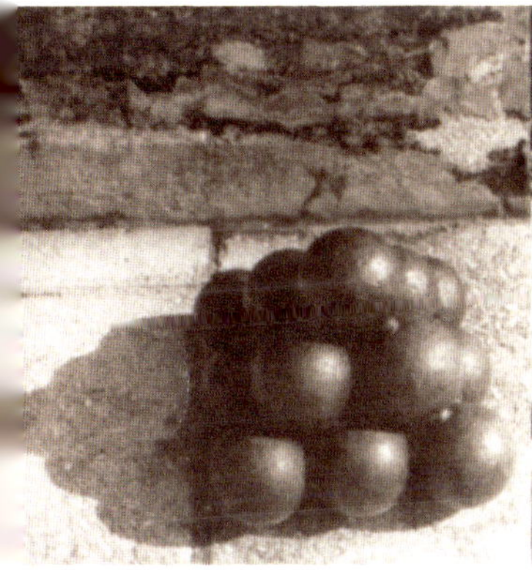
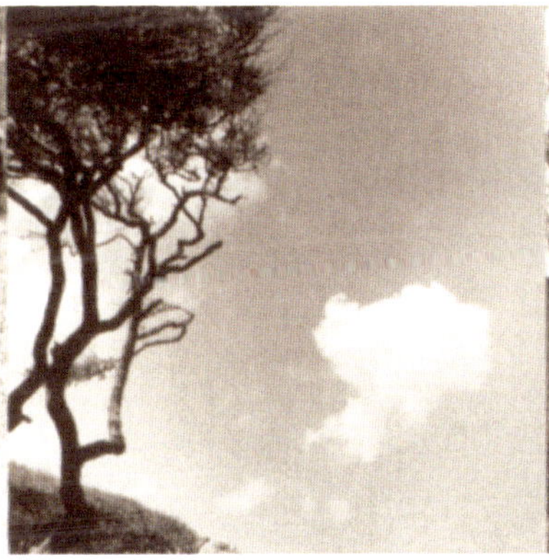
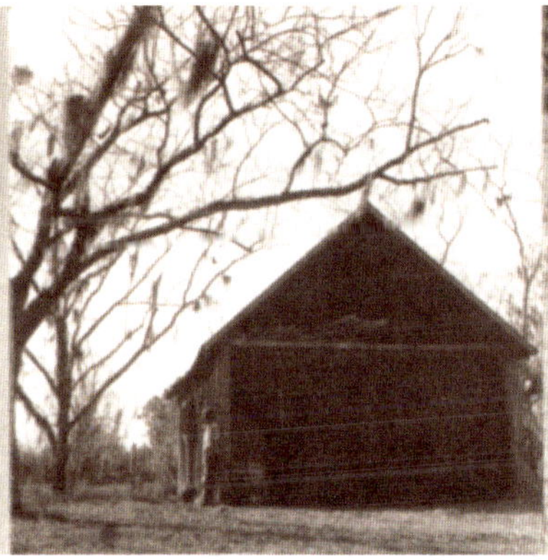
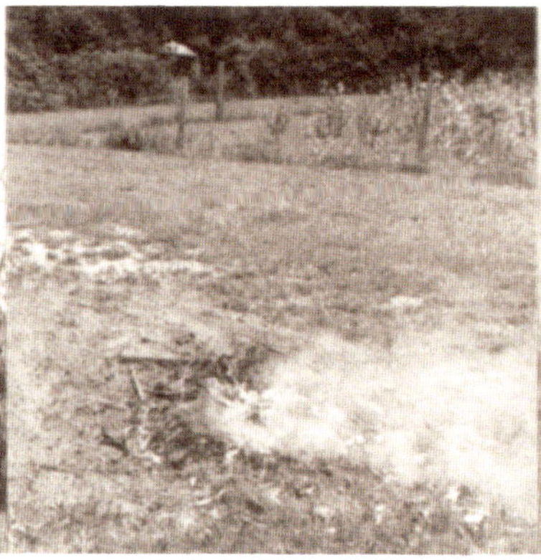
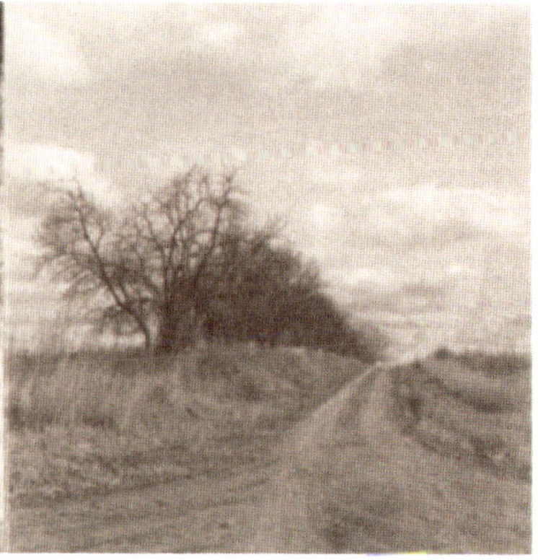
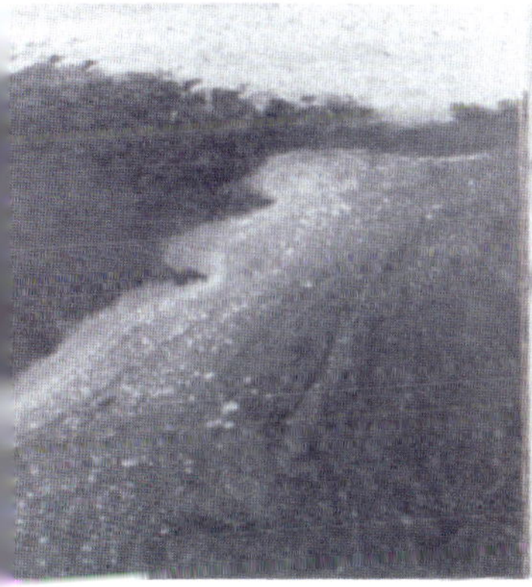
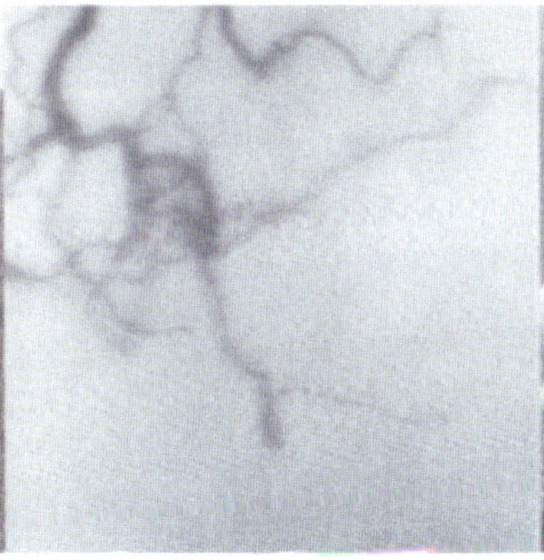
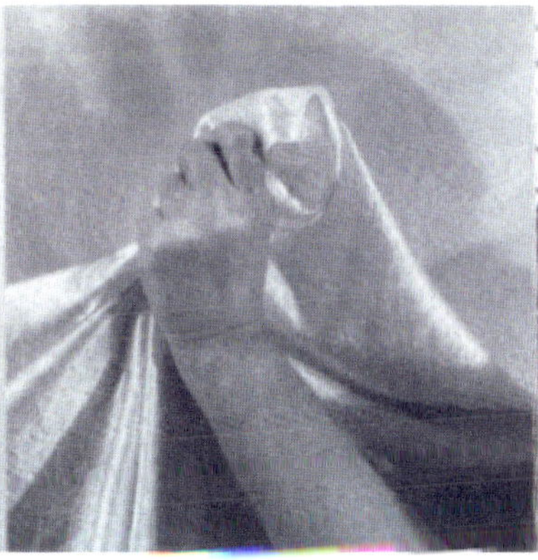
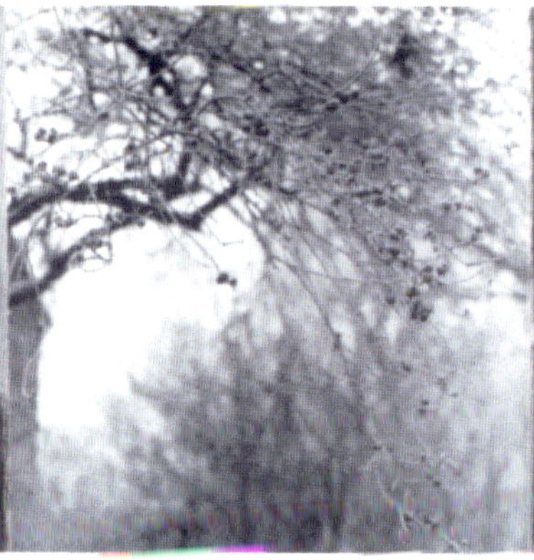
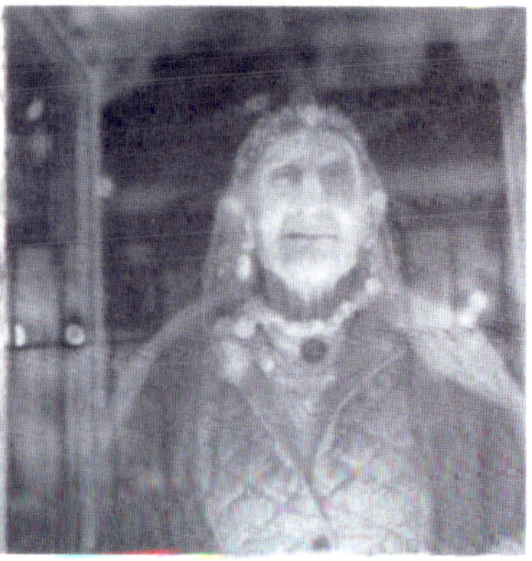

> ***Return Trips***

*Birdbath*, 1999,
inkjet print

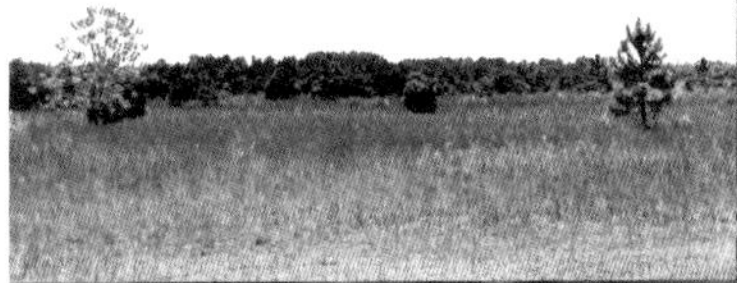
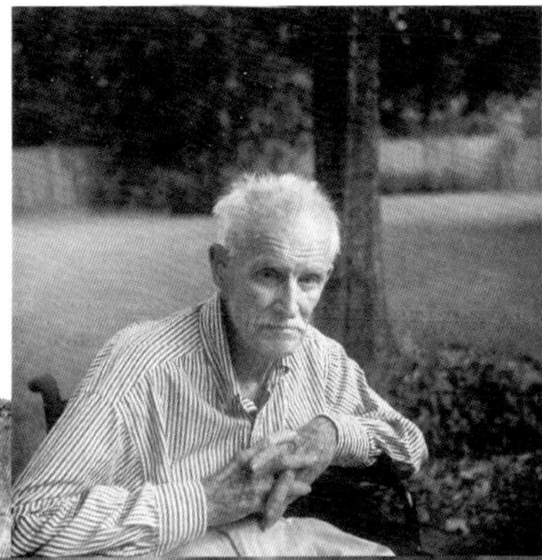
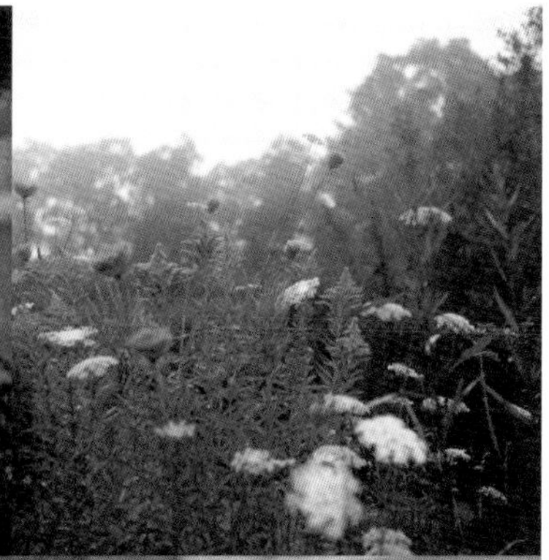
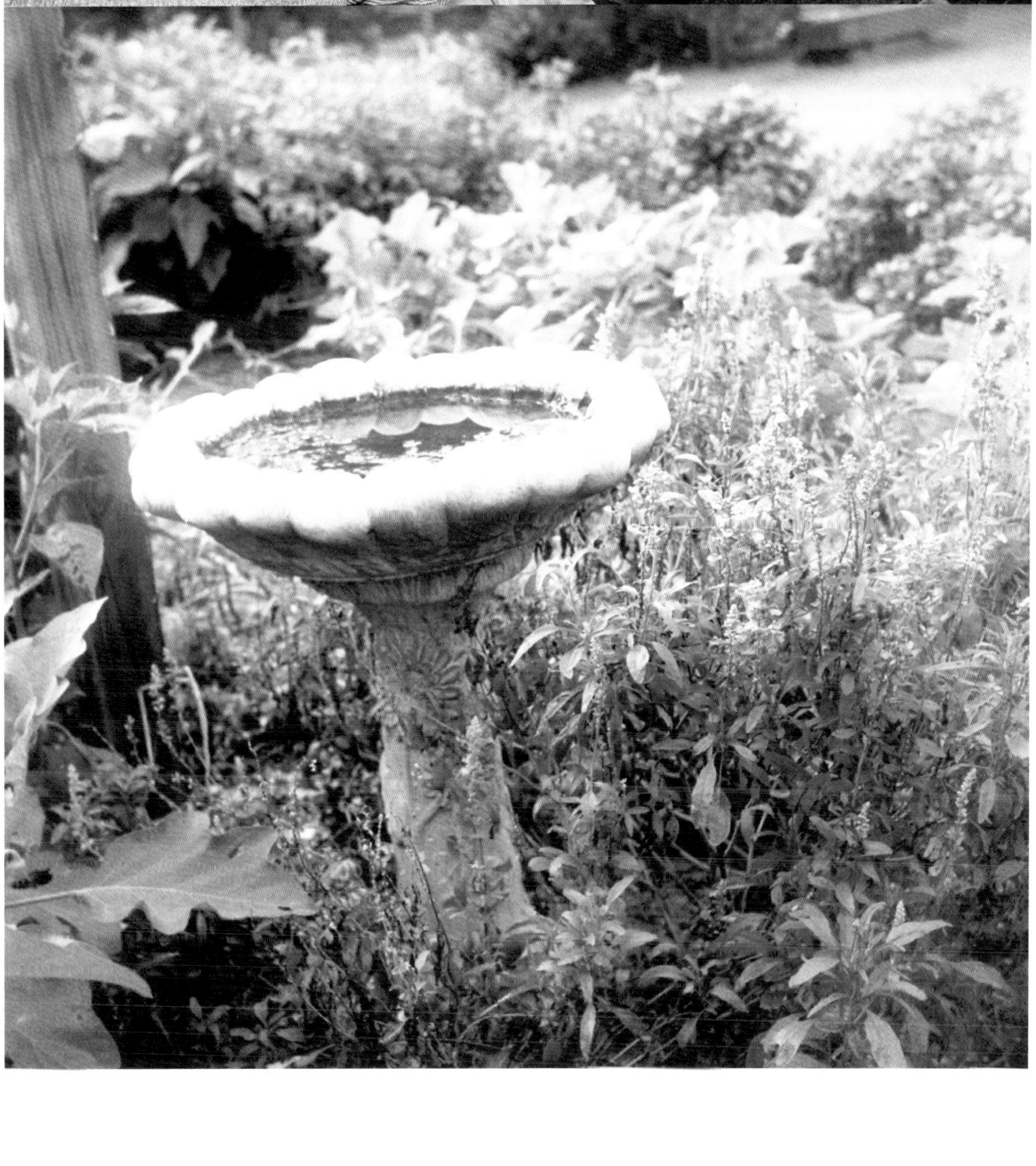

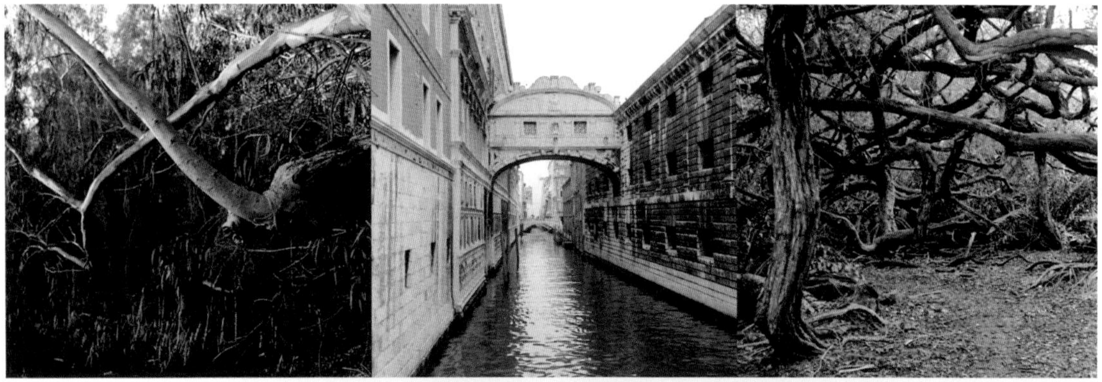

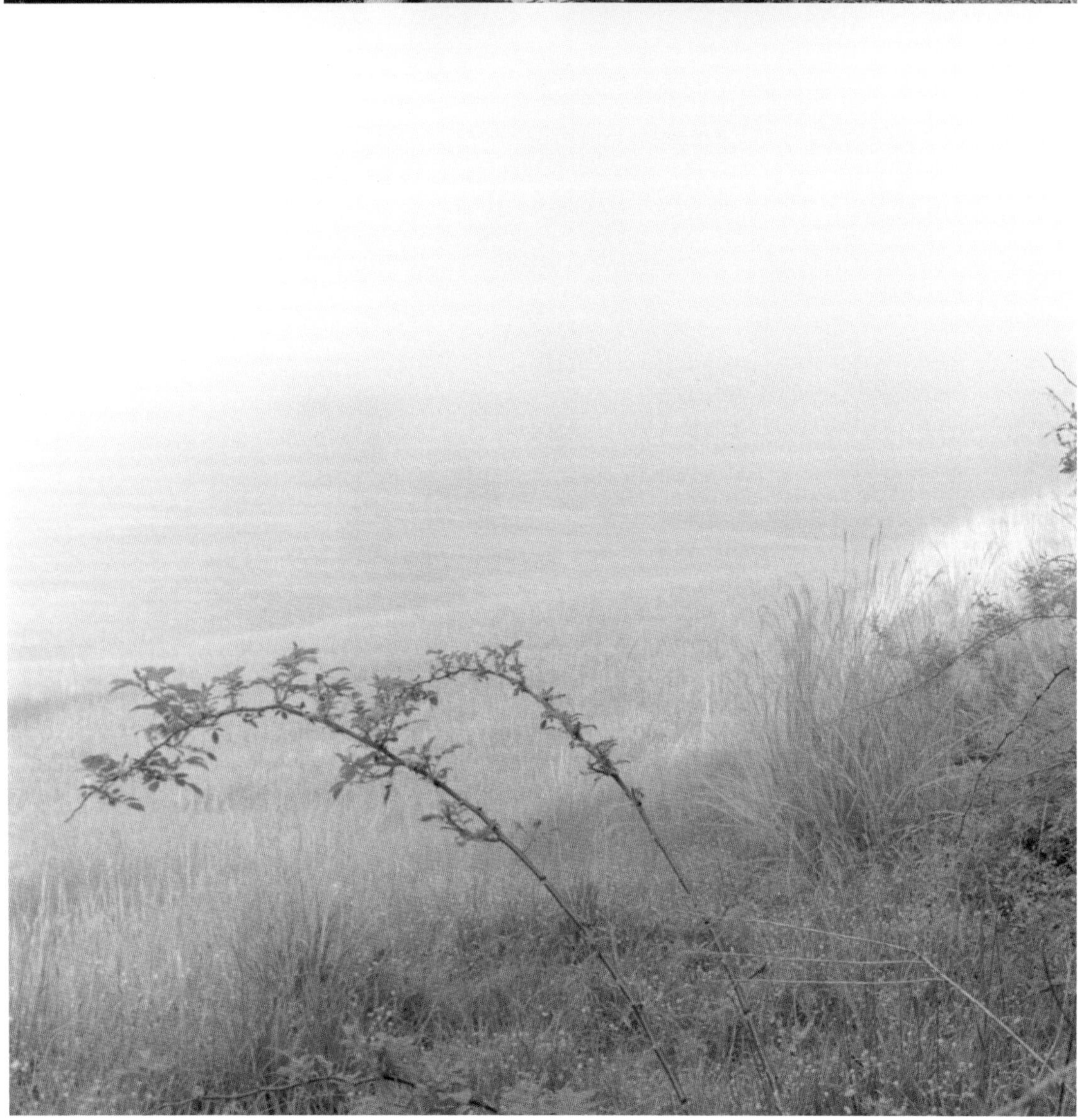

> ***Return Trips***

*Bridge of Sighs*, 1999, inkjet print

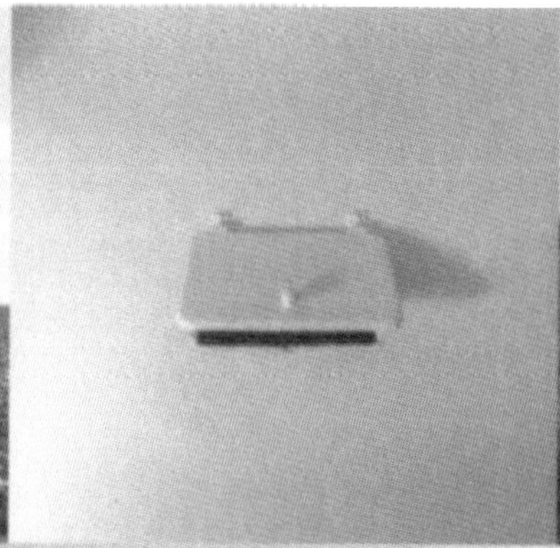

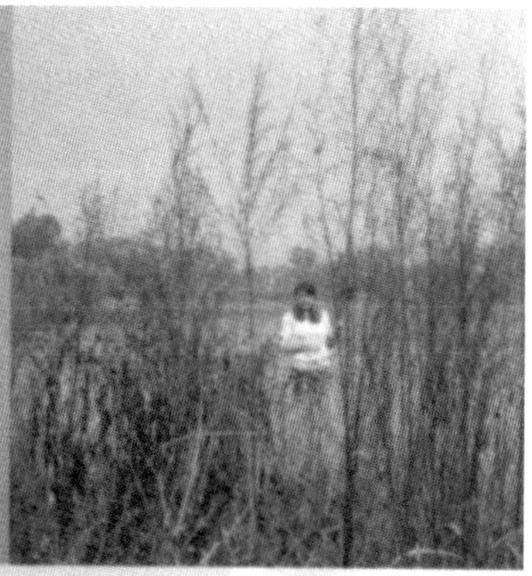

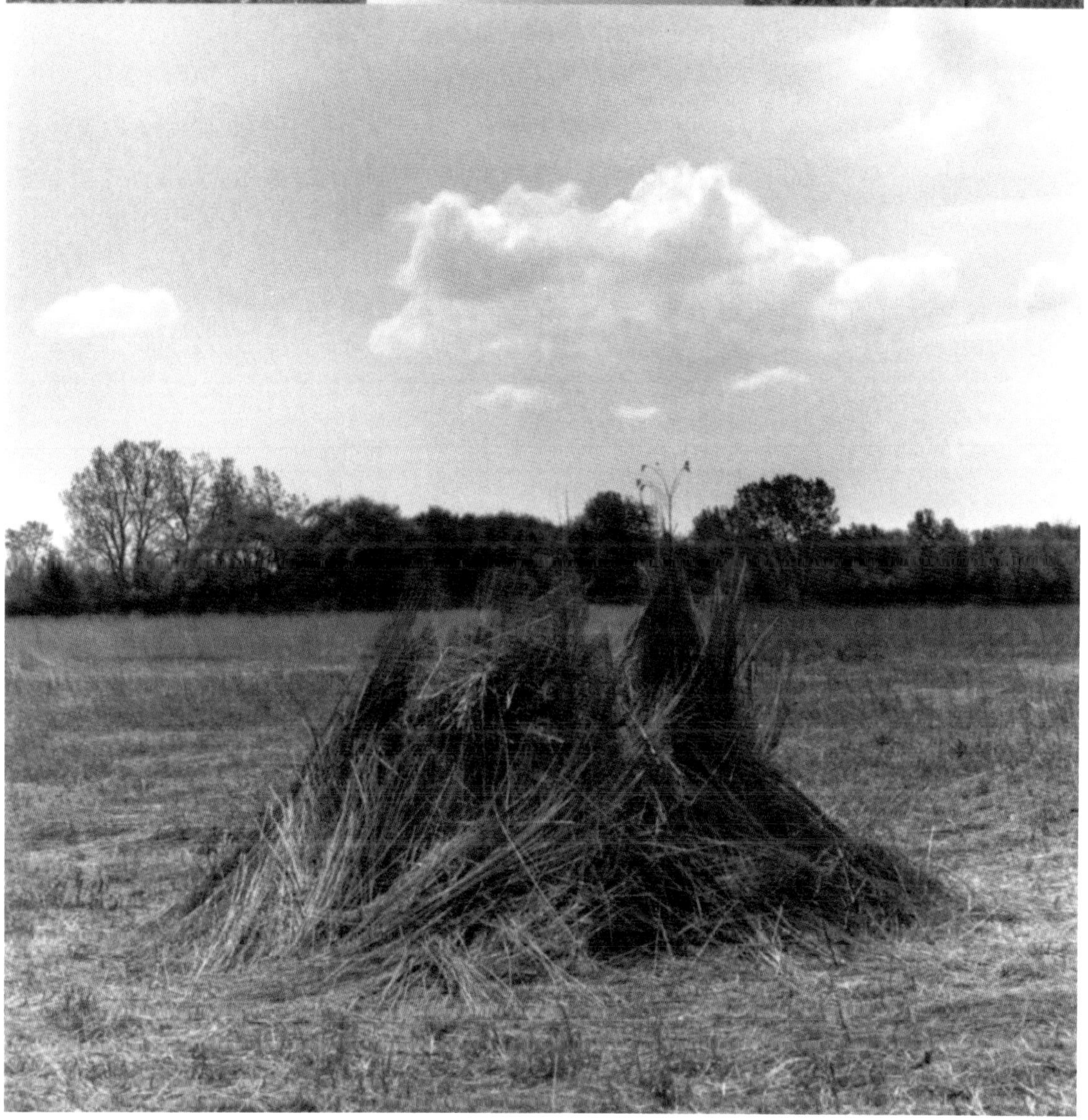

*Prairie Grass*, 1999,
gelatin silver print

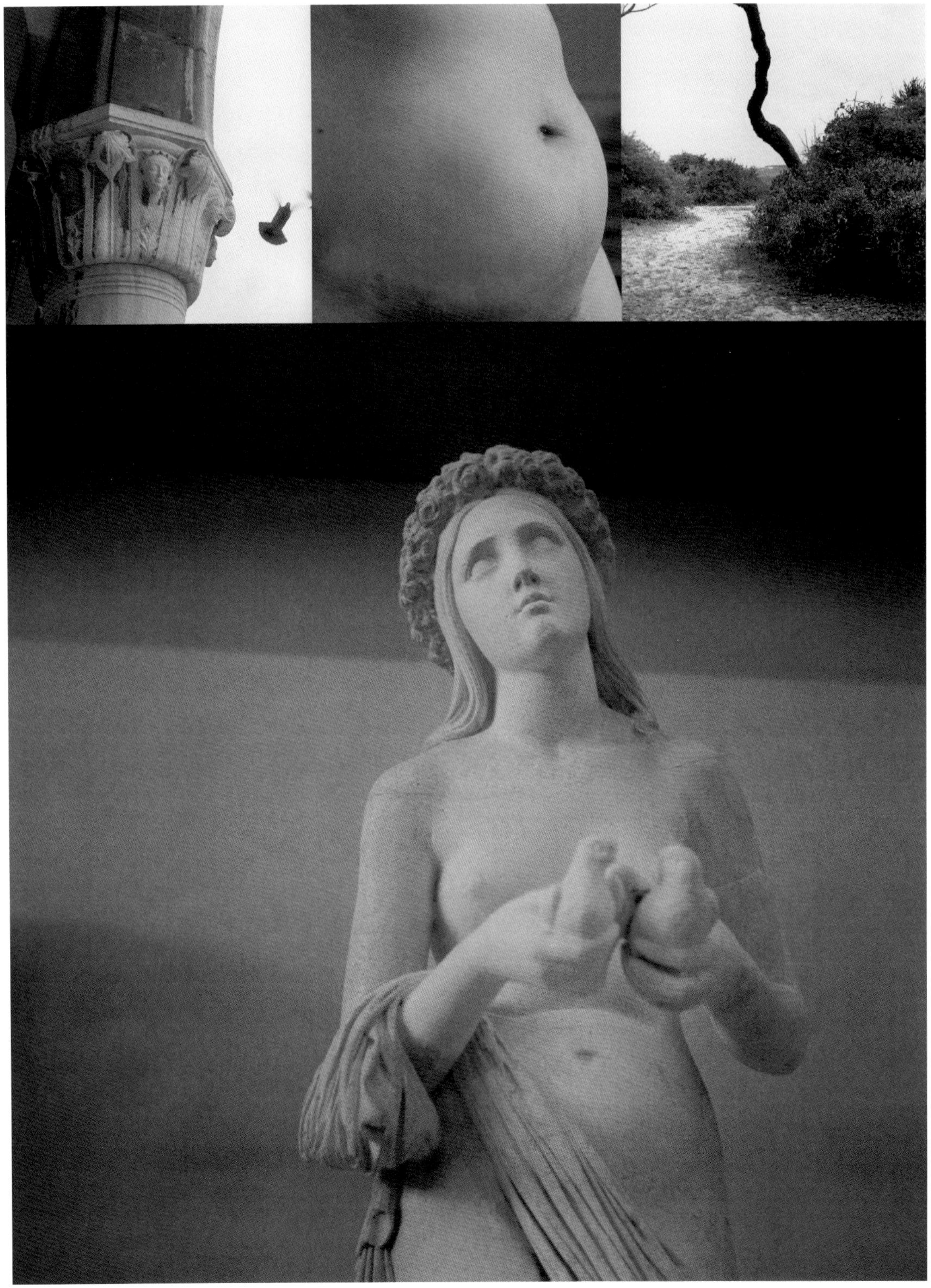

> **_Return Trips_**

*Two Doves*, 1999,
inkjet print

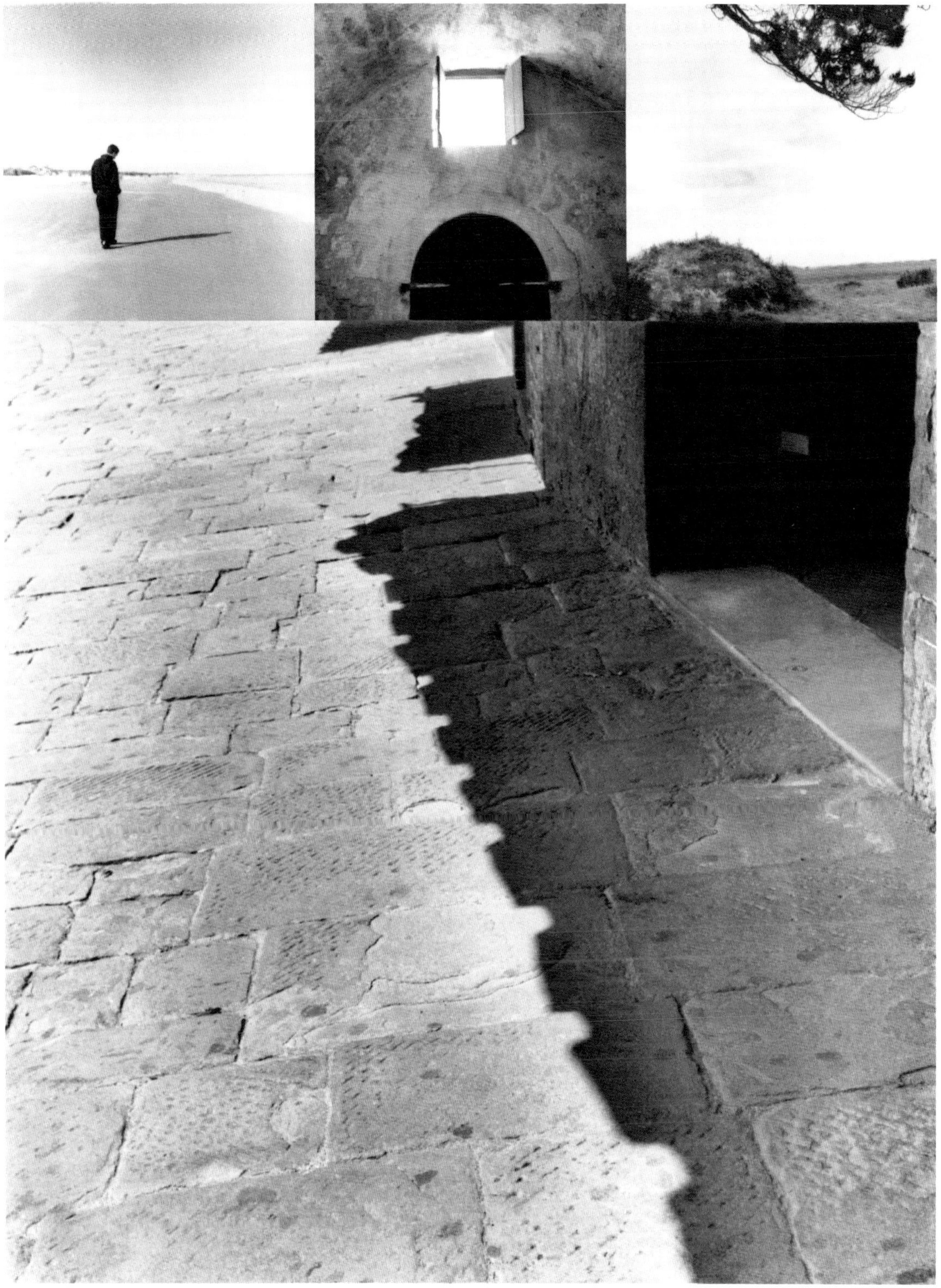

*St. Augustine*, 2000,
inkjet print

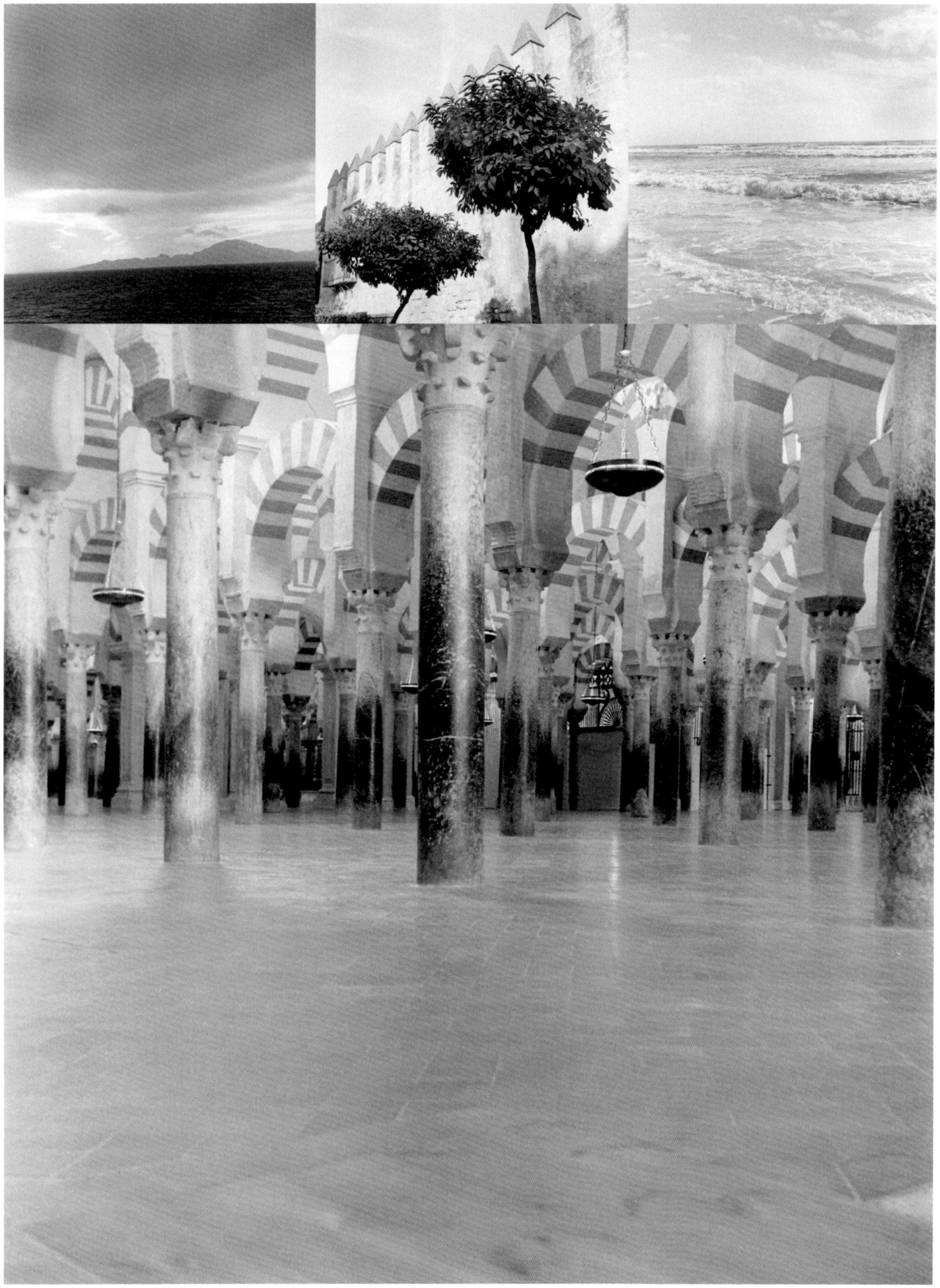

> ***Return Trips***

*Cordoba*, 2000, inkjet print

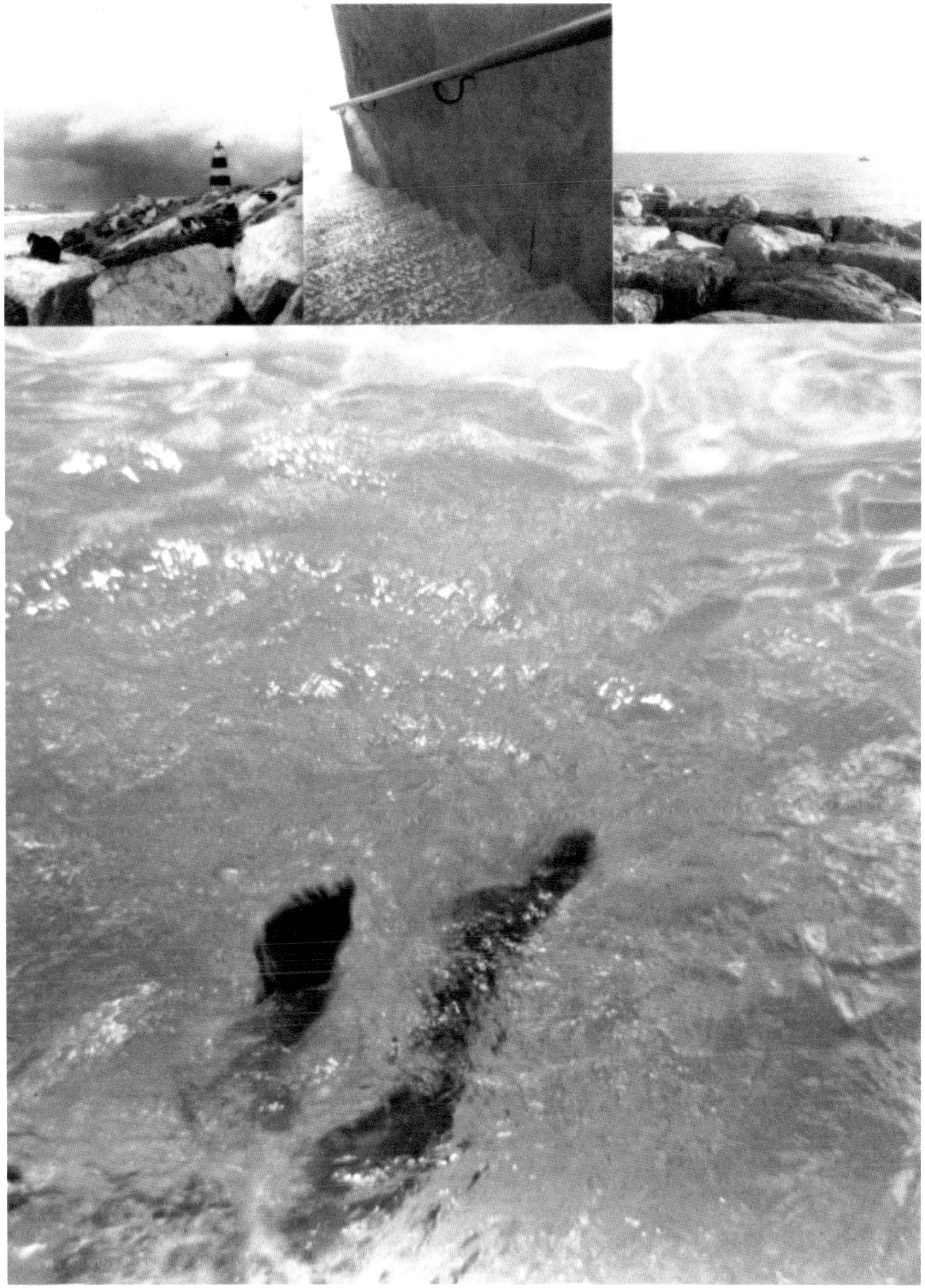

*Light House*, 2001,
gelatin silver print

## The Worn Shell

*See how the tumbling water and the sand*
*Abstracted this from nature into art*
*Into that dream of shape that floats*
*Beyond the sculptor's chisel*

*The tumbling sand and water yes*
*And time*
*Destruction death disintegration*
*Time.*

*Is art then just the consciousness of time*
*And what it does?*
*Not that alone.*

*The special charm of this worn shell*
*Comes from a calm acceptance*
*From a wise rolling with the punches of the tides*
*From a soft settling in the sun*
*And from some gentle flirting*
*With the edges of the waves.*

**GRACE NOBLE NETTLES**
1975

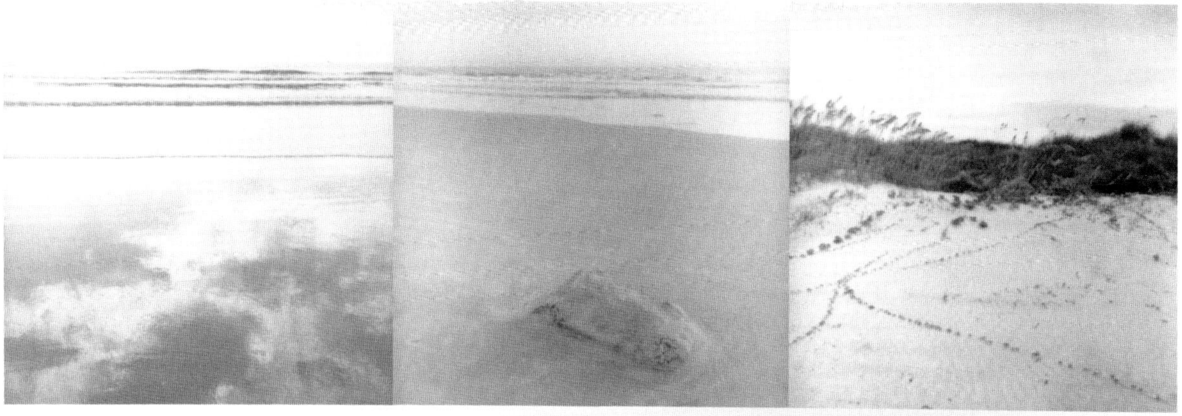

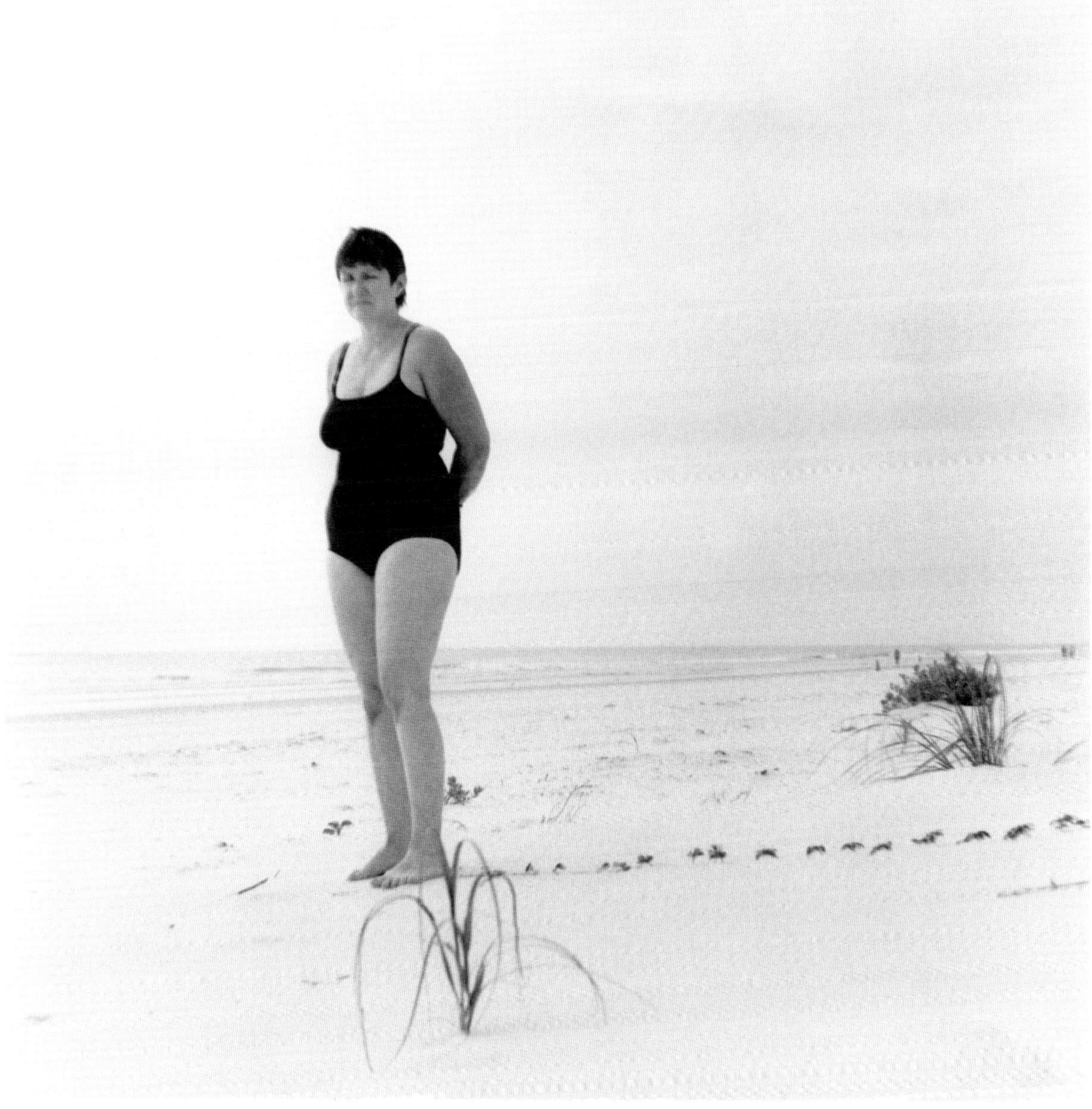

→ ***Return Trips***

*Crescent Beach*, 2002,
inkjet print

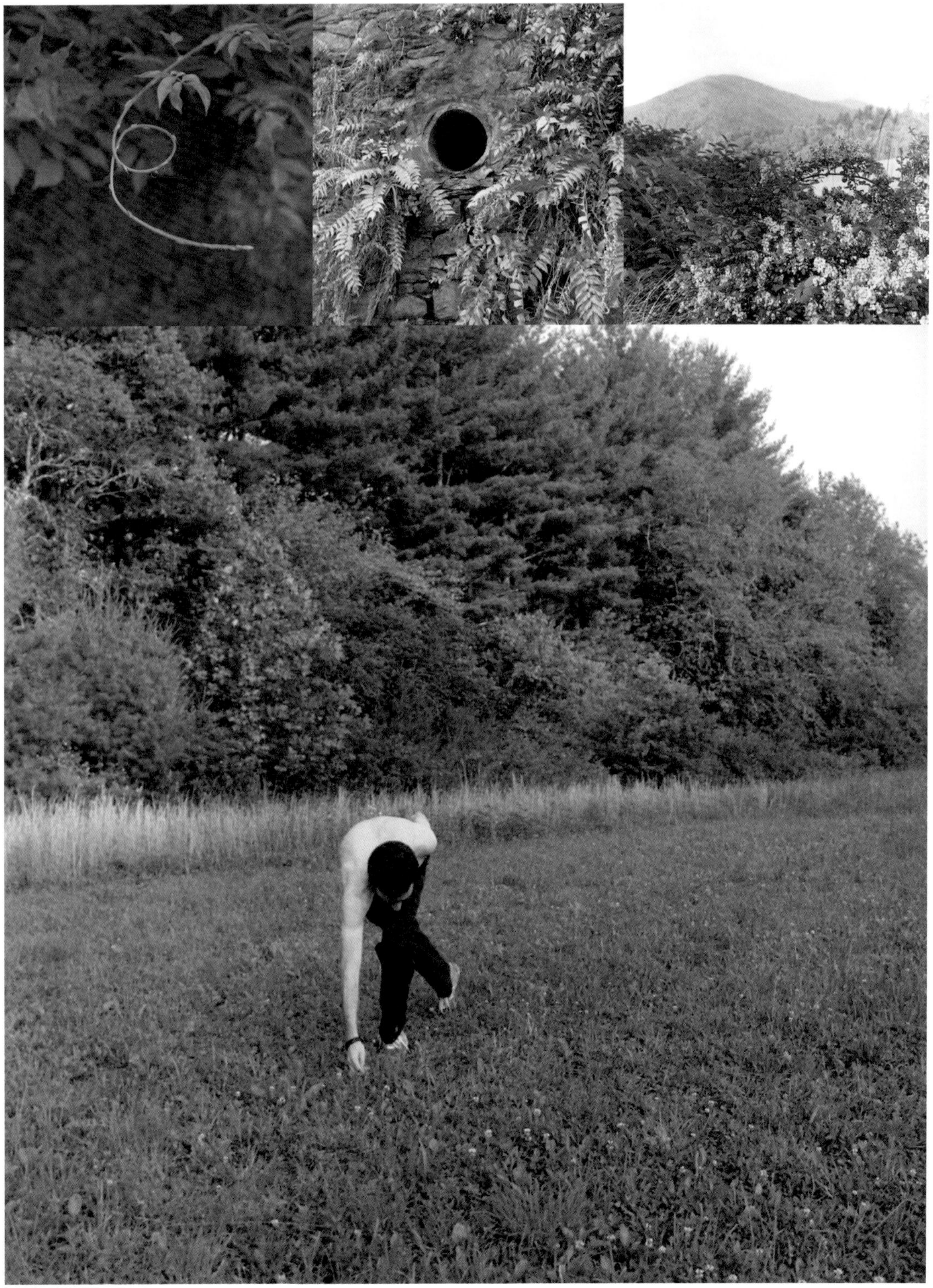

> ***Return Trips***

*Dance*, 2001,
inkjet print

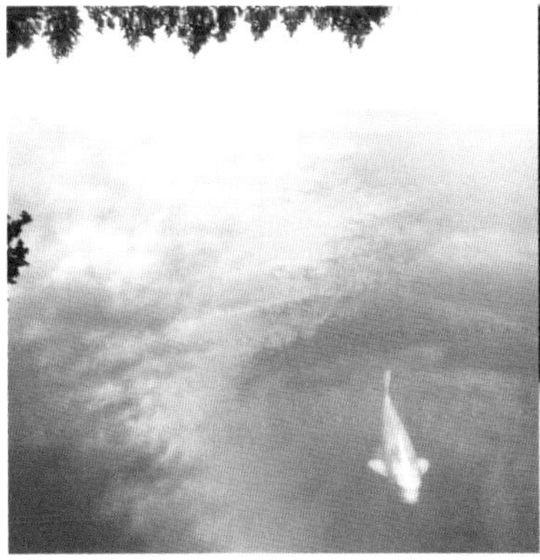

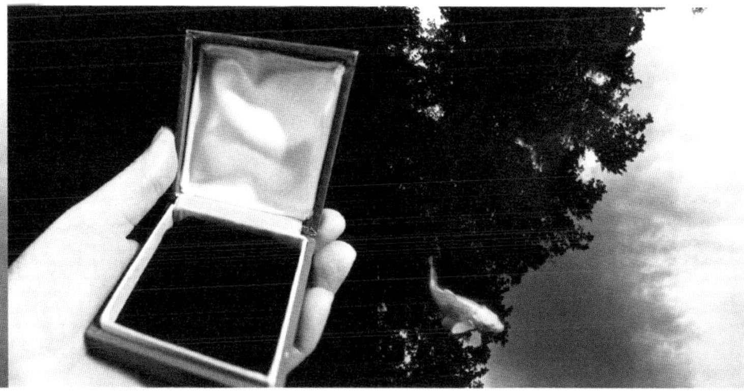

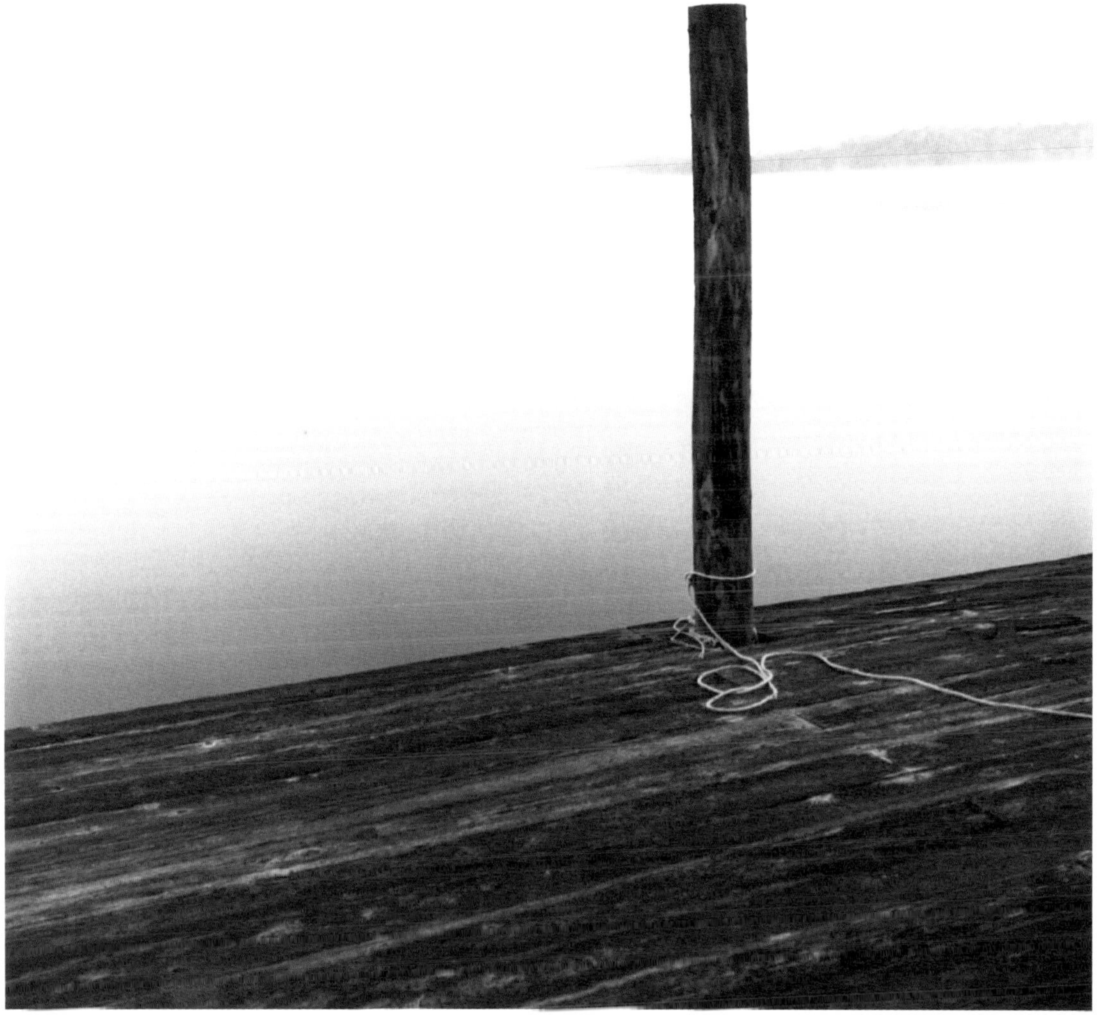

*Goldfish*, 2003, from
inkjet print

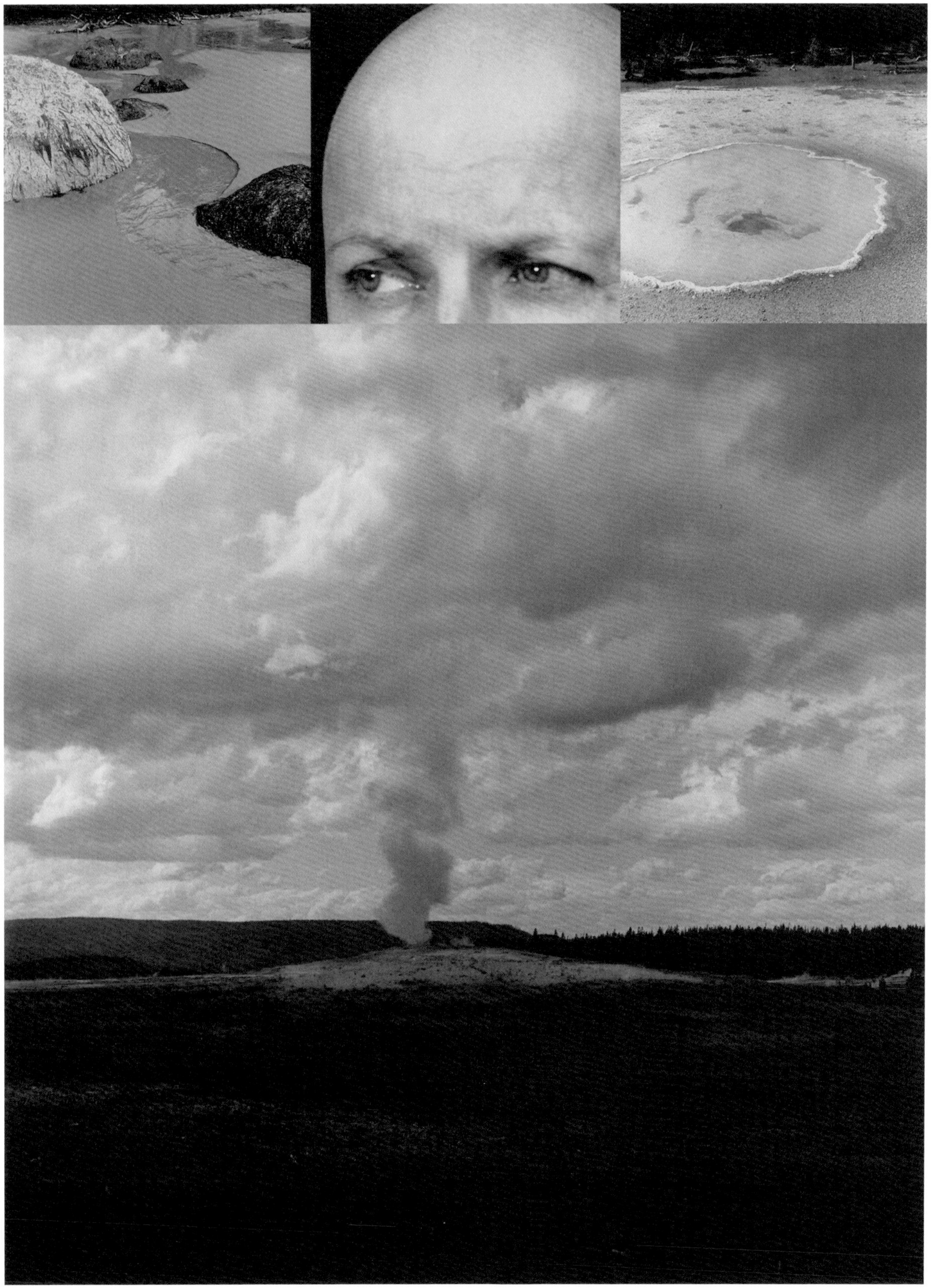

< **Return Trips**

*Hole*, 2005, inkjet print

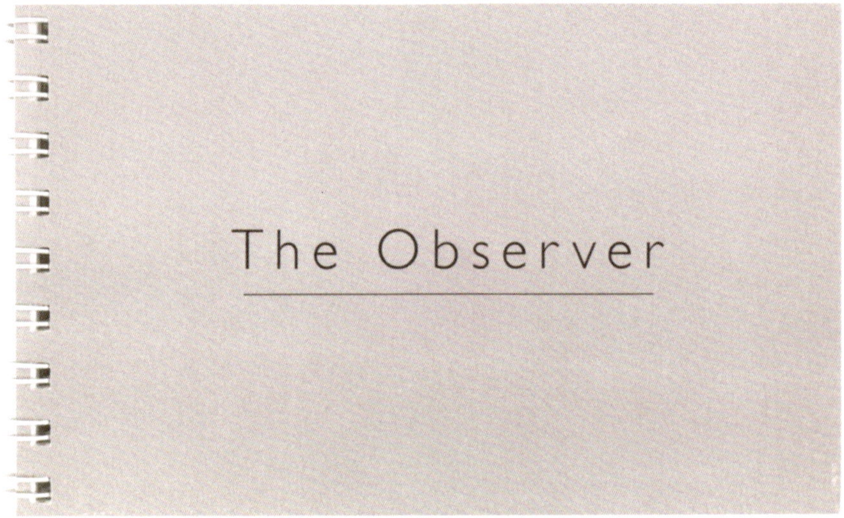


> *The Observer*, 2005, book with offset lithographs

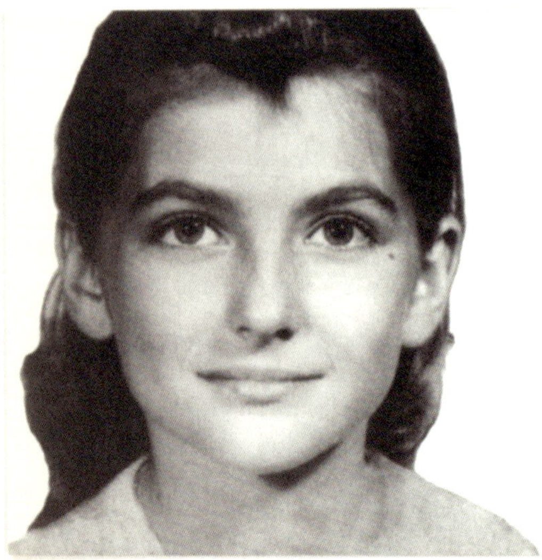

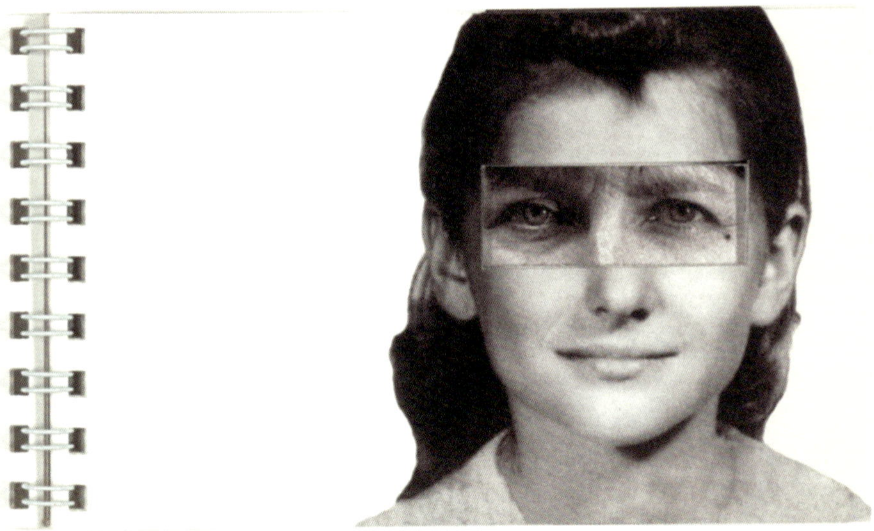

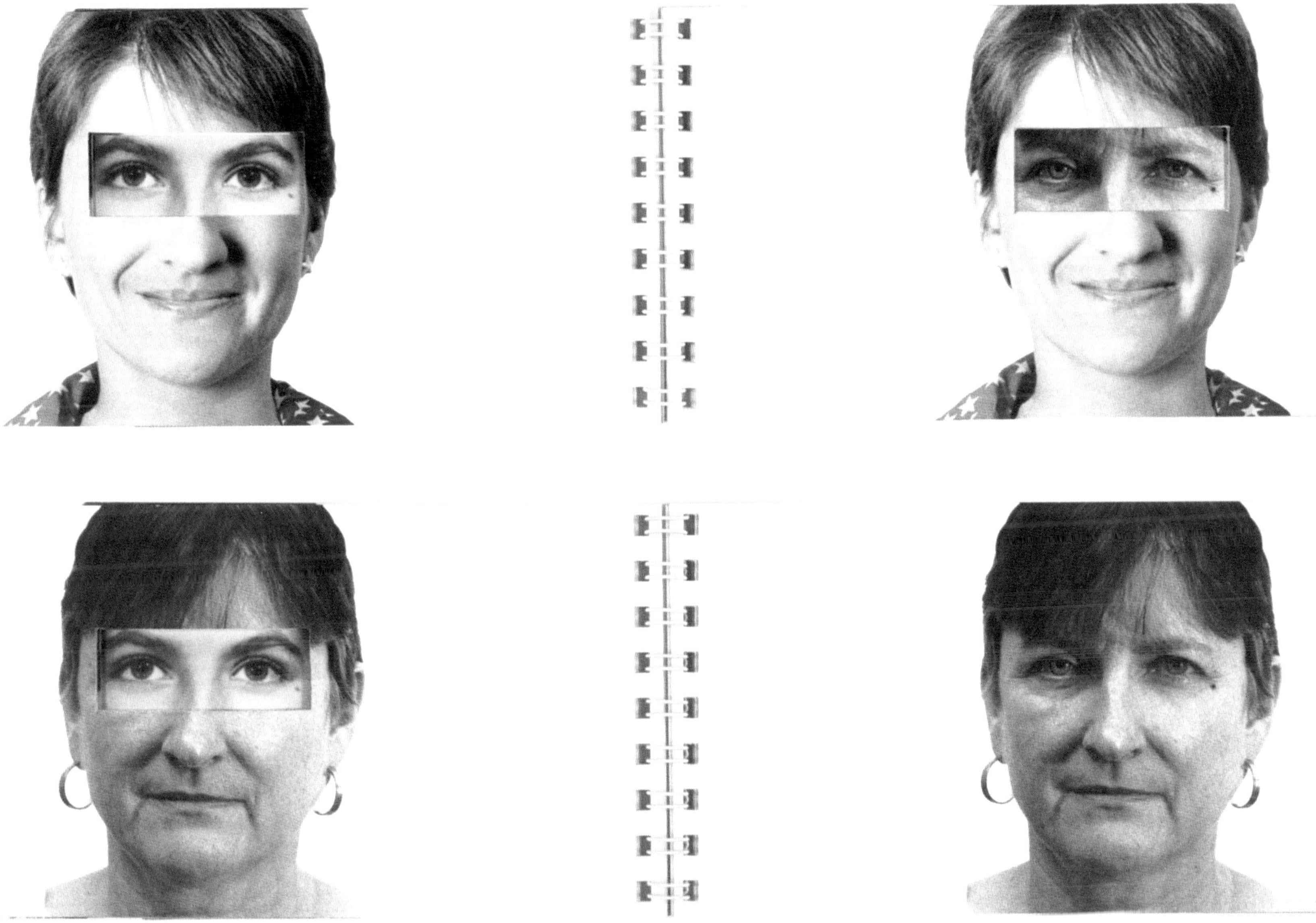

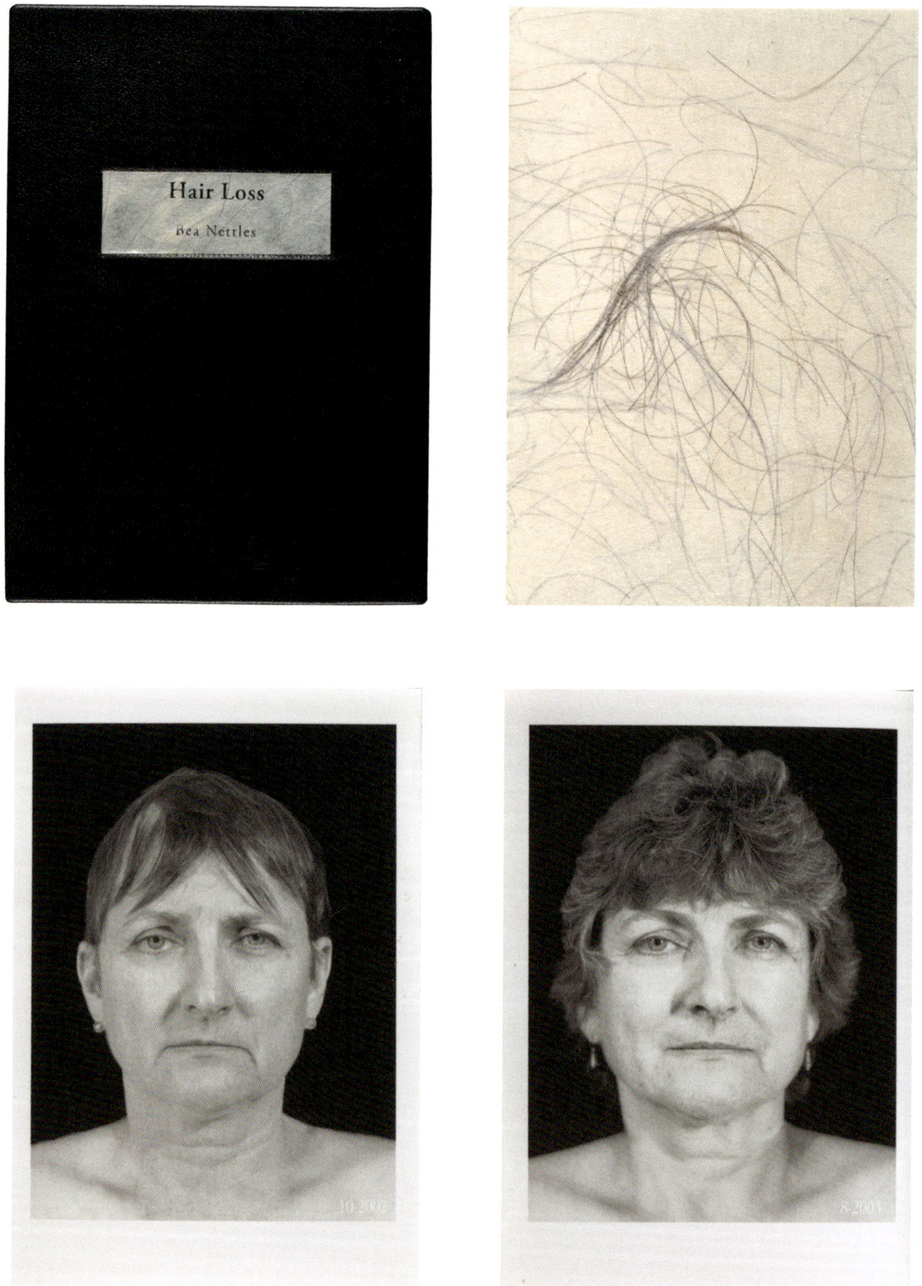


> *Hair Loss*, 2007, book with inkjet prints, leather, and abaca with embedded hair

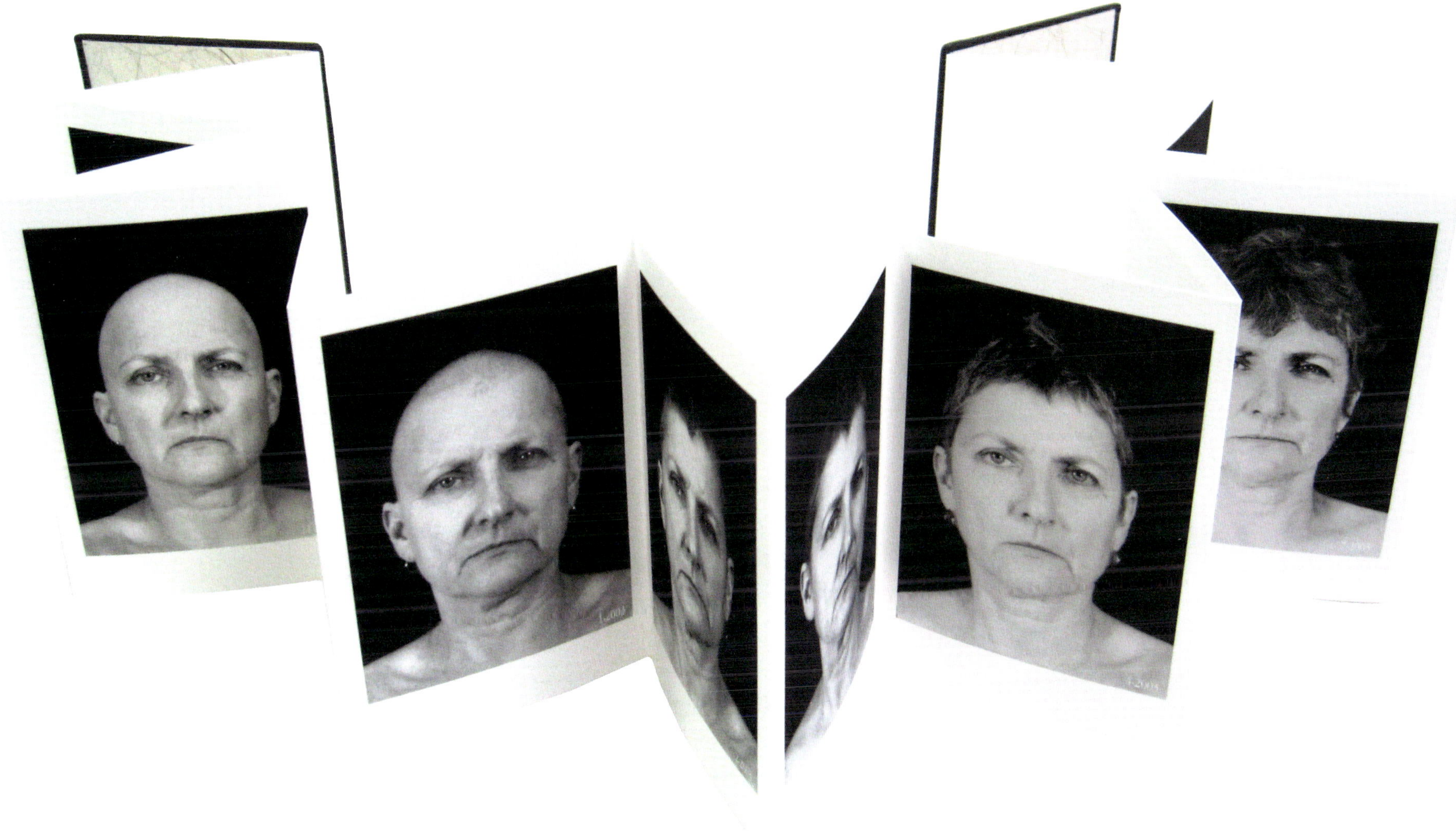

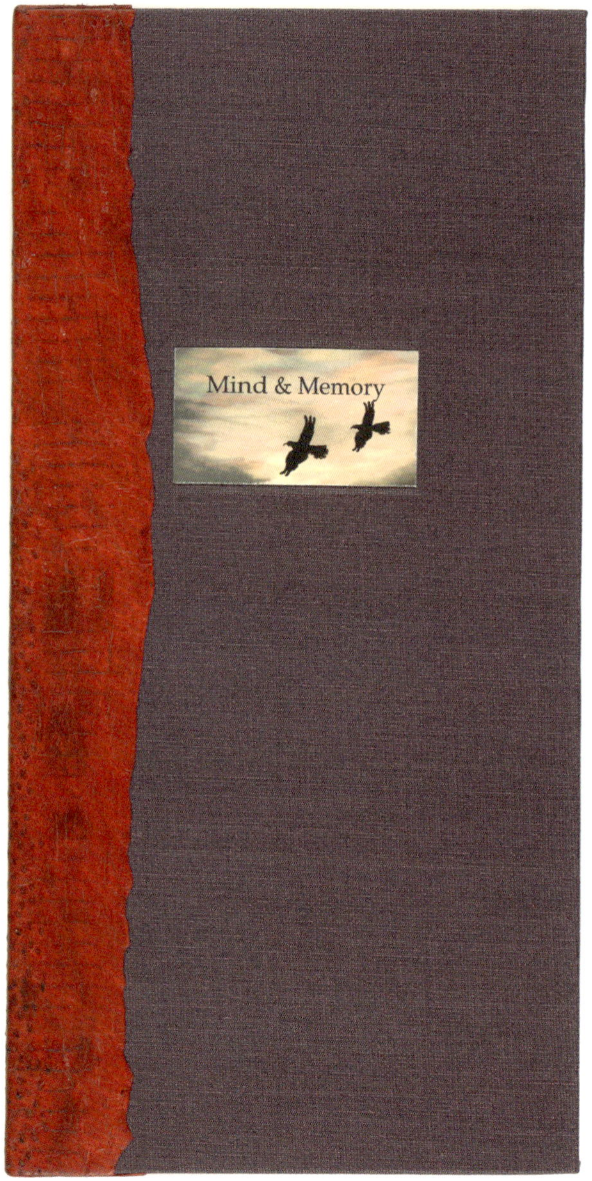


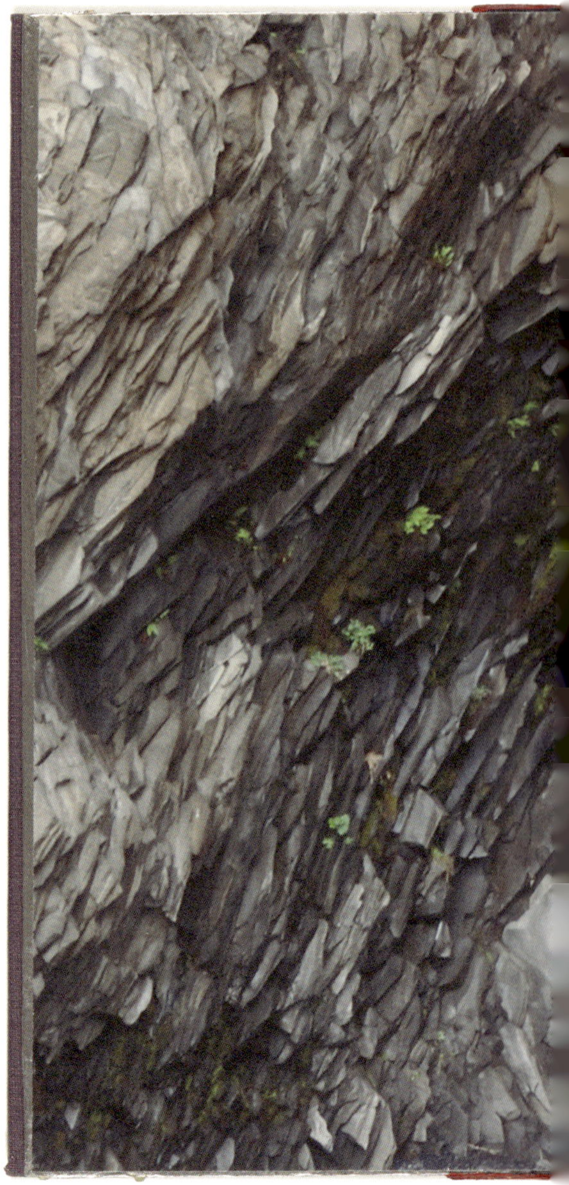

> *Mind & Memory*, 2008, book with Icelandic fish leather spine binding and inkjet prints

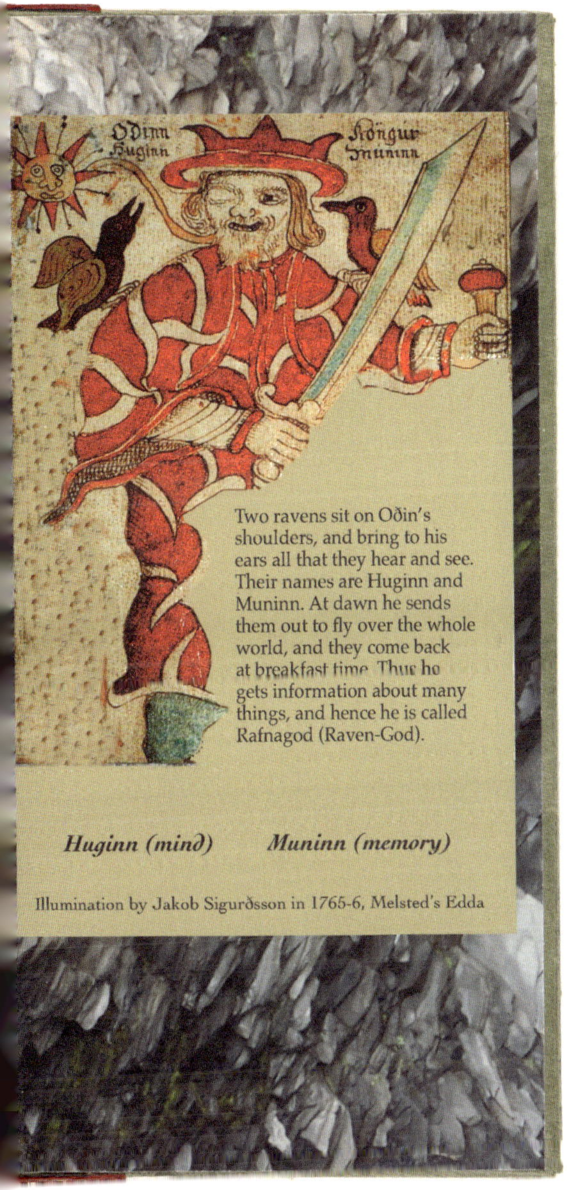
Two ravens sit on Oðin's shoulders, and bring to his ears all that they hear and see. Their names are Huginn and Muninn. At dawn he sends them out to fly over the whole world, and they come back at breakfast time. Thus he gets information about many things, and hence he is called Rafnagod (Raven-God).
Huginn (mind)
Muninn (memory)
Illumination by Jakob Sigurðsson in 1765-6, Melsted's Edda

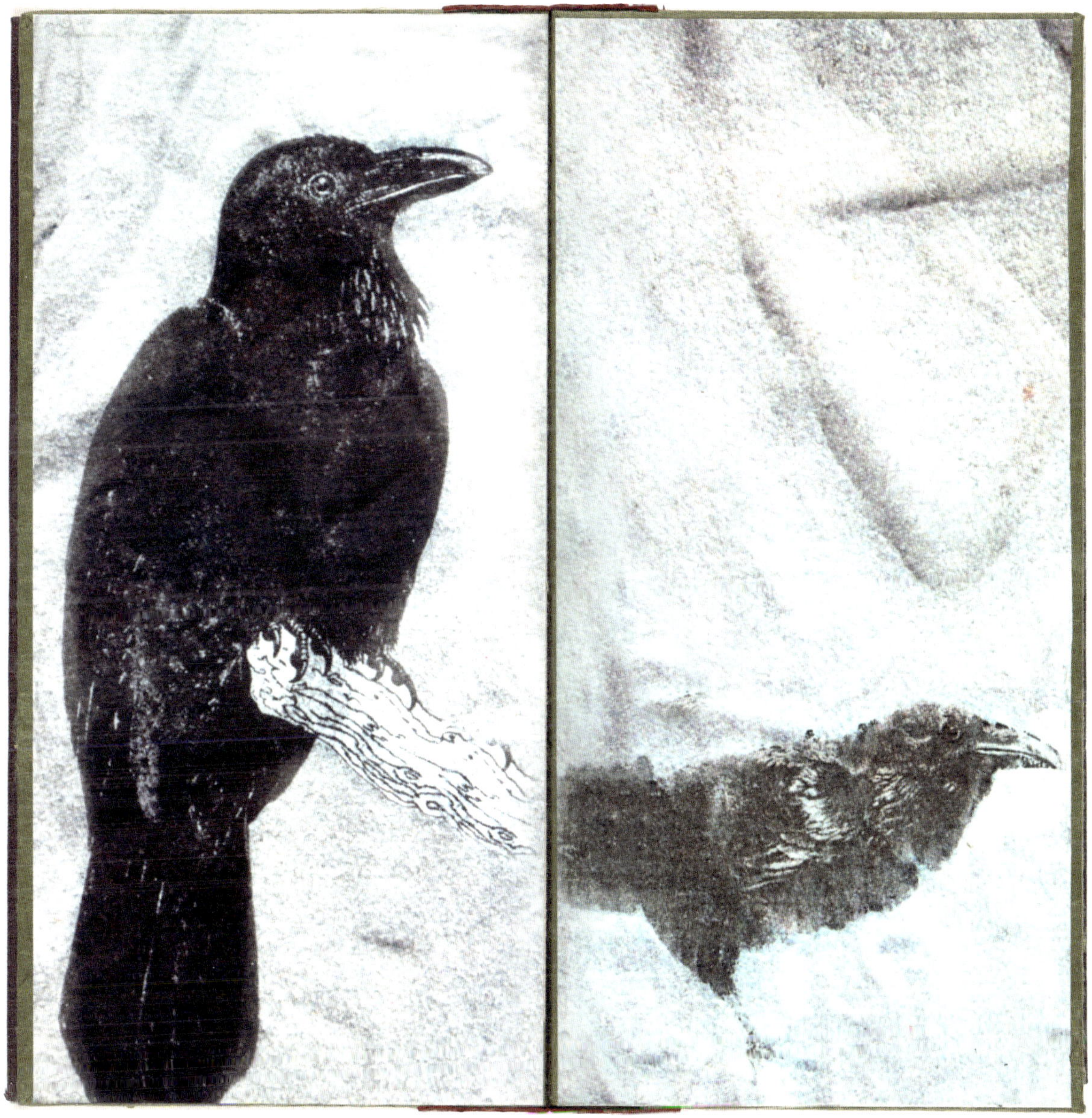

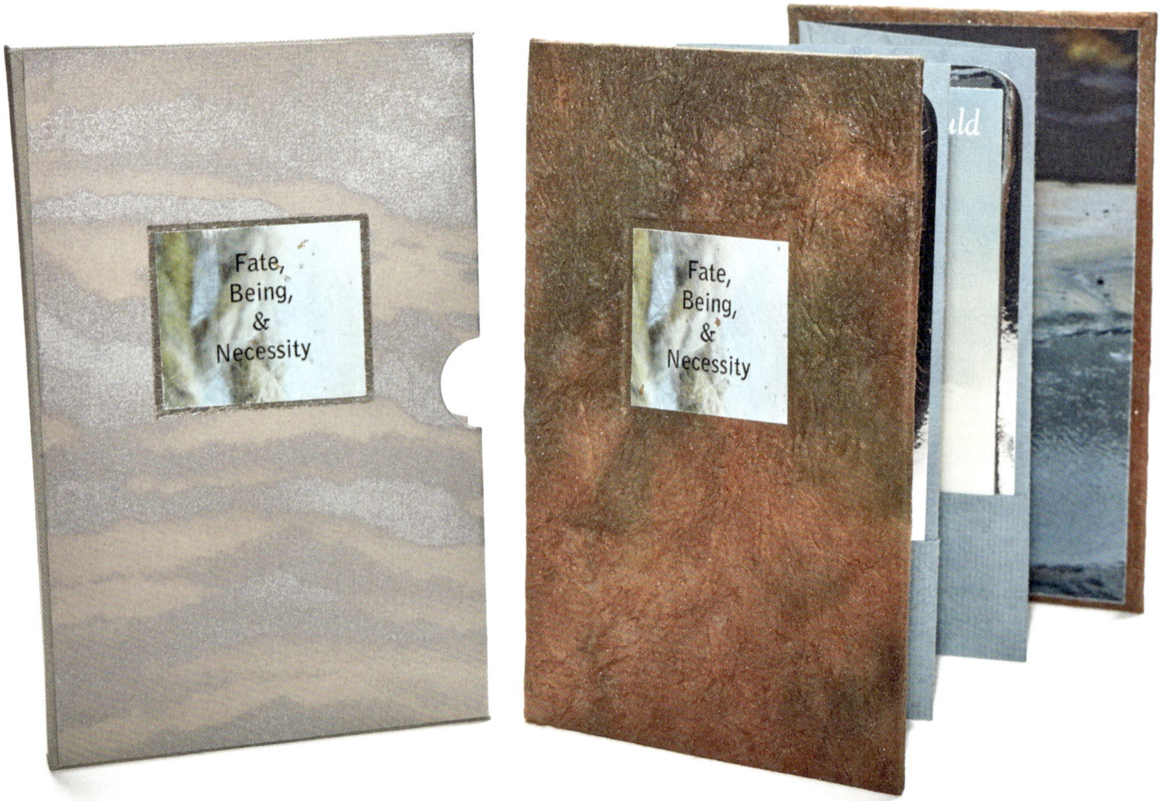


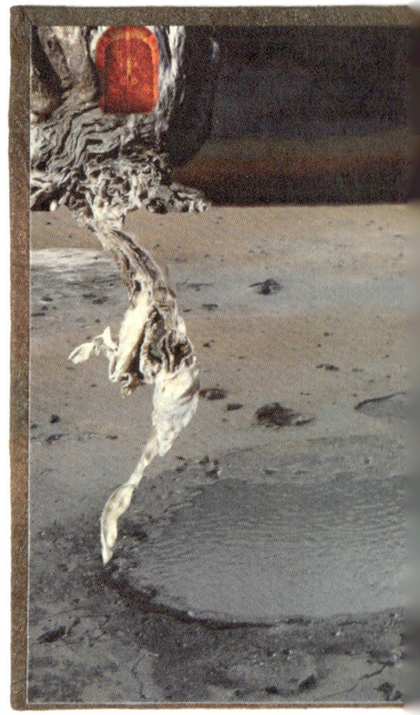

> *Fate, Being, & Necessity*,
2008, book with inkjet prints

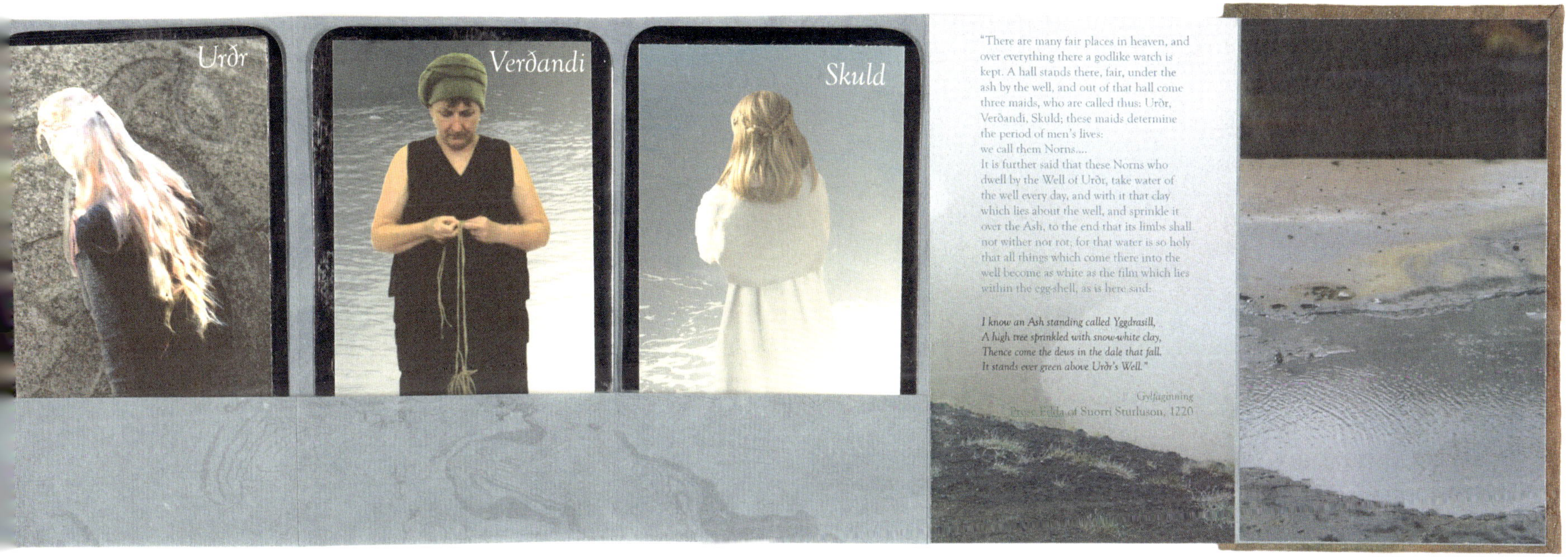
Urðr
Verðandi
Skuld
"There are many fair places in heaven, and over everything there a godlike watch is kept. A hall stands there, fair, under the ash by the well, and out of that hall come three maids, who are called thus: Urðr, Verðandi, Skuld; these maids determine the period of men's lives:
we call them Norns....
It is further said that these Norns who dwell by the Well of Urðr, take water of the well every day, and with it that clay which lies about the well, and sprinkle it over the Ash, to the end that its limbs shall not wither nor rot; for that water is so holy that all things which come there into the well become as white as the film which lies within the egg-shell, as is here said:
I know an Ash standing called Yggdrasill,
A high tree sprinkled with snow-white clay,
Thence come the dews in the dale that fall.
It stands ever green above Urðr's Well."
Gylfaginning
Prose Edda of Snorri Sturluson, 1220

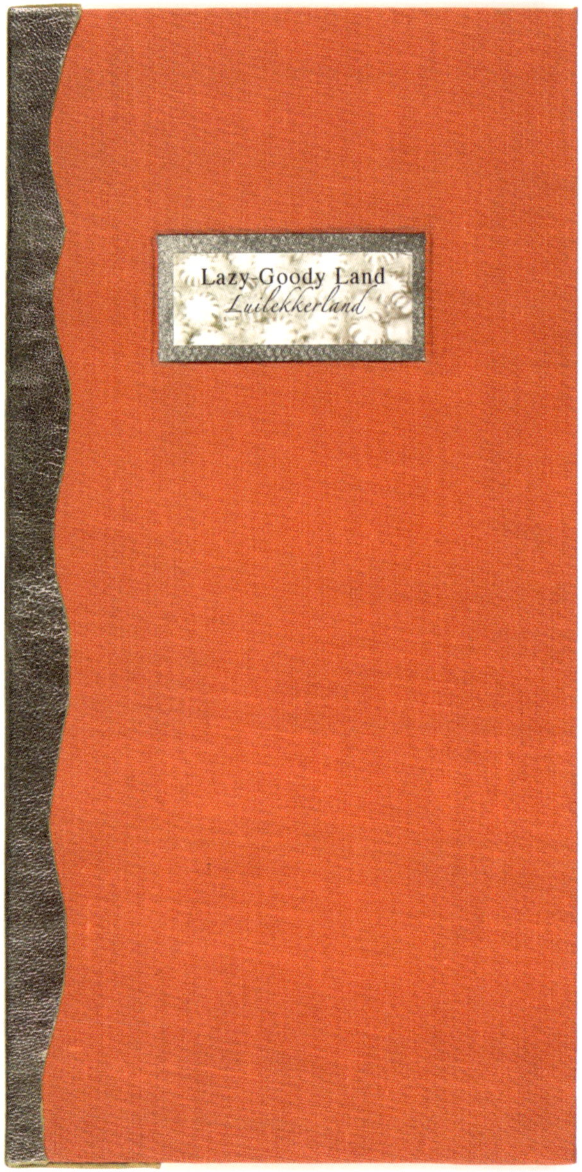


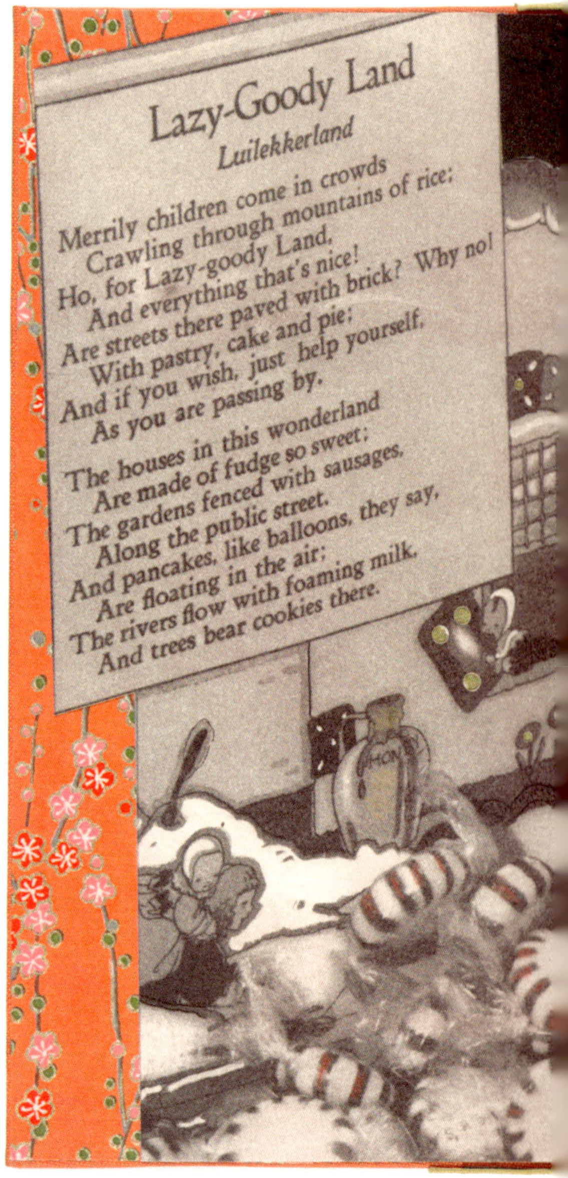


> *Lazy Goody Land / Luilekkerland*, 2008, book with photographic etching collages

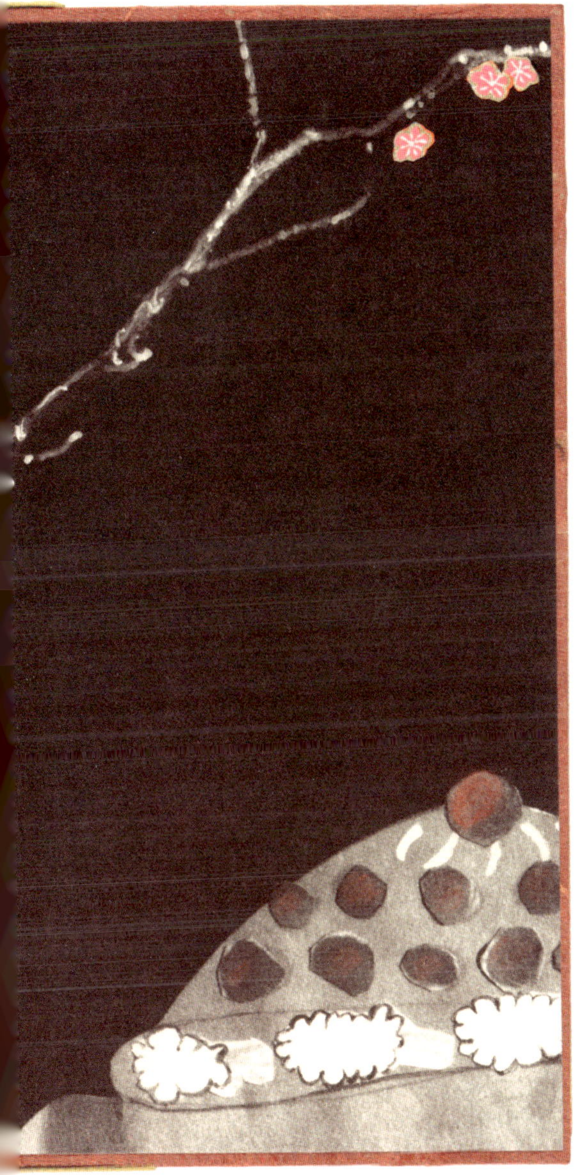

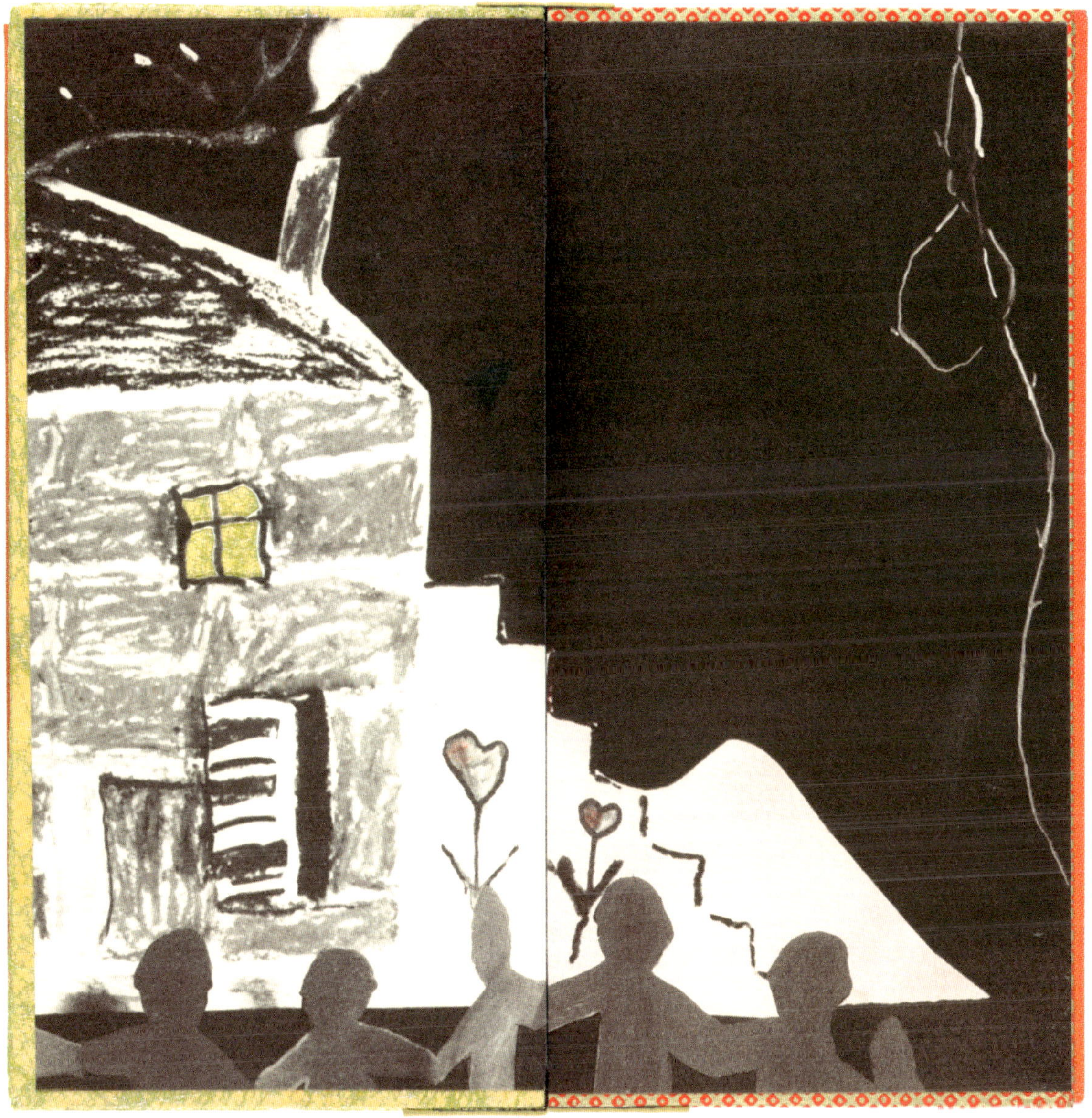

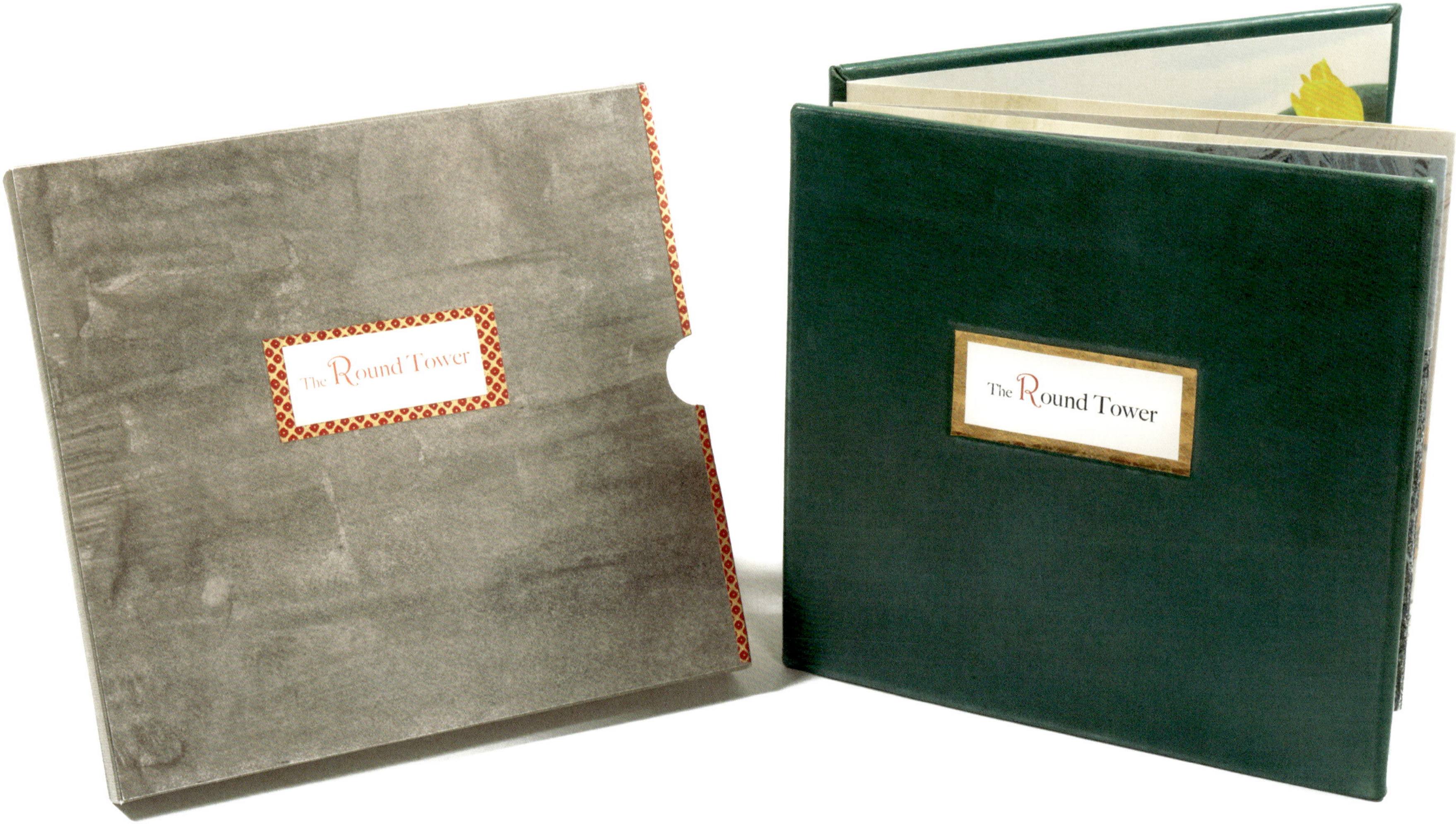


> *The Round Tower*, 2010, leather-bound accordion book with paste papers, digital photographs, decorative papers, and slipcase

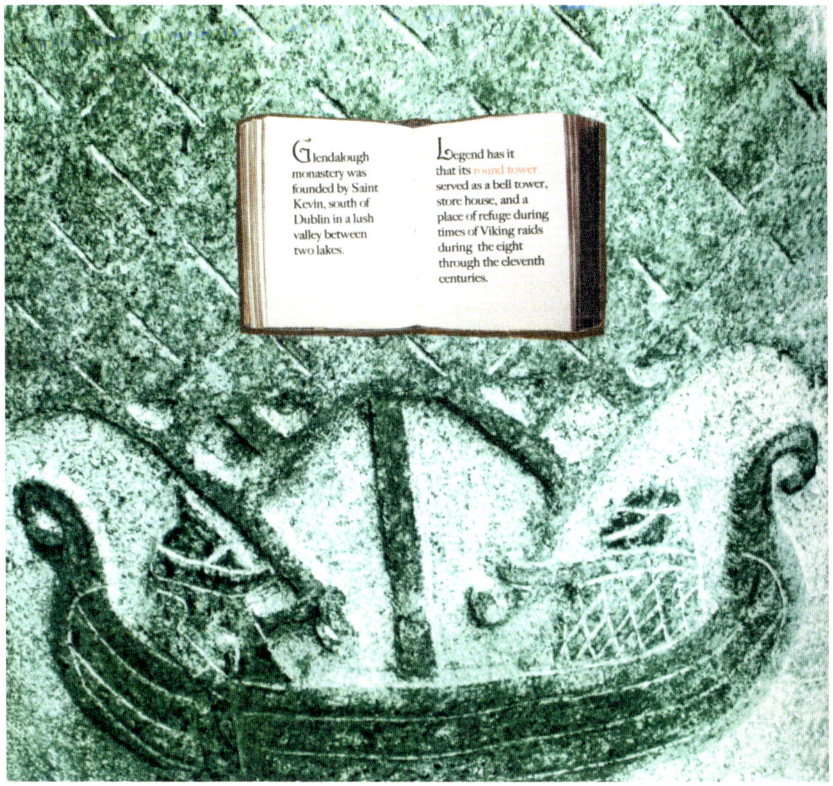
Glendalough monastery was founded by Saint Kevin, south of Dublin in a lush valley between two lakes.
Legend has it that its round tower served as a bell tower, store house, and a place of refuge during times of Viking raids during the eight through the eleventh centuries.

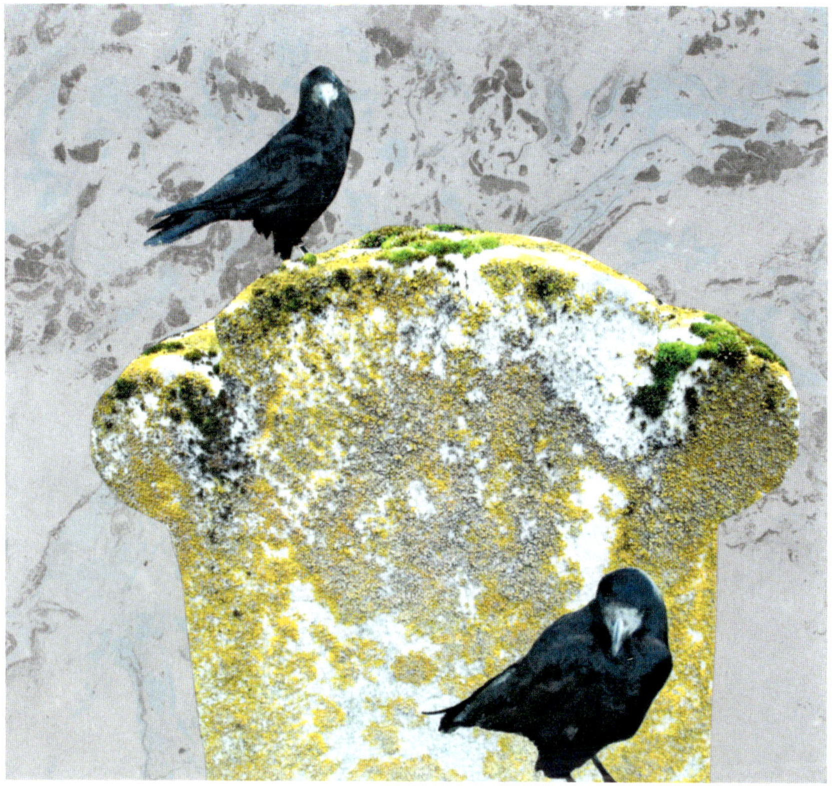

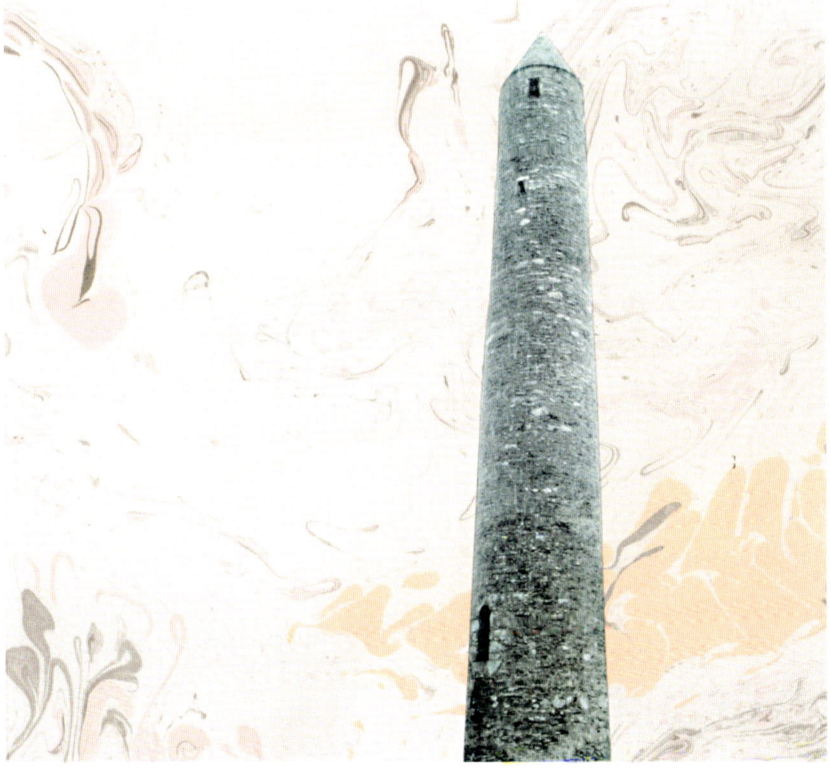

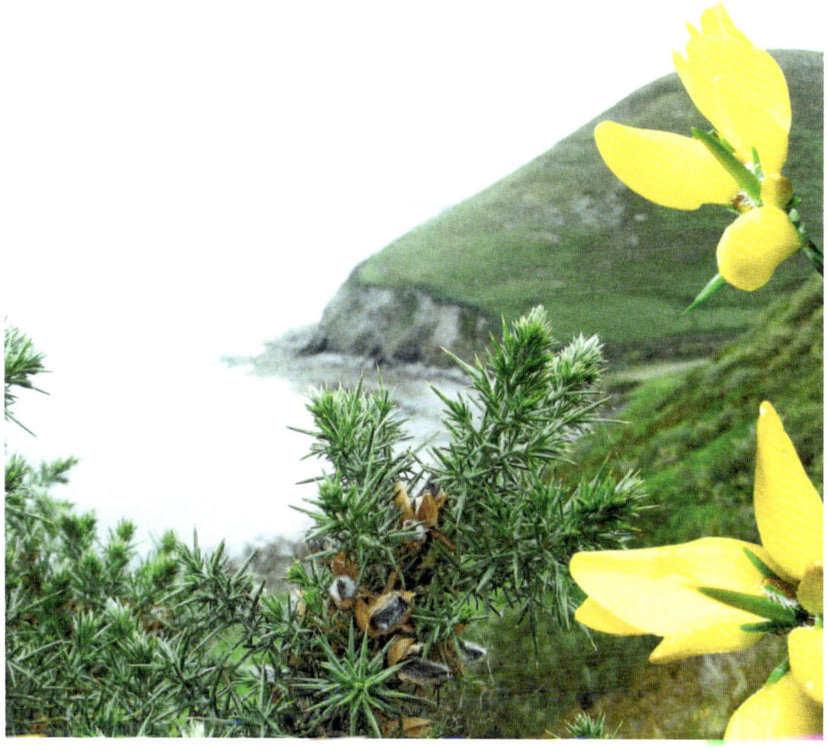

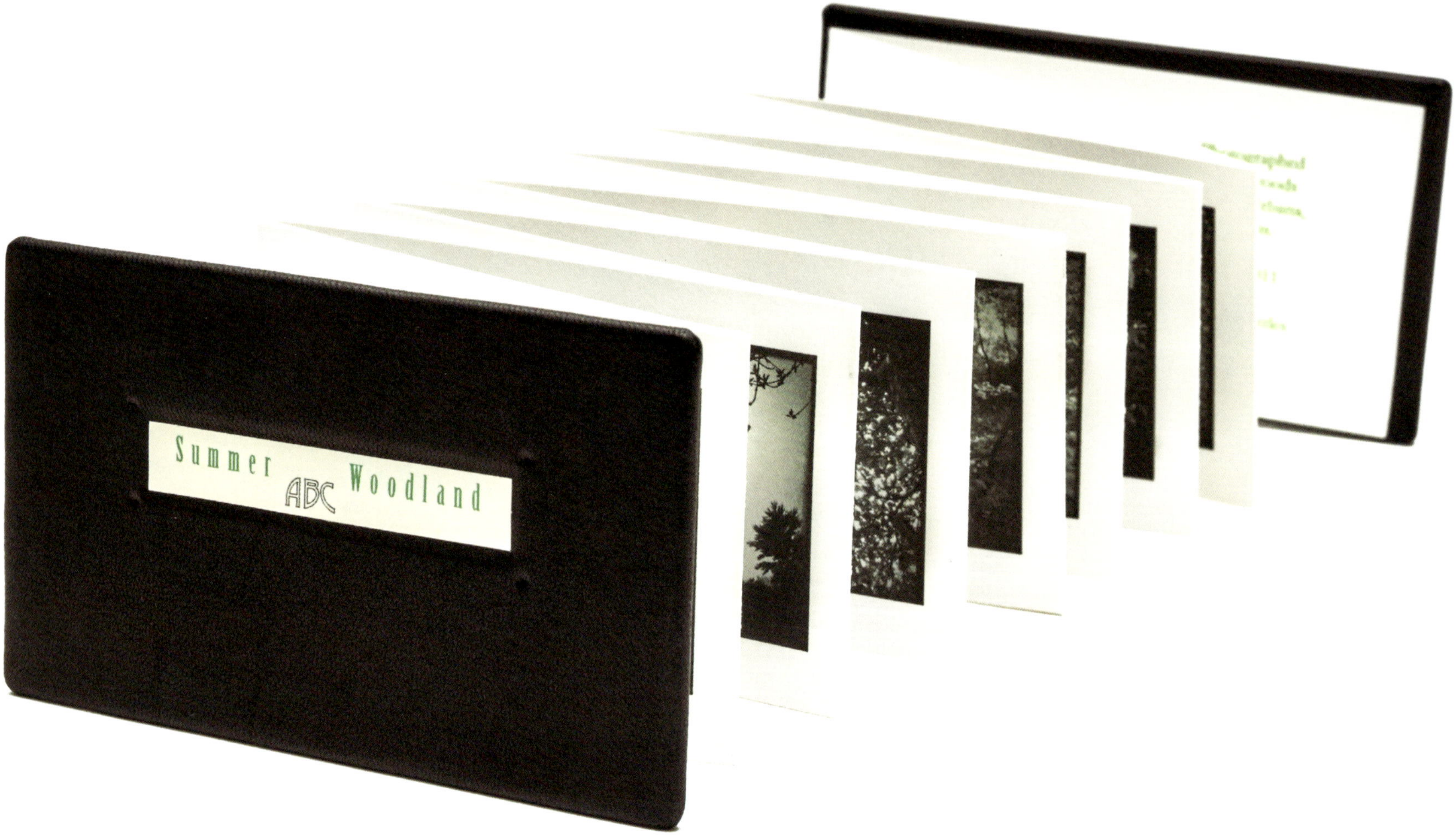


> *Summer Woodland ABC*, 2011, book with inkjet prints and leather covers

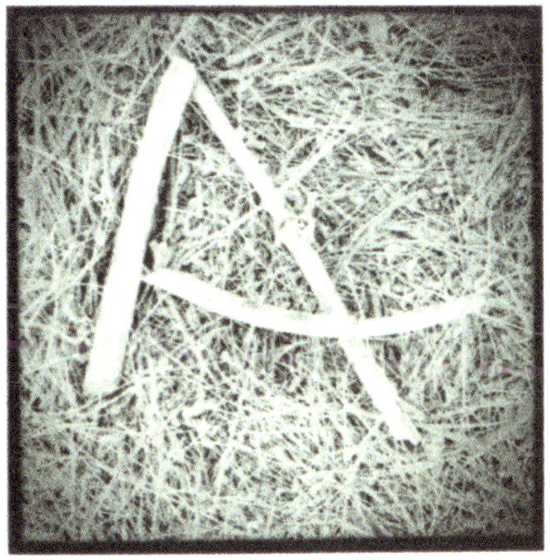
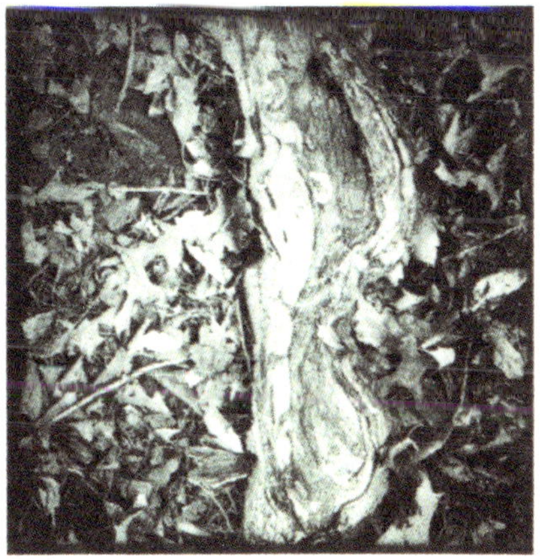
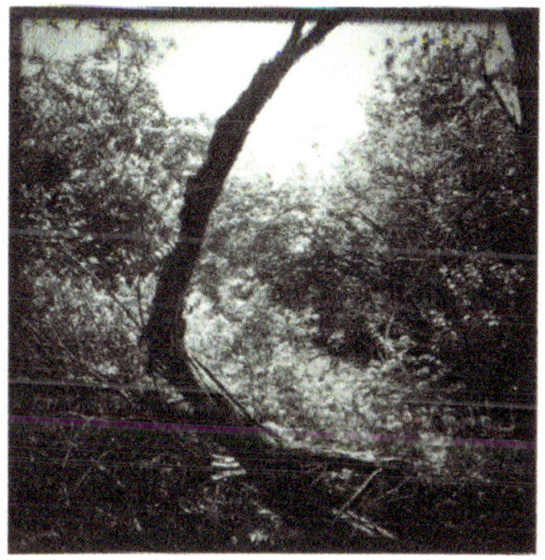
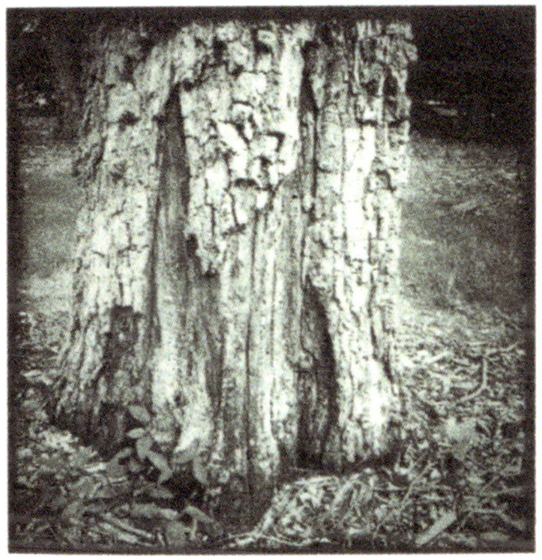
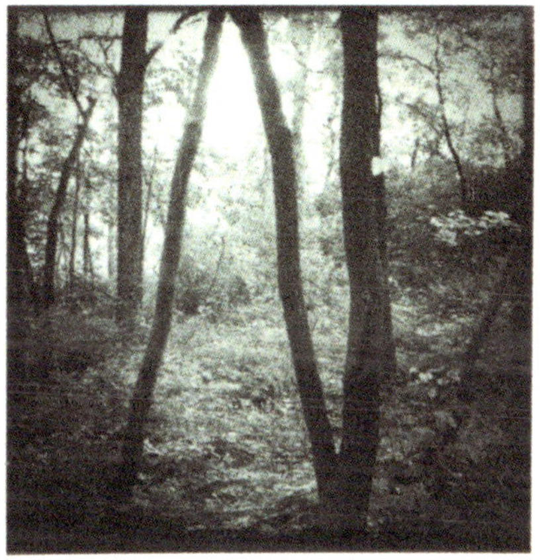
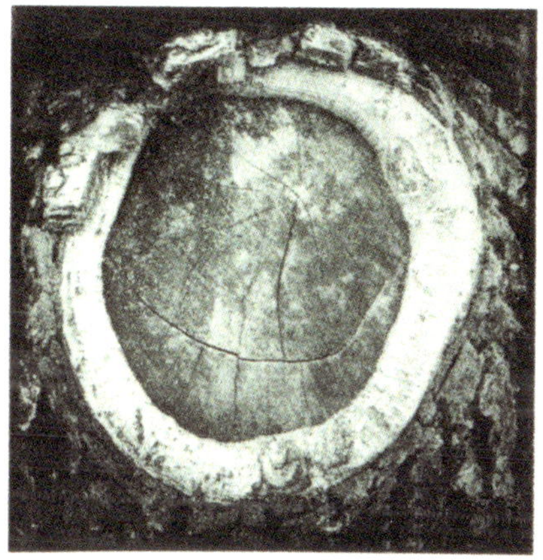
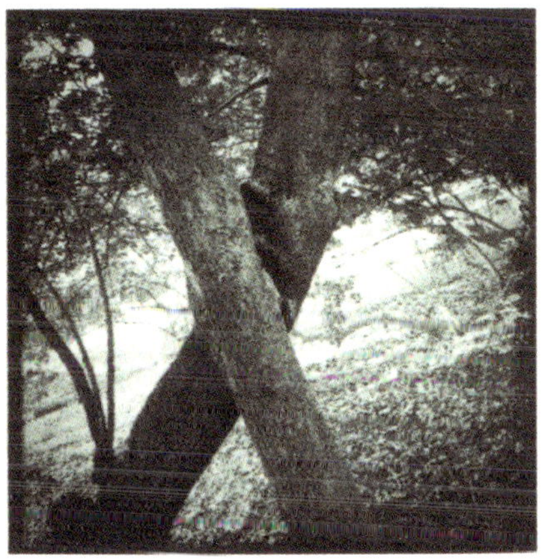
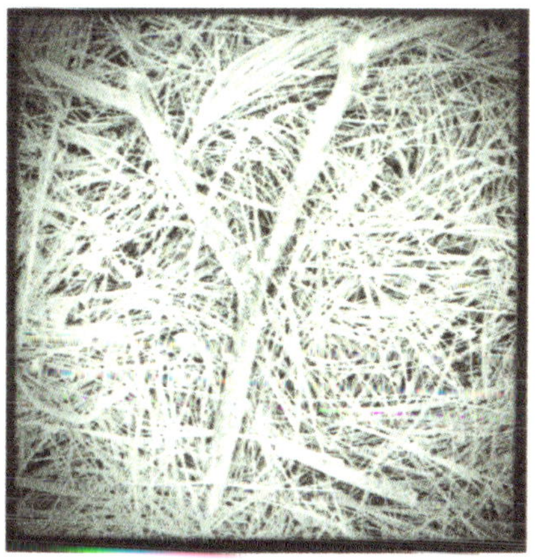
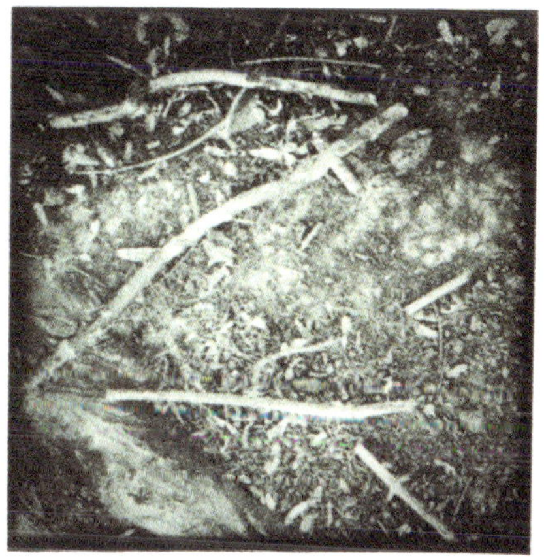

# GRAVESTONE POETRY

Since 2010, I have photographed over six thousand headstones bearing surnames that also work as parts of speech. For sometimes obvious but also curious reasons, people have been named for places, occupations, plants, animals, colors, and personalities. Using these words, I create works that investigate language, mythology, history, life events, time, memory, aging, and travel to unknown places.

The project began, as many of mine do, because something struck me as amusing. I walked through a cemetery at Salem College in North Carolina, where I confronted a large granite stone with a single surname on it: SOUTHERN. It struck me as apt, and I pulled out my cellphone. The following spring I visited another cemetery on my hometown campus. Here I was struck by several "name words," including *keen*, *bull*, *furry*, *lavender*, and *treat*. I had never given much thought to names serving as parts of speech, but of course my own name, Nettles, can function as a noun, a verb, and in a pinch, an adjective. I photographed more and determined to write about the four seasons using these images. This became *Stonecipher: A Book of Seasons*, for which I used headstones located thirty minutes from home. More projects followed as I allowed myself to wander. The next book was *Place*, American history written in the four cardinal directions. *Hawk/Dove* is a poem about war and peace written entirely in veterans' headstones.

I took a break from writing poetry to design numerous card decks, utilizing their two-sided nature to create decks of antonyms, homonyms, aptonyms, and famous pairs, including *Dante* and *Beatrice*. Those names inspired me to write *Dante Enters Hell*, my interpretation of the *Inferno*. Collecting the names *Kore*, *Demeter*, *Neptune*, *Hermes*, *Jupiter*, and *Hades* led me to *Springs Victory—Kore Comes Back*, a compelling explanation for the return of spring and a story of a powerful mother-daughter bond. In this tale, *corn*, *wheat*, *barley*, and *oats* appear, as do abundant birds. Winter is filled with *wind storms*, *frost*, *sleet*, *ice*, and *snow*.

With all these projects, I have set constraints, which I find a helpful practice. I use only surnames, I do not edit the spelling, and the grammar must be correct (my mother was an English teacher, and she would have been proud). I encourage the occasional collaborators and have sometimes sent them in search of particular names on stones that I locate online but can't travel to myself. If possible, I enlist friends to walk with me and help me shoot. This is more fun and saves my strength, for each photograph requires a deep knee bend. I continue to collect marvelously descriptive words with no immediate end in sight!

**BEA NETTLES**

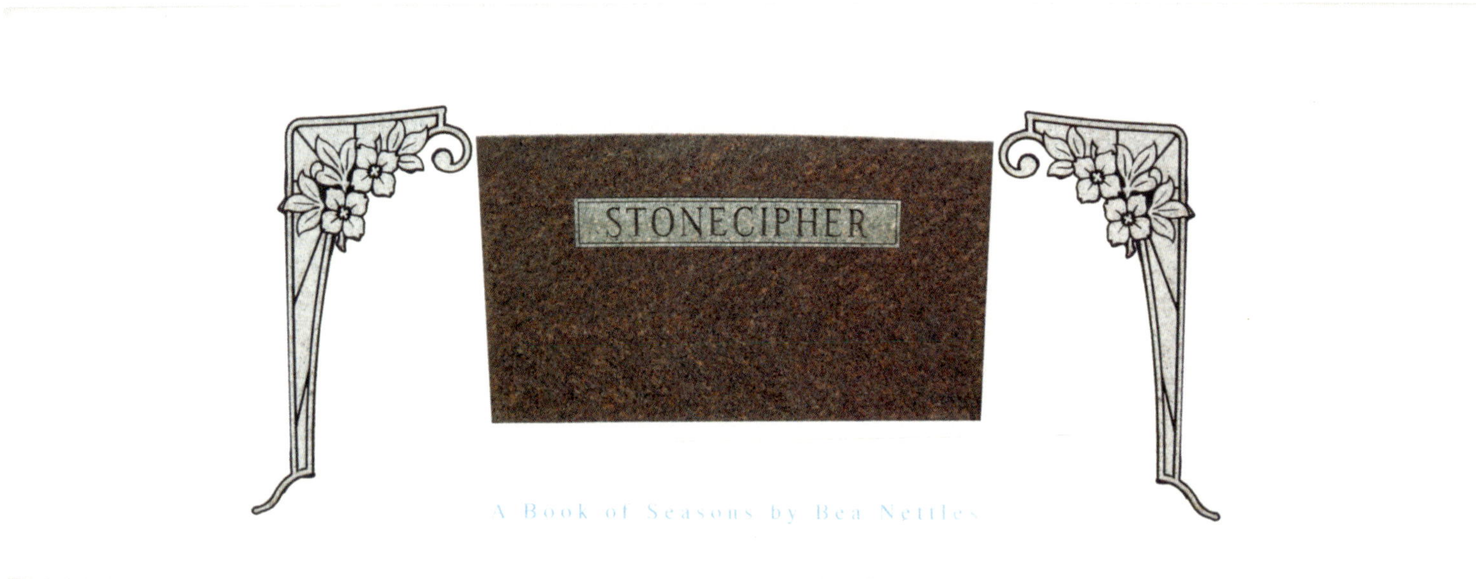


> *Stonecipher*, 2011, book with electrostatic prints

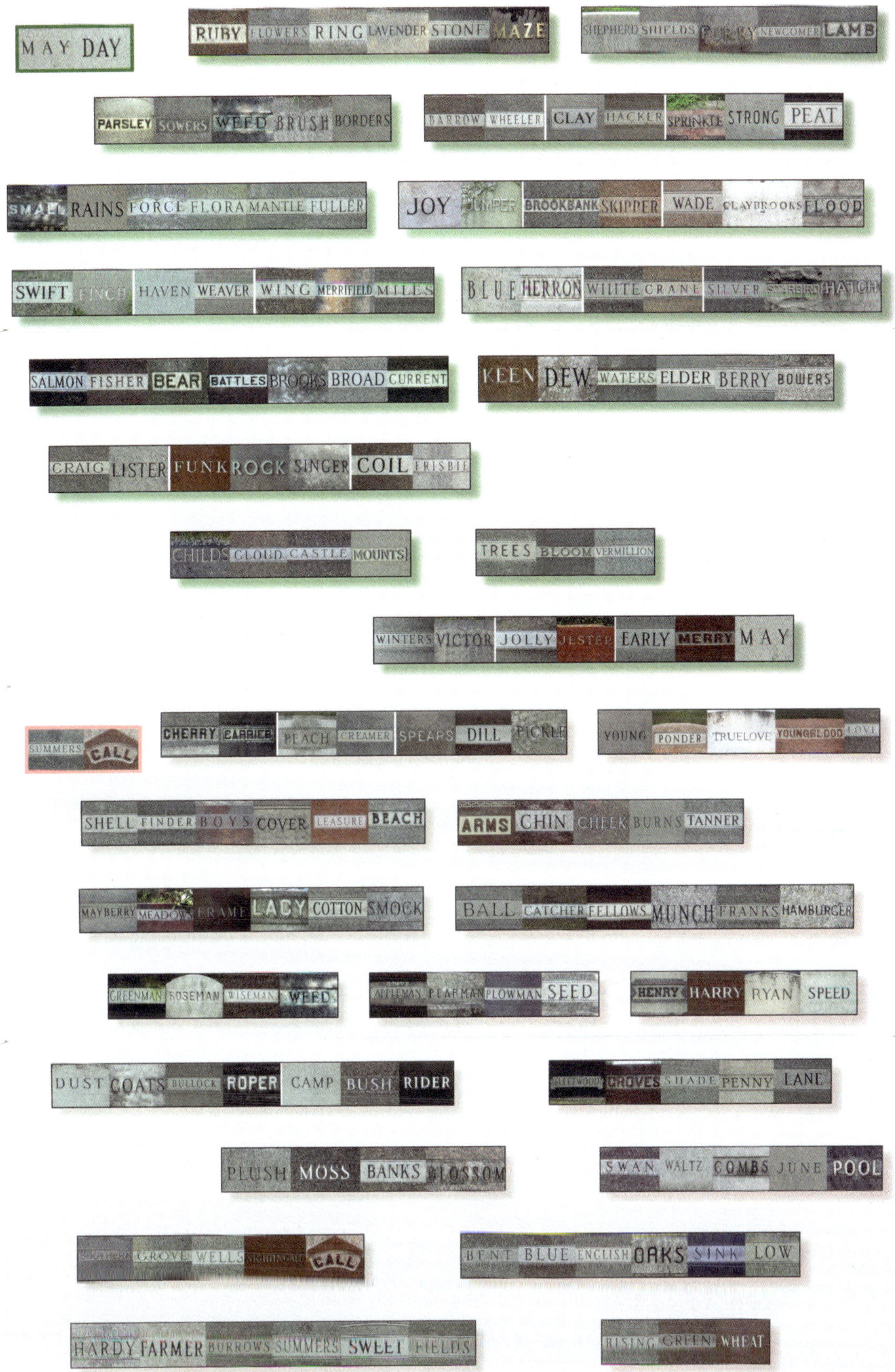
MAY DAY
RUBY FLOWERS RING LAVENDER STONE MAZE
SHEPHERD SHIELDS NEWCOMER LAMB
PARSLEY SOWERS WEED BRUSH BORDERS
BARROW WHEELER CLAY HACKER SPRINKLE STRONG PEAT
SMALL RAINS FORCE FLORA MANTLE FULLER
JOY BROOKBANK SKIPPER WADE CLAYBROOKS FLOOD
SWIFT FINCH HAVEN WEAVER WING MERRIFIELD MILES
BLUE HERRON WHITE CRANE SILVER HATCH
SALMON FISHER BEAR BATTLES BROOKS BROAD CURRENT
KEEN DEW WATERS ELDER BERRY BOWERS
CRAIG LISTER FUNK ROCK SINGER COIL FRISBIE
CHILDS CLOUD CASTLE MOUNTS
TREES BLOOM VERMILLION
WINTERS VICTOR JOLLY JESTER EARLY MERRY MAY
SUMMERS CALL
CHERRY CARRIER PEACH CREAMER SPEARS DILL PICKLE
YOUNG PONDER TRUELOVE YOUNGBLOOD LOVE
SHELL FINDER BOYS COVER LEASURE BEACH
ARMS CHIN CHEEK BURNS TANNER
MAYBERRY MEADOWS FRAME LACY COTTON SMOCK
BALL CATCHER FELLOWS MUNCH FRANKS HAMBURGER
GREENMAN ROSEMAN WISEMAN WEED
APPLEMAN PEARMAN PLOWMAN SEED
HENRY HARRY RYAN SPEED
DUST COATS BULLOCK ROPER CAMP BUSH RIDER
GROVES SHADE PENNY LANE
PLUSH MOSS BANKS BLOSSOM
SWAN WALTZ COMBS JUNE POOL
GROVE WELLS CALL
BENT BLUE ENGLISH OAKS SINK LOW
HARDY FARMER BURROWS SUMMERS SWEET FIELDS
RISING GREEN WHEAT

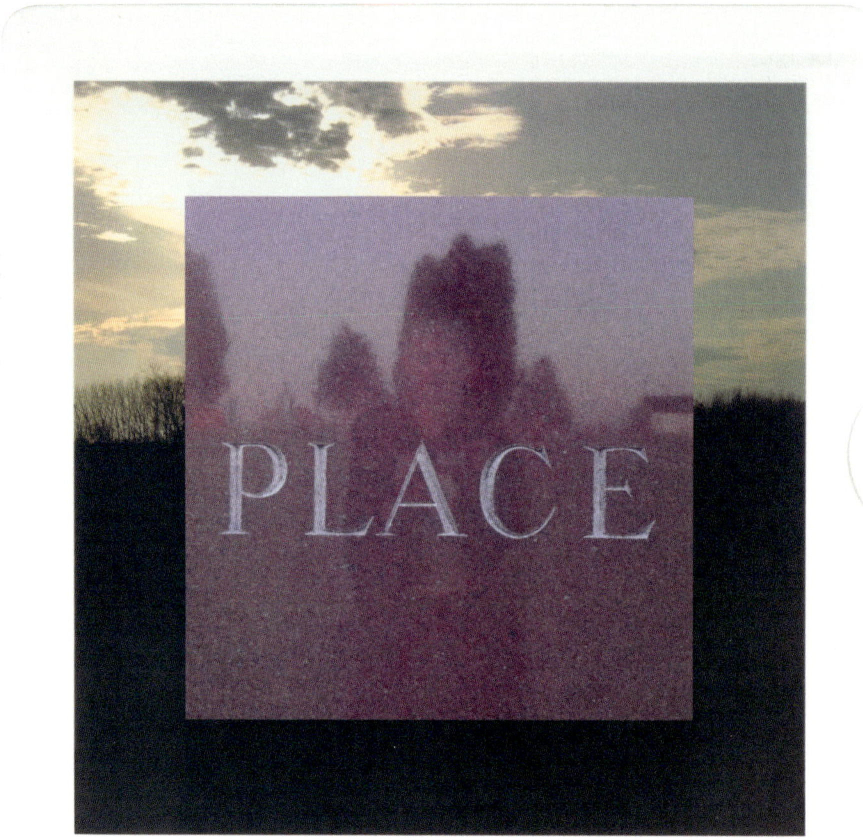


> *Place*, 2013, book with electrostatic prints

W WESTMORELAND WEST WARD HO WEST WINDERS WANTLAND MORELAND MOREFIELD
LEWIS CLARK CROSS CUMBERLAND OVERFIELD ABLE FISHER HOOKS RAINBOW TROUT
ROCK CLINGER SCALES SHEER SUMMIT SIDES CHITTY BIRD PIPES TICK TICK TICK
BLUE BONNET VIOLET THISTLE TUFTS STRETCH MILES
DEER STALKER TRAIL WALKER SETTLE WINTER CAMPS BOATRIGHT FELLS TIMBERS
CREWS ROW OVER CLEARWATER SNAKE COLUMBIA RIVERS SHELLY BEACH WAITS WOOD BURNER
DEW COATS HIGH PINE TREES DAMP SPRAY WATERS HAZY SHORE

◇

MILLMAN SPIES GOLDEN FLECK
CLEARWATER STRIKE SPARKS GOLD RUSH LUCKY FELLOWS REGISTER MINES
PLACE NUMBERS DROVER BUSHWACKER SADDLER SKINNER TANNER TROTTER DICE THROWER WINNER
BOOMER TOWNS PROSPER OUTLAW BEER BREWER HUSSEY PROFIT
FORTUNE JUMPER FEARS ROUGH JUSTICE MARSHALL BUYS DERRINGER DOWNS SILVER DOLLAR DRAM
WILDER TOWNS LYNCH BURY COFFIN NAILER WORKS
STARK CROSS MARKS HASTY GRAVES LAWLESS SANDS BLOW FREE

WORK CREWS LAY STEEL GAGE
RICE EATER POUNDS SHARP SPIKES IRISH BOYS GANDY DANCE OVER TIMBERS
GRANT BLESSING GOLDEN SPIKES LINK
DARING DRIVER WORKS LEVERS COKE LOADER STOKES HOPPER
ASH LADEN BILLOW SMOTHERS
EAST LANDERS HURDLE SHOCK RUMBLE ROCK NATION LINKER Showers SPARKS
HUFFER PUFFER MOUNTS RIDGE ROUNDS HIGH MOUNTAIN PASS

◇

EAGLE FEATHERS CROWN RIDGE RIDER WAGONER FEARS CREE CREEK CROW
FLINT POINT FELLS WHITEMAN HORSEMAN COUNTS COUP GRABS HAIR HANKS
CUSTER SPIES BLACK HILLS CAMPS WINCHESTER BANGS HORSEFALLS OVER
BLUE COATS SLAUGHTER BUFFALO LARGE BONES LEACH
WHITELAW WILLS FIRST NATION BARREN LAND
BUFFALO BILLS WILD WEST HIRES PEACE PIPER NOBLE SAVAGE
ELDER OLDFATHER GRIEVE GRANDE MARCH TOPPING EAST COAST BILLINGS

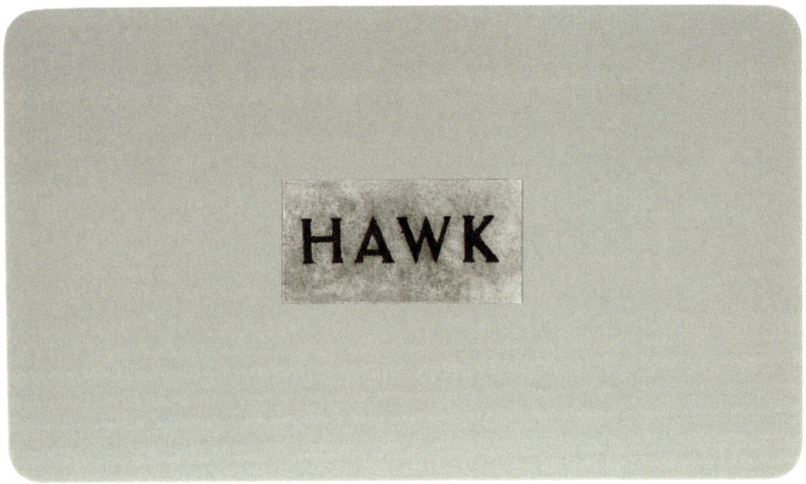


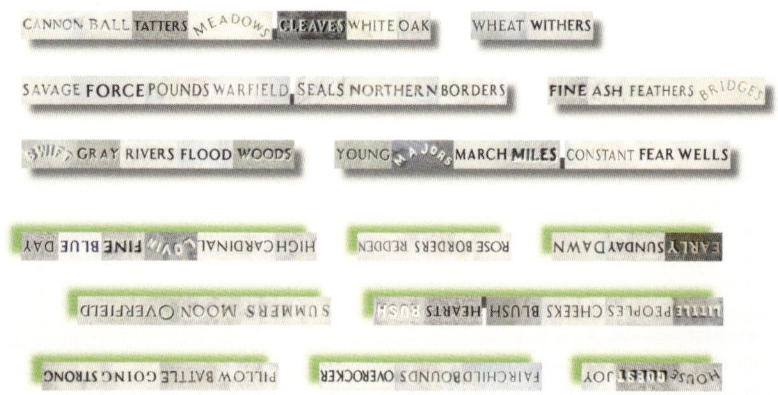


> *Hawk/Dove*, 2013, book with digital prints

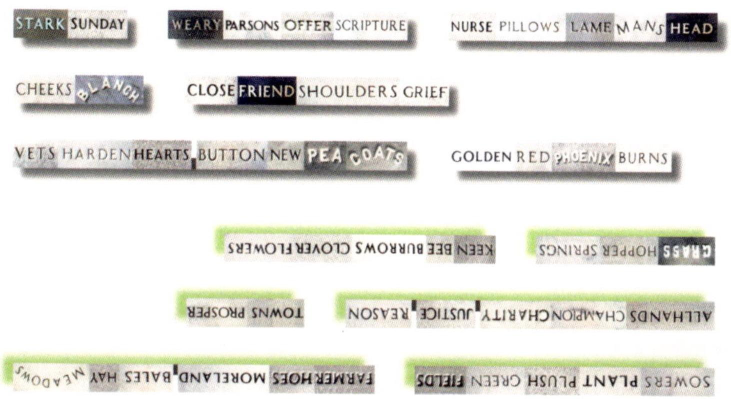
STARK SUNDAY
WEARY PARSONS OFFER SCRIPTURE
NURSE PILLOWS LAME MANS HEAD
CHEEKS BLANCH
CLOSE FRIEND SHOULDERS GRIEF
VETS HARDEN HEARTS BUTTON NEW PEA COATS
GOLDEN RED PHOENIX BURNS

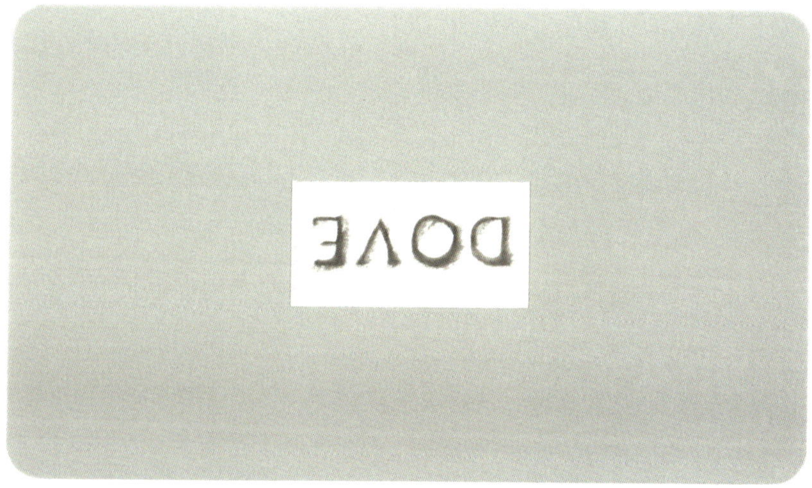

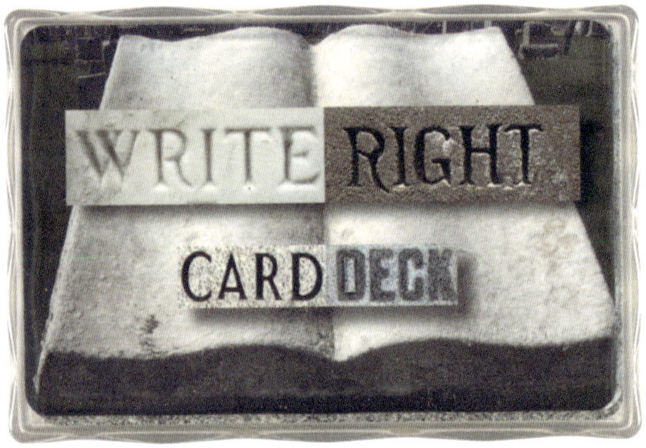


> *Write Right: Card Deck*, 2015, print-on-demand deck of two-sided cards

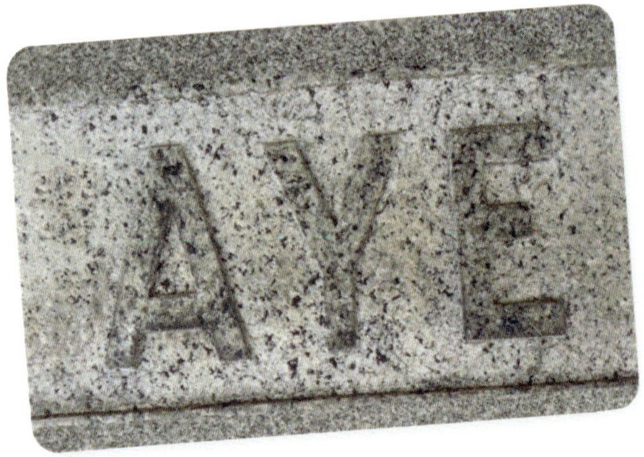


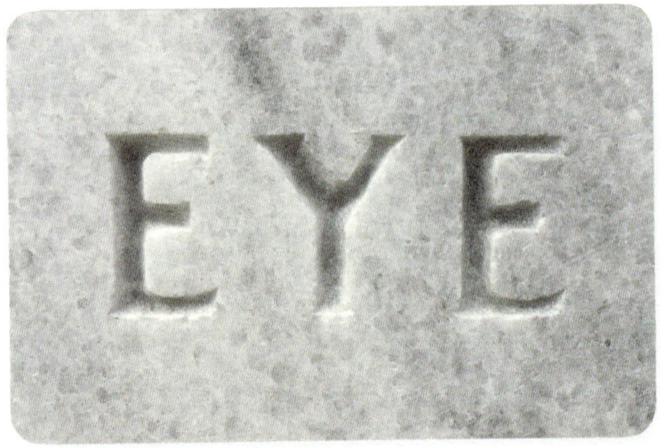


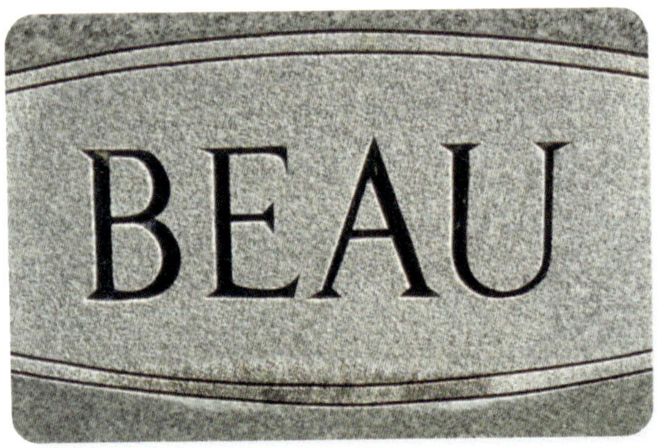


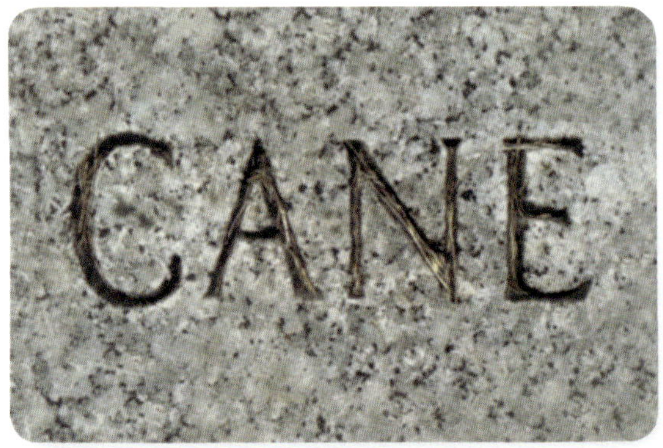


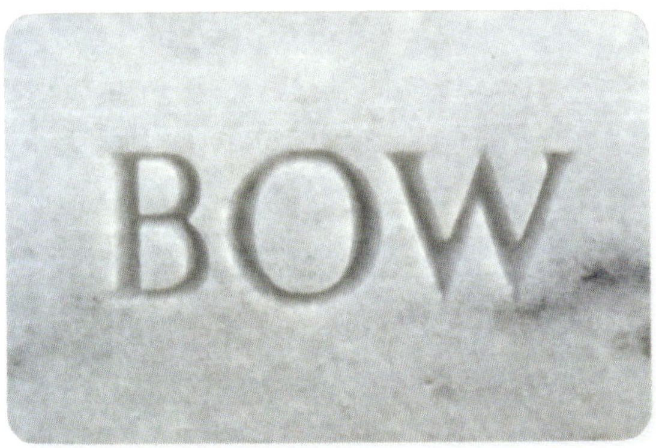


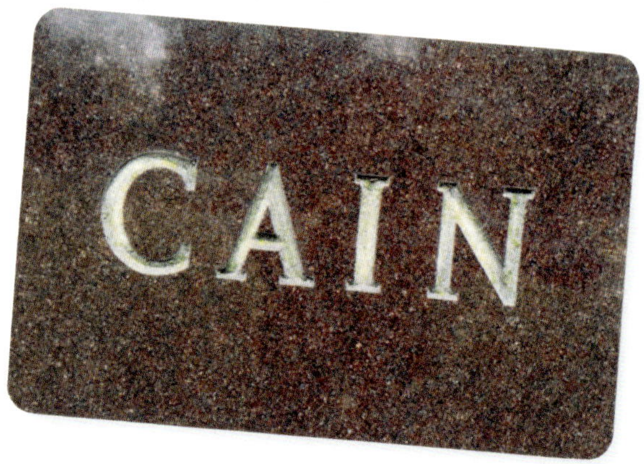

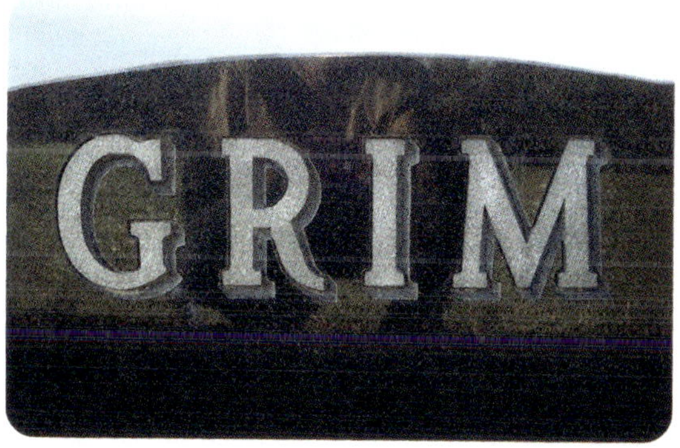
GRIM
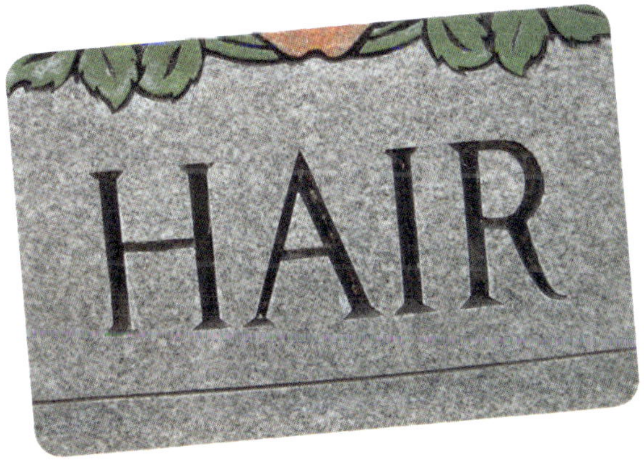
HAIR

PRAY
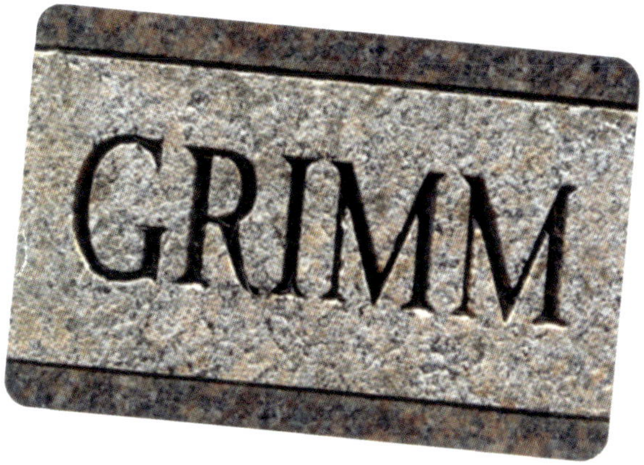
GRIMM
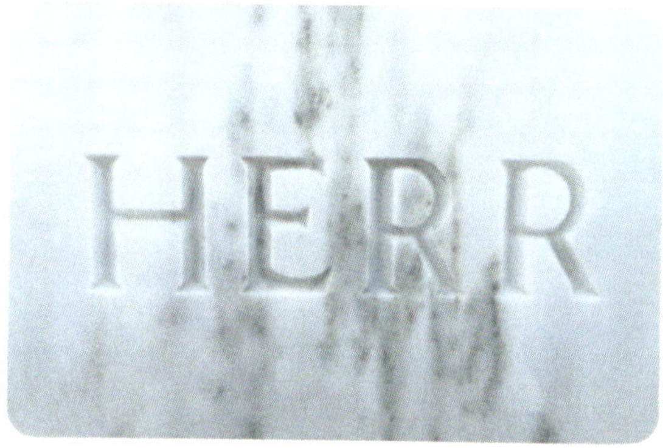
HERR
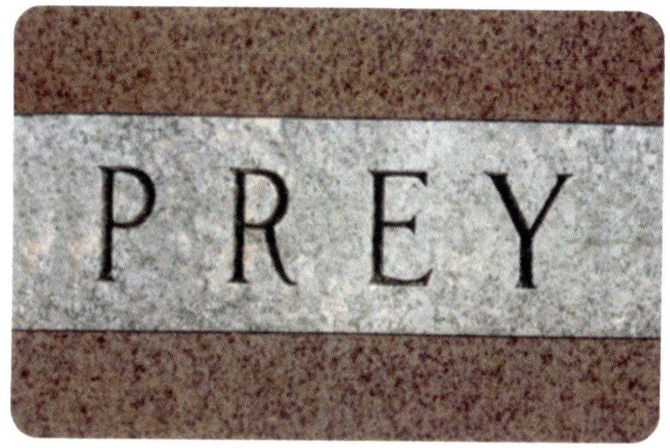
PREY
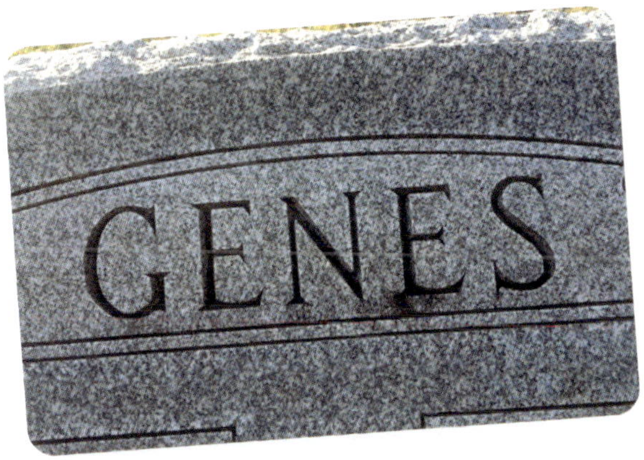
GENES
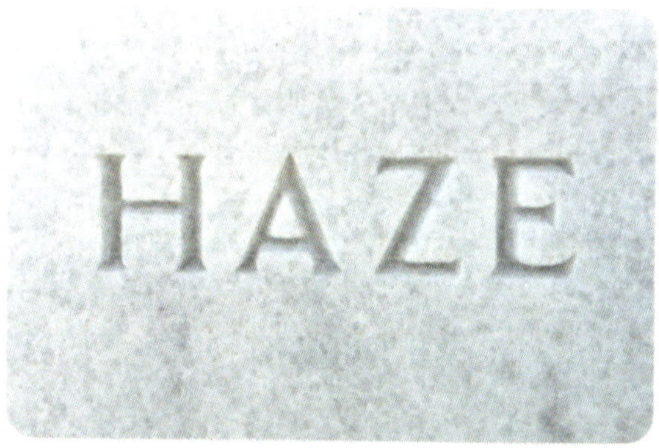
HAZE
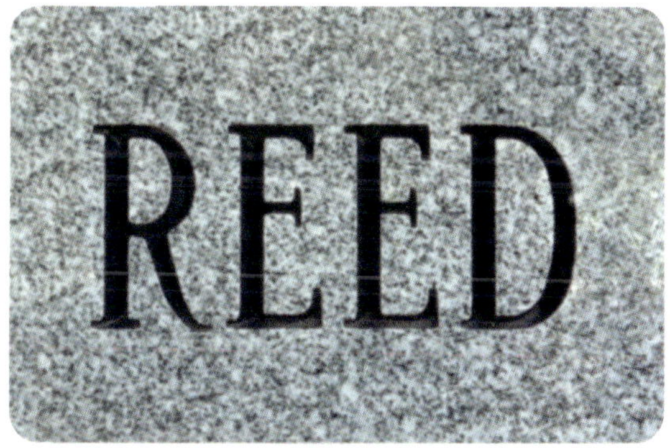
REED
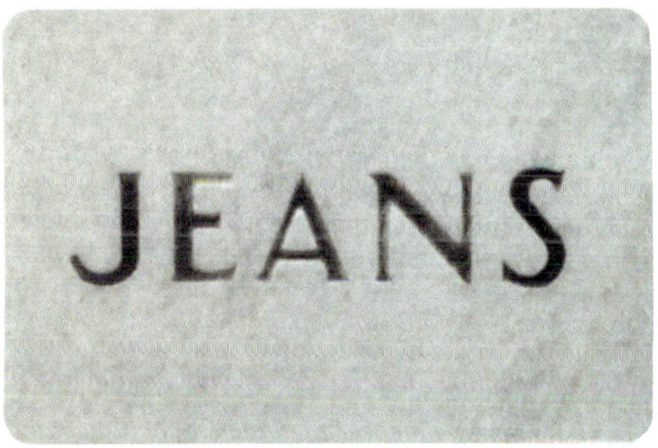
JEANS
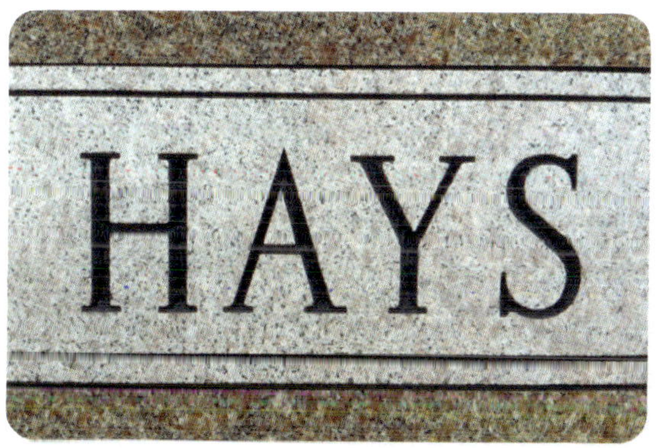
HAYS

READ

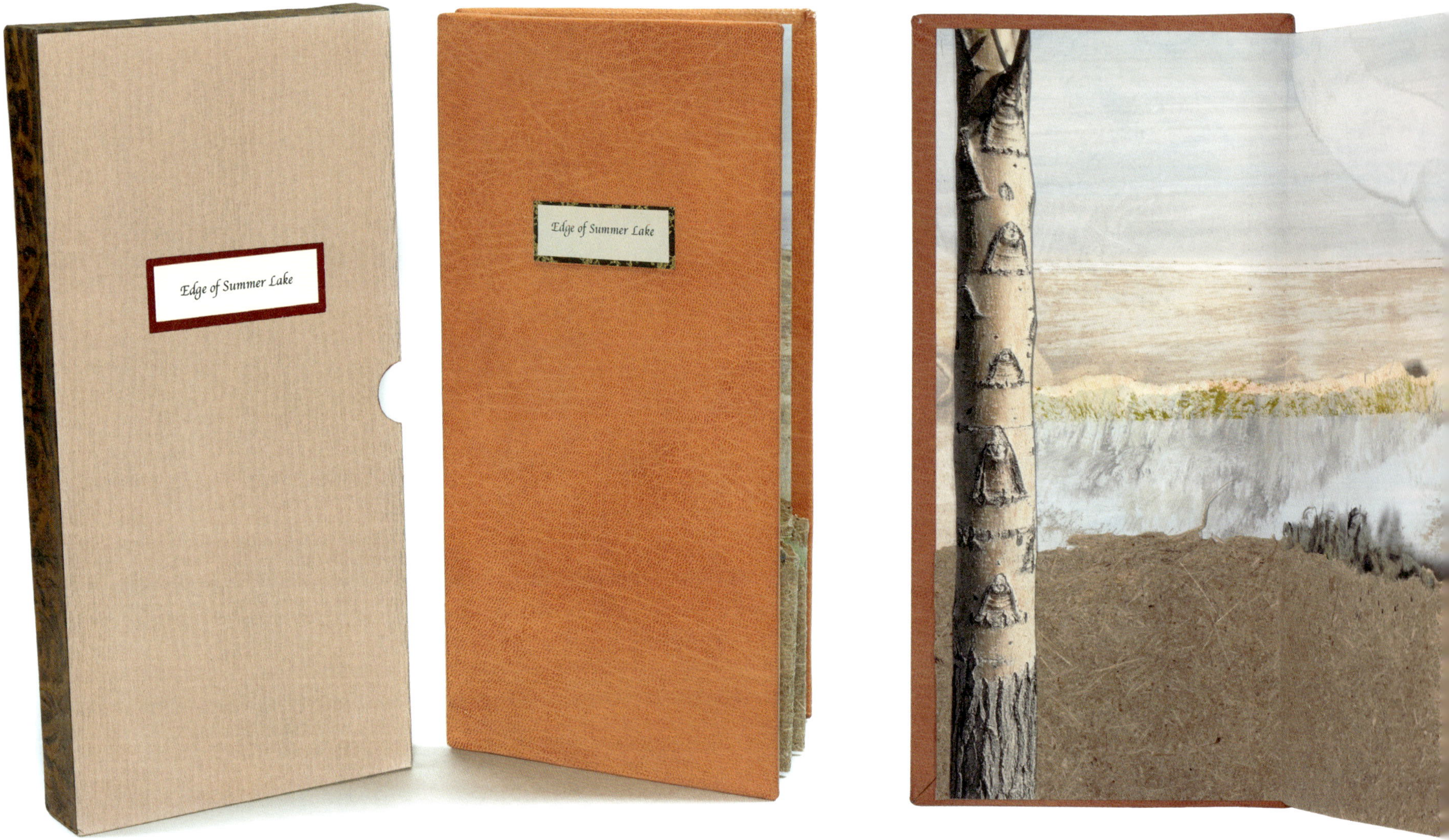


> *Edge of Summer Lake*, 2015, leather-bound book with collage of digital prints, paintings, and artist papers

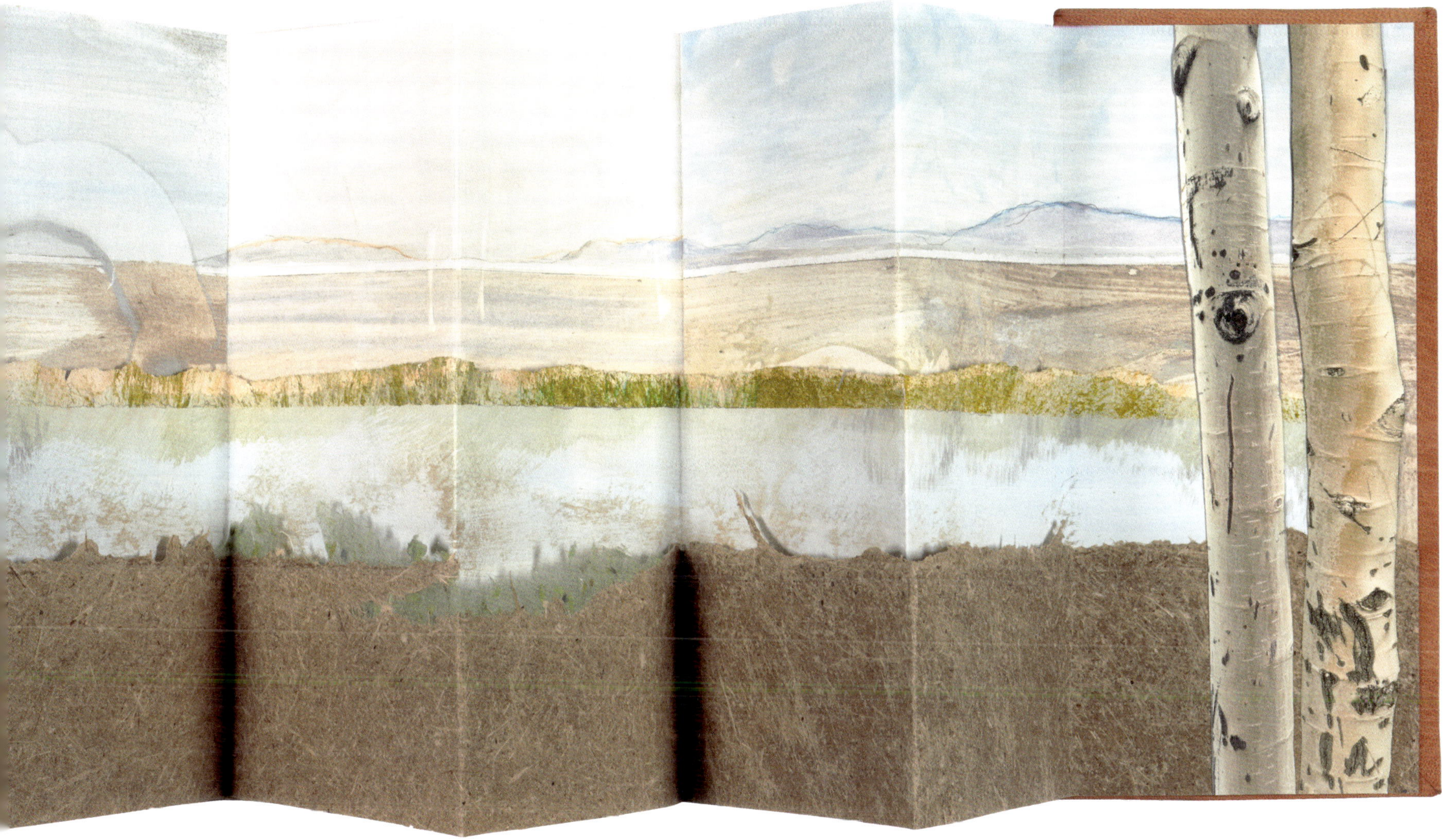

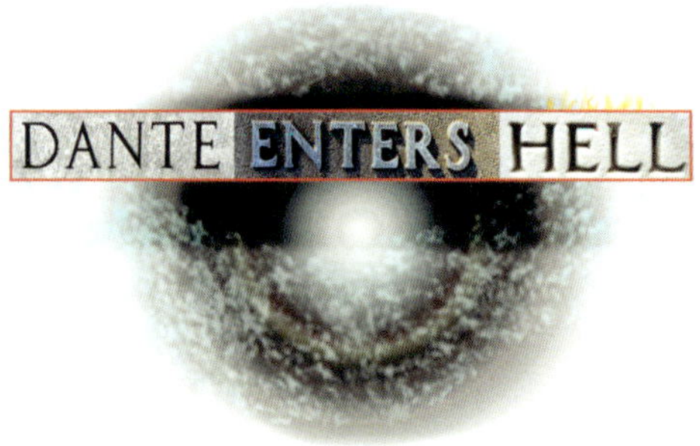


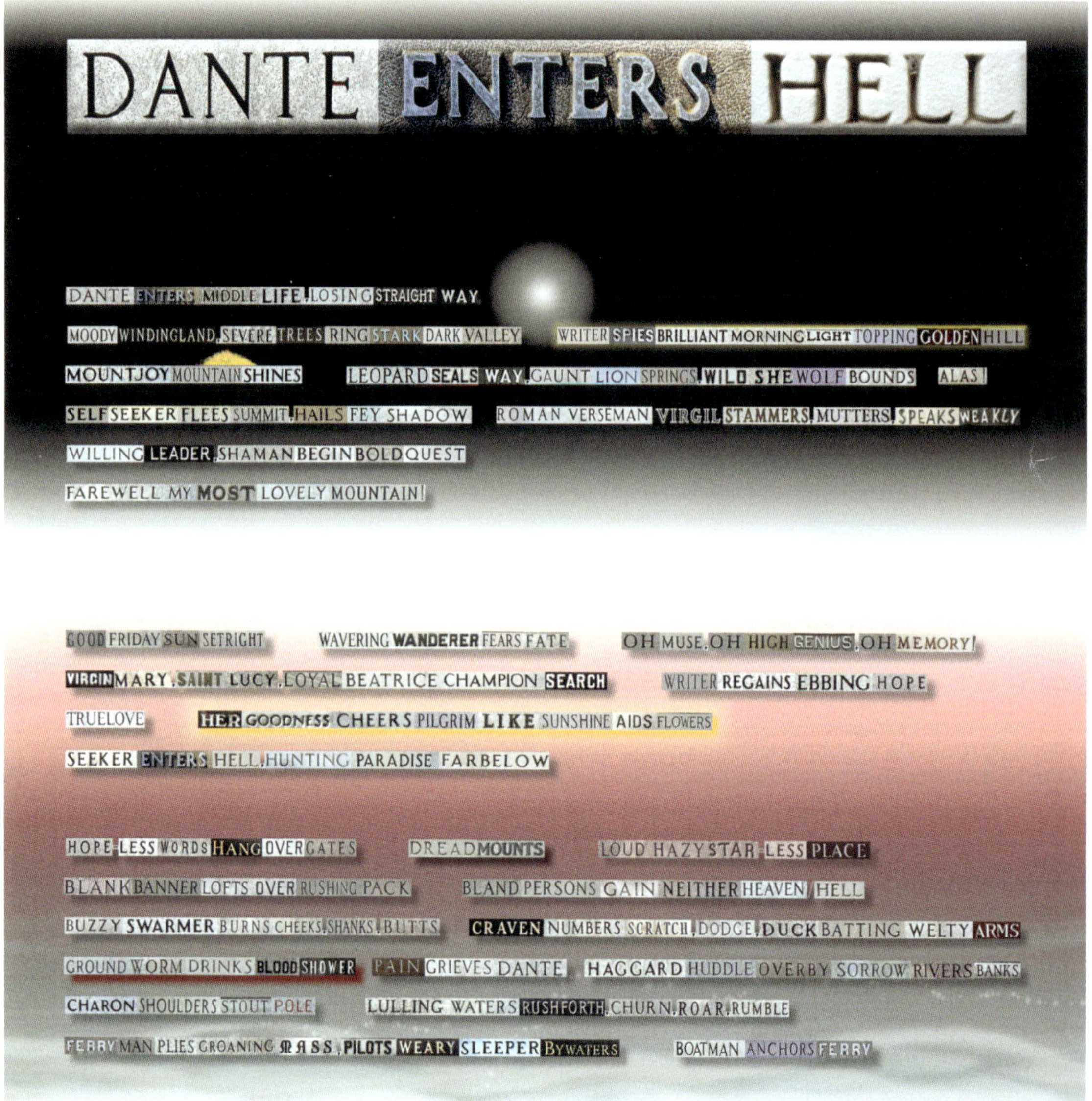


> *Dante Enters Hell*, 2016, book with digital offset prints

CIRCLE 1 VERBOOM! LOUDER BOOMS ROUSE DANTE GRUMBLING TONE RISING OVER SHEER Cliff
NEWCOMER WONDERS PAIR ENTERS FAITH-LACKER WOODS PAGAN ELDERS WELCOME VIRGIL HOME
ALL HONORABLE MALES GOFORTH LUSH GREEN MEADOWS BORDER GRAND CASTLE WALLS
BOTH CROSS LITTLE STREAM. PASSMORE GATES. MOUNT HALFHILL
PLATO, HECTOR, JULIUS CAESAR PASS PLEASANT DULL DAYS. ALL HOPES FADE

CIRCLE 2 WAITERS WAIT DUE JUSTICE DIMMER WORMLIGHT
TEMPEST DRONE BANNING PEACE HELL-SORTER SCREWS CIRCLE OVER BEASTY SIDES
GROSS JUDGE NAMES CIRCLE CHOICE! COIL NUMBERS SETTLE SINNING PERSONS FINAL FATE
GALES BLOW CUTTING WIND! HURLING CRASS SINNER! LUST-BOUND LECH! LIKE OPENSKY ROOKS
HARSH AIRS BELT TROJAN PRINCE! WANTON TART CARNAL DEED FETTERS YOUNG LOVER PAIR
ARTHURS KNIGHTS RACY STORY STOKES LOVING HUG, KISS, ALL AMISS FIE! INNOCENT BOOK READING DONE
LAST DARING MEMORY SHAMES GENTLE LADY STRAYER DANTE FALLS FAINT

CIRCLE 3 WETTER SLEET FALLS ROT STORM DROWNS SWINEY CLUSTER LARGE WAY-BLOCKER BARKS
CUTTING, GUTTING BLIND LARD-BUTTS FLESH HACKER HARMS STEINER-CHILLER, WINER-FILLER
CONSTANT HUNGER PANG! HOGSHEAD SPILLERS SUCK MUCK, CHURN, SWALLOW BRINEY BROTH BRINE FEASTER SINKS
KEEN ODOR RISING WAY WINDERS LOB CRAP BALL. GUARD Sopper STILLING WARDEN GOERS SCURRY OVERALL FALLEN FORMS

CIRCLE 4 MONEY-MISER, MONEY-LOSER ROLLING STONES
FACE-LESS FORMS CIRCLE, WHACK, BUMP, SMACK POW! POW!
MONEY-STOWERS BATTLE LAVISH-LIVERS PUFF, BLOW, START WHEELING
SINNING PRIEST BANGS BALDING MONKS BODY HASSLER BICKERS, BITTER HECKLER RILES
ROCK BUMPERS SPRAIN, ROCKENSOCK, ARGUE, CHANGE PLACE

# CLOSING STATEMENT

There are parallels to making art and tending one's garden. Sharing is the key. It is reassuring to think that sometimes something that I have nurtured and grown, and here I mean an image or an idea, can be split up, shared, and even better yet, transplanted into someone else's garden.

**BEA NETTLES** *THE SKIRTED GARDEN: FORTY YEARS OF IMAGES* (2011)

# SELECTED CHRONOLOGY

Jamie M. Allen with Bea Nettles

**Note to the Reader**

The following chronology is adapted from Bea Nettles's book *The Skirted Garden: Forty-Five Years of Images*, which documents the artist's reflections on her life and career. Additional information was supplied by the artist to expand on years not covered in that publication.

## 1946

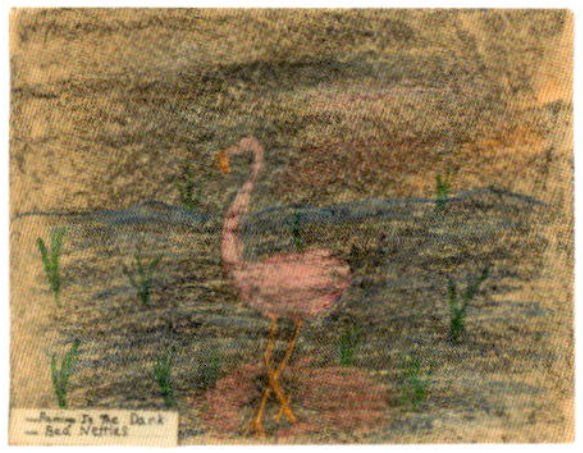

*Flamingo in the Dark*, drawing by Bea Nettles created in elementary school

Bea Nettles is born on October 17 in Gainesville, Florida, to Victor and Grace Nettles

## 1956

Receives her first camera and makes her first photographic images, which she will use later in various projects

## 1959

Wins a Kodak Brownie camera

## 1964

Begins studies at the University of Florida, Gainesville (UF)

## 1967

Attends a lithography course at the Penland School of Crafts, Penland, North Carolina

## 1968

Earns bachelor of fine arts degree in painting from UF

Spends the summer at Penland and teaches there for the first time

Moves to Champaign, Illinois, to begin studies at the University of Illinois at Urbana-Champaign (UIUC)

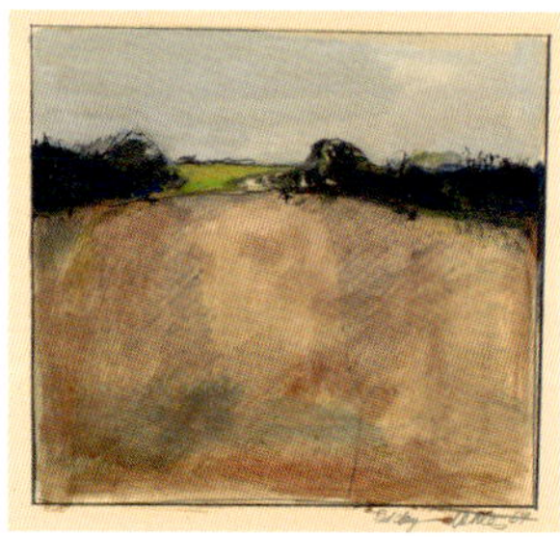

*Red Clay*, 1969, paint and pencil

## 1969

Makes her first stitched photograph in July

## 1970

Attends a Society for Photographic Education (SPE) conference in Indianapolis, Indiana, reconnecting with Robert Fichter and meeting Harold Jones

One group exhibition, *Photography into Sculpture*, Museum of Modern Art (MoMA), New York

Earns master of arts degree in painting from UIUC

Moves to Ionia, New York, and begins teaching at Nazareth College, Rochester, New York, holding a full-time position during the 1970–1971 school year (teaches part-time 1971–1972)

Begins making three-ring binder books

First solo exhibition, *Images and Swamp Dreams . . .*, George Eastman House, Rochester, New York

## 1971

Featured in *13 Photographers*, the first exhibition at Light Gallery in New York, New York

Begins teaching at Rochester Institute of Technology (RIT), holding this position through June 1972

Three solo exhibitions, including *Plastic Mythology & Ecology Apology*, Light Impressions, Rochester

Three group exhibitions, including *Photo Media*, Museum of Contemporary Crafts, New York, New York

## 1972

One solo exhibition, *Heart Attacks & Photo Fantasies*, Light Gallery, New York, New York

Teaches at the Center of the Eye, Aspen, Colorado; returns to teach here in 1973 after it merges with the Center of the Hand to become the Anderson Ranch Arts Center, Snowmass Village, Colorado

Begins using a 3M Revere Automatic 500 camera

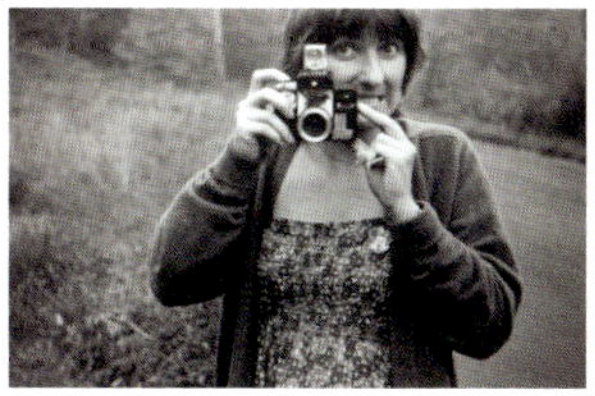

Linda Connor (American, b. 1944), Bea Nettles with her 3M Revere Automatic 500 camera at Apeiron (women in photography workshop co-taught with Linda Connor and Anne Tucker), Millerton, New York, 1973

Moves to Philadelphia, Pennsylvania, to teach at the Tyler School of Art at the invitation of William Larson, holding this position through June 1974

Three solo exhibitions

Eleven group exhibitions, including *60's Continuum*, George Eastman House (this exhibition travels through 1973 to four additional venues); and a faculty exhibition at Tyler

## 1973

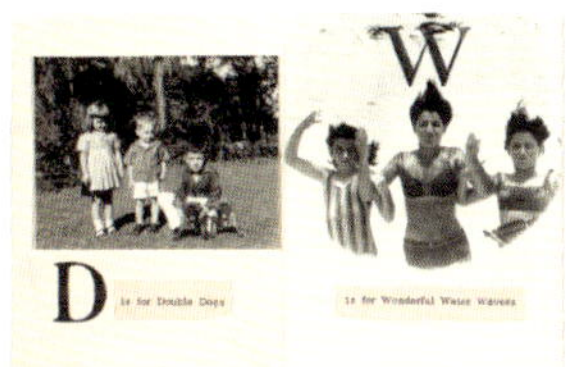


Pasteup for *A is for Applebiting Alligators*, ca. 1973

Begins making limited-edition books with offset lithographs and screen prints

Teaches with Linda Connor and Anne Tucker at Apeiron Workshops, Millerton, New York

Has work included in Anne Tucker's book *The Woman's Eye*

Two solo exhibitions

Seven group exhibitions, including *Multiple Sculptures/Unique Photographs*, MoMA

## 1974

Marries Lionel Suntop while attending an SPE conference in Rochester, New York

Continues to teach numerous workshops throughout the United States, including courses at Penland, where she teaches periodically through 2012; Sun Valley Center for the Arts and Humanities, Ketchum, Idaho, where she teaches again in 1975; and the University of Minnesota, Minneapolis

Moves to Rochester, New York

Begins to teach at the Visual Studies Workshop (VSW), Rochester, New York, holding this position through June 1975

Begins printing books with VSW Press but continues to hand-assemble the final books

One solo exhibition

Four group exhibitions, including *10 American Photographers*, the Photographers' Gallery, London, UK

## 1975

Joins Witkin Gallery, New York, New York

Prints first card decks, including *Swamp Lady* and *Mountain Dream Tarot*

Participates in *Colors*, a portfolio of offset lithographs produced by Florida State University; the portfolio includes her card deck *Swamp Lady*

Makes a series of cyanotype and Van Dyke prints in her backyard

Teaches at University of California, Los Angeles, for one week

Prints her book *Of Loss and Love* on a press at Light Impressions

Two solo exhibitions

Five group exhibitions

## 1976

Returns to teaching at RIT, first as a sabbatical replacement for Betty Hahn and then as full-time faculty through June 1984

Receives a Creative Artists Public Service (CAPS) grant from the New York State Council on the Arts

Begins to use Kwik-Print materials (originally known as Kwik-Proof; referred to as gum bichromate on vinyl in the plate section)

Teaches with Lucas Samaras at the International Center of Photography (ICP), New York, New York

Two solo exhibitions

Six group exhibitions

## 1977

Teaches with Ansel Adams, Jerry Uelsmann, Eikoh Hosoe, and Lewis Baltz at Friends of Photography, Carmel, California, and at VSW

Publishes her book *Breaking the Rules: A Photo Media Cookbook*

Two solo exhibitions

Three group exhibitions

## 1978

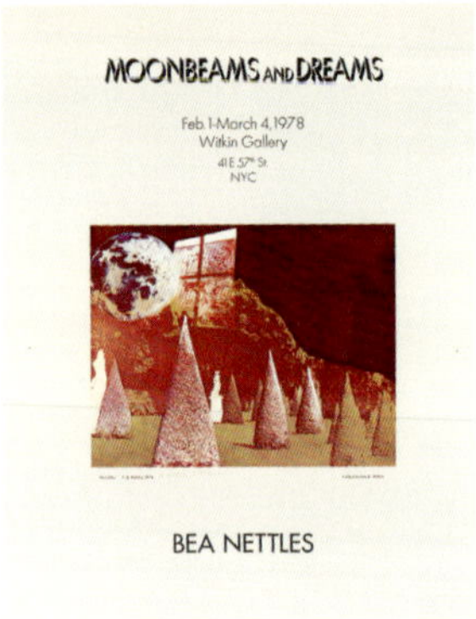


Exhibition poster for *Moonbeams and Dreams*, Witkin Gallery, New York, New York, February 1–March 4, 1978

Her daughter, Rachel, is born on May 7

Teaches at Essex Photo, Essex, Massachusetts, and the Photographer's Place, Philadelphia, Pennsylvania

One solo exhibition, *Moonbeams and Dreams*, Witkin Gallery

Four group exhibitions

## 1979

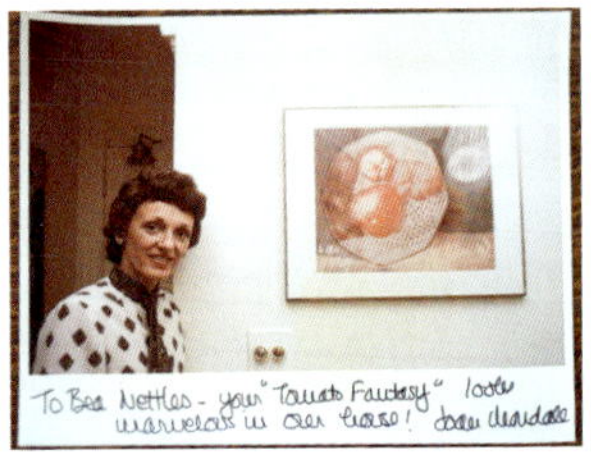

Photograph from Joan Mondale, taken while Bea Nettles's *Tomato Fantasy* (May 1976), from *Flamingo in the Dark*, was on display at the vice president's house for a year, 1979–1980

Receives Visual Artist Fellowship from the National Endowment for the Arts; uses funds to publish the book *Flamingo in the Dark*

One solo exhibition, *Flamingo in the Dark*, Orange Coast College, Costa Mesa, California (this body of work travels to ten additional venues between 1984 and 1986)

Six group exhibitions, including one displayed at the home of Vice President Walter Mondale

## 1980

Begins to use pinhole camera to photograph still lifes at her home, starting her series *Close to Home*

One solo exhibition

Four group exhibitions

## 1981

Her son, Gavin, is born May 31

Takes sabbatical from RIT for the fall 1981 and spring 1982 semesters

Two solo exhibitions

Nine group exhibitions

## 1982

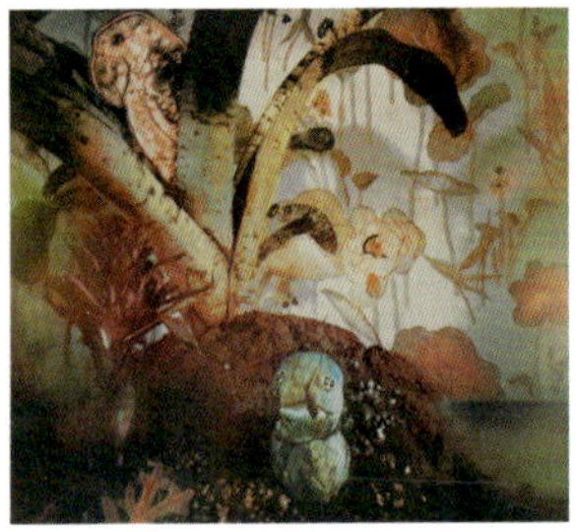

Exhibition poster for *Close to Home*, MFA Gallery, Rochester Institute of Technology, Rochester, New York, 1983

Her husband, Lionel, is voted out of Light Impressions by his business partner and their investors; as a result, Nettles stops using Kwik-Print products

One solo exhibition, *Close to Home*, Robert Samuel Gallery, New York, New York (this body of work travels through 1985 to seven additional venues)

Ten group exhibitions

## 1983

Takes a color photography class at RIT resulting in her use of the dye imbibition process

One solo exhibition, *Gifts: A Retrospective*, Frank E. and Seba B. Payne Gallery, Moravian College, Bethlehem, Pennsylvania

Three group exhibitions

## 1984

Moves to Champaign, Illinois, to teach at UIUC; establishes the undergraduate photography program, serving as the chair until 1999 and as a professor until May 2008 (she is now a professor emerita)

Two solo exhibitions

Five group exhibitions

## 1985

Begins participation in Polaroid Corporation's Artist Support Program, receiving five years of support, including 4 x 5 Type 55 film

Begins printing work as photographic etchings, producing the series *Landscapes of Innocence*

Two group exhibitions

## 1986

Receives an Artist Fellowship from the Illinois Arts Council

Begins making triptychs with her photographic etchings, beginning her series *Life's Lessons*

Moves to a house in Urbana, Illinois, with space for a darkroom and studio in the basement

Two solo exhibitions: *Bea Nettles*, Museum of Contemporary Photography, Columbia College Chicago, Illinois, and *Landscapes of Innocence*, University of Dayton, Ohio (this body of work travels in 1989 to one additional venue)

Three group exhibitions

## 1987

Invited to use the 20 x 24 Polaroid camera in New York, New York; has her first session with the camera in April

Teaches with Sheila Pinkel, Kenda North, and Jerry Burchfield at Light Explorations, Friends of Photography, Carmel, California

One solo exhibition, *Rachel's Holidays*, Mitchell Museum, Mt. Vernon, Illinois

Four group exhibitions, including *True Stories & Photofictions*, the Ffotogallery, Cardiff, UK (this exhibition travels through 1989 to four additional venues)

## 1988

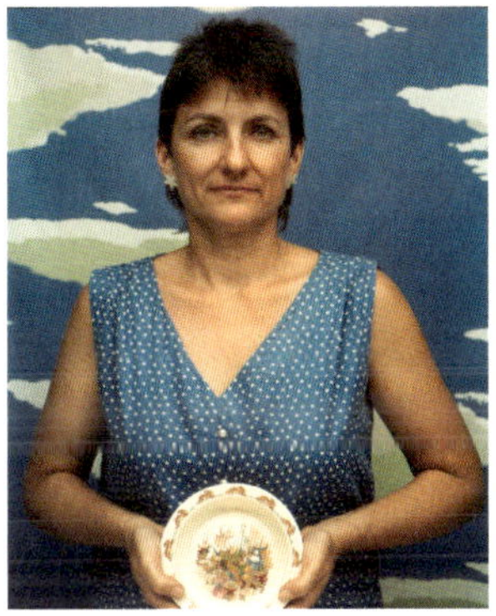

*Star Dress*, 1988, dye diffusion transfer print

Returns to New York to use the 20 x 24 Polaroid camera in August

Receives Artist's Fellowship Grant from the National Endowment for the Arts; uses funds to publish the book *Life's Lessons: A Mother's Journal* (1990)

Publishes two books: *Corners*, with poems by her mother, Grace Nettles, and the second edition of *Breaking the Rules: A Photo Media Cookbook*

Three group exhibitions

## 1989

Teaches at Pyramid Atlantic Art Center, Washington, DC, where she also teaches in 1993

Works as visiting artist at the Rhode Island School of Design, Providence

Two solo exhibitions, including *Life's Lessons*, Rhode Island School of Design (this body of work travels through 1995 to six additional venues)

Eight group exhibitions

## 1990

Named Senior University Scholar, UIUC; uses the funds received to support her book projects

Works with Matsuda, a Japanese fashion firm, on a series of images to promote their men's clothing line; the resulting images are self-published in her book *Knights of Assisi: A Journey through the Tarot*

Publishes her book *The Skirted Garden: 20 Years of Images*

Two group exhibitions

## 1991

Publishes her card deck *28 Days: A Deck of Cards*

Joins Women, Information, Technology & Scholarship (WITS) group at UIUC (remains a member through 1996)

Takes sabbatical from UIUC for the fall semester

Works as artist in residence for two weeks at Penland

Five group exhibitions, including *Photographic Book Art in the United States*, College of Liberal and Fine Arts, University of Texas at San Antonio (this exhibition travels through 1995 to sixteen venues)

## 1992

Delivers a lecture at the SPE national conference in Alexandria, Virginia; this lecture is published as the foreword to her book *Complexities* (1992), selections of which appear in this book (p. 298)

Teaches at ICP

Publishes two books: *Complexities* and the third, revised edition of *Breaking the Rules: A Photo Media Cookbook*

Two group exhibitions, including *Three Decades of Midwestern Photography: 1960–1990*, Davenport Museum of Art (now the Figge Art Museum), Davenport, Iowa

## 1993

Begins making strips of images that became a series in her book *Turning 50* and influenced how she worked with images in her series *Return Trips*

One solo exhibition, *Photo Etchings*, Heuser Art Center Gallery, Bradley University, Peoria, Illinois

Two group exhibitions

## 1994

Works as artist in residence for two weeks at Penland

Publishes her book *Grace's Daughter*

Teaches at the Women's Studio Workshop in Rosendale, New York

Has work included in Naomi Rosenblum's book *A History of Women Photographers*

Seven group exhibitions

## 1995

Publishes her book *Turning 50*

Has work included in Jonathan Feinberg's book *Art since 1940: Strategies of Being*

Reprints the third edition of her book *Breaking the Rules: A Photo Media Cookbook*

One solo exhibition, *Complexities*, Toledo Museum of Art, Ohio

Three group exhibitions

## 1996

One solo exhibition, *Turning 50*, I-Space Gallery, Chicago, Illinois

Seven group exhibitions, including *A History of Women Photographers*, New York Public Library, New York, New York (this exhibition travels to three additional venues that year)

## 1997

Awarded Honored Educator by SPE Midwest Region

Publishes her book *Memory Loss*

Three group exhibitions, including *Eye of the Beholder*, ICP

## 1998

Begins her series *Return Trips*

Publishes her book *Seasonal Turns*

Reprints the third edition of her book *Breaking the Rules: A Photo Media Cookbook* for the final time

Takes sabbatical from UIUC for the spring semester

One group exhibition

## 1999

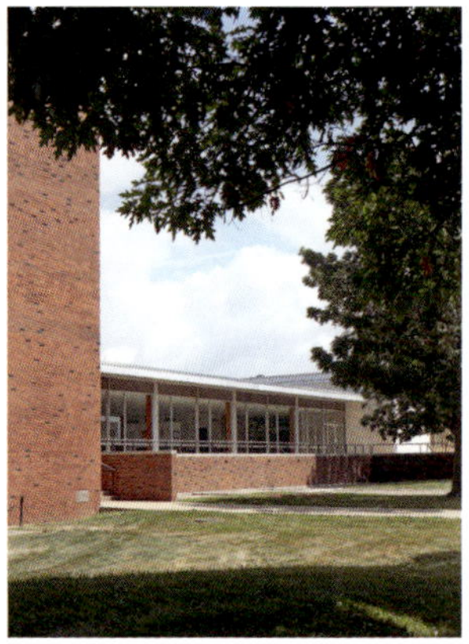

School of Art + Design at the University of Illinois, August 2018

Continues to teach after stepping down as chair of the program in photography, School of Art + Design, UIUC

One group exhibition

## 2000

Receives Artist Fellowship from Illinois Arts Council

Teaches at ICP

Reprints her card deck *28 Days*

One solo exhibition, *Return Trips*, Manchester Craftsmen's Guild, Pittsburgh, Pennsylvania (this body of work travels through 2012 to nine venues)

Three group exhibitions

## 2001

Resumes making unique artists' books

Publishes second edition of her card deck *Mountain Dream Tarot*

Teaches at Peters Valley School of Craft, Layton, New Jersey, and Society for Contemporary Photography, Kansas City, Missouri

One group exhibition

## 2002

Attends her first Paper and Book Intensive, with participation continuing through the present day

Diagnosed with breast cancer; has lumpectomy, chemotherapy, and radiation treatments

Two group exhibitions, including *Sun Works: Contemporary Alternative Photography*, Art Institute of Boston, Massachusetts

## 2003

Attends box-making workshop at Haystack Mountain School of Crafts (Haystack), Deer Isle, Maine

Three group exhibitions

## 2004

Takes sabbatical from UIUC for the fall semester

Attends bookmaking workshop with Hedi Kyle at Haystack

Two group exhibitions, including *Six from the Seventies: The Last Years of Modern Photography*, Howard Greenberg Gallery, New York, New York

## 2005

Publishes her book *The Observer* while working as visiting artist at Borowsky Center for Publication Arts, University of the Arts, Philadelphia, Pennsylvania

Teaches at the Paper and Book Intensive, Steamboat Springs, Colorado

Three group exhibitions

## 2006

Begins teaching a broader range of courses, including book binding

Publishes her book *Family Resemblances: 50 Years of Florida Family Portraits*

Exhibits her books for the first time at Pyramid Atlantic Book Arts Fair, Silver Spring, Maryland

One group exhibition

## 2007

Publishes her book *Hair Loss*

Works as artist in residence for two months at Hafnarborg Center of Culture and Fine Art, Hafnarfjördur, Iceland

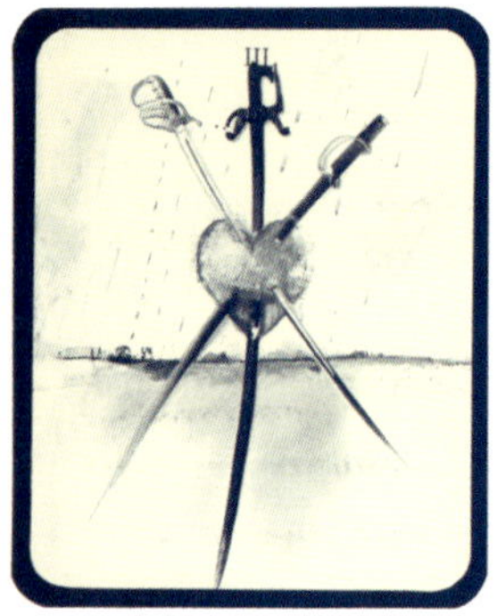

*Three of Swords*, 1975, from *Mountain Dream Tarot*, offset lithograph card

Nettles's *Three of Swords* from *Mountain Dream Tarot* used on the packaging and promotion for Bruce Springsteen's album *Magic*

Four group exhibitions

## 2008

Retires from UIUC, named professor emerita at UIUC

Continues to teach at the Graduate School of Library and Information Science (later School of Information Sciences), UIUC, through 2014

Publishes her books *Cooking the Books: A Concise Guide to Bookbinding* and a Lulu edition of *Corners*

Four group exhibitions, including *University of Florida's Photographic Legacy*, Harn Museum of Art, UF

## 2009

Teaches book arts course with the University of Georgia study abroad program in Cortona, Italy

Teaches a workshop at University of Alaska

One solo exhibition, *Memory Theaters: Photographs and Books*, University of Alaska, Anchorage

Four group exhibitions

## 2010

Teaches at Cincinnati Book Arts Society, Cincinnati, Ohio

One solo exhibition, *Life's Lessons*, Harn Museum of Art

Six group exhibitions

## 2011

Begins gravestone work

Begins making a series of alphabet books

Creates collaborative book *Cropwork Orange* with Robert Fichter and Denise Bookwalter

Donates her darkroom equipment to a local high school, moving her art practice to digital photography and artist books

Four group exhibitions, including *Photography into Sculpture*, Cherry and Martin Gallery, Los Angeles, California (this exhibition travels under the title *The Photographic Object 1970* to Le Consortium, Dijon, France, in 2013 and to Hauser & Wirth, New York, New York, in 2014)

## 2012

Receives National Conference Travel Grant from the College Book Art Association to participate in a panel discussion in San Francisco, California

Publishes third edition of her card deck *Mountain Dream Tarot*

Teaches at Jaffe Center for Book Arts, Florida Atlantic University, Boca Raton

One solo exhibition, *String of Hearts*, Akron Art Museum, Ohio

Five group exhibitions

## 2013

Publishes her books *Place* and *Hawk/Dove*

Publishes *Stone Turner: A Deck of Cards*, her first gravestone-based card deck

Teaches at Newspace Center for Photography, Portland, Oregon

One solo exhibition, *Memory Theaters*, 23 Sandy Gallery, Portland, Oregon

Three group exhibitions, including *The Power of Pictures*, Beinecke Rare Book and Manuscript Library, Yale University, New Haven, Connecticut

## 2014

Works as invited artist in residence at PLAYA, Summer Lake, Oregon

Awarded "Honored Alumna" designation from PK Yonge Developmental Research School, UF

Four group exhibitions, including *Transformational Imagemaking: Handmade Photography since 1960*, CEPA Gallery, Buffalo, New York (this exhibition travels in 2016 to two additional venues)

## 2015

Works as artist in residence at PLAYA

Teaches bookbinding at School of Art + Design, UIUC, for one month

Three group exhibitions, including *Attachment*, Krannert Art Museum, UIUC

## 2016

Publishes her book *Dante Enters Hell*

Work included in Mary Statzer's book *The Photographic Object 1970*

Ten group exhibitions, including *Dream States*, Metropolitan Museum of Art, New York

## 2017

Five group exhibitions, including *The Good 70s*, San Francisco Museum of Modern Art, San Francisco, California

## 2018

Publishes her book *Springs Victory: Kore Comes Back*

Four group exhibitions, including *The Logic of the Copy: Four Decades of Photography in Print*, Phoenix Art Museum, Phoenix, Arizona

## 2019

Retrospective exhibition, *Bea Nettles: Harvest of Memory*, opens at Sheldon Art Galleries, St. Louis, Missouri; scheduled to travel in 2020 to the George Eastman Museum, Rochester, New York, and the Krannert Art Museum, UIUC

# SELECTED BIBLIOGRAPHY

Jamie M. Allen

**Note to the Reader**

Nettles's career as a bookmaker has been prolific, to say the least. She has self-published unique and limited edition books since 1973, and as of 2009, her artistic output has focused on books and card decks. This bibliography concentrates on Nettles's books and card decks printed in runs of more than one hundred, as well as sources that illuminate her career. Note that many of her self-published books are published under the name Inky Press Productions. Bracketed text indicates information that may not be found in the cited publication.

## Books by Bea Nettles


*Events in the Water.* [Philadelphia, PA]: self-published, 1973. Edition of 100.

*Events in the Sky.* [Philadelphia, PA]: self-published, 1973. Edition of 100.

*The Imaginary Blowtorch.* Poetry by Grace Nettles. Images by Bea Nettles. [Philadelphia, PA]: self-published, 1973. Edition of 100.

*The Elsewhere Bird.* Poetry by Grace Nettles. Images by Bea Nettles. [Philadelphia, PA]: self-published, 1974. Edition of 120.

*A is for Applebiting Alligators.* Rochester, NY: self-published, 1974. Printed at Visual Studies Workshop, Rochester, NY. Edition of 200.

*The Nymph of the Highlands.* Story by Connie Nettles. Images by Bea Nettles. Rochester, NY: self-published, 1974. Printed at Visual Studies Workshop, Rochester, NY. Edition of 200.

*Swamp Lady: A Card Deck.* [Rochester, NY]: Inky Press Productions, 1975. Printed by Nettles at Light Impressions, Rochester, NY. Edition of 150.

*Dream Pages.* [Rochester, NY]: self-published, 1975. Printed at Visual Studies Workshop, Rochester, NY. Edition of 100.

*Mountain Dream Tarot: A Deck of 78 Photographic Cards.* [Rochester, NY]: self-published, 1975. Edition of 850.

*Of Loss and Love.* Poetry by Grace Nettles. Imagery by Bea Nettles. Rochester, NY: Inky Press Productions, 1975. Printed by Nettles at Light Impressions, Rochester, NY. Edition of 100.

*Breaking the Rules: A Photo Media Cookbook.* Rochester, NY: Inky Press Productions, 1977.

*Flamingo in the Dark.* Rochester, NY: Inky Press Productions, 1979.

*Breaking the Rules: A Photo Media Cookbook.* 2nd ed. Urbana, IL: Inky Press Productions, 1987.

*Corners.* Poetry by Grace Nettles. Urbana, IL: Inky Press Productions, 1988. Edition of 1,000.

*The Moon Sisters.* Text and images by Bea Nettles. Poem by Grace Nettles. [Urbana, IL]: self-published, 1990.

*Knights of Assisi: A Journey through the Tarot.* Urbana, IL: Inky Press Productions, 1990. Approximately 3,000 copies printed.

*The Skirted Garden: 20 Years of Images.* Urbana, IL: Inky Press Productions, 1990.

*Life's Lessons: A Mother's Journal.* Introduction by Sandra Matthews. Preface by Terry Suhre. Urbana, IL: Inky Press Productions, 1990.

*28 Days: A Deck of Cards.* Urbana, IL: Inky Press Productions, 1991. Edition of 1,000.

*Breaking the Rules: A Photo Media Cookbook.* 3rd ed. Urbana, IL: Inky Press Productions, 1992.

*Complexities.* Urbana, IL: Inky Press Productions, 1992.

*Grace's Daughter.* Urbana, IL: Inky Press Productions 1994.

*Turning 50.* Urbana, IL: Inky Press Productions, 1995.

*Memory Loss.* Urbana, IL: Inky Press Productions, 1997.

*Seasonal Turns: Four Accordion Books.* Urbana, IL: Inky Press Productions, 1998.

*28 Days: A Deck of Cards.* 2nd ed. Urbana, IL: Inky Press Productions, 2000. Edition of 1,000.

*Mountain Dream Tarot: A Deck of 78 Photographic Cards.* 2nd ed. [Urbana, IL]: self-published, 2001. Edition of 1,000.

*The Observer.* [Urbana, IL]: self-published, 2005. Printed at the Borowsky Center for Publication Arts at the University of Arts, Philadelphia, PA. Edition of 300.

*Corners.* Poetry by Grace Nettles. 2nd ed. Urbana, IL: Inky Press Productions, 2008; distribution, Morrisville, NC: Lulu.

*Cooking the Books: A Concise Guide to Bookbinding.* Urbana, Illinois: Inky Press Productions, 2008; distribution, Morrisville, NC: Lulu.

*Return Trips.* [Urbana, IL]: self-published, 2009; distribution, Morrisville, NC: Lulu.

*The Skirted Garden: Forty Years of Images.* 2nd ed. [Urbana, IL]: self-published, 2011; distribution, Morrisville, NC: Lulu.

*Mountain Dream Tarot: A Deck of 78 Photographic Cards.* 3rd ed. [Urbana, IL]: self-published, 2012. Open edition.

*The Skirted Garden: Forty-Five Years of Images.* 3rd edition. [Urbana, IL]: self-published, 2015; distribution, Morrisville, NC: Lulu.

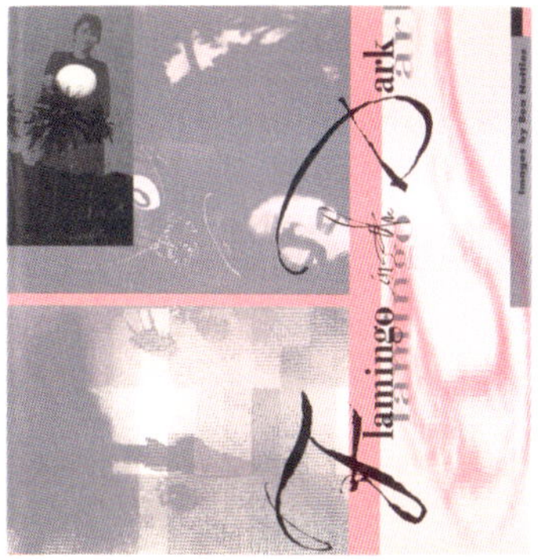


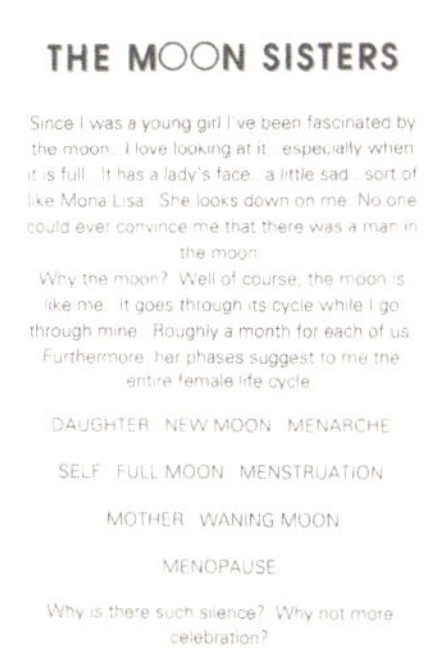


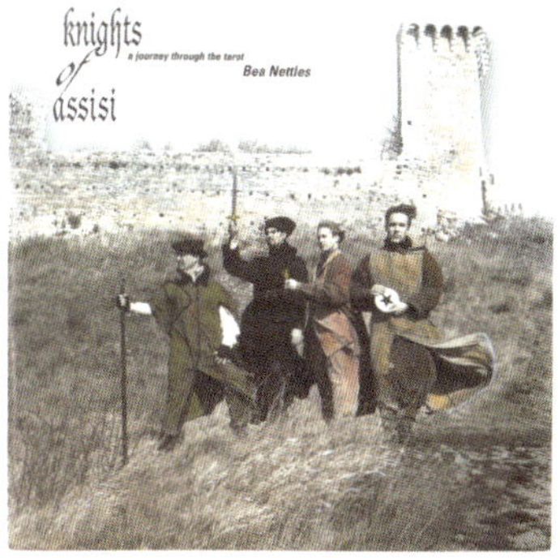


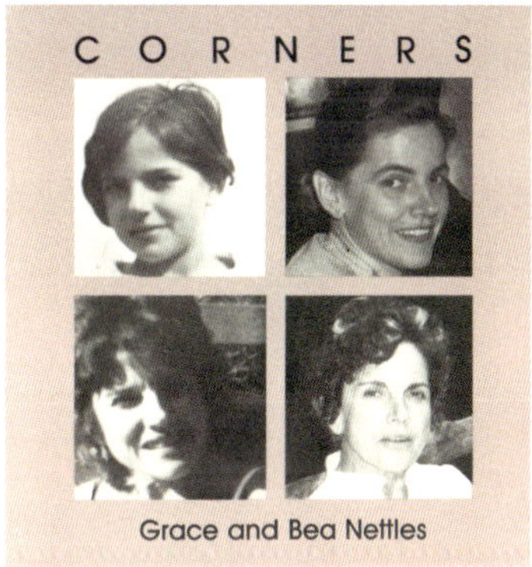


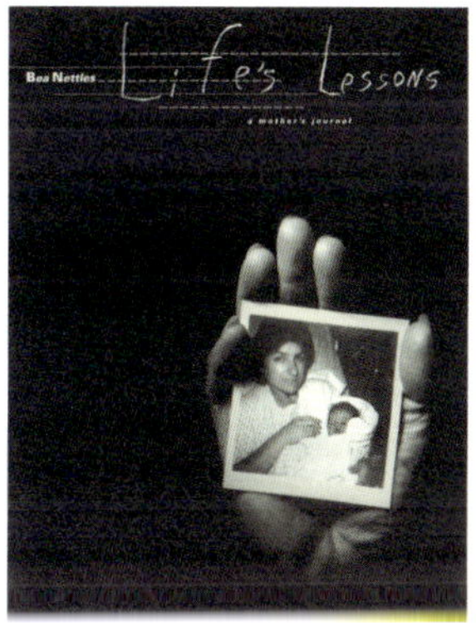


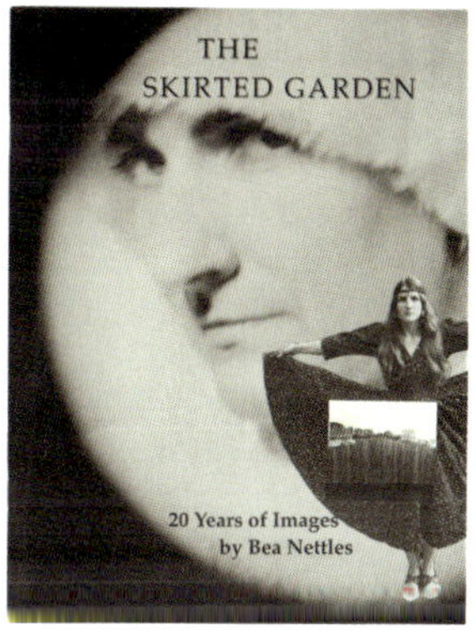


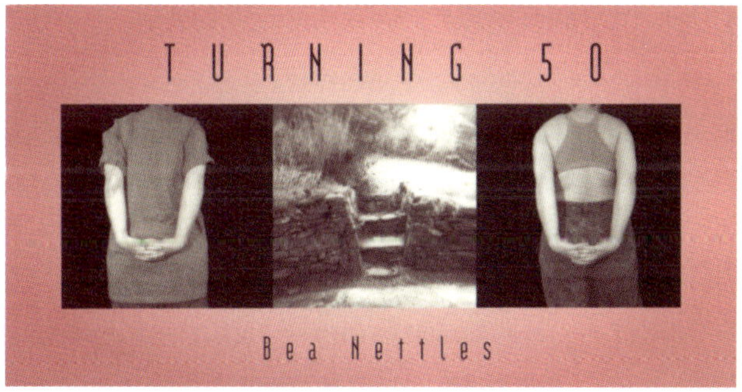


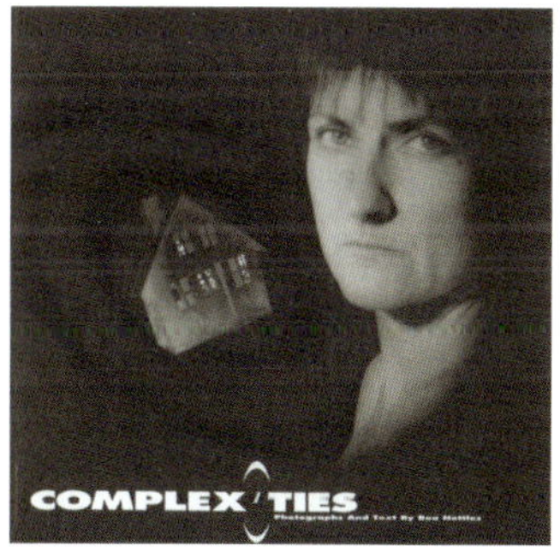


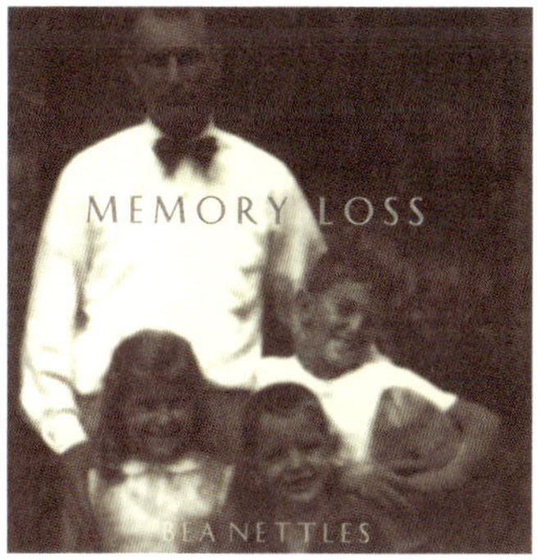


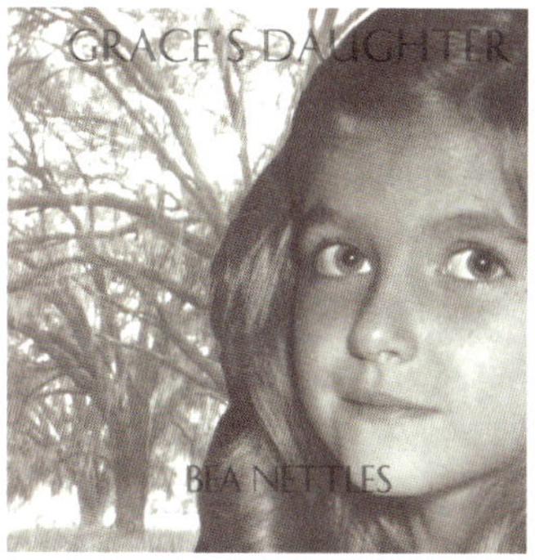


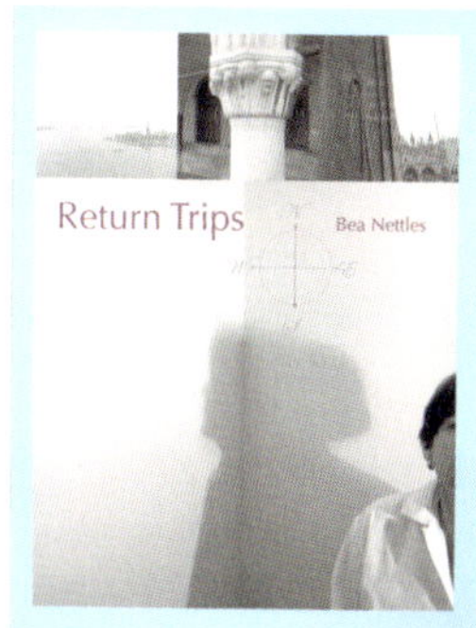


*Flamingo in the Dark*, 1979

*The Moon Sisters*, 1990

*Knights of Assisi: A Journey through the Tarot*, 1990

*Corners*, 1988

*Life's Lessons: A Mother's Journal*, 1990

*The Skirted Garden: 20 Years of Images*, 1990

*Turning 50*, 1995

*Complexities*, 1992

*Memory Loss*, 1997

*Grace's Daughter*, 1994

*Return Trips*, 2009

# Resources about Bea Nettles


**1972**

Chase, William D. "Reviews: New York Galleries." *Arts Magazine*, Summer 1972, 61–63.

**1973**

Tucker, Anne, ed. *The Woman's Eye*. New York: Knopf, 1973.

**1974**

Lambert, Bonnie. "Guided Daydreams: The Imaginary Blowtorch." *Afterimage*, February 1974, 11.

**1976**

*Aspects of American Photography 1976*. Introduction by Jean S. Tucker. St. Louis: University of Missouri–St. Louis, 1976. Exhibition catalog.

**1977**

"Bea Nettles." *Le Nouveau Photocinéma*, July–August 1977, 28–37.

**1978**

Cohen, Joyce Tenneson, ed. *In/Sights: Self-Portraits by Women*. Essay by Patricia Meyer Spacks. Boston: David R. Godine, 1978.

DiGrappa, Carol. "Bea Nettles Dreams On." *Village Voice*, February 6, 1978.

Eauclaire, Sally. "A Space-Age Print System That Makes Fantasies Visible." *Democrat and Chronicle*, March 5, 1978, 68.

Honigsfeld, Carole G. "Book Reviews." *PSA Journal*, June 1978, 26–27.

"Kwik-Print: An Interview with Bea Nettles." *Afterimage*, February 1978, 27–29.

Manella, Douglas. "Bookshelf: Breaking the Rules: A Photo Media Cookbook." *Amateur Photographer*, September 27, 1978, 113.

O'Grady, Mary. "What's What: Nettles Cooks Up a Media Main Dish." *Modern Photography*, May 1978, 89–90.

"Photopourri: Mixed Media and Other Marble Cakes." *Camera 35*, April 1978, 15.

Rice, Shelley. "Bea Nettles at Witkin." *Art in America*, May–June 1978, 111.

**1979**

Dugan, Thomas. "Bea Nettles." *Photography Between Covers: Interviews with Photo-Bookmakers*. Rochester, NY: Light Impressions, 1979.

Nettles, Bea. "Kwik-Print: A New Color Process," *Darkroom Photography*, March–April 1979, 82–83.

**1980**

Goldberg, Vicki. "Books: A Touch of Surrealism." *American Photographer*, June 1980, 14, 16.

Sheldon, James. *Aspects of the 70's—Photography: Recent Directions*. Lincoln, MA: the [Decordova] Museum, [1980]. Exhibition catalog.

**1981**

Coleman, A. D. "What Happens When You Cross a Photograph with a Rock?" *ARTnews*, April 1981, 152–156.

"In Brief (Flamingo in the Dark)." *Photo Communiqué*, Spring 1981, 28.

Seigel, Judy. "Crooked Photography: Good, Bad or Obnoxious?" *Women Artists News*, Fall 1981, 7–8.

**1982**

Samuel, Robert. "Bea Nettles." *ARTnews*, Summer 1982, 198.

**1983**

Engel, Charlene. *Gifts: A Retrospective of Works by Bea Nettles 1969–1983*. Includes artist's statement and catalog entries by Bea Nettles. Bethlehem, PA: Payne Gallery of Moravian College, 1983. Exhibition catalog.

John Michael Kohler Arts Center. *The Alternative Image: An Aesthetic and Technical Exploration of Nonconventional Photographic Printing Processes*. Sheboygan, WI: John Michael Kohler Arts Center, 1983. Exhibition catalog.

Nettles, Bea. "Processes: Kwik-Print." *Modern Photography*, November 1983, 110+.

**1984**

John Michael Kohler Arts Center. *The Alternative Image II: Photography on Nonconventional Supports*. Sheboygan, WI: John Michael Kohler Arts Center, 1984. Exhibition catalog.

Nettles, Bea. "Close to Home: The Pinhole Project." *Lens On Campus*, March 1984.

**1985**

Canavor, Natalie. "Rachel's Holidays." *Popular Photography*, January 1985, 24+.

Hornstein, Henry. "Gumming Up Their Works." *American Photographer*, August 1985, 66–75.

**1986**

Foerstner, Abigail. "Printing the Old-Fashioned Way—with the Help of the Sun." *Chicago Tribune*, May 9, 1986.

———. "Two Artists' Mixed Media Works are Slices of Their Lives." *Chicago Tribune*, September 5, 1986.

Noah, Toni. "News: Bea Nettles." *Views: The Journal of Photography in New England*, Spring 1986, 4–5.

University of Illinois and Bea Nettles. "Bea Nettles MFA 1970." *Alumni Newsletter*, 1986, 15.

**1987**

Beardmore, Susan. *True Stories and Photofictions*. Cardiff, UK: Ffotogallery, 1987. Exhibition catalog.

Bellon-Fisher, Linda. "Photographers on Process and Idea: A Through-the-Mail Dialogue." *Re:view* (Newsletter of the Friends of Photography), April 1987, unpaginated.

Logan, Daniel. "She Can Work It Out: Bea Nettles at Catskill Center for Photography." *Woodstock Times*, April 9, 1987.

Olsen, Tillie, Julie Olsen Edwards, and Estelle Jussim, eds. *Mothers and Daughters: That Special Quality*. New York: Aperture, 1987.

**1988**

Bernier, Elizabeth. "New Dimensions in Photography." *The Heights*, March 21, 1988, 22.

Wise, Kelly. "Paying Attention to Form, Craft and Content." *Boston Globe*, March 31, 1988.

**1989**

Dahlberg, Laurie Virginia. *Our Corner of the World: Seventeen Illinois Artists*. Normal: University Galleries, Illinois State University, 1989. Exhibition catalog.

Donato, Debora Duez, and Terry Suhre. *Photography Illinois*. Springfield: Illinois State Museum, 1989. Exhibition catalog.

Mitchell, Melissa. "Celebrating Mother's Day in a Special Way." *Illini Week* (University of Illinois at Urbana-Champaign), May 11, 1989.

Thall, Larry. "'Photography Illinois': A Fresh Look at Some Familiar Names." *Chicago Tribune*, April 1989.

### 1990

Gironda, Belle. "The Unavoidable Context." *Arts Journal*, June 1990, 14–15.

McGreevy, Linda. "Life's Lessons: A Nurturing Mother's Thoughts." *Port Folio Magazine*, May 22, 1990.

Rooney, Peter. "UI Faculty Rewarded for Scholarly Pursuits." *Champaign-Urbana News-Gazette*, October 13, 1990.

Ruehlmann, Bill. "Images of Ambiguity, Dread Hunt Exhibit of 'Mother's Journal.'" *Norfolk Virginian-Pilot*, April 24, 1990.

Shellcliffe, S. E. "Chrysler Presents *Life's Lessons*: Works by Photographer Bea Nettles." *On Stage*, May 1990.

Towner, Mark. *Three Decades of Midwestern Photography: 1960–1990*. [Davenport, IA]: Davenport Museum of Art, 1990. Exhibition catalog.

### 1991

Ivey, Sue. "Lives of Women Celebrated in Photographer's Collection." *Yankton [SD] Daily Press and Dakotan*, April 11, 1991.

Foerstner, Abigail. "Photography: Bea Nettles Views Motherhood from Many Perspectives." *Chicago Tribune*, November 22, 1991.

Mitchell, Melissa. "Nettles Draws on Themes Close to Heart, Home for Photography." *Inside Illinois*, April 18, 1991.

### 1994

Krantz, Claire Wolf. "Bea Nettles (State of Illinois Art Gallery)." *New Art Examiner*, April 1992, 34–35.

Meyers, Jenny. "Photographer Contemplates Motherhood." *The Observer* (Augustana College, Rock Island, IL), January 21, 1994.

Rosenblum, Naomi. *A History of Women Photographers*. New York: Abbeville Press, 1994.

Towner, Mark. "Visual Arts." *River Cities' Reader* (Davenport, IA), January 1994.

### 1995

Braff, Phyllis. "Monochromes, Motherhood and Scrimshaw." *New York Times*, February 26, 1995.

Corinne, Tee A. "Art Books: What's Available." *Women's Caucus for Art*, Summer 1995, 8.

Fineberg, Jonathan. *Art since 1940: Strategies of Being*. New York: Harry N. Abrams, 1995.

### 1998

"Artist Books: Books by Bea Nettles." *Umbrella*, December 1998, 123–124.

### 1999

Drucker, Johanna. "Experimental Narrative and Artists' Books." *Journal of Artists' Books*, Fall 1999, 3–25.

Nettles, Bea. Artist's statement. *Journal of Artists' Books*, Fall 1999, 10.

### 2004

Merli, Melissa. "Corners." *Champaign-Urbana News-Gazette*, May 9, 2004.

### 2005

"Current Shows: Bea Nettles: Return Trips." *St. Louis Riverfront Times*, March 16, 2005, 39.

Lee, Ginny. "'Merge' Photographers Featured at UIS reception." *Illinois Times* (Springfield), March 3, 2005.

Wiegand, Gabrielle. "Merge Is a Celebration." *UIS Journal* (University of Illinois at Springfield), March 9, 2005.

### 2006

Hares, Amber. "Turning 50." *Afterimage*, March–April 2006, 54.

### 2007

Des Garennes, Christine "The Art of Books." *Champaign-Urbana News-Gazette*, 2007.

Merli, Melissa. "I Dream of Genius." *Champaign-Urbana News-Gazette*, December 30, 2007.

### 2009

Ganis, William V. "String Theories: Annegret Soltau's Transitional, Fetishistic Photocollages." *Afterimage*, January–February 2009, 6–14.

### 2010

Curry, Lashonda Stinson. "A Mom's Journey." *Gainesville Sun*, March 14, 2010.

Levin, Samantha. "Bea Nettles: Myths behind the Woman." Posted February 17, 2010. samanthalevinfineart.com/2010/02/17/bea-nettles-myths-behind-the-woman.

### 2011

Hubbard, Karen [Kitty]. "Art and Science." *Afterimage*, May 2011, 7–8.

### 2012

Cress, Sarah. "Love, Loss, and Everything in Between: The Artwork of Bea Nettles." *Art Education*, May 2012, 25–32.

Jones, Harold. "Voices of Photography: Bea Nettles." Tucson, AZ: Center for Creative Photography. Skype interview recorded March 9, 2012.

### 2015

Moreno, Julia. "Bea Nettles on Display at Milner Library." *The Daily Vidette* (Illinois State University, Normal), April 7, 2015.

### 2016

"Bea Nettles Presents Retrospective of Work at Fine Arts Library." *Indiana Daily Student* (Indiana University, Bloomington), October 27, 2016.

Statzer, Mary. *The Photographic Object 1970*. Oakland: University of California Press, 2016.

### 2017

Edgington, Colin. "In Dream and Soil: A Conversation with Bea Nettles." *Afterimage*, March–April 2017, 15–19.

Johnson, Kelsey Halliday. *Light and Matter: The Photographic Object*. Doylestown, PA: James A. Michener Art Museum, 2017. Exhibition catalog.

### 2018

Emerson, Melanie E. "Bea Nettles: Performing Identity through Mystical Storytelling." *Journal of Artists' Books*, Spring 2018, 14–17.

# CONTRIBUTORS

**Jamie M. Allen** is the Stephen B. and Janice G. Ashley Associate Curator in the Department of Photography at the George Eastman Museum. She has curated exhibitions such as *Nathan Lyons: In Pursuit of Magic* (2019), *#LarsonShindelman #Mobilize* (2019), *Photography and America's National Parks* (2016), *In the Garden* (2015), *Astro-Visions* (2013), *Between the States: Photographs of the American Civil War* (2011), *Portrait* (2010), and *The Photograph Collection: An Introduction* (2008). Her books include *Nathan Lyons: In Pursuit of Magic* (University of Texas Press, 2019), *The Photographer in the Garden* (Aperture, 2018), *Picturing America's National Parks* (Aperture, 2016), and the essay "From Vision to Reality: A Transition from Pictorialism to Modernism" in *Imogen Cunningham* (TF Editores/D.A.P., 2012/2013). Allen holds an MA in photographic preservation and collections management from Ryerson University in coordination with the George Eastman Museum, as well as a BA in art history and a BFA in photography from the University of Arizona, Tucson.

**Olivia Lahs-Gonzales** served as director of the Sheldon Art Galleries in St. Louis, from 2001 to 2019, where she curated exhibitions and directed educational programs for six exhibit spaces. Previously, she worked at the Saint Louis Art Museum (SLAM) as an assistant curator of prints, drawings, and photographs. Her publications include *My Nature: Works with Paper by Kiki Smith* (SLAM, 1999); *Defining Eye: Women Photographers of the 20th Century* (SLAM, 1997); "To Unseal the Deeper Nature," in *Inge Morath* (Prestel and Kunsthalle, Vienna, 1999); *Secrets of Real Estate: John Gossage* (Sheldon, 2008); "Lewis Baltz," in the Detroit Institute of Arts *Bulletin* (2010); and *Larry Fink: Attraction and Desire—50 years in Photography* (Sheldon, 2011). Her traveling exhibitions with publications include *Josephine Baker: Image and Icon* (2006) and *Ralston Crawford and Jazz* (2012), among others. Lahs-Gonzales has an MFA from Columbia College, Chicago, where she worked at the Museum of Contemporary Photography, and a BA Honors from West Surrey College of Art and Design, Farnham, Surrey, United Kingdom.

**Amy L. Powell** is the curator of modern and contemporary art at Krannert Art Museum at the University of Illinois at Urbana-Champaign. Her research engages contemporary art with a commitment to university art museums as sites for knowledge production and experimentation. Her exhibitions at KAM have included *And yet my mask is powerful*, with Basel Abbas and Ruanne Abou-Rahme; *Autumn Knight: In Rehearsal*; *Time / Image*; and *Zina Saro-Wiwa: Did You Know We Taught Them How to Dance?* Her work has been supported by the Andy Warhol Foundation for the Visual Arts, the Smithsonian Institution, and the Institute for Research in the Humanities at the University of Wisconsin-Madison, where she earned a PhD in art history in 2012.

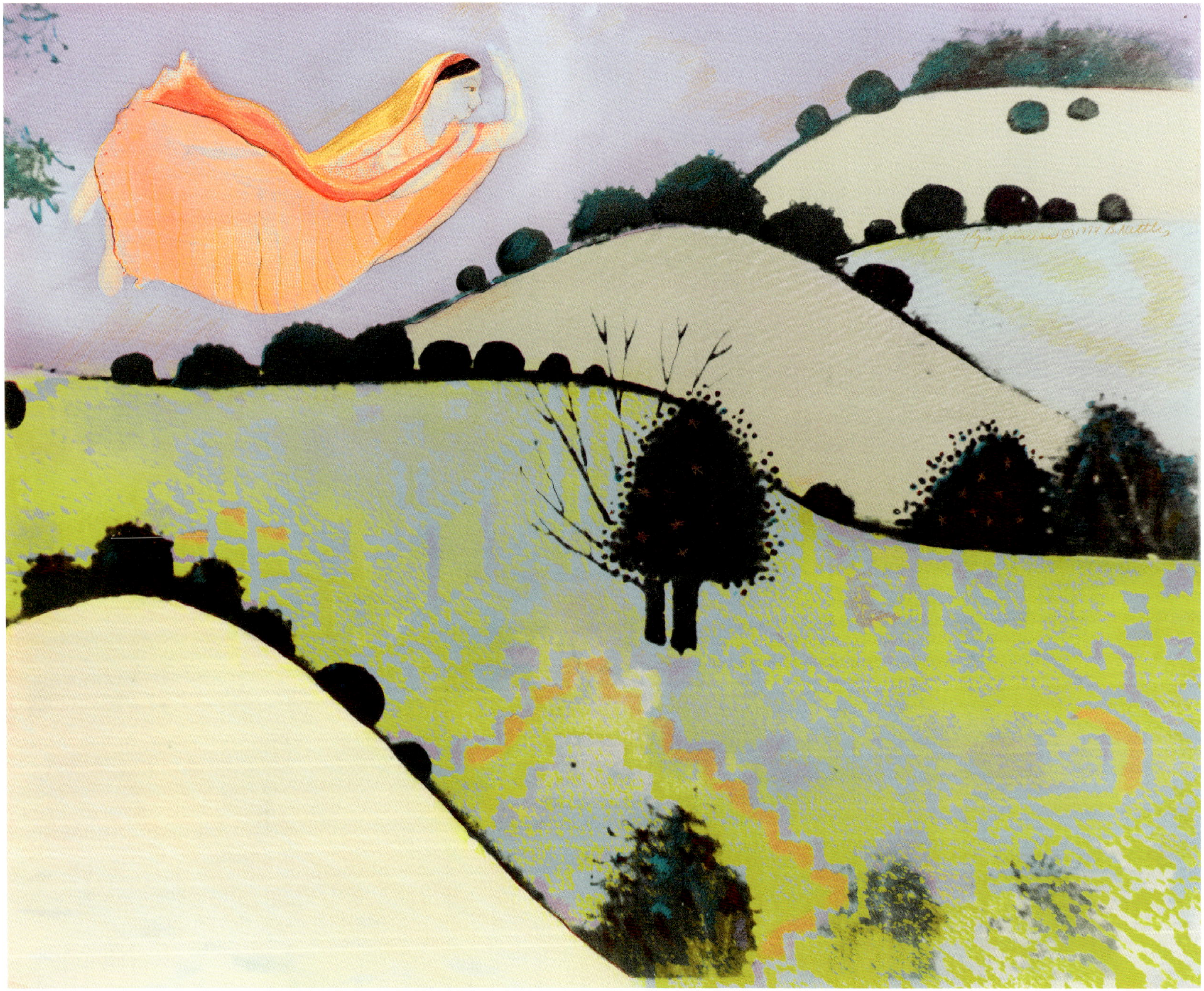

*Flyin Princess*, 1978, from *Flamingo in the Dark*, gum bichromate print with applied color, 16 × 20 in. Collection of the artist

# PHOTOGRAPHY CREDITS

**Note to the Reader**

Unless otherwise noted, all images are by Bea Nettles (American, b. 1946). All Bea Nettles images are copyright © Bea Nettles.

## Title Page

**2–3** Detail of image on page 141

## Foreword

**7** George Eastman Museum, exhibition file. © George Eastman Museum

## Preface

**9** Collection of the artist

## Acknowledgments

**10** George Eastman Museum, gift of the artist

## Part I: Essays

**14–15** Detail of image on page 18

## Overcoming Constraints

**16** Fig. 1.1. Collection of the artist

**17** Fig. 1.2. Robert Fichter. *Untitled*, 1967. George Eastman Museum, purchase. © Robert Fichter

**18** Fig. 1.3. George Eastman Museum, gift of the artist

**19** Fig. 1.4. Joseph Cornell. *Untitled (Palais de Cristal)*, ca. 1953. Crystal Bridges Museum of American Art, Bentonville, Arkansas (2014.28). 13 × 9 ½ × 4 ¼ inches. Photography by Edward C. Robison III. © 2018 The Joseph and Robert Cornell Memorial Foundation / Licensed by VAGA at Artists Rights Society (ARS), NY

**19** Fig. 1.5. Detail of image on page 68

**20** Fig. 1.6. Negative in the collection of the artist

**22** Fig. 1.7. Image file provided by the artist

**23** Fig. 1.8. Image file provided by the artist

**24** Fig. 1.9. George Eastman Museum, gift of Elizabeth Clark

**25** Fig. 1.10. George Eastman Museum, gift of the artist

## Bea Nettles: Artist/Mother

**29** Fig. 2.1. Statuette of a woman, steatopygous, ca. 4500–4000 B.C. Metropolitan Museum of Art, Bequest of Walter C. Baker, 1971 (1972.118.104). Image copyright © The Metropolitan Museum of Art. Image source: Art Resource, NY

**30** Fig. 2.2. Collection of the artist

**31** Fig. 2.3. Image file provided by the artist

**31** Fig. 2.4. John E. James. *William Wallace Shirley*, ca. 1865. George Eastman Museum

**32** Figs. 2.5–2.7. Collection of the artist

**33** Figs. 2.8–2.9. Collection of the artist

**34** Fig. 2.10. George Eastman Museum, gift of the artist

**35** Fig. 2.11. George Eastman Museum, gift of the artist

**37** Fig. 2.12. Image file provided by the artist

**38** Fig. 2.13. Image file provided by the artist

**40** Fig. 2.14. Image file provided by the artist

## Photographic Objects/Institutional Artifacts: Bea Nettles in Context

**43** Fig. 3.1. Betty Hahn. *Greenhouse Portrait (Bea Nettles)*, 1972. Purchase through the Julius L. Rolshoven Memorial Fund, University of New Mexico Art Museum, Albuquerque (74.58). © Betty Hahn

**44** Fig. 3.2. Calvin J. Sumsion with John Cage, Gary Viskupic, and David Eisenman, event poster for *HPSCHD*. Board of Trustees of the University of Illinois on behalf of its Krannert Art Museum. Museum Purchase through the Art Acquisition Fund (2001-10-2)

**44** Fig. 3.3. Robert Fichter. *Astronaut Still Life*, ca. 1974. George Eastman Museum, purchase with funds from National Endowment for the Arts. © Robert Fichter

**45** Fig. 3.4. Joanne Leonard. *Roots and Wings*, 1988. Collection of Barbara Raymond. Image file provided by the artist. © Joanne Leonard

**46** Fig. 3.5. George Eastman Museum, gift of the artist

**47** Fig. 3.6. Board of Trustees on behalf of its Krannert Art Museum. Gift of the artist (2018-17-1)

**48** Figs. 3.7–3.9. George Eastman Museum, Richard and Ronay Menschel Library

**48–49** Fig. 3.10. Rochester Institute of Technology art faculty exhibition announcement. RIT Archive Collections, Rochester Institute of Technology

**50** Figs. 3.11—3.13. Collection Center for Creative Photography, The University of Arizona

**51** Fig. 3.14. Collection Center for Creative Photography, The University of Arizona

## Part II: Plates and Texts

**54–55** Detail of image on page 140

## Plates: 1968–1975

**58** 9 15/16 × 8 1/16 in. George Eastman Museum, gift of the artist

**59** 9 ¾ × 7 ¼ in. George Eastman Museum, gift of the artist

**60** 72 × 60 in. Collection of the artist

**61** 48 × 54 in. Board of Trustees of the University of Illinois on behalf of its Krannert Art Museum. Gift of the artist (2017-20-2)

**62** 27 × 63 × 2 in. Board of Trustees of the University of Illinois on behalf of its Krannert Art Museum. Gift of the artist (2017-20-1)

**64** 10 13/16 × 7 5/16 in. George Eastman Museum, gift of the artist

**65** 9 3/16 × 7 5/16 in. George Eastman Museum, gift of the artist

**66** 10 × 22 ½ in. George Eastman Museum, gift of the artist

**68** 58 × 18 × 10 in. Collection of the artist

**69** 10 3/16 × 7 11/16 × 1 ¾ in. Frame: 14 ⅛ × 11 5/16 × 1 1 ¾ in. Purchased 1971. National Gallery of Canada, Ottawa

**70–75** Binder: 11 7/16 × 11 × 2 ⅜ in. Each page: 11 × 8 ½ in. George Eastman Museum, purchase with funds from the Horace W. Goldsmith Foundation

**77** 9 13/16 × 7 9/16 in. George Eastman Museum, purchase

**78** 14 ¾ × 10 ⅜ in. Collection of the artist

**79** 9 ¾ × 7 11/16 in. George Eastman Museum, gift of the artist

**80** 10 5/16 × 7 ¾ in. George Eastman Museum, gift of John Pfahl and Bonnie Gordon

**81** 10 13/16 × 7 ⅝ in. Collection of the artist

**82** 11 × 8 9/16 in. Collection of the artist

**83** 9 ¾ × 7 ⅝ in. George Eastman Museum, gift of the artist

**84** 14 × 10 ⅞ in. George Eastman Museum, gift of the artist

**85** 13 ⅞ × 10 ⅞ in. Collection of the artist

**86** 11 × 6 9/16 in. Collection of the artist

**87** 21 × 33 ⅞ × 2 5/16 in. Collection of the artist

**88** 20 × 16 in. Collection of the artist

**89** 16 5/16 × 11 ⅝ × 1 13/16 in. Collection of the artist

**90–91** Each image: 6 × 6 in. George Eastman Museum, gift of the artist

**92(l)** Closed: 10 ⅞ × 8 7/16 × ⅛ in. George Eastman Museum, Richard and Ronay Menschel Library

**92(r)–95** Each image: 6 × 5 ⅞ in. Collection of the artist

**96(l)** Closed: 10 ⅝ × 8 ¼ × ⅛ in. George Eastman Museum, Richard and Ronay Menschel Library

**96(r)–99** Each image: 6 × 5 7/8 in. George Eastman Museum, gift of the artist

**100–103** Each image: 6 × 6 in. George Eastman Museum, purchase with funds from National Endowment for the Arts

**104–105** Closed: 10 1/2 × 8 1/4 × 3/16 in. George Eastman Museum, Richard and Ronay Menschel Library

**106–107** Closed: 10 7/16 × 8 1/4 × 3/8 in. Collection of the artist

**108–109** Closed: 5 1/8 × 4 1/8 × 1/4 in. Collection of the artist

**110–111** Closed: 5 1/2 × 4 1/2 × 1/8 in. George Eastman Museum, Richard and Ronay Menschel Library

**112–113** Closed: 9 1/4 × 7 1/4 × 1/8 in. George Eastman Museum, Richard and Ronay Menschel Library

**114–115** Closed: 9 13/16 × 7 3/16 × 3/16 in. George Eastman Museum, Richard and Ronay Menschel Library

## Mountain Dream Tarot

**118–121** Box: 5 × 4 × 1 in. Each card: 4 1/2 × 3 5/8 in. George Eastman Museum, Richard and Ronay Menschel Library

## Plates: 1975–1992

**122** 18 7/8 × 25 9/16 in. Collection of the artist

**124** 18 7/8 × 25 9/16 in. Collection of the artist

**125** 18 7/8 × 25 9/16 in. George Eastman Museum, gift of the artist

**126** 21 7/8 × 29 3/4 in. George Eastman Museum, purchase

**128** 10 1/16 × 9 15/16 in. Collection of the artist

**129–130** Each image: 10 1/16 × 10 3/16 in. George Eastman Museum, gift of the artist

**131** 10 3/16 × 10 3/16 in. Collection of the artist

**132** Frame: 10 1/4 × 30 1/16 × 1 3/4 in. George Eastman Museum, gift of the artist

**134** 30 1/4 × 51 1/4 in. Purchased with funds from the Morton R. Hirschberg Bequest (AP.2005.3.1). The Cummer Museum of Art & Gardens

**136** 15 1/16 × 17 15/16 in. George Eastman Museum, purchase

**137** 14 15/16 × 18 in. Collection of the artist

**138–139** Each image: 24 × 20 in. Collection of the artist

**140–141** Each image: 26 × 20 in. George Eastman Museum, purchase with funds from the Charina Foundation

**143** 19 3/4 × 23 15/16 in. Collection of the artist

**144** 15 × 18 in. George Eastman Museum, gift of the artist

**145** 23 3/4 × 19 3/4 in. Collection of the artist

**146** 15 × 18 in. George Eastman Museum, gift of the artist

**147** 24 × 20 in. Collection of the artist

**148** 16 × 20 in. Collection of the artist

**149** 19 13/16 × 23 15/16 in. George Eastman Museum, gift of the artist

**150** 15 15/16 × 19 15/16 in. George Eastman Museum, gift of the artist

**153** 16 × 20 1/16 in. George Eastman Museum, gift of the artist

**154** 16 × 20 in. Collection of the artist

**155** 16 × 19 15/16 in. George Eastman Museum, gift of the artist

**156–160** Each image: 16 × 20 in. Collection of the artist

**162** 8 1/2 × 9 7/16 in. George Eastman Museum, gift of the artist

**163** 9 3/4 × 9 3/4 in. Collection of the artist

**165–169** Each image: 9 1/2 × 9 1/4 in. George Eastman Museum, gift of the artist

**171** 9 1/2 × 9 1/2 in. George Eastman Museum, gift of Elizabeth Clark

**172–173** Each image: 9 1/2 × 9 1/2 in. George Eastman Museum, gift of the artist

**174(l)** 9 3/4 × 9 5/8 in. George Eastman Museum, gift of the artist

**174(r)** 9 1/2 × 9 1/2 in. Board of Trustees of the University of Illinois on behalf of its Krannert Art Museum. Gift of the artist (2015-15-1.11)

**175(l)** 9 1/2 × 9 1/2 in. Board of Trustees of the University of Illinois on behalf of its Krannert Art Museum. Gift of the artist (2015-15-1.13)

**175(r)** 9 ½ × 9 ½ in. Board of Trustees of the University of Illinois on behalf of its Krannert Art Museum. Gift of the artist (2015-15-1.15)

**176–177** Each image: 9 ½ × 9 ½ in. George Eastman Museum, gift of the artist

**178(l)** 9 ½ × 9 ½ in. George Eastman Museum, gift of the artist

**178(r)** 9 ½ × 9 ½ in. RIT Archive Collections, Rochester Institute of Technology

**180–181** Each image: 10 13/16 × 13 9/16 in. George Eastman Museum, gift of the artist

**182–183** Each image: 10 ¾ × 13 7/16 in. George Eastman Museum, gift of the artist

**184–185** Each image: 10 ¾ × 13 7/16 in. George Eastman Museum, gift of the artist

**186** 24 × 20 in. Samuel P. Harn Museum of Art, University of Florida

**187** 24 × 20 in. Samuel P. Harn Museum of Art, University of Florida

**189** 20 × 15 ⅞ in. George Eastman Museum, gift of the artist

**190** 19 5/16 × 23 7/16 in. George Eastman Museum, gift of the artist

**191** 23 3/16 × 19 in. George Eastman Museum, gift of the artist

**193** 24 ¼ × 21 in. George Eastman Museum, gift of the artist

**194** 25 × 21 in. George Eastman Museum, gift of the artist

**196–197** Box: 4 ⅝ × 3 9/16 × ⅜ in. Each card: 4 ½ × 3 ½ in. George Eastman Museum, Richard and Ronay Menschel Library

## Plates: 1995–2011

**200** 12 × 32 in. Illinois Legacy Collection, Illinois State Museum, Springfield

**202** 5 × 14 9/16 in. Collection of the artist

**204** 4 13/16 × 14 ⅝ in. Collection of the artist

**206** 5 × 14 ⅝ in. George Eastman Museum, gift of the artist

**208–209** Closed: 4 ⅜ × 4 7/16 × 1 3/16 in. George Eastman Museum, Richard and Ronay Menschel Library

**211** 16 × 12 in. George Eastman Museum, gift of the artist

**212** 16 9/16 × 12 3/16 in. Collection of the artist

**213** 8 15/16 × 6 ¾ in. Collection of the artist

**214** 16 ⅜ × 12 5/16 in. George Eastman Museum, gift of the artist

**215–216** Each image: 16 9/16 × 12 ⅜ in. Collection of the artist

**217** 8 15/16 × 6 11/16 in. George Eastman Museum, gift of the artist

**219–221** Each image: 16 ¼ × 12 ⅜ in. Collection of the artist

**222** 16 9/16 × 12 ⅜ in. George Eastman Museum, gift of the artist

**224–225** Closed: 3 × 5 3/16 × ⅛ in. George Eastman Museum, Richard and Ronay Menschel Library

**226** Closed: 5 × 4 in. Courtesy of The Rare Book & Manuscript Library, University of Illinois at Urbana-Champaign

**227** Image supplied by the artist

**228–229** Closed: 8 ⅛ × 4 ⅛ × 1 ⅜ in. George Eastman Museum, Richard and Ronay Menschel Library

**230–231** Closed: 6 × 3 ⅞ × 7/16 in. George Eastman Museum, Richard and Ronay Menschel Library

**232–233** Closed: 8 × 4 × ⅞ in. George Eastman Museum, Richard and Ronay Menschel Library

**234–235** Slipcase: 6 ½ × 7 1/16 × ¾ in. Collection of the artist

**236–237** Closed: 2 ½ × 4 7/16 × 9/16 in. George Eastman Museum, Richard and Ronay Menschel Library

## Plates: 2011–2016

**240–241** Slipcase: 4 ¼ × 11 × ⅛ in. George Eastman Museum, Richard and Ronay Menschel Library

**242–243** Slipcase: 10 3/16 × 10 3/16 × ⅛ in. George Eastman Museum, Richard and Ronay Menschel Library

**244–245** Closed: 5 ½ × 9 ½ × ⅜ in. George Eastman Museum, Richard and Ronay Menschel Library

**246–247** Box: 2 ½ × 3 ¾ × 1 in. Each card: 2 ¼ × 3 ½ in. George Eastman Museum, Richard and Ronay Menschel Library

**248–249** Slipcase: 9 7/16 × 4 13/16 × 1 ⅛ in. Collection of the artist

**250–251** Slipcase: 5 × 8 ½ × ⅛ in. George Eastman Museum, Richard and Ronay Menschel Library

## Selected Chronology

**254** Both images: Collection of the artist

**255(t)** Linda Connor. Bea Nettles with her 3M Revere Automatic 500 camera. Collection of Bea Nettles. © Linda Connor

**255(b)** Collection of the artist

**256(l)** Exhibition poster for *Moonbeams and Dreams*, Witkin Gallery, New York. Collection of Bea Nettles

**256(c)** Photograph from Joan Mondale. Collection of Bea Nettles

**256(r)** Exhibition poster for *Close to Home*, MFA Gallery, Rochester Institute of Technology. Collection of Bea Nettles

**257** George Eastman Museum, gift of the artist

**258(l)** Photograph by Elizabeth Chiang © George Eastman Museum

**258(r)** George Eastman Museum, Richard and Ronay Menschel Library

## Selected Bibliography

**261** All images: George Eastman Museum, Richard and Ronay Menschel Library